A SHORT HISTORY OF THE WESTERN WORLD

A Short History
of the Western World

JOHN E. RODES

OCCIDENTAL COLLEGE

CHARLES SCRIBNER'S SONS · New York

TO ELIZABETH AND JENNIFER

PREFACE

When writing about the past, value judgments are unavoidable. Whether consciously or not, the historian approaches his task with ingrained preconceptions. He strives to be objective and accurate in asserting that particular events occurred at specified times and in a given sequence. But when causal relationships come into focus, the historian's description becomes enmeshed with his personal views on historical developments, for the very pattern he imposes on history affects his conclusions. The need for focusing on certain aspects of man's past influences his interpretation and often imposes an apparent causal pattern which may or may not have existed in actuality. His selection of materials from the vast past is bound to make it a personal history. In this respect, history is still an art rather than a science. Value judgments also enter when the historian must deal with such questions as progress or stagnation, the achievements of a ruler, or the efficiency of an institution. We may believe that the liberalization of Czechoslovakia in 1968 is "good," whereas Castro's revolutionary dictatorship is "bad"; we may deplore the rigidity of the reign of King Philip II of Spain in the sixteenth century or applaud Beaumarchais' condemnation of social injustice in the eighteenth century. Such judgments are unavoidable, since the historian is just as human as any other political and moral human being. Let us just remember that the result is *our* history and not necessarily history as such.

When dealing with vast stretches of history, the writer is easily tempted to become encyclopaedic in his approach and produce catalogues of names of people and battles, which in the end only confuse the reader. I have sought assiduously to avoid this temptation. This book stresses trends, events, and people which I deem to have been especially important in giving direction to a particular development or typifying the mood of a given age. Many names are therefore indicated only in parentheses for purposes of identification. Moreover, I have purposely stressed certain aspects of Western history, in particular socio-political developments and prominent ideas that shaped man's thinking in the past. The arts, literature, and philosophy are introduced *passim* in order to depict the temper of an era or the character of a civilization. No attempt has been made here to include all of man's cultural achievements.

Such a study of the past, for which this is only a skeleton, must be supplemented with specialized treatments of particular historical periods, as well as aspects of philosophy, literature, art, sociology, economics, religion and other facets of human existence. For this purpose, each chapter is provided with a brief bibliography of more detailed analyses of specific periods, cultural developments, and source materials. A list of more general books and source collections is appended at the end of the book. With few exceptions, all books listed are available in paperback. Having familiarized himself with the major aspects of the development of the Western world, the reader should select materials suggested in these bibliographies in order to add depth to his understanding and acquire greater appreciation for differing historical points of view. The skeleton presented in this book will thus acquire flesh and dimension.

I am grateful to the numerous colleagues, students, editors, and friends who helped me with this book. Among the many I might mention, let me thank two in particular: my late mother, who worked on many phases of the book, and Miss Kathleen Grantham, who labored assiduously on the bibliography and other aspects of the manuscript.

                                                                    JER

Altadena, California

CONTENTS

A WORD ABOUT DATES AND CHRONOLOGY

Dates in this book appearing in parentheses following names of people refer to life spans except in cases of kings, emperors, and popes when they indicate the period of their reign. Since this history is written from a Western point of view, the dates used are based on the by now traditional Christian calendar. Yet, it is worth recalling that the use of this Christian chronological scheme, no matter how convenient, colors historical accounts in a very subjective way. To put it bluntly, why should one say, for instance, that Confucius, Pericles, or Mohammed lived so and so many years *before* or *after* Christ, rather than indicate that Christ lived some five centuries after Buddha?

Most civilizations developed their own systems of chronology and their own calendars, based on lunar, solar, or other calculations, and even within the Christian community there were different systems of chronology. One major problem in setting up a calendar involved the choice of units of measurement (such as years, months, weeks, cycles, or other divisions) and their relationship to the seasons and the revolutions of planets and stars. A great variety of measurements was developed, based on the moon (Babylon), the sun and the moon (Greece), the star Sirius, or Sothis (Egypt), or other celestial configurations.

In Western chronology, the calendar decreed by Julius Caesar (about 45 B.C.) became the preferred yardstick for many centuries. This Julian calendar, based on the sun, fixed the year at 365 days, with an extra day intercalated every fourth year. However, since this scheme deviated slightly from actual solar years, a time lag developed between solar circumvolutions and the Julian calendar. Hence, a "new style" calendar was proposed by Pope Gregory XIII in 1582. To bring the calendar up to date with the sun, the pope suggested a one-time omission of ten days and the future abolition of certain leap years. This Gregorian calendar was soon adopted in most Catholic states, whereas the Protestant countries in general (Germany, Scandinavia, and England) retained the "old style" or Julian calendar until the eighteenth century. Russia stayed with the older system until it was abolished by the Bolsheviks in the 1920's. Since the difference between the Julian and Gregorian calendars had increased to thirteen days by the twentieth century, the discrepancy between Russian and Western European dates had by then become considerable.

Besides variations in the length of a year—differences which by themselves make chronological correlation difficult—an even greater problem in establishing historical contemporaneity results from the differences in historical base points among the civilizations. The precise correlation between different timetables still remains a serious problem for chronologists.

The Chinese, for example, first used cycles of sixty days, months, and years, and later (second century B.C.) began to date by the names of ruling emperors. "Eras" were used in India, "lists of rulers" in Babylon, "names of pharaohs" and later of "dynasties" in Egypt. The Greeks initially employed no continuous counting but named each year by incumbent kings, priests, or magistrates—differing, of course, in the various city-states. Eventually some Greeks arbitrarily selected the supposed year of the first Olympic Games (776 B.C.) as the year 1 of a continuous calendar. The Romans, similarly, at first dated by consulships and later added a system of continuous accounting by taking as base point the year when Rome was presumably founded (753 B.C.). The Moslems, on the other hand, at an early date took 622 A.D., marking Mohammed's flight from Mecca to Medina (the Hegira), as the initial point for their calendar. The immense difficulty in correlating such diverse chronological systems can readily be seen. The chronologist must determine, for example, that "the year of the consulship of Cinna and Marius" in Rome, "the 690th year of the Olympiad" in Greece, "the third year of the reign of Ptolemy VIII" in Egypt, and "the era of the late Sunga dynasty" in the Ganges Valley all presumably refer to the same year 86 B.C.

The development of the Christian calendar itself took a long time. The early Christians used the local Roman or Greek calendars. Then, Christian writers began to date events starting with the Creation (set at first at 5499 B.C. and later changed to 4004 B.C.) or with the Flood. When Eusebius of Caesarea in his *Chronicle* (fourth century A.D.) attempted to correlate Hebrew, Christian, and pagan histories, he used as his base point the birth of Abraham (2016 B.C.) Despite its faults and the credulity of its author who inserted dates for such mythological characters as Bacchus, Oedipus, and Orpheus, Eusebius' book dominated Christian chronological calculations down to early modern times. Meanwhile the new practice of dating events in relation to the birth of Christ (i.e. B.C. and A.D.) was introduced in the sixth century and made more widely accepted by the Venerable Bede in the eighth century. Even this system, however, turned out to be not without flaws, since chronologists eventually concluded that Christ was probably born four years "before Christ."

A SHORT HISTORY OF THE WESTERN WORLD

CHAPTER I

❧ *Introduction:* *The Study of Civilizations*

The term "civilization" has acquired three different meanings. In a basic sense, it simply designates a society developed beyond the stage of primitive barbarism. In a larger context, the term "civilization" refers to the total complex of philosophical and spiritual beliefs, artistic achievements, and political, social, and economic institutions of a people, regardless of their state of development. Such a definition usually embraces large geographic areas and long spans of time, as in reference to "Western" or "Eastern" civilization. In the third meaning of the word, "civilization" denotes a relatively homogeneous state of culture, either of a people or of a period, characterized by a particular *Zeitgeist* (spirit of the times). In this sense the larger term "Western civilization," for instance, can be subdivided into smaller divisions, each of which can also be called "civilization," such as the civilization of the Middle Ages, of the Renaissance, or of the nineteenth century. In this book we are interested in "civilization" in both the second and third meanings of the word.

Much history written during the past two centuries was less concerned with the civilizations of particular periods—an approach one might call horizontal since it cuts across boundaries—than with the national development of a given people. Thus we have numerous histories of France or Germany, using the chronological or vertical approach. The vertical approach furnishes a convenient framework for historical study, since it offers a well-defined focus, but it also embodies dangers. By concentrating on the nation-state as a frame for analysis, it is all too easy to implant implied national cohesion on periods when the national ideal did not yet exist. Can one, for instance, really speak of France during the earlier Middle Ages? Similarly, the vertical approach often gives an impression of the cultural isolation of a given people when in fact there was constant cultural interchange with others. To give an example, it is probable that the aristocratic Frenchman of the eighteenth century felt considerably more affinity for his aristocratic contemporary across the Rhine than for a French peasant, so that one should probably not generalize about the French people in the eighteenth century but rather about European aristocracy of that period.

The vertical approach involves another danger for those readers who may conceive of events as occurring consecutively rather than simultaneously, simply because of the order in which they are presented. It is customary, for example, to study the histories of Judea, Persia, Greece, and Rome in this given order. We could conclude that the Jews should be associated with the tenth through sixth centuries B.C., the Persians with the sixth, the Greeks with the fifth, and the Romans with a later period. Yet, if we were to examine the fifth century horizontally we should find that the high point of Hellenic civilization coincided with the continued flowering of Persian civilization, that the Hebrews were then still developing their influential religion, and that Rome was already at work building its famous constitutional structure. More importantly, even, the reader would realize that all four peoples were constantly influencing one another.

Ideally the area of historical analysis for a given period should be determined by the range of contact, or what one might call the horizon, of the people studied. As the centuries passed, changes in transportation and communication as well as the growth of populations obviously created a widening horizon for individuals and a greater interchange of ideas, goods, and peoples. Hence, a logical unit for historical analysis during the year 500 A.D., for example, might be no more than the portion of an area occupied by a single Germanic tribe. In the early tenth century, it might be as small as an isolated manor. By the time of the Renaissance, it might be a province of France or the bulk of the Italian Peninsula. And in later times, the framework widens to most of the European continent, then to Europe and the Americas, and ultimately to the known world.

A history based on a people's "horizon" would inevitably expand to a history of mankind as contact between populations increases—manifestly an unmanageable task for the historian. Hence, we must compromise between the ideal and the practical. In our study of civilizations we shall use the horizontal approach wherever appropriate but retain the vertical, more traditional, analysis where such treatment might aid the reader.

Historic periodization

The history of man and in particular of Western civilization has traditionally been divided into chronological periods. The basic two periods are (1) prehistoric, or preliterate, times, and (2) historic, or literate, times.

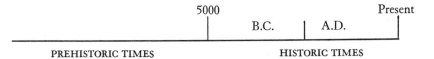

The prehistoric or preliterate period is the age which preceded the invention of writing, or—more accurately speaking—the era of man's earlier life from which we possess no written sources. The historic or literate age comprises those centuries from which we have written records. The dividing line between the two periods naturally occurs at different times in different areas of the world. Since we have no written records of certain American tribes prior to the arrival of the Spanish conquerors, the period before the fifteenth century A.D. in some areas of America is properly called the preliterate or prehistoric age. With most civilizations, the dividing line recedes as archaeologists make new discoveries of inscriptions and other written records. A few decades ago, it was customary to assume that the historic age in Egypt and Mesopotamia started about 3000 B.C. Recent discoveries have pushed the date back to about 5000 B.C., while for China it is now about 1500 B.C.

In this brief survey, we cannot study the endless millennia of the prehistoric age, a period encompassing a seemingly infinite span of time in contrast to the brief period of so-called history. Yet we should recognize that man's accomplishments during the prehistoric age in his evolution toward civilization probably involved greater changes and more relative progress than anything achieved since the beginning of historic times. Man's initial conquest of nature, his adaptation of fire and tools for his own benefit, his acquisition of dominance over animals and plants (sometimes called the "Neolithic Revolution," which took place some seven or eight thousand years before Christ) were possibly even greater feats than what was accomplished in the recent industrial and atomic revolutions.

The historic, or literate, age (the last seven thousand years) in turn is commonly divided into at least three periods: ancient times from 5000 B.C. to 500 A.D., medieval times from 500 A.D. to 1500 A.D., and modern times after 1500 A.D. Such dates are, of course, mere conventions, since no particular period ended precisely at a given point.

Traditional and convenient as these subdivisions are, they should be used with caution. First of all these divisions are applicable only to parts of Europe and distort the history of mankind because they are seen only from a Western point of view. They do not refer to the Far East, Africa, or America. While an understandable distortion for a book dealing with the Western world and written in America, it is important to keep in mind that they are distortions. Moreover, such periodization evokes an unwarranted impression of enormous gulfs between the different periods. Culture, after all, is a continuum. One generation passes its achievements on to the next, and it would be misleading to assert that medieval society is of a totally different fabric than that of ancient times, or that modern times have little in common with the Middle Ages. Finally this periodization has led to the dubious practice of endowing the label for a period with almost magic powers. Once the label is applied, the period is cast into a mold which supposes a homogeneous quality for all its subperiods. Such terms as "ancient," "medieval," or "modern" assume static conditions and constant characteristics in defiance of evolutionary reality. For the sake of convenience we shall use this traditional periodization, trusting that the reader will remain cognizant of its pitfalls.

Each of the three major historical periods is in turn traditionally divided into various phases. These subdivisions are based on differences between civilizations and peoples, or on chronology and geography. Although these artificial categories further distort history, their usefulness gained them a seemingly indelible place in historiography.

Ancient history is usually divided into three subdivisions: (1) the civilizations of the Near and Middle East, (2) the Pre-Hellenic civilizations of the Aegean, and (3) the Classical civilizations of Greece and Rome. The first of these concentrated along the shores of the eastern Mediterranean and in the so-called Fertile Crescent along the Tigris and Euphrates rivers during the period from about 5000 B.C. to 300 B.C. when it merged with Greek culture to form the Hellenistic civilization. The second flourished on the islands and the shores of the Aegean from about 3000 B.C. to 1200 B.C., when it gradually succumbed to invaders from the North. The third and last originated in the Aegean basin and the Greek mainland, spread to the Italian Peninsula and ultimately most of the Mediterranean, and flourished from about 800 B.C. to 500 A.D. These historical divisions should not obscure the fact that there was much cultural diffusion between the various regions and that, at the same time, other civilizations developed with relatively little or no contact with the Mediterranean basin, in India, China, and America.

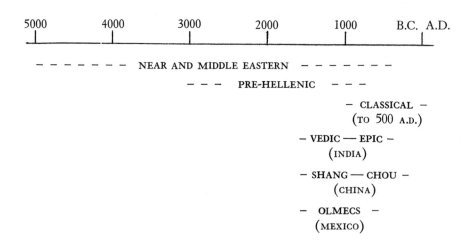

The civilizations of the Near and Middle East were developed by numerous peoples, many of whom became important to the stream of later history. One by one, various peoples rose to prominence, created a civilization of their own, and then sank into lethargy or servitude, or disappeared altogether from the accountable path of history. Among the more important peoples were the Egyptians, Sumerians, Akkadians, Babylonians, Phoenicians, Hebrews, Assyrians, Chaldeans or Neo-Babylonians, and Persians.

```
5000        4000         3000         2000         1000     B.C.   A.D.
 |           |            |            |            |            |

 – – – – – – – – –  EGYPTIANS  – – – – – – – – –
 – – SUMERIANS AND AKKADIANS – –
         – – – BABYLONIANS  – – –
                 – – PHOENICIANS – –
                 – – ASSYRIANS  – –
                     – KASSITES –
                     – – HEBREWS  – –
                         – PERSIANS –
                             CHALDEANS
```

The Pre-Hellenic period—sometimes called the Pre-Greek, or Aegean, Age—includes the Minoan civilization of the island of Crete as well as the cultures of Mycenae and of the Homeric period. Whereas a few decades ago little was known about these civilizations, recent archaeological excavations and the gradual deciphering of Minoan inscriptions have brought to light a brilliant and highly developed culture. For a long time this period was considered largely a developmental state in the foundation of Classical Greek civilization. However, as new discoveries are made, it becomes increasingly evident that there was a considerable break between the Pre-Hellenic and the Classical cultures, occasioned presumably by the large-scale invasions of northern peoples which took place after 1200 B.C.

The Classical period has usually been given fewer subdivisions because it is shorter and because fewer diverse peoples dominated the age culturally and politically. The customary divisions of this period are: one, the Hellenic civilization, centering in Greece, and spreading throughout the Mediterranean shores between the eighth and fourth centuries B.C.; two, the Hellenistic civilizations, based largely on a mixture of Greek and Near Eastern characteristics, which started in the eastern Mediterranean in the fourth century B.C. and developed into the partial basis of later Roman and even medieval times; and, three, the Roman civilization, by far the longest in duration and geographically the most widespread.

The second major traditional period, the Middle Ages, is in turn sometimes divided into several subdivisions, which however do not apply equally

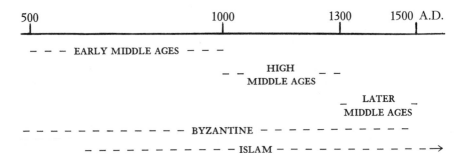

well to all parts of Western civilization. In Northern, Western, and Southern Europe, the centuries following the disintegration of the Roman Empire are often divided into three periods: one, the Early Middle Ages, from about the fifth to the tenth centuries; two, the High Middle Ages, from the eleventh to the thirteenth centuries; and, three, the Later Middle Ages, the fourteenth and fifteenth centuries.

These categories, however, are inappropriate for Eastern Europe and the eastern and southern parts of the Mediterranean. The Byzantine civilization, which lasted from 500 A.D. to the fifteenth century, was in many respects more a continuation of Hellenistic characteristics than a medieval period. And to the Southeast arose the Islamic civilization, originating with the Arabs in the seventh century and rapidly enveloping the Near East and most of the Mediterranean coastal lands. When we look at America or Asia proper, these divisions become entirely inappropriate.

Finally the Modern Age, starting in the fifteenth century, lends itself to an infinite variety of subdivisions, each series deriving its usefulness from the particular objective of the respective historical study.

The study of civilizations

Since this book discusses the history of the Western world, we must attempt to define the concept "Western." In its geographic sense, the term may apply to Europe alone, or to Europe and America, or to the Western Hemisphere. In its ethnologic sense in which we speak of "Western" peoples, the term is more puzzling. It may refer to Europeans or also to former Europeans, no matter where they live or how long ago their ancestors left Europe.

The term "Western" perhaps becomes clearest when used in the expression "Western civilization," evoking almost intuitively the picture of a particular way of life with relative similarity in people's outlook on most social, political, economic, aesthetic, and spiritual questions. Yet, even such a vague definition entails arbitrary judgment. Since civilizations change and develop with the passing of generations, one would have to determine how many centuries one can go back in time and still find that people's views resemble those of our present Western civilization. At what point do the differences between Western culture today and the culture of earlier centuries become so great that we can no longer apply the term "Western civilization?" Unquestionably, medieval France is an integral component of Western civilization. But what about the Babylonians of the twentieth century B.C., for example, or the Etruscans of the sixth century B.C., both of whom contributed to the development of Western civilization? Was their overall outlook and way of life not so much different from our own, so that the Babylonian and Etruscan civilizations should not be called a part of Western civilization? The answers are altogether arbitrary.

Much of the fabric of Ancient civilization, in particular Classical times, became a part of the web of Western civilization. But the peculiarity of medieval and modern times, which distinguishes them from Ancient and non-Western civilizations, is the mixture of Classical strands with Hebrew-Christian ideals and, to some extent, Germanic customs. Only after these streams merged do we have the complete basis for Western civilization.

By this definition then, Western civilization is no more than some fifteen centuries old, starting in some parts of Europe as early as the fourth century A.D., in others—particularly Northern Europe—only in the tenth century because of the later introduction of both Classical and Hebrew-Christian ideals.

Yet, in order to understand Western man's heritage, one must study the antecedents of Western civilization, particularly the Classical civilizations of Greece and Rome and the religions of the Near East. Moreover, a study of Western civilization cannot totally ignore such contemporaneous civilizations as those of Islam, India, and China, which on occasion have exerted profound influence on the development of the West.

Once the area of study has been delineated, there remains the question of how such a vast panorama as the history of the Western world can best be studied. Since one cannot study all aspects of Western civilization in a book of limited size, I have concentrated on the socio-political and intellectual development of the Western world. Certain themes predominate in this study, foremost among them the question of historical change. Throughout most eras one finds a surprising continuity of development side by side with a pattern of action and reaction. In the latter case, one period seems to react against the main stream of its predecessor as in some form of a dialectic. In this theme of change through slow continuity, through reversal of previous trends, or even through the application of violence, the struggle between liberals and conservatives naturally looms large in all periods.

Another theme involves the discovery of the *Zeitgeist* of a given period. One need not accept the views of many Romantic historians of the nineteenth century who endowed the *Zeitgeist* with well-nigh spiritual powers to direct the lives of people. Yet, it seems undeniable that the total ambience of a given period profoundly affects as well as reflects the lives of the people. Surely in our own day there is an ambience of freedom which is reflected in most phases of our culture, be that experimentation in painting and sculpture, improvisation in music and dance, greater sexual freedom, or more permissiveness in education. It is this ambience or *Zeitgeist* that we shall try to analyze in the various periods of Western history.

A further theme deals with church-state relations. The dichotomy between the city of man and the city of God, which existed in most civilizations, beckoned for reconciliation during most periods of history, in Christian as well as non-Christian societies. It involved not merely relations between ecclesiastical and secular authorities but also the conflict between the spiritual and worldly aspirations of the people.

Finally, there are various fundamental questions—not all of which could be analyzed in this book—which the student should keep in mind when pursuing his own investigation of past civilizations. Throughout the ages civilized man has felt impelled to satisfy certain fundamental needs within the framework of his community. It is therefore important, when analyzing a cultural epoch, to ascertain how men satisfied their basic physical, social, political, economic, aesthetic, and spiritual requirements. An analysis of the economic base of society, for example, might show the existence of a mere subsistence economy or, on the contrary, it might reveal substantial surpluses and the consequent presence of a leisure class. Equally important is an examination of the role of law in a given period. Whether law is God-given or formulated by man, whether it is imposed from above in arbitrary fashion or legislated from below in accordance with established custom or the desires of the people is of vital consequence for the functioning of a society. Our understanding of a society is also greatly enhanced if we know its ideals of the "good life," people's aspirations, and their concepts of the ultimate goals of existence.

SUGGESTED READINGS

NOTE: All books are paperbacks except for those marked with an asterisk. Some dates of publication are not available in reprints.

Historiography

Aron, Raymond, *Introduction to the Philosophy of History* (Beacon, 1961).
Berdyaev, Nicolas, *The Meaning of History* (World).
Butterfield, Herbert, *Man on His Past: The Study of His History of Historical Scholarship* (Beacon, 1960).
Collingwood, R. G., *The Idea of History* (Oxford, 1956).
Gustavson, Carl G., *A Preface to History* (McGraw, 1955).
Kahler, Erich, *The Meaning of History* (World, 1968).
Nevins, Allan, *Gateway to History* (Quadrangle, 1963).
Seligman, Edwin R. A., *The Economic Interpretation of History* (Columbia, 1963).
Shotwell, James Thomson, *The Story of Ancient History* (Columbia, 1961). On historical writings from ancient Egypt to St. Augustine.

Prehistory

Clark, John G. D., *World Prehistory—An Outline* (Cambridge U. P., 1961).
Day, Michael H., *Guide to Fossil Man, A Handbook of Human Palaeontology* (World, 1966).
Gabel, Creighton, ed., *Man Before History* (Prentice-Hall, 1964).
Koenigswald, G. H. R. von, *The Evolution of Man* (U. of Michigan, 1962).
*Levy, G. R., *Religious Conceptions of the Stone Age and Their Influence Upon European Thought* (Peter Smith).
*Lowie, Robert H., *Primitive Society* (Liveright, 1947).
Oakley, Kenneth P., *Man the Tool-maker* (U. of Chicago, 1959).
Ucko, Peter J., and Rosenfeld, Andrée, *Palaeolithic Cave Art* (McGraw, 1967).

Social Sciences

Bagby, Philip, *Culture and History: Prolegomena to the Comparative Study of Civilizations* (U. of California, 1960).
Benedict, Ruth, *Patterns of Culture* (Houghton, 1961). Description of three primitive societies.
Childe, V. Gordon, *Social Evolution* (World).
Dawson, Christopher H., *The Dynamics of World History* (New American Library, 1962). On the interaction of biology, geography, economy, and religion.
Hook, Sidney, *The Hero in History: A Study in Limitations and Possibility* (Beacon, 1955). Evaluation of nineteenth and twentieth century theories of society.
Huntington, Ellsworth, *Mainsprings of Civilization* (New American Library, 1959). Influences of geography and climate on history.
Kroeber, A. L., *Style and Civilizations* (U. of California, 1957).
Maine, Henry J. S., *Ancient Law: Its Connection with the Early History of Society and Its Relation to Modern Ideas* (Oxford U. P., 1931).
*Mitchell, J. B., *Historical Geography* (Dover).
Sapir, Edward, *Culture, Language and Personality* (U. of California, 1949).
Weber, Max, *Basic Concepts of Sociology* (Citadel, 1962).
Wendt, Herbert, *It Began in Babel* (Dell, 1964).

CHAPTER II

✻ *The Ancient Near East*

At present, it is generally estimated that man emerged some 600,000 years ago during the Lower Palaeolithic period. During these early millennia, man supported himself by hunting and used tools made from chipped stone. Assuming all human beings to have descended from a single prototype, palaeontologists formerly theorized that man originated in one region and gradually migrated to other areas of the globe. Central Asia had been regarded as the so-called cradle of later civilizations. Yet, recent findings in Saharan and sub-Saharan Africa as well as additional discoveries in Western Europe, particularly in France, make it possible that early Palaeolithic cultures existed in all three places simultaneously. The question as to where, if anywhere, the cradle of mankind might be discovered, if indeed it existed, is thus reopened.

Only during the Neolithic era, or New Stone Age, did man settle down in organized communities that approached the status of civilization. The fabrication of knives, hatchets, and axes from polished stone allowed him greater control over nature; domestication of animals and the development of agriculture assured him a more constant supply of food. Once surpluses had been achieved, man could spend time beyond merely assuring survival and thus develop different civilizations.

The dates for the Neolithic Age vary from one region to another. In Egypt, it may have started as early as 10,000 B.C., while in northern Europe probably no earlier than 5000 B.C. Recent archaeological discoveries have shown that the precursors of the Olmecs of Central America entered this stage about 6000 B.C. The Neolithic Era in turn ended when the use of metals was introduced, around 5000 B.C. in Egypt, but only about 500 B.C. in some areas of Europe. Even today people in some Arctic regions and in some jungles of South America and Africa live under essentially Neolithic conditions.

Although no decipherable writing from this age has been found, we have uncovered numerous paintings, burial places, jewelry, and artifacts which enable archaeologists to reconstruct legends, rites, and institutions of Neolithic peoples. Unless the archaeologists' vision has been blurred by seeing the past too much through the eyes of the present, these reconstructions emphasize a remarkable continuity in man's development. Marriage, burial rites, codes of conduct, and socio-religious institutions of Neolithic man, as well as physical facilities such as farm implements, appear to be similar to those found in later historic periods.

The third millennium

We know today that the literate period started at least around 5000 B.C., if not earlier. Yet our information on the first two thousand years of man's "history" is still sketchy. Only from the third millennium on can we speak with some certainty.

Egypt

Some time around 3000 B.C., the regions of Lower and Upper Egypt were brought under the control of a single ruler, or pharaoh, who established the first of a long series of hereditary dynasties that were to rule the united Egyptian kingdom for centuries. To control this area—about six hundred miles long and one hundred miles wide—the monarchs and their agents developed a fairly elaborate administrative machinery, instituted tribunals, and collected taxes. At first, the Egyptians enjoyed relative isolation and peace, and apparently saw no need for an army or a class of warriors. After the middle of the millennium, however, troops were required to repel invasions from the South, to keep open the routes to the valuable mines on the Sinai Peninsula, and to repress rebellious Nubian tribes.

Material achievements and intellectual progress reached high standards during this period of the so-called Old Kingdom. Elaborate irrigation canals were constructed to take advantage of the precious waters of the Nile. Gigantic pyramids, built from the twenty-seventh century on, served as tombs and memorials for the pharaohs, who were considered to be descendants of gods. Hieroglyphic writing was perfected, and mathematics and astronomy were used to establish a solar calendar. As late as the fifth century B.C., the Greek historian Herodotus wrote that he believed the Egyptians "contrive their year much more cleverly than the Greeks; for the latter intercalate every other year a whole month, but the Egyptians, dividing the year into twelve months of thirty days each, add every year a space of five days, whereby the circuit of the seasons is made to return with uniformity."

During these early centuries, certain problems that have persisted throughout much of history are already discernible. One is the relationship between secular and religious powers. In theory, Egypt was a theocracy. As the son of a god, the pharaoh ruled in the name of that deity and was himself his chief priest. In practice, however, the monarch was surrounded by a powerful priestly class, jealously guarding its prerogatives and frequently acting against the secular interests of the state. This rivalry between the two powers whose jurisdiction overlapped brought frequent strife to the kingdom. Since religion played such a large role in the social life of the Egyptians, whom Herodotus called "religious to excess, far beyond any other race of men," this problem was particularly severe in their history.

Another problem was the threat of feudalism. The kingdom was divided into many districts, each under the rule of a governor, or nomarch, appointed by the king as superintendent of canals, collector of taxes, local judge, and leader of the local militia. Like the counts of medieval times, the nomarchs gradually made their positions hereditary, developed local roots, and usurped the power of the pharaohs in their own districts. So long as the pharaoh alone enjoyed the respect devoted to divinity, centralized rule remained possible. By the latter part of the third millennium, however, the Egyptians began to believe that immortality, and with it a spark of the divine, resided in every soul and not only in that of the pharaoh. As a result, the prestige and power of the ruler declined, whereas that of the nomarchs and landed aristocracy grew. By about 2200 B.C., feudal atomization and disorder characterized Egyptian politics.

Mesopotamia

During this same third millennium, a highly developed civilization emerged in Mesopotamia, the land adjacent to the Tigris and Euphrates rivers. Here the Sumerians formed small theocratic city-states, each ruled by a *patesi,* a high priest who governed in the name of a local god and for the benefit of a strong priestly class. Occasionally the individual city-states became leagued in military confederations, and around 2300 B.C. they were united into a large kingdom under the Akkadian ruler Sargon I. During most of the third millennium, however, Mesopotamia remained more decentralized and preserved more local autonomy than Egypt, although no feudal tendencies developed.

Unlike Egypt, which was relatively sheltered, Mesopotamia was open to invasion. This geographic difference may explain why Mesopotamian religion was, on the whole, more pessimistic, with its gods pictured as angry and wrathful, and its legends of the Creation and the Flood colored with vengeance and deceit. The Mesopotamians did not mummify their dead and at first showed little faith in an afterlife, a fact which may account for their later fascination with the myths of death and resurrection. At the same time, they placed great emphasis on obedience to the gods and on fertility rites, both of which influenced the later Hebrews.

Mesopotamia's position astride the trade routes between the Mediterranean, Persia, and India, as well as its own abundant agricultural production, led to the development of a flourishing commerce. To support this trade, the Mesopotamians built roads and canals for communication and transport, and developed mathematics, bookkeeping, and cuneiform writing, a form of wedge-shaped ciphers pressed into clay tablets. They also placed great emphasis on laws, particularly property laws, which were later codified and exerted much influence on Babylonian and Hebraic legislation.

India and China

Simultaneously with those of Egypt and Mesopotamia, civilizations flourished in the Indus River valley of India and somewhat later also in the Huang River valley of northern China. Although writing existed in both areas, inscriptions so far discovered are few in number and have not yet been deciphered, so that our knowledge of this period is legendary. Technically therefore the third millennium B.C. for India and China must still be considered as prehistory. Recent excavations at Mohenjo-Daro in India have produced evidence of an advanced urban society that enjoyed extensive trade with Mesopotamia.

Indo-European invasions and the second millennium

Some time around 2000 B.C., great movements of peoples fundamentally affected most civilizations known to us. Numerous Indo-European tribes gradually established themselves in Russia, Central Europe, the Balkans, Greece, and the Italian Peninsula, invaded Egypt, overran the Near East, and settled in Persia and India. Among them were the Aryans, the Hittites, Kassites, Mitanni, Ionians, and a host of other peoples important in ancient history.

The newcomers

We do not know the areas where these Indo-European tribes originated. They apparently stemmed from various ethnic groups and appeared everywhere under different names, although they spoke related languages and shared many fundamental beliefs and customs. Well armed with bronze axes, they also benefited from great mobility in battle, since they were equipped with horses and chariots, both unknown until then in the Mediterranean. Organized into tight groups under ambitious leaders, they usually succeeded in dominating the populations of areas they overran.

In some regions, such as northern India, the invaders mixed and intermarried with the local peoples; in Greece and other areas, they formed an elite of conquerors; almost everywhere, they perpetuated beliefs and rituals that were common to most Indo-European tribes. Although these ancient beliefs and rituals were later altered by changes in thought and institutions, their remnants became an inherent part of the behavioral patterns in Western civilization. Similarly, most of the peoples of the conquered areas retained the basic Indo-European language, and hence similar modes of expression. Thus, the Indo-European invasions furnished common links that help explain parallel traits in the cultures of Europe, North Africa, and the Near and Middle East.

Among the common beliefs, a few are of special interest. The Indo-Europeans believed that the soul was immortal and that after death it lived underground near the buried body from which it had departed. The earliest Vedas of the Aryans in India, later Egyptian legends, and many Greek and Roman practices echoed this belief. Since the soul lived in or near the tomb, it needed food, even slaves and horses. Egyptian, Greek, Roman, and Norse tombs, for example, were filled with ample supplies. Moreover, elaborate burial services were instituted, less for the sake of the dead body than of the living soul. If a soul was not properly buried, it wandered about the earth and became an evil spirit. Sophocles' drama *Antigone* is merely one of many examples from ancient history and literature stressing the importance of proper burial. Even though the Hindus soon turned to cremating their dead and introduced the concept of the transmigration of souls (theory of reincarnation), and the later Greeks and Christians believed in a special Elysium, or Heaven, for souls, much of the Indo-European thought pattern remained in Western civilization. When burying our dead, we still entomb relatives in adjacent tombs to permit family souls to be together after death, and we chant *requiescat in pace* (may he rest in peace), surely an enjoinment to a living soul rather than to an inanimate body.

Similarly, the Indo-Europeans worshiped all the dead, not merely dead heroes. Hindus still worship their forebears; Greeks and Romans venerated the spirits of departed ancestors in the form of *demons* and *lares;* today, we pay reverence to our forefathers as an essential part of social behavior.

Fire, according to the Indo-Europeans, was sacred, not merely useful or destructive. The hearth in most households was considered a sacrosanct place, as is so well illustrated in the *Iliad*. The Hindus worshiped the god of fire Agni, whose Indo-European name is still preserved in such words as "ignite." The Greeks venerated Prometheus and honored their Olympic flame, while the Romans revered the vestal virgins tending the sacred fire in the Roman forum. Today we still speak of the hearth of the household and burn candles in church.

Even some of our marriage ceremonies originated with the Indo-Europeans, who worshiped family gods. The young bride had to be introduced to the gods of her husband's family through a religious ceremony. Hence marriage came to be regarded as a sacred institution. Other marriage customs may hark back to Indo-European times: the bride wears white robes to show her purity; the husband carries her, seemingly by force, over the threshold of their new house, to introduce her to his family gods; the new couple participates in the ceremonial sharing of bread or cake in front of the sacred hearth.

Egypt and the empire

After about two centuries of feudal disorder and political division, Egyptian unity was gradually restored around 2000 B.C., opening the period of the Middle Kingdom. With their capital at Thebes—the center of the Old Kingdom had been further north around Memphis—the pharaohs recast administrative institutions and created a large civil service in order to gain more control over the independent nomarchs. A standing army was set up and military expeditions were launched south into Nubia and east into Canaan. Egypt's former isolation began to end. Considerable trade, carried mostly in Egyptian ships, developed with Crete, Syria, and Phoenicia. More-over, Egypt permitted the immigration of small groups of foreigners and their settlement in the Delta region. Conceivably Abraham's tribe was among those which settled in northern Egypt sometime during the eight-eenth century. Gradually, Egypt grew immensely wealthy, her cultural basis broadened, and art and literature flourished.

However, the pharaohs of the Middle Kingdom could not reassume all the powers held by their predecessors of the Old Kingdom. Feudal pockets remained. Moreover, unlike the Mesopotamians whose class divisions resem-bled castes, the Egyptians had developed a surprising sense of equality among men, especially before the law. Such incipient "democratization" made the re-establishment of absolutism more difficult. The same is also no-ticeable in the role played by women in political and economic life and in the sudden popularity of the Osiris legend, a religious myth of death and resurrection that promised immortality for everybody and a day of final judgment with equal treatment for all.

Since Egypt lay further removed from the initial point of impact of the Indo-European invasions, it was at first not much affected by the newcomers. Hittites, Kassites, and Mitanni overran much of the Near East during the eighteenth century and temporarily established strong states. But they de-voted almost the same energy to fighting each other as to suppressing local populations. Then, around 1650 B.C., the Hyksos, a mixture of Semitic and Indo-European peoples, began to infiltrate into northern Egypt, and estab-lished themselves as masters of most of the country. The result was a pro-found change in Egyptian life.

Resenting domination by outsiders, the Egyptians gradually discarded their preference for individualistic independence and became willing to unite behind a common leader. From the Hyksos they adopted the horse and new methods of warfare. The rulers of Thebes once again took the initiative, and by 1550 B.C. they had freed Egypt of Hyksos domination. The new pharaohs promptly re-established centralized rule over all of Egypt. Their power and glory was such that they could eliminate local resistance by the nomarchs. Moreover, with their appetite whetted by the successful campaigns against the Hyksos, the pharaohs became imperialistic and thus inaugurated another period in Egyptian history, the New Kingdom or Empire.

Under the Empire, which lasted from about 1550 to the eleventh century, Egypt was ruled by a number of skilled pharaohs, many of whom exercised absolute power at home and gloried in military conquests abroad. Thutmose III (about 1500–1450), for example—sometimes called the Napoleon of Egypt—conquered Palestine, Phoenicia, and Syria, and extended Egyptian domination to the upper Euphrates River. Details of his military exploits can still be read today inscribed along the walls of the great temple at Karnak. With wealth and tribute flowing in from conquered lands and neighbors, Egypt further prospered in material splendor, in magnificent temples, tombs, paintings, and sculptures. Some pharaohs, like the famous Ramses II (1292–1225), devoted much of their resources to building vast edifices along the Nile Valley.

The power of the pharaohs did not remain unchallenged. The priests of the Theban god Ammon, to whom they attributed the victory over the Hyksos, soon gained in wealth and influence. They demanded tribute from conquered peoples, tried to undermine the importance of Osiris and other gods, and further enriched themselves by selling magical formulas designed to ensure salvation. Some of these formulas have been preserved in the *Book of the Dead*. By the fourteenth century, a power struggle had developed between the pharaohs and Ammon's priestly class.

The pharaoh Amenhotep IV (1375–1358), whose wife, Nefertiti, is so well known from existing sculptures, attempted to undermine the power of Ammon's priests through a religious revolution. He proclaimed a new sun god, Aton, the source of all creation, changed his own name to Ikhnaton, meaning "pleasing to Aton," and founded a new capital, Akhetaton, in order to escape the influence of the Theban priests. The new religion was clearly monotheistic. Beautiful hymns, some resembling the later songs of the Hebrews in adoration of Jehovah, were composed in worship of the new omnipotent deity. "Thy works are prodigious, and hidden from us, sole God, to whom no other is likened." Ethical behavior was stressed, and painting suddenly took on a naturalistic tone. Historians wonder whether this religious revolution was primarily Amenhotep's instrument for reducing the political and economic power of the Ammon priesthood, whether it was an attempt to unify his large empire under a single new god, or whether the pharaoh was reacting against the prevalent concepts of mechanical salvation. Similarly, it is debatable whether the Aton worship influenced the Hebrews, since we are not certain whether they were still in Egypt or had already crossed the Red Sea on their way to Palestine.

Amenhotep's religious reforms hardly survived his short reign. Am-

mon's' priests soon regained power and attempted to extirpate the very name
of Ihknaton. Then, after two more centuries of relative political stability and
order, Egypt declined. The empire was gradually lost, Libyans and Ethiopians raided the land, and Ammon's priests ruled in the name of ever
weaker pharaohs. During the last millennium before Christ, Egypt suffered
from intermittent foreign invasions until the Persians finally conquered the
country in the sixth century. Thereafter, Egyptian culture became stagnant
while the land remained under foreign occupation—Persian, Macedonian,
Roman, Arab, Turk, French, English—and did not regain its independence
until the present century.

Mesopotamia

The history of Mesopotamia, Asia Minor, and the coastal regions of the
eastern Mediterranean during the second millennium is more complex than
that of Egypt. Kingdoms and civilizations, some Indo-European, some
Semitic, rose and fell in bewildering order. Babylonians conquered Assyrians, Kassites routed Babylonians, Mitanni battled Egyptians over possession
of Phoenicia, and Hittites fought with their many neighbors. Each people
had its own religion, invented its own writing—some of which has not yet
been deciphered—developed its own customs, while at the same time engaging in commercial and cultural exchanges with other groups.

Among the most influential of these civilizations was the first Babylonian Empire (nineteenth to seventeenth centuries). The kings of Babylon
extinguished the independent power of the local *patesi* and established a single system of government supported by an efficient tax structure. To enhance
their authority they claimed partial divine powers for themselves.

One of their kings, Hammurabi (about 1700), promulgated a famous
code of 285 laws as a basis for uniform legislation and judicial procedure for
the entire kingdom. These laws, which Hammurabi claimed had been dictated to him by the god of justice, reveal the existence of a fairly complex
society. In parts, the code was still based on the harsh concept of retaliation—
an eye for an eye—and prescribed the death penalty for what we would call
lesser offenses. It was however not always so strict as later Hebraic law.
Whereas Hammurabi stipulated that "if a son strike his father, they shall cut
off his fingers," *Exodus* (21:15) proclaimed that "he that smiteth his father,
or his mother, shall be surely put to death." Hammurabi's code placed great
stress on rights of women, on property rights in general, and the sanctity of
commercial contracts. It also prescribed the duty of the state to succor the
individual and protect him against loss. One law stated that "if the brigand
be not captured, the man who has been robbed, shall, in the presence of god,
make an itemized statement of his loss, and the city and the governor, in
whose province and jurisdiction the robbery was committed, shall compensate him for whatever was lost."

The Babylonians preserved much of their writing in archives, so that we are fairly well informed about the high order of their civilization. Artistic achievements reveal a highly prosperous society. Around 1600, Babylon was conquered by the Kassites and remained under their occupation for some four centuries. Nevertheless its culture, especially its religion, with its stories of the Creation, its fertility rites, and its predilection for magic and divination, left a strong impact on the subsequent history of the region.

The Aegean basin

The peoples inhabiting the island and shores of the Aegean also made important progress during the third millennium. By 2000 B.C., commercial and artistic leadership of the area had been assumed by the inhabitants of the island of Crete. This Minoan civilization, so named after the legendary King Minos, derived its wealth from the production of pottery and from extensive trade throughout the eastern Mediterranean. A new type of linear script was developed which experts are now beginning to decipher. The Minoan kings built vast, elaborate palaces, such as the one at Cnossus, supplied with plumbing conveniences and adorned with brilliant frescoes.

As a commercial power, backed by a strong fleet, Crete spread its influence over the Aegean Sea and the east coast of Greece. After 1600 B.C., it attained temporary ascendance over the peoples around Mycenae in the Peloponnesus. Around 1400 B.C., however, the Mycenaeans assumed power in their own right. They destroyed Crete's commercial supremacy, sacked the Cretan palaces, and set up their own settlements on various islands of the Aegean Sea. Possibly in one of their raids they also attacked and pillaged the city of Troy, an event celebrated in Homer's *Iliad*. The Mycenaeans remained masters of the Aegean for over two centuries and, together with the Cretans, laid the substructure for later Greek civilization. In the end, the Mycenaeans, too, were overwhelmed by new invaders from the North, the Dorians who started to penetrate into the Greek Peninsula in the twelfth century. The arrival of the Dorians marked the beginning of Greek history as such.

India and China

During the first half of the second millennium, Indo-European peoples, the Aryans, conquered the Iranian plateau, where they became the ancestors of the Persians. They also settled in the fertile plains of northern India between the Indus and Ganges rivers. For the early centuries after their arrival, we have no written historical accounts. This period, 1500 to 800 B.C., is often called the Vedic Age.

The Vedas, at first transmitted orally and later recorded in Indo-Aryan (Sanskrit) writing, were collections of prayers, hymns, chants, and sacred formulas, mixed with homilies and folklore. Together with archaeological findings, the Vedas reveal how much the Aryans assimilated the art and culture of pre-invasion India. Religious imagery was retained, among them certain fertility symbols, the sacredness of animals such as bulls, elephants, snakes, and monkeys, and the swastika as a token of good luck. On the other hand, the Aryans introduced their own Indo-European gods—which accounts for the similarity of the pantheons of India, Persia, Greece, and Rome. The Persian gods Mithras and Ahura were the same as Mitra and Asura in India. The Indo-Aryan god of the sky Dyaus (related to the Latin word *deus*) was the same as Zeus, the Greek god of light and sky. Just as the Romans later changed this lord of the bright heaven into Jovis (Djovis or Jove) and ultimately into Jupiter (Jovis-pater), so the Aryan Dyaus in the Upanishads gave way to *Prajāpati* (Almighty Jupiter), the supreme god, ultimately representing the All.

During the early Vedic Age, the Aryans of India converted their gods into abstract, spiritual forces more in consonance with the religious instincts of the Pre-Aryans. This fusion resulted in early Hinduism, an ethical and religious system similar to those of other Indo-Europeans in the West, optimistic and affirmative, and not yet colored by preoccupation with reincarnation and the World Soul.

Unlike the other areas discussed, China was apparently not affected by Indo-European invasions, and its history during the second millennium remains shrouded in mystery. From about 1500 to about 1000 B.C., the so-called Shang emperors probably extended their political control to the South, East, and West from the Huang River valley and thus widened the area of Chinese civilization. Pictographic and ideographic inscriptions appear similar to later Chinese writing and the bronze vessels from this period show an extraordinarily vivid style.

The era of small states and the new imperialism

Despite the seeming confusion in the rise and fall of civilizations, there was a parallelism which fascinates those historians who assume some underlying historical spirit or an organic force that moves history. Almost everywhere, the second millennium of large states was followed after 1000 B.C. by an era of small states: China under the Chou dynasty consisted of numerous feudal entities; northern India was divided into many small Aryan states; Iran split into Elamite, Medic, and Persian kingdoms; the narrow shorelands of the eastern Mediterranean were crowded with tiny kingdoms (Judah, Israel, Tyre, Syria, Damascus, and others); the former Hittite empire of Asia Minor was now occupied by Phrygia, Lydia, and Armenia; and small political units dotted the Greek and Italian peninsulas.

Between about 700 B.C. and the Christian era, the centuries of small states were followed by a period of new and ever vaster empires: Assyria (eighth to seventh centuries), Chaldea (sixth century), Persia (sixth to fourth centuries), Macedonia (fourth century), the Maurya empire of India (fourth to second centuries), and the Ch'in empire in China (third century).

Similarly, historians are struck by the inexplicable parallelism in the development of the great new ethical movements that so profoundly affected later history: Confucius, Lao-tse, Buddha, Ezekiel, and perhaps Isaiah II and Zoroaster all lived during the sixth century before Christ.

Phoenicia and Palestine

Among the many small states of this period—apart from those in Greece and on the Italian Peninsula—those of the Phoenicians and of the Hebrews exerted particular long-range influence because of their exceptional contributions to the development of Western civilization.

The coastal cities of Phoenicia, ranging about 250 miles north from Mt. Carmel and inhabited primarily by Semitic people, had become wealthy centers of trade as early as the third millennium. As long as Egypt and later Crete dominated the seas, the naval prowess of the Phoenicians could not make itself fully felt. Starting in the twelfth century, however, they threw off foreign domination and turned their region into independent and powerful city-states. For the next five centuries, the Phoenicians were the most active traders and navigators of the Mediterranean. They established colonies and trading posts along the shores of the Mediterranean, on Cyprus, Sicily, and Sardinia, in southern Spain, and in Africa, where they founded the city of Carthage. The Phoenicians exported glass, metal, and wood—the famous cedars of Lebanon. Their trade in purple dye may have acquired for them the name "Phoenician" from the Greek word "*φοινιξ*" meaning red. Although primarily interested in commerce, they also achieved importance in the interchange of ideas. Possibly they played a significant role in the development of the alphabet that was eventually adopted by the Greeks. Based on sounds rather than pictographs or syllables, and thus simplifying the art of writing, the Phoenician-Greek alphabet furnished the basis for all later Western scripts.

Starting in the eighth century, the Phoenicians suffered from pressure by the new rising empires in the East—Assyria, Chaldea, and Persia. Four hundred years later, after their conquest by Alexander the Great, they disappeared from history as an independent people, except for their colony in Carthage.

Details concerning the history of the Hebrews before they settled in Palestine are still in dispute, especially in regard to dates. Presumably they first lived in the Arabian desert, then wandered to Mesopotamia, and later to Canaan. From there some of the tribes went to Egypt where they remained for several centuries. After Moses led the Exodus from Egypt, the Israelites settled in the Sinai Peninsula before gradually infiltrating and conquering the Promised Land. By the eleventh century, the various tribes, led by

Judges, were in control of most of Palestine except for the coastal strip which had been seized by non-Semitic peoples, the Philistines. Between about 1020 and 933 B.C., the tribes were tenuously united under a monarchy founded by Saul (about 1020–1013). His successor, King David (1013–973), the victor over the Philistines, established his capital at Jerusalem and attempted to give cohesion to his loosely knit state, while Solomon (973–933), the last king of the united monarchy, tried to make himself an absolute ruler, surrounded by luxurious splendor, including vast palaces, temples, and his legendary one thousand wives and concubines. But neither monarchical institution nor fear of enemies could really unite the tribes. After Solomon's death political unity disappeared. (See Map 1.)

The northern tribes, eventually called the Ten Lost Tribes, formed the Kingdom of Israel which survived for two centuries before its destruction and absorption by the Assyrians in 722 B.C. The two southern tribes around Jerusalem, as the Kingdom of Judah, remained independent for over three centuries of almost constant warfare with neighboring states, until Jerusalem was finally seized by the Chaldean Nebuchadnezzar in 586 B.C. and some of its people were taken into captivity in Babylon.

The Jews of Judah and those in Babylon, who under Persian rule in the late sixth century were allowed to return to Jerusalem and rebuild the temple, were the perpetuators of the Hebrew religion. This religion had undergone vast changes over the centuries. In the days of Moses, the worship of Jehovah, or Yahweh, as a supreme law giver had begun to supplant tribal worship of spirits and anthropomorphic gods. As the Pentateuch, the first five books of the Old Testament shows, Hebrew religion taught a code of moral and social behavior rather than a way of salvation. The laws of Exodus, perhaps influenced in part by Hammurabi's code, reveal a great sense of equity and justice—although frequently extremely harsh—but they promise no rewards in life after death. Moreover, the Hebraic religion was as yet henotheistic, proclaiming Yahweh to be the sole god of the Jews, but not denying the possible existence of other gods for other peoples.

During the period of the prophets, from the ninth to the sixth centuries, especially during the Babylonian captivity, monotheism gradually supplanted henotheism. Yahweh became the sole, omnipotent god of the universe, not just of Judah; his image was spiritualized; his thoughts became unfathomable, as shown in the Book of Job.

After the Jews came under Chaldean and later Persian domination, they attempted to safeguard their identity by keeping their religion pure and insisting on strict observance of special rituals, such as circumcision. Nonetheless their religion continued to change under the impact of Chaldean, Persian, and ultimately Greek ideas. The experience of the Babylonian captivity added a touch of pessimistic fatalism, and it is probably under Persian influence that the Jews began to conceive of evil as a real power, to stress salvation, and, above all, to long for a redeemer, or Messiah.

Assyria, Chaldea, and Persia

First of the new great empires to rise was that of the Assyrians whose civilization near the headwaters of the Tigris River dated back to the third millennium. Under constant attack by neighbors, the Assyrians developed a formidable army, equipped mostly with iron weapons and considered well-nigh invincible during the height of Assyrian power (eighth to seventh centuries). By 650 B.C. the Assyrian Empire stretched from the Egyptian delta to the highlands of Armenia, from the Taurus Mountains to lower Mesopotamia. At their capital of Nineveh, the Assyrian rulers collected an extensive library of cuneiform tablets, dealing with religion, laws, medicine, and mathematics, knowledge they had largely gathered from the peoples they had conquered. Assyria thus furthered the process of disseminating and amalgamating diverse cultures, a trend which ultimately consolidated Near Eastern civilization. Although the Assyrians tried to rule their vast empire through an elaborate system of provincial administration, through the establishment of good communications and the ever present threat of reprisals by the army, they had to face frequent revolts by subject peoples. The empire turned out to be a fragile structure, which was easily destroyed by the Chaldeans who demolished Nineveh in 612 B.C.

The Chaldean or Neo-Babylonian Empire that followed was consolidated around Babylon in 625 B.C. and spread to include all of Mesopotamia and the shores of the eastern Mediterranean. Under Nebuchadnezzar (605–561), Babylon was turned into a resplendent capital, with its hanging gardens and sumptuous palaces. The Chaldeans were much interested in astronomy and practiced astrology for purposes of divination. Their gods, although similar to earlier Babylonian deities, were likened to stars and hence became far removed from humans. This may account for the Chaldeans' fatalistic attitude, for their awe of divinity and their humility before their gods—an attitude unknown to the Indo-Europeans, but later shared by Hebrews and Christians. Despite its cultural brilliance, the Chaldean Empire was short-lived and fell to Persian conquest in 538 B.C.

Its successor, the Persian Empire, was larger than any of its predecessors. In the span of a few decades during the late sixth century, the Persian rulers (Cyrus, Cambyses, and Darius I) extended their domination from Libya, on the western fringes of Egypt, and the Hellespont to Afghanistan and the Indus Valley in India. To administer such a vast empire, they placed special governors (satraps) in charge of each province and had these in turn supervised by royal inspectors. To bind the empire together, they constructed an excellent road system, connecting the various capitals with outlying provinces; special relay horse stations every few miles expedited royal messengers. (See Map 3.)

Unlike the Assyrians, the Persians treated subject peoples with some respect, permitting them their own customs and religion, while levying tribute and retaining for themselves political and military power. Although continuing the process of amalgamating Near Eastern culture, they exerted little innovating influence except in the field of religion.

The Persian prophet Zoroaster (sixth century?) taught a dualistic belief, in which Ahura-Mazda, the god of light and goodness, was locked in vital struggle with Ahriman, the god of evil. Ahura was destined to win some day over Ahriman, and Zoroaster taught that it was man's duty to side with the god of goodness so that on the day of judgment he would be found on the "right" side. These Persian concepts of dualism and of an ultimate day of judgment influenced the Hebrews, Romans, and later the Christians.

During the fifth century, the Persian Empire became engaged in a contest with the independent city-states of Greece, and it ultimately succumbed to the conquests of Alexander the Great in the fourth century. In a sense, Alexander's empire was a continuation of the Persian Empire with Greek-Macedonian overtones. After its dissolution, the western areas of the former Persian state were gradually absorbed by Rome, but east of the Tigris, on the Iranian plateau, a new Parthian Empire arose which succeeded in maintaining its independence against Roman pressure and remained an important bridge between the Mediterranean and India. This Parthian or Neo-Persian Empire existed for another thousand years until its destruction by Moslem Arabs in the seventh century A.D.

The parallels of India and China

The Vedic Age in India was followed by the Brahman or Epic Age (800–300 B.C.), a period during which changes in Hinduism gradually took India out of the mainstream of Indo-European cultures. This religious and social development, encouraged by the Brahmans (priests) in an effort to increase their power, can be seen in the Brahmanas and Upanishads, treatises on the nature of man and the cosmos as well as reinterpretations of the older Vedas. Written over a period of centuries after about 800 B.C., these writings show the earlier optimism of the Aryans to have given way to the mood of resignation more typical of later Hinduism. The doctrine of reincarnation through the transmigration of souls in accordance with the law of *karma,* which rewards good or bad action by determining the stage of existence in the next life, had become an integral part of Hinduism. The material world was belittled and stress was laid on the world soul of which every individual soul was a part. Many new gods had been added or granted more importance, such as the fearsome Shiva, "who danced upon an infant." Moreover, a hierarchical caste system was developed and strictly enforced by the Brahmans.

Many of these new concepts may also be found in India's great epics, the *Mahabharata* and the *Ramayana,* orally composed during an earlier age, but gradually altered and written down in Sanskrit toward the end of the Epic Age. Somewhat like the Homeric epics, the *Mahabharata* and *Ramayana* contained panoramic stories of heroes and gods and represent a storehouse of information on social and ethical practices.

During the Brahman Age, the Indians continued to expand their domination to the East and South but failed to achieve political unity. Numerous kingdoms existed in a relatively small area. Disunity also characterized religion, for Brahmanism did not remain unchallenged. During the sixth and fifth centuries, many religious teachers were active, perhaps motivated by a desire to break the power of the Brahman class. Some taught Jainism, a strict asceticism which ultimately became an integral part of Hindu civilization. Others advocated communal property as a way to salvation, while still others proclaimed the sanctity of all life, including that of the lowest form of animals, a concept that has also remained popular in India to this day.

Among these reformers was Gautama (about 563–483), later called the Buddha, "the enlightened one," who rejected Brahmanism as well as asceticism. He founded a community where his disciples could practice his new doctrine of salvation—the attainment of Nirvana—through meditation and personal religious experience and through the abandonment of all craving. Buddha advocated "the middle path" where nothing in human conduct was done in excess, and man led a simple, selfless, moral life. He accepted the Hindu concept of reincarnation but asserted that man could escape from this endless suffering by leading a pure and simple life.

Although Buddha's teachings were meant to be a philosophy of life, after his death Buddhism was turned into a religion which was spread through India and abroad by missionary monks. A split among Buddhists soon occurred. Hinayana Buddhism, a more strict and orthodox version, was accepted primarily in Ceylon, Burma, and Thailand; Mahayana, a looser interpretation that deified the Buddha himself became popular in most of Asia, particularly Tibet.

During Buddha's lifetime, Indian disunity made the area a tempting prey to its neighbors. Around 500 B.C. Darius I of Persia invaded the Indus Valley and added it to his empire, and during the fourth century, Alexander the Great assumed control of the area. Chafing under foreign control, the Indians finally accepted the idea of political unity and launched their first experiment in imperialism.

After Alexander's empire fell apart, the Indians under the Maurya dynasty (321–184) expelled the Persians and Macedonians and consolidated a unified state of their own. Yet they kept close cultural contact with Persia and Greece, an influence which can be seen in their sculpture and architecture. The Maurya dynasty produced two eminent rulers, Chandragupta (321–297), its founder, and his grandson Asoka (274–236), a truly remarkable king. Most of India was brought under a single, fairly efficient government. Asoka was a devout Buddhist who not only tried to bring peace and prosperity to his subjects but also expected them to lead a moral life in accordance with Buddha's teaching. At the same time he sent missionaries in all directions to convert India's neighbors to the new faith. Yet he remained tolerant at home and made no effort to extirpate Brahmanism. (See Map 11.)

The Maurya dynasty was short-lived and upon its extinction, Indian political unity collapsed. Moreover, there followed a strong Brahman Hindu reaction. In the end, Asoka's missionary zeal abroad and his failure to weaken the Brahman class at home may account for the fact that Buddhism, although originating in India, ultimately became important in Ceylon, Southeast Asia, Tibet, China, and Japan, whereas Hinduism triumphed in India.

Just as India was rent by disunity during this period, so China was divided by feudal decentralization despite the existence of a superficial imperial framework under the Chou dynasty (about 1020–221 B.C.). The Chou emperors made the monarchy hereditary and like rulers in western Asia claimed to be sacred "sons of heaven." Their nominal power extended south to the Yangtze Valley; yet, real political control resided in local rulers and feudal aristocrats, who engaged in frequent civil wars.

Despite this decentralization, the Chou period was one of great prosperity. The fertile soil, improved by elaborate irrigation and cultivated by hand with primitive tools, furnished ample rice and vegetable crops. Silk and other textiles were manufactured and traded on a large scale, with camel and donkey caravans crossing vast areas of Asia. At first using stamped leather as currency, they turned to coined copper around the fifth century B.C., only a few decades after coins were introduced in Lydia in Asia Minor. This commercial activity helped spread Chinese influence as far south as Indo-China.

The Chou period, particularly from the sixth to the fourth centuries B.C., was also the age of China's great philosophers. More concerned with ethics and social cooperation than with metaphysics, these philosophers left an indelible imprint on Chinese culture. Lao-tse (sixth century), about whose life little is known, stressed love and kindness in human relations. Like the eighteenth-century French writer Rousseau, he pleaded for a return to a more natural and hence happier life. His teachings were later turned into a religion called Taoism.

Confucius (about 551–479 B.C.) differed on many points with Lao-tse. Like Socrates, Confucius stressed the importance of knowledge as virtue and as a path to happiness, whereas Lao-tse thought that knowledge might corrupt man's pure existence. Lao-tse was mostly concerned with nature and emotions; Confucius however dealt with man and the intellect. He advocated the golden mean as a standard of conduct. Proper ceremonial behavior was to help man achieve self-discipline and altruistic social cooperation. Believing in the essential goodness and brotherhood of man, Confucius urged family solidarity as the surest basis for a viable society. While Lao-tse distrusted governmental institutions and believed people to be better off without government interference, Confucius advocated a strong, centralized but benevolent government devoted to the well-being of its subjects—a paternalism rarely found in ancient times.

After Confucius, Mo Ti (late fifth century B.C.), an early devotee of utilitarianism, preached the blessings of a simple, plain life and universal pacifism. His social concern was aimed primarily at raising the living standard of the poor. Finally the philosopher Mencius (about 372–289 B.C.), an ardent follower of Confucianism, advocated a type of welfare state as a solution to China's social problems.

Unlike the Indians, the Chinese did not develop comprehensive religious systems and had no strong priestly caste. They worshiped many deities and spirits, including those of their ancestors, but religion tended to be a family ritual rather than adherence to an organized institution.

The legacy of the ancient Near East

Although initially the various civilizations developed in relative isolation, improved communications and transportation, as well as the increased movement of peoples after the second millennium, provided so much cultural contact and interchange that it is futile to speculate whether later ages owed a specific legacy to this or that civilization. One could draw an endless list of such legacies and debate fruitlessly whether their origin has been pinpointed correctly: Did the Egyptians originate architectural columns? Did the Chaldeans invent the twelve signs of the zodiac?

Rather it is important to acknowledge the vast development achieved in pre-Greek and pre-Roman times—in jurisprudence, commercial relations, astronomy, medicine, engineering, agriculture, architecture, ethics, in fact in almost every area of human endeavor—that formed the basis on which the new Mediterranean as well as Asian cultures could flourish. Moreover it is worth recalling that the different cultures from the Nile to the Huang River, despite their outward differences, held many ideas and practices in common. Rather than ascribing this common heritage merely to cultural contact, to a common neolithic substructure, or to the Indo-European invasions, which in any case did not penetrate China, it is perhaps safest to assume that men in society have similar needs and similar ways of satisfying them.

SUGGESTED READINGS

Egypt

Aldred, Cyril, *Egypt to the End of the Old Kingdom* (McGraw, 1965).
Edwards, I. E. S., *The Pyramids of Egypt* (Penguin, 1961).
Fairservis, Walter A., Jr., *Ancient Kingdoms of the Nile* (New American Library).
Frankfort, Henri, *Ancient Egyptian Religion: An Interpretation* (Harper).

Mertz, Barbara, *Temples, Tombs and Hieroglyphs: The Story of Egyptology* (Dell).
Piankoff, Alexandre, *The Shrines of Tut-Ankh-Amon* (Harper, 1962).
Wilson, John A., *The Culture of Ancient Egypt* (U. of Chicago, 1956).

Mesopotamia

Chiera, Edward, *They Wrote on Clay* (U. of Chicago, 1955).
Contenau, Georges, *Everyday Life in Babylon and Assyria* (Norton, 1966). Mesopotamian civilization between 700 and 530 B.C.
Covensky, Milton, *The Ancient Near Eastern Tradition* (Harper, 1966). Deals with Egyptian and Mesopotamian civilizations.
Frye, Richard N., *The Heritage of Persia* (New American Library, 1962).
Gordon, Cyrus, *Hammurabi's Code: Quaint or Forward Looking?* (Holt, 1957).
Gurney, Oliver R., *The Hittites* (Penguin, 1961).
Harden, Donald, *The Phoenicians* (Praeger, 1962).
Heidel, Alexander, *Babylonian Genesis* (U. of Chicago). Translations of cuneiform tablets of the various Babylonian creation stories.
*Kramer, Samuel Noah, *The Sumerians, Their History, Culture, and Character* (U. of Chicago, 1963).
Mallowan, M. E. L., *Early Mesopotamia and Iran* (McGraw, 1966).
Olmstead, A. T., *A History of the Persian Empire, Achaemenid Period* (U. of Chicago, 1948).

Asia

Arvon, Henri, *Buddhism* (Walker, 1963). A general history.
Benda, Harry J., and Larkin, John A., eds., *World of Southeast Asia: Selected Historical Readings* (Harper, 1967).
Chai, Ch'u and Winberg, *Story of Chinese Philosophy* (Simon and Schuster, 1961).
Conze, Edward, *Buddhism: Its Essence and Development* (Harper).
Creel, Herrlee Glessner, *Confucius and the Chinese Way* (Harper, 1960).
Fairservis, Walter A., Jr., *The Origins of Oriental Civilization* (New American Library, 1959).
Fung, Yu-Lan, *A Short History of Chinese Philosophy* (Macmillan, 1960).
Gard, Richard A., ed., *Buddhism* (Simon and Schuster, 1961).
Grousset, René, *Rise and Splendor of the Chinese Empire* (U. of California, 1953).
*Osgood, Cornelius, *The Koreans and Their Culture* (Ronald, 1951).
Radhakrishnan, Sarvepalli, *Hindu View of Life.* (Macmillan, 1927).
Renou, Louis, ed., *Hinduism* (Simon and Schuster, 1963). Collection of Hindu writings.
Renou, Louis, *The Nature of Hinduism* (Walker, 1962).
Rowland, Benjamin, ed., *Ajanta Caves: Early Buddhist Paintings from India* (New American Library).
Storry, Richard, *Japan* (Oxford U. P., 1965).
Watson, William, *Early Civilization in China* (McGraw, 1966).
Welch, Holmes, *Taoism: The Parting of the Way* (Beacon, 1966).
Wheeler, Robert E. M., *The Indus Civilization* (Cambridge U. P.).

The Aegean

Cottrell, Leonard, *Bull of Minos* (Grossett, 1958). On Cretan civilization.
*Davis, Simon, *Decipherment of the Minoan Linear Photographic Scripts* (Humanities, 1967).
Pendlebury, John D. S., *The Archaeology of Crete* (Norton, 1965).
Samuel, Alan E., *The Mycenaeans in History* (Prentice-Hall, 1966).

The Hebrews

Albright, William, *Biblical Period from Abraham to Ezra: An Historical Survey* (Harper).

Allegro, John M., *Dead Sea Scrolls* (Penguin, 1956).

Bickerman, Elias, *From Ezra to the Last of the Maccabees: Foundations of Post-Biblical Judaism* (Schocken, 1962).

Chouraqui, André, *A History of Judaism* (Walker, 1963). Mostly after the Diaspora.

De Vaux, Roland, *Ancient Israel,* Vol. I, "Social Institutions"; Vol. II, "Religious Institutions" (McGraw).

Gray, John, *Archaeology and the Old Testament World* (Harper, 1965).

Heidel, Alexander, *The Gilgamesh Epic and Old Testament Parallels* (U. of Chicago, 1949).

Hertzberg, Arthur, ed., *Judaism* (Simon and Schuster, 1963). Collection of writings of the Jewish tradition.

Moscati, Sabatino, *Ancient Semitic Civilizations* (Putnam, 1960).

Orlinsky, Harry M., *Ancient Israel* (Cornell, 1954).

Schonfield, Hugh J., *A History of Biblical Literature* (New American Library, 1962).

Ancient Culture

Gaster, Theodor H., ed., *The Oldest Stories in the World* (Beacon, 1958). Myths and legends of the Babylonians, Hittites, and Canaanites.

Gordon, Cyrus H., *The Ancient Near East* (Norton, 1965).

Groenewegen-Frankfort, H. A. and Ashmole, Bernard, *The Ancient World,* Vol. I (New American Library). An account of ancient art.

James, E. O., *The Ancient Gods* (Putnam, 1960).

*Muller, Herbert J., *Freedom in the Ancient World* (Harper, 1961). Deals with the Near East, Greece and Rome.

Neugebauer, Otto, *The Exact Sciences in Antiquity* (Harper).

CHAPTER III

❧ *Greece*
(Eighth to Third Centuries B.C.)

Greece today extends over some 51,000 square miles—about the size of Alabama. The ancient Greek city-states, occupying the mainland and numerous islands in the Aegean and Ionian seas, covered only about half that area. On the mainland, Greece stretched some two hundred and fifty miles from Mount Olympus in the north to the southern tip of the Peloponnesus, with a maximum width of two hundred miles. Yet, from this small area the Greeks spread their influence and settlements throughout the Mediterranean coastline and developed a civilization which became the basis of the Western world in thought, art, and even political organization. (See Map 2.)

The soil of Greece, although it produced wheat, was generally arid, adequate for growing olives and grapes and for raising goats, but insufficient for feeding a growing population. Unlike the Egyptians and Mesopotamians, the Greeks experienced food shortages at an early date and found themselves compelled to import food, expand commerce by exporting pottery, olive oil, and wine, and dispatch their excess population to colonize new areas. Fortunately, Greece, like Great Britain, was aided by geography. Deep inlets provided easy access to the sea and permitted the Greeks to develop sizable commercial fleets.

The formative years to 500 B.C.

The early periods of Greek history—from the Ionian settlements (around 2000 B.C.) through the Dorian invasions to the end of the seventh century—are largely shrouded in mythology. The historian must rely on archaeological data, Homeric legends, the poetic works of Hesiod (eighth century), and fragmentary descriptions from the seventh century. The paucity of written sources is somewhat offset by the work of later Greek historians, such as Herodotus and Thucydides (fifth century), who wrote in part about earlier times and showed remarkable knowledge, as corroborated by archaeological findings. These Greek historians displayed a strikingly modern sense of history and, in many ways, remain models of historiography down to our own day.

The Homeric Age

The Homeric legends of the Trojan War and of the adventures of Ulysses, probably composed in the ninth century B.C., depict events reaching back to the twelfth century and thus contain elements from late Minoan and Mycenaean times as well as Homer's own period (see p. 20). Homer's *Iliad* and *Odyssey* furnish the historian with insight into the formative years of Greek history. At the same time, these works served as literary prototypes for later epics and provided the Greeks with a pantheon of Olympian gods and with much stock material for their dramas.

The *Iliad* shows that from earliest times, the Greeks cherished individualism and were disunited in tribal rivalry even in times of crisis. During the Trojan War, according to Homer, the tribes fought separately under their respective leaders, just as in later centuries each city-state sought to retain its independence. In fact, the separation between the various city-states was such that rather than speak of a political history of Greece, it would be more accurate to write separately about each of the city-states. In part, this disunity derived from tribal allegiances as well as religious conservatism, since each city-state venerated its own god or demigod as the founding father of the land. The rugged mountain chains, dividing the Greek Peninsula into small, isolated units, and the concomitant need for local defense and administration must also have contributed to keeping the various states politically separated from one another.

Despite this pronounced political individualism, the Greeks early developed a cultural unity which allows us to speak of Greek civilization as a single entity. The various Greek peoples shared a common language, believed in the same Olympian gods and Homeric legends, and heeded the same oracles, particularly that of Apollo at Delphi. To harmonize relations between the city-states which were so frequently locked in war, the Greeks developed several joint activities. Fiercely competitive, they naturally enjoyed interstate games. The Olympics, begun in 776 B.C. and held every four years thereafter in honor of Zeus, were soon supplemented by the Corinthian and the Pythian games in Delphi, in honor of Apollo. The Delian festivals, designed primarily for Ionian city-states, included athletic, music, and dance contests, while other festivals, such as those at Corinth, included poetry and drama competitions. A possible binding element among the Greeks may also have been the amphictyonic councils, in which delegates from many city-states met twice a year to deliberate on public affairs and the guardianship of important temples, particularly those of Apollo and Demeter.

According to the Homeric epics, the Greeks early developed their political unit of the city-state which became typical for ancient Greek history. These city-states were small, usually built around a fortified citadel or acropolis. At its height, the Athenian state, for example, was only twice the size of Los Angeles. The government of these city-states was usually in the hands of kings, but Homer's frequent references to councils makes it probable that even these early rulers were never absolute. Power and prestige were apparently vested in a landholding aristocracy which advised the king, who acted primarily as a commander-in-chief of the army. Homer's preoccupation with the life of the nobility, although merely mirroring the social structure of his age, furnished Western culture with the epic and dramatic tradition that associated heroes with the deeds of nobles.

The mores of Homeric Greece present an interesting mixture of family blood feuds and superstition with the strong rational overtones which became the trademark of Greek civilization. Since the Olympian gods demanded obedience from mortals, divination and soothsaying guided the actions of men; yet, the gods were presented in human forms and with human foibles, and heroes could trick them and even become demigods themselves. Although respectful of the higher powers on Mt. Olympus, the Homeric Greeks already displayed that self-reliance and this-worldliness that was to become characteristic of classical thought.

Governmental and social development

From the eighth to the sixth centuries, the various city-states developed a variety of political frameworks which turned Greece into an ideal field of observation for later political scientists. The city-state of Sparta retained the monarchical edifice, but implemented a system of dual kingship in which two hereditary kings balanced each other's power and were themselves supervised by an elected council. In most other city-states, monarchy was gradually replaced by the rule of landholding nobles, who were the defenders of the state in times of war. Actually, effective power usually passed into the hands of a small ruling group or oligarchy, rather than of the aristocracy in general. As a result, a few rich families dominated most city-states. In such timocracies, the cleavage between rich and poor increased until, according to Aristotle, "the poorer classes, men, women, and children, were in absolute slavery to the rich."

Concern over this growing social cleavage was noticeable by the eighth century. While Homer had shown interest only in the nobility, Hesiod in his *Works and Days* discussed the life of ordinary people, especially farmers. Homer's insistence on vengeance and honor gave way to Hesiod's stress on justice. As the latter wrote, "For whoever knows the right and is ready to speak it, farseeing Zeus gives him prosperity." During the seventh century, the lower classes gained further safeguards, especially in Athens, for which we have the best historical sources. The powers formerly held by kings were delegated to nine *archons,* elected annually: one to act as the executive, one as the religious representative of the state, one as the commander of the army in time of war, and the remaining six to be the guardians of the law. The emphasis on law and justice as a safeguard against arbitrary rule, elaborated during these formative centuries, was to be one of the most far-reaching Greek contributions to Western civilization. It is typified by the Athenian Draco who, during the late seventh century, codified the law and once and for all established the supremacy of public justice over private vengeance.

Of course, laws alone did not pacify the lower classes who aspired to political and social equality, especially those peasants who were enslaved for debts. Starting in the early sixth century, the poorer citizens in many city-states were attracted by the promises of *tyrants* to secure for them additional rights. Such *tyrants,* who became a familiar phenomenon in Greek history, were not necessarily cruel rulers as the word implies today, but were politi-cians who gained power by extralegal means or who maintained themselves in dominant positions by appealing to the mob, frequently in demagogic fashion. Despite the questionable motives of some tyrants, they helped in many city-states curtail the power of the aristocracy and prepare the way for limited democracy—limited, since it always was restricted to a small number of citizens and never extended to slaves or countless resident aliens.

Colonization

From the eighth century on, the Greeks sent out expeditions to establish colonies on the northern Aegean Islands and along the coasts of the Black Sea and the Mediterranean. These colonies maintained close cultural and economic contacts with the founding cities and shared the same gods, but became independent political units—again demonstrating the political indi-vidualism of the Greeks. Besides stimulating commerce and spreading Greek culture, these colonies affected the city-states themselves. The conquering colonists gathered large contingents of slaves which they sold to their mother city-states, and returning colonists brought new and diverse ideas to their compatriots, thereby infusing the Greeks with an unusually cosmopolitan outlook.

Sparta and Athens

By the sixth century, the differences between two of the most important city-states, Sparta and Athens, appeared considerable, with Sparta conserva-tive and culturally isolationist, and Athens increasingly dynamic and cosmo-politan. But the picture one often finds, describing the Spartans as militaris-tic aggressors and the Athenians as peaceful artists and philosophers, needs retouching. One must recall that the Spartans left little literature and that most of our data comes from Athenian writers.

In the course of the eighth and seventh centuries, the Spartans conquered populous neighboring Messina and enslaved its population. Eager to exploit the conquered lands and afraid of slave rebellions, the Spartans revised their constitution toward the end of the seventh century, establishing strict state control over the population and tightening up a caste-like class structure. The slaves (*helots*) were to till the land and perform hard labor. The middle class (*perioeci,* or dwellers around), free men of non-Spartan cities, were given exclusive rights over commerce and business; they paid taxes, served in the lower echelons of the army, but had no rights of citizenship. A small group of Spartan citizens, the only ones to enjoy some limited leisure time, were trained primarily to govern and fight. Young Spartans were educated by and for the state; communal life transcended family ties. The state owned the land and in turn furnished the citizens with the means of livelihood, so that the Spartans were free to devote their energy to administrative and military endeavors.

This strict system transformed Sparta into the foremost power on the Peloponnesus, enabling her in the course of the sixth century to turn most of her neighbors into tributary or allied states, loosely bound together in a Peloponnesian League. Sparta had previously established some colonies, but preoccupation with the Peloponnesus had lessened her interest in colonial, commercial, and naval matters, turning her predominantly into a land power. Her conservative frame also affected her foreign policy among the Greek states. Wars with other states, including particularly Athens, were no longer motivated solely by economic rivalry or a desire for territorial gain, but frequently had ideological overtones. As a champion of conservatism, Sparta interfered in the affairs of other states to block the growing power of the lower classes or unseat a tyrant who displayed democratic tendencies.

Athens, for her part, was frequently rocked by class strife and was politically quite unstable. Yet she never abandoned her dynamic outlook. She, too, interfered in other states and constantly expanded her far-reaching colonial and commercial empire, frequently by force, and widened her intellectual and political horizon to embrace many peoples of the Mediterranean shore. But she remained an open city, diversified in her population. Her famous statesman Solon (640?–558?) encouraged immigration by foreign craftsmen; and, according to Thucydides, Pericles in the fifth century asserted proudly: "Our city is thrown open to the world, and we never expel a foreigner or prevent him from seeing or learning anything."

Class distinctions in Athens were less rigid than in Sparta. As in many states, there were the citizens who alone enjoyed full political rights; the resident aliens (*metics*) were active in the commercial and intellectual life of the city but could neither vote nor own land; and finally there were the slaves. In contrast to the relatively few classes among Spartan citizens, there were numerous subdivisions within the Athenian citizen class, based on the amount of land owned as well as economic interest. Differentiation was made, for instance, between the rich farmers living in the more fertile plains, the artisans, fishermen, and naval entrepreneurs of the seashore, and the impoverished peasants and shepherds of the arid hills. Since these distinctions involved different political rights, the reforms of the sixth and fifth centuries entailed many social and legal changes in the Athenians' quest for greater democracy.

The first major reforms after Draco were initiated in 594 B.C. by Solon, a statesman and poet renowned for his wisdom. Solon was made archon and, according to the historian Plutarch (first century A.D.), was "empowered to be an arbitrator and lawgiver; the rich consenting because he was wealthy, the poor because he was honest." Awarded special powers to change the constitution and implement socio-economic reforms, Solon canceled all debts on real estate and set a maximum quota for land ownership. He freed all who had been enslaved for debts and made it illegal henceforth to sell people into slavery for indebtedness. To combat inflation and economic crises, he devalued the currency and encouraged the expansion of manufacture. Besides passing legislation dealing with agriculture, education, and the legal system, Solon divided all citizens into four classes on the basis of wealth and assigned special rights and duties to each class. While members of all four classes could attend the popular assembly (*ecclesia*)—a rare example of direct democracy—only those of the upper three classes could belong to the Council of Four Hundred, and only those of the first class could be elected archons. Similarly, each class had different duties. Members of the first two classes, for instance, could serve in the cavalry, while oarsmen in the navy were taken from the lowest class.

Solon's constitution neither eliminated poverty nor made it impossible for a tyrant to seize power. Hence, taking advantage of his popularity as a successful general and appealing to the hopes of the landless peasants, Peisistratus made himself tyrant in 560. Twice exiled and twice returned to full power, Peisistratus governed Athens for twenty-three years. "His administration was temperate," according to Aristotle, "more like constitutional government, . . . in every respect mild and humane." Peisistratus aided the poor, kept the peace, although interfering in other states to help set up tyrannies, spent much on public works, such as road building and the beautification of Athens. His was a type of tyranny not many objected to. The few who opposed him he exiled, confiscating their property and awarding it to landless peasants.

In 527 B.C., two of Peisistratus' sons inherited their father's tyrannical powers, but their harsher and more arbitrary rule soon alienated many Athenians. They were finally overthrown in 510 B.C. by a group of political exiles who returned to Athens with the support of Spartan forces and with

the blessing of the Delphic Oracle, which by that time had assumed considerable importance not only in legend and literature but also in political influence.

From the chaos which followed the overthrow of the tyrants arose a
new leader of the lower classes, Cleisthenes. To break the power of the aristocracy, he rewrote the constitution. All citizens were divided into ten units
called *demes,* each containing members from the city of Athens, from the
coastal regions, and from the interior. Each deme was to send fifty delegates,
chosen by lot, to the council whose total membership was raised from four
hundred to five hundred. Management of the executive affairs of the council
was to rotate among the *demes* at regular intervals. Election to some offices,
such as archon and *strategoi* (general), was retained, but most important
administrative officers were chosen by lot. Cleisthenes' democratic reforms
naturally encountered opposition. To safeguard his new constitution, he initiated the practice of ostracism, by which a majority of the assembly (*ecclesia*) could vote by secret ballot to force any person suspected of endangering the safety of the state to exile himself from Athens for ten years.

Cleisthenes' constitution, which dated from the end of the sixth century,
did not establish a fully developed democracy. Yet, the reforms were so far-
reaching that Cleisthenes became known as the father of Athenian democracy.

The fifth century

The fifth century, for which much source material is available—in fact
more than for the fourth—is usually called the Golden Age since it saw the
flowering of Greek drama, sculpture, architecture, philosophy, and historical
writing. Rightly or wrongly, we have come to associate Greek classical
thought with that of the fifth century. Yet, it is conceivable that the self-
reliant, rational-minded Greek with his anthropomorphic deities, his analytic
questioning nature, and his dramatic concept of life, the Greek whom Western civilization has so much admired and so often attempted to imitate, is
merely the synthesis of a group of Athenians during the fifth century, possibly quite atypical of the main stream of Greek history.

The Persian Wars

Between 550 and 530 B.C., the Persians conquered the Ionian colonies of
Asia Minor, the hub of Greek intellectual life during much of the sixth century. Thereafter the cultural center of gravity shifted to Athens, and the
Greek city-states faced a redoubtable empire on the opposite shores of the
Aegean. The inevitable struggle between the individualistic Greeks and the
empire-minded Persians which was then initiated lasted almost two centuries. The contemporary Greek historian, Herodotus, saw in it a symbolic
struggle between East and West. In the end, despite victories on both sides,

the long fight resulted in an amalgamation of the two civilizations after the conquests of Alexander, during what is usually called the Hellenistic era (see p. 45).

The first and most famous of the Persian Wars opened in 499 with a revolt of some Ionian colonies against their Persian conquerors. The rebellion was eventually crushed, but King Darius I of Persia decided to punish those Greek states, particularly Athens, which had aided the rebels. In 490, he sent an expeditionary force across the Aegean, expecting to receive support from discontented factions within some of the Greek states. The Athenians, however, aided only by the neighboring Plataeans, inflicted a resounding defeat on the Persians in the battle of Marathon. The Spartans had offered their assistance to Athens but for religious reasons had waited until "after the full of the moon," and had then rushed north in three days, arriving in time to view the Persians slain on the battlefield.

The victory of Marathon, in which tiny Athens defeated the mighty Persian Empire, removed the Persian threat for a few years and imbued the Athenians with a new self-confidence which is clearly recognizable in their artistic achievements. At the same time, the Athenian general and statesman, Themistocles (527?–459), in an effort to prepare Athens for the next Persian onslaught, sought to assuage party strife by further democratizing the Athenian government. Even the archons were to be chosen by lot from among candidates elected by the demes. Themistocles also forced wealthy citizens to contribute to the construction of a new fleet of triremes, a measure which not only helped Athens' survival during the second Persian attack but also increased the power of the poorer citizens who had to row in the galleys.

In 480 B.C., the Persians reinvaded Greece under their new king, Xerxes (486–465). This time the Athenians were aided by Sparta and many other Greek states but were defeated, partly through treachery, at the battle of Thermopylae. Athens was taken by the Persians and destroyed, but thanks to a rearguard action by the Spartans, the bulk of the Greek army was able to retreat to the Peloponnesus, while Themistocles' new navy defeated the Persian fleet in the battle of Salamis. As a result, two-thirds of the Persian forces retreated to Asia Minor and the remainder was routed by the Spartans in the battle of Plataea in 479 B.C. The Greek states had thus decisively beaten back two attempts by the Persians to subjugate them, and Athens was launched on her glorious century.

The Periclean Age

For several decades after the Persian Wars, Athens remained at her zenith in wealth, commercial activity, military and political power, as well as in her vibrant artistic and intellectual life. In domestic affairs the trend of democratization continued, while abroad the Athenians became imperialistic.

In 479 B.C., Themistocles, leader of the popular party, and General Cimon (507?-449), the head of the aristocratic party, agreed on the need for continuing the war against Persia in order to free Asia Minor from Persian control. On domestic policy and on relations with Sparta, however, the two disagreed. The conservatives sought an understanding with Sparta which would allow the Greeks to present a common front to the Persians; the democrats were hostile to Sparta as well as to all other oligarchies. They believed that Athenian democracy would not be safe so long as other Greek states were ruled by oligarchies. This belief was to cause much internecine warfare among the Greek states and was one of the causes of the long Peloponnesian War and the ultimate decline of Greece.

After Themistocles' ostracism in 471 and a ten-year rule by Cimon, who in turn was ostracized in 461, the popular party, then led by Pericles (? - 429), seized power. The new rulers at once initiated further constitutional reforms to benefit the lower classes. The conservative high court (*areopagus*) was deprived of all power over magistrates, education, and political matters in general, retaining jurisdiction only over cases involving murder. To favor the rising merchant elements, class divisions were henceforth based on total income instead of merely on produce of the land. Members of the third class were allowed to become archons, and finally Pericles instituted pay for jury service to enable even the poor to serve.

Periclean democracy, which the Greek historian Thucydides called "an aristocratic government, that went by the name of democracy, but was, indeed, the supremacy of a single great man," involved more than mere constitutional reforms. Pericles, by nature aloof and reserved, the son of a rich noble family, probably was a democrat by calculation rather than by instinct. He appealed to the masses in demagogic fashion in order to remain in power, which he did longer than any other Greek statesman (461-429). He paid the poor to attend festivals and devoted huge sums to public works, in particular the reconstruction and embellishment of Athens. Nicknamed "the Olympian" because of his aloofness, he was yet able to charm the masses through his great rhetorical powers which Thucydides tried to portray in his *History of the Peloponnesian War*.

Since Pericles himself left no writing except for a few law decrees, we know little of his own political ideas. Some contemporary writers criticized his demagoguery; yet they agreed that his benevolent rule was to a large extent responsible for the flourishing of Athens.

Soon after the Persian Wars, Athens became imperialistic. It is a fairly common historical phenomenon that a normally peaceful state, once it has experienced the shock of invasion, begins to push beyond its borders and becomes imperialistic. This phenomenon had occurred in Egypt after the invasion of the Hyksos just as it happened with Athens after her destruction by the Persians.

Leadership of the Greek drive, by sea and land, to oust the Persians from Asia Minor soon passed from the Spartans to the Athenians. The latter fashioned an anti-Persian alliance with most of the Aegean island states and the Ionian cities in Asia Minor, with headquarters on the island of Delos. This Delian League, at first a religious union of equal states under the protection of Apollo of Delos, was then transformed into an Athenian Empire. Pericles forcefully prevented member states from withdrawing from the so-called alliance and added new members by conquest. The allies were made tributary states, with Athens stationing garrisons on their territory, assuming control over their domestic and foreign policies, and forcing their citizens to bring their law cases before Athenian courts. Ultimately Pericles even moved the common treasury from Delos to Athens and used its funds on the beautification of Athens. He defended his action with the argument that it was just that the other states should pay tribute since the Athenian fleet defended them against Persia. The historian, Xenophon (430?– ?), thought the whole arrangement wonderful since it brought court fees, tourism, employment, and prestige to Athens.

Pericles' imperialism reached beyond this newly acquired empire. During his administration, Athens sent military expeditions over wide areas and interfered particularly in Corinth and Sparta, in Egypt and Cyprus, and as far away as the Black Sea and the island of Sicily.

The Peloponnesian War

Rivalry between the Athenian Empire and the Spartan League had led to several wars before. In 431 B.C. it brought about a new, bitter conflict which, except for a truce of seven years, lasted until 404 and so weakened both contestants as to permanently undermine the independent viability of the Greek states. The Peloponnesian War, the earlier phases of which were analyzed by Thucydides in great detail, was in part an ideological struggle between "efficiency through discipline" and "efficiency through freedom," as Pericles supposedly described it. It was also a commercial war, provoked by Athens' attempt to dominate the eastern Mediterranean trade routes; and it represented a foretaste of a struggle repeated several times in later history, a battle between Leviathan in the form of the Athenian navy and Behemoth as represented by Spartan land power.

The war was fought over wide areas ranging from Sicily to Thrace and Asia Minor. Athens and Sparta continuously sought to subvert their opponent's respective allies, and within many of the cities democrats and oligarchs fought fierce civil wars. Whole cities were destroyed, entire populations slaughtered or sold into slavery. The Spartans repeatedly invaded Attica and ravaged the countryside in the hope of starving out the Athenians, while the latter, safe behind their walls, secured food supplies by sea.

Athens' prospects for victory began to dim after a disastrous expedition to Sicily (415–413) in which she lost over a hundred ships and thousands of soldiers. Hereafter, the Peloponnesian fleet, supported by Persian money, posed an ever-increasing threat to the commercial lifelines of the Athenian Empire. In Athens itself, the Sicilian disaster shattered the relative political stability which had persisted even after the death of Pericles, who perished in a plague which swept the city in 429. The oligarchs ousted the democrats and seized power for a year, insisting that they could attract Persian aid away from the Spartans and that their party was better equipped to fight the war. But neither the oligarchs nor the democrats, who shortly returned to power, could stay ultimate defeat.

In 405 B.C., the Athenian fleet was defeated by the Peloponnesians and Persians, and Athens was forced to surrender in the following year. Her empire was dismantled and oligarchies were established everywhere under supervision of Spartan military governors. Athens had to give up her remaining fleet and tear down her fortified walls, so that in future she would be at the mercy of Sparta or other invaders. Once again democracy was abolished, when the oligarchs exiled the democratic leaders and sought to restrict full citizenship rights to a mere three thousand rich Athenians. Yet, democracy seemed by then so ingrained in Athenian political life that the popular party soon returned to rule, without however being able to regain for Athens her vast power and self-confidence.

The fourth century

As a result of the Peloponnesian War, the exhausted Greek city-states declined in political influence. To the East, Persia regained temporary dominance over the Aegean, to the North, Macedonia started to consolidate into a powerful rival, and in the West, Carthage and the nascent Roman Republic began to vie over control of the western Mediterranean. The appearance of these new forces, coupled with continued disunity among the Greek states, ultimately caused the Greeks to lose their political independence.

Changing ideals

The Greeks' altered political position was reflected in a change of philosophical, religious, and artistic ideals. During the height of the Golden Age, the Athenians in particular had been sublimely self-confident and vibrantly optimistic. The Athenian dramatist Aeschylus (525–456), for example, had presented grand Homeric, mythological themes in which humanlike gods or godlike humans battled majestically with the powers of fate. Life in his dramas carried an impressive spiritual dignity. The playwright Sophocles (496?–406) generally retained this idealism. His dramatic characters remained heroic, and religious traditions stayed untouched.

The same majestic grandeur can be seen in Herodotus' history of the struggle between Persians and Greeks from the early sixth century to the end of the Great Persian Wars. The Greeks' self-sufficiency and their comfortable relations with the gods are equally revealed in the temples of the Athenian

Acropolis which were rebuilt after their destruction by the Persians, particularly in the imposing Parthenon. Similarly in sculpture, the friezes of the Parthenon, designed by the sculptor Phidias (500?–432?), or Polyclitus' (? –420?) *Spear Bearer* show a remarkable idealism and sense of aesthetic certainty.

In philosophy, too, the Greeks of the Golden Age prided themselves in their analytical powers which might enable them, unlike the Hebraic Job, to understand the universe. Philosophers, like Parmenides (early fifth century), continued the naturalist tradition of the previous century which sought to investigate the natural universe. Parmenides felt that change was illusory and that reality was changeless. Sophists, such as Protagoras (middle fifth century), exaggerated this self-confident tendency by intimating that all knowledge could be taught and that rhetoric and argumentation were ultimately more important than "true" knowledge. By thus making "man the measure of all things," the sophists were among the first in Western civilization to introduce the concept of relativity in standards of morals as well as truth.

All this evokes a picture of what we have come to look upon as the prototype of classical Greece: a man confident of his own rational powers, vaguely conscious of but not intimidated by cosmic forces; a worshiper of idealized physical beauty; a noble convinced that human suffering, where it exists, is in essence self-inflicted through human flaws, such as overweening pride.

During the Peloponnesian Wars and the early fourth century, however, the Greeks began to abandon their aesthetic idealism and reject the Homeric tradition. It is perhaps symptomatic that Euripides (480–406), the last of the three great Greek dramatist, who toward the end of his life emigrated from his native Attica and died in Macedonia, depicted characters that were more human and ordinary than Aeschylus' over-life-sized heroes. Like the comic poet Aristophanes (448?–380?), Euripides was critical of accepted morality and showed less reverence for the traditional gods. Aristophanes, in fact, ridiculed everything in the Athenian way of life, democracy and war, social mores and philosophic certainty.

Greek religion of the sixth and fifth centuries, although not spiritual and other-worldly in the Christian sense, must have provided the Greeks with a comforting relationship with the unknown and easy explanations for the unknowable. The decline of this religious tradition may well be related to the decay of the city-state. To be sure, unlike the Near East, Greece was not plagued by church-state conflicts, for the Greeks had no strong, organized class of priests. But religion and politics had become closely intertwined in the form of patriotism, with each city rendering homage to a patron deity. As the glory of the city declined, it must have undermined the prestige of its protecting deity and aroused distrust in the old gods. The same incipient diffidence is seen in the treatment of the oracles which were still consulted *pro forma* in the fourth century, but whose advice was rarely heeded.

A similar trend is noticeable in other phases of Greek culture. Thucydides forsook the larger idealized historical themes of Herodotus. In his treatment, gods, fate, and myths receded and man, less sure of himself, emerged as the agent in history. The historian Xenophon, who in his *Hellenica* continued Thucydides' history of Greece down to the battle of Mantinaea (362), finally abandoned most ideals and presented man as primarily a political being.

In the arts, the trend toward realism is particularly evident in sculpture, a foretaste of the Hellenistic era to follow. Statues of goddesses, such as Praxiteles' *Aphrodite* (around 330) are more lifelike in proportion and texture, more human in their nudity than the draped, majestic figures of the preceding century. It is also interesting that the great public buildings of the fifth century had generally been dedicated to the honor of a god or goddess, whereas in the fourth century we find—what we saw in Egypt and will again encounter in later eras—vast edifices, such as the Mausoleum of Halicarnassus, erected in memory of a single man.

In philosophy, Socrates (469–399), through his method of question and answer, later termed "Socratic dialogue," attacked the shallowness of the sophists and the general ignorance of those about him. In his search for knowledge he was interested in morality rather than in speculation about the physical universe, as had been earlier philosophers. The search for knowledge, to him, would lead to virtue and happiness. Unlike the sophists who saw no need for standards outside of man, Socrates believed in some sort of divine spark within man. He intimated that the human soul was immortal and that an eternal justice existed above and apart from human justice.

This quest for eternal values was taken up by one of Socrates' disciples, Plato (427–348), who, together with his own pupil Aristotle (384–322), became the most influential philosophers in Western civilization. Plato argued that "ideas" were timeless concepts, existing in the mind only and not in the world of matter. Man, he contended, uses general nouns to refer to such ideas, but his sense-perception grasps only imperfect and transitory reflections. The ideas themselves range from those referred to by the simplest general nouns to the most complete and supreme, the idea of the Good. Like Socrates, he believed virtue to consist of knowing this supreme idea, a knowledge to be attained by rational thought and not by appeal to the senses. Hence, virtue and morality were stressed in most of Plato's numerous writings, including the famous *Republic*. Plato's confidence in man's rationality places him squarely into the tradition of fifth century Greece; but his elevation of an ideal goodness in contrast to human imperfection also makes him the herald of a new era and an influential forerunner of Christian theology.

The era of leagues

For three decades after the end of the Peloponnesian Wars, Sparta and her allies attempted to dominate the Greek city-states and to assume Athens' former role as chief antagonist of Persia. Athenians, Corinthians, Thebans, and others formed a series of leagues to fight Spartan hegemony, while Persia, interested in keeping Greece disunited, supported now this, now that protagonist. The result was a period of almost uninterrupted warfare.

By 370 B.C., Sparta's hegemony was broken. Thebes and her league allies defeated the Spartans (at Leuctra), invaded the Peloponnesus, and freed the Messenian slaves from Spartan control, thereby permanently undermining Spartan military power. Consequently Thebes emerged temporarily as Greece's most powerful state, a position owed partly to the military tactics invented by its brilliant general Epaminondas (420–362). His phalanx, a tightly assembled mass of soldiers armed with long spears, capable of crushing the then common lighter formations of infantry, was later adopted by Alexander the Great and helped make his armies well-nigh invincible.

After Thebes' decline, Athens briefly regained a measure of leadership, but the Greek states remained arranged in a bewildering, constantly shifting array of leagues and alliances, exhausting their resources in frequent wars. In consequence, the Greek Peninsula presented a tempting prey to the Macedonians who began their rise to power when Philip II became king in 356 B.C.

The growth of Macedonia

Philip II, a ruthless ruler, skillful diplomat, and excellent general who had learned military tactics from Epaminondas in Thebes, was the first to consolidate the Macedonian monarchy into a centralized, quasi-absolute state, capable of exerting a powerful role in foreign affairs. After imposing tighter control on his subjects and modernizing his army along Theban lines, he extended Macedonian might over neighboring states. Using bribery, trickery, and military force, he expanded his state to almost twice its size within a few years. Almost everywhere, this Macedonian expansion clashed with the commercial and political interests of Athens, Thebes, and other major Greek states.

The Greeks' attitude toward Philip was ambivalent. Some looked upon him as a dangerous barbarian; others saw in him a kindred Greek. As early as 380, the Athenian orator and philosopher Isocrates (436–338) had pled in his famous *Panegyric* for an end to warfare among the Greeks and had urged Greek cooperation in a united effort against Persia. Thereafter he continued to admonish his compatriots to search for a leader capable of uniting Greece against "the Great King" (Persia) who, as he put it, treated the Greeks "as though we were captives of his spear." In 346, he publicly appealed to Philip of Macedonia "to reconcile Argos and Lacedaemon and

Thebes and Athens" and "to extend your power over the greatest possible number of the barbarians." Others, however, led by the Athenian orator and statesman Demosthenes (385?–322), regarded Philip with the same antipathy as they did the Persians. In a series of inflammatory orations, the *Philippics,* Demosthenes tried to arouse the Athenians and Thebans to form a common front against Philip's interference in Greece.

King Philip, however, successfully bought and fought his way ever deeper into Greece. Some cities (Olynthus, for example) he treated with extreme harshness, selling entire populations into slavery; others he attracted to his side with charm and promises. When Athens and Thebes finally joined in a belated attempt to halt the Macedonian advance, their forces were crushed in the battle of Chaeronea (338). This event marked the end of Greek independence and the termination of the Hellenic age. Philip promptly dissolved all local leagues and at a congress in Corinth forced all states except Sparta to unite in a Hellenic league under the protective leadership of Macedonia. Greece seemed at last united, but the Greek states had in reality become tributaries to Macedonia.

In the following year, Philip declared war on Persia, thus fulfilling the hope cherished by Isocrates. However, before the invasion of Persia could be launched in full force, Philip was murdered (336), leaving the throne to his twenty-year-old son, Alexander.

Alexander and the Hellenistic era

That Greece had not lost her cultural influence when she forfeited her political independence is well seen in the life of the philosopher Aristotle (384–322). Born in Stagira, which was conquered by the Macedonians in 347 B.C., and making his temporary home in Athens, Aristotle became tutor to Alexander the Great. More interested in the analytical, systematic, empirical examination of matter and form than in Plato's rationalistic speculations about eternal ideas, Aristotle wrote extensively on logic, ethics, natural science, as well as politics. His ultimate influence on Western civilization—be it in philosophy or literature, in physics, theology, political theory, or even economics—can hardly be exaggerated. Yet during the fourth century, his greatest importance perhaps was that he helped so convincingly to convert Alexander the Great into a champion of Greek culture and thus assisted indirectly in the initiation of the Hellenistic era, as the four centuries after Alexander's conquests are called.

The conquest of the Near East

The exploits of the youthful Alexander the Great, who ruled a mere thirteen years from 336 to 323 B.C., are so shrouded in legend that it is difficult to disentangle fact from myth. Typically, one statue (by Lysippus) depicted him with mellow features and with what Plutarch called "melting eyes"; another showed him with thunderbolts in his hands; on a contemporary coin, he was drawn with the curved horns of a ram protruding from his head, to denote his affinity with the Egyptian god Ammon.

Unquestionably Alexander was a great general and an efficient organizer, a man of vast ambition, apparently unbridled in his temper and incontinent in the enjoyment of physical pleasures. It is difficult to ascertain whether Alexander had indeed clearly conceived plans for the creation of a Macedonian-Persian empire and the reconciliatory fusion of East and West, or whether the stages of his conquests were rather the result of timely seized opportunities and his vision of a new society largely the retroactive creation of admirers. For, like the Napoleonic legend, the myth of Alexander blossomed even during his life time. A few centuries later, the Greek historian Arrian (95?–175 A.D.), in a serious discussion of Alexander, insisted "that a hero unlike any other human being could not have been born without the agency of the deity."

Soon after his accession to the throne, the young Alexander demonstrated that he had inherited his father's ruthlessness and military genius. He quickly crushed a revolt of several Greek states and razed the city of Thebes as a warning to the Greeks. Athens and others thereupon gave Alexander half-hearted support for his planned attack on Asia, although probably more Greeks flocked as mercenaries to the aid of the Persians than joined Alexander's Macedonian armies.

In 334 B.C., Alexander crossed the Hellespont and initiated the conquest of Asia Minor. At Troy, he supposedly sacrificed to Minerva, "honored the memory of the heroes who were buried there," especially that of Achilles, and "with his friends, as the ancient custom is, ran naked about his sepulchre." A year later, he routed the numerically superior Persian forces under King Darius III (336–330) at the battle of Issus (333), opening vast stretches of the Near East to easy conquest. The legendary prophecy that he would conquer Asia after having cut the Gordian knot with his sword was approaching fulfillment, barely a year after he had left Macedonia. (See Map 3.)

With Darius' wife and children his prisoners, Alexander in rapid succession occupied Phoenicia, Palestine, and Egypt, all tributaries of Persia's vast empire. Not far from the mouth of the Nile in Egypt, he founded a new city, appropriately named Alexandria, that soon became one of the most important centers of Hellenistic culture. Throughout his reign, he retained this practice of founding new cities which were to be populated with Greek and Macedonian inhabitants, and could thus help spread Greek culture and at the same time serve as military outposts. In Egypt, he also worshiped at the temple of Ammon and agreed to have himself recognized as a son of that god. Motivated in part by vanity and in part by his desire to fuse Eastern and Western traditions, his action foreshadowed his later elevation to a level above that of ordinary humans.

In 331 B.C., Alexander resumed his attack on Darius and defeated him decisively in the battle of Gaugamela near the Tigris River. Babylon, Susa, and Persepolis, with their vast treasures, were now easily seized by the Macedonian conqueror. After a drunken orgy at Persepolis, the great palace of Xerxes was burned, supposedly set aflame by a Greek courtesan to avenge the burning of Athens, a century and a half earlier; others report that the fire was set by Macedonian generals, while the intoxicated king himself, garlanded with flowers, danced around the burning palace, holding a torch. The generals presumably hoped to dissuade Alexander from lingering in Persia and to entice him to return to Macedonia.

Insatiable in his quest for further conquests, Alexander then pushed north and east into Parthia and Bactria as far as Samarkand. In 327, he crossed the mountains into India. During these years, he became increasingly alienated from his Macedonian followers. Dressing himself in Persian fashion, he began to demand the reverence due to an Oriental despot and assumed the prerogatives of a semidivine ruler. Those of his companions who did not cherish such un-Greek elevation of a living mortal and who questioned his authority, he had murdered or executed on charges of treason. At the same time he continued to found new Alexandrias, absorbed native Asians into his armies and his administrative system, encouraged intermarriage between Greeks and Persians, and himself married Roxane, a girl from Sogdiana.

By 326 B.C., Alexander had conquered the lands along the Indus River, corresponding more or less to modern western Pakistan. His intrusion into the Indian subcontinent, which strongly affected Indian politics and culture, was to be his last conquest. His soldiers were unwilling to follow Alexander in further drives to the East and finally forced him to return westward. After descending the Indus River to its mouth, a part of his army regained Persia by sea, while Alexander with the remainder of his forces crossed the desert to return to Susa, where he arrived in 324.

Finding that some of the governors he had left to administer outlying provinces had not remained loyal to him, he began to reorganize the administrative machinery of his vast empire and sought to strengthen the ties between Europeans and Asians by inducing some ten thousand of his followers to take local brides. He himself set the example by taking as his second wife a daughter of the late King Darius. Yet Alexander was hardly given the time to consolidate his vast conquests. During a visit to Babylon in 323, he died at the age of thirty-two.

Hellenistic civilization

Alexander's vast empire was a transitory creation. The attempt to preserve the integrity of the empire for his posthumous son proved abortive. For several decades, rival generals fought over the spoils of the inheritance, while the Athenians attempted in vain to rebel against Macedonian overlordship.

Finally, three kingdoms emerged as successor states to Alexander's empire, each ruled by a dynasty descendent from a Macedonian general.

Egypt and nearby lands, once again enjoying wealth and prodigious trade, were governed by general Ptolemy and his successors. This Ptolemaic Kingdom finally lost its independence to Rome during the first century B.C. The bulk of the former Persian Empire was initially ruled by the Seleucid dynasty, but northwestern India, under Chandragupta and his son Asoka, soon regained her independence and the Parthians gradually extended their rule over a vast part of former Persia. After a brief resurgence in the later third century B.C., the Seleucid Kingdom, with its capital at Antioch in Syria, shrank slowly through the defection of outlying districts and almost incessant warfare until it, too, was destroyed by the Romans during the first century B.C. The third area—Macedonia, Thrace, and Greece—fell under the nominal rule of yet another dynasty (the Antigonids).

The restive Greek city-states, for their part, resumed their customary wars and intrigues, which kept the peninsula in turmoil and reduced the effectiveness of Macedonian control. In the end, some of the Greeks, foremost among them the Spartans, allied themselves with Rome in hopes of escaping Macedonian overlordship. Thus drawn east, Rome subdued Macedonia in a series of four major wars (between 215 and 146 B.C.) and converted her into a Roman province. In the course of these wars most of the Greek states slipped into the orbit of the irresistibly expanding Roman Empire.

Whereas Alexander's political creation was ephemeral, the cultural repercussions of his exploits were lasting. The Hellenistic age which his conquests initiated became a significant transitional phase between Near Eastern and Western civilization. It became the seedbed for Christianity, molded the later Roman Empire, and formed the basis of the Byzantine Empire which lasted until the fifteenth century A.D.

In essence, the Hellenistic Age was based on the fusion of two cultures, that of Greece and that of the Near East. Macedonians and Greeks acted as the ruling class in the Ptolemaic and Seleucid kingdoms and dominated the trade of the East, while slowly adopting local customs. On the other hand, oriental ideas infiltrated into Greece—and later Rome. East and West both contributed generously to the new civilization.

During this era, the individualism, fierce love of independence, and veneration of the city-state of the Greeks were stifled by the emergence of large kingdoms, dominated by rulers who in oriental fashion considered themselves semidivine. The gulf between ruler and ruled widened with each century. The democratic ideal of self-rule vanished, but a new feeling of cosmopolitan brotherhood rendered those in power more generous in granting citizenship as well as legal and social rights to foreigners and even slaves. Under the new paternal despotism, there tended to be more social equality among the masses, although a few rich ascended to heights of prosperity hitherto unknown in the West. Tapping the wealth of Asia, which produced this prosperity, also entailed inflation. The resulting increase in poverty greatly widened the cleavage between the very rich and the masses. Perhaps in compensation for their lost sense of belonging to a local political unit, people increasingly joined social and religious organizations.

The need to adjust to new socio-political realities is seen in philosophy and religion. If man is but an insignificant speck in a vast kingdom or lives in miserable poverty, he is not likely to share the sense of this-worldly self-importance which had prevailed among the citizens of fifth-century Athens. Two possible solutions emerged, both more or less influenced by the East and both stressing the brotherhood of man.

The philosophers Zeno (336?–264?) and Epicurus (341?–270) presented the educated with theories designed to suggest ways of life rather than to aid the search for ultimate truths. Zeno's Stoicism, which became one of the main philosophies of Rome and highly influential in the formation of early Christian doctrine, stressed universal brotherhood and the importance of living in harmony with nature. The universe, according to Zeno, functioned on the basis of rational or divine law. If man, himself endowed with a spark of this divine rationality, would but attempt to understand this law of the universe and refrain from seeking the irrational, he would be happy. In practice, Stoicism led its followers to a sense of detachment from the world about them, a mood analogous to Indian philosophy and to later medieval asceticism.

Epicurus, on the other hand, produced an essentially materialistic doctrine to help his followers lead the good life. Epicureanism, which some Romans later perverted into hedonism, sought to teach men to avoid pain as a means to happiness and to reject all notions of god and an afterlife in order to rid themselves of fear and anxiety.

Stoicism and Epicureanism appealed primarily to the educated. For the masses, the East provided easier remedies, less dependent on self-discipline, more imbued with emotion. Mystery cults, such as those at Eleusis, celebrating the fertility of the soil and of humans, had existed for some time in Greece, practiced on a relatively small scale. In the spread of the Egyptian cult of Osiris and Persian Mithraism, as well as similar eastern cults involving emotional celebrations of the mysteries of death and resurrection, the impoverished masses could find solace in the hope that their baneful existence might some day terminate by entrance into a glorious paradise. These Hellenistic cults, which later spread to Rome as forerunners or rivals of Christianity, with their emotional stress on salvation and strong suggestions of monotheism, represent a typical fusion of East and West.

Although largely Greek inspired, literary, artistic, and intellectual developments flourished mostly elsewhere than on the Greek Peninsula—in Alexandria, Egypt, in Syracuse, Sicily, or on the Island of Rhodes, for example. Education was emphasized, and libraries and new theaters were constructed.

It was also a fertile period in literature. More readers and more patrons called for a vastly increased output of a cosmopolitan nature. Less vibrant in epic and tragedy, the period was fruitful in the composition of didactic poetry and epigrams, of pastorals (Theocritus, third century), history (Polybius, 202?–120?), and comedy (Menander, 342?–292?)—the so-called New Comedy which dealt with comical situations rather than character satire and became the model for Rome and Hollywood. This literature, more emotional and cosmopolitan than heroic and superhuman, also revealed a widely expanded geographic knowledge of the world from the Indus to the North Sea.

Realism and emotionalism characterize the art of the period. Statues of idealized heroes seemed out of place in Hellenistic times. Instead, sculptors portrayed common people, everyday scenes, and nature. Whereas the fifth century sculptors had made their figures appear above human emotions, those of the Hellenistic era delighted in the realistic portraiture of suffering, as in the statue of *The Dying Gaul.* And goddesses, such as *Venus* (de Medici) or *The Victory of Samothrace,* were carved as humans, with even a touch of the erotic.

The realistic Hellenistic Age was also a period of pragmatism, again an aspect easily assimilated by the Romans. The Hellenists generally preferred to assemble knowledge—of East or West—as in the vast library of Alexandria in Egypt—and to work on applied science. Speculation seemed less important to them than applied knowledge. Their discoveries in geometry (Euclid), in astronomy (Aristarchus' heliocentric theory), in physics (Archimedes), and anatomy were so advanced that they were again lost during the late Roman and medieval periods. Similarly, Hellenistic scientists invented steam engines, pumps, and other practical devices which soon sank into oblivion, either because people were not ready to accept them or because cheap slave labor made their general introduction economically impractical.

The legacy of Greece

It is difficult to summarize the legacy of Greece in a few paragraphs. As Edith Hamilton wrote, we in the West "think and feel differently because of what a little Greek town [Athens] did during a century or two, twenty-four hundred years ago."

Greek achievements in law and politics, in literature, art, and philosophy, as well as in science left an indelible impact on Western civilization. Even today, aesthetics is influenced by notions of Greek classicism, and much of our scientific language uses Greek prototypes. At the same time, Greek mythology made a pervasive and enriching mark on Western literature and thought.

To be sure, like all other peoples, the Greeks lived in a chain of cultural transmission. They borrowed from their predecessors and adapted ideas from the Near East. Moreover, much that has come down to us from Greece came through the filter of Near Eastern, Roman, or Arab transmitters.

The primary contributions of this fertile civilization to the development of Western man probably are its regard for the importance of law, its concepts of the dignity of the individual, and its achievements in the realm of analytical and speculative philosophy.

SUGGESTED READINGS

Greek Political History

Andrewes, Antony, *The Greek Tyrants* (Harper, 1963).
Burn, A. R., *Pericles and Athens* (Macmillan, 1962).
Burn, A. R., *Persia and the Greeks: The Defense of the West 546–478 B.C.* (Funk, 1962).
Claster, Jill N., *Athenian Democracy: Triumph or Travesty?* (Holt, 1967).
Ehrenberg, Victor, *The Greek State* (Norton, 1964).
Forrest, W. G., *The Emergence of Greek Democracy: 800–400 B.C.* (McGraw, 1966).
Forsdyke, John, *Greece Before Homer* (Norton, 1957).
Freeman, Kathleen, *Greek City-States* (Norton, 1963).
Hamilton, Edith, *The Echo of Greece* (Norton, 1957). A study of fourth-century B.C. Athens.
Havelock, Eric A., *The Liberal Temper in Greek Politics* (Yale, 1957).
Michell, Humphrey, *Sparta* (Cambridge U. P., 1952).

Greek Philosophy

Grube, G. M. A., *Plato's Thought* (Beacon, 1958).
Guthrie, W. K. C., *The Greek Philosophers: From Thales to Aristotle* (Harper, 1960).
Hadas, Moses, *The Greek Ideal and Its Survival* (Harper, 1960).
Kirk, G. S., and Raven, J. E., *The Presocratic Philosophers* (Cambridge U. P., 1957).
Levin, Richard, *The Question of Socrates* (Harcourt). Source book on the trial of Socrates.
Lloyd, G. E. R., *Aristotle, The Growth and Structure of His Thought* (Cambridge U. P., 1968).
Randall, John Herman, Jr., *Aristotle* (Columbia, 1960).
Sinclair, T. A., *A History of Greek Political Thought* (World, 1967). From Homer to the beginning of the Christian era.
Snell, Bruno, *The Discovery of the Mind: The Greek Origins of European Thought* (Harper, 1960).
Taylor, Alfred E., *The Mind of Plato* (U. of Michigan, 1960).

Greek Culture

Barron, John, *Greek Sculpture* (Dutton, 1965). Seventh to second century B.C.
Bury, John Bagnell, *The Ancient Greek Historians* (Dover).
Dickinson, G. Lowes, *The Greek View of Life* (U. of Michigan, 1958).
Farrington, Benjamin, *Greek Science* (Penguin, 1961).
Glotz, Gustave, *Ancient Greece at Work* (Norton, 1967). Economic history from Homer to the Roman conquest.

Guthrie, W. K. C., *The Greeks and Their Gods* (Beacon, 1955).
Hadas, Moses, *A History of Greek Literature* (Columbia, 1954).
Hamilton, Edith, *The Greek Way* (Norton, 1930).
Kagan, Donald, ed., *Sources in Greek Political Thought from Homer to Polybius* (Macmillan, 1965).
Kitto, H. D. F., *The Greeks* (Penguin, 1957).
Nilsson, Martin P., *A History of Greek Religion* (Norton, 1964).
Robinson, Charles A., Jr., *Selections from Greek and Roman Historians* (Holt, 1957).
Seltman, Charles, *Approach to Greek Art* (Dutton).

Alexander and the Hellenistic Age

Burn, Andrew R., *Alexander the Great and the Hellenistic Empire* (Macmillan, 1966).
Grant, F. C., ed., *Hellenistic Religions: The Age of Syncretism* (Bobbs, 1953).
*Hadas, Moses, *Hellenistic Culture: Fusion and Diffusion* (Columbia, 1959).
Tarn, William W., *Alexander the Great* (Beacon, 1956).
Tarn, William W., *Hellenistic Civilization* (World, 1961).

CHAPTER IV

❧ *Rome*

(753 B.C. to 180 A.D.)

From its myth-shrouded beginnings in the eighth century B.C. to its final destruction with the fall of Constantinople in the fifteenth century A.D., the Roman state enjoyed a longer continuous history than most known civilizations. Because of the Romans' sense of history and their efficient devotion to keeping records, we are also better informed about most periods of their development than about other ancient civilizations.

Formation and consolidation of the Roman state

From the middle of the second millennium B.C. successive waves of Indo-European invaders passed into Italy through the Alps which, despite their height and ruggedness, never presented an effective barrier against invasions. The newcomers gradually penetrated into the fertile valleys of central Italy, where they became the ancestors of the Latin and related Italic tribes who eventually dominated all of Italy and the Mediterranean.

Then, sometime before the eighth century, another group of invaders, the Etruscans, conquered the area of modern Tuscany, while Greek colonists began to settle Sicily and the coasts of southern Italy as far north as Naples. Until the fifth century B.C. or later, Etruscans and Greek colonists were more powerful and influential than the Latins living around Rome.

The period of the Monarchy

According to tradition and legend, Rome was founded in 753 B.C. by Romulus, with the aid of his father, the god Mars, and his grandmother, the goddess Venus. The year 753 was therefore made the beginning of the Roman calendar.

Actually, various Latin tribes of shepherds living on hills near a ford in the river Tiber gradually merged their villages during the eighth century. To cooperate in matters of defense, the Romans set up a joint meeting place, the forum, encircled their growing "city" by walls, and elected a king. These early kings apparently ruled like Greek tyrants, appealing to the poor against the rich, although their power was presumably checked by the Senate, a council of elders. Sometime during the seventh century—we do not know whether by conquest or election—the kingship of Rome passed into the hands of Etruscan rulers.

The origin of the Etruscans is as yet unknown. Since they settled inland, some historians believed they came from Central Europe. Most archaeologists now believe they migrated from Asia Minor. The orator Cicero (106–43 B.C.), who like all other patriotic Romans despised the Etruscans, thought they had arrived by sea, "for no barbarians were originally seafaring except the Etruscans and the Carthaginians, of which the former voyaged for the sake of commerce, the latter for the sake of piracy." The Etruscans developed an advanced civilization, which was rediscovered only recently. Apparently quite religious, they believed in anthropomorphic gods—deities with human forms and qualities—who played important roles in the political life of their cities. They also used divination to determine public or private decisions, a practice inherited by the Romans.

After seizing control of Latium in the seventh century, the Etruscans continued their expansion. As allies of Carthage, they successfully battled the Greeks in the Tyrrhenian Sea; to the north they extended their domination over the Po Valley. Presumably in 509 B.C., however, they were expelled from the city of Rome. During the succeeding century, they were defeated by the Greeks of Syracuse and expelled from southern Italy, and in the course of the fourth century they were crushed by simultaneous pressure from Romans and invading Gauls. Thereafter the Etruscans became lost in the mainstream of Roman history.

During the period of the Monarchy (753–509 B.C.), the Romans developed political and social institutions which survived the fall of the kingdom and remained an integral part of Roman life. The people were divided into two classes: the wealthy, landowning patricians and the plebeians. Among the patricians much stress was placed on family and clan relationships. Within the family, the paterfamilias was all powerful, and the dispensing of justice rested largely in his hands. To preserve family unity, the death masks of all male ancestors, together with inscribed tablets listing their names and honors, were kept in the home and carried in solemn procession during funerals. The clans were composed of all who worshiped a common ancestor and hence bore the same clan name. The patricians' wealth, their military monopoly, and their strong clan organization assured them of sole political power for a long time. The plebeians, on the other hand, at first with few clan ties, without unity and weapons lacked political rights. Their hope was to appeal to the king or to become "clients" to patricians. In return for a patrician's protection, aid, and legal advice, the "client" followed his patron into battle, performed honorable service, and swelled his entourage at assemblies in the manner of a bodyguard. In this way some plebeians could gradually become identified with a patron's clan.

Roman religion was similar to that of the Greeks and Etruscans. It tended to be pragmatic and tied to the needs of the state. No special class or caste of priests emerged. Rather, priests were government officials, appointed for several years or for life. New gods, new cults, or new temples had to be approved by the Senate. According to Plutarch, the Pontifex Maximus, the highest religious leader, "interpreted the divine law, or, rather, presided over sacred rites." He "regulated the sacrifices of private persons" and, above all, "prescribed rules for public ceremony." Divination played an important role in Roman religious life.

The Romans early displayed much political ability, a characteristic they preserved throughout their history. Besides setting up functional governmental bodies, such as the Senate and the Assembly, they developed a keen sense of distinction between private and public (or governmental) matters, a distinction rarely made in ancient times. The power to command or order, in civil or military matters, called by the Romans *imperium,* was not automatically assumed by the kings, but was a special honor conferred by the Assembly.

Under the Monarchy, the Romans also demonstrated their skill at territorial expansion. They increased their influence and resources by contracting alliances with neighboring Latin tribes. Supposedly all partners in these arrangements enjoyed equal status. Yet the Romans soon assumed the right to speak for their Latin allies. In a treaty of friendship with Carthage (508 B.C.), for example, one clause—according to the historian Polybius (second century B.C.)—referred to Rome's allies as "people of the Latins that are subject to Rome."

Establishment of republican institutions

The expulsion of the Etruscan kings from Rome ended the period of the Monarchy. From 509 to 31 B.C., Rome remained a Republic. Essentially two main themes pervaded the five centuries of republican history: one, the struggle of the plebeians for political equality with the patricians, including the later concomitant attempts of the lower classes to enhance their social and economic status; and two, Rome's continuous expansion from a small city-state to mistress of the Mediterranean and of Western Europe.

For information concerning the earlier period of the Republic, the historian must rely on archaeology and on the often fabulous renditions of later Roman historians. Actually, the Pontifex Maximus maintained yearly records of main events and of the names of magistrates, but these *Annales Pon-tificum,* inscribed on tablets affixed to public buildings, which some Roman historians used as source material, were later destroyed. Similarly, not much remains of the biographical sketches attached to the family death masks, which, although probably embellished out of family pride, would have furnished much data. After the third century B.C., several Roman and Greek historians provided fairly reliable accounts of their times, making the last two centuries of the Republic a period rich in historical material.

In 509 B.C., the power of *imperium* formerly held by the king was transferred to two annually elected consuls, sharing equal authority. This ingenious system of checks and balances, where one consul could veto the decisions of the other, worked very smoothly but provided little comfort for the plebeians who previously had obtained some protection from the kings. The patricians, with their monopoly of power, oppressed the plebeians, many of whom suffered poverty and unemployment, while some were enslaved for debts. The resulting discontent made the plebeians all the more determined to seek ways of obtaining redress.

The plebeians' struggle for political equality, which lasted from 509 to 287 B.C., was conducted without the violence accompanying most class war. In fact, until the last century of the republic, the Romans' genius for political maneuvering and sense for law and order enabled them, like the British in later centuries, to solve most problems by slow compromise.

As weapons in this struggle the plebeians relied heavily on their own elected officials, especially the tribunes who were plebeian representatives and whose primary task was to protect individuals from arbitrary acts by the government or by patricians. To exert pressure for their demands, the plebeians several times organized a boycott by withdrawing to one of Rome's seven hills, the Aventine, and refusing to leave until they had been granted concessions.

The first major step in the plebeian drive for legal equality (about 450 B.C.) was the codification of the laws in the so-called *Law of the Twelve Tables.* The purpose was not, as the historian Livy (59 B.C.–17 A.D.) later asserted, "to equalize the rights of all, both the highest and the lowest," but rather to avoid arbitrary application of justice, a change which would benefit primarily the plebeians. The laws remained harsh, based on an eye for an eye retribution. Enslavement for debt was still authorized, but the creditor now had to feed the debtor at least "one pound of grits a day." While marriage between plebeians and patricians remained outlawed, Romans were permitted to marry foreigners; and the law made a distinction between armed and unarmed robbery. Soon thereafter, marriages between plebeians and patricians were also legalized (about 445 B.C.) and several governmental positions, such as that of quaestor, embodying judicial and financial functions, were opened to plebeians.

Despite these measures, it is symptomatic that when Rome was raided by Gauls in about 390 B.C., Livy reports, probably correctly, that most of the patricians, some soldiers, the vestal virgins, and sacred religious objects were safely ensconced in the impregnable citadel of the Capitoline Hill, while the old men and the plebeians, unable to fit within its limited area, were left in the city below to be slaughtered and plundered by the invaders. Yet progress toward equality continued. A second major step occurred in 367 B.C. when plebeians were made eligible to become consuls. Soon thereafter, they were given access to all offices, including those of priests. A law of 287 B.C. finally allowed the tribunes, then ten in number, to attend Senate meetings and awarded the popular assembly the power to pass on all legislation proposed by the Senate. Rome thus had achieved democratic institutions, although the senatorial class still retained firm control over the machinery of government. As a result, the Romans benefited from political stability during the height of the republican era.

Roman expansion

After the expulsion of the Etruscans, Rome continued to expand and to develop the governmental system for dependent areas which enabled her to unite the peoples of Italy under her suzerainty and retain their loyalty. In the course of numerous wars—not all of which terminated in Roman victories—the Romans acquired power first over nearby Latin states, then, by the third century B.C., over all of central Italy.

Some neighboring areas were simply annexed to Rome, but most were induced to join the League of Latin States in which all supposedly enjoyed equal power. In 340 B.C., however, the Latin allies revolted against Rome since they had not in fact been granted equality. After defeating the rebels, the Romans discontinued the fiction of a league of equals and set up a system in which every area was treated according to its political development and presumed loyalty to Rome. Five Latin towns were incorporated into the Roman state and their inhabitants granted citizenship. Some regions were allowed their own local government, could trade in Rome and intermarry with Romans, but were not awarded full rights of Roman citizenship. Some were given the status of self-governing allies, who had to accept Rome's dictates in foreign policy and furnish troops in time of war. Others were turned into Roman colonies, administered more or less directly by Rome and guarded by Roman garrisons. Beyond these were still other categories with varying degrees of self-rule.

While this system was admirably flexible, it contained a flaw that became a weakness in Rome's imperial system. Although full citizenship was granted to some allied communities, the Romans were generally reluctant to bestow such rights to the people under their control. Hence, Rome tended to remain a small city-state with an ever growing appended empire. Ultimately the dependent peoples were to press increasingly for the privileges of Roman citizenship. The Roman institutions, designed for governing a small area, were to prove inadequate for the administration of a large empire. Although the allied and subject states remained on the whole surprisingly loyal, the Romans apparently were in no mood to take chances after the Latin revolt of 340 B.C. During the succeeding decades, they began to construct their famous roads which led from Rome directly to many dependent areas and permitted Roman armies to march speedily to the aid of any embattled local garrison.

Until the third century B.C., Roman expansion confined itself to central Italy. Northern Italy was dominated by the powerful Gauls, and the Greek settlements in southern Italy and Sicily were then at the height of their cultural and political might. During the fifth and fourth centuries, the city-state of Syracuse on the island of Sicily, ruled by a series of tyrannical rulers, was not merely a center of Greek culture but also a formidable power, locked in frequent strife with Carthage. Rome as yet could hardly have dared challenge such a power.

The height of the Republic and internal disorder

With internal antagonisms temporarily lessened, Rome launched her conquest of the Mediterranean. It is futile to speculate whether these conquests were deliberate imperialistic moves or—as has been asserted—reluctant defensive responses to foreign pressures. In the course of a century and a half during the height of the republican period, the Romans extended their domination first over the western, then over the eastern, Mediterranean.

Conquest of the Mediterranean

In 282 B.C., Rome became involved in a costly, ten-year war against the ambitious king (Pyrrhus) of Epirus, a state in northwestern Greece which exerted much influence on the "heel" of the Italian Peninsula. Successful conclusion of the war allowed Rome to acquire all of southern Italy. Thus planted across the Straits of Messina from Sicily, the Romans became embroiled in the quarrel between Syracuse and Carthage both of which sought to dominate all of the island.

Rome's intervention in Sicily led to a life and death struggle with Carthage. The ensuing three Punic Wars (264–241, 218–201, 149–146 B.C.) were probably the most important undertaken by the Romans in their rise to a world power. Spectacular campaigns were fought in Italy, Spain, Sicily, and North Africa, directed by such military geniuses as the Carthaginian Hannibal (247–183 B.C.) and the Roman Scipio Africanus (237–183 B.C.). Large-scale sea battles took place throughout the western Mediterranean, and states as far away as Macedonia and Pergamum in Asia Minor became involved in this prototype of a world war. Despite severe reverses suffered alternately by each side, both protagonists showed surprising perseverance. Yet in the end, Carthage succumbed.

The direct and indirect consequences of the three Punic Wars for the development of the Roman state are significant. As a result of the first war, Rome annexed Sicily and turned it into a conquered province, the property of the Roman state. Its people became neither allies nor Roman citizens, but tax-paying subjects, contributing one-tenth of their annual crop of grain and one-fifth of all other produce. Soon thereafter, the Romans seized Corsica and Sardinia. In the treaty ending the Second Punic War, Carthage ceded Spain to Rome, agreed to pay an indemnity for a period of fifty years, to surrender all of her famous elephants, and to dismantle her navy except for ten warships. The third war finally ended with the physical destruction of the city of Carthage and with the surrounding territory made a new Roman province.

This territorial accretion was merely the most spectacular evidence of the vast transformation which Rome experienced as a result of the Punic Wars. In the span of a few generations, Rome was catapulted from a small, agricultural state into an imperialistic maritime power. This development in turn affected most phases of Roman life. The devastation of the Italian countryside, particularly during the second war, and the subsequent ample supply of cheap grain from Sicily and Spain necessitated a readjustment of Italian agriculture and almost destroyed the livelihood of the small Roman peasants. On the other hand, more government officials were required to administer the conquered areas, where many of them found tempting opportunities for becoming rich. Moreover Rome now needed a standing army based on long-term enlistments, which in turn produced a new social group of army veterans who after some twenty years of military service had to be reabsorbed into civilian life. Finally, the conquests, particularly in southern Italy and Sicily, brought the Romans into closer contact with Greek culture —a fact readily noticeable in art and literature; they also increased the number of slaves available to rich Romans and produced the need for new laws to regulate relationships between conquered and conquerors.

While fighting Carthage, Rome also expanded northward and eastward. Under pretext of clearing the Adriatic of pirates, the Romans established a protectorate over Illyricum (modern Dalmatia), an act applauded by the Greek city-states. Before the Second Punic War they gained control over the Po Valley by establishing garrisoned colonies among the hostile Gauls. After the war, this area was turned into a new province, Cisalpine Gaul. Supported by most of the Greek states, the Romans fought four wars against Macedonia between 215 and 148 B.C. In the end, Macedonia as well as Greece passed under Roman control, with some Greek states permitted to retain partial self-rule. Since the Seleucids of Asia Minor frequently intervened in Greece, the Romans were drawn into Near Eastern affairs. By 133 B.C., Rome had conquered the entire western coast of Asia Minor and seized control of the Dardanelles.

As a result, Rome commanded the Mediterranean from modern Turkey to the Straits of Gibraltar. Even the peoples of the non-occupied areas began to look upon Rome as the logical arbiter of international disputes and thereby encouraged the Romans to play a role which easily led to further conquests.

The beginning of internal friction

During the second half of the second century B.C., the Roman socio-political system was beset by problems which could not be solved by the traditional methods of patient compromise. These internal problems essentially resulted from Rome's acquisition of a vast overseas empire and her simultaneous failure to alter her political forms from those of a city-state.

The class structure had changed. Instead of two, there were now three classes: the rich senatorial class, comprised of wealthy landholders, old patrician families, former consuls, provincial governors, and other office-holders; the knights (equites), rich financiers aspiring to high office but considered parvenus by the traditional upper strata; and the vast masses of the plebs, poor and often unemployed, flocking to the large cities—especially Rome—in ever greater numbers.

Rome's increased wealth, furnished by tribute from the provinces and by the influx of gold from the East, caused inflation and a widening gap between the rich and the poor. Closer contact with newly conquered provinces brought increased Hellenistic and Oriental influences. To court the plebs and secure the loyalty of soldiers and veterans, ambitious politicians resorted to demagoguery, providing free grain and amusements to the masses and offering booty and land to soldiers.

Rome's tradition of peaceful solutions to socio-economic problems was replaced by violence, illegality, murder, and banishment. During the last century of the Republic, the customary respect for law and order gave way to dictatorship and the rule of private armies, ultimately culminating in the demise of republican institutions. At the same time, the peoples of Italy increased their agitation for an extension of Roman citizenship.

The period of internal violence opened in 133 B.C. during the tribuneship of Tiberius Gracchus (163–133 B.C.), who sought to remedy the cleavage between rich and poor by limiting individual ownership of public lands and distributing some of them to the poor. In violation of tradition, the ambitious Tiberius had a rival tribune deposed and himself re-elected for a second consecutive term as tribune. In retaliation, the frightened upper classes had him murdered. An era of illegality and political assassination was inaugurated.

Ten years later, Tiberius' brother Gaius Gracchus (153–121 B.C.) attempted to use his office as tribune to effect even more far-reaching social, economic, and political reforms. To gain a better base of power, he sided with the knights against the senators. He proposed further land reform measures, reduction of grain prices, free uniforms for soldiers, and the extension of voting rights to all Italic peoples. To annul the Senate's exclusive judicial rights, he suggested the seating of knights in the law courts. Although largely unsuccessful, Gaius Gracchus' reform program pinpointed the social ills of his time. But his methods were revolutionary. It is symptomatic that when haranguing the crowd he abandoned the tradition of turning toward the Senate house. Instead he addressed the people, "a change of posture," according to Plutarch, which indicated "somewhat of a revolution in state affairs." In the end, Gaius, like his brother, was assassinated.

Soon after the attempted Gracchan social revolution, Rome fell under the dominance of the ambitious general Gaius Marius (155?–86 B.C.). The historian Sallust (86–34 B.C.) called him a man of "diligence, sense of honor, and great military knowledge," who later "fell headlong because of ambition." Successful in military campaigns in Africa, southern France, and Spain, Marius had himself re-elected to six illegal consecutive terms as consul between 107 and 100 B.C., by appealing to the plebeians in opposition to the Senate. By permitting volunteers without property to enlist in his armies and enticing them to join by the promise of booty and land, he created a "new army," loyal to him rather than to the state, and inaugurated the era of private armies that ultimately signaled the end of Roman republican government. Street-fighting henceforth became commonplace in Rome and ultimately degenerated into outright civil war between the armies of Marius and his followers and those of the more conservative Sulla (138–78 B.C.), who was to dominate Rome from 88 to 82 B.C. Thereafter, the dying years of the Republic were marked by almost incessant warfare between the private armies of ambitious politicians, fighting all over Italy and in the provinces of the empire.

After Marius' death, Sulla tried to reinstate the Senate in its prerogatives of power and began to act "like a dictator over the consuls." According to the Roman historian Appian (second century A.D.), Sulla walked about like an ancient king with "twenty-four axes borne in front of him." To obtain plebeian support, he awarded freedom and citizenship to many slaves and distributed free land to his legionnaires. But his attempted conservative reforms failed to stem the avalanche of internal disorder and corruption in provincial administration. Sallust's contemporary complaint, "I am disgusted with the morals of my state," was echoed many times in Cicero's frequent public denunciations of thievery and depredation, the plundering of public funds and sanctuaries, the increase of piracy and the embezzlement by provincial governors.

By Sulla's time, the question of the franchise could no longer be overlooked. When a bill to extend voting rights was once again defeated by the Senate in 91 B.C., many Italic communities rose in revolt. The ensuing struggle between Rome and its allies, sometimes labeled the Social War, lasted three bitter years. To entice the rebels into surrender, the Romans finally offered citizenship to all Italic peoples who laid down their arms—the

first significant extension of the privileges and protection of citizenship beyond Rome's environs. Yet Rome remained essentially a city-state, since no
provincial assemblies or representative system was created.

The decline in the political system was accompanied by changes in religious tradition. The state cults were neglected or degenerated into mere
forms largely devoted to divination. Some temples fell into ruins and priest-
hoods were often left vacant. Instead, Hellenistic philosophies—Stoicism and
Epicureanism—became favored by the upper classes. From Greece and the
eastern Mediterranean emotional religions were introduced, stressing the
theme of death and resurrection—among them vegetation and mystery cults,
the worship of Isis and of the Great Mother. Their emphasis on an afterlife
appealed to the downtrodden, while their emotional ceremonies furnished an
outlet for discontent. Senators and the upper classes generally objected to
these new cults as being un-Roman and leading to immorality, just as later
they opposed the spread of Christianity. Yet the Hellenization of Roman
thought continued.

Disintegration of the republican structure

During the last four decades of the Republic, all sense of legality and
devotion to the welfare of the state was overshadowed by the political and
military maneuvers of ambitious politicians. Taking advantage of existing
class hatreds, shifting their political flirtations between the popular and the
senatorial factions, and using semiprivate armies to conquer foreign lands and
acquire wealth and power, Pompey, Crassus, Caesar, Antony, Octavius, and
others plunged Rome into almost incessant civil wars. The hapless Senate
bestowed emergency powers now on this and now on that contestant, while
consulships were gained by bribery or military pressure rather than by election. Governmental authority was often exercised through cynical power
compacts, such as the triumvirate of 60 B.C. among Pompey, Crassus, and
Caesar. Political reputations were made through spectacular conquests
abroad, followed by grandiose triumphs celebrated in Rome, with booty for
the senatorial treasury and amusements for the masses. Dominion over parts
of the empire was divided and redivided, as though provinces had become
parcels of private real estate. Yet every military triumph unleashed a new civil
war, and every political success ultimately ended in defeat, murder, or suicide. In addition, this internecine strife of ambitious titans was made almost
legendary by the enigmatic role played during its last two decades by the
young queen of Egypt, Cleopatra (69–30 B.C.).

In 73 B.C., a serious slave rebellion, the third in five decades, erupted in
southern Italy under the leadership of the gladiator Spartacus (?–71 B.C.).
The wealthy financier Crassus (115?–53 B.C.) and the brilliant, young
general Pompey (106–48 B.C.), already famous through his military victories in Spain, were asked to suppress the uprising, a task that required
three years. Having thus gained added fame, Pompey and Crassus had

themselves illegally elected consuls (70 B.C.) and abolished the remaining portions of Sulla's conservative constitution. During the sixties, Crassus continued his financial speculations and supported ambitious politicians such as Julius Caesar (100–44 B.C.), while the orator and lawyer Cicero, initially a supporter of Pompey, sought to rid Rome of corruption and demagogic conspiracies. Meanwhile Pompey rose to unrivaled power, foreshadowing the era of one-man rule. He was entrusted with special authority over the Mediterranean coasts to enable him to clear the seas of piracy. After successful accomplishment of this task, he was given *imperium* without time limit over Asia, which he used to consolidate Roman domination from Jerusalem to the Black Sea and to reorganize the administration of the area.

Upon his return to Italy in 61 B.C., Pompey split with the Senate because of its refusal to ratify his Asian decrees and to provide for his veterans. But instead of using his army and his reputation to achieve his demands, he dismissed his forces and thus forfeited his chance of becoming sole ruler of Rome. A year later, Crassus and Caesar drew Pompey back into the center of the political stage by joining with him in the first triumvirate, designed to enable each participant to satisfy his personal aspirations.

Julius Caesar, too, had won military fame in Spain and had identified himself with the popular faction. According to the historian Suetonius (70–121?), Sulla had clearly recognized the potential of the young general by asserting that "in this Caesar there is more than one Marius." Caesar was even more ambitious and self-assertive than Pompey, possessed of a clearer vision of his future destiny. Even as a young official he claimed in a public oration that his aunt Julia was the descendant of kings and gods, including Venus. "Our stock therefore has at once the sanctity of kings, who among men are most powerful, and the claim to reverence which attaches to the gods, to whom kings themselves are subject." To gain more prestige and the support of a loyal army, Caesar obtained for himself command over Gaul, both south and north of the Alps. For nine years (58–49 B.C.) he campaigned in Gaul, adding the area between the Rhine and the Atlantic Ocean to the Roman Empire and making two descents on Britain. Through his own reporting on the Gallic Wars which he had published and circulated in Rome, he made sure that his exploits were brought before the eyes of his countrymen.

The first triumvirate lasted for six years, giving the three leaders controlling power over the empire. But in 53 B.C., Crassus was killed in Mesopotamia in battle against the Parthians. Meanwhile Pompey, less resolute and active than before, shifted his allegiance back to the senatorial faction in anticipation of an eventual showdown with Caesar. When the Senate became alarmed at Caesar's growing power and finally ordered his return to Rome without his armies (49 B.C.), he decided that the time had come to settle accounts with Pompey who remained his sole rival for supreme power. As the poet Lucan (39–65 A.D.) wrote, "Caesar could no longer endure a superior, nor Pompey an equal." Contrary to established custom, he crossed the Rubicon River and entered central Italy with his legions. Pompey's attempt to rally his disbanded armies with the aid of the Senate proved futile. He went to Greece where he was defeated by the pursuing Caesar (48 B.C.), and thence fled to Egypt. By the time Caesar reached Egypt, Pompey had been murdered.

After spending a few months with Queen Cleopatra, Caesar routed some followers of Pompey, reconquered the province of Syria, and finally made his triumphant return to Rome in 46 B.C. As sole ruler of the state, he was awarded numerous titles and powers, including that of dictator for life. He instituted many governmental reforms, some designed to aid the people of the provinces. But his reforms were haphazard. He neither permitted the Senate and the traditional officers to run the country nor took the ultimate step toward one-man rule by making himself king or emperor. It is impossible to say whether he lacked the requisite political vision or whether, as his admirers assert, he simply did not have the time needed to make order out of chaos and to formalize the new system of one-man rule which was to inaugurate the Empire. To be sure, there was not much time, for after his return to Rome, he soon had to rush to Africa and Spain in order to fight Pompey's sons and their various supporters, and in March, 44 B.C., he was assassinated.

Transition from Republic to Empire

Caesar's assassination opened a period of thirteen more years of civil war, during which Caesar's great-nephew and adopted heir, the young Octavius (63 B.C.–14 A.D.), gradually seized all power. Aided by the Senate and senatorial supporters, Caesar's murderers fled to the provinces to raise troops, while the consul Mark Antony (83?–30 B.C.) secured Rome with the good will of the popular faction and Octavius began recruiting an army among Caesar's veterans. This triple split of power lasted a year. In 43 B.C., Antony and Octavius agreed to collaborate. Together with General Lepidus (?–13 B.C.) they set up the second triumvirate, a formal agreement for sharing control of the empire. To eliminate personal enemies and obtain funds—Italy was exhausted and the tribute money from the East was being intercepted by the conspirators—the triumvirs then sentenced hundreds of senators and knights to death and confiscated their property. In the following year, they crossed over to Macedonia and defeated the armies of the chief conspirators, Brutus and Cassius.

The triumvirate was supposed to last for at least a decade. Actually the Roman Empire was soon divided between two rulers, with Lepidus imprisoned in 36 B.C. Octavius, in control of Italy and the West, was busily securing increased power and privileges. Antony ruled the East from his headquarters in Egypt where in 36 B.C. he married Queen Cleopatra. Antony's domain was the wealthier and on several occasions he even furnished aid to

Octavius, but he lost power when much of his army disintegrated during an unsuccessful war against the Parthians. Whether he was less ambitious than his younger rival, Octavius, and whether, as has been asserted, it was largely Cleopatra's aspirations which drove Antony into the final struggle against Octavius, is a matter of conjecture. In the late thirties, Antony adopted some Hellenistic customs and bestowed favors on Cleopatra's children, actions which Octavius exaggerated in his propagandistic efforts to undermine Antony's reputation in the West. Antony and Cleopatra, it was rumored, aspired to become eastern despots.

In 32 B.C., finally, Octavius asked the people of Italy and the western provinces to pledge him an oath of fealty. He then declared war on Cleopatra and set out for the East. After three battles, the last a naval engagement off Actium in northwestern Greece (31 B.C.), Antony's remaining forces were lost. He and Cleopatra committed suicide in the following year, leaving Octavius free to obtain the allegiance of the East and to complete Rome's transformation from Republic to Empire.

Life under the Republic

Despite internal friction and political chaos, all was not decline during the last century of the Republic. Popular government collapsed and provincial administration became corrupt, yet Rome continued to grow as a state and as a civilization.

Between 133 and 31 B.C., Rome rounded out her possessions in North Africa by incorporating into the empire the entire coast from the Atlantic to the Red Sea. In addition, Syria, large areas of modern Turkey, as well as all of Gaul were placed under Roman control. Continued territorial expansion required further refinement of Roman law, particularly the *ius gentium* which defined legal relations between individuals belonging to different subject peoples. This *ius gentium,* largely unwritten and concerned largely with commercial matters, was based on what later in the eighteenth century was to be called natural law. Common sense and practical considerations had to furnish solutions since the customs of every subject people differed.

Roman law itself, that is, law for Roman citizens, tended to be legislated a priori rather than based on precedents. Theoretically all citizens were equal before the law and the accused was deemed innocent until proven guilty. The Romans even sensed that equity was sometimes more important than strict legality—a feature normally associated with common law in the Middle Ages. These and other legal advances allowed the Romans to develop an elaborate system of jurisprudence and legislation which ultimately became a fundamental part of Western civilization.

Besides this excellence in law, the Romans became famous engineers and constructed aqueducts, roads, and bridges, some of which are still in use today. In the arts, letters, and philosophy, there is some controversy concerning Roman achievements. The Romans were profoundly influenced by

Greek culture. Study with Greek tutors was considered proper upbringing among the upper classes of Rome, and many intellectuals, architects, historians, and artists in Rome were in fact Greeks. In philosophy, the Romans were not very speculative and undertook instead practical adaptations of Greek ideas. Thus Cicero sketched a modified Stoicism in *Scipio's Dream,* with its emphasis on man's duty to the state and the promise of future fame in the form of an afterlife in heaven rather than reputation among men. The poet Lucretius (98?–55 B.C.) expounded a form of Epicureanism in his poem *On the Nature of Things* in which the universe was shown as an agglomeration of atoms. According to many critics, therefore, the Romans were primarily adaptors, assimilators, and transmitters of Greek art and thought.

Since much Greek sculpture and writing has been preserved for us primarily in Roman copies, such a role of transmitter should actually not be belittled. Moreover in art and in literature, the Romans were also originators. In pottery and mosaics, in the architectural organization of space as exemplified in the various forums, in the enclosure of vast areas for public buildings through the use of arches and domes, in wall painting and sculptured friezes, and above all in realistic sculptures—the so-called speaking likeness portraits—the Romans were indeed creative and original. Similarly, Cicero's numerous writings on politics, rhetoric, and law, the lyric poems of Catullus (87–54 B.C.), or the histories of Sallust can hardly be labeled imitations.

The early Empire

Octavius' victory over his rivals in 31 B.C. initiated one-man rule in Rome and, by tradition, marked the beginning of the Empire, although there was no formal establishment of imperial institutions. This "Empire"— a term which refers only to a form of government under a single sovereign and not to "empire" in terms of colonial possessions—lasted until 476 A.D. in the West and 1453 A.D. in the East. During the first two centuries, there was considerable prosperity and order, and the emperors enjoyed normal tenures of office (thirteen emperors in 211 years from 31 B.C. to 180 A.D., not counting an exceptional year of civil war with four emperors). However the last three centuries in the West were marked by the gradual shrinkage of the empire and by short reigns of the emperors, most of them terminated by murder (sixty-two emperors in 296 years from 180 A.D. to 476 A.D.).

Pax Romana

When the victorious Octavius returned to Rome in 29 B.C., he ordered the closing of the doors to the temple of Janus at the base of the Capitoline Hill, an act which by tradition signified the advent of peace. This propagandistic gesture hardly meant that the empire ushered in centuries of peace. The closing of the temple of Janus merely underscored the temporary end of the long period of civil wars. Actually, intra-Roman fighting occurred again in the next century, and there was almost constant skirmishing at the confines of the empire, especially in Europe and Asia.

To pacify and stabilize Rome, Octavius needed a rare combination of skill, tact, and ruthlessness. Under the guise of restoring republican institutions and mollifying the conservative groups, he created the substance of monarchic rule without the outer forms. By having himself elected or appointed to numerous offices simultaneously, he preserved the democratic forms while in reality establishing firm one-man rule.

His official title, among others, soon became "Imperator Caesar Augustus divi Juli filius." "Imperator," a term which in romance languages came to mean "emperor," denoted that he had the proconsular powers of *imperium* and that he was a victorious general. "Caesar," at first a family name, soon designated a ruler, and ultimately, in the Germanic and Slavic languages also came to mean an "emperor." "Augustus" was a special title with religious connotations of gratitude and consecration, conferred upon Octavius in 27 B.C. And "divi Juli filius"—son of the divine Julius—showed the tendency of the emperors to claim descent from divinity, although the early emperors demanded the worship of their genius (guiding spirit) rather than their living person. To ensure himself specific powers, Augustus first assumed the positions of consul and of tribune, to obtain the power of legislation, then of censor, to determine the make-up of the Senate, and, ultimately of Pontifex Maximus (13 B.C.). Above all, Augustus secured supreme judicial powers and gained sole control over the army even in the provinces. To retain their loyalty, he paid regular pensions to veterans. The title which he himself preferred was that of *princeps,* or first citizen, a term which later became "prince."

On the basis of these combined powers, Augustus reorganized the state. To eliminate embezzlement in the provinces, he paid regular salaries to provincial officials. He launched an imperial civil service, dependent solely on the Emperor. Although courting the good will of the senators, Augustus gradually reduced the functions of the Senate. Remaining for some time as a law court, it was reduced in later centuries to no more than the municipal government of the city of Rome.

Augustus was also intent on reviving Roman morality. Laws were passed discriminating against bachelors and encouraging parents to have more children. Through the writings of his protégé, the poet Virgil (70–19 B.C.), he aspired to revive such Roman virtues as love of fatherland, faithfulness, honesty, and respect for one's ancestors—all of which are exemplified in the *Aeneid*. Virgil's works also helped to glorify Augustus' reign and bestow splendor on Roman history.

The political edifice constructed by Augustus was strange indeed. It was so personal that none of his successors could make it operate quite as smoothly as he had; yet it was solid enough to last for centuries. Its main weakness was the absence of a set system of succession. New emperors were chosen by a mixture of adoption, inheritance, and interference by the Praetorian, or Imperial, Guard and later by the armies in the field.

Emperor Tiberius (14–37 A.D.), more conservative and despotic than Augustus, further weakened the power of the popular assembly and allowed the Praetorian Guard to assume greater importance. Under his reign, there was some fighting along the Rhine and the Danube, while at home court intrigues shattered the more dignified atmosphere that had characterized the Augustan era. Perhaps afraid of assassination, Tiberius ruled during the last decade of his life from a villa on the island of Capri.

A strangely uneven succession of emperors followed from 37 to 98 A.D. The mentally disturbed grandnephew of Tiberius and great-grandson of Mark Antony, Caligula (37–41), who demanded to be worshiped as a god, was followed by his shrewd uncle, Claudius (41–54), under whom the civil service was vastly expanded and the conquest of England begun. Nero (54–68), another great-grandson of Antony, son-in-law and adopted son of his predecessor, was an unpopular ruler, although his repute as a mad fiddler while Rome burned in 64 A.D. is perhaps undeserved and may be attributed to the fact that he was the first emperor to order the persecution of Christians in the city of Rome. Nero's unpopularity finally led to rebellion and to his suicide, marking the end of the direct descendants of Octavius (the Julian dynasty). The nebulousness of the system of succession became obvious when in one year (69 A.D.) four different rulers were chosen by four different armies. Murder and civil war finally eliminated all but one of the candidates.

The emperorship of Trajan (98–117 A.D.) opened a series of relatively successful reigns under the Flavian dynasty, when the principate was reconsolidated. Trajan came from Spain, the first non-Italian on the imperial throne. His interest in building, furtherance of public works, and his conquests of Mesopotamia and Rumania required an increase in the centralization of government and finances, with the consequent breakdown of local administration. His military exploits were recorded on the famous victory column in Trajan's Forum. The learned Emperor Hadrian (117–138 A.D.), less warlike than his predecessor, but even more intent on raising the material splendor of the empire through a large building program, stressed the special status of the person of the emperor. He built for himself a sumptuous villa at Tivoli, outside of Rome and, like a Hellenistic ruler, had a large tomb constructed on the banks of the Tiber, an edifice which in the Middle Ages became the papal fortress of Castel San Angelo. Imperial edicts then became the source of legislation, pointing toward the day when the ruler's word had the force of law. Like other emperors of this period, Hadrian experienced financial difficulties and was unable to erect an equitable and efficient tax system. Although a lenient ruler, he acted with severity against the Jews. After a revolt of the Jews in 70 A.D., the Romans had destroyed the city of Jerusalem. When the Jews rebelled again against Roman overlordship, Hadrian simply ordered their dispersion, thus completing the Diaspora which lasted until the creation of Israel in the twentieth century.

The prosperous period of the Empire ended with the reign of Marcus Aurelius (161–180 A.D.), best known perhaps for his Stoic philosophical *Meditations*. Under him there was almost constant fighting in Asia and the upper Balkans, as increased barbarian pressure on the Roman frontiers foreshadowed the gradual shrinkage of the empire during subsequent centuries.

Problems of further expansion

After the accession of Augustus, Roman territorial expansion continued for over a century until the empire reached its largest extent under Trajan. England, southern Germany, Palestine, and parts of Arabia were added. In the Balkans, the border was advanced to the Danube and for a time even beyond to include modern Rumania. Mesopotamia, Assyria, and most of Armenia were occupied temporarily. Repeated attempts to seize the German lands between the Rhine and Elbe were however frustrated by the fierce resistance of the Germanic tribes. (See Map 4.)

Pressure by tribes along the confines of the Empire was almost continuous and led to frequent wars which produced occasional serious defeats for the Roman legions. One wonders whether the tribute paid by the new provinces adequately paid for the cost of such constant wars. To keep out marauding tribes, the Romans built fortified walls, guarded by frontier detachments, across Germany from the Rhine to the Danube and across southern Scotland. These walls lent a temporary stability to the Roman frontiers, however, without preventing gradual barbarian infringement on the borders of the empire.

Expansion also added urgency to the question of extending Roman citizenship. Although the people of the provinces demanded the legal and tax privileges connected with Roman citizenship, the early emperors feared that wholesale extension of such rights might swamp Rome with alien elements. Under the Flavians, citizenship was granted more generously, but only in 212 A.D. were all free men throughout the empire made citizens.

At the same time, one must recognize the immense contribution made by Rome to the conquered areas, particularly northern Africa and Europe. The Romans built cities, constructed roads and bridges, improved agriculture, introduced new entertainments, and implanted new socio-political structures. Almost everywhere, Romanization left its imprint on later civilizations.

Imperial Rome

Literature and art flourished during the Augustan, or Golden, Age, encouraged and subsidized by the emperor himself. Virgil's love of the countryside (as in his *Eclogues, Bucolics* and *Georgics*) well suited Augustus' desire to encourage agriculture and the simpler country life as opposed to the luxury of the cities. Similarly, Augustus was delighted with Livy's (59 B.C.–17 A.D.) *History of Rome,* an account from the founding of the city to the age of Augustus, filled with legends and replete with glorification of Rome and of the new emperor. Belonging to the same circle were the poets Horace (65–8 B.C.) with his *Odes* and *Satires,* and Ovid (43 B.C.– 17 A.D.) with his love poems. The remaining period of the early Empire, sometimes called the Silver Age, continued to be very productive in satire (Juvenal, 60?–130? A.D.), drama (Seneca, 4 B.C.–65 A.D.), history (Tacitus, 55?–120? A.D.), and philosophy (Epictetus, 60–140 A.D.).

Sculpture under the Empire abandoned the realism of the Republic and became more idealistic and symbolic. Architecture flourished: the Pantheon, Colosseum, Altar of Peace, and Arch of Titus are all famous examples of Roman edifices in the early imperial period.

In his attempt to revive republican virtues and instill patriotism, Augustus discouraged the spread of foreign cults, built new temples to the traditional gods—Jupiter, Apollo, and Venus—and attempted to resuscitate the old state religion. Yet, the traditional gods failed to satisfy the lower classes, and Roman religious ideas continued to become more Orientalized. A new problem arose over the issue of emperor worship. In 29 B.C., some cities in Asia Minor received permission to pay divine homage to Augustus. However, such practices, though customary in the East, were disliked by the upper classes of Rome. Hence Augustus forbade emperor worship in Italy but did nothing to hinder its spread in the eastern provinces. Soon these rites became established also in Gaul and Germany, and eventually in Spain and Roman Africa. The trend thus started gradually altered the role of the ruler in the West and led to a major problem in Western civilization: the relations between the secular and the religious arms of society.

Contemporary events in Asia

While Rome rose to ascendancy in the Mediterranean, equally brilliant civilizations flourished in Asia. Indeed, one can observe interesting parallels between these civilizations, notwithstanding the geographic distance that separated them.

In the late third century B.C., the Chou dynasty was replaced by the rulers of Ch'in, often called the first Chinese emperors, who supposedly gave China her name. Although lasting less than two decades (221–207 B.C.), their rule exerted a deep influence on Chinese history. The Ch'in rulers suppressed feudalism and successfully centralized the administration and the army. To unify the people, they imposed a single style of writing. Eager to combat tradition and to construct a new society, the government even ordered the burning of the books of the great philosophers. During the Ch'in dynasty various forts in the northwest were connected into the famous Great

Wall, some fourteen hundred miles in length, for the purpose of restraining the constant inroads of tribes from Central Asia—a device similar to that used three centuries later by the Romans to prevent Germanic invaders from penetrating into Roman territory.

After the fall of Ch'in, China was ruled for four centuries (about 206 B.C. to 220 A.D.) by the less authoritarian Han dynasty. Based on a well-trained civil service, government administration remained fairly stable, with social policies resembling those of the modern welfare state. High taxes and government monopolies, coupled with price-fixing, enabled the rulers to engage in extensive public-works projects, particularly the construction of roads and canals. At the same time, there was a great cultural flourishing. Buddhist missionaries spread the new faith and Confucianism was again taught. The powerful Han dynasty also expanded Chinese domination northward to Korea, southward to Indochina, and westward as far as Turkestan, permitting direct overland contact with India and trade with the eastern Mediterranean.

Just as the Roman Empire started to decline in the western Mediterranean during the third century A.D., so China then entered a period of disorder. Commercial prosperity and cultural activity remained at a relatively high level, but the lack of political cohesion from the third to the seventh centuries A.D. made China a tempting prey for invading tribes from Central Asia. Northern China was gradually overrun by Hunnish and Turkish peoples from Mongolia.

In the face of these disorders, many Chinese hoped to preserve their way of life by stressing philosophical tradition. But change can never be prevented over a long period of time. Perhaps it is symptomatic that in place of the customary tunics many Chinese began to wear trousers of the type worn by the invading Huns. Such garments also made it easier to fight on horseback. At the same time, Buddhism flourished in greater strength and, for the lower classes, Lao-tse's philosophy was changed into mystic Taoism which emphasized immortality for the faithful and recommended a life of monastic simplicity—at a time when many poorer Romans also sought consolation in the immortality promised by Christianity.

After the fall of the Maurya dynasty in the second century B.C., India also suffered almost five centuries of disunity and foreign invasions. It was an age about which not much accurate historical information is available. Southern India resumed its independence, Greek dynasties and Greek influence dominated the northwest, and Turkish tribes infiltrated into various parts of the north. Despite political disunity, however, much art as well as Hindu and Buddhist literature was produced, although many of the writings survived only in Chinese translations.

After northern India was reunited under the Gupta dynasty (320–535 A.D.), Indian sculpture, poetry, and drama written in classical Sanskrit flourished for two centuries. The invention of the concept of zero and of the decimal point sped progress in mathematics. Yet, like China's Han dynasty, the Gupta rulers were overcome in the late fifth century A.D. by invading Huns who seized northern India and Afghanistan, where they became gradually assimilated to the local population.

During this era, particularly in the two centuries before and after the birth of Christ, there was much contact between the Far East and the Mediterranean by land and by sea. Chinese silk and Indian jewels found their way to Rome via Persia and Arabia. China and India exchanged missionaries, while northern India and Rome were influenced by the same Hellenistic thought. The Romans thus had some acquaintance with all the known civilizations of their day, except for those in the Western Hemisphere (the Zapotecs, Teotihuacans, and Mayas of Mexico and Central America, as well as the Paracas, Mochicas, and others in South America).

Moreover, Rome, India, and China shared the fate of having to face repeated onslaughts by invaders from Central Asia. The early history of these nomadic invaders and their interrelationship is only dimly known. Huns, Turks, and Tatars, all Mongolian tribes, probably lived in Central Asia as early as 2000 B.C. By the third century B.C., Turks and Huns, sometimes called Hsiung-nu, had become powerful in Mongolia and were frequently raiding northern China. Two centuries later, another Mongolian tribe, the Avars, or Juan-juan, obtained domination over the Huns, Turks, and Tatars and ruled such a wide area that their reign is often called the first Mongol Empire. (For the second Mongol Empire, see p. 166). But rather than submit to Avar domination, some Huns moved into northern China, others crossed the mountains into India, while a third group pushed through the Ural gap into Europe where, under the leadership of King Attila (433?–453 A.D.), it raided and plundered as far as central France and the gates of Rome (see p. 81). In the sixth century A.D., Avar power in turn was broken by rebellious Turks. The defeated Avars moved westward and during the succeeding two centuries established themselves in the Balkans whence their further advance was stopped by the Franks in the eighth century (see p. 113). The Turks, for their part, set up their own empire which soon split. The western Turks became embroiled in fights with Persia and the Byzantine Empire, and the eastern Turks attacked China. By the early ninth century this first long wave of Turkish power had subsided: the Chinese T'ang emperors defeated the eastern Turks (see p. 109); the Arabs blocked the advance of the western Turks.

SUGGESTED READINGS

Political History

Boren, Henry C., *The Roman Republic* (Van Nostrand, 1965).

Cowell, F. R., *Cicero and the Roman Republic* (Penguin, 1948).

Ferrero, Guglielmo, and Barbagallo, Corrado, *A Short History of Rome,* Vol. I, "Monarchy and Republic: 754–44 B.C."; Vol. II, "The Empire: 44 B.C.–476 A.D." (Putnam, 1964).

*Lamb, Harold, *Hannibal: One Man Against Rome* (Doubleday, 1958).

Mommsen, Theodor, *The History of Rome* (World, 1958). From the fall of Carthage to Caesar.

Nilsson, Martin, *Imperial Rome* (Schocken, 1962).

Richmond, Ian, *Roman Britain* (Penguin, 1962).

Rowell, Henry T., *Rome in the Augustan Age* (U. of Oklahoma, 1962).

Scullard, Howard H., *From the Gracchi to Nero: A History of Rome from 133 B.C. to A.D. 68* (Barnes and Noble, 1966).

Syme, Ronald, *The Roman Revolution* (Oxford U. P., 1960). The change from republic to empire.

Taylor, Lily Ross, *Party Politics in the Age of Caesar* (U. of California, 1949).

Warmington, Brian Herbert, *Carthage* (Penguin, 1965).

Culture

Adcock, Frank E., *Roman Political Ideas and Practice* (U. of Michigan, 1964).

Barrow, R. H., *The Romans* (Penguin). Rome's contribution to Western civilization.

Davenport, Basil, ed., *The Portable Roman Reader* (Viking). Selections of Roman literature.

Duff, John Wight, *A Literary History of Rome from the Origins to the Close of the Golden Age* (Barnes and Noble, 1963).

*Fowler, William Warde, *Rome* (Oxford U. P., 1947). Rome's influence on modern civilization.

Grant, Frederick C., ed., *Ancient Roman Religion* (Bobbs, 1957).

Hadas, Moses, *A History of Latin Literature* (Columbia, 1964).

Hamilton, Edith, *The Roman Way* (Norton, 1932).

Laistner, Max L. W., *The Greater Roman Historians* (U. of California, 1963).

Lewis, Naphtali, ed., *Roman Civilization; Selected Readings,* Vol. I, "The Republic"; Vol. II, "The Empire" (Harper, 1951, 1955).

*Paoli, Ugo Enrico, *Rome: Its People, Life and Customs* (McKay, 1963).

Von Vacano, Otto-Wilhelm, *The Etruscans in the Ancient World* (Indiana, 1965).

CHAPTER V

❧ *Transition to the Middle Ages* (180-565 A.D.)

The popular term "the fall of Rome" is misleading, since it evokes the picture of a cataclysmic change. Rather than collapsing suddenly, parts of the Roman Empire slowly decayed economically and financially, its administrative machinery became increasingly corroded, barbarian tribes infiltrated into the empire and acquired power in army and government, the frontiers of the empire were pushed in, and intellectual life changed under the impact of Christianization from within and barbarian influence from without. This process took three centuries. Moreover Rome did not "fall" like Carthage in that she disappeared from the earth. In the East, the Roman (or Byzantine) Empire survived for another millennium. Even in the West, after the centralized political control of the Latins had been shattered, significant aspects of Roman civilization—urban centers, land tenure, the Latin language, Roman law, to mention but a few—were incorporated in medieval society.

Growing influence of the East

Throughout most Roman history, the eastern Mediterranean—wealthier and intellectually more active—exerted much influence on the West. Greek and Hellenistic culture, Near Eastern religions, the influx of slaves from the East, the pomp and luxury of Oriental court life, all increasingly affected the West. In fact, during the fourth and fifth centuries A.D., the East became the more important part of the empire, considered by some emperors more worthwhile defending than the West.

The spread of Christianity

Palestine, the cradle of Christianity, had passed from Persian domination to the rule of Alexander the Great and then to his Hellenistic successors, the Egyptian Ptolemies and later the Seleucids. The Jews thus absorbed a good deal of Hellenistic culture. After a century of independence (168–63 B.C.), Palestine was conquered by Rome and ruled first by local kings—such as Herod—appointed by the Roman Senate, and later by Roman administrators. It was one of the latter, Pontius Pilate, who faced the task of trying Jesus, whom some Jews had expected to be the Messiah, but with whom they had become disenchanted, perhaps on realizing that he had no intention of freeing them from Roman rule.

After Christ's crucifixion—around 34 A.D., during the reign of Tiberius —his disciples and followers, particularly the Hellenized Paul, undertook the missionary task of helping to organize Christian communities. The new faith stressed love, inner purity, and salvation, but its rites aroused suspicion, and the Christians' all-absorbing devotion to Christ and God led some Romans to question their loyalty to the state. The first government-sponsored harassment of Christians occurred under Emperor Nero. St. Peter and St. Paul probably perished during these early persecutions. Soon thereafter it was made a capital offense to be a Christian, although the law was enforced only sporadically during the next two and a half centuries.

Christian beliefs spread with surprising speed. Local groups organized themselves into churches and elected their own leaders (presbyters or priests). Gradually a network arose, linking the various churches along Roman administrative lines, with bishops or metropolitans in the provincial capitals exerting primary influence. During these early centuries the leaders of the Christians faced three main problems. They had to determine the relationship of this new institution, the church, to the state—a new issue for the Romans in general who had not experienced any conflict with priestly classes. Secondly, they had to agree on an organizational framework, either a democratic or a hierarchical one. Finally, they had to decide how questions of dogma were to be settled, whether by a church council, by a single bishop, or by the emperor, and what was to be done with those who would not abide by the established dogma.

Economic and intellectual trends aided the spread of the new faith. As poverty increased, the poor flocked to the comfort of salvation promised by Christianity. Among the educated classes, Neoplatonism, with its equation of Plato's idea of the Good with God and its preference for spiritual over physical experience, provided a basis for the diffusion of Christianity, even though Neoplatonism later came into conflict with Christian dogma. Moreover many people must have seen in the Church, and later particularly in the monasteries, a haven of refuge from growing political chaos and financial disarray. Finally, the organizational growth of the church was also helped by political developments. As the emperors increasingly shunned Rome and lived in fortified Italian cities like Ravenna, or in the East, the bishop of Rome assumed greater responsibilities and power, thus undergirding his claim to leadership of the Catholic Church (see p. 90).

Division of the Roman Empire

During the third century, the imperial crown became a prize fought for by ambitious generals. Rulers, many not Italian by birth or upbringing, were frequently murdered. Wives, mothers, and concubines of emperors vied for power. Class distinctions again increased and the ideal of equality before the law was abandoned. Government became more and more a military dictatorship. The armies justified their financial exactions and political interference by pointing to the constant barbarian pressure on the frontiers in Germany and the Middle East. During the third century, the danger was particularly acute in the East after the Sassanians revived the Persian Empire and fought four major wars with Rome in seven decades.

At the end of the third century, Rome was governed by a strong ruler who sought to recast the empire on a firmer footing. Diocletian (284–305) divided the empire into two parts, with the dividing line running from east of Belgrade to Cattaro on the Adriatic. Each half was to be ruled by an Augustus, coequal to his partner and supreme like an Oriental despot over his own area, although Diocletian reserved over-all pre-eminence for himself. Under each Augustus was to be a junior emperor entitled Caesar to assist in the defense of the empire and be the official successor in his part of the realm. Each half of the empire was in turn divided into prefectures, dioceses, and provinces ruled respectively by prefects, vicars, and governors. By raising himself to a place of sacred eminence and insisting on emperor worship—a practice already common in many areas—Diocletian hoped to endow the imperial institutions with greater stability. Yet, the new administrative system did not prove viable.

Diocletian undertook many other reforms. He divided his armies, including hired troops of barbarians, into smaller units and scattered them all over the empire. He further enlarged the bureaucratic machinery, without however abolishing outmoded offices. Since military and administrative requirements were costly, taxes, though already oppressive, were raised, and in an unsuccessful attempt at stabilizing the economy the emperor decreed a limitation on prices and wages.

Diocletian's reforms hardly cured Rome's social and economic ills. Nor did the Christian persecutions which he ordered throughout the East divert attention from the continuing decay. Yet indirectly he may have contributed to the preservation of the eastern part of the empire by de-emphasizing the importance of Rome and enunciating guidelines for the division of the empire. For much of his reign he resided at Nicomedia on the Sea of Marmora and finally retired to his palace at Split on the Dalmatian coast, giving the rare example of an emperor abdicating.

This abdication was followed by almost nineteen years of strife and civil wars before Emperor Constantine (306–337), another influential ruler of the later empire, could exert effective power over the state. Under Constantine, the division between East and West was further accented. Perhaps because the location was safer from barbarian invasions and more strategically placed to watch the Danubian and eastern fronts, Constantine built a new capital at Byzantium and named it Constantinople. Although he eventually abandoned Diocletian's system of co-rulership and ruled alone, since he did not trust any partners, the founding of Constantinople gave much impetus to the division of the empire.

In economics, Constantine faced the same problems as Diocletian. With the decline of the currency, barter was becoming the preferred medium of exchange, and taxes were collected largely in produce—a foretaste of the natural economy that was to characterize the Middle Ages. To escape oppressive taxation, many freemen were engaging themselves on large estates as *coloni,* the prototype of the medieval serf. Constantine attempted to halt this social defection by legislating a caste system that fixed people in their profession and seemed to foreshadow the socially static Middle Ages.

Most important was Constantine's attitude toward Christianity. According to tradition, he was converted to Christianity in 312 when, before a battle, he saw in the sky a cross with the letters *in hoc signo vinces* (thou shalt win under this symbol). Actually, historians dispute as to when, if ever, Constantine became a Christian. There is no question, however, that he took a vital interest in Christian affairs. In 313, he promulgated the Edict of Milan, awarding freedom of worship to all religions. It stipulated "that the Christians and all others should have liberty to follow that mode of religion which to each of them appeared best." The arguments advanced in the Edict appear surprisingly modern: "For it befits the well-ordered state and the tranquility of our times that each individual be allowed, according to his own choice, to worship the Divinity; and we mean not to derogate aught from the honor due to any religion or its votaries." The Edict also stipulated restoration of confiscated Christian property.

Constantine soon became more intimately involved with Christianity. In 316, he was asked to judge, though he failed to settle, the assertion of one Christian group, the Donatists, that a sacrament such as holy mass if performed by a sinful priest was not valid, whereas most clergymen insisted that no man, no matter how imperfect, could impair the validity of a sacrament. Nine years later, Constantine interfered even more actively in ecclesiastical matters. In 325, he convoked the Church Council of Nicaea and presided over its sessions to decide another point of dogma. The Arians (followers of Arius, a priest at Alexandria) asserted that Christ and God were made of different substances, since they rejected the possibility that human beings could have crucified a part of God. The followers of Athanasius, the patriarch of Alexandria, on the other hand, believed that Christ and God were of the same substance, since otherwise God would not have sacrificed a part of Himself for the redemption of mankind. Constantine and the Church Council opted in favor of Athanasianism which became accepted dogma, although the emperor later reversed himself and urged the Eastern churches to adopt Arianism, thus increasing dissension within the Church.

Dogmatically important as the decision against Arius was, it did not obviate subsequent prolonged debates on the nature of Christ. Significant also was the fact that the Council of Nicaea was called by the emperor and sat under his direction. It provided a vital precedent for the imperial claim to leadership over the Church, as practiced in the East Roman (Byzantine) Empire, and later in Czarist Russia. It also increased differences between East and West, since the bishops of Rome, further removed from Constantinople's imperial influence, tended to reject secular interference in ecclesiastical matters.

The end of the Roman Empire in the West

During the fourth and fifth centuries, the socio-economic decline accelerated, particularly in the western provinces. By itself this decline was not fatal. What ultimately caused the western areas to be detached from the empire while imperial rule continued in the East was the simple fact that the West was overrun by barbarian peoples who established a number of new kingdoms on former Roman territory.

Internal disarray

Constantine's death in 337 was followed by almost three decades of civil wars among his descendants. Of his eight sons and nephews who successively claimed the roles of Augustus or Caesar, only two died a natural death—the others were murdered, died in battle, or committed suicide. The emperorship was at times in the hands of a single ruler and then again divided between two or more.

The wars ruined the countryside and further lowered agricultural production. Inflation worsened and the lack of coinage—gold and silver specie was draining to the East—affected trade, foreshadowing the localized economy of the Middle Ages. Communication between parts of the empire became less efficient, giving the separate regions the impression that they had to fend for themselves. Afraid of barbarian incursions or plundering by roving troops, many communities began to surround themselves by defensive walls. At the same time it became more difficult to field effective armies. Apart from lack of funds, manpower was scarce. The impoverished peasants had little incentive to fight for a decaying system which merely oppressed

them. Hence more and more of the fighting was done by barbarian mercenary troops, often led by their own generals who thus acquired considerable
political power.

While engaged in civil wars over imperial prerogatives, the rulers also
had to rush from one frontier to another to ward off invasions. Outside pressure became particularly acute in Mesopotamia (the Persians), along the
Danube (the Goths), and in Belgium (the Franks).

During the last decades of the fourth century, a few fairly skilled rulers
attempted to make the Diocletian system of co-rulership function effectively.
These emperors were however generally unsuccessful against the invading
barbarians along the Danube. Theodosius I (379-395), probably the
strongest ruler of the period, tried a somewhat different policy. Groups of
baptized Visigoths had previously been allowed to settle south of the Danube, but when large numbers had sought to enter the empire under arms,
Emperor Valens had tried to stop them. However, Valens had been defeated
and killed at the battle of Adrianople (378). Theodosius then made a treaty
with the Visigoths. He gave them land in Thrace and Macedonia as well as
regular payment, in return for which they were to defend the Balkan frontier against other invading tribes. Turning imperial land over to an organized barbarian people under its own king—not simply allowing them to
serve as mercenaries—proved a dangerous precedent. It was more than retrenchment of the frontiers, as had already been done when Mesopotamia,
Rumania, Swabia, and Scotland had been abandoned. Theodosius' action
initiated the dismemberment of the empire.

Theodosius also changed relations with the Christian Church. With one
notable exception, when Emperor Julian "the Apostate" tried to revive paganism, the rulers after Constantine found it advantageous to cooperate with
the Church. Emperor Gratian (375-383) even closed down pagan altars in
Rome and relinquished the title *Pontifex Maximus* which was later assumed
by the popes. Yet prior to Theodosius the Roman government was not officially committed to one particular religion. Theodosius, however, became
deeply involved in Christian affairs. He supported strong antipagan measures and tried to bring harmony between rival sees in the East, particularly
the patriarchs of Constantinople, Antioch, and Alexandria. He also convoked a Church Council at Constantinople (381) in order to heal continued
dissension over dogma. The Athanasian creed was reaffirmed and eradication of Arianism ordered—at a time when most of the barbarians knock-
ing at the doors of the empire had been converted to Arianism.

Significant also was Theodosius' attitude toward the powerful bishop of
Milan, St. Ambrose (bishop, 374-397). After a revolt in Thessalonica during which thousands were massacred presumably on orders of the emperor,
Bishop Ambrose withheld communion from Theodosius for eight months
until the emperor had done penance. Such humiliation of an emperor was a
curious rehearsal for medieval times, when popes were to excommunicate

emperors. It also gave the appearance that, at least in the West, the ecclesiastic powers were superior to those of the emperor.

Emperor Constantine, one might say, had turned the Roman state toward the Christian Church. With Theodosius, the final step was taken of turning Rome into a Christian state.

External pressures

The permanent division of the empire occurred in 395 with the reigns of Theodosius' sons, one married to a Frankish princess, the other under the influence of his father-in-law, a Vandal. It was symptomatic that barbarian princes frequently married into Rome's ruling families and actually ran imperial affairs or imposed their own puppet rulers. Hence, when the invasions of the empire were launched in full force, one barbarian chief with mercenary troops often found himself fighting other barbarians. Moreover the division of Rome made it more difficult to present a united front. The East was less threatened than the West. In theory each Augustus was responsible for the defense of the entire empire, but some emperors in Byzantium were not averse to see the barbarians threaten Italy while sparing the East.

Marauding tribes had existed before. During its long history, the Roman state had frequently been raided by barbarians, especially by the Celtic Gauls. For several centuries after about 375 A.D., these barbarian invasions assumed the proportions of human avalanches as wave after wave of tribes breached the frontiers of the Roman Empire. Most of these tribes spoke related Germanic languages—for example the Goths, Franks, Burgundians, Vandals, and Saxons. They were thus related to the tribes whom the Romans had battled for centuries along the Rhine and the Danube, the people of whom the historian Tacitus (first century A.D.) had written that "they all have fierce blue eyes, reddish hair, and large bodies fit only for sudden exertion." The Huns, on the other hand, who had been pushed out of Central Asia, came from an entirely different ethnic stock (see p. 72).

We do not know precisely what caused these gigantic migrations. Some historians believe it was largely a chain reaction caused by the appearance of the Huns. As a sixth century historian (Jordanes) wrote, "the race of the Huns, fiercer than ferocity itself, flamed forth against the Goths." The Huns pushed the Ostrogoths who in turn pressed on the Visigoths. Plausible as this explanation is, it is also possible that equal barbarian pressure along the frontiers had existed for some time but that conditions in the western part of the empire now made resistance impossible. To put it simply, the frontiers caved in.

Soon after the beginning of the fifth century, the Romans felt forced to abandon Britain which was then gradually taken over by Germanic invaders from the Continent: Saxons, Angles, and Jutes. Simultaneously, Franks, Burgundians, Vandals, and others raided Gaul and took large parts of it from Roman control.

Meanwhile the Visigoths were once again on the move. Expelled from Greece in 397, they were led by their energetic King Alaric (395–410) to Italy where, after initial reverses, they seized Rome and plundered it (410). After Alaric's death, the Visigoths occupied southern Gaul and made their headquarters at Toulouse. From there they fought with the Vandals over possession of Spain where they finally established an independent Visigothic Kingdom.

The Vandals, having ravaged parts of Gaul and established themselves in southern Spain, crossed to Africa in 429 under their King Gaiseric (428–477). They carved out a large kingdom from Tangiers to Tripolis, with its center at ancient Carthage, acquired a navy, and in 455 made an expedition to Italy and sacked the city of Rome.

Finally, the Huns began to raid the empire. After leaving the Ukraine and remaining for some time in the Danube Valley, a large horde of Huns, led by King Attila and supported by various Germanic groups, raided Central Europe as far as northeastern France, until they were defeated by a motley force of Romans, Gauls, Visigoths, and Franks (451). Still seeking to acquire a share of Roman territory, Attila then rushed through southern Germany and Austria and invaded Italy in the following year. Afraid of the Huns, the people along the northeastern shores of the Adriatic fled to some offshore islands where they founded the city of Venice. Attila seemed ready to turn south and occupy Rome itself. But after negotiating with an imperial delegation which included Pope Leo I (440–461), he abruptly withdrew to Austria. Historians will never know whether it was papal persuasiveness, newly arrived Roman reinforcements, a plague among his own troops, or some other reason, which determined the feared Hunnish king to reverse his steps. Attila died in the following year (453), and some of his people eventually settled present-day Hungary. Although actually unsuccessful in his exploits, Attila's fame was such that he retained an important place in medieval epics. (See Map 5.)

The significance of the year 476

The barbarian invasions resulted in a shrinkage of the empire. By the middle of the fifth century, much territory had simply slipped out of the political, economic, or financial control of the emperors. The Roman government extended official recognition to the Visigothic Kingdom in Spain, the Vandal Kingdom in Africa, and others, while theoretically retaining jurisdiction over the Roman citizens in these areas. In practice, local barbarians soon assumed control over most of the western regions of the Roman Empire.

During the first half of the fifth century, the western empire experienced two long, though weak, reigns (of Honorius and Valentinian III), providing at least a semblance of continuity. Thereafter the western rulers, residing in Ravenna rather than in Rome, tended to be puppets installed by barbarian chieftains or by ambitious women. In the East, however, the empire suffered less loss of territory, had a better paid administrative system, and profited from longer reigns after the mid-century.

In 475, the western emperor—Emperor Nepos, the sixth ruler in the West in sixteen years—was overthrown in favor of Romulus Augustulus, whose name was a curious reminder of the birth of Rome and of the first emperor. In the following year, the barbarian chieftain Odoacer (476–493) in turn deposed Romulus Augustulus. But instead of installing a new puppet ruler in the West, Odoacer assumed control over much of Italy more or less as an independent king. He sent the imperial emblems to the eastern emperor (Zeno), as if to indicate that there was no more need for two Augusti. The emperor at Constantinople, in turn, recognized Odoacer as *patricius,* a title which soon came to mean the protector of Rome.

After this, no new co-ruler was appointed for the West. The year 476 therefore marked the end of the period of emperors in the West and has, by tradition, come to mean the end of the Roman Empire in the West. But it is important to recognize that the absence of emperors in Italy simply signified that the emperors in Byzantium henceforth ruled the entire empire. Actually, consuls continued to be appointed in both parts—in Rome only until 534—and theoretically the same Roman Empire persisted, with its capital at Constantinople, the so-called Second Rome. The year 476 therefore signified only the discontinuance of the co-emperorship in the West. Seen from Constantinople, 476—or 480, the year the deposed Emperor Nepos died—in fact symbolized the reunification of the empire. The loss of the western provinces was looked upon as a temporary political and military setback. There seemed no reason why the western parts could not be reconquered and reincorporated into the empire.

Continuation of the Roman Empire in the East

By the end of the fifth century, the political map of the Mediterranean had changed considerably. North Africa, Spain, Gaul, and Italy had become independent kingdoms. These will be discussed in the next chapter since they reflect the problems of the dawning Middle Ages more than those of declining ancient times. The eastern Mediterranean—Egypt, Greece, Thrace, Asia Minor, Syria, and Palestine—remained firmly under the control of the emperor at Constantinople. Although this empire in the East was a direct continuation of the Roman Empire and was officially known as such, it is usually referred to as the Byzantine Empire to stress differences which had actually existed from the beginning between the Hellenistic East and the Latin West. The difference was more than one of language, between Greek and Latin. In the East, thought was more speculative and art more abstract; there was more wealth and trade, hence a more active middle class and more sumptuous cities. Moreover the East was more accustomed to theocratic rule.

Many of these differences between the Byzantine Empire and the defunct Roman Empire in the West were gradually also reflected in the differences between Greek Orthodox and Roman Catholic Christianity.

From 527 to 565, Byzantium was ruled by an extraordinary team, the intelligent and sometimes dreamy Justinian and his forceful wife Theodora (508?–548). Justinian was determined to recreate the old Roman Empire in all its splendor and extension, on the basis of the new Christian framework, solidified by imperial absolutism. In the Balkans, he faced constant inroads by Slavish and Hunnish tribes. In the East, his reign more or less coincided with that of one of the strongest rulers of the revived Persian Empire, Khosru I (531–579), under whose firm leadership the Sassanid Empire flourished and attained its greatest extent. Although he would have preferred not to get militarily embroiled in this region, Justinian fought two major wars against the Persians and in the end agreed to pay annual tribute in order to obtain their benevolent neutrality.

Justinian's main interest was concentrated on the West. In a relatively brief campaign in 534, his highly gifted general Belisarius (505?–565) conquered the Vandal Kingdom of North Africa. Within a few years, the area had been reincorporated into the Roman administrative system. With the aid of German mercenary troops, Belisarius then launched the long and difficult reconquest of Italy (535–554). Justinian, who looked upon the barbarian kings as no more than vice-regents for Constantinople, justified the attack by asserting that his troops came to avenge the murder of the Ostrogothic regent of Italy. In the process of the reconquest, the Ostrogothic Kingdom was destroyed (see p. 95) and Italy returned to imperial rule as the Exarchate of Ravenna. In 554, southeastern Spain was also conquered and added to Justinian's possessions. With the exception of northern Spain, southern France, and a few places in Italy, Byzantium thus once again controlled the entire coast line of the Mediterranean. (See Map 6.)

It has been argued that these costly conquests were of no consequence and that Justinian merely wasted precious resources, since Byzantium hardly possessed the strength to defend such an extended empire. In fact, the Byzantines were unable to retain most of the conquests for long. The destruction of the Ostrogothic Kingdom opened Italy to new barbarian invaders, the Lombards, who gradually gained control of much of the peninsula. The Spanish possessions were reconquered by the Visigoths at the beginning of the seventh century and a little later North Africa fell to the Arabs. Nonetheless, Justinian's conquests bore many long-term fruits.

In Italy, Byzantium retained Venice, Ravenna, Rome, Naples, and the southern tip of Italy—much of it for many centuries. Constantinople thus retained over Italy some influence, which is particularly noticeable in architecture and art. Moreover the emperors were able to exert occasional pressure on the popes at Rome, while the popes could now and then use the Byzantines as convenient counterweights to other threats. Justinian's conquests had also confirmed Byzantium as a strong naval power—important not merely for the protection of trade but for defense against the Arabs in the following century.

Ruling like a despot, surrounded by luxurious pomp and awe-inspiring court etiquette in order to raise his position far above that of ordinary mortals, Justinian devoted much energy to internal reforms. He sought to purify the administrative machinery by punishing bribery, forbidding the sale of offices, and improving salaries. Although unable to eradicate embezzlement, he fashioned a good civil service which later helped hold the state together even when civil wars over disputed successions rent the empire. He launched a vast building program in Constantinople and the provinces—imperial palaces, monasteries and churches (among them the incomparable Church of Holy Wisdom or St. Sophia), aqueducts, roads, bridges, fortresses, public baths, and decorative fountains. Whether built for his own benefit, for use by the Church, or as public works, all edifices served to glorify the emperor and spread the fame of Byzantium.

The wars, the vast court expenses, and the emperor's building program required increased revenues. Taxes and tariffs were raised and new state monopolies established. Attempts were made to gain more profits from the flourishing trade in silks, spices, and other luxury goods that came to the empire from China and Ceylon. Yet despite oppressive taxes, there was little abject poverty and no flight into serfdom as in the West. Similarly, large scale commerce and an economy based on money rather than land never disappeared.

Justinian also assumed tight control over the armies. Although consisting largely of Germanic, Hunnish, and other mercenaries, they were loyal and obedient to the emperor. Except for a few mutinies in later reigns, the Byzantine army remained a state army and hence a pillar of the government and did not again become the instrument of private war lords.

Justinian was particularly interested in law. Coincidentally, this was a period of general progress in jurisprudence. In the barbarian kingdoms, where no written laws existed, a statement of valid legislation was clearly needed. Visigoths, Burgundians, and Franks all codified their laws around the turn from the fifth to the sixth century. Within the empire, too, many legal questions remained to be clarified. Hence, Justinian ordered a group of jurists to work on this task. Four major collections were issued in the course of his reign, all together loosely labeled the Justinian Code. The *Codex* itself contained imperial edicts issued since the days of Hadrian, after elimination of contradictions and repealed items. The lengthy *Digest,* like a reference book, included legal statements of famous jurists on important points of law. The third, the *Institutes,* was a law textbook; and Justinian's own legislation was gathered at the end of his reign in a volume entitled *Novellae.*

By preserving Roman legislation and making it more useable for jurists, Justinian made possible its great influence in Western civilization. The Code, frequently amended, henceforth served as the basis for law in Byzantium and soon made itself felt in the growing ecclesiastical law of the Church. In the kingdoms of the West, as we shall see, concepts of law were at first more influenced by Germanic customs. But when the study of law was revived during the eleventh and twelfth centuries and actively promoted at Italian universities, and when political advisers sought to bolster their theories for reviving centralized states by imitating Roman absolutism, Justinian's Code became the legal bible for professors, jurists, and politicians alike. Perhaps the most influential concept in the Code was the enunciated notion that the voice of the ruler was to be law, surely a basis for later absolutism.

Justinian was almost obsessively interested in religion, including problems of dogma. For political as well as religious reasons, he sought to restore harmony within the Church by ending the quarrels between the papacy and various bishops over questions of dogma and authority. Yet neither force nor persuasion ultimately helped him achieve this task. To be sure, he extended the influence of the Church by dispatching missionaries among the Slavs and to Africa as far as Abyssinia. Within the empire, he tried to eliminate paganism and proceeded harshly against heretics such as the Donatists and the Arians. But he was unable to reconcile the pope and the heretic Monophysites of Egypt and the Near East, who believed that Christ had only one nature and not two (one human and one divine), as had been stipulated by the Council of Chalcedon in 451.

His treatment of the pope and the patriarchs as strict subordinates ultimately helped to disunite the eastern and western churches rather than create harmony. For the patriarchs in the East could not escape the direct supervision of the emperor. In Italy, however, although Belisarius' reconquest allowed Justinian to control the papacy, the emperor found it expedient to award more and more secular powers to the pope as a sort of civil governor in central Italy, a position which assured the papacy greater independence. Thus the Church was soon split even more between the dependent patriarchs in the East and the quasi-independent pope in the West.

Justinian's reign of almost four decades left the Byzantine Empire in financial straits and militarily over-extended. But it also had turned Byzantium into a resplendent, vibrant state which was to accomplish far more than merely preserve the Graeco-Roman heritage while Western Europe slumbered during the Early Middle Ages. Byzantium acted as the primary civilizing agent for most of the Slavic peoples of Eastern Europe, converting them to Christianity, providing them with an alphabet, and teaching them Roman governmental ideas. Finally, Byzantium was to serve for centuries as a bulwark against Moslem penetration into southeastern Europe (see p. 106).

SUGGESTED READINGS

Religion

Bainton, Roland H., *Early Christianity* (Van Nostrand, 1960). To the fifth century A.D.

Bultmann, Rudolf, *Primitive Christianity* (World, 1956).

Glover, Terrot R., *The Conflict of Religions in the Early Roman Empire* (Beacon, 1960).

Hatch, Edwin, *The Influence of Greek Ideas on Christianity* (Harper, 1958).

Klausner, Joseph, *From Jesus to Paul* (Beacon).

Parkes, Henry Bamford, *Gods and Men: The Origins of Western Culture* (Random, 1959). An evaluation of the Judaeo-Hellenic origins of Western culture.

Mattingly, Harold, *Christianity in the Roman Empire* (Norton, 1967).

Weiss, Johannes, *Earliest Christianity: A History of the Period A.D. 30–150,* two vols. (Harper).

Disintegration of the Roman Empire

Barker, John W., *Justinian and the Later Roman Empire* (U. of Wisconsin, 1966).

Burkhardt, Jacob, *The Age of Constantine the Great* (Random, 1967).

Bury, John Bagnell, *The History of the Later Roman Empire; From the Death of Theodosius I to the Death of Justinian,* 2 vols. (Dover, 1910).

Bury, John Bagnell, *The Invasion of Europe by the Barbarians* (Norton, 1967).

Chambers, Mortimer, *The Fall of Rome: Can It Be Explained?* (Holt, 1963). Collection of essays.

Gibbon, Edward, *The History of the Decline and Fall of the Roman Empire* (Simon and Schuster, 1962). An eighteenth-century classic.

Gordon, C. D., *The Age of Attila, Fifth-Century Byzantium and the Barbarians* (U. of Michigan, 1960).

Kagan, Donald, *Decline and Fall of the Roman Empire—Why Did It Collapse?* (Heath, 1962).

Katz, Solomon, *The Decline of Rome and the Rise of Mediaeval Europe* (Cornell, 1955).

Lot, Ferdinand, *The End of the Ancient World and the Beginnings of the Middle Ages* (Harper, 1961).

Starr, Chester G., *Civilization and the Caesars* (Norton, 1965). On the decline of classical civilization.

CHAPTER VI

※ *The Dawning of the Middle Ages*
(Fourth to Eighth Centuries)

In Western civilization, the term "Middle Ages"—a label first used in this connotation in the seventeenth century—denotes a span of time between the end of ancient times in the Mediterranean area (300–500 A.D.) and the beginning of the modern era in Europe (1300–1500 A.D.). By the early nineteenth century, however, historians of the Romantic school, who were interested in analyzing the spirit of an age (*Zeitgeist*) rather than ascertaining chronological sequences, began to use the adjective "medieval" as referring to a particular type of civilization. The Middle Ages thus became less a chronological period than an era with a particular way of life. The essence of this medieval civilization was based on a fusion of Hebraic-Christian, Greco-Roman, and Germanic elements. Generally speaking, medieval man was strongly influenced by the Christian faith, by Germanic notions of personal loyalty, and by Greek rationalism. His relatively static life rested on a predominantly agricultural economy, rather simple trade, and a feudal class structure.

Beyond those areas of Europe where such a medieval civilization developed, the term "Middle Ages" has little meaning. When speaking of the Near East or Asia during medieval times, the reference should be understood to be a chronological one, taken from the frame of Western history; it should not imply "medieval" characteristics in these non-Western areas.

Growth of the Church

In the beginning, "the Christian Church" consisted of a handful of disciples and followers of Christ loosely joined by the common belief in His resurrection. They had little organization and no property. Centuries later, the Church had become a fully developed institution, with its own laws and courts, its own taxes and resources, its own administrative machinery and large landed possessions. Popes, bishops, and abbots had assumed not only spiritual powers over the peoples of Europe but also significant secular jurisdiction. In essence, the difference between these two periods denotes the growth of the Christian Church from its humble origins into the most powerful institution of medieval times. For the sake of clarity, this development can be analyzed under four different aspects: (1) the growth of the Church as an institution, (2) the ascendancy of the bishop of Rome, (3) the acquisition of secular power, and (4) the development of the new faith.

The Church as an institution

By the beginning of the second century, the Christian communities, scattered over the Roman Empire, were still autonomous, administered by elected and consecrated bishops who were assisted in their work by presbyters, or elders. The community's funds were derived from gifts and self-taxation (the tithe). The bishops had some judicial powers, being able to exclude from the community those who violated its rules—a precedent for excommunication. A loose association was gradually fashioned between these autonomous communities to supplement their common belief in the Scriptures. Bishops exchanged letters and visits, and began to hold joint meetings to discuss common problems. Ultimately, this practice led to the gathering of church councils, usually convoked by the emperor for the purpose of settling questions of dogma and of relations between the communities.

Meetings of synods and councils raised vital organizational questions. For instance, one had to decide whether the five patriarchs (Constantinople, Rome, Jerusalem, Antioch, and Alexandria) should have a greater voice at such gatherings, and whether metropolitans (archbishops) who administered the large sees of former provincial capitals should have power over ordinary bishops. In answer to such questions a hierarchical church structure was gradually developed. As vertical administrative lines were drawn, with their implicit channels of command, the democratic basis of the bishoprics was abandoned, the practice of electing bishops being replaced by appointment from above.

The growing wealth and power of individual churches as well as the frequent disputes over dogma between groups of churches also required clarification of the corporate nature of the institution. In accordance with Roman law, the local churches soon assumed corporate status. They owned property as a group and it was presumed that the bishop could speak for the community. At the level of the "catholic" church, meaning all the Christian churches combined, it took considerably longer to establish corporate guidelines and to determine who was to be entitled to speak for the Church.

While establishing an organization to tie the separate communities together, the Church acquired "immunities" which called for further institutionalization. The churches received immunity from taxation by the local rulers, as well as exemption from military service. Collecting its own revenues and administering its own services required an ever growing administrative organization. Soon bishops also obtained judicial immunity: the right to judge members of the clergy, first only on ecclesiastical business and later also in civil matters. Such legal duties which eventually led to the development of a complete body of canon law required further institutional innovations, as did the acquisition of landed properties, armies, and eventually sovereign status.

In a loose sense, the concept "church" referred to all the believers in Christ. A more restricted definition included only the institutionalized church with its ordained members, the "secular" clergy, who tended to the needs of the community. By the sixth century, however, a new branch had been added in the form of the "regular" clergy, those living by a *regula* (rule) in a monastery. Monasticism had originated in the East in the form of hermitages. Later, St. Anthony (250?–350?) and St. Jerome (340?–420) had organized hermits into monastic communities, which attracted many brilliant people. Monastic institutions gradually spread to the West, but fell into disrepute because of a lack of discipline. During the sixth century, St. Benedict (480?–543?) introduced a new type of Western monasticism, based on strict rules—including vows of obedience—which he wrote for the monastery at Monte Cassino. People flocked to these new monasteries in answer to spiritual needs as well as to escape the devastation of the period, for, by the sixth century, even the city of Rome resembled an empty shell. Gone were the days of luxury, of public games, and of free bread.

Eastern monasticism had been devoted to the ascetic salvation of the individual hermit. Although still more concerned with the self than with society, monasticism under St. Benedict acquired more social and intellectual aspects. Like most churchmen of the period, Benedict considered that knowledge for knowledge's sake was sinful and that man's activities should further salvation. At the same time he believed that "leisure is the enemy of the soul," and urged that monks be kept busy. The labors undertaken by monks proved invaluable to society. They studied and copied manuscripts, thus preserving much of antique learning and amassing priceless libraries; they practiced agriculture and viniculture, staffed hospitals, and tended to the poor. With their better schooling, they soon came to be used at court as special envoys, advisors, and educators of princes. The "regular clergy" thus became an important addition to the institutionalized church.

Papal ascendancy

Starting in the second century, the bishop of Rome aspired to the headship of the entire Church and sought to speak for it. For example, Pope Victor I (189–198), or to be more technically correct, Bishop Victor of Rome, since the distinction between bishops and popes did not yet exist, made a unilateral decision regarding the date for Easter and insisted that all good Christians accept it.

There are many reasons why Rome should have aspired to pre-eminence. It was considered a holy city, since Peter and Paul had presumably been martyred there. As the Church developed along Roman administrative patterns, there was a natural tendency for ecclesiastical lines of communication to centralize on the capital. Moreover Rome benefited from a lack of competition. The East was dotted with powerful bishoprics, many of which could boast apostolic fame; in the West, however, before the emergence of Milan in the fourth century, no bishop was strong or wealthy enough to challenge Rome. Finally there was the Petrine theory of apostolic succession, which was frequently hinted at during the fourth century but fully proclaimed only during the fifth century by Pope Leo I. According to the Petrine theory (Matthew 16:18–19), Christ had built His Church on Peter, the Rock, and had given him the keys to the Kingdom. As leader of the Christian community, and hence first bishop of Rome, Peter had bequeathed "the power to bind and loose" to his successor and thence through apostolic succession to all subsequent bishops of Rome. The bishop of Rome was therefore to be considered superior in power and responsibility to all other bishops.

When Constantine moved his capital to Constantinople, the question arose whether the capital of Christendom—if indeed one can speak of such a capital at this time—should also be shifted east. Constantinople, which lacked the spiritual prestige of other patriarchal sees, since it had not even existed at the time of Christ's crucifixion, soon launched a struggle for power against Rome as well as against its rivals in the East, Antioch and Alexandria. With the Church rent by heresies and by quarrels among bishops during the fourth century, not much progress was made in effective administrative centralization.

The emperorship of Theodosius I introduced new problems. At the Church Council of Constantinople (381), it was proclaimed that the patriarch of Constantinople, a city to be considered "the new Rome," was to rank in power and prestige immediately below the bishop of Rome. Although this decision affirmed the supremacy of Rome, it made the patriarch of Constantinople feel entitled to pre-eminence at least over all eastern bishops, including his archrival in Alexandria. The possibility thus loomed that a divided Roman Empire would entail a divided Christian Church, one ruled by

Rome, the other by Constantinople, foreshadowing the eventual split between the Roman Catholic and Greek Orthodox churches. Theodosius' reign
also opened another problem. With Christianity the official religion of the
state, the emperor tended to look upon the Church as a state institution for
which he was responsible, although Bishop Ambrose warned that "the
emperor is within the Church, not over it." The implied union of Church
and state in one ruler threatened the independence of the Church and
ultimately produced a new array of difficulties.

With no strong emperors in the West during the fifth century, the bishops of Rome were called upon to assume more secular power, especially
when the barbarians threatened Rome while the emperors remained safely
ensconced in well-fortified Ravenna. The patriarchs of Constantinople
lacked such opportunities for gaining prestige. The highly skilled Pope Leo
I, often named Leo the Great, was probably the first to take full advantage
of this development for the purpose of advancing the power of Rome. He
claimed the power to adjudicate between contending bishops and freely accepted appeals from local synods. He insisted that he could promulgate
dogma, for the time being with imperial consent. On the basis of the Petrine
theory, he assumed apostolic powers over the "universal" church and intimated that there could be no salvation outside the Church. One might say
that Leo I was the first pope in the modern sense of the word and that with
him papal ascendancy became the established desideratum for the Church—
at least in the West—although it was to take many centuries before the theories of papal supremacy could be put into effective practice.

Justinian's reconquest of Italy in the sixth century endangered the position of the Roman papacy. The newly appointed exarch of Ravenna claimed
powers superior to those of the pope since he was the representative of the
emperor. Ironic though it appears, the Lombard invasions of Italy (see p.
112) may have helped preserve papal power, at least in the West. Pope
Gregory I, the Great (590–604), possibly the strongest and most influential
pope of the first millennium, was able to regain considerable freedom of action by playing off the Lombards against the imperial forces. He reorganized
the financial structure of the Roman see and increased the papacy's temporal
powers in central Italy. Greater papal influence in some countries of the
West was also gained by intensified missionary activity. Parts of southern
England, for example, were Christianized during Gregory's pontificate.
Himself a Benedictine monk, he recognized the potential value of monasticism and attempted to bring the regular clergy under control of the papacy.
The monastics, in turn, became useful tools for the extension of papal influ-
ence.

The secular power of the Church

Vital for the inauguration of the Middle Ages was the growth of the
temporal power of the Church, both at the level of ordinary bishops and that
of the papacy in particular.

As the Roman administrative system began to falter, many bishops in outlying provinces assumed the role of government officials, either by default or because of political ambitions. Bishops administered cities, collected tolls and supervised markets, fed the people, and even led troops in defense of their community. In Italy, it became common for an elected tribune and the local bishop to share the privileges and responsibilities of municipal government.

The Church also became a major landholder in Western Europe. In gratitude for salvation, the faithful deeded land to the Church, and the weak lent her their land—as so-called *precaria*—in return for its lifetime use and protection. As bishoprics thus acquired title to more land, more cities became the possessions of local churches, ruled by a bishop as other rulers governed their own state. Ecclesiastical landholdings in turn required a larger administrative machinery. The Church needed serfs and slaves, bailiffs and supervisors, financial officers and defensive troops. The many ecclesiastical states governed by bishops and abbots, which thus arose during the Middle Ages, represented an important phenomenon in involving the Church in secular affairs.

The powers of the papacy during these centuries present a more complicated problem. As the richest see, Rome was also given vast stretches of land in the vicinity of the city. Such lands belonged to the bishopric of Rome and before the days when centralized taxation was perfected, the pope derived his revenue from them. When during the fifth century and again after the Lombard invasions, the pope came to administer parts of central Italy—partly by default of other authority and partly upon the specific request of the emperor—the question loomed whether he ruled these areas solely for the emperor or whether he might eventually establish claims in the name of the bishop of Rome or of the Church as an institution. The so-called Donation of Constantine, by which Emperor Constantine supposedly gave to the papacy temporal rule over Rome, Italy, and "the provinces, places, and *civitates* of the western regions," was not yet referred to. Yet, in essence, the popes already claimed sovereign status in central Italy, acknowledging merely a vague obedience to the emperor in Constantinople. The Church had thus progressed beyond the position of a mere institution within the state and was on the way to becoming a state in itself.

The new faith

Christianity, needless to say, was more than an institution. It represented a set of beliefs, a way of life, which vastly affected peoples' outlook. There is no need to describe here the teachings of the Gospel. Yet it is worth recalling that churchmen were plagued for centuries by the problem of defining specific aspects of dogma, a task engendering frequent accusations of heresy and splits within the Church.

Another problem for Christians was the determination of their attitude toward classical learning and philosophy. At first there was a tendency among some Christian apologists to adapt Christian thought to the existing Hellenistic-Roman framework. Such an attitude, however, involved the danger of losing sight of Christianity's central meaning and of producing many differing interpretations. Gradually it became clear that new moral and philosophical problems should not necessarily be considered in light of the old classical learning. On the contrary, the triumph of Christianity called for the accommodation of pagan thought to Christian dogma, a reconciliation in which Christian theology was to be paramount. Origen of Alexandria and of Caesarea (182?–251?), whose numerous writings and widespread influence made him one of the Greek Fathers of the Church, was one of the first to attempt such a reconciliation between pagan learning and Christian theology. Later, the patristic writers in the West—primarily the four Western Fathers of the Church, Ambrose, Jerome, Augustine, and Gregory—continued the process of adapting pagan learning to the new Christian universe. Their writings became so important that, together with the Scriptures, they were incorporated in the *traditio ecclesiae,* a basic part of Catholic teachings. St. Ambrose, the powerful bishop of Milan, wrote about ethics in an attempt to reconcile Stoicism with Christian thought. St. Jerome translated the Bible into Latin in the so-called Vulgate which became for centuries the standard version for Roman Catholicism.

A Church Father of greater originality was St. Augustine (354–430), who served for almost half of his life as bishop of Hippo in North Africa. Augustine did not merely adapt pagan thought to Christian requirements. Although influenced by Plato and Neoplatonism, he was an original thinker who deeply imprinted his concept of Christianity on medieval times and beyond. His view of an all-powerful God, the sole source of grace and salvation, made a strong impact on Luther; his ideas on divine predestination were rejected by most medieval churchmen but exerted considerable influence on Calvin. Augustine's *City of God* left a profound mark on medieval society with its distinction between the eternal, blissful city of God, and the ephemeral, sinful, terrestrial city of man. Together with his *Confessions*—an autobiography in which earthly pleasures are in the end considered sinful —Augustine's *City of God* reinforced the ascetic tendency bequeathed by St. Paul and helped set the prevailing mood for the Middle Ages.

Finally, Pope Gregory I, the last of the Church Fathers, sought to do more than merely reorganize the administration of the Church. Eager to educate the clergy and to improve the morals of all believers, he wrote extensively on many aspects of Christian life. Some of his writings, such as the *Dialogues* and *Magna Moralia,* an analysis of the Book of Job, became more or less standard reading in the Middle Ages. A comparison of the writings of Gregory with those of his predecessors, particularly St. Augustine, reveals the change in the level of learning from late classic to medieval times. Although insisting that the true value of all knowledge resided in its ability to help man attain salvation and that love of knowledge for any other purpose involved the danger of turning man away from God, St. Augustine had still harbored the profoundest respect for Greek and Roman thought. With Gregory however, as with most of his contemporaries, one finds a distrust of pagan learning and a rejection of inquiry and investigation. Sophisticated logic and arguments had given way to credulity and allegorical explanations.

Meanwhile the question had also arisen as to how to treat pagan history in relation to Christian chronology. Eusebius (260?–340?), bishop of Caesarea, the author of a history of the Church down to his own day, attempted to tackle this problem. In his *Chronicle,* he constructed a sort of universal timetable, consisting of parallel columns of royal succession in different countries, with notes on historical events. He thus sought to give perspective to the Christian era.

The Germanic kingdoms

From the fifth to the eighth centuries, the western Mediterranean and Western Europe went through an era of small states. Various independent political units occupied the area once ruled by the Roman Empire. Yet by the eighth century, the smaller states had again disappeared—except in the British Isles—and three major powers, the Byzantine, Moslem, and Frankish empires, dominated the area.

The short-lived states

Of the more important Germanic kingdoms of the period, only the Franks and Anglo-Saxons ultimately retained their independence. The others all succumbed within a few centuries. (See Map 6.)

By the middle of the fifth century, the Vandal Kingdom of North Africa seemed solidly established (see p. 81). Possession of a navy enabled the Vandals to conquer Corsica and Sardinia and to import food from Italy. The emperor in Ravenna (Valentinian III) even signed a treaty with Gaiseric in 442, recognizing him as an independent king in Africa and betrothing his daughter to the Vandal's son. But in Africa, the scattered Vandal settlements were plagued by constant raids by unruly Berber tribes. Moreover the local Christian population, despite the prevalence of heresies such as Donatism and Manichaeanism—the belief in the existence of evil as a force in itself—distrusted the Arianism of the Vandals. When Justinian undertook the reconquest of North Africa, Vandal rule proved to be a thin veneer. The century-old kingdom (429–534) collapsed and the Vandals disappeared from history.

The Kingdom of the Visigoths lasted longer—until 711. After their exploits in the Balkans and in Italy (see p. 81), the Visigoths seized southern Gaul under the leadership of Alaric's brother-in-law who married the emperor's half-sister (Galla Placidia). The emperor (Honorius) then awarded the Goths parts of Aquitaine to be administered as a kingdom under Roman suzerainty. Two-thirds of the land was to belong to the Visigoths, with the rest remaining in Roman hands. Urged by the emperor to clear the province of Spain of barbarian invaders, the Goths soon set out to conquer Spain. Thus, by the late fifth century their kingdom stretched from Gibraltar to the Loire, and from the Alps to the Atlantic. Like the Vandals in Africa, the Visigoths enjoyed a somewhat colonial existence. The local population retained Roman law, spoke Latin, and adhered to the Athanasian creed, whereas the conquerors lived according to their own law code—based on a mixture of Germanic and Roman law—and stubbornly defended their Arian beliefs.

In 507, the Franks expelled the Goths from southern Gaul. With the center of their kingdom moved from Toulouse to Toledo, the Goths next lost southeastern Spain to Justinian's reconquest. Although reduced in size, this Visigothic Kingdom in Spain lasted another two centuries (507–711), and even proved strong enough to reconquer the lands taken by Justinian and to overrun the Sueves who had occupied the northwestern part of the Spanish Peninsula. Yet, weakened by internal rivalry, the Goths succumbed to Arab invaders in 711.

The Kingdom of the Ostrogoths (489–553) in Italy was the most short-lived and yet in many respects the most interesting. The Ostrogothic King Theodoric the Great (489–526), who in Germanic legends was glorified as "Dietrich von Bern," was partly educated at Constantinople and became a general in the Roman army. When the Ostrogoths became inconveniently powerful in the Balkans, the Byzantine emperor commissioned Theodoric and his Goths to seize Italy where Odoacer had assumed too much independence (see p. 82). The Ostrogoths thereupon conquered Italy. Supposedly, Theodoric killed Odoacer himself by cleaving his body with a sword.

The Ostrogothic Kingdom which Theodoric then established was an interesting mixture of Germanic and Roman elements. As a Roman citizen, Theodoric ruled Italy according to Roman law with the aid of the Roman civil service, used only imperial coins, surrounded himself with Roman officials at his court in Ravenna, and maintained the fiction that he served under Constantinople. But his own Gothic subjects were guided by Germanic laws.

Although ruthless as were most of his contemporaries, Theodoric was a wise ruler, perhaps the most skilled of the barbarian kings. In Italy, he tried to prevent the exploitation of the local population by his own people and attempted to restore whatever he found decaying. Among his barbarian colleagues he tried to act as mediator and advisor. His diplomatic contacts were augmented by marriage ties with many important Germanic ruling families: the Vandals, Visigoths, Franks, and Burgundians. Theodoric's transitional position between ancient Rome and the Middle Ages is well illustrated by his choice of two advisers: the philosopher Boëthius (480?–524?) and the churchman Cassiodorus (480–575). Boëthius is sometimes called "the last Roman," since his book, *Consolation of Philosophy,* still preserved the Stoic tradition. One might also call him the last Roman senator in that he represented the dying Roman aristocracy. Ultimately, Theodoric had him executed on charges of treason. Cassiodorus, on the other hand, with his monastic preoccupation and his devotion to encyclopaedic knowledge laced with allegorical meanings, was a typical forerunner of the Middle Ages. Soon after Theodoric's death, the Byzantine general Belisarius initiated the reconquest of Italy, an act leading eventually to the annihilation of the Ostrogothic Kingdom (see p. 83).

There were other Germanic kingdoms that were shortlived, such as those of the Burgundians in eastern France and of the Lombards in Italy, both of which were destroyed by the Franks. One might speculate why such large kingdoms as those of the Vandals, Visigoths, and Ostrogoths did not survive, since they might have "Germanized" the entire western Mediterranean. It is hardly enough to assert that they fell because they were conquered by the Byzantines and Moslems respectively. Had the kingdoms been more viable, they might have successfully resisted such attacks.

One important factor no doubt can be found in the religious issue. All three peoples were Arians at a time when the Arian heresy had been largely stamped out in the empire. During the fourth century, the missionary bishop Ulfilas (311?–381) had brought Arian Christianity to the Goths along the Danube, had composed for them an alphabet from a mixture of Greek letters and Gothic runes, and had translated the Bible into Gothic. From the Goths, Arian Christianity had rapidly spread to most other Germanic tribes —except those which still remained pagan, like the Franks and Anglo-Saxons. The differences between Germanic Arianism and orthodox Christianity within the empire were more than doctrinal. Since the barbarians did not live in the Roman Empire, their churches could hardly be expected to be organized along Roman lines. Their services were simple, performed in the vernacular language. Their ecclesiastic organization was subject to the tribal king, not to the authority of any pope. After settling within the empire, the barbarians, who were at any rate not much interested in dogmatic discussions about the nature of Christ, saw no reason for changing either their beliefs or their ecclesiastical organization.

From the moment they set foot on Roman soil, therefore, the barbarians had to face the organized resistance of the Church. Most Romans looked upon the barbarians not merely as intruders but, worse, as heretics. Although the policy of the barbarian kings was not to interfere with the local Roman Church, Germanic Arians and Roman Athanasians frequently persecuted each other, especially when the struggle involved possible political advantage or the prospect for confiscating the loser's property.

There were other reasons why the three kingdoms lacked viability. The barbarians had not entered the empire to destroy Roman civilization but to share in it. Yet they lived essentially like colonial rulers, mixing little with the local populations. With their troops acting like an army of occupation, they tended to live by their own laws, despite the attempted compromise between Roman and Germanic law in some of the law codes. While Roman loyalties had been territorial or, as it were, directed to the abstract ideal of the state, Germanic loyalties tended to be personal, to a leader. Hence herein, too, there was little meeting of minds.

Theodoric was perhaps the only one who consciously tried to "Romanize" his Goths, possibly because he occupied Italy itself and not merely the provinces, or because of his upbringing and the influence of such advisors as Boëthius. Yet even Theodoric did not succeed. Moreover, one must keep in mind that the barbarians were few in number. The average tribe can be estimated at about one hundred thousand people, including women and children. Their success in battle against the Romans was probably due to their superior use of cavalry and certainly not superiority in numbers. The barbarian occupation represented a thin layer and it is hardly a coincidence that the barbarian kingdoms failed in the most Romanized areas of the empire (Italy, Spain, Africa), whereas the Franks and Anglo-Saxons survived in northern Gaul and Britain.

A final factor explaining their failure to survive was the lack of cooperation between tribes. Encouraged by Rome and later by Constantinople, which stood to profit from such dissension, the barbarians constantly fought among each other. Here, too, Theodoric was an exception with his unsuccessful attempts to cement friendly relations between the barbarian kingdoms. In the end each kingdom sought only its own advantage, and they perished separately.

The viable kingdoms

Whereas the three southern kingdoms disintegrated, the Franks in northwestern Europe created a viable kingdom which was to become a major center of medieval culture. Support by the Church of Rome was important in ensuring Frankish survival. Of equal significance were geographic and demographic factors. In their settlements between the Seine and the Rhine, the Franks were relatively numerous, and by amalgamating with Alemani, Burgundians, Goths, and other Germanic tribes, they avoided being submerged among the Gallo-Roman population. Moreover they lived at the limits of the Roman Empire, not at its heart, and could easily remain in contact with related Germanic tribes across the Rhine. The Alemani, Bavarians, and Anglo-Saxons probably survived for similar reasons.

The Franks were fortunate in having a very skilled leader at a crucial point in their history. King Clovis (481–511) of the Merovingian dynasty may have been brutal and cunning as legends describe him, but he was highly successful. Most of our knowledge of him comes from a single admiring source, his biographer, Bishop Gregory of Tours (538–593). In three decades, Clovis changed the Franks from allied status within the empire to complete independence, united his dissident people under his rule, and more than tripled the territory they controlled by defeating Gallo-Romans, Alemani, Visigoths, and Burgundians. His most decisive step was his adoption of Roman Catholicism, followed by the conversion of all his Franks. This step at once evoked a friendlier attitude among the local Gallo-Roman population. His wars against the Arian Burgundians and Visigoths were turned into holy wars against heresy. Even the emperor at Byzantium looked favorably upon this new outpost of orthodoxy. Above all, conversion to Athanasianism meant that the Merovingian dynasty could count upon the active support of the Church. This cooperation between the papacy and the Frankish (and later French) monarchy was to help on various occasions ensure the survival of both partners.

Clovis' Frankish Kingdom was so well founded that it survived despite the vast problems it faced during the succeeding centuries of transition to feudalism. Like many barbarians, the Franks did not know the concept of the "state," of *res publica,* which had been so thoroughly developed by the Romans. The Merovingian rulers, who did not practice primogeniture (the sole inheritance right of the eldest son), tended to look upon the kingdom as their personal possession which they could divide among their sons, a custom which frequently entailed civil wars among the heirs.

Furthermore, administrative power began to slip from the control of weak kings and became decentralized at lower levels. Some local officials—counts and dukes—acquired immunity from royal interference and began to assume judicial and military responsibilities normally belonging to the government. Since money was in short supply, grants of land came to be used as reward for services. The Church naturally was involved in this gradual feudalization of society (see p. 118). As large land owners, the bishops not only became landed aristocrats but acquired secular functions. Even though by the eighth century some ecclesiastical lands were taken by the kings and awarded as benefices to public officials and military leaders, the Church probably gained more from the system than it lost.

England experienced a rather different development. After the Roman legions were withdrawn in the early fifth century, tribes of Angles, Saxons, and Jutes from present-day Denmark and northern Germany gradually occupied much of the island in the course of the next two hundred years. Meanwhile the Celts, who had been subdued by the Romans, resumed their independence in the hills of Cornwall, Wales, and Scotland. The Germanic invaders established seven small kingdoms which fought one another for preeminence during the seventh century. Dense forests tended to separate the various tribes, and jealousies among the rulers made amalgamation of the kingdoms difficult.

Although Christianity had penetrated into England under Roman occupation, paganism had reasserted itself after the withdrawal of the Romans. Southern England was again Christianized after the monk Augustine, dispatched by Pope Gregory I (596), established a mission at Canterbury. Thereafter there was a brief struggle between Irish and Roman missionaries for domination over England, until the English churches were reorganized under the primacy of Rome in the late seventh century. With its growing episcopal organization and frequent synodal meetings, the Church helped bridge the gap between the seven separate kingdoms.

Unlike many of the other Germanic tribes, the Anglo-Saxons had not lived on the borders of the Roman Empire. This may explain why they retained so much confidence in tribal customs and had relatively little knowledge of Roman governmental institutions. As a result, the Church had an opportunity to make herself important in law and government, much more so than in Gaul. In a way, the Church in England represented not only Christianity but also the Greco-Roman heritage, whereas the local rulers were more purely Germanic in outlook. A good example was the new archbishopric of York which during the eighth century became a famous center of learning. At York "the Venerable Bede" (673–735) taught Greek and Hebrew and wrote on physical science as well as history.

During the late eighth century, Danish foragers raided the coasts of England, Scotland, and Ireland. Soon thereafter, one of the seven kingdoms, Wessex, began to dominate the others, thereby initiating the unifying process which was to lead to a single English kingdom.

Neither Scotland nor Ireland were settled by Germanic tribes and hence cannot be considered as "viable Germanic kingdoms." Yet both survived the Early Middle Ages as distinct cultures. Inhabited mostly by Celtic tribes, Ireland had not been touched by the Roman occupation. It became converted in the fifth century by St. Patrick and thereafter grew quickly into a vital outpost of Christianity, with monks and bishops acting rather independently from Rome. Monasticism proved particularly popular with the Irish. Monastery schools became important repositories of learning and fostered interest in Gaelic poetry as well as in art (for example, the *Book of Kells*). Irish monks sent missionaries to Scotland and England and established numerous monasteries on the Continent, some of which became important institutions (Luxeuil, St. Gall, Würzburg, Salzburg, and others). Despite their contributions to the growth of Christianity, however, the Irish remained politically and economically backward and did not form a kingdom as such.

The disunited clans of Scotland were converted by Irish missionaries during the sixth century. Two hundred years later, a more or less united Scottish Kingdom emerged (under King Kenneth I, ?–858). Soon thereafter, the English claimed overlordship over Scotland and initiated the Anglo-Scottish struggle which lasted intermittently for almost a thousand years, until both countries were merged as "Great Britain" in 1707.

SUGGESTED READINGS

Church

Deane, Herbert A., *Political and Social Ideas of St. Augustine* (Columbia, 1963).

Duckett, Eleanor Shipley, *The Gateway to the Middle Ages: Monasticism,* Vol. III (U. of Michigan, 1961).

Laistner, M. L. W., *Christianity and Pagan Culture in the Later Roman Empire* (Cornell, 1951).

Lietzmann, Hans, *A History of the Early Church* (World, 1961). From its founding through the early Church Fathers.

Taylor, Henry Osborn, *The Emergence of Christian Culture in the West: The Classical Heritage of the Middle Ages* (Harper, 1958).

Workman, Herbert B., *The Evolution of the Monastic Ideal* (Beacon, 1962).

Germanic Kingdoms

Blair, Peter Hunter, *Roman Britain and Early England, 55 B.C.–A.D. 871* (Norton, 1966).

Dill, Samuel, *Roman Society in Gaul in the Merovingian Age* (Barnes and Noble, 1966).

Duckett, Eleanor Shipley, *Gateway to the Middle Ages,* Vol. I, "Italy"; Vol. II, "France and Britain" (U. of Michigan, 1961). On the Goths.

*Gregory, Bishop of Tours, *History of the Franks* (Octagon, 1916). Contemporary source on early Merovingians.

*Thompson, E. A., *The Early Germans* (Oxford U. P., 1965). On Germanic tribes.

CHAPTER VII

❧ *The Early Middle Ages*
(Seventh to Tenth Centuries)

After the seventh century, parts of Europe began to develop the institutions and intellectual climate which marked the beginning of the Early Middle Ages. Elsewhere, however, no similar transition to a medieval period occurred. To be sure, the flourishing civilization in the Byzantine Empire bore some resemblance to developments in early medieval Western Europe, since both shared the common heritage of Christianity and classical thought. But Byzantium experienced no Germanic influence, did not develop the feudal institutions characteristic of Western Europe, and hence did not go through a "medieval" stage.

In Asia and Northern Africa also, significant changes took place during the seventh century, changes which, however, bore no relationship to the concept of a Middle Age. Most of the Mediterranean and Near Eastern lands were set on an entirely new course by the spread of the new religion of Islam. During the same period, Japan entered an era of reform, Korea first emerged as a unified state, and China became strengthened under the new and effective rule of the T'ang dynasty.

Byzantium to the eleventh century

After Justinian's death, internal disorder and external pressure almost caused the collapse of the Byzantine Empire. Spain and most of Italy were again lost. Avar tribes took the eastern Balkans and several times besieged Constantinople, while Slavic peoples infiltrated the western Balkans and gradually severed Constantinople's land contact with the West. There were frequent wars against Persia which in the early seventh century resulted in Persian conquest of the entire area from Egypt to Chalcedon, across the Bosporus from Constantinople. With most of its territory lost, the empire seemed doomed.

Yet Byzantium was saved by the imaginative energy of a new emperor, Heraclius (610–641), the son of a general from Carthage. While Persians and Avars were besieging his capital of Constantinople, he rallied his people and led a bold offensive into the heart of the Persian Empire. His gamble was successful: Persia surrendered and Byzantium regained her former territories.

Hardly had Heraclius restored the empire when a new and more formidable menace arose in the South. In 632, the Moslems burst forth from Arabia and in rapid order seized Syria, Mesopotamia, Persia, Egypt, and eventually the entire coast of North Africa. By mid-century, they had acquired a fleet and were threatening the city of Constantinople itself. Their conquests were facilitated by the Monophysites in the Near East who were not unhappy to see the arrival of the Moslems, whose strict monotheism appealed to them more than the orthodox Christian dogma of the two natures of Christ (see p. 85). Although the emperor belatedly granted doctrinal concessions, the Arab advance was not slowed down, and Byzantium's losses in the southeastern Mediterranean remained permanent.

While the Arabs advanced in the South, another threat to the empire loomed in the Balkans. Bulgarian tribes defeated the Avars and settled the area of modern Bulgaria, where they established a strong and expanding kingdom. During the next four centuries, they fought sixteen major wars and innumerable minor skirmishes against Byzantium. At the same time, the pope of Rome and the patriarch of Constantinople vied for spiritual influence over the pagan Bulgarians. When the Bulgarian King Boris I (852–889) finally consented to the baptism of his people, they embraced the Christianity of Constantinople, thereby reopening Bulgaria to the penetration of Byzantine influence. By the tenth century, the Bulgarian rulers had become so powerful that they called themselves "Tsars" and even presumed to supersede Byzantium by styling themselves "Tsars of the Romans and Bulgars." Yet, weakened by struggles against the Serbs in the West and against the newly arrived Magyars and Russians in the North, Bulgaria finally succumbed to Byzantium (1018), and its territory was reabsorbed into the empire. Then in the course of the eleventh and twelfth centuries, frequent rebellions again gave Bulgaria partial independence. When Byzantium collapsed temporarily after seizure by the crusaders in 1204, Bulgaria regained complete independence with the assistance of the Roman pope and established the so-called second Bulgarian Kingdom or Empire. The Bulgarians defeated the Venetians and even captured Count Baldwin of Flanders, whom the crusaders had proclaimed emperor of Byzantium. For several decades thereafter, Bulgaria predominated in the Balkans, while

Greece and Byzantium were split into numerous Latin and Greek states (see p. 177). In the end, the Bulgarians succumbed to the invading Ottoman Turks in the fourteenth century, and did not regain their autonomy until 1878.

For a century after Heraclius, Byzantium was governed intermittently by weak and strong rulers, with an occasional lapse into anarchy. Over half the emperors were placed on the throne by the army. That Byzantium survived and even prospered under such conditions shows the miraculous resiliency of its governmental system, its continued wealth, its adequate supply of manpower from Anatolia and Thrace, and the almost impregnable position of Constantinople, which was frequently invested but never fell to the enemy. Moreover Byzantium retained an active middle class and what one might call a commercial aristocracy. Unlike in medieval Western Europe, commercial wealth was never disparaged in Constantinople.

Internal peace was to some extent restored through the governmental and financial reorganization undertaken by the strong Emperor Leo III (717–741). But Leo also created new friction by his concerted attack on the monks, whom he considered too powerful and too numerous, and by his decision to prohibit the worship of religious images or "icons." The resulting bitter iconoclastic controversy and the struggle between the imperial and monkish parties lasted intermittently for over a century. The prohibition of image worship was particularly resented by the popes, and by the Italians and Greeks. By the middle of the ninth century, icon worship was again permitted—a vindication of sorts of the papal point of view. Yet, the creation of free-standing sculptures and of images of God was still discouraged. The iconoclastic controversy greatly added to the growing split between the Roman Catholic and the Orthodox churches. Relations between the pope and the patriarch of Constantinople were severed and re-established several times during the ninth and tenth centuries until the final split in 1054.

Some of the differences between the eastern and western parts of the Church have been mentioned before. They were doctrinal and cultural as well as political. After the Arab occupation of the Near East, the three powerful patriarchates of Antioch, Jerusalem, and Alexandria were clearly eliminated from the struggle for pre-eminence in the Church, leaving only Constantinople and Rome to wage the final duel. As Italy slipped from the domination of the Byzantine Empire and acquired new masters—first the Lombards, then the Franks, and finally the Germans—the emperor in the East lost all authority over the pope, whereas he continued to control his own patriarch of Constantinople. The Orthodox Church thus remained subordinate to the state, a department of the state so to speak, with the bishops' duties primarily sacramental rather than legislative or administrative. The Roman Catholic Church in the West, on the other hand, tried to remain independent of the state. As part of an independent institution, the bishops in the West also retained extensive administrative responsibilities.

Furthermore, free-standing sculptures of saints and martyrs were venerated in the West, whereas the flat mosaics and paintings in the East were considered only symbolic, with no power of intercession between the worshiper and God. There were differences in interpretation of the Eucharist, of the Holy Spirit, and many other points of dogma. It is perhaps indicative of the two cultures during the Middle Ages that the Greeks preferred to depict the resurrection of Christ, whereas the Latins concentrated on Christ the Judge and later on the crucified Christ. Finally, differences in customs and rites arose, such as the more elaborate, mystical church services in the East, or the gradual insistence on celibacy of the clergy in the West, which was not practiced in the East.

This East-West rivalry had a profound effect on the cultural development of the rest of Europe. Roman Catholicism with its Latin background spread to the British Isles, to Germany, Bohemia, Poland, and ultimately to Scandinavia. During the ninth and tenth centuries, on the other hand, missionaries from the Byzantine Empire took Christianity to many of the Slavic tribes from Moravia to the Ukraine, provided the Slavs with the Cyrillic alphabet, and thus acquired a strong civilizing influence in Eastern Europe. The result was a cleavage in Europe's development.

Islam

Few events in history affected the course of world civilization as profoundly as the birth of Islam. Although this new religion was extensively influenced by Judaism and Christianity, and although Arab culture came to incorporate much Hellenistic learning, the spread of Moslem civilization opened a new historical era and signified the first major breakaway in the development of Western civilization.

The faith

The word Islam means "to surrender oneself to God." The religion was founded by Mohammed (570?–632) of Mecca, about whose life little is known. His knowledge of Christianity and Judaism, together with frequently experienced visions during which he heard heavenly voices, inspired him to reform the social and religious morals of his countrymen. Unable to gain ascendancy among the traders of Mecca, he moved with a few followers to the city of Yathrib, whose name he soon changed to Medina, "city of the prophet." This so-called flight (Hegira) to Medina, traditionally thought to have occurred in 622, is regarded by Moslems as the starting date of the faith and marks the beginning of their calendar.

The Medinans were quickly converted, and Mohammed's fame began to spread throughout the Arabian Peninsula. He continued to relate his visions and revelations to his followers who, after his death, were to write them down in the Koran. As the spiritual leader as well as the political and military ruler of Medina, Mohammed spoke authoritatively about all sorts of secular matters. These admonishments were also included in the Koran, which thus did not remain merely a guide to worship, but became a civil and penal code and a rule book for social conduct for Moslem society as a whole.

From Medina, Mohammed tried to unite the various feuding tribes of nomadic shepherds, and attempted to bridge the enmity between the backward Bedouins and the sophisticated merchants of the towns. After several years of war against Mecca, Mohammed was finally able to return to his native city, which he then turned into the center of the new faith. The Arabs had long looked upon Mecca as a holy city, since the Kaaba contained the famous Black Stone which was supposed to have been miraculously sent from heaven. Thereafter Mohammed converted most of the remaining Arabs. He died in 632, in the tenth year of the new Moslem calendar.

The tenets of Islam are relatively easy to understand. Mohammed accepted as valid, although incomplete, the revelations of the Old Testament prophets as well as the prophecies of Jesus. As the last and the greatest of the prophets, he considered himself destined to complete the process of revelation. In many aspects, therefore, the Koran parallels the Bible. As in the Old Testament, the omnipotence of a single God, Allah, was made central to the new faith, but the concept of a Trinity was rejected as not being truly monotheistic. The veneration of images was prohibited—a prohibition which greatly affected Moslem art. As among the Biblical Jews, polygamy was allowed.

Like Jesus, Mohammed urged love of one's neighbor, and preached the need for inner piety and not merely outward observance of ritual. The Koran also stressed the belief in resurrection and a Last Judgment. Mohammed believed in angels as Allah's helpers, but in view of God's omnipotence, he left no room for saints as possible intercessors between God and man.

These similarities between Christianity and Islam should be kept in mind, for the Western view of Moslems has been warped by medieval legends and by the enmity engendered by the Crusades. Actually Moslems respected Christians and Jews as believers in revealed books, and they scorned only those who worshiped idols. In Christian eyes, Moslems after all were not looked upon as pagans but as "infidels," people "unfaithful to Christianity." Dante, in his *Inferno,* called them "schismatic," a term in this sense equivalent to heretic.

Islam required of its adherents certain obligations. Above all, they had to believe in Allah and had to accept Mohammed as the last of the prophets. They were to drink no alcohol, eat no pork, and fast during daytime in the month of Ramadan which roughly corresponds to the Christian Lent. Five times a day they were to pray and bow in the direction of Mecca. If possible, they were to undertake a pilgrimage to Mecca at least once in their lifetime, and if called upon, they were to fight in defense of their faith—a demand which has been differently interpreted over the centuries. Some of the faithful believed that the concept of a "holy war" necessarily involved physical violence, while others sought to limit it to spreading the faith by persuasion. Moreover, Moslems were enjoined to give alms to the poor, to feed the hungry, and to take care of orphans. But Mohammed's commandments were not strict and unyielding. Belief was always stressed more than good works. For the latter, the Koran always provided alternatives, while no substitute was offered for faith. If, for instance, a Moslem could not fast during Ramadan because he was sick or was on a journey, the Koran advised him to fast at another time.

Since the prophet himself and the caliphs, his successors, were religious as well as political leaders, no distinction was made between the Arab state and a Moslem "church." Similarly, no priesthood was created, since Islam involved no sacraments to be performed by ordained people and permitted no intercessors between Allah and the worshiper. Islam thus was to remain a "secular" religion.

Moslem expansion

Moslem inroads into neighboring Syria began even before Mohammed's death. Thereafter, with a speed reminiscent of Alexander the Great's campaigns, the Arabs completely destroyed the political structure of the Persian Empire and deprived Byzantium of all its eastern and southern provinces. Within a century after 632, they had conquered Morocco and Spain in the West, Georgia in the North, and in the East modern Afghanistan, western Pakistan, Kashmir, Turkistan, and Kazakhstan. From there, the Moslems soon spread their religious, commercial, and cultural influence to the Turks of Central Asia, beyond the Indus River into the Punjab, to the borders of China—then under the T'ang dynasty—and ultimately further east to the Indonesian Archipelago and in the Southwest into sub-Saharan Africa. (See Map 8.)

This rapid acquisition of one of the largest empires known in the history of civilization was due partly to the Moslems' military prowess and their courage, reinforced as it was by a measure of fatalism, for those who died for the faith were to be rewarded on Judgment Day. Moreover, the Moslems were often welcomed by the local population as liberators from religious or financial oppression. Contrary to the prevalent Western image, the Arabs were hardly wanton destroyers. Except by accident or in the course of a battle, the Moslems did not destroy what they found. During the first generations of conquests, they were not even particularly eager to convert the conquered to the religion of Islam. They preferred to maintain their separate identity as conquerors, forcing the local non-believers to pay a special tax.

Moslem (or Saracen) civilization was at first dominated by Arabs. By the early eighth century, however, more and more subject peoples, such as

Persians, Syrians, Jews, and Berbers, became converts to Islam—to satisfy religious needs or to gain preferential tax status—and began to mix with their Arab masters to form a new ruling class. Purely demographic considerations could in any case hardly have permitted such a small group of Arabs to dominate so vast an area. The mixing of peoples thus engendered led to a more cosmopolitan Saracen civilization.

The question of succession to Mohammed presented a difficult problem, since the position of caliph ("successor to the prophet") involved spiritual as well as political powers. The Sunnites, a sect of Moslems who believed that only Mohammed had the power to define dogma, asserted that caliphs should be elected. The Shiites, on the other hand, insisting that caliphs could define dogma, held that only descendants of Mohammed, by blood or marriage, were eligible for succession. Besides these, other sects developed, among them the ascetic fakirs who even today sit on pedestals and fast for months in hope of releasing the soul from physical bondage; the fakirs, however, gained no influence on the choice of caliphs. Finally, the question of succession was frequently affected by personal and group jealousies. Of the first four caliphs (632–661), three died by assassination.

From 661 to 750, there was a semblance of a dynastic succession in the Omayyad caliphate, with its center at Damascus. The Omayyads were able to retain control over the ever growing Arab Empire, despite frequent rebellions and civil wars as well as doctrinal disputes over such questions as whether one could be a true Moslem without performing good works.

However, under the Abbasid caliphate established by Shiites in 750, the administrative unity of the empire began to wane. Ruling in glorious splendor at their new capital of Baghdad, the caliphs lost spiritual as well as political control over some outlying districts, permitting the caliph of Cordova and the emir of Morocco, among others, to become independent Moslem princes.

Despite political splintering, Arab civilization continued to flourish as a splendid amalgamation of other civilizations under the aegis of Moslem and Arab culture. With Arabic serving as a common means of communication from Toledo in Spain to Samarkand in Central Asia, knowledge could be exchanged, compared, and combined as never before, not even under the Romans. Building on Indian, Persian, Hellenistic, Roman, Germanic, and Arab bases, the Moslems could thus establish a brilliant civilization, far more advanced than that of contemporary Europe. In fact, after the enmity between Christians and Moslems ebbed, the latter became one of the major civilizing agents for Western Europe. (See Map 9.)

This brilliant civilization was made possible in part by the enormous wealth of the empire. The Arabs themselves were excellent merchants and wherever they went they encouraged industry. Trade fairs were set up, caravan routes improved, and new cities founded at crucial commercial intersections. The Arabs profited not only from the vast market they dominated within their empire but also from external trade. They alone controlled the main trade routes to the wealthy East, by land and by sea, just as they dominated the approaches to sub-Saharan Africa. Soon they even set up trading colonies in T'ang China, Ceylon, and Korea. Although their trade embraced varied goods, much of it was concentrated on luxury items—either imported (spices and perfumes from the East; ivory from Africa) or produced within the empire (tapestries, tooled leather, gold-inlaid metalwork from Damascus, or specialized steel from Toledo).

As they spread over the former Hellenistic and Roman areas, Arabs gathered the knowledge they found, translated it, collected it in encyclopaedias, and placed it in libraries. Greek philosophy, Indian mathematics, Hellenistic engineering, Babylonian astronomy all interested them. From the bases they rediscovered, they soon made brilliant advances, particularly in mathematics, the treatment of contagious diseases, surgery, the use of well-ordered hospitals, astronomy, optics, physics, and chemistry.

Excellent in the sciences, the Moslems were less productive in literature. Probably under Persian influence, they wrote much romantic poetry such as *The Rubaiyat* by Omar Khayyam and tales of adventure such as *A Thousand and One Nights,* but belles-lettres as such were not their forte. On the other hand, they wrote much on law and philosophy, both types of treatises often being exegeses of the Koran. Avicenna (980–1037), a prodigious philosopher and skilled physician, who may have written as many as one hundred books, issued a set of medical "canons" which for centuries remained a standard medical textbook in Asia and Europe. An avid student of Aristotle and Neoplatonism, he also broached the problem—which Western scholars faced two centuries later in regard to Christian theology—of how to reconcile Greek reason and logic with revelation and authority as embodied in the Koran. Later, Averroës of Cordova (1126–1198), also a physician, lawyer, and philosopher, wrote commentaries on Aristotle and Plato. He, too, attacked the problem of "reason" versus "revelation." Translated into Latin, his commentaries became highly influential at the University of Paris in helping to revive knowledge of Aristotle, and in paving the way for medieval scholasticism: the philosophical system which sought to harmonize pagan and secular truths with Christian truth.

Since most Arabs had little experience with art before Mohammed, Moslem architecture became eclectic, reflecting the myriad influences of the people they dominated. Syrian arches, Persian mural designs, Byzantine domes and mosaics, and geometric floral patterns (arabesques) influenced by Persian decorations and Arabic script, were somehow molded into a new, harmonious Moslem style of art. Despite such eclectic cosmopolitanism, Arab art preserved some local characteristics. The shape of minarets, for instance, differed from region to region; yet everywhere they performed the same function of permitting a muezzin (crier) to call the people to prayer. Although the Koran prohibited the representation of humans and animals, an exception was made in Syria and Persia.

Affluent and eager to enjoy new comforts, conscious of their social obligations, and highly energetic, the Arabs became prodigious builders. Mosques and vast palaces, schools and hospitals, cool gardens with fountains and pools, and entire new cities were built in profusion from Cordova, Granada, Fez, and Cairo to Damascus, Baghdad, Bokhara, and Samarkand.

The East

During the late sixth century China recovered from the experience of partial Hunnish occupation (see p. 72). The empire was reunited under an effective, highly developed central administration ruled by the T'ang dynasty (618–907). The T'ang emperors resumed the expansionist policy of the Han dynasty. They subdued most of the eastern Turks, and regained control over Tibet and Turkistan. Thus they again achieved direct contact with Persia and India at a time when Moslems were infiltrating from the West. In fact, the Arabs seized Turkistan from the Chinese in 751. T'ang acquisition of parts of the island of Sumatra also helped keep open the sea lanes to India.

Relatively easy access between China and India, active commercial relations, and widespread reciprocal missionary interest led to strong cultural influences. Buddhism became even stronger and almost dominant in China, despite determined opposition by Confucians and by the Taoist priesthood. A somewhat modified Buddhism was also introduced into Tibet. Indian Buddhist texts were translated into Chinese, and even T'ang pottery showed in its forms the clear influence of Persian and Indian models. In this dialogue between India and China, India at this time tended to be the more influential—probably because of the afterglow of the brilliant Gupta period and because of the continued dynamic growth of Buddhism. In her cultural contacts to the northeast, on the other hand, China clearly exerted the dominant influence. Korea and Japan both were cultural dependencies of China during this era. At the same time, Moslem and Christian missionaries were spreading their faiths in parts of China.

Like Byzantium and the Moslem Empire, but unlike Western Europe of the Early Middle Ages, China under the T'ang emperors enjoyed a splendid cultural period. Universities were stirring with activity and the rulers sought to establish schools in every district of the empire. Education was placed on an exalted pedestal—long before the Italian Renaissance and eighteenth-century Enlightenment engendered a similar esteem for the educated man in Western society. However, since Chinese writing is so complex and difficult to learn, only intelligent people with sufficient leisure could hope to become literate and learned. By means of strict civil service examinations, the T'ang rulers tried to staff government posts primarily with educated people and, where possible, advance them by merit rather than by favoritism. In the seventh and eighth centuries, there was a veritable renaissance in the arts and letters, particularly in the writing of poetry, history, and encyclopaedias as well as in painting. By the late T'ang period, the Chinese had also perfected various devices for printing on paper by using carved wooden blocks.

The last decades of T'ang rule were marred by civil wars and religious persecution, with Taoists suddenly trying to eliminate Buddhism as well as all traces of other religions. Yet Buddhism survived. During the early tenth century, the T'ang Empire collapsed, as various Mongolian tribes infiltrated into northern China while the South splintered temporarily among· numerous contending minor princes.

The next major dynasty, that of the Sung (960–1279), made a new, successful attempt at centralization. The Sung emperors experimented with a type of state socialism and attempted to make education more pragmatic. They also encouraged philosophic writing, especially the formalization of Confucianism, and the compilation of all knowledge in large encyclopaedias. Landscape painting reached a high point under the Sungs. But the emperors gradually lost control over the area north of the Huang River to successive waves of Mongolian invaders (K'itan, Hsi Hsia, Chin Tatars), until the last and most successful of the aggressors, Genghis Khan, seized all of northern China in the early thirteenth century (see p. 165). Half a century later, the southern Sungs also fell under Mongolian domination.

In India meanwhile, intellectual life continued at a brilliant level even after the fall of the Gupta dynasty (see p. 71). Politically however, India was again divided into many smaller states. Northwestern India remained under Hunnish occupation for over five centuries (the sixth to eleventh), and the western regions experienced frequent Arab incursions. Most of India was ruled by local dynasties, which constantly battled one another for possession of a few square miles. Two characteristics mark the period: southern India became culturally more developed and politically more important; Buddhism and Jainism began to lose ground throughout India to the advantage of Hinduism.

Up to this time, no Korean state as such had arisen. The Korean peninsula had been invaded by the Chinese before the Christian era (see p. 71); later it was subject to sporadic occupation by the Japanese. In the seventh century, the area was first unified into a single Korean state. For almost six centuries thereafter, Korea enjoyed a relatively flourishing civilization, strongly influenced by Chinese Buddhism, until during the thirteenth century it slipped under Mongol control and with it indirectly under Chinese overlordship.

Japan, about which we know little prior to the second century A.D., emerged during the T'ang period as China's "best pupil." From the third to the sixth century, the Japanese had come in touch with Chinese civilization largely through contacts in Korea. They had adopted Buddhism, Chinese writing, and Chinese governmental practices. Chinese influence in Japan reached its height during the seventh and eighth centuries. The Japanese sent agents to China to study and to bring back new ideas and new methods. Even the new capital, Heian (modern Kyoto), which was to remain Japan's capital until 1868, was built on a Chinese model. Imitation of China lessened after 900, and the Japanese then began to develop a civilization more distinctly their own. Aided by a simplified system of phonetic writing, Japanese literature and scholarship prospered. Slowly the socio-political system also changed. A landed, military aristocracy assumed preponderant power and developed the shogunate, an arrangement whereby certain nobles, acting like hereditary military governors, exercised dominance over the emperor. This system lasted down to 1868.

The Carolingian Empire

While the eastern and southern Mediterranean areas experienced the opulent centuries of the Byzantine and Moslem empires, most of Europe suffered from economic stagnation and intellectual anaemia. The peoples of Northern and Eastern Europe remained unsettled until the tenth century and little is known about their history. Thus it was in Western and Southern Europe that medieval civilization was born. By fusing a large area of Western Europe into a single political unit and by solidifying the social and political structure of society, the Carolingian Empire became a vital factor in shaping this medieval civilization.

Carolingian institutions

Since the later Merovingian rulers of the Frankish Kingdom (see p. 98) did little to check the growing power of the landed nobility, their royal prestige gradually waned. Controlling power was eventually usurped by one noble family, the Carolingians, whose members held the office of Mayor (superintendent) of the Palace almost uninterruptedly for a century. In the early eighth century, the tottering kingdom was saved from dissolution by the Carolingian Charles Martel (714–741), who assumed the real power in the realm. He suppressed those nobles who had acquired too much independence, while gaining the fealty of others by awarding them lands taken from the Church. Increased wealth from their new landholdings and the introduction of the stirrup enabled these vassals to form a new type of cavalry which heightened the military power of the Franks. The creation of this cavalry, a prototype of medieval knighthood, also furthered the growing feudal distinctions between the wealthy who could become mounted knights and the poor who lost their legal and social equality.

Charles Martel conquered the Frisians, brought Bavaria and other outlying regions back into subjection, and confronted the invading Moslems between Poitiers and Tours in central France in a battle that took place in either 732 or 733. Although the Arabs may have retreated more for lack of food and supplies than for fear of the ferocious Franks, some historians later hailed Charles "the Hammer" as the savior of Western Europe from potential Moslem domination.

Charles' son Pepin drew the logical consequences from the heightened power of his family. He deposed the last Merovingian king and had himself elected in his stead (751). To gain further prestige and support, Pepin then made an arrangement with the papacy. Pope Stephen (752–757) at the time needed a military counterweight to the Lombards who had entered Italy in the sixth century and had assumed control over much of inland Italy. Although the Lombards had become friendly toward the Roman Church and had adopted the Italo-Roman language, Pope Stephen feared their growing political might and therefore asked Pepin to check their power. After prolonged negotiations, the pope visited Pepin in Gaul, anointed him as king, and bestowed on him the Roman title of *patricius* (see p. 82). In return, the Frankish king defeated the Lombards and in the Donation of Pepin (756) bestowed on the pope parts of central Italy.

These events of the mid-eighth century were precedent-setting. Anointed by the pope, Pepin could claim to be the legitimate king of the Franks, and as *patricius,* he could intervene in Italian affairs at his discretion. In theory, the act of anointment did not necessarily imply any superiority on the part of the pope, who performed the sacrament merely as an intermediary at the behest of Christ. Yet, the pope could assert that his action had made a legitimate king out of the usurper Pepin, thereby implying that popes had the power to make or depose kings. Moreover, the papacy could conclude that the Donation of Pepin gave it a legal basis for the establishment of the Papal States. In essence, both king and pope gained from the arrangement which further sealed the friendship between the Franks and the papacy. Only distant Byzantium lost, since the pope had bestowed titles and rights which only the emperor had the prerogative to award, while Pepin had given away land which theoretically still belonged to the Byzantine Empire.

From 768 to 814, the Frankish Kingdom was ruled by Charlemagne, one of the most influential figures of early medieval Western Europe. Charlemagne was important not merely because of his accomplishments but also because of the nimbus which came to surround his reign and his person. He became the archetype of the ruler. His image fired popular imagination, and his reign served as a political model and inspiration for later kings. Coins were struck depicting him as a Roman emperor with a crown of laurel. In legends he appeared as the grandson of Hector or as a two-hundred-year-old warrior with a flowing beard, surrounded by his twelve palatines, striking his enemies with the lightning of his eyes. Soon after Charlemagne's death, Western Europe passed through a period of chaos and disintegration—often called the Dark Ages. The legendary splendor of his reign was probably heightened by this contrast. Whatever the explanation, the image of Charlemagne cast its spell over many medieval centuries.

According to his contemporary biographer Einhard (770?–840), Charlemagne's "expression was brisk and cheerful," "his eyes were very large and piercing," and "his appearance was dignified and impressive." He was interested in learning and architecture and personally supervised royal legislation and ecclesiastical matters. Moreover he devoted a great amount of time to his large family—he probably married five times, kept many concubines, and produced numerous legitimate and illegitimate offspring. He seemed particularly enthralled with his daughters, none of whom he permitted to marry during his lifetime. Yet most of his time must have been absorbed by wars, since during his reign of forty-six years he conducted fifty-five military campaigns.

In the course of these wars, Charlemagne extended the borders of the kingdom in all directions and almost doubled its size. In Italy he defeated the Lombards and made himself their king, while reconfirming Pepin's Donation to the papacy (774). The Papal States were thereby included within the sphere of Frankish influence. Consequently, the papacy slipped further from the control of Constantinople, while on the other hand new problems arose in the changed relationship between the pope and the Frankish ruler.

In Spain, seven bitter campaigns—one of which gave rise to the *Chanson de Roland*—enabled Charlemagne to dislodge the Moslems from the southern slopes of the Pyrenees as far as the river Ebro. The resulting Frankish border district, the Spanish March, became the basis for the later *reconquista* of Spain (see p. 134). In northeastern Europe, Charlemagne conducted eighteen campaigns against the heathen Saxons and gradually succeeded in conquering all lands between the Rhine and the Elbe. At the same time he fought Slavs and Avars in the East. To secure the newly conquered areas, Charlemagne established marches (or marks), specially fortified border districts administered by a count of the march or margrave. The names of some of these districts—such as the Dane Mark or the Ost Mark (Austria)—became permanently attached to the areas. As a result of this northern and eastern expansion, most Germanic tribes on the Continent were brought under a single rule. Charlemagne thus laid the basis for later German and French history. His campaigns also reversed the movement of the Germanic tribes, who for centuries had been moving west and henceforth started to push east against the Slavs. (See Map 7.)

These conquests conferred tremendous prestige on Charlemagne. Contemporaries esteemed him more highly than ordinary rulers. The king of Asturias voluntarily called himself Charlemagne's vassal. The caliph of Baghdad exchanged presents and messages of friendship with the Frankish king, and even the emperor at Constantinople felt constrained to deal with him as an equal. Charlemagne's greatest prestige probably derived from his imperial coronation in the year 800.

His theoretical re-establishment of the Roman Empire in the West created precedents which colored much of medieval history. The act was a conscious reversion to ancient times: the coronation took place at Rome and Charlemagne assumed the titles of imperator and augustus. Although in geographic extent as well as in socio-political construction the Frankish Empire was obviously not a resurrected version of the western part of the Roman Empire, still the revived imperial title resuscitated memories of Roman imperial pretensions to universal obedience. Relations between the two emperors, the Byzantine and the Frank, had to be clarified. The two could not return to the spirit of the fifth century when two augusti supposedly shared dominion over a single empire. After Charlemagne applied successful military pressure, Byzantium begrudgingly recognized him as a "brother-king" in the West; yet the official relations between the two always remained cool.

The most serious effect of Charlemagne's imperial coronation concerned church-state relations. On the one hand, it was the pope (Leo III) who crowned Charles, as though the pope had the prerogative of bestowing the imperial crown. Yet, the pope was so weak that he had been evicted from Rome and had been restored to his see only with the aid of Frankish troops, an event that had shown the importance of the temporal power of the Franks for the safety of the papacy. Whether under such conditions pope or emperor was superior remained to be fought out in subsequent centuries. During Charlemagne's reign, of course, the powerful emperor was clearly the stronger of the two. The papacy, however, gained in another direction. Having crowned his own emperor in the West and having found protectors in the Franks, the pope could assert greater freedom from Constantinople, an action which further intensified the split between Greek Orthodox and Roman Catholic Christianity (see p. 103).

To control such a large empire, Charlemagne resorted to many devices which depended on his personal prestige rather than on a clear concept of the state. He sought to bind all important nobles to himself by making them take an oath of fealty and placed designated regions of his realm under the supervision of counts, subject to his appointment and removal. The counts were to act as military leaders, chief judges, tax collectors, and generally represented the emperor. They in turn were supervised by special imperial inspectors, the *missi dominici,* teams usually consisting of a bishop and a count who toured the country to check on the activities of the local counts. Charlemagne's legislation, issued in capitularies, revealed the emperor's paternalism and showed how far private and public matters were intertwined in those days. A typical capitulary might specify how much smoked meat to store at one of Charlemagne's estates and how much cabbage to plant at another; it might urge the counts to ascertain that the people said their prayers, gave alms, and observed fasting; or it might list the type of weapons soldiers were to bring along when reporting for military service.

Similarly there was no real division of functions at his own court between what concerned the "state" and what concerned the royal household—just as the government's revenue consisted primarily of the ruler's income from his private estates, supplemented by feudal dues, highway tolls, customs, and court fines.

Carolingian cultural revival

After the end of the patristic period which closed with the death of Pope Gregory I in 604 (see p. 93), the level of learning in the West sunk woefully low. Even supposedly literate monks and clerics understood the Scriptures and the writings of the Fathers only at the simplest allegorical level. As ruler over a Christian society, Charlemagne considered himself responsible for the spiritual well-being of his people. Hence he encouraged learning among the clergy and tried to improve the level of literacy at least at his own court. For this purpose he attracted to his entourage several relatively good scholars, including the Saxon Alcuin of York (735–804) and Paul the Deacon (720?–800?), the author of *History of the Lombards*. This group of scholars is sometimes referred to as Charlemagne's palace school.

At this so-called school students and teachers collected, copied, and attempted to interpret manuscripts. Their own works were mostly commentaries on the Scriptures and collections of miscellaneous information, usually not conceived at a very high level. In the long run, the greatest influence of this group was the development of the beautiful Carolingian minuscule, a style of small lettering—as opposed to the usual capital letters used by the Romans—which became the basis of Western writing and printing.

There was also a renaissance in the arts, as can be seen from book bindings and book illuminations that have been preserved. Moreover Charlemagne was interested in architecture. His buildings were scattered over the empire, since no "capital" as such was ever developed. Late in his reign, Aix-la-Chapelle, west of the Rhine near the present-day Belgian border, tended to become the center of the empire. Here he built a large palace, whose octagonal chapel with its mosaics and dome reveals considerable Byzantine influence. Because of the nature of the economy, however, his court remained itinerant, moving from villa to villa to consume the produce of his private estates—a custom by necessity retained by the kings of France to some extent until the sixteenth century.

Seeds for the future

In his relations with the Church, Charlemagne considered himself supreme. He appointed bishops, presided over synods, and even pronounced on questions of dogma. The pope himself he treated as no higher than an important bishop. He granted political rights and immunities to bishops and abbots, used church land to reward military service, and drew high ecclesiastics into his administrative system, so that church and state became inextricably intertwined. Under his strong rule, relations with the Church presented no problems; but after his death, much friction was to stem from this mixing of church and state.

Charlemagne's conquests did not lessen the economic stagnation that had set in under the Merovingians. Trade with the Mediterranean and the East had been sharply reduced by the Arab conquests, and even within the Frankish Empire, commercial life languished and towns decayed economically. Silver and gold were scarce and the localized economy came to be based more and more on land and service. Unable to support themselves, small freeholders became serfs on larger estates or "manors," where they paid for the use of land by surrendering produce to the lord of the manor or by performing menial services for him. Similarly, it became customary for the ruler to pay for services through grants of land or through recognition of immunity to those who already were large landholders. In the long run, such immunities had the effect of diminishing the financial, judicial, and military power of the government.

At the same time, the Germanic practice of commendation increased. Commendation signified an honorable relationship whereby a weaker freeman commended or entrusted himself to the protection of a stronger noble, in return for performing some honorable services for him. This personal tie between vassal and lord threatened to weaken the control of the ruler over the people in his realm. By insisting on direct allegiance to himself and trying to supervise all areas of government, Charlemagne attempted to diminish the effect of these centrifugal forces. Yet even under his strong regime, the feudalization of society continued apace.

Moreover the emperor left some important problems unresolved. He retained the Frankish practice of dividing the kingdom among the male heirs, without rights of primogeniture, thus helping to set the stage for a century of wars among his heirs. He made no attempt to establish a clear relationship between imperial and royal prerogatives. When he first divided the empire among his sons (806), he did not assign the imperial title to anyone, as though the emperorship had been a personal honor rather than an inheritable position. In the end, after all but one of his sons had died, he arranged for his surviving son Louis to be crowned emperor without papal blessing. It remained to be seen whether the imperial title was largely an honorific designation, gave its bearer limited rights over Italy, entrusted him with protective responsibilities over the papacy, with power over other kings, or even with universal rule over Western Christendom. Much fighting was to ensue and many centuries pass before these questions would be answered.

Disintegration of the Carolingian Empire

Charlemagne's empire survived his death less than three decades. After years of intrafamily war, his grandsons divided it (843) into three parts. During the next century, it was further dissolved into numerous feudal entities. This dismemberment of the empire had many causes besides the rivalry among Charlemagne's descendants: constant enemy raids along the borders that required local defense; economic decline resulting in the need for regional self-sufficiency; or—given the poor state of communications—the simple fact that the empire had grown too vast to be ruled by a single person.

The breakup of the empire

During the struggles over territorial inheritances between Charlemagne's son, Emperor Louis the Pious (814–840), and his grandsons, the Church sided first with Louis and then with his eldest son Lothair, who obtained the imperial title after his father. In both cases, the Church thus supported the emperor against "lesser" princes. This attitude was not motivated solely by the circumstances that Louis was devout and consented to have himself crowned by the pope, although he had already previously crowned himself emperor. Rather the Church sought peace, and the popes hopefully saw in the emperorship a guarantee of internal law and order. Popes and emperors recognized early that they could benefit from mutual support, and it was hardly coincidental that the emperorship decayed in the late ninth century at the same time that the papacy plunged to its nadir—a time when the popes were little more than puppets of the local Roman aristocracy.

When Charlemagne's three surviving grandsons divided the empire in 843, one (Louis) received the lands east of the Rhine, the basis for later Germany; another (Charles) obtained the western portion of Roman Gaul, the core for medieval France; and Lothair (840–855) was allotted a strip of land from Holland to south of Rome, an area over which the French and Germans were to fight for centuries. While the land was being divided and redivided, the imperial title was fought over like booty. Hence the emperorship temporarily lost all meaning and prerogatives, until the office was revived on a new basis in the second half of the tenth century. (See Map 7.)

With the government weak and paralyzed by dissension, there was little chance for effective defense against foreign raiders. Charlemagne had fortified the mouths of rivers against their raids and had either bought off the invaders or warded them off in open battle. But now Europe lay open to what amounted to a second wave of invasions. In the South, the Arabs raided the coasts of Italy and southern France and established piratical colonies to intercept transient trade. In the East, the Magyars launched forays for half a century until finally defeated in 955 by Emperor Otto I and forced to settle in modern Hungary. Further east, Scandinavians, locally called Russ, penetrated into Russia and gradually established settlements from the Baltic to the Black Sea. In the North, West, and South, Europe was raided by Norsemen, or Vikings. Norwegians settled parts of Ireland and pushed on to Iceland, Greenland, and perhaps even the North American coast; Danes attacked England and gradually seized the northeastern portions of the island;

and various Viking tribes raided the coasts of Europe from the Baltic to the Mediterranean, pushing their plundering expeditions far inland.

The feudal substitute

The rulers of the Frankish kingdoms showed little ability in defending cities and monasteries against the Vikings who sailed and rowed up the Seine, Loire, Garonne, and Rhone, and other rivers as far as Burgundy, Auvergne, Toulouse, and Valence. With the economy already shrunk, and communications between areas increasingly disrupted, the needs for defense, administration, and justice had to be satisfied at the local level. This, in essence, was the feudal substitute for the central state which had disappeared.

The lords of large estates built defensive palisades and small wooden towers—the crude prototypes for later fortified castles. To assemble a small corps of fighters, they engaged freemen as vassals. There was nothing degrading about vassalage. Only a freeman, later in fact only a noble, could become a vassal. The vassal assumed toward his lord certain obligations, which in later centuries were usually written down contractually. Among the vassal's usual duties were fighting for the lord a certain number of days a year, helping him dispense justice in court, and raising ransom money in case of his capture. The lord in turn owed protection to his vassal, and he might bestow on him a fief in the form of an estate or manor, the revenue of which would support the vassal.

While large landholders sought vassals, many small proprietors found themselves too weak to defend their land against constant pillage and too poor to attract help. Hence they gave their land to a stronger lord, or an abbot or a bishop, and commended themselves as his vassals. At the other end of the social scale, even strong lords found it prudent to become vassals of still more powerful lords, giving birth to an entire ladder of lord-vassal relationships.

This feudal structure, which determined the relations among nobles, was based on the manorial system of agricultural organization, which had gradually evolved from the landed estates of late Roman times. A manor was a more or less self-sufficient agricultural estate, normally owned or controlled by a single lord. It consisted of plow land, meadows, woods, a stream or wells, a village for the peasants, a manor house for the lord, usually a parish chapel, and the most essential implements such as ovens, flour mills, a wine press and a loom. Most of the peasants and laborers working on the manor had lost their free status and had accepted servile tenure. As serfs they were not free to leave the manor, were socially inferior to freemen, and obligated for various menial services. The noble lord of the manor, for his part, was supposed to protect and not abuse his serfs. But since the lord's manorial court was the only source of justice, the serfs in effect had no recourse except to the generosity of the lord.

Feudalism and manorialism evolved in part from Germanic and Roman institutions—such as the Germanic custom of commendation and the

Roman system of agricultural tenure. In part, the feudal and manorial systems were also improvised to meet local military, economic, and social needs. In some respects, feudalism was consciously encouraged by the Frankish rulers to supplement their own weak administration. In 847, for instance, the Frankish king (Charles the Bald) ordered all freemen to commend themselves to a lord and to accompany him in battle—a military measure which greatly encouraged the process of infeudation. In 877, Charles further guaranteed the counts that their sons could succeed them in office, thus making the position of count hereditary and losing control over its incumbents. The establishment of the great fiefs or duchies, such as Burgundy, Anjou, and Normandy also dates from this period. Theoretically these fiefs were granted to great lords for the sake of better local defense, and remained dependent on the king as supreme suzerain. In practice, powerful ducal dynasties developed, sometimes stronger and richer than the king himself. The history of the French monarchy from the eleventh to the sixteenth century in fact is the story of the gradual reabsorption of these fiefs by the central crown.

As a result of the solidification of manorial and feudal institutions, Western European society was transformed. Cities declined or even disappeared, unless stoutly defended by a bishop; towns languished or decayed, unless some special local reason permitted a modicum of economic life. Consequently the class of burghers diminished even further, just as relatively few freeholders survived the economic and military pressures of the century. Henceforth, essentially two classes remained: the vast number of serfs who tilled the soil and performed all menial work; and the small number of nobles who governed, fought, enjoyed leisure, and were not supposed to engage in manual labor. Beyond these two were the members of the clergy, themselves socially divided between the hard-working, lowly parish priests and the landowning bishops and abbots who were as powerful and influential as other nobles.

The fortified castle of the nobleman, separated from the nearest manor by miles of mysterious forests, led to new cultural interests. Myths of strong heroes, tales of adventure and love, stories of miracles seemed more important than refined theological argument on the nature of Christ or philosophical discussions of logic. Hence, the level of learning sank even further to suit the mentality of the fortified castle.

SUGGESTED READINGS

Early Middle Ages

Brentano, Robert, *The Early Middle Ages, 500–1000,* Vol. IV (Macmillan, 1964). Sources.

Duckett, Eleanor Shipley, *Alfred the Great, the King and His England* (U. of Chicago, 1956).

Laistner, M. L. W., *Thought and Letters in Western Europe, A.D. 500 to 900* (Cornell, 1957).

Lewis, Archibald, *An Emerging Medieval Europe, A.D. 400–1000* (Knopf, 1967).

Linklater, Eric, *The Conquest of England* (Dell, 1966).

Moss, H. St. L. B., *The Birth of the Middle Ages, 395–814* (Oxford U. P., 1964).

Southern, Richard W., *The Making of the Middle Ages* (Yale, 1953).

Wallace-Hadrill, J. M., *The Barbarian West: The Early Middle Ages, A.D. 400–1000* (Harper, 1962).

Byzantium

Baynes, Norman H., and Moss, H. St. L. B., *Byzantium: An Introduction to East Roman Civilization* (Oxford U. P., 1948).

Guerdan, René, *Byzantium, Its Triumphs and Tragedy* (Putnam, 1962).

Hussey, Joan M., *The Byzantine World* (Harper, 1961). From 330 to 1453.

Miller, D. A., *The Byzantine Tradition* (Harper, 1966).

Rice, David Talbot, *Art of the Byzantine Era* (Praeger, 1963).

Runciman, Steven, *Byzantine Civilization* (World, 1956).

Vasiliev, Alexander A., *History of the Byzantine Empire, 324–1453* (Wisconsin, 1952).

Islam

Andrae, Tor, *Mohammed, the Man and His Faith* (Harper, 1960).

Hitti, Philip K., *The Arabs: A Short History* (Regnery, 1956).

——, *The Meaning of the Glorious Koran* (New American Library). An annotated translation of the Koran.

Pirenne, Henri, *Mohammed and Charlemagne* (World, 1955).

Sourdel, Dominique, *Islam* (Walker, 1962).

Von Grunebaum, Gustave E., *Medieval Islam* (U. of Chicago, 1953). A study in cultural orientation.

Asia

*Eberhard, Wolfram, *Conquerors and Rulers: Social Forces in Medieval China* (Heineman, 1965).

*Kosambi, D. D., *Ancient India* (Pantheon, 1966).

*Sansom, George B., *A History of Japan*, Vol. I, "To 1334" (Stanford, 1958).

Carolingians

Einhard, *The Life of Charlemagne* (U. of Michigan, 1960). Written by Charlemagne's contemporary.

Fichtenau, Heinrich, *The Carolingian Empire: The Age of Charlemagne* (Harper, 1963).

Havighurst, Alfred F., ed., *The Pirenne Thesis—Analysis, Criticism, and Revision* (Heath, 1958).

Hinks, Roger, *Carolingian Art: A Study of Early Medieval Painting and Sculpture in Western Europe* (U. of Michigan, 1962).

Lamb, Harold, *Charlemagne: The Legend and the Man* (Bantam, 1954).

Sullivan, Richard, *The Coronation of Charlemagne: What Did It Signify?* (Heath, 1959).

Winston, Richard, *Charlemagne: From the Hammer to the Cross* (Random).

Feudalism

Bloch, Marc, *Feudal Society,* Vol. I, "The Growth of Ties of Dependence"; Vol. II, "Social Classes and Political Organization" (U. of Chicago, 1961).

Ganshof, F. L., *Feudalism* (Harper, 1961).

Hoyt, Robert S., *Feudal Institutions: Cause or Consequence of Decentralization?* (Holt, 1961).

Lopez, Robert S., *The Tenth Century: How Dark the Dark Ages?* (Holt, 1959).

Stephenson, Carl, *Medieval Feudalism* (Cornell, 1966).

CHAPTER VIII

❧❧ *The Awakening of New Forces*
(Tenth to Twelfth Centuries)

The so-called Dark Ages were followed by a slow but noticeable recovery which started in the middle of the tenth century. Norse, Magyar, and Arab raiders settled down, new political units began to consolidate, and there was a slight economic upswing.

Revitalization of the Church

The political and economic decay of the ninth century had affected the Church as much as it had the secular states. The papacy had lost power and prestige and had become subject to the whim of local Roman noble families, while bishops were involved in feudal power struggles. Supported by the Saxon emperors (see p. 123), however, and by a host of monks whom one historian aptly labeled "the militia of the Church," the latter recovered more rapidly than other institutions. Despite occasional periods when the papacy again became the pawn of ambitious nobles, the Church gradually attained dominant status.

Churchmen retained a measure of learning and a sense for law. They harbored a strong desire for peace and saw the advantage of consolidating larger areas under a single political control. Unlike most feudal lords, they had some understanding of Roman administrative theories and of the advantages of distinguishing between private and public matters in government. Hence the Church supported local efforts to organize political units in Northern and Eastern Europe. During the second half of the tenth century, Catholic missionaries helped establish Christian kingdoms in Bohemia,

Poland, and Hungary. In the early eleventh century, the newly consolidated Danish monarchy (under Canute the Great, 1014–1035) extended its power over Norway and over parts of England, where it received the aid of the Anglo-Saxon clergy to spread Christianity as well as Danish influence. Sweden, at the same time, emerged as a new, although as yet weak, Christian monarchy. Meanwhile, further east, Byzantine and Roman missionaries rivaled over the conversion of the Serbs, and Byzantine priests preached among the Russians. By the late ninth century, the Kievan state had extended its rule from Novgorod in the North to the Danube in the South. Once Christianized under Prince Vladimir at the end of the tenth century, Kiev became a powerful state. In all these areas, conversion to Christianity and the concomitant assistance of clerics and monks helped lay the foundation for viable monarchical institutions. This important civilizing and missionary work was made possible through the revitalization of the Church during the tenth and eleventh centuries.

Reform of the Church

The initial impetus for reform came largely from monastic groups, particularly from the Cluniac monks. The Abbey of Cluny, founded in 910 on the basis of the Benedictine rule and later placed directly under the authority of the papacy, was not subject to control or interference by a local bishop or feudal lord. Thus fairly free from secular influences, the monks reformed monastic life by insisting on pure living and strict obedience to the rules of the monastery. Cluny quickly became famous and other monasteries adopted its system. Soon some three hundred monastic houses, spread over many parts of Europe, had ranged themselves under the control of Cluny, thus forming a large and influential monastic order. The monks were primarily concerned with improving the pious character of monastic life and showed little interest in pushing for reforms in the Church in general. Yet this heightened piety helped awaken determination among certain nobles and clergymen to undertake similar reforms in the Church as a whole.

Following prior attempts to purify the structure of the Church and the morals of clerics, reform-minded clerics concentrated their attention during the eleventh century on emancipating the Church from secular influences. To this effect, they sought to take ecclesiastical appointments out of lay hands by eliminating outside interference in papal elections and in the investiture of bishops and abbots—investiture being the act of conferring the spiritual and secular prerogatives of an office. They also hoped to abolish simony, the prevalent custom of selling Church offices, and to enforce celibacy of the clergy, so that ecclesiastics would no longer be tempted to turn bishoprics and abbeys into hereditary possessions.

Demands for reform were echoed at various synods and were actively supported by the first three Saxon emperors (Otto I, II, and III), who tried to aid the movement by appointing several reform-minded popes. Yet the very fact that the emperors appointed the popes showed that lay influence on the Church would not be eliminated unless the system of papal selection itself were changed. A first major step in this direction was taken in 1059 when the Lateran Council decreed that papal elections were to be performed by a college of cardinals. The custom of locking up the cardinals in conclave for the duration of the election, in order to prevent possible outside interference, started only in the late thirteenth century.

Meanwhile ecclesiastics and monks attempted to lessen feudal chaos by other means. By decrees usually labeled "Peace of God," they threatened with excommunication those knights who in their forays harmed defenseless peasants, widows, nuns, or monks. Later, by the additional "Truce of God," they prohibited fighting among knights between Thursdays and Sundays and during the Christmas and Easter seasons. Except where enforced by secular rulers, such injunctions were of course more hopeful than effective, but they typify the Church's attempt to assert moral leadership.

The Church at the height of power

After the middle of the eleventh century, the papacy successfully assumed leadership of the Church and promptly became involved in a drawn-out struggle with some lay rulers, at first primarily with the emperors, later also with other powers including the kings of France and England.

Pope Gregory VII (1073–1085), the determined monk who inspired and dominated the papacy for twenty years before his own elevation, fastened on the question of investiture as the focal issue for emancipating the prelates from secular authority, a complicated task since the Church's vast landed possessions had deeply enmeshed it in the feudal system. Feudal lords in many areas looked upon local monasteries as their personal possessions and were therefore intent on controlling the abbots. Similarly, the lands of bishops, although in practice under their sole control, were theoretically also under the jurisdiction of some king or duke or other magnate. The local lay ruler therefore sought to retain power over the appointment and investiture of such ecclesiastics. Hence the struggle between Pope Gregory and certain feudal lords.

To underscore papal power vis-à-vis lay rulers and regain control over the appointment of bishops, Gregory in 1075 decreed excommunication for "any emperor, king, duke, margrave, count, any power or layman who dared invest another with a bishopric or an ecclesiastical office." These decrees, which the pope soon supplemented by the assertion that he alone had the authority to depose emperors, led to the famous investiture controversy with Emperor Henry IV (1056–1106), including the emperor's humiliation at Canossa (see p. 127).

The first phase of this controversy ended with a compromise between the papacy and Emperor Henry V (1106–1125) in the Concordat of Worms (1122). The emperor was granted a voice in the election of bishops and the privilege of investing them with their lay powers and demanding their homage, while the pope was assured the right to grant or withhold spiritual investiture. Soon thereafter, the struggle resumed between the papacy and the powerful Emperor Frederick I Barbarossa (1152–1190), with its focus not only on further questions of investiture but also on the control over northern Italy. Finally, during the thirteenth century, the quarrel was reopened between the popes and Emperor Frederick II (1211–1250) essentially on the issue of papal or imperial domination of Italy. Although each particular quarrel fastened on a specific issue, in essence there was but one fundamental question: whether empire or Church was to be supreme.

In each case, the Church faced formidable opponents. Emperors Henry IV, Frederick Barbarossa, and Frederick II were all strong and resourceful rulers. Yet in one way or another, they all lost out to the Church which usually was able to find opportune allies—German princes, Lombard communes, or Norman kings. The papacy, in fact, normally commanded more weapons and resources than lay rulers. In addition to its wealth, its reservoir of learned assistants, and armed support, it commanded the spiritual weapons of excommunication and interdict which it alone possessed. Excommunication was the act of excluding an offender from the sacraments and banning him from the companionship of fellow Christians; an interdict debarred all residents of a particular area from ecclesiastical functions and privileges.

The power of the papacy soon assumed remarkable proportions. Pope Urban II (1088–1099), for example, not only preached the first crusade against the Seljuk Turks but also organized it, a feat requiring the solution of serious financial and logistical problems. Later popes guaranteed the crusaders suspension of interest obligations on debts and assurance of inheritance rights for their children, measures which seemed purely secular. By the time of Pope Innocent III (1198–1216), the power of the Church reached its zenith. Innocent asserted the prerogative of deciding on the legitimacy of imperial elections and of excommunicating such powerful monarchs as the kings of France and England. Acting like an emperor, he received Aragon, Denmark, England, Hungary, Poland, and other states as papal fiefs, claiming political as well as spiritual power over these lands. At the Fourth Lateran Council (1215) he decreed the universality of the Church and intimated that there could be no salvation outside the Church. Innocent's power over the Church and over Western Christendom made him indeed the dominant figure of the Western world.

The Holy Roman Empire

From the fifth to the ninth century, the areas of former Roman Gaul and of southern and western Germany had usually been ruled by a single Frankish king. After the division of 843 (see p. 117), the three kingdoms—reduced to two in 870—continued to be governed by descendants of Charlemagne. In 911, however, the East Frankish lords elected as king one of their own dukes. "France" and "Germany" henceforth started their separate histories.

The kings of the Saxon dynasty, who ruled the German lands from 919 to 1024, were kept occupied with the defense of the eastern borders of their kingdom against incursions by Slavs and Magyars and used these raids as an excuse for resuming Charlemagne's policy of eastward expansion. Most of them were skillful rulers who, with the stout support of the bishops, tried to weld the independent duchies that made up their kingdom into some sort of a state. But from the very beginning, Germany remained disunited and German history was to be a long roll call of civil wars and rebellions.

The strongest of the Saxon rulers was Otto I (936–973), who during his reign led three military expeditions to Italy. In 962, Otto permitted the pope to crown him emperor, thereby reviving the empire of Charlemagne. This new Roman Empire in the West, which later was given the name of Holy Roman Empire, was to last from 962 to 1806. Its creation gave the German rulers control over central and northern Italy—an economic and financial advantage but also the cause of frequent military and political setbacks south of the Alps. Although German domination of Rome led to repeated struggles between popes and emperors, the two powers were not necessarily irreconcilable rivals. The emperor benefited from a friendly papacy in order to have better control over the German bishops. The pope needed military protection and could use imperial aid to spread Roman Catholicism to Eastern Europe.

Just as ancient Rome recognized no rivals, so the Holy Roman Empire was in theory universal. Otto I tried to impress his contemporaries with splendid court ceremonial; his grandson (Otto III) moved to Rome, built himself a palace on the Aventine Hill, and adopted Byzantine customs. On many occasions, distant rulers paid respect to the emperor as a special suzerain, higher than ordinary kings. In practice, however, the new empire was far from universal. In fact it was smaller in extent than the empire of Charlemagne, and vast areas of Europe were never under its jurisdiction.

From the very beginning, the evolution of the Holy Roman Empire was complicated by the existence of the German Kingdom. For, the Saxon rulers did not convert the kingdom into an empire as Augustus had gradually transformed the Roman Republic into the Roman Empire. Rather they let both kingdom and empire exist side by side, united in the person of the ruler. The German Kingdom, reaching from the North Sea to Trieste on the Adriatic, was smaller than the Holy Roman Empire which, besides comprising the territory of the kingdom, included north and central Italy and later added territories in the East and in what is today southeastern France. Separate elections were used to choose incumbents for the royal and the imperial throne, though most of the time the person elected as German king was also later chosen as emperor. (See Map 10.)

The fact that both crowns remained elective presented another problem.

Successful rulers like the Saxons were able to ensure dynastic succession for several generations by having their sons elected during the father's lifetime. However, when in the twelfth and thirteenth centuries other states tackled the task of converting their loose feudal systems into more centralized monarchies, the German custom of electing their rulers proved to be a major weakness for the Holy Roman Empire.

Under the Salian dynasty (1024–1125), the empire grew in size and prestige, while at the same time continued feudalization sapped the potential strength of the emperors. During the investiture controversy, most of the bishops and abbots sided with Emperor Henry IV, since they were imperial appointees and stood to lose power from the proposed papal reforms. The German magnates (dukes, counts, margraves and other important nobles), on the other hand, tended to support Pope Gregory VII and his successors, since they were wary of the growing power of the emperor. In the course of the controversy, Gregory twice declared the deposition and excommunication of Henry IV and supported an antiking. Henry, in return, at one point had Gregory deposed and named his own antipope. In the later struggle, Emperor Henry V once even imprisoned the pope (Paschal II) and his cardinals in order to force them into concessions.

After these prolonged fights between the Salians and the papacy, the Holy Roman Empire rose to new glory under Emperor Frederick I Barbarossa of the house of Hohenstaufen. Frederick took full advantage of the tenets of Roman law, which were then being revived at the Italian universities, in order to exalt the position of the ruler as supreme sovereign and lawgiver. Within Germany he was greatly respected and even popular, and he was strong enough to deal with rebellions more summarily than his predecessors. At a series of imposing meetings of the imperial Diet (the assembly of German magnates, ecclesiastical lords, and representatives of some towns), the emperor surrounded himself with majestic pomp and accepted honors presented to him by envoys from rulers beyond the confines of the empire, including King Henry II of England.

In the course of his long reign, Frederick Barbarossa conducted six military campaigns south of the Alps in order to gain better control of central and northern Italy. In these attempts he was steadfastly opposed by the papacy—particularly Pope Alexander III (1159–1181). The popes could usually rely on military aid from their vassals, the Norman kings of Sicily, who objected to imperial domination of Italy. The papacy had also found new allies in the North in the prospering towns of Lombardy, which banded together in the Lombard League in order to extract greater concessions from the emperor. Already largely self-governing, these communes (municipal associations bound together for the defense of their liberties) sought maximum freedom from all imperial interference. Finally, the popes could count on occasional assistance from rebellious German princes, particularly from the Guelf family who were rivals to the Hohenstaufen dynasty.

Although Frederick was powerful and in command of a strong feudal army, he could not prevail over his combined opponents. In 1176, he was defeated by the Lombard cities at the battle of Legnano, an early instance in which mounted knights were routed by foot soldiers armed with pikes. Hence in the end Frederick was forced to compromise his differences with the papacy and to grant virtual autonomy to the Lombard communes. Unable to defeat the Normans, he married his son to the heiress of Sicily. He thus prepared for the union of Sicily and the empire during the reign of his son (Henry VI). Having arranged for peace through compromise, Frederick Barbarossa led the imperial forces on the Third Crusade, in which kings Richard the Lion-Hearted of England and Philip II Augustus of France also participated. The lack of military success of the crusade did not detract from Barbarossa's glory since he drowned before reaching the Holy Land. After his death he immediately became a legendary hero.

Consolidation of feudal monarchies

In Western Europe, the Holy Roman Empire had been the first to arise as a state of some influence. In other regions, in France, England, and Spain, the feudal monarchies that were to serve as forerunners of national states were established later.

France

In the West Frankish Kingdom, the Carolingian rulers had become woefully weak toward the end of the ninth century. They remained inconspicuous for a century until 987 when the crown was given to a new dynasty with the election of Hugh Capet. The Capetians were not a particularly strong family. Their domains, concentrated in the Ile de France around the Seine and the Loire, gave them fewer resources than those held by several of the other powerful dukes. But the family had acquired a reputation for recognizing the importance of fulfilling royal obligations. Hence the Capetians became the nucleus around which the French monarchy, or France, was to be built and along with their indirect heirs ruled France for almost nine hundred years.

In view of the dukes' jealous guarding of their independence, it is perhaps surprising that they elected a king at all. They could simply have let every duke and count become his own sovereign. There obviously existed no "national" feeling for a French state which guided the magnates. Rather, they needed a leader in time of war and must have seen the value of having some impartial judge to adjudicate differences among themselves. Moreover, there was the Germanic tradition of kingship, powerfully supplemented by the Hebrew-Christian thaumaturgic theory which endowed an anointed king with special powers and thus placed him above the ranks of ordinary nobles. Finally, the Church favored retention of monarchy as a guarantor of a modicum of peace and order.

During the eleventh century, the French monarchy remained weak and relatively unimportant. A history of "France" for the period would really be a history of the separate duchies and counties, since the Capetian kings exerted little control over the dukes and counts. Capetian power depended primarily on the royal domain—the private holdings of the kings—and on ecclesiastical patronage. The kings concentrated their attention on getting from their own domain all rights and revenues that they could demand on the basis of feudal customs. They also succeeded in gradually making the crown hereditary, a step of vast importance for the stability of the monarchy. Although briefly involved in the investiture controversy, they were not yet strong enough to engage in a very active "foreign" policy. While they were busy consolidating the Ile de France, most of the former Lotharingian lands —the territory assigned to Lothair in 843, or the so-called middle kingdom between the Saône and the Rhine, from Holland to Italy, including present-day Alsace-Lorraine—were incorporated into the Holy Roman Empire. For centuries thereafter, the French were to fight to acquire these territories.

By the twelfth century, the French feudal monarchy began to consolidate. The *curia regis,* or king's council, came to be staffed more with learned clerics rather than feudal nobles, assuring the king more power over his administration. Having obtained a firm grip over his own domain, the king attempted to expand the area under his control. He began to reduce the independent power of the lesser vassals, especially north of the Loire, and granted charters to some communes, guaranteeing certain privileges to their bouregois inhabitants. This marriage of convenience between king and rising bourgeoisie characterized French politics for several centuries. The growing communes gained royal protection against petty oppression by local nobles. The monarch for his part usually received financial rewards, extended his influence, and undermined the power of the landed nobles, who tried to obstruct the growth of royal authority for fear of losing their independence.

By the time of King Louis VII (1137–1180), the French monarchy was stable enough to allow the king to go on the Second Crusade and leave the administration of the realm in the hands of a skillful adviser (Suger, the abbot of St. Denis), without fearing rebellion by the great feudatories. Through his young wife Eleanor (1122?–1204), Louis acquired the greater part of Aquitaine, south of the Loire. But Eleanor bore him only daughters and the ponderous Louis finally divorced the gay and intelligent Eleanor, despite the personal attempts of the pope to prolong the marriage. After her departure from Paris, Eleanor of Aquitaine promptly married the young count of Anjou, Henry Plantagenet, who two years later became king of England as Henry II (1154–1189). Having already lost control of Normandy and the western provinces to England, Louis thus also forfeited Aquitaine. Hence the French suddenly faced the prospect of remaining a minor, landlocked kingdom, wedged between the Holy Roman Empire in the east and a strong Anglo-Norman kingdom in the west, covering the Atlantic coast from the Channel to the Pyrenees.

Henry II and Louis VII fought for over two decades without changing the territorial division between England and France. Under their successors, however, there was a sudden turn in favor of France. Philip II Augustus (1180–1223), a determined and skilled ruler, who greatly added to the prestige and power of the French crown, more than doubled the French holdings—mostly at the expense of England. At first unsuccessful in his attempt to seize England's Continental possessions from Richard the Lion-Hearted, Philip's opportunities improved when John I of England became king in 1199. As duke of Normandy, John was a vassal to the king of France, and Philip took full advantage of these feudal ties. He accused John of disobedience and even of murder, and when the English king did not appear for judgment in Philip's court, the French king condemned him to forfeiture of all his fiefs. In execution of this judgment, Philip then conquered all Angevin holdings north of the Loire River—Normandy, Anjou, and Maine.

In the territories he acquired by conquest or marriage, Philip usually retained the local laws and customs, making France the patchwork of provinces it was to remain until the French Revolution. In his older possessions, however, he attempted a measure of administrative centralization. The bailiffs he dispatched were salaried royal agents, directly responsible to the king for supervising local administration and collecting what little revenue there was. Philip also sought to replace feudal courts with royal justice as a basis for the extension of political power and the acquisition of more revenues. Moreover, he added to his income by permitting people to pay monetary contributions in lieu of performing military service.

In his relations with the powerful Pope Innocent III, Philip fared generally better than most contemporary monarchs. By placing an interdict on France, the pontiff was able to force the king to take back his wife whom he had repudiated in favor of another woman. Unlike King John I of England, however, Philip succeeded in arranging a compromise with the pope without turning France into a fief of the papacy.

England

By the early ninth century, the small Anglo-Saxon kingdoms of England had all come under the control of Wessex, which had attained prominence under King Alfred the Great (871–889). Alfred had faced increased pressure from Danish raiders, who finally settled in northeastern England, in the so-called Danelaw. During the subsequent century and a half, Wessex extended its control northward and absorbed these Danish territories. Thus arose a new Anglo-Saxon monarchy which was more solidly founded than the contemporary Continental kingdoms. Despite some feudalization, the Anglo-Saxon kings retained more direct control over the land than did the kings of France. They also kept alive the tradition that all propertied free-men owed military service, and they were able to obtain fairly adequate revenues from the royal domains and from feudal dues. Long before the French kings used bailiffs as agents of the crown, the Anglo-Saxons were using sheriffs for essentially similar purposes. Even the Danish interlude in the early eleventh century, when England was ruled by the Danish King Canute, did not detract from the inherent strength of the monarchy.

Hence, when William of Normandy conquered England in 1066, he acquired a well-organized kingdom. William I (1066–1087) claimed the English throne by inheritance (as cousin of King Edward the Confessor), but he had to implement his claim through conquest. At Hastings near the English Channel, some seven thousand Norman knights, footsoldiers, and archers defeated an Anglo-Saxon force of less than five thousand, which included only footsoldiers and very few archers. The famous tapestries woven at Bayeux in Normandy preserve a picture of this memorable Battle of Hastings which changed the history of England. However, it took many more years before all Anglo-Saxon and Danish opposition to William was suppressed.

William the Conqueror assumed the right to seize all land and keep it as royal domain or distribute it at his discretion. He also enjoyed the support of the papacy, since he had promised to introduce reforms in the Church. He was thus in an ideal position for imposing feudalism from above, a feudalism based on strict royal control. From the beginning, he insisted that all Norman nobles who received fiefs from him had to be his direct vassals, had to serve at his call, train knights for him, and remain subject to his justice. Similarly, he retained control over ecclesiastical appointments in England, despite Pope Gregory VII's attempt to eliminate such lay influence over the Church.

Toward the end of his reign, William ordered a state-wide census, the results of which were recorded in the *Domesday Book*. The survey contained data on land ownership, estimated value of the land, size of woods, and the number of mills, carts, and other implements. It furnished William invaluable information for purposes of taxation and for estimating the resources of his realm. For the historian it represents a unique source of medieval history.

Like the Norsemen, from whom they descended, the Normans proved to be highly skilled state builders. In Normandy and Kievan Russia, where they had settled in the ninth century, as well as in southern Italy, Sicily, and later in the Near East, the Norsemen demonstrated their political skill and their adaptability. They were good organizers and usually introduced their own governmental ideas. At the same time, they tended to preserve much of the local culture. In most areas they even adopted the local language. It is curious that they made no effort to remain in contact with each other. Only England and Normandy, which at first were under separate though related rulers, remained joined until 1204. In this Anglo-Norman combination, the Continental possessions tended to be the more important. Hence, French constituted the language of government and of the educated in England during the twelfth century, while the poor and uneducated continued to speak Anglo-Saxon. Only when England lost Normandy and most of her Continental possessions at the beginning of the thirteenth century did Anglo-Saxon and French begin to merge.

William I's successors were not spectacular rulers. They quarreled with the Church over questions of investiture and engaged in internecine family feuds. Yet England continued to prosper and Norman rule became firmly established.

After a period of disorder, the throne was assumed in 1154 by Henry II Plantagenet, whose family is usually called "Angevin," since his father was duke of Anjou. Henry ruled over vast territories, stretching for almost one thousand miles from the borders of Scotland to those of Catalonia. From his father he inherited Anjou, Maine, and Touraine, from his mother Normandy and England. His wife Eleanor of Aquitaine's dowry included Poitou, Guienne, Gascony, and claims on Toulouse. In addition he established feudal claims on Brittany, Scotland, Wales, and eastern Ireland. Henry was more "French" than "English." Of his thirty-five years as king of England, he spent only sixteen on the island. Like the early Hanoverian rulers of England in the eighteenth century (see p. 318), who were to value their Duchy of Hanover more than the Kingdom of England, so Henry and his sons remained essentially Continental. England served them as a convenient reservoir of soldiers and tax revenue, and provided them with a royal title. (See Map 12.)

Despite this Continental attitude and the fact that he spent so much time quarreling with the Church and fighting Louis VII of France, Henry was a successful ruler in England, ranking among those who did most to build up the English monarchy. He struck at the power of the great nobles, who had grown unruly during the period of disorder, by having some of their fortified castles demolished. The revenue of the crown was increased by reclaiming alienated royal land. To help finance the Third Crusade, Parliament granted Henry the so-called Saladin tithe, the first tax levied on personal property in England. Above all, he expanded royal justice through greater use of royal courts and itinerant justices and the extension of the jury system. These efforts, which helped the gradual development of English common law, served to increase the power of the crown while weakening that of the feudal nobles. The extension of royal justice also provided a good source of revenue and ultimately helped unify England.

Henry's determination to expand the jurisdiction of royal courts led to a spectacular clash with the Church, which was attempting to widen the traditional "benefit of clergy" that permitted members of the clergy to be tried in ecclesiastical courts and exempted them from the jurisdiction of civil courts.

Henry demanded that ecclesiastics be subject to royal courts, at least in criminal cases, and that appeals to the pope in Rome be discontinued. Over this issue he fought a determined battle with his friend and former chancellor, Archbishop Thomas Becket (1118?–1170). Becket's murder near the altar of his own cathedral of Canterbury did not solve the problem. Indignation over the murder which had been committed by knights from Henry's entourage forced the king to desist from further attempts to undermine "benefit of clergy."

Henry's son and successor, Richard I the Lion-Hearted, was a dashing knight, better known for heroic exploits than for statesmanship. In his youth, he intrigued against his father with Philip II Augustus of France. After becoming king, he spent three years on the Third Crusade, winning knightly fame in the siege and capture of Acre, and was then imprisoned and held for ransom for two years by the German emperor (Henry VI). During his absence, his brother John plotted against him, and the kingdom was administered by the queen mother Eleanor. Under such circumstances, the great barons again assumed some independence at the expense of the royal power. After his release, he spent five years fighting Philip II over England's Continental possessions and finally died from a wound received in battle.

Richard's brother, John I "Lackland" (1199–1216) is usually characterized as mean and faithless. While this indictment is probably correct, one should keep in mind that his position was difficult and his enemies formidable. The barons and high ecclesiastics were restless, the treasury was depleted from constant warfare in France, and John faced two powerful opponents abroad in Pope Innocent III and King Philip II of France.

In his struggle with Innocent III, John showed less flexibility than had been demonstrated by Philip II in similar circumstances. The quarrel centered on the electoral procedure used in the choice of a new archbishop of Canterbury. Innocent used all the weapons at his disposal: he stirred up the English baronage against their king, placed England under an interdict, and excommunicated John, thereby releasing his subjects from fealty to their king. He then urged Philip II of France to conquer England and place his own son on the English throne. John resisted for eight years, displaying considerable strength. Perhaps he resisted too long, for in the end he had to submit unconditionally. He restored all Church property he had confiscated during the quarrel, agreed to the pope's procedure for electing the new archbishop of Canterbury, and accepted England and Ireland as a fief from the papacy, thus becoming a vassal to the pope.

Meanwhile, as we saw (see p. 130), he lost all Continental possessions north of the Loire to Philip and failed in an attempt to reconquer them at the Battle of Bouvines, 1214, in which England, some imperial princes, and Flanders were defeated by Philip and the young Frederick II of Hohenstaufen. These humiliations by the pope and the king of France ruined what remained of John's prestige. Heretofore worried about the king's attempt to increase the powers of the crown, barons, churchmen, and some towns rose in revolt and presented John with the famous Magna Carta which the king felt forced to seal in 1215.

Magna Carta is subject to differing interpretations. Seen in the context of the thirteenth century, it is a conservative document by which John promised to respect feudal customs, to reform taxes mostly in favor of the feudal lords, to guarantee the preservation of town liberties, and not to interfere in free Church elections. On the other hand, Magna Carta contained clauses which in later times could be construed as harbingers of democracy. The Great Council, consisting of government officials, heads of the royal household, and the great lords, was to have some control over taxation—a vague forerunner of parliamentary control over the state's finances. Freedom of travel was guaranteed. Moreover, there were to be no arbitrary arrests or banishments of any freeman "except by the legal judgment of his peers or by the law of the land"—a clause establishing due process of law.

No matter how Magna Carta is interpreted, it contains an element that is almost revolutionary. Tired of arbitrary royal rule, particularly as exhibited by John I, the barons noted specific grievances and forced the king to promise to redress them. Such an act limited the potential power of the rulers. In this light, the Great Charter was less a seed of democracy than an affirmation of the need for rule under law. The pope's attitude was instructive. As John's suzerain, Innocent III annulled it and instructed John to disregard its provisions, since it checked not only royal power but also papal absolutism. Before his death in 1216, King John himself disavowed his seal to the charter.

Spain

The creation of Christian feudal monarchies on the Iberian Peninsula resulted from the success of what Spaniards proudly call *la reconquista.* When the Moslems conquered Visigothic Spain, only a small area in the Northwest (Asturias) and some border districts in the Pyrenees escaped their occupation. *La reconquista,* or the Christian reconquest of Spain, was launched by Charlemagne when he established the Spanish March south of the Pyrenees. Thereafter the liberation of the peninsula from Moslem control continued by fits and starts. Small Christian kingdoms were created by local nobles or adventurous knights from the North—among them Galicia, León, Castile, Navarre, and Aragon. These states often fought with one another, but their primary goal remained southward expansion at the expense of the Moslems. The greatest progress of the *reconquista* occurred during the eleventh and twelfth centuries. After Castile's decisive victory at Las Navas de Tolosa (1212), Moslem power in Spain was reduced to the southeastern corner of the peninsula, the province of Granada, where it held out for over two more centuries. (See Map 12.)

By the early thirteenth century, the many Christian kingdoms in the Iberian Peninsula had merged into only four: Portugal, Castile, Navarre, and Aragon. Portugal had been founded in the eleventh century as a fief of León in northern Spain and had gradually expanded southward with the aid of Burgundian knights. In the mid-twelfth century, the Burgundian dynasty of Portugal gained royal prerogatives and independence from León—which by that time had been absorbed by Castile—in return for turning Portugal into a fief of the papacy. With the aid of knights who stopped in Portugal on their way to join the Second Crusade, Lisbon was taken from the Moslems and added to the growing Portuguese Kingdom.

Meanwhile the Kingdom of Castile, with its center at Burgos, had acquired León and Asturias and had begun its expansion southward. Ruled from the late eleventh to the thirteenth century by a series of skilled kings, Castile assumed the forefront in the *reconquista*. The prowess of her kings furthered the fighting *élan* of the Castilians. Several of them called themselves "emperors," one in the thirteenth century even claiming the crown of the Holy Roman Empire. The legends of *El Cid,* who in real life had been an unscrupulous knight changing colors to suit his ambition, provided the country with unifying inspiration.

During this period, the small Kingdom of Navarre in the Basque country between Pamplona and the Bay of Biscay changed in size almost every generation, increasing or decreasing in contest with its neighbors. When Castile and Aragon obtained a common border in the twelfth century, Navarre was cut off from direct participation in the *reconquista* and lost her vitality. Passing first into the French orbit, Navarre was ultimately absorbed by the united Spanish Kingdom in the early sixteenth century (1512).

Aragon, the fourth of the Iberian kingdoms, emerged as an independent realm only in the eleventh century. After uniting with the county of Barcelona—the territory of Charlemagne's former Spanish March with added holdings north of the Pyrenees—Aragon rapidly acquired power. Possession of the Mediterranean shore with the rich harbor of Barcelona, followed by acquisition of the Balearic Islands in the early thirteenth century, turned Aragon into a strong state that occupied an important place in late medieval Europe.

The four kingdoms shared common characteristics. Based on conquest, their feudalism centered on the king. The riches confiscated from the Moors swelled the royal treasuries and attracted venturesome knights to join the campaigns against the Moors. *La reconquista* in fact took on the fervor of a crusade. The kings also received support and encouragement from the Church and awarded her a good share of the conquered lands. Cooperation between king and Catholic primate became a permanent feature of Spanish history. But the expanding kingdoms were not based exclusively on military centralism. The anti-Moorish campaigns permitted great vassals to pre-empt huge, entrenched fiefs that made them quasi-independent of the monarchy;

similarly, the towns, founded and chartered by the kings in the course of the *reconquista,* remained fiercely independent.

The greatest influence on the Iberian kingdoms came perhaps from the Moors themselves. When the Abbasid caliphs overthrew the Omayyad dynasty in Baghdad in 750, descendants of the Omayyads retained control of Spain, where they founded an independent kingdom at Cordova which flourished in economic and intellectual brilliance until the eleventh century and extended its power over Morocco. Cordova became one of the great centers of art and learning and an invaluable repository for transmitting Greek, Roman, and Arabic knowledge to the Christian world. Despite the *reconquista,* there was much cultural and economic exchange between the Moorish and Christian states. They carried on active diplomatic relations and occasionally even supported one another against unruly subjects. During the eleventh century, after the end of the Omayyad dynasty, the Cordovan caliphate split into numerous small states until Berber tribes from Morocco (Almoravids and later Almohades) seized power in Spain and slowed down Christian expansion until the Battle of Las Navas de Tolosa (1212). As the reconquest progressed, the captured cities—notwithstanding occasional Christian vandalism—served as new transmitters of Moslem culture to the Spanish kingdoms and beyond to the Christian West.

The Norman Kingdom of Sicily

As indicated before (see p. 122), the late tenth and eleventh centuries saw the birth of Christian feudal monarchies in many areas—Denmark, Norway, Sweden, Bohemia, Poland, Hungary, and Russia. In some of the new states, however, little feudalism emerged. The Norman state in southern Italy and Sicily, for example, although marked with feudal trappings, was relatively centralized and "modern."

In the early eleventh century, Norman adventurers conquered southern Italy from Byzantium. After trying unsuccessfully to dislodge them, the popes recognized the advantage of using the Normans as a counterweight to the German emperors. In 1059 therefore, the pope made an alliance with the Norman leader Robert Guiscard (1015–1085), invested him with southern Italy, accepted him as his vassal, and urged him to conquer Sicily from the Saracens and keep it as a papal fief.

Robert Guiscard and his brother Roger I (1031–1101) then undertook the conquest of Sicily. Later, Roger seized the island of Malta and challenged the Byzantine emperor with his ambitions for a Norman Mediterranean empire. In 1130, his son, Roger II (1101–1154), was recognized as king. The Kingdom of the Two Sicilies, as his realm later came to be called, stretched from the vicinity of Rome to the southern tip of Sicily. Nominally vassals of the papacy, the Norman kings were actually strong and wealthy enough to follow an independent policy that was sometimes pro-papal and at times anti-papal. Their state was tightly administered by a centralized civil service. Thanks to their adaptability, the Normans developed a culture that was a fruitful mixture of Roman, Greek, Byzantine, Arab, and Norman elements.

In 1194, the Norman Kingdom lost its independence when it was inherited by the house of Hohenstaufen (see p. 128). But as the home of Emperor Frederick II and the wealthiest, best-developed part of his empire, the Kingdom of the Two Sicilies retained its importance for another half century.

Economic and intellectual resurgence

The consolidation of feudal monarchies, which permitted rulers to extend their political control over ever wider areas, was made possible by the economic upturn of the eleventh century and by a noticeable improvement in communications. Political order for its part benefited commerce and accelerated the pulse of town life. Both factors in turn facilitated monarchical growth. These political and economic changes were so intertwined that it seems futile to speculate on their particular causal relationship.

Socio-economic changes

In the eleventh, and particularly in the twelfth century, there was a marked increase in available money—that is, in the supply of gold and silver —and in the speed with which it circulated. Availability of specie stimulated trade and affected the structure of society, with feudal and manorial relationships gradually giving way to hiring and renting. Landlords, who preferred cash to payment in produce, could purchase luxury items that were imported from the East and, with less need for local self-sufficiency, they could specialize in sheep raising, viticulture, or the growing of grain. Serfs, on the other hand, could become free by buying up servile contracts with money earned from the sale of excess produce in nearby towns.

In the eleventh century, sea trade with Byzantium and the Arab world was reopened on a large scale. Increased trade as well as a noticeable increase in the population of Western Europe helped restore vitality to towns. It is popular to speak of the "revival" of trade and towns during this period; yet this expression may convey the erroneous idea that towns had been "dead" during the earlier Middle Ages. To be sure, many Roman towns had simply disappeared into the realm of archaeological curiosities; but just as many survived through the "darkest" periods, although economically they had been reduced to mere shells.

Those areas which benefited from the new trade routes—in the Mediterranean or near the mouth of important inland waterways such as the Rhine —were the first to see the regeneration of town life. Venice, Genoa, Pisa, Barcelona, and the cities of Flanders became particularly active during the eleventh century. After 1100, towns began to prosper in many other areas. In

Italy, the commercial aristocracy tended to dominate the towns until the lower classes gained some influence in the later Middle Ages. Most of the Italian towns also gained dominance over surrounding lands and thus became city-states. Many bishoprics north of the Alps, built around a bishop's city, also became city-states; but most towns in the north usually did not control much area beyond the city walls. The northern nobility generally retained the land, while bourgeois merchants, eventually constituting a new patrician aristocracy, controlled the towns.

As towns grew in population and economic vigor, they sought rights and privileges: self-government, control over their own tolls and taxes, over their own police and law courts, and in some cases the right to strike their own coins. The merchants and upper classes of these towns had new interests, different from those of the landed aristocracy. This new bourgeois class which now began to grow in size and importance did not fit into the feudal scheme socially or economically; it was a "middle" class, between peasants and serfs on the one hand and the landed nobility on the other.

New contacts with the East

This period of resurgence was also the age of the crusades. Because historians have numbered the crusades, from the first launched by Pope Urban II in 1095 to the eighth and last undertaken by King Louis IX of France in 1270, we frequently picture them as eight separate events between 1095 and 1270. Actually the crusades were part of a general movement to reconquer Moslem lands that started in the late tenth century—when the Byzantines temporarily reconquered Damascus and Beirut and almost captured Jerusalem—and continued long after 1270 in campaigns against the Turks. One might mention Amadeus of Savoy's attempt to liberate Gallipoli (1366), two crusades undertaken by the Hungarians (1396 and 1443), or the many Venetian-Turkish wars of the fifteenth century. Moreover, even between 1095 and 1270, there were more than just the numbered crusades—for instance those of 1100–1101, 1123–1124, and 1240–1241. And between the more spectacular campaigns, there was a steady flow of reinforcements and supplies to the East, as well as a return of crusaders to the West. In this constant stream rather than in the spurts of organized campaigns lies the importance of the crusades for cultural exchanges, for trade, for enlarging the Western horizon, and, one might add, for Italian shipping.

Many reasons may account for the crusades and may explain why the movement became so widespread in the eleventh century. Jerusalem had remained accessible to pilgrims even after the Arab conquest of Palestine. During the ninth and tenth centuries, the papacy had been allowed to exercise an honorary protectorship over the holy places. Then, in the early eleventh century, the Greek Orthodox Church seized the guardianship of the shrines in Jerusalem and made access difficult for Catholic pilgrims. When the Seljuk

Turks conquered Jerusalem in 1070, Palestine became almost inaccessible to the West.

This closing off of the Holy Land occurred at the moment when both the revitalization of religious fervor in the West—as seen in the Cluniac reforms—and improved communications were making pilgrimages more popular. To join a pilgrimage, or better yet, to join a crusade, was considered an act of penance. One should not cynically underestimate the religious motivation of countless crusaders. Many knights "took the cross" out of purely spiritual conviction. The bands of thousands of disorganized pilgrims who marched toward the Holy Land after Pope Urban's call for a crusade, and who either died en route of famine or disease or were slaughtered by the Turks in Asia Minor, attest to the strength of religious conviction.

Crusades also appealed to the popes who sought to purify the secular world and to gain control over its politics. The Church had previously attempted to lessen chaos in Europe by promoting the "Peace" and the "Truce of God." Now Pope Urban II urged the knights to stop their fratricidal wars on the Continent and to turn their fighting skills against the infidels. The nascent chivalric ideals fitted admirably into this picture with their admonishments to the knights to protect the weak (pilgrims), to fight for the good (the Church), and to destroy evil (the infidel). Pope Urban was able to dominate the First Crusade, which was led mostly by French nobles without the participation of kings or emperor. In later crusades, the papacy could no longer retain such control.

Even before the fall of Jerusalem to the Turks, campaigns against the Moslems had been launched in many areas, for the sake of religion, trade, or territorial gains. The Spanish *reconquista* was in full swing, Pisans and Genoans had conquered Sardinia, and the Normans had begun their conquest of Sicily. Fighting the Saracens had become popular with Mediterranean sailors as well as Norman and French knights. As the Italians gradually reopened the sea, new possibilities for trade and conquest appeared, rekindling the desire to reactivate the trade routes to Asia—in itself a contributing factor to the crusades.

Another reason for the crusades was a reawakening of the East-West rivalry, sharpened by the final break between the Greek Orthodox and Roman Catholic churches in 1054. The failure of the Byzantine Empire to stem the Turkish onslaught opened a chance for the Latins to reconquer the East. The Eastern emperor (Alexius Comnenus) obviously feared such a possibility, since he forced most leaders of the First Crusade to swear that the territory they might conquer from the Turks would be restored to the Byzantine Empire. That these fears were well founded became clear during the twelfth century, when Norman and French crusaders carved out several feudal states in the eastern Mediterranean—among them the kingdoms of Jerusalem and of Armenia, and the counties of Edessa, Tripoli, and Antioch.

Even better proof was furnished by the Fourth Crusade (1202–1204) which, instead of going to the Holy Land, terminated with the capture and sack of Constantinople and the establishment of a Latin empire in Byzantium (until 1261), soon followed by the creation of many French feudal realms in Greece, most of which lasted throughout a good part of the thirteenth century. At the same time, the papacy sought to regain control over Jerusalem, while the Venetians pocketed scattered holdings on the islands and coasts of the Adriatic, Aegean, and eastern Mediterranean at the expense of the Byzantine Empire, in order to expand their commercial operations.

Ironic as it may seem, the First Crusade was undertaken at the specific request of the emperor of Byzantium who appealed to the papacy and to the French nobility for aid against the Seljuk Turks. The Turks had come out of Asia in the early eleventh century, had adopted Islam, and captured Baghdad. Soon they replaced the Arabs as rulers, defeated the Byzantine armies (in the Battle of Manzikert, 1071), and seized most of the Near East from the Dead Sea to the Caucasus Mountains. Having lost their remaining holdings in Asia, the Byzantines hoped that the West could help save Byzantium itself, although their appeal for assistance was clothed in the more dignified form of a call to rescue the Holy places from the infidel.

The consequences of the crusades went far beyond the temporary establishment of shaky feudal states in the Near East, such as the Kingdom of Jerusalem which lasted from 1099 to 1187. The Mediterranean bustled with trade and naval expansion that brought further wealth to the Italian city-states of Venice, Genoa, and Pisa, and then stimulated commercial activity throughout many areas of Europe. The adventures of the crusaders brought glory and often riches to the knights and helped develop chivalric codes under the influence of such organized religious orders as the Teutonic Knights and the Knights Templar, even though the crusades as such were replete with acts of excessive cruelty. Reports of heroic acts also revived interest in epics. And there were countless instances where the death or absence of a crusading lord had a profound influence on a ruling family or an entire region.

Less measurable is the extent to which the European horizon widened through cultural contacts with the East. The crusading knights were presumably more concerned with material luxuries than with intellectual matters. The "Franks," as the Moslems called all crusaders who settled in the new Latin principalities in the East, apparently lived peacefully among the local Moslems, whom they taxed heavily but whom they did not try to convert to Christianity. There is little evidence of intellectual contact between the native Moslems and the Western settlers, although some families remained for two or three generations before returning to the West. It seems probable that cultural interchange at the highest intellectual level between Moslems and Christians took place in Spain rather than in the Near East.

The twelfth-century "renaissance"

The term "renaissance" usually designates the cultural and political changes of the fifteenth and sixteenth centuries. But over the past decades, historians have applied this term also to the twelfth century, a period in which vast changes were noticeable in most cultural fields. Indeed, there was then perhaps more of a "rebirth" than in the fifteenth century.

In architecture, for example, the increased wealth of the twelfth century permitted more building in stone and more refinement in craftsmanship. Fortified castles no longer consisted largely of massive walls but were built with some thought for the comfort of their occupants. The Romanesque style of church architecture spread rapidly over Europe. Based on the Roman basilica plan, with the addition of a transverse aisle as transept and of side aisles to provide more space, these churches were constructed with heavy walls and round arches. Inside, they tended to be dark. Soon towns, bishoprics, and abbeys vied with one another in the construction of more elaborate and magnificent churches and cathedrals. The Romanesque style was lightened. Radiating and side chapels were added for the veneration of saints and more side aisles provided greater space for worshipers. The profuse addition of sculptures and stained glass windows, the use of ribbed vaulting that permitted an increase in the height of the building, and buttressing that allowed for thinner walls and more windows, prepared for the gradual transition to the Gothic style during the twelfth century.

In the Early Middle Ages, a few important literary works had been produced, most of them epics such as the Anglo-Saxon tale about the warrior *Beowulf* (eighth century), the story of *Hildebrand,* composed in Charlemagne's era, and *Walter of Aquitaine,* written during the reign of Emperor Otto I. But on the whole, these early centuries had not been a fruitful period for belletristic literature. Most of the legends of heroes and gods, based on events from the era of migrations or on the deeds of such rulers as Charlemagne and King Arthur, had been transmitted orally. In the eleventh century, there was an increase in literary activity, especially in historical descriptions, annals, and theological disputations.

Beginning in the second half of the twelfth century literature flourished, stimulated by the exotic reports of the crusaders and the demands of a feudal aristocracy with more wealth and leisure. Most literary products went hand in hand with the growing chivalric ideals. The period was particularly rich in poetry and epic. Inspired by the troubadours (poet-musicians of southern France) and the jongleurs who wandered from court to castle, reciting ballads and epic songs, poets in France, England, Germany and Scandinavia transformed into literary style the epics and legends which had hitherto been transmitted in popular form. In many cases they added Christian overtones to stories essentially pagan in content. The written forms of the Icelandic *Eddas,* the Arthurian romances, the early versions of *Parsifal,* of *Tristan,* and of the *Niebelungenlied* all date from this period, as do many tales of love and adventure, such as *Aucassin and Nicolette* and valuable lyric poems by Walther von der Vogelweide. The imaginative quality of this literature of the twelfth and thirteenth century was such that, next to Greek mythology and the Bible, it ranks among the largest sources for the inspiration of later Western writers.

There was also a significant change in thought and education. Scholars increasingly tried to summarize existing knowledge, particularly in theology, law, and medicine. By the twelfth century, the greater availability of Greek and Roman works, especially of Aristotle and his Arab commentators, added to this intellectual ferment. A few old schools of rhetoric had survived in Italy, but most existing educational facilities were ecclesiastical, connected with monasteries or cathedrals. The need for more educated clerics and for improved training in law and medicine gave impetus to the expansion of higher education. Hence more cathedral schools were created and universities were founded at Salerno, Bologna, Padua, Oxford, Paris, Valencia, and several other towns. These early universities began as corporations of masters or of students, or of both combined, organized for the protection of their mutual interests. Most universities tended to specialize: Salerno became known for medicine, Bologna for law, and Paris for theology and philosophy.

Increased interest in learning and a more sophisticated level of understanding revived the great theological and philosophical debates among bishops, abbots, and university professors. By the twelfth century, such debates reverberated throughout the theological world of the West. As new knowledge in mathematics, medicine, and astronomy was made available by the Arabs, and as more of Aristotle's works were rediscovered—largely at first through Avicenna and Averroës (see p. 108)—the question of how to reconcile this secular knowledge with Church tradition became more and more pressing.

In essence, it was the same question which Saint Augustine had asked and which in one form or another was debated throughout the High Middle Ages. "Whence shall we begin? With authority or with reason?" Those who were mystically inclined like St. Augustine and St. Bernard of Clairvaux (1091–1153) tended to place uncritical faith in revelation and showed little confidence in the powers of human reason, if unaided by the divine. Others, like Peter Abelard (1079–1142), teacher and philosopher, while not rejecting the basic assumption that revelation or authority is "the foundation of all good," would have man reason his beliefs critically. Convinced that "by doubting we are led to inquiry, and from inquiry we perceive truth," he analyzed the writings of the Church Fathers to demonstrate contradictions in some of their answers to fundamental questions. St. Bernard fulminated against him as a "fabricator of heresies" who "deems himself able by human reasons to comprehend God altogether," and ultimately succeeded in having him condemned for error. Several generations later, St. Thomas Aquinas (1225-1274) was to attempt a reconciliation between reason and revelation (see p. 149).

Renewed interest in science, the rediscovery of Aristotle, and the emphasis on human reason led to further challenges to St. Augustine. John of Salisbury (?-1180) boldly asserted that physical phenomena were worth studying in themselves and that such study was not sinful, even if it did not contribute to salvation. It was a modest attempt toward separating "science" from religion and making the investigation of nature acceptable in the eyes of the Church, an attempt which was to be taken up in the next century by Roger Bacon (1214-1294).

SUGGESTED READINGS

Church Reform

Baldwin, Marshall W., *Mediaeval Church* (Cornell, 1953).

Duggan, Alfred, *The Falcon and the Dove: A Life of Thomas Becket of Canterbury* (Pantheon, 1966).

*Knowles, David, *The Monastic Order in England* (Cambridge U.P., 1963).

Powell, James M., *Innocent III—Vicar of Christ or Lord of the World?* (Heath, 1963).

*Tellenbach, Gerd, *Church, State and Christian Society at the Time of the Investiture Contest* (Humanities, 1959).

Tierney, Brian, *The Crisis of Church and State, 1050-1300* (Prentice-Hall, 1964). With translated sources.

*Ullmann, Walter, *Growth of Papal Government in the Middle Ages* (Barnes and Noble, 1963).

Williams, Schafer, ed., *The Gregorian Epoch: Reformation, Revolution, Reaction?* (Heath, 1964).

Holy Roman Empire

Benson, L., ed., *Imperial Lives and Letters of the Eleventh Century* (Columbia, 1962). Sources.

Hertzstein, Robert E., ed., *The Holy Roman Empire in the Middle Ages—Universal State or German Catastrophe?* (Heath, 1965).

Otto of Freising, *The Deeds of Frederick Barbarossa* (Norton, 1966). Contemporary account of his early reign.

*Tout, T. F., *Empire and the Papacy, 918-1273* (Barnes and Noble, 1965).

Feudal Monarchy

Brooke, Christopher, *From Alfred to Henry III, 871-1272* (Norton, 1966).

Fawtier, Robert, *The Capetian Kings of France, Monarchy and Nation 987-1328* (St. Martins, 1960).

Haskins, Charles Homer, *The Normans in European History* (Norton, 1966). From the ninth to the thirteenth century.

Hassall, W. O., ed., *Medieval England: As Viewed by Contemporaries* (Harper, 1965). Sources up to the fifteenth century.

Kelly, Amy, *Eleanor of Aquitaine and the Four Kings* (Random, 1957).

Luchaire, Achille, *Social France at the Time of Philip Augustus* (Harper, 1967).

Painter, Sidney, *The Rise of the Feudal Monarchies* (Cornell, 1951). France, England, and Germany from the tenth to the fifteenth century.

Petit-Dutaillis, Charles, *The Feudal Monarchy in France and England: From the Tenth to the Thirteenth Century* (Harper, 1964).

Thorne, Samuel E., and Dunham, William H., and others, *The Great Charter* (New American Library, 1966).

Crusades

Brundage, James A., ed., *The Crusades: Motives and Achievements* (Heath, 1964).

Joinville, Jean de, and Villehardouin, Geoffrey de, *Chronicles of the Crusades* (Penguin, 1963).

Newhall, Richard A., *The Crusades* (Holt, 1963). A cursory survey of main events.

Runciman, Steven, *A History of the Crusades,* Vol. I, "The First Crusade and the Foundation of the Kingdom of Jerusalem" (Harper, 1964).

Treece, Henry, *The Crusades* (New American Library, 1964).

Social and Cultural Revival

*Brophy, Liam, *Marvelous Doctor* (Franciscan Herald, 1963). On Roger Bacon.

Clagett, Marshall, Post, Gaines, and Reynolds, Robert L., eds., *Twelfth-Century Europe and the Foundations of Modern Society* (U. of Wisconsin, 1961). Collection of Essays.

Coulton, G. G., *Medieval Village, Manor, and Monastery* (Harper, 1960). Somewhat dated but still illuminating.

*Focillon, Henri, *Art of the West in the Middle Ages,* Vol. I, "Romanesque" (Phaidon, 1963).

Haskins, Charles Homer, *The Renaissance of the Twelfth Century* (World).

Holmes, Urban T., *Daily Living in the Twelfth Century: Based on the Observations of Alexander Neckam in London and Paris* (U. of Wisconsin, 1952).

Knowles, David, *The Evolution of Medieval Thought* (Random).

Pirenne, Henri, *Economic and Social History of Medieval Europe* (Harcourt, 1956).

——, *Medieval Cities* (Doubleday, 1956).

*Vinogradoff, Paul, *Roman Law in Medieval Europe* (Barnes and Noble, 1967).

White, Lynn, Jr., *Medieval Technology and Social Change* (Oxford U.P., 1962).

CHAPTER IX

✤ *Height and Decline of the Middle Ages*
(Thirteenth and Fourteenth Centuries)

Medieval civilization with its special *Zeitgeist* became most fully expressed by the thirteenth century, a period called by some historians the "High Middle Ages." During the fourteenth century, however, often called the "Later Middle Ages," many new phenomena appeared which did not fit into the socio-political and cultural pattern of medieval civilization and thus prepared for the transition to a new age.

The temper of the thirteenth century

One tends to think of the Middle Ages as dominated by the Church. Yet even at its height, medievalism was not unmitigated otherworldliness. The "typical" medieval man was not preoccupied solely with the salvation of his soul, nor was his life totally guided by spiritual considerations. Medievalism rather represented a mixture of worldly and spiritual concerns, always guided heavily by the moral and emotional influences of religion. The thirteenth century, one must recall, produced such diverse contemporaries as the mystic and ascetic St. Francis of Assisi (see p. 148) and the worldly and rational Emperor Frederick II (see p. 149), whose metaphysical speculations were quite impersonal and not concerned with salvation.

To understand the temper of the thirteenth century, let us look at the reign of King Louis IX of France, at feudalism and chivalry, at the Gothic cathedral, the new mendicant orders, and the teachings of St. Thomas Aquinas.

St. Louis IX of France (1226–1270) may serve as the model of a feudal monarch. "This holy man loved God with all his heart," wrote his contemporary biographer Joinville, whose hero worship may have been influenced by the fact that King Louis had already been canonized by the Church (1297) when Joinville completed his biography in 1309. Louis was modest in taste, in fact somewhat ascetic. According to Joinville, "he watered his wine," was "temperate in language," and was humble to the point of ceremoniously washing the feet of the poor. He tended the sick, endowed hospitals, and was a model of Christian charity.

King Louis maintained most cordial relations with the Church. He faithfully supported the Inquisition, which the papacy and the Dominican Friars had turned into an organized institution for ferreting out and eliminating heretics. Twice he took the cross. On his first crusade (1248-1254), he lost his entire army, was captured in Egypt, and was finally ransomed after four years of confinement in Syria. He died on his second crusade in Tunis. Furthermore, he arranged for the construction of Sainte Chapelle in Paris, an exquisite Gothic chapel built to house Christ's crown of thorns and other relics which he had bought from the impecunious emperor of Byzantium.

St. Louis bestowed dignity on the French crown by stressing morality in politics. His decisions were generally guided by Christian humility and a strong sense of equity. Yet he never forgot the self-interest of the French monarchy. Notwithstanding harmonious relations with the Church, he firmly insisted on the crown's prerogatives. Nor did he hesitate to profit from the Albigensian Crusade (1208-1226), which had been waged by Pope Innocent III and by Louis' father against heretics in southern France. Upon its conclusion, he acquired the large county of Toulouse, which was annexed to the royal domain in 1271.

Louis IX's devotion to justice became legendary. Like all rulers who sought to increase the crown's power and revenue, he expanded the system of royal justice; he also tried to make the ordinances he issued from time to time respected over wider areas of the kingdom. He considered it the duty of a king to dispense justice personally and to arbitrate between litigants, preferring to reconcile and mediate rather than condemn. His fame as arbiter became such that even the barons of England asked him to judge their case against King Henry III, probably not suspecting that he would side in favor of the king.

But Louis was no humble weakling. Personally a valiant knight, he insisted on obedience and respect to the majesty of a king. He suppressed unruly nobles and tightened royal control through firmness and improvement of the governmental machinery. During his reign, specialization within the court grew apace. Some members dealt with financial matters; others, constituting the *parlement,* discussed and registered new laws. Under the impact of revived Roman legal concepts, there was also a growing awareness of the distinction between the king's public and private affairs.

With England St. Louis negotiated settlements whereby he relinquished claims to lands conquered by his predecessors. In return, he obtained English renunciation of Poitou and all Continental lands north of the Loire. Besides demonstrating the application of Christian principles to international politics, such abandonment of territorial claims also represented a sound retrenchment between periods of expansion.

All in all, St. Louis added moral *élan* to the growth of the French monarchy, and most later French monarchs proudly called themselves descendants of St. Louis. But he also left a harmful legacy by continuing his father's practice of granting appanages in the form of large duchies to royal brothers and sons. Such splintering of the royal domain into great fiefs was potentially dangerous, since it encouraged the formation of rival branches of the royal dynasty (see p. 173).

Feudalism and chivalry also typify medieval civilization. By the thirteenth century, French feudalism was no longer the patchwork of personal relations it had been in the tenth century. It had developed into a highly structured and ritualized socio-political system. Through plural vassalage, overlapping jurisdiction of suzerainty, and subinfeudation—the subdivision of fiefs into smaller holdings—the system had also become enormously complicated. As in contemporary Gothic cathedrals, where by means of ribbed vaulting one buttress supported several arches and every arch in itself had several supports, so most vassals served several lords. Such plural vassalage produced complications when two lords of the same vassal fought each other and both requested his aid.

Feudal ceremonies had been coated with religious overtones. The oath of fidelity tendered by the vassal to his lord during the act of homage had become quasi-religious, and popes claimed the power to nullify such oaths. Before a young man was knighted, he not merely had to prove his skill at arms, but he had to fast, pray, confess, and take communion, so that he might become a "pure" knight. The code of chivalry, which was partly inspired by the epic literature of the day, enjoined knights to fight for a noble lady or for the Virgin Mary. The duty of a vassal was of course to fight for his lord, but chivalric ideals made it clear that it was even better to fight for the Church.

The numerous orders of crusading knights, most of which were founded and confirmed by the papacy in the later twelfth century, were based on a mixture of chivalry and monasticism. Most orders required their members to take the monastic vows of poverty, chastity, and obedience. Over their armor, the knights wore a wide cape with an embroidered cross; their shields were embossed with crosses. Their aims and activities also mixed worldliness and religion. The Knights of the Temple, organized to protect pilgrims in the Holy Land, became wealthy bankers, transferring funds for the crusaders. Fighting for pope and emperor against heathens along the Baltic shore, the Teutonic Knights acquired a vast commercial and landed empire, just as the Spanish Order of Alcántara, ostensibly founded to aid the *reconquista,* rapidly became a rich, aristocratic organization. Finally, it is worth recalling that by the thirteenth century, abbots, bishops, and popes had become so enmeshed in the feudal system as suzerains and vassals that it was often hard to determine whether a given bishop was supporting worldly aims or whether a duke was fighting for the Church.

The Gothic cathedral was also a mixture of the spiritual and the secular in that it was built for the glory of God and for the glorification of the city. The vast array of statues which adorned it depicted saints and burghers, apostles and kings, as well as demons and animals. Heaven and earth could truly meet under its spiraling height, made solemn by the inspiring colors of its stained glass windows. More than a symbol of the city, the Gothic cathedral also became a center of its activities, with miracle and morality plays performed on its steps, plays which in themselves were earthy, even bawdy, although they served to inspire the audience to seek the path to salvation.

Conditions in the thirteenth century also produced new religious orders more attuned to the needs of city life than the existing monastic orders, whose monasteries usually lay isolated in rural communities. The new mendicant orders established their houses in the center of cities. Unlike the older monastics, the mendicants (or friars) did not withdraw from the world. Rather they sought to help the poor and the sick, to spread love and charity, and to eradicate heresy. Most important among the mendicant orders were the Franciscans (or Little Brothers) and the Dominicans.

The Franciscans—often called Gray Friars, because of the color of their coarse robe—were founded by St. Francis of Assisi (1181–1226), a man of the sincerest religious convictions who abandoned his father's inheritance to became a beggar and devote his life to helping others. Suspicious of the value of scholarly theology, St. Francis was imbued with a deep concern for the suffering of the wretched and with a loving, almost pantheistic reverence for animals and the forces of nature. In all men and all things he saw God's creation. Himself attempting to lead a Christlike life, he had an immense faith in the goodness of humanity. His life left a profound impression on his followers, and the Little Brothers, authorized by the pope as an order in 1223 and operating under the direct control of the papacy, quickly acquired an influential voice in medieval Christendom. By 1350 already, some 1450 Franciscan houses had been formed.

The Dominicans, or Black Friars, were founded by the learned Spaniard, St. Dominic (1170–1221), as an Order of Preachers with the primary aim of service to the Church. At first less concerned with helping the poor than the Gray Friars, the Dominicans preached, taught, and became skilled administrators of the Inquisition. Although the two mendicant orders were rivals who initially espoused different goals, both became vital contributors to the intellectual revival occurring in the universities of the thirteenth century.

Finally, medieval thought was epitomized by the teachings of Thomas Aquinas, who attempted to resolve the dichotomy between reason and revelation, or as it were between Aristotle and Holy Scriptures. A synthesis of these two was essential for medieval civilization, since it would herald the final reconciliation between the Greco-Roman and Hebrew-Christian heritage. St. Thomas reasoned away the dichotomy in logical steps. Reason and revelation, he asserted, were simply different roads to the same end of knowledge. Some revealed truths could easily be verified by human reason. But some truths were above human reason and could be apprehended only through revelation. Reason thus supported revelation rather than contradicting it. Even this slight acknowledgment of the power of human reason shocked some of Thomas' contemporaries like St. Bonaventure who followed in the tradition of St. Augustine and St. Bernard. Yet, ultimately, Aquinas' synthesis became the official philosophy of the Catholic Church.

The universals: from zenith to decline

In the thirteenth century, empire and papacy, the two institutions that aspired to universal recognition if not predominance, both passed their zenith. By the middle of the century, the Holy Roman Empire began to disintegrate; even its slight recovery at the end of the century left it greatly reduced in power and prestige. The papacy, after an undulating course of power during the century, suddenly took a similar plunge after the pontificate of Boniface VIII (1294–1303).

The Holy Roman Empire

Emperor Frederick II began his career as a ward of Pope Innocent III and came to the throne only after a prolonged period of civil wars. Half Norman and half Hohenstaufen by birth, Frederick was perhaps the best educated medieval emperor, skilled in diplomacy and a patron of learning. He spoke fluent Arabic, kept a harem, and was more interested in the Saracen culture of his native Sicily than in his German lands. His realm was larger and wealthier than that of other medieval emperors, since he also owned southern Italy and Sicily, and indirectly ruled the Kingdom of Jerusalem as well as East Prussia, which was conquered by the Teutonic Knights during his reign.

Since he was not much interested in his possessions north of the Alps, so long as they remained obedient and paid taxes, he ceded much power to the princes and bishops of Germany. By granting them authority to collect their own taxes and tolls, to control their own police systems, strike their own coins, and set up their own courts, Frederick accelerated the decentralization of the empire. (See Map 12.)

His desire to gain control of central Italy involved him in an interminable struggle with the papacy, a struggle which neither was able to win. As husband of the heiress to the Kingdom of Jerusalem, Frederick undertook a crusade (the Sixth, 1228–1229) to the Holy Land, although he was under the ban of papal excommunication. Instead of conquering the Holy Land by force of arms, he negotiated a settlement with the Moslems and thereby gained for the Christians free access to Jerusalem, Nazareth, and Bethlehem. To see an excommunicated emperor obtain access to the Holy Land horrified devout Christian believers while delighting the antipapal factions. This ambivalence helps explain Frederick's reputation: with some he ranked as the greatest of emperors; others looked upon him as anti-Christ.

After Frederick's death, the imperial structure collapsed. The popes waged a relentless struggle to keep Frederick's descendants from retaining control of southern Italy. To help extirpate the house of Hohenstaufen, the papacy invited the French Charles of Anjou (1226–1285), St. Louis' brother, to seize the Kingdom of the Two Sicilies. The ambitious Charles complied gladly. He defeated the Hohenstaufen forces, had the last surviving male heir, Emperor Frederick's fifteen year old grandson (Conradin) beheaded in Naples, and assumed the Sicilian crown. But Charles of Anjou, who dreamt of creating a Sicilian Mediterranean empire at the expense of Byzantium, soon became as unwelcome a neighbor to the papacy as the Hohenstaufen had been. In 1282, the Sicilians themselves rose in rebellion, massacred their French masters, and awarded the Sicilian crown to the King of Aragon (Peter III, the husband of Frederick II's granddaughter). The Angevins succeeded in retaining only Naples. Thereafter, Sicily and Naples remained divided between Aragon and Anjou until the mid-fifteenth century.

Meanwhile, during the so-called Interregnum (1254–1273), there was no effective ruler for the Holy Roman Empire. The Italian city-states acted like sovereign bodies, and north of the Alps individual princes and bishops gained ever greater independence. The political splintering of Italy and Germany thus increased at a time when the French monarchy was growing more unified and centralized.

In 1273, the German electors ended the Interregnum by choosing as ruler Duke Rudolf of Hapsburg (1273–1291). The election had taken place under pressure of the papacy which recognized the need for re-establishing order in Germany and which was already casting about for a possible ally against the unruly Charles of Anjou who had barely established himself in Naples. Despite centuries of fighting between emperors and popes, the papacy realized that the two needed each other.

With the election of Rudolf of Hapsburg, the Holy Roman Empire entered a new era. Gone was the relative dynastic stability which before had left the crown in the same family for several generations at a time. For the next two centuries, the imperial crown was continually passed from one ducal house to another. The center of the empire as well as of the royal domains that provided the primary income of the ruler shifted erratically from southern Germany (Hapsburg) to central Germany (Nassau), to western Germany (Luxemburg), to Bavaria (Wittelsbach), to the East (Luxemburgs of Bohemia), and to Austria (later Hapsburgs). As a result, the crown was seriously weakened while the territorial princes gained in strength.

Emperor Charles IV (1347–1378) of the Luxemburg-Bohemian dynasty sought to put some order into the electoral process. In the Golden Bull of 1356, Charles awarded sole rights to elect the king as well as the emperor to seven electors—four lay lords and three ecclesiastical princes—and stipulated that the lay electorates should be inherited by primogeniture and be indivisible. This scheme did not provide for greater stability but merely guaranteed more power to the seven electors. Meanwhile the German princes, aided by pamphleteers and antipapal ecclesiastics such as the Spiritual Franciscans, who believed in apostolic poverty and objected to the wealth of the Church and to the worldly possessions acquired by the Franciscan Order, had proceeded to secularize the imperial crown. Through edicts by the German imperial Diet they stipulated that the imperial crown was henceforth to be bestowed by the German electors without papal approval or intervention.

During this period, the empire shrank in size and gradually shifted its center of gravity eastward. Control over Italy was lost despite occasional fruitless attempts to reclaim the peninsula. The Swiss cantons declared their independence (see p. 156); Provence, Burgundy, and the Low Countries slipped from imperial control. While the empire shrank in the south and west, its influence expanded in the east and north. Hungary, Bohemia, and Silesia became closely associated with it, and the Hapsburgs shifted their basis of operation from southern Germany and Switzerland to the newly acquired Austrian hereditary lands. Meanwhile German settlers, lay and ecclesiastic, noble and peasant, continued to push east along the Danube Valley and northeast along the shores of the Baltic, extending German commercial and cultural influence.

Two organizations were particularly active in this movement. During the thirteenth and fourteenth centuries, the Teutonic Knights acquired a vast principality, stretching from west of the Vistula River to the Gulf of Finland. Although these lands did not remain within the official imperial frontiers after 1250 and their extent shrank considerably after the Knights' several defeats by the Poles and Lithuanians between 1410 and 1466, the Teutonic conquests in Prussia formed the political basis for the later Kingdom of Prussia.

At the same time, the Hanseatic League extended German influence from Bruges and London in the west through the Scandinavian lands to Novgorod in Russia. The League was a loose association of north German trading cities for the purpose of protecting their trade, safeguarding common warehouses in foreign lands, and, if necessary, imposing favorable commercial settlements on other states through joint military action. By the late fourteenth century, the Hanseatic League had become so strong that it was able to defeat the Kingdom of Denmark.

Thus the Holy Roman Empire survived as a weak secularized state north of the Alps. Until the sixteenth century, most emperors still dreamt of reconquering Italy and some actually attempted it. But, in fact, the claim to universality had ceased to be meaningful with the end of the Hohenstaufen dynasty, with the rise of territorial states within the empire, and with the growth of more centralized monarchies elsewhere in Europe.

The Church

After the powerful pontificate of Innocent III, the papacy spent the first half of the thirteenth century in bitter fight against Frederick II; much of the second half of the century was taken up by the problems of Naples and of anarchy in Rome. Meanwhile the papacy lost control over the crusades. Even some of the mendicant orders, although organized to spread the faith and to combat heresy, complicated the work of the popes. The Spiritual Franciscans alarmed the prelates of the Church through their insistence on apostolic poverty, while the Dominican friars became embroiled in the scholastic quarrel over the relative importance of reason and faith.

During the late thirteenth century, the papacy became quite secularized. Noble Roman families, supported by outside forces, particularly the Angevins of Naples, fought to determine whom to make pope. Yet the papacy retained much prestige. Pope Boniface VIII (1294–1303) attempted once more to raise the papacy to the level of universal authority and to recapture the glory of the pontificate of Innocent III. His failure has been attributed to many causes: he was too tactless in his maneuvers and too much interested in the advancement of his own family; his opponents, Edward I of England and Philip IV of France, were much stronger than had been Innocent III's antagonists, John I and Philip II; moreover, the temper of the times no longer left room for claims of universal power.

Boniface's fight with the kings of England and France centered primarily on tax exemption of the clergy (see p. 161). The pope was unsuccessful, since the English and French clergy generally sided with their king. Finally Boniface issued the bull *Unam Sanctam* (1302), an anachronistic statement of papal supremacy over the rising national monarchies. "Outside this [Catholic and Apostolic] Church," the bull stated, "there is neither salvation nor remission of sins," and "both are in the power of the Church, the spiritual sword as well as the material." Such claims to superiority were clearly out of tune with the time. The papal bull aroused the wrath of the French monarchy. Confident in the support of public opinion—a strong term for this period, but perhaps justified—the French king dispatched agents who captured Boniface with the aid of local enemies of the papacy. Although they were supposed to bring the pope back to France for trial, the French had to release him after a few days, when the local populace rose in his support. Soon thereafter Pope Boniface died, and with his death ebbed the power of the medieval papacy.

For well over a hundred years after Boniface's death, the papacy floundered, embroiled in national quarrels, its political power low, its moral prestige in danger. Afraid of the anarchy in Italy, especially in Rome itself, and pressured by the kings of France, the popes took up residence at Avignon in southern France from 1309 to 1376. The Italian poet Petrarch (1304-1374) called this period "the Babylonian Captivity of the Papacy."

While at Avignon, the popes succeeded in centralizing papal administration and improving the tax collection system. At the same time, they unwittingly endangered papal power. Some unwisely continued to fight with the Holy Roman emperors at a time when they had lost the power to conduct such a struggle effectively. Moreover, the financial exactions and the pomp of the Avignonese court aroused the ire of kings and religious reformers—such as John Wyclif (1320?-1384). Above all, it was risky for the papacy to abandon its universal character and to become identified with national politics, particularly during the Hundred Years' War (1337-1453). For during this prolonged struggle against France, the English naturally distrusted a French pope, surrounded by French cardinals and residing in the confines of the French kingdom.

Worse problems faced the papacy after 1378. The cardinals first elected an Italian pope who took up residence at Rome. Soon thereafter, some changed their support and chose a French pope to re-establish the Avignonese line. The resulting schism in the Church lasted until 1417. With Christians able to choose between two popes, obedience to, or rather support of, the one or the other depended heavily on political considerations. England, for example, still at war with France, sided with the Italian pope, whereas Scotland, as an ally of France, supported Avignon.

The papal schism further lowered the prestige of the papacy and stirred demands for reform both within and outside of the Church. As early as 1324, Marsiglio of Padua (1290-1343) in his book *The Defender of the Peace,* used in part by the emperor in his fight against the Avignon popes, had advocated the separation of church and state and had rejected the Petrine theory of apostolic succession. He had also urged that within the Church a general council should always be superior to the pope. This concept of conciliar supremacy within the Church, which harked back to the early centuries of Christianity before papal centralization, gained momentum after 1378, since the schism could only be ended if an authority *higher* than the popes determined which one was the legitimate pontiff. The conciliar movement was strongly supported by the theologians of the University of Paris and ultimately by various lay rulers, cardinals, lawyers, and reformers. Moreover it corresponded to a similar phenomenon in the secular world of the fourteenth century when corporate or representative bodies attempted to gain control over the monarchs (see p. 158).

When the conciliarists finally succeeded in forcing the convocation of a Church council (Pisa, 1409), the result was disastrous. The council deposed the two popes and chose one (Martin V); as no incumbents resigned, a triple schism resulted. A new council convened five years later at Constance (1414–1418) (see p. 204). By then France was more than half occupied by English troops and was in no position to aid the Avignon pope. As in earlier centuries, the Holy Roman Emperor (Sigismund, 1411–1437) assumed control. The council then ended the schism by deposing all three popes and electing a new one. At the same time, the council of Constance passed several decrees which threatened the centralized, hierarchical structure of the Church. One (*Sacrosancta*) spelled out conciliar superiority over the papacy; the other (*Frequens*) asserted the right of Church councils to meet at regular intervals, without waiting to be convoked by a pope.

Consolidation of new political and economic forces

While the Holy Roman Empire and the papacy declined, new political and economic forces were consolidating and new or reawakened concepts were arising, some of which ran counter to the medieval way of life.

The creation of new political units

Developments in Italy were particularly interesting, since the peninsula, like ancient Greece, came to resemble a political laboratory. Southern and central Italy remained monarchical, although even in Rome several attempts were made in the days of the Avignonese papacy to substitute a republican system for rule by the great noble families. But in the north, widely different systems arose—oligarchic, despotic, and republican. Among the northern states, Venice, Milan, and Florence eventually emerged as the most powerful.

The city of Venice was presumably founded during the Hunnish invasions of the fifth century or soon thereafter. Its location in the off-shore lagoons gave it an enviably safe position. During the first five centuries, the city's orientation was primarily toward Byzantium. Venice was, in fact, officially a part of the Byzantine Empire, and Byzantine influence was especially noticeable in art, as for instance in St. Mark's Basilica. During the ninth and tenth centuries, Venice extended her control over the Dalmatian islands and began the expansion which soon made her mistress of the Adriatic. With her merchants being rivals of Byzantium and the lower classes preferring closer ties with the Roman Catholic Church, Venice slipped out of the orbit of the Eastern Empire and became completely independent.

Starting in the eleventh century and taking advantage of the opportunities offered by the crusades, Venice set up colonies and trading posts all over the eastern Mediterranean. This spectacular growth which added to the small city-state the appendage of a large empire led to frequent wars with its trade rivals, Byzantium and Genoa, and later with the Ottoman Turks. It also produced great wealth from trade and shipping. The new wealth in turn made the commercial aristocracy strong enough by the thirteenth century to convert the government into a hereditary oligarchy. A Senate and a Council, both composed exclusively of members of wealthy families, aided a doge who acted as executive and was elected to his position for life. Although this oligarchic system allowed no voice to the middle and lower classes, Venetian government was a remarkably stable albeit rather oppressive system.

The history of Milan differed considerably from that of Venice. Milan was strategically located near the main passes through the Alps and was surrounded by a rich agricultural area; but it was hopelessly landlocked and had to turn to manufacture and banking as added sources of wealth. Already an important center in late Roman times, it became one of the most influential bishoprics during the early Middle Ages and the city itself remained for centuries under the control of its archbishops. As in many other episcopal cities, Milanese political development therefore took the form of a struggle of the bourgeois and the lower classes against the bishop.

During the eleventh century, as elsewhere in northern Italy, the government of Milan developed into a commune, with elected consuls running the city in the name of a council. Soon Milan became a leader of the powerful Lombard League which successfully defied Emperor Barbarossa. Although the city was completely destroyed by the imperial armies in 1162, it was promptly rebuilt with the aid of its Lombard neighbors. By the thirteenth century, the city had acquired great power and wealth, and started to expand by swallowing up nearby communities. At the same time, it became involved in the struggle between Guelfs (pro-papal) and Ghibellines (pro-imperial), and within the city there was strife between the nobles and the masses, a phenomenon common to most north Italian city-states. By appealing to the masses like ancient Greek tyrants, ambitious demagogues acquired power. At the end of the century, one such family, the Visconti, attained so much influence that its members ruled Milan for almost two hundred years, first as "imperial vicars" and after 1395 as "hereditary dukes." In terms of wealth, influence, and international connections, the Visconti acted like kings of northern Italy, marrying their sons and daughters into the great monarchical houses of Europe.

Florence, also founded in late Roman times, meanwhile became rich from trade and banking, and developed into a large city-state by conquest and purchase of its neighbors. During the twelfth and thirteenth centuries it, too, became embroiled in the Guelf-Ghibelline struggle. The Guelf faction, pro-papal and pro-French, came largely from the middle class; the pro-imperial Ghibellines stemmed more from the nobility. Social antagonism, factional strife, and international complications thus became intertwined and brought turmoil to Florentine politics, as parties traded power and exiled their opponents after each successful coup.

Florence became a republic in 1115, ruled by elected consuls who were chosen by the nobility. As the city grew wealthy, the productive, commercial

and financial guilds began to wrest power from the nobles. By the late fourteenth century, when Florence had developed into one of the wealthiest of
the Mediterranean states, great merchant and banking families, appealing to
the lower classes, emerged as leaders of the city. Soon one of these, the
Medici, attained dominant status.

North of the Alps, too, new political constellations arose during the thirteenth and fourteenth centuries. Unusual in view of their forms of government were the Teutonic Knights and the Swiss Confederation. The Knights
were a monastic order that became a political state under its own Grand-
master (see p. 151). The Swiss League was a confederation based on republican principles.

During the thirteenth century, three Swiss regions (Uri, Schwyz, and
Unterwalden), which belonged to the Hapsburgs and which had acquired
strategic and commercial importance after the opening of the St. Gotthard
Pass, obtained imperial protection against their lords, who, it was alleged,
treated them too harshly and taxed them too heavily. Imperial protection
served its purpose under Emperor Frederick II, but it hardly helped during
the Interregnum, or when their own lord, Rudolf I of Hapsburg, became
emperor. Hence the three areas or cantons began to organize politically and
band together. In 1291, they took an oath of mutual protection (as in the
legend of William Tell), and in 1315 they took advantage of one of the
many civil wars in the empire to renounce all allegiance to the Hapsburgs.
When the latter came to subdue the rebellious areas, the Swiss soundly defeated their army.

Once more or less free of Hapsburg control, the cantons formed a league
which expanded during the fourteenth century through adherence by neighboring cantons. By 1389, the league had grown into a confederation of eight
cantons, strong, self-reliant, and quite wealthy. Technically the confederation
remained within the Holy Roman Empire, and its legal independence received international recognition only in 1648. However, after the Hapsburgs
failed in several attempts to reconquer their lost provinces during the fourteenth century, the cantons were in fact independent and formed a new,
fairly important state.

In the North and East, there were other major political changes besides
the growth of the Scandinavian monarchies, the appearance of the Mongols,
and the arrival of the Ottoman Turks (see p. 166 and p. 178). In the
Balkans, for instance, the small principality of Serbia suddenly expanded in
the fourteenth century and extended its domination over northern Greece,
Macedonia, Albania, and parts of Bulgaria. These conquests were soon lost
to the Venetians in the West and the Turks in the South. Serbia even lost her
own independence to the Turks in the mid-fifteenth century. Yet the memory of such a moment of expansive glory added much to Serbian pride and
nationalism when the Serbian state was re-created in the nineteenth century.

Lithuania, too, grew rather rapidly. Its history as an organized state began only in the thirteenth century, and it became permanently Christian-ized in the fourteenth. Yet, the Lithuanian duchy, with its capital at Vilna, quickly expanded into a powerful state. Unsuccessful in its challenge of the Teutonic Knights and therefore blocked from access to the Baltic, Lithuania expanded toward Russia and the Ukraine. Joined to Poland in a personal union between the two ruling houses in the late fourteenth century, its domination soon reached as far south as the mouth of the Danube.

Poland during this time experienced frequent reversals, increasing and decreasing in size and in the power of its rulers, losing and gaining access to the Baltic Sea. By the early eleventh century, the Poles occupied almost iden-tically the same area that they were to control after 1945, with the western borders of the state running more or less along the Oder-Neisse rivers. Most of the lands east of the Oder-Neisse that were seized by Poland after World War II were in medieval times held by the Poles as fiefs of the German crown (see p. 536).

Some early tendencies of Polish history foreshadowed the future. The great landlords assumed much power to the detriment of the monarchy, which suffered from disputed successions and from the elective system that became ultimately entrenched. The Roman Catholic Church gained great strength and independence, and there was an almost constant penetration of German settlers. During the twelfth century, Poland lost the western prov-inces to the German Kingdom and soon thereafter the Teutonic Knights seized the Baltic shoreland. Thus landlocked, the Poles turned south and be-came an important inland kingdom. But various dynastic marriages with the ruling houses of Lithuania, Bohemia, and Hungary always ended with ad-vantages to the other party, so that Poland remained potentially great but not truly powerful.

In Russia, too, there were considerable changes. The Kievan state (see p. 123), much influenced by Byzantium in art and religion, continued to prosper until the twelfth century. But frequent civil wars among the great noble families and constant splintering of political power sapped the impor-tance of Kiev. By the following century, Novgorod in the north, rich in trade and flourishing in art, had become quasi-independent. Its ruling prince (Alexander Nevsky, 1236–1263) was strong enough to defeat the Swedes as well as the Teutonic Knights and thereby safeguarded Novgorod's inde-pendence at the very time when southern Russia was being overrun by the Tatars (see p. 166).

When the Khans of the Golden Horde, or Tatars, established their kingdom after 1242 with its center on the lower Volga—a rule that was to last for over two hundred years—Russia was cut off from Byzantine and Western developments. Poland seized Galicia, Lithuania took White Russia, while the rest of Russia fell physically or nominally under control of the Tatars. The Russians had to furnish tribute on the basis of a Tatar census, and the Tatars enforced their rule by occasional military punitive raids and by appointing local princes who usually vied for Tatar favors. Consonant with Mongolian religious tolerance, they left the Orthodox Church free and independent—perhaps an explanation for the Church's considerable power at a time when ecclesiastical influence began to wane in the West. The north, however, was not occupied by the Tatars. Novgorod paid tribute, and its rulers rendered obeisance to the Khan, but their state remained free. To the east, the Duchy of Moscow also remained unoccupied. By the late fourteenth century, Moscow assumed the offensive against the Tatars and became important as the kernel of a state which within a century was to dominate all of northern Russia, including Novgorod.

Corporate and representative ideals

A corporate framework as seen in the Church, the guilds, or the universities, was not uncommon in medieval times. Yet when the corporate structure invaded the political field, it undermined the feudal order of personal relationships. Corporate organization permitted the monarchs to legislate for and bargain with semiorganized groups in society. On the other hand, a corporate sense of solidarity enabled groups of barons to impose their will on the king. In either case, the balance of a feudal monarchy was altered. In England, such a movement in the form of a parliament was gradually used to limit the powers of the crown; in France, the king himself initially shaped the Estates General as a sounding board of "public opinion" and as a support to the monarchy. Almost everywhere, except in England, attempts to set up corporate political structures in order to limit the powers of the monarchs aborted and ultimately succumbed to royal absolutism. Yet during the fourteenth century, these corporate movements endangered the medieval structure and set precedents that were revived in later times.

After the death of King John I, the English crown recovered considerable strength during the minority of Henry III (1216–1272), thanks to the skill of his regents. But once himself in the saddle, Henry became increasingly unpopular until there was outright rebellion against him. Resentment stemmed from various causes. Henry continued the centralizing tradition of his father. He tried to add to his power by ruling through his household staff, which was subject to his command, rather than ruling through the traditional officers, the more independent minded great barons. With great abandon, he bestowed favors on relatives and friends, many of whom came from England's Continental possessions. The nobility resented the ubiquitous royal agents; the clergy disliked Henry's submissiveness to the papacy, for he did not prevent the popes from staffing English church offices with foreign candidates nor did he protect English ecclesiastics from papal exactions. Finally the bourgeois and the Great Council balked at Henry's reckless spending, particularly for unsuccessful foreign ventures: attempting to subdue Wales, trying to reconquer lost French lands, supporting his brother's

(Richard) effort to become Holy Roman Emperor, and aiding his son (Edmund) in a futile endeavor to conquer Sicily.

When King Henry demanded extraordinary financial aid from the Great Council—to get such approval was becoming customary—it insisted on reforms as a condition for any grant of money. A commission then drew up the Provisions of Oxford (1258) and initiated an inquiry into general abuses. Within this commission opinion was divided: the barons sought to limit the king's prerogatives, whereas more radical reformers wanted a wider distribution of power. The leader of the latter was Simon de Montfort (1208?–1265), Henry's French brother-in-law, an ambitious noble who championed the cause of the lesser landowners and the bourgeois.

The Provisions of Oxford which the King was forced to accept, although he repudiated them three years later, attest to the baronial victory. A council of fifteen was to supervise the king's actions and select the high government officials, such as the chancellor and the treasurer. The prospect of government by a baronial oligarchy displeased the lower nobility and the bourgeois and led to civil war. Simon de Montfort emerged victorious. Henry and his son Edward were imprisoned for a time, and Simon governed the kingdom for a year, until he was killed during a renewal of hostilities. This one year was crucial for English institutions. Simon reinstituted the Provisions of Oxford. In the parliament he convoked for 1265, he summoned, in addition to the usual barons and high ecclesiastics, two knights from each shire—which had been done before—and two burgesses from the boroughs. Bringing townsmen, or as it were the middle class, into parliament was a step of consequence which eventually led to more parliamentary control of the monarchy.

Under Edward I (1272–1307) Parliament grew in importance. Actually, Edward was a strong ruler who reorganized the administrative and judicial system in favor of greater royal power, and who, without destroying feudalism, tried to circumvent it by insisting on direct vassalage to the king. His strength assured him easy victory over Pope Boniface VIII (see p. 152) and enabled him to subdue Wales and temporarily conquer Scotland. But his great needs for funds, largely to obtain supplies and mercenary troops for his wars, could not be satisfied by normal revenue and by such devices as confiscating the property of the Jews whom he expelled from the kingdom. He therefore had to convoke Parliament frequently, for, although he could legislate without recourse to Parliament, parliamentary approval of money grants had become established custom. In 1297, in fact, the king had to give his official, albeit reluctant, agreement that Parliament had to authorize the collection of all new non-feudal taxes.

Membership and purpose of Parliament at this time were still unclear and changed from meeting to meeting. The king summoned those he needed to act as a court, to help legislate, to discuss financial matters, or "to provision for remedies against the dangers which . . . threaten the king-dom." Sometimes he called two sessions a year with only the great lords attending; but when money was required or non-feudal issues were discussed, the burgesses were also invited. The so-called Model Parliament of 1295 set a standard for membership for many centuries, when the king required the sheriff of each county "to cause two knights from the aforesaid county, two citizens from each city in the same county, and two burgesses from each borough, of those who are especially discreet and capable of learning, to be elected without delay." During the fourteenth century, the clergy, except for the prelates, separated to form its own convocation. Moreover, the prelates and lay lords withdrew to a distinct meeting place from that used by the knights and burgesses, thus marking the beginning of the separation between the House of Lords and the House of Commons.

Parliament gained added status under Edward I's unskilled and unpopular successor (Edward II, 1307–1327). After the barons had forced new limiting ordinances on the king, Parliament annulled them on the significant grounds that only a full Parliament, including the burgesses, could legislate for the realm. In 1327, Parliament became involved in an even more far-reaching step, after the Queen (Isabella of France) had gone to France, fallen in love with one of the king's chief enemies (Roger Mortimer), and returned with her lover to conquer England and capture her husband. With the king in prison, Parliament voted for his deposition; and, soon after his abdication, the king was murdered. It was the first time that Parliament had pronounced the deposition of a monarch.

The Hundred Years' War (see p. 171) afforded Parliament the opportunity for a further increase in power. King Edward III's (1327–1377) need for money to prosecute the war gave it added leverage. By lavish use of petitions and by assuming some control over legislation and even over spending, Parliament began to act as though it represented the interests of the state as a whole in relation to the king.

It may seem strange that France received her first taste of a "nation-wide" assembly under King Philip IV (1285–1314), a powerful and ruthless monarch who created a highly centralized, almost "national" monarchy, unless one keeps in mind that the assembly in France did not grow out of an antiroyal body as in England, but was started as a support of the monarchy. The highly skilled Philip, aided by effective ministers, turned France into the strongest European state of his day. He expanded royal justice and increased the royal domain. To gain funds he instituted new taxes, collected war contributions without going to war, debased coinage, and confiscated the property of the Jews and the Italian bankers, whom he expelled, and of the Templars whom he accused of heresy and whose order he forced the pope to dissolve (1312). His wars against Edward I of England and against the Count of Flanders, which foreshadowed the Hundred Years' War, were not successful; but he showed great skill in expanding France's eastern borders at the expense of the floundering Holy Roman Empire, particularly in the acquisition of Franche-Comté and Lyons.

Philip IV's fight with Pope Boniface VIII (see p. 152) showed how many new weapons lay rulers had acquired since the twelfth century. When Philip taxed the clergy (1296) to help pay for the war against England and the pope prohibited such taxation without papal consent (in the bull *Clericis laicos*), the French king countered by stopping the export of gold from France, thus forcing Boniface's capitulation. A few years later, the quarrel reopened when a French royal court condemned an unruly bishop and asked Boniface to strip him of his office so that lay authorities could punish him. The pope replied with a series of haughty bulls against Philip, implying that a bishop could be tried only in Rome. Philip reacted by inciting anticlerical feeling with forged documents, and, confident of public opinion, he did not hesitate to have one of the bulls (*Ausculta fili*) publicly burned. In the end, after the pope's last bull on papal supremacy (*Unam Sanctam*), Philip had him accused of heresy and crimes and sent French agents to capture him.

To gain support against Pope Boniface, Philip summoned the Estates General in 1302. Provincial assemblies of separate orders had been convened before during the thirteenth century. But in 1302, Philip called all three orders from all over France. Naturally, the corporate sense of the estates had not yet fully developed. The bishops who attended spoke for themselves as territorial lords, although in a way they represented the entire French clergy. The great nobles, however, stood largely for themselves, and the delegates from the towns were certainly not fully empowered representatives. Yet each of the three orders complied with the king's wishes and dispatched an insulting letter to the pope, as if the Estates General represented "French opinion." King Philip obviously considered the experiment a success, for during the remainder of his reign, he repeatedly summoned the Estates General, particularly to support him in his attack on the Templars and to grant him funds for war on England.

Thereafter the Estates General met occasionally to discuss tax levies. But when the direct Capetian line died out in 1328 with the death of all three of Philip IV's sons, it was an assembly of nobles and not the Estates General which proclaimed the so-called Salic Law to the effect that no woman could reign in France nor pass the crown on to her son. Hence the nobles awarded the throne to the nearest male heir through the male line (Philip VI of Valois, the nephew of Philip IV) rather than to King Edward III of England who, as Philip IV's grandson, was a nearer heir but through the female line. Edward disputed this decision and laid claim to the kingship of France, a claim which was partially responsible for the outbreak of the Hundred Years' War.

French defeats during the first decade of the war—the French fleet was destroyed at the Battle of Sluys and the French knighthood decimated at Crécy—coupled with the king's constant need for money again gave greater importance to the Estates General. In 1346, the Estates from the provinces north of the Loire even refused to grant money. The disasters of the second decade further weakened the monarchy. Calais was lost to the English (who kept it over two hundred years), the Black Death ravaged France, and an idealistic knight-errant (John II) became king of France. In addition, the king's cousin deserted and claimed the throne, and, finally, the French were once again disastrously defeated at the Battle of Poitiers (1356) in which the king himself was captured and sent to prison in London.

Under these circumstances, the northern Estates General, dominated by Etienne Marcel (?–1358), the provost of the merchants of Paris, sought to gain control over the eighteen-year-old dauphin, the future King Charles V. Before granting funds to continue the war or ransom the king, they forced the dauphin to sign the Great Ordinance (1357), the "magna carta" of France. The Ordinance stipulated frequent meetings of the Estates General without need for royal summons, reserved to the Estates the sole right to grant new taxes and to supervise collection and disbursement of revenue, and established a commission of nine selected by the Estates to reform the administration. Unlike Magna Carta, the Great Ordinance did not deal with civil rights. It appeared as if control of the monarchy by the Estates General had been achieved. But the Estates that had passed the Great Ordinance hardly "represented France." With the nobility discredited at Crécy and Poitiers, the Estates were largely the voice of Marcel and the rebellious commune of Paris. In the following year, Marcel was murdered and the dauphin subdued Paris in a short civil war. As Charles V the Wise (1364–1380), he gradually regained control of France, successfully turned the tide of war against the English, and the Great Ordinance remained a dead letter.

Corporate and representative systems also arose at this time in other areas of Europe. The imperial Diet (*Reichstag*) of the Holy Roman Empire remained ill-defined in its purposes and failed to gain cohesion, although it became a permanent institution. Within the territories of the empire however, in the duchies, counties, margraviates, and smaller entities, local estates coalesced and gained considerable power by the end of the fourteenth century. When two centuries later the rulers of these lands tried to become absolute, their main task was to overcome these provincial estates.

The many leagues originating at this time in the empire were based more on cooperation than on corporate structures. The Hanseatic League of merchant towns (see p. 151) never developed into a formal corporate organization; yet in times of crisis, the League's spokesmen—usually the more important towns such as Lübeck or Bremen—could speak for the League. As disorder increased after 1250, protective leagues multiplied. The League of Swiss Cantons developed corporate and representative features; but most others, such as the League of Swabian Cities, the League of Rhenish Cities, or various leagues of knights, remained at the cooperative level.

In the Iberian kingdoms, assemblies of large landholders and high ecclesiastics had existed for some time. When towns grew powerful during the twelfth century, particularly in León, the burghers sent delegates to these cortes, as the assemblies were called. By the thirteenth century, the cortes were strong in all Iberian kingdoms except in Navarre. In Aragon and Catalonia, the king could not even legislate without consent of the cortes, and in Castile as well as in Aragon, the government was supervised by committees of the cortes. In this respect, the cortes were almost more powerful than similar bodies in other parts of Europe; but deep-seated distrust between nobles and townsmen prevented the formation of any "national" consensus such as seen in the emerging House of Commons in England.

Distortion of the medieval structure

During the fourteenth century, the medieval structure was disturbed by growing secularization and by the vague awakening of "national" consciousness. Simultaneously, the broadening geographic and intellectual horizon burst the medieval frame and called for readjustments—some of which were made during the Renaissance, while others, especially in science, had to wait until the seventeenth century.

Changing attitudes

When examining the fourteenth century, one can point to many phenomena that seem to disjoint the medieval frame. The use of professional mercenary troops was undermining feudal vassalage; the introduction of the longbow and the appearance of artillery were threatening the knighthood; the wealth of merchants was endangering the social monopoly of the landed nobility. Rather than compose a long list, one might select two phenomena which in themselves touched many areas: the progress of secularization and the crystallization of a vague "national" consciousness.

Secularization occurred in two ways: institutional and ideological. Imperial elections became independent of the papacy; national monarchs, as in England and France, emancipated themselves from papal control. The Gallican (French) Church emerged, dominated by the king rather than the pope. The English monarchs legislated against all appeals to Rome (Statute of Praemunire, 1353), while in the Holy Roman Empire the great bishops became largely secular territorial lords. In social matters, there began a gradual transference of power, rights, and responsibilities from church to state, although the degree of this change should not be exaggerated, since the Church continued to operate most of the social services and educational institutions for many centuries.

Secularization of thought was equally noticeable as asceticism and otherworldliness paled. In its symbolism, its concern for salvation, and its elaboration of a world scheme, the *Divine Comedy* by Dante (1265–1321) was still medieval. But Dante's medievalism was already tempered by strong individualism. He did not hesitate to deride the papacy or to assign Pope Boniface VIII to hell in his *Divine Comedy*. In *De Monarchia* he extolled the advantages of a secular and imperial Italy. Petrarch, who was crowned poet laureate in 1341 and who is sometimes called the first humanist, revered the classics, especially Virgil and Cicero, almost more than the Bible. Like the ancient Greeks, he asserted that education of the mind had to be supplemented by training of the body, and he astounded his contemporaries by climbing mountains and glorifying their beauty, not as evidence of God's beneficence but simply as beautiful in themselves. Boccaccio's (1313-1375) *Decameron,* the best known work from the pen of a prolific author—like Chaucer's (1340?-1400) *Canterbury Tales* which were influenced by Boccaccio—was worldly to the point of ribaldry.

Similar changes of attitude can be observed in areas other than literature. There seemed to be less fear of God; the threat of excommunication was losing some effectiveness. In Italy, the painter Giotto (?-1337) infused his frescoes of Christ and the Madonna with more human traits, abandoning the more purely symbolic style of the Byzantine school. Similarly, some religious reformers, such as John Wyclif, seemed to search for a religion designed more for man rather than for God and the Church.

Hand in hand with secularization appeared a vague "national" consciousness. To be sure, the ideal of a united, Latin-speaking Christendom prospering under the twin umbrellas of papacy and empire had never been implemented. Yet around 1200, large areas of Europe enjoyed considerable unity, with most rulers acknowledging papal suzerainty, with knights fighting their petty quarrels under the same code of chivalry, and with philosophers and theologians writing in the same Latin language. Likewise all Europeans lived supposedly for the same purpose, the greater glorification of God. This unity began to shatter in the fourteenth century.

The Church itself split into "national" churches with local rulers assuming more control over the clergy in their state. Wars went beyond the usual feudal overtones, as "national" animosities appeared: the Scots launched a popular resistance against English intrusion; English sailors and fishermen during the Hundred Years' War hated their French counterparts across the Channel, not just as commercial rivals but as "national" enemies; and the Germans began to inveigh against "foreigners" in general. Above all, the growing use of vernacular languages helped to accent differences between cultures and peoples. Some poetry, epics, and legends had been written in the vernacular before, but this trend became more pronounced in the fourteenth century. The great poets, Dante, Petrarch, Boccaccio, and Chaucer, wrote part of their works in the vernacular, thus giving form and style to the language of their country. In most areas, the vernacular started to be used in chronicles and legal works. Under Emperor Frederick II, the first imperial decree was written in the German language (1235); Wyclif translated the

Bible into English; and by the late fourteenth century, English was used in court and even for debate in Parliament.

Broadening geographic horizons

In Hellenistic and Roman times, the West had traded with India and China, yet, judging from maps and descriptions, the ancients possessed little precise geographic knowledge about Asia beyond the Caspian Sea and the Tigris River. Even the maps and geographic notes of Ptolemy of Alexandria (second century A.D.), perhaps the most "scientific" of the ancient cartographers, embodied serious mistakes, such as showing the Indian Ocean as a closed lake. Much of even this scanty geographic knowledge was lost during the Middle Ages, when Ptolemy's work was forgotten in Western Europe until translated into Latin in 1410.

This shrinking horizon was caused partly by the low level of intellectual curiosity and the attitude of the Church, which discouraged investigation of the physical world. The content of medieval maps was largely based on Scripture, with heavy overtones of symbolic considerations. Many maps were schematic diagrams, artistically drawn around a centrally located Holy Land; or they were slavish copies of traditional models, rarely adjusted to incorporate reports of actual observations. Ptolemy had described the earth as spherical, and some medieval intellectuals also held that the earth was a globe. Yet most medieval maps depicted it as flat. Similarly, after the eleventh century, many a sailor's chart showed a much wider and more accurate knowledge of the world than the maps of the academicians. According to a recently discovered sketch, the sailors of the twelfth century may have known about the existence of America. Moreover, they apparently knew by the late thirteenth century that the Indian Ocean could be reached by circumnavigating Africa and possibly were aware of the Azores and Madeiras before these islands were discovered in the fourteenth century.

The medieval horizon had shrunk also because of loss of trade and because of the Islamic curtain which had descended in the East during the seventh century. When trade with farther Asia revived after the tenth century, it was conducted through middlemen. The rich Italian of the twelfth century enjoyed spices from Java, silk from China, or carpets from Persia, but his knowledge of these exotic lands was minimal. His traders could sail to the eastern Mediterranean or the Black Sea ports but were not allowed to go far inland.

The view toward the East suddenly opened in the thirteenth century when, within the span of three generations, the Mongols conquered Asia from Baghdad to Korea and permitted the West to establish direct contact with China and India.

During the late twelfth century, a Mongol tribal chief (Temujin, 1167–1227), an excellent general and organizer, united under his rule the Mongolian and Turkish tribes living between Lake Baikal and the Altai Mountains. After 1206, he called himself Genghis Khan, "the very mighty lord." Since one of the Turkish tribes was called Tatars, Europeans later frequently referred to all Mongols as "Tatars." The newly united Mongol or Tatar Empire expanded rapidly through conquest and voluntary submission of other peoples. Northern China was attacked and absorbed between 1213 and 1234; meanwhile Turkistan and Persia were conquered and southern Russia invaded. Under Genghis Khan's sons and grandsons, Mongol expansion continued unabated. The Mongols seized the Ukraine, ravaged Poland, Silesia, Moravia, Hungary, and Serbia, defeated the Poles, the Teutonic Knights, and the Hungarians, but could not take Novgorod. Other Mongol armies defeated the Seljuk Turks, stormed Baghdad and Damascus, and occupied parts of Asia Minor, while Genghis Khan's grandson, Kublai Khan (1216–1294), destroyed the Sung dynasty of southern China and established himself as Chinese emperor of the Yüan dynasty (1279–1368), with his capital at modern Peking. (See Map 11.)

This vast empire, perhaps the largest ever assembled, was loosely organized and soon subdivided into four khanates, each adapting itself culturally to local conditions. Kublai Khan became a Buddhist, while the Mongols in the southwest embraced Islam. Despite this diversity and despite the destruction and slaughter which accompanied its creation, the Mongol Empire offered to the West a vast area for travel, trade, and possible conversion to Christianity. The Mongol rulers, especially Kublai Khan, were tolerant in religious matters and hospitable to new intellectual ideas. Kublai also supported a public works program—canals, roads, and public transport—financing some of it through the issue of paper money, and he encouraged art and literature.

As a result, there was an influx of Western merchants and missionaries. They traveled through the Black Sea and then through Central Asia, a route by which they could reach China in a mere six weeks; or they passed via Syria and Persia, and then by sea to India and China, a trip which usually took up to two years. The merchants, largely Genoese, were attracted by the prospect of great profits, facilitated by the Mongols' insistence on low tariffs, safe roads, and protection to foreigners. They established trade posts in Persia, along the Indian coasts, and in China. The missionaries were encouraged by the fact that the Mongols were heathens rather than infidels. The pope (Innocent IV) and St. Louis of France sent envoys to the khan in the hope of negotiating a Mongol-Christian alliance against the Turks in the Holy Land. Christian colonies were established in India and China, and Franciscan missionaries flocked east in such numbers that it was deemed advisable to set up a Catholic archbishopric in Peking.

The merchants and missionaries who returned from their voyages to the khan related what they had seen among the Mongols. Best known among these was the Venetian Marco Polo (1254?–1324?) who spent almost two decades in the service of Kublai Khan, traveled widely throughout the Mongol Empire, and later wrote down his impressions.

The sudden acquaintance with China raised the Western horizon and transfused new ideas to the West, in governmental practices and in the use of gunpowder and the magnetic compass. Better knowledge of the Mongols, who in the beginning had only been feared as merciless destroyers, also raised new problems for Christians: churchmen had to account for the moral behavior of the Mongols who as heathens had not benefited from revelation and Christian instruction.

This widened horizon lasted less than a century. After the middle of the fourteenth century, the Ming rulers of China expelled the Mongols, thereby breaking the contact between China and the other khanates, while Tamerlane and the Ottoman Turks in the Near East again cut the land routes from the Mediterranean. Europe fell back on itself until, during the fifteenth century, the Europeans pushed south and west and thus found new routes to the East.

Expanding intellectual concepts

Stimulated by new ideas permeating into Western Europe from the Arab world, furthered by better communications and by greater leisure, European intellectual life deepened not only south but also north of the Alps. Greater interest in learning required new centers of study, and numerous new universities were opened.

A precursor of this awakening was the Franciscan Roger Bacon (1214–1294). Although not the first to advocate experimentation, Bacon showed unabashed interest in the world about him and placed such trust in experimentation that he insisted experiential knowledge was more important than scholastic or scholarly tradition. Most of his experiments dealt with optics, but his emphasis on experimentation could be applied to any science and undercut the medieval respect for authority. William of Ockham (1300?–1349?), an English Franciscan who aided Marsiglio of Padua in his defense of the secular aspects of the emperorship, was deeply imbued with the interest in science and mathematics then prevalent at the University of Oxford. By rejecting the rationalism of Thomas Aquinas, he further separated reason from faith and prepared the way for the eventual divorce of philosophy from theology. While retaining a firm faith in divinely revealed truth, he undermined the Neoplatonic position that universal ideas are real by asserting that only particular objects possess reality and being. Such ideas disturbed the medieval scholastic synthesis as much as his notion that nature would always choose the simplest and most direct path, a concept which implied a God with logic similar to man's.

SUGGESTED READINGS

Thirteenth- and Fourteenth-century Society

Boissonnade, Prosper, *Life and Work in Medieval Europe: The Evolution of Medieval Economy from the Fifth to the Fifteenth Century* (Harper, 1964).
*De Roover, Raymond, *Money, Banking and Credit in Medieval Bruges* (Mediaeval Academy of America, 1948).
D'Haucourt, Geneviève, *Life in the Middle Ages* (Walker, 1963).
Labarge, Margaret W., *Baronial Household of the Thirteenth Century* (Barnes and Noble, 1966).
Mundy, John H., and Riesenberg, Peter, *The Medieval Town* (Van Nostrand, 1958).
Painter, Sidney, *French Chivalry, Chivalric Ideas and Practices in Mediaeval France* (Cornell, 1957).
———, *Mediaeval Society* (Cornell, 1951).
Scheville, Ferdinand, *Siena: The History of a Medieval Commune* (Harper).
Thrupp, Sylvia L., *The Merchant Class of Medieval London* (U. of Michigan, 1962).

The Church and Theology

*Almedingen, E. M., *St. Francis of Assisi* (Knopf, 1967).
Coulton, George Gordon, *Inquisition and Liberty* (Beacon, 1959).
DeWulf, Maurice, *Philosophy and Civilization in the Middle Ages* (Dover, 1922).
Eckhardt, Johannes, *Meister Eckhardt; a Modern Translation,* transl. by Raymond B. Blakeney (Harper, 1957).
Freeman, Eugene, and Owens, Joseph, *The Wisdom and Ideas of St. Thomas Aquinas* (Fawcett, 1968). Selected writings.
Haskins, Charles Homer, *The Rise of Universities* (Cornell, 1923).
Leff, Gordon, *Medieval Thought from St. Augustine to Ockham* (Penguin).
*Loomis, Louise R., *Council of Constance* (Columbia, 1961).
Mollat, G., *The Popes at Avignon, 1305–1378* (Harper, 1965).

Political Developments

Barraclough, Geoffrey, *The Origins of Modern Germany* (Putnam, 1963).
*Bonjour, Edgar, *et al., A Short History of Switzerland* (Oxford, 1952).
Fedotov, Georgii P., *The Russian Religious Mind: Kievan Christianity, the Tenth to the Thirteenth Centuries* (Harper, 1960).
Froissart, Jean, *The Chronicles of England, France, and Spain* (Dutton, 1961). Contemporary account of the sixteenth century.
Kantorowicz, Ernst H., *Frederick the Second, 1194–1250* (Ungar, 1957).
Joinville, Jean de, and Villehardouin, Geoffrey de, *Chronicles of the Crusades* (Penguin, 1963). Joinville discusses life of St. Louis.
Lyon, Bryce, *The High Middle Ages: 1000–1300,* Vol. V (Macmillan, 1964). Sources.
Stenton, Doris M., *After Runnymede: Magna Carta in the Middle Ages* (U. of Virginia, 1965).
Trevelyan, George M., *England in the Age of Wycliffe* (Harper, 1963).
Wood, Charles T., ed., *Philip the Fair and Boniface VIII, State vs. Papacy* (Holt, 1967).

Political Thought

D'Entreves, Alexander P., *Medieval Contributions to Political Thought* (Humanities, 1939). Mostly on Marsiglio of Padua.

Gierke, Otto, *Political Theories of the Middle Ages* (Beacon, 1958).
Marsilius of Padua, *Defensor Pacis* (Harper).
*Sigmund, Paul E., *Nicholas of Cusa and Medieval Political Thought* (Harvard, 1964).
    On the conciliar theory.

Early Explorations

Diffie, Bailey W., *Prelude to Empire: Portugal Overseas before Henry the Navigator*
    (U. of Nebraska, 1960).
Lamb, Harold, *Genghis Khan* (Bantam, 1952).
*Olsehki, Leonardo, *Marco Polo's Asia* (U. of California, 1960).
Rugoff, Milton, ed., *The Travels of Marco Polo* (New American Library, 1962).
Wright, John Kirtland, *The Geographical Lore of the Time of the Crusades, A Study
    in the History of Medieval Science and Tradition in Western Europe* (Dover,
    1925).

Art and Literature

Barbi, Michele, *Life of Dante* (U. of California, 1954).
Cawley, A. C., *Everyman and Medieval Miracle Plays* (Dutton).
Curtius, Ernst Robért, *European Literature and the Latin Middle Ages* (Harper).
*Grandgent, Charles H., *Dante Aligheri* (Ungar).
Meiss, Millard, *Painting in Florence and Siena after the Black Death* (Harper).
Panofsky, Erwin, *Gothic Architecture and Scholasticism* (World).
Rickert, Edith, *et al.,* eds., *Chaucer's World* (Columbia, 1962).
Von Simson, Otto, *The Gothic Cathedral: Origins of Gothic Architecture and the Me-
    dieval Concept of Order* (Harper, 1962).

CHAPTER X

❧ *The Beginning of National Consolidation*
(Fifteenth Century)

In many respects, the fifteenth century was a watershed between medieval and modern times. It was both the last century with strong medieval elements and the first with pronounced modern overtones. For instance, a new upper middle class was growing rich and influential from trade and banking, yet socially the landed nobility remained the upper class. Armor-clad knights were still the idealized warriors, although gunpowder and artillery were beginning to render armor obsolete. The Catholic Church attempted to become more centralized at a time when national monarchies were gaining in strength. In many areas, traditional ideas and practices stood side by side with new ones, sometimes uneasily, sometimes harmoniously.

In politics, thought, art, religion, and other fields of human endeavor, the fifteenth century was replete with changes, some of which will be discussed in the subsequent chapter. These changes resulted from the acceleration of trends started in late medieval times, such as the process of secularization and the emergence of national consciousness (see p. 163). Their impetus also derived from a new interest in classical antiquity, as seen in the Renaissance. The building of nation-states in the fifteenth century, in France, England, and the Iberian Peninsula, for example, was a continuation of late medieval developments with the addition of revived classical political concepts.

Dynasticism

One area in which medieval customs still prevailed was the place of dynastic considerations in the political life of states. Not concerned with distinctions between public and private matters, medieval rulers had looked upon land and people as the personal property of a dynastic family. Such possessions could be inherited or divided among heirs, given as dowry in marriage, sold, or bartered. Even in early modern times, when more differentiation was introduced between the ruler's personal needs, prerogatives, and possessions and the public domain, dynasticism remained the accepted determinant of national and international relations until the American and French revolutions in the eighteenth century. Many wars were fought, kingdoms enlarged or decreased, and duchies destroyed or created, not on the basis of economic needs, geographic requirements, ethnic considerations, linguistic preferences, or popular demand, but because a ruler happened to marry a particular princess or because a dynastic marriage produced too many or too few heirs.

The Hundred Years' War

The fundamental causes for the Hundred Years' War, for example, were directly or indirectly dynastic. To be sure, this long war—in reality a series of campaigns, raids, and skirmishes interspersed by long truces—had many causes, some of which seem quite modern: fishing disputes in the English Channel, contested tariffs on wine exports from Guienne to England, control over the Flemish wool trade, and an almost chauvinistic antagonism between French and English. Yet, if the English kings had not inherited Guienne, there would have been no need for a French campaign to oust them from the Continent. Similarly, the disorders in France which complicated and prolonged the Hundred Years' War in the fifteenth century were largely dynastic in origin—the claims of the English Kings Henry V and VI to the French kingship and the rise of Burgundy to the status of a separate duchy (see p. 173).

The first phase of the long war ended in favor of England (Peace of Brétigny, 1360). Three major English victories—Sluys, Crécy, and Poitiers —had given Edward III the advantage. France, moreover, was weakened by peasant uprisings, subjected to plunder by roving companies of freebooters, and had for a while been torn between allegiance to an absentee king, to a hesitant dauphin, or to the usurping Estates (see p. 162). But soon France recovered some strength. The dauphin matured into the skilled and intelligent Charles V. By avoiding open battles and engaging only in small harassing skirmishes, he reconquered large areas from the English. Charles also began to free the government from control by the Estates General, and he established a more regular tax structure (including a tax on salt, the *gabelle,* which was levied until the French Revolution). He attempted to professionalize the army, developed a corps of artillery, and rebuilt the fleet. Reacquisition of a navy allowed the French to weaken England by aiding the Scots and Welsh as well as English rebels who opposed the English monarchy.

After the death of Edward III and of Charles V, the Hundred Years' War lapsed into temporary quiescence, while England and France were both preoccupied by domestic problems. England (under Richard II, 1377–1399) suffered from civil strife, peasant revolts, and religious ferment caused by the Lollards, followers of Wyclif, who preached in the open air and urged the disestablishment of the Church (see p. 203). When Henry IV (1399–1413) overthrew and imprisoned the king, the English monarchy hardly gained in stability. Called upon to legalize Henry's usurpation of the crown, Parliament acquired more power, and rebellions by Welsh, Scotch, and English barons further weakened Henry's reign.

France, at the same time, suffered from the rule of a king (Charles VI, 1380–1422) who was intermittently incapable of exercising command because of attacks of insanity. There were tax revolts and fights between those who sought governmental reforms and those who opposed them. The kingdom was rent by rivalry between the king's brother, Louis of Orléans—the founder of the later Orléans dynasty—and the king's uncle, Philip of Burgundy (1363–1404) (see p. 174). After Orléans had been murdered (1407) on orders of the new Duke of Burgundy (John, 1404–1419), the rivalry deteriorated into outright civil war. The Orléans (or Armagnac) party, fiercely anti-English and supported mainly by the southern aristocrats, fought the Burgundians, whose strength lay north of the Loire and who favored cooperation if not outright alliance with the English. To avenge the murder of Orléans, the Duke of Burgundy (John) was assassinated in 1419. Murder seemed to become an accepted political tool.

The complexion of the war changed again with the succession of the strong and determined King Henry V (1413–1422) in England. In alliance with Burgundy, he reopened the war. His spectacular victory at Agincourt (1415)—over numerically superior French knights who, despite the lessons of Crécy and Poitiers, charged the English foot soldiers in the heroic but suicidal tradition of a frontal assault—enabled him to conquer northern France. Some cities, protected by artillery, endured long sieges. In the end, even Rouen surrendered after a siege of seven months and such a famine that dead mice fetched a good price. By 1420, Henry V had seemingly triumphed. The mad French king disinherited his own son, the future Charles VII (1422–1461), and instead recognized the English Henry V as his heir (Treaty of Troyes), a decision approved by the Estates General. When two years later both the French king and Henry V died, Henry's baby son (the nine months old Henry VI) was therefore declared to be king of both France and England.

English success in extending the conquest of France continued for a few years with the disinherited, irresolute Dauphin Charles barely holding his own south of the Loire. Then, in 1429, the initiative suddenly passed into the hands of the French, who gradually expelled the English forces from the Continent until at war's end, in 1453, only Calais in northern France remained in English hands. These French successes can be explained in many ways: England suffered from the gradual defection of its ally Burgundy and from the reappearance of internal disorder, while France was strengthened by successful governmental, financial, and military reforms (see p. 183). The primary reason for the turn in French affairs, however, was the appearance of a seventeen-year-old, mystically inclined peasant girl from Lorraine, Joan of Arc (1412–1431).

Buoyant with determination and self-assurance, Joan felt inspired to help the dauphin "boot the English out of France." After having her examined by theologians to ascertain that the young visionary was not a sorceress, Dauphin Charles allowed her to lead a small army to the relief of the city of Orléans, which was being besieged by the English. Within nine days of her arrival at Orléans, the heartened soldiers and citizens had forced the English to lift the siege, and Orléans was freed. Joan's fame as a miracle worker promptly evoked a patriotic and religious revival among many segments of the French population.

Soon thereafter, Joan's army won another battle over the English, and a month later, Joan induced Charles to go to Rheims for his coronation as Charles VII. France was now divided between two kings, the infant Henry and Charles VII. Joan favored maintaining French momentum while morale was high, although she failed in a premature attempt to storm Paris. But the lethargic Charles, perhaps ill advised by unscrupulous ministers, preferred a slower pace. Hence he made no effort to aid Joan or to ransom her when she was captured by Burgundian troops in 1430.

Sold to the English for ten thousand gold francs, Joan was tried under English supervision by the Church in Rouen. Since she had become a symbol of French confidence in ultimate victory and had been instrumental in getting the rival King Charles crowned, the English could benefit more from having Joan discredited by seeing her declared a heretic than from simply having her killed. In the course of a four months' long trial, she was accused of being a heretic, an idolatress, a schismatic, a consort of demons, and of being "wholly forgetful of womanly honesty" since she wore "immodest garments belonging to the male sex." In 1431, a year after her capture, she was condemned and burnt at the stake. The Church had acquired a new saint and the French a symbol of national purpose.

The rise and fall of Burgundy

Dynasticism was also the basis for the state of Burgundy, which in the fifteenth century extended from the Alps to the North Sea. The appanage system, begun in the thirteenth century—whereby kings endowed their relatives with large fiefs—was a typical by-product of feudal practices. In the case of the appanage of Anjou, created for St. Louis' brother Charles, the French monarchy was not endangered, since the dukes of Anjou sought their fortunes elsewhere, in Naples and Hungary, and the French county of

Anjou ultimately reverted to the French crown in 1480. But when in 1363, the king of France (John II) awarded Burgundy as an appanage to his son Philip, the result proved disastrous for France.

Through his marriage with the heiress of Flanders and later inheritances, Duke Philip and his descendants acquired a vast personal realm. But their political status was unclear, for in Holland the Burgundian dukes were technically vassals of the Holy Roman emperor, whereas in Burgundy they were subjects of the king of France. Nevertheless, the wealth of their possessions, their alliance with England, and their strategic position between France and the empire made Burgundy so powerful that Charles VII of France in 1435 recognized its duke (Philip the Good, 1419–1467) as an independent sovereign.

The high point of Burgundy's rise came under its last duke, Charles the Bold (1467–1477). To obtain a bridge between his northern and southern possessions, he seized Lorraine. He also bargained, though unsuccessfully, with Emperor Frederick III (1440–1493) for recognition of a royal title. But Charles' power and ruthless behavior provoked rebellion among his own subjects and a combined attack by the French, Swiss, and Rhineland states that terminated in his defeat and death. Dynastic considerations again decided the future of the Burgundian lands. Charles left only a daughter (Mary), who, at first betrothed to the dauphin of France, later, after much diplomatic maneuvering, married Maximilian of Hapsburg, the future emperor. After the death of Charles the Bold therefore, the bulk of the Burgundian estates went to the Hapsburgs, while France was able to acquire only the Duchy of Burgundy, Artois, and Picardy.

The hundred years' history of Burgundy is notable for several reasons. Through marriage and inheritance, the Burgundian dukes attempted to recreate the northern half of the Lotharingian Kingdom in the zone of fragmentation between France and Germany, despite the lack of linguistic cohesion. Moreover, during the early fifteenth century, the Anglo-Burgundian alliance had almost crushed France. Finally, the outcome of the Burgundian marriage maneuvers awarded many French-speaking border districts to the Hapsburgs, laying the ground for centuries of conflict during which the French conquered some though not all of these areas.

The Holy Roman Empire

Dynasticism was also at work in the Holy Roman Empire. The duchies and smaller states in the empire, some of which had originally been based on tribal allegiances, became the creations and possessions of noble families. A typical state of the period, such as Saxony, might be composed of numerous holdings scattered over considerable distances, held together on the basis of family ownership.

While the German Kingdom was thus splintered into territorial dynasties, each of which sought to attain absolute sovereignty, the imperial prerogatives themselves were used by the emperors primarily to acquire wealth and status and to enlarge their family possessions. Such dynastic expansion had been skillfully practiced by the house of Bohemia in the fourteenth century. But even more adept at this endeavor were the Hapsburgs, of whom it was said that while others gained land by fighting wars, they obtained it through marriage.

The Hapsburg Emperor Frederick III typified this trend. He had no interest in the German Kingdom, which he rarely visited. So long as the popes did not obstruct Hapsburg expansion, he even sided with the papacy against those German reformers who sought to "Germanize" the Church in Germany by diminishing papal control over the German bishoprics. With the Hapsburgs' center of power now established in Austria, imperial interests, according to Frederick, had become identified with those of Austria. His official motto was "AEIOU," meaning *Austriae est imperare orbi universo* (Austria's role is to rule over the world). Such Hapsburg dynasticism hurt the institutional development of the German Kingdom, but it paid handsome dividends to the Hapsburg family during the reigns of Frederick's sons and grandsons.

His son, Maximilian I (1493–1519), an intelligent and well-educated Renaissance prince, inherited most of the Burgundian lands through his wife, the daughter of Charles the Bold. Through marriages arranged for his children and grandchildren, his family within a few decades acquired Bohemia, Hungary, Castile, Aragon, and Naples, as well as the American territories claimed by Spain. This dynastic success, which suddenly propelled the Hapsburgs to the forefront of European royalty, hardly benefited the Germans. In view of their multi-ethnic empire, the Hapsburg rulers had to be cosmopolitan in outlook. Yet, like the contemporary English and French, the Germans were then experiencing a wave of cultural nationalism.

Ironically, Maximilian became a German "national" hero, although he did little for the German Kingdom. In order to obtain financial contributions and soldiers for his many wars, he finally acceded to the demands of those in the imperial diet who sought to give some substance to the imperial superstructure in matters of taxes and justice. He agreed that the levying of regular taxes should be supervised by a committee of the imperial diet, and that an imperial court of justice should be set up to enforce civil peace and end private warfare. Yet these measures remained essentially a dead letter. Maximilian was too busy pacifying his inherited Low Countries, fighting the French over possession of northern Italy, meeting the first Turkish onslaught (see p. 179), or adding to Hapsburg possessions to pay much attention to Germany or to notice that toward the end of his reign Martin Luther had taken the first steps that were to initiate the Reformation.

The East

There were many other states in Europe which were founded on, or were heavily influenced by, dynasticism. But some states during this period were shaped rather by conquest, as for instance the Duchy of Moscow, the Ottoman Empire, and the Mongol states in Asia.

Russia

When the Tatars overran southern Russia in the thirteenth century, Moscow and Novgorod remained semi-independent, both paying tribute to the khans but remaining free from Tatar occupation (see p. 166). Of the two, Moscow became the more powerful during the fourteenth century. The dukes of Moscow gradually increased their holdings at the expense of surrounding minor princedoms, and they became wealthy and disliked as tribute collectors for the khans. By the late fourteenth century, the dukes felt confident enough to challenge the Lithuanians and the Tatars. When the Greek Orthodox patriarch of Constantinople and the pope agreed to reunite their churches (at the Council of Florence, 1439), the Russian Orthodox clergy was irritated. Although the attempted reunion of the churches failed (see p. 179), the Russian Church, led by its metropolitan who had moved from Kiev to Moscow in the fourteenth century, henceforth assumed a more nationalistic tone and began to make itself more independent of Constantinople. The new stance of the Church in turn enhanced the power and prestige of the Muscovite dukes. Meanwhile Novgorod, Moscow's former rival, lost some of its trade and was beginning to feel the pressure from Lithuania in the west and from Moscow in the southeast.

Under Ivan III the Great (1462–1505), Moscow emerged as a major power. Ivan married the heiress (Sophia) of the last emperor of Constantinople. Together with Byzantine customs and ideas, his wife brought to Moscow Greek and Italian advisers and artisans. Ivan henceforth asserted that his duchy had become the political and religious successor to the Byzantine Empire. He adopted Byzantine court ceremonial and changed the Russian emblem to the double-headed eagle. As rulers of the "Third Roman Empire," the dukes of Moscow thereafter adopted the title of Tsar (Caesar or emperor) and endeavored to assume authority over the Orthodox Church, just as the emperors at Constantinople had controlled the patriarchate.

Within his duchy, Ivan vigorously suppressed all opposition to his power. Abroad, he was able to defeat and annex Novgorod and its dependencies. Taking advantage of a decline in the power of the Tatar khanate, he stopped paying tribute to the Tatars as if to signal that Muscovy was resuming its sovereignty, and in a war against Lithuania he acquired some lands in the West.

Soon after the Duchy of Moscow emerged thus strengthened, the Tatars of southern Russia along the shores of the Black Sea fell under the domination of the powerful Ottoman Turks. Moscow therefore remained blocked from further growth toward the south. Yet, the decline of the Tatars and the growth of Muscovy in the north and west was to bring Russia back into the Western stream during the sixteenth century, allowing increased contact, active diplomatic relations, and considerable trade between Moscow and the rest of Europe.

The Ottoman Empire and the end of Byzantium

In the Balkans and the Near East, numerous states were created, and destroyed, by warfare. Most of the wars during this period, from the Danube to the Nile and from the Adriatic to the Tigris River, directly or indirectly involved the Byzantine Empire.

During the eleventh century, Byzantium's power and prosperity had ebbed and flowed, while its territorial holdings were shrinking in the Balkans, in southern Italy and Greece (through losses to the Normans), and in Asia (through conquests by the Seljuk Turks). Internal political life was characterized by strife among ecclesiastical elements, civil authorities, and the military. Murder and palace revolutions often determined succession to the imperial throne, which was frequently occupied by women rulers. In these civil wars, the Seljuk Turks were occasionally invited by one party to furnish aid against the other, a practice which helped the Seljuks extend their conquests in Asia Minor.

After the First Crusade had brought the West commercially and militarily into the Near East, the Byzantines found themselves fighting not merely against the Turks but also against Venetians, Normans, Hungarians, and at times against the new Latin states of the Near East. The West, in fact, was often considered a greater foe than the Moslem Turks. It is characteristic that when Jerusalem was reconquered by Sultan Saladin in 1187, the Byzantine emperor made an alliance with the infidel sultan as safeguard against a possible new Western crusade. Despite these foreign involvements, there was a brief recovery in the middle of the twelfth century (under the strong Emperor Manuel Comnenus, 1143–1180).

After the sack and seizure of Constantinople by the crusaders in 1204, the empire almost ceased to exist. Its territory was split into smaller units, most of them ruled by Venetian or Frankish nobles, each tending to the interests of his own family. Constantinople itself was in the hands of Roman Catholic Flemish counts, the so-called Latin emperors, while across the Sea of Marmora at Nicaea reigned a Greek Orthodox emperor who controlled no more than a small enclave. While battling Turks and Bulgars the two emperors and their successors fought each other for half a century (1206–1261). In the end, the Greek emperors carried the day. Taking advantage of the defeat of the Seljuk Turks by invading Mongol tribes, they retook parts of Anatolia. Finally, the Greek emperors seized Constantinople with the aid of Bulgarians and Genoese. The Byzantine Empire was thus reunited (1261).

After this resurrection of Byzantium, its history continued to be marked by surprising resilience for two more centuries. Despite a steady decline in size and power, it experienced intermittent periods of political importance and economic prosperity.

Soon after its reconstitution, the empire was attacked by the insatiable Charles of Anjou who had already become king of Sicily, had seized control of parts of Greece, and who posed a well-organized threat to Byzantium (see p. 150). To gain the support of the Latins and the papacy, the Byzantine emperor suddenly embraced Roman Catholicism (1274). Theoretically, Roman Catholicism and the Orthodox Church were thus reunited. Actually, there was so much resistance to the Latins in Byzantine territory.that the emperor's decision could not be implemented.

Meanwhile a new danger to Byzantium appeared in Asia Minor with the appearance of various new Turkish tribes in the wake of the Mongol invasion. One tribe, under Osman (1290–1326), soon imposed its dominion over others and successfully expanded its control into the nucleus of a new empire. Its people were named after its leader "Ottoman Turks" or "Osmanlis."

With the Byzantine Empire again distracted by civil wars and palace revolutions, the Ottomans could expand rapidly. To defend the empire, the emperors hired Spanish, French, German, Tatar, and Vlach mercenaries, only to find that the different groups also enjoyed fighting one another and that some ravaged the country more than the Turks might have. Yet the need for mercenaries was so great that the Byzantine rulers even engaged Turkish volunteers. To counter the Byzantine mercenary system, Osman's son (Orkhan, 1326–1359) established the corps of Janissaries which he staffed with hired Christian troops. Within a generation, the Turks further developed this system by taking captive Christian boys and raising them as devoted Moslem soldiers or civil servants, thereby augmenting their own ranks while weakening those of the subject population. At the same time the Ottoman Turks gained adherents by taxing their subjects less than the Byzantine emperors and by permitting Christians to worship freely so long as they did not thereby undermine Turkish domination.

During the first half of the fourteenth century, Byzantium lost more than half of its European territory to Serbia and Bulgaria, while its remaining holdings in Asia Minor were seized by the Turks. In 1354, the Ottomans acquired their first permanent foothold in continental Europe with the seizure of Gallipoli at the entrance to the Dardanelles. Led by a succession of skilled sultans (Murad I, 1359–1389, and Bajazet, 1389–1403), the Turks then conquered Thrace, Bulgaria, and Macedonia, reduced Serbia, and forced the shrunken Byzantine Empire to recognize Turkish suzerainty.

Repeatedly the emperors appealed for help to the West. The Knights Hospitalers, Venice, France and Savoy sent occasional support. In 1396, the Burgundians and the Hungarians—the latter were then assuming their role as Europe's defenders against the Turkish menace—mounted a full-fledged anti-Turkish crusade which ended disastrously with the slaughter of the Burgundian knighthood. Constantinople would have fallen then, had it not been saved by help from an unexpected direction. The Mongol Tamerlane (1370–1405) suddenly burst forth from the East and crushed the Ottoman Turks in Asia Minor. As a result, the Turkish Empire split momentarily into several smaller states fighting one another for supremacy, and Byzantium was given a respite of several decades.

By 1430, the Turkish Empire was reunited and ready to resume the attack on Constantinople. Again the Hungarians, aided by the Poles, attempted an unsuccessful crusade. The Byzantine emperor even journeyed to Italy to attend a Church council (Florence, 1439), at which it was once again decided to merge the Orthodox and Catholic churches and to subordinate the Eastern Church to the dictates of the pope. Instead of strengthening Byzantium, this decision caused disunity. Anti-Catholic feeling among some Orthodox believers was so strong that they preferred the sultan to the pope.

The final assault on Constantinople came in 1453 under the command of Sultan Mohammed II (1451–1481), called Mohammed the Conqueror. French knights, Venetians, and Genoese helped man the defenses of the city, which was besieged by land and sea for seven weeks before finally surrendering to the Turks. After the fall of Constantinople, Mohammed II went on to conquer Serbia, Bosnia, most of Greece, Albania, Rumania, and the Crimea, leaving only scattered Venetian outposts of what had once been the Byzantine Empire.

The victory of the Ottoman Turks introduced a new power into European history. From the fifteenth to the eighteenth century, the Ottoman Empire was to be one of the strongest states in Europe, almost constantly trying to expand its holdings. During these years "the Turkish menace" figured prominently in European diplomatic calculations. The Ottomans' great antagonists, Venice, Hungary, the Hapsburgs, Poland, Russia, and Persia, could hardly undertake any major foreign ventures without ascertaining the attitude of the sultan. Some other states, particularly France, welcomed them as allies who could apply pressure on the Holy Roman Empire from the East, whenever such a diversion appeared useful to the French.

The Turkish occupation of the Balkans, which in some parts lasted until the nineteenth century, in most other areas until shortly before World War I, naturally left a deep impact on the development of this region. While elsewhere Europeans fashioned their culture and their political institutions according to their own dictates, the people in the Balkans lived under the whim of their Moslem overlords.

Finally, the success of the Ottomans ended an era of history. The year 1453, marking the fall of Constantinople—as well as the end of the Hundred Years' War—is sometimes used to designate the end of the Middle Ages. It also signified the real termination of the Hellenistic age, which, overlaid with a Christian cover, had largely survived in Byzantium. Turkish interests were different. Since the Koran prohibited the representation of the human figure, the Turks whitewashed the Byzantine mosaics, and they added minarets to St. Sophia. Soon they built new mosques and palaces and developed a Greco-Turkish culture of their own.

With the curtain drawn on Greek and Roman culture in the East, the survival of the ancient heritage became all the more dependent on the revived interest in the classics evinced by the humanistic movements of the Renaissance in the West.

Asia

There were certain parallels between developments in Europe and those in Asia. Feudalism was followed by attempts at national consolidation in Japan as well as in the West; Chinese maritime explorations toward the West in some ways resembled Portuguese explorations toward the East less than a century later. But on the whole, East and West as yet followed different paths.

An important feature dominating Indian history during the Middle Ages was the confrontation between Hindus and Moslems. The Arabs themselves had not invaded India except for the Sind region, in the lower valley of the Indus River. Yet, after the tenth century, Moslems, mostly of Turkish descent, expanded from their political center in what is today Western Pakistan and extended their power into northwestern India. In 1193, they conquered Delhi and founded the Kingdom of Delhi. Under various Turkish and native Moslem dynasties, this kingdom lasted until 1526. Most of the time under the nominal rule of the caliph of Baghdad, it was in practice an independent sultanate, on occasion strong enough to extend its control over northeastern India and into Kashmir. In the late thirteenth century, it succeeded in repelling the attempted Mongol invasions from the North. Moslem domination, however, was never extended into southern India which remained largely Hindu.

The Moslem conquerors of northern India were at first quite destructive in their attacks on Hindu temples. Contrasts between the two faiths were indeed great. The Moslems' strict monotheism, rejection of images, and emphasis on the brotherhood of all believers were diametrically opposed to the Hindus' polytheism, reverence for statuary, and stratification of society into castes. Even their eating habits contrasted: Moslems ate beef whereas Hindus looked upon cows as sacred. As a result, there were frequent religious massacres. Yet in the long run, many Moslem rulers recognized the need for living at peace with the Hindu majority they governed. An interesting attempt at accommodation can be seen in the architecture of the period with its amalgamation of Hindu elements with Moslem arches and domes.

At the end of the fourteenth century, northern India was suddenly raided by the Mongol Tamerlane, who ravaged the Kingdom of Delhi in a destructive year-long campaign and then withdrew to continue his plunder toward the West. A few decades later, the Moslem kingdom began to show signs of decline. In 1526, it was conquered by a new wave of Moslem Mongol invaders who set up the Mogul Empire, founded by a descendant of Tamerlane. The Mongols gradually extended their domination also over southern India, except for certain coastal areas which were seized by European traders and conquerors. The great mogul Akbar (1556–1605), an excellent organizer and avid builder, finally attempted a policy of almost forced religious toleration, hoping to find, if not a common religion for his subjects, at least religious peace among Hindus, Moslems, Jainists, Parsi fire worshipers, and Jesuit priests from Portuguese Goa.

In China, the Mongol, or Yüan, dynasty (see p. 166) was overthrown in the middle of the fourteenth century, soon followed by the ouster of the Mongols from Korea which, although governed locally from Seoul, remained under Chinese overlordship. The new Chinese Ming dynasty (1368–1644), founded by an orphaned beggar who helped organize the rebellion against the Mongols and then ensured control for his dynasty by eliminating all possible rivals in a series of bloody purges, ushered in a prosperous but culturally less vibrant period. The Ming emperors encouraged schooling and further developed civil service examinations in order to improve the conduct of government, but their rule became more and more of a personal autocracy, with even the prime ministership abolished in the early fifteenth century. Artistically the period became famous for the production of exquisite porcelain, bronze sculptures, and printing in color.

With their capital first at Nanking and later again at Peking, the early Ming rulers embarked on a remarkable expansion of Chinese influence. Military expeditions were sent into Outer Mongolia while Chinese navies sailed to Sumatra and Ceylon and as far as the Gulf of Aden and the east coast of Africa. These expeditions of the early fifteenth century stimulated trade, but the Chinese were content with gathering tribute and increasing their prestige in Asia and made no attempt to create an overseas empire as was to be done by the Europeans in the following century.

The Ming dynasty declined after the middle of the fifteenth century. Weak emperors occupied the throne while powerful eunuchs of the imperial palace usurped political authority. Chinese influence abroad lessened and there was a general reaction against foreigners in China, particularly the Moslems and Christians. Hence, when the Portuguese first arrived on the Chinese shores in the early sixteenth century, they were not welcomed and were restricted to the coasts, where they eventually established the colony of Macao.

In Japan, feudalism continued to spread during the thirteenth century. Government was in the hands of warriors and military shoguns. Yet the emperorship was retained and the emperors continued to be considered of divine origin, in accordance with the Shinto cult which demanded the veneration of ancestral spirits, particularly those of the imperial family. The military class developed the code of the *samurai* with its insistence on stanch self-discipline. The sword, as a symbol of manliness, became the focus of this cult which persisted down to modern times. Besides the warrior class, organized monks, some supported by their own military troops, grew in power as new variations of Buddhism made their appearance, including Zen with its teaching of calm acquiescence in the world. And as warriors and monks rose in prestige, women were placed on a lower and lower status.

In the late thirteenth century, the Japanese succeeded in defeating two attempted invasions by the Mongols, and soon thereafter, particularly after the Ming dynasty supplanted the Mongols, increased contact between China and Japan was again established. Although safe from invasion, Japan suffered at the time and for several succeeding centuries from internal chaos and civil wars.

The political disorder did not prevent the growing cultural and artistic refinement which marked the fifteenth century. Graceful social behavior was stressed, as in the famous Japanese tea ceremony. Often much influenced by Buddhism, art flourished, particularly architecture and painting. Moreover Japan was growing more nationalistic and more prosperous from increasing trade. This nationalism was to be important in the sixteenth century, when Japan, like many states in the West, began the task of national consolidation. At first, the civil wars worsened when great territorial lords attempted to seize more control for themselves. Then, when the Portuguese arrived eager for trade in the 1540's, Japan suddenly found itself in direct contact with the West. While the Portuguese sold firearms, Jesuit missionaries, soon followed by Franciscans and Dominicans, began the teaching of Christianity. Although some Buddhist monks were less than hospitable to the new faith, quite a number of converts were made within a few decades.

After 1568, the government's drive for unifying the country bore results. Without abolishing feudalism, the government achieved greater control over the great feudatories as well as over the Buddhist monks, and Japan became more consolidated.

Toward the creation of national states

At a time when the Italian states were thriving in Renaissance splendor but remained politically disunited (see p. 189) and when Germany was splintering into ever more dynastic units, four western states—France, England, Spain, and Portugal—took the path of national consolidation that made them the foremost powers of the world during the sixteenth century.

France

King Charles VII (see p. 173) not only expelled the English from France and successfully concluded the Hundred Years' War, but also continued the work begun by Charles V (see p. 162) of turning France into a nation-state and laying the bases on which later royal absolutism could be built. He succeeded in making the taille, a land tax, permanent, thus further freeing the government from the need to refer to the Estates General for revenues; he organized a standing army that made the king the single most powerful lord in the realm; and he established the so-called Gallican Church through his support of the Pragmatic Sanction of Bourges (1438). At the Church Council of Basel, the reformers once again sought to impose conciliar supremacy on the papacy. Charles VII joined this struggle within the Church by supporting the French conciliarists against the papists. In the Pragmatic Sanction, he subscribed to most of the antipapal measures of Basel, including the suppression of appeals to Rome and of annates (the first year's revenue from a Church benefice, usually remitted to the papacy). The French clergy was given more self-rule, and the Gallican Church was placed under control of the king rather than of the pope. An important step toward French royal absolutism had been accomplished.

Despite this increase in royal power, France was not unified. A vital part of the royal task from Charles VII to Francis I (1515–1547) was to round out and consolidate the kingdom by regaining the royal appanages (Anjou, Burgundy, Orléans, and Bourbon) and acquiring possession of such provinces as Brittany. Charles' son Louis XI (1461–1483) made a start in this direction when he inherited Anjou and its dependencies. Simple in dress and manner, Louis XI was in fact a skilled intriguer, so perfidious that his enemies nicknamed him "the spider," since he preferred to trap his opponents rather than fight them in open battle. He was able to defeat several rebellions of nobles in France and cement friendly relations with the bourgeoisie. But his drawn-out fight with Burgundy fell short of success, since after the death of Charles the Bold he obtained only a small portion of the Burgundian inheritance.

By the time of Charles VIII (1483–1498), who inherited Brittany through his wife, the French monarchy was fairly well consolidated. Instead of devoting more efforts to integrating the recently acquired provinces into the kingdom, the adventuresome, young Charles dreamt of grandiose crusades. Perhaps he felt challenged by the exploits of his ambitious contemporaries, Ferdinand and Isabella of Spain.

In 1494, Charles claimed Naples by inheritance and launched an invasion of Italy. His act unleashed a series of twelve wars. The first, the so-called Italian wars (1494–1519), pitted France against Spain and the Hapsburgs over possession of Naples and Milan, with the Italian city-states ranged now on one, now on the other side. The second series, the so-called

Hapsburg-Valois wars (1519–1559), fought largely on Italian and German soil, resulted primarily from French attempts to break the Hapsburg encirclement of France, and at times involved Turkey, England, and the German states (see p. 222).

Charles VIII's Italian invasion was like a Viennese operetta. In the course of a triumphant military parade of five months, his armies entered Milan, Florence, and Rome. Everywhere the young king was received with fanfares. After a brief skirmish, he entered Naples wearing an imperial crown and acclaimed by the multitude as emperor of Constantinople and king of Jerusalem. Three months later, the Venetians and Milanese joined Maximilian I, Ferdinand, and Isabella in an attempt to cut off Charles' lines of communications. With his troops weakened by an epidemic, the French king effected a hasty retreat.

The results of the French invasion of Italy have been much debated. It initiated a long period of wars, and the loot which Charles brought back from Italy may have whetted French appetite for further conquests. For the Italian city-states, it marked an end to their independent political development. But the assertion that Charles VIII discovered the Renaissance in Italy and brought it across the Alps should not be overemphasized. The dawn of the northern Renaissance occurred well before the French invasion of Italy.

England

While the French monarchy became more consolidated and less dependent on the Estates General, England was wracked by civil wars and the English Parliament grew in power. Yet by the end of the fifteenth century, England, too, was to emerge as a consolidated nation-state.

Ruled by a weak king (Henry VI, 1422–1461), who was incapacitated by occasional attacks of insanity, England suffered frequent disorder. The private armies of the great nobles plunged the country into domestic warfare, which ultimately led to the thirty-year-long War of the Roses (1455–1485) between the houses of Lancaster and of York. This long bloodletting weakened the traditional ruling nobility. The War of the Roses finally terminated when the Lancastrian Henry VII (1485–1509) defeated the last York king (Richard III), married the heiress (Elizabeth) of York, and founded the Tudor dynasty.

During the long period of chaos, Parliament had gained in power and prestige. It had acquired greater financial initiative as well as legislative prerogatives. Subject to royal approval, its petitions could now become legal statutes. Moreover, Parliament was repeatedly asked to validate claims to the throne, first by the Yorkists (Edward IV and Richard III), then by the Lancastrian Henry VII. Although not preventing absolutism in England, this growth of parliamentary power signified that English absolutism, unlike its French counterpart, would always have to reckon with the existence of a strong parliamentary tradition, a condition well recognized by all but one of the Tudor rulers.

Henry VII, a strong and determined ruler, laid the basis for Tudor absolutism. Although he had to fight various pretenders who disputed his right to the crown, he successfully re-established royal authority by abolishing the private armies of the surviving big nobles and curbing disorder through proceedings of the revived Court of Star Chamber. More than previous rulers, Henry also sought to identify the interests of the merchant class and shape his policies in its favor, thus initiating the alliance between court and middle class that became characteristic of Tudor rule.

Henry resumed a more active foreign policy on the Continent as well as in the British Isles. English rulers had repeatedly attempted to gain Scotland, by conquest or marriage, and had on several occasions come close to success. But Scottish love of independence, often supported by French troops and money, had always foiled English plans for annexation. After an unsuccessful war with Scotland, Henry VII married his eldest daughter (Margaret) to the Scottish king (James IV). He could hardly have known that within a century the Tudor dynasty would die out and that his daughter's great-grandson, James, would finally unite the crowns of England and Scotland and prepare the way for ultimate union.

Henry also attacked the problem of Ireland, to which the English had laid claim since the days of Henry II. The Irish, ruled by an English viceroy, had generally been treated like colonial subjects. Different in language from the Irish, the English in Ireland formed a small colony and did not mix with the local population. From the fourteenth century, the Irish had begun to seek greater independence, and the English had dispatched frequent punitive expeditions to keep Ireland under control. Henry VII continued this policy of suppression by insisting that English law be applied automatically to Ireland and that the Irish Parliament could not act without special permission from the king of England.

Spain and Portugal

During this period, Spain entered the last stages of the *reconquista*. From the late thirteenth century on, the *reconquista* had been almost quiescent. Castile had suffered from intermittent dynastic struggles and repeated wars with Portugal. The Aragonese meanwhile had been occupied with the conquest of Sicily and Sardinia, as well as Naples which was seized in 1442. The wealthy and luxuriant Moslem kingdom of Granada in southeastern Spain had thus been able to survive for another two centuries.

When Ferdinand of Aragon and Isabella of Castile married in 1469, the basis was laid for the final emergence of a united Spanish Kingdom. After her death in 1504, Ferdinand added his wife's possessions to his own. Moreover, in 1492 he had conquered the Kingdom of Granada, putting an end to the Moslem toehold in Spain; and in 1512, he acquired Navarre. Except for Portugal, the Iberian Peninsula thus came under the control of a single ruler, and next to the Ottoman Turks, the Spanish monarchy emerged as the strongest Mediterranean power.

Ferdinand and Isabella, who came to be known as *Los Reyes Catolicos* (The Catholic Monarchs), were extremely powerful rulers. They emancipated themselves from control by the Cortes by becoming financially more independent. Property confiscated from Jews and Moslems, contributions from a grateful merchant class, and gold from the newly discovered Americas temporarily gave the crown sufficient resources. To counterbalance the power of the great nobles, the rulers struck an alliance with the towns, which sought protection from the rapacious nobility. In Castile, this alliance took an organized form as the Holy Brotherhood (*Santa Hermandad*), a league of towns bound by oath to aid the king against the great nobles.

Royal power, derived in part from Spain's sudden prosperity, was also based on relations with the Church. As victors over the infidels of Granada and those responsible for bringing Christianity to millions of heathens in the New World, the Catholic Monarchs were deemed the most pious of rulers. Yet they were no pawns in the hands of the Church. A concordat with the papacy allowed the king to exercise wide powers over the Church in Spain. When the Inquisition was introduced (1478), staffed mostly by Dominican monks, it was kept under royal control and thus became another prop to royal power. Moreover, the Catholic Monarchs launched a new policy of intolerance that became almost a hallmark of Spanish politics thereafter. Moors and Jews were expelled or killed and their property confiscated. Converts who retained former religious practices were persecuted. The subjection of the American Indians was proclaimed a moral necessity for the propagation of the faith. As in the days of Charlemagne, politics and conquests were conducted under the Christian banner, providing more power for Church and state.

Portugal meanwhile had secured her complete independence from Castile in the fourteenth century, developed her own navy, and established an alliance with England (1386) that created a long friendship between the two states and is technically still valid today. While its kings concentrated on consolidating the powers of the crown, its sailors began the exploration and conquest of Africa, Asia, and America, the results of which quickly elevated tiny Portugal to the status of a world power.

SUGGESTED READINGS

General Coverage

Aston, Margaret, *The Fifteenth Century: The Prospect of Europe* (Harcourt, 1968).
Cheyney, Edward P., *The Dawn of a New Era: 1250–1453* (Harper, 1962).

Mattingly, Garrett, *Renaissance Diplomacy* (Penguin, 1963).
Oman, Charles W. C., *The Art of War in the Middle Ages: A.D. 378–1515* (Cornell, 1960).
Perroy, Edouard, *The Hundred Years War* (Putnam's Sons, 1965).

Asia

*Hookham, Hilda, *Tamburlaine the Conqueror* (Verry, 1962). On Tamerlane.
Hucker, Charles O., *The Traditional Chinese State in Ming Times 1368–1644* (U. of Arizona, 1961).
*Mahajan, Vidya D., *Muslim Rule in India*, 2 vols. (Verry, 1965).
*Sansom, George B., *A History of Japan, 1334–1615* (Stanford, 1961).
Vucinich, Wayne S., *The Ottoman Empire, Its Record and Legacy* (Van Nostrand, 1965).

Europe

Baron, Hans, *The Crisis of the Early Italian Renaissance: Civic Humanism and Republican Liberty in an Age of Classicism and Tyranny* (Princeton, 1966).
*Calmette, Joseph, *Golden Age of Burgundy* (Norton, 1963).
Elliott, John Huxtable, *Imperial Spain, 1469–1716* (New American Library, 1963).
Grey, Ian, *Ivan III and the Unification of Russia* (Macmillan, 1967).
Holmes, George, *The Later Middle Ages, 1272–1485* (Norton, 1966). On England.
Hunt, Percival, *Fifteenth Century England* (U. of Pittsburgh, 1962).
*Pernoud, Régine, *Joan of Arc* (Stein and Day, 1966).
Roth, Cecil, *The Spanish Inquisition* (Norton, 1964).
*Vaughan, Richard, *John the Fearless: The Growth of Burgundian Power* (Barnes and Noble, 1966).
*Waas, Glenn E., *Legendary Character of Kaiser Maximilian* (AMS, 1941).

CHAPTER XI

❧ *The Renaissance Era*
(Fifteenth and Sixteenth Centuries)

The dates for the Renaissance, as for all such periods, are a matter of convention and subject to varying interpretations. Moreover they differ in various fields and between certain areas of Europe. In literature and in politics, for example, the Renaissance started in Italy in the fourteenth century. In painting, sculpture, and architecture, it began only in the fifteenth century. By the first half of the sixteenth century, Italy had reached the stage of the high, or later, Renaissance. North of the Alps, however, the Renaissance generally occurred later. In France, for instance, it flourished in the first half of the sixteenth century, whereas in England it attained full fruition during the reign of Queen Elizabeth I (1558–1603).

The Renaissance was strongly influenced by classical times. While artists tried to recapture the aesthetic concepts of the ancients, humanists sought to break with the medieval past by attempting to return to an earlier, "purer" age. Classical humanists longed for the golden days of Greece and Rome; Christian humanists sought the untarnished text and ideals of the original Bible. In this respect, the Renaissance or "rebirth" was looking backward rather than anticipating "modern" times. This tendency to look for the golden age in the past rather than in the future remained a strong ingredient in Western thought until the eighteenth century.

Renaissance thinkers, however, were no slavish imitators of antiquity. Rather, the creative Renaissance artist was inspired by the classics and adapted some classical aesthetic principles to the requirements of his own Christian heritage, with a particular stress on humanistic elements. The importance of the Renaissance, therefore, lies not merely in the revived interest in classical antiquity, but in the way this classicism was adapted to late medieval ideas and practices as an eventual basis for the modern age.

The Renaissance

The Renaissance was a European phenomenon, although it was probably felt more intensely in north and central Italy than in other areas. Many factors may help explain why the Renaissance began in Italy: the wealth and competitive atmosphere of the city-states, a propitious interplay between bourgeois tastes and aristocratic patronage, the influence of Byzantium and of the memory of classical Rome, and the cosmopolitanism provided by trade contacts and by a hospitable atmosphere. Yet such explanations do not necessarily describe causal relationships. Unless one is prepared to accept the historian Jacob Burckhardt's romantic thesis that fundamentally the Renaissance was the product of the fusion of revived antiquity "with the genius [*Volksgeist*] of the Italian people," one must wait until sociologists, social psychologists, and cultural historians develop better analytical tools before attempting to decide why cultural flourishing occurs.

North of the Alps, especially in painting and architecture, but also in literature, Renaissance art tended to contain more distinct Gothic elements. Despite its cosmopolitan nature, there were thus distinct regional differences, particularly between the northern and southern Renaissance.

Political life of the Italian city-states

As we noted (see p. 154), the city-states of northern and central Italy achieved wealth, power, and independence when the Holy Roman Empire and the papacy declined. Relatively free from foreign interference, they reached the height of their political development during the fourteenth and fifteenth centuries. During this same period, they also fought numerous wars against one another. After 1454, a pattern of alliances developed among the larger states that ensured relative stability for forty years: upon the urging of Cosimo de Medici, Florence, Milan, and Naples became aligned against Venice and the papacy. Still, each state stood essentially by itself, for no ally could be trusted to fulfill its obligations. Such political individualism and the inability to unite made it easy for outside forces eventually to gain influence over Italy. After the French invasion of 1494 (see p. 183), France, Spain, and the Hapsburgs struggled over the peninsula for almost four hundred years, a rivalry that terminated only when a united Italian Kingdom was formed and the last French troops departed from Rome in 1870. (See Map 20.)

The wars and shifting alliances of the city-states required armies as well as diplomacy. When it became customary in the fourteenth century for citizens to absolve themselves from required military service by payment of a special fee, the city-states hired mercenary armies for their campaigns. This practice gave rise to the *condottieri,* the famous mercenary generals who gathered private armies and fought for whatever state met their financial demands. The *condottieri,* of course, felt allegiance to no state and were interested solely in their own advancement, a fact which further complicated interstate relations in Italy. Thus Francesco Sforza, a successful *condottiere,* was able to conquer Milan, marry into the Visconti family, and make himself its reigning duke (1450–1466). The *condottieri* system lasted from about 1350 to 1500; thereafter Swiss mercenaries generally supplied the military needs of Italy.

To supplement the work of their hired armies, the Italians developed diplomacy to a fine art. The Venetians in particular set up an elaborate diplomatic service, with ambassadors permanently accredited to foreign governments. Such ambassadors, who soon enjoyed diplomatic immunity, submitted regular reports to their home governments and were well supplied with secret instructions to intrigue and interfere in the host country. Furthermore, there was a constant need for special envoys, sent out to influence a possible associate or to spy on the intentions of a distrusted ally. Many famous humanists, such as Petrarch, Lorenzo Valla, and Machiavelli, served from time to time as such special envoys.

If the Renaissance became famous for the refinement of diplomatic practices, it also became infamous for its political amorality. The age produced its share of despots who became almost legendary for unscrupulous behavior toward their own subjects and for their conduct of foreign relations (for example: Ferdinand I of Naples, 1458–1494; Ludovico Sforza of Milan, 1481–1499; and Cesare Borgia, 1476–1507). Torture, rat-infested dungeons, poison and assassination, false promises, and counterintrigues symbolize the reigns of these tyrants. To be sure, these were not new phenomena. The medieval Inquisition had freely used torture, and political murder had been common in the Roman Empire. But Renaissance Italy provided a particularly fertile ground for the practice of political amorality.

It would be wrong to attribute this new political philosophy of expediency simply to the weakening of religion that is often—and not always correctly—associated with the Renaissance. Rather the notion that the end justifies the means in political action was a by-product of the separation of public from private morality. Perhaps it was a natural sequel to the renewed differentiation between public and private matters in government. The duty of a ruler was to advance the fortunes of his state, without regard to the moral scruples that normally governed the lives of private individuals. This amoral scheme of politics was analyzed by Niccolo Machiavelli (1469–1527) in *The Prince* (1513). "You must realize," he wrote, "that a Prince . . . cannot observe all those rules of conduct on the basis of which men are judged good; for in order to preserve his Princedom, he is often forced to act in opposition to good faith, charity, humanity, and religion." Machiavelli, who was also a historian and an active government official in republican

Florence, merely observed the actions of such astute practitioners of Renaissance politics as Cesare Borgia, who firmly believed that whatever served the prince _as_ ruler was justified. If one substitutes the concept of "the state" for "the prince," this political philosophy is the precursor of the idea of _raison d'état_ ("the interest of the state") which became important in international affairs in the seventeenth century.

Such secular politics were practiced not only by the city-states but also by the Renaissance papacy. In theory, a papal state had existed since the Donation of Pepin in 756 (see p. 112). In practice, the land controlled directly by the popes had alternately grown and shrunk over the centuries, with the papacy at times even losing control over the city of Rome. When Pope Pius II (1458–1464) succeeded in recasting the centralized authority of the papacy, he also laid the administrative basis for a real papal state. The Borgia Pope Alexander VI (1492–1503), although primarily interested in helping his son Cesare acquire a larger princedom, started the territorial expansion which was consolidated by his bellicose successor, Julius II (1503–1513). Although suffering from continued feuds among the great noble families, the papal states thus became a bona fide political state, extending across central Italy. As such, the papal states engaged in wars, alliances, and diplomatic maneuvers like any other Italian state, until their destruction in 1860.

Humanism

Much of the spadework for the Renaissance was done by the so-called humanists, a relatively small group of intellectuals who studied, collected libraries, wrote voluminously, and eagerly corresponded with one another. Originating in Italy in the late fourteenth century, humanism soon spread to many areas of Europe and affected the views of a part of the aristocracy and of the upper middle classes.

As the term implies, humanistic ideals were concerned with man. The secular world was again emphasized; knowledge and education were deemed good in themselves and not merely as pillars of religion. Like the Romans whom they revered, the humanists valued human dignity, admired the hero and the many-sided creative genius, and saw no reproachable vanity in men seeking fame among mortals. Like the Renaissance artists, they sought beauty for beauty's sake, finding it in the human body, in nature, in friendship, and in love.

In view of their secularism and their reverence for pre-Christian times, humanists have sometimes been called pagan. Moreover, because of their preoccupation with the classics, the humanists of Italy have often been referred to as literary or classical humanists; those in the North were looked upon as Christian humanists, in view of their interest in biblical studies. A statistical analysis might indeed reveal that more biblical investigations were undertaken north of the Alps, while more work on the classics was done in

Italy. Yet, no such clear distinction between classical and Christian humanism existed in fact. Most humanists were Christian in outlook. Petrarch,
Marsilio Ficino (1433–1499), and many other Italian humanists were ordained members of the clergy, even Machiavelli was a devout Christian, and
on the other hand many important classical studies were accomplished in the
North.

Looking upon classical times as an age when man had expressed his
potential to the fullest, humanists devoted their ingenuity to recovering
classical texts, gathering them in libraries, and translating them. Some humanists roamed the monasteries of Europe to buy or beg for copies of
ancient works. One of the most successful of these collectors (Giovanni
Poggio Bracciolini, 1380–1459) recovered works by Cicero, Lucretius,
Plautus, Tacitus, and others. It is said of him that when he could not
persuade a hesitant monk to part with a document or to let it be copied, he
would stealthily pull a sharp dagger, cut out the desired sheets, and slip
them under his wide mantle.

The humanists also resumed the study and teaching of ancient Greek,
which had been neglected during the Middle Ages. A professorship of
Greek was established at the University of Florence in the late fourteenth
century, a step soon imitated by other universities. The ability to go directly
to Greek sources evoked much new interest in Greek philosophy, particularly in Plato. Commissioned by his patron, Cosimo de Medici the Elder
(1389–1464), the ruler of the Florentine republic, Marsilio Ficino translated Plato and some Neoplatonists into Latin, and thereby helped launch a
strong Neoplatonic revival.

Aided by their knowledge of Greek, other humanists engaged in biblical
studies in order to retrieve a more intense, personal Christianity by stripping
medieval encumbrances away from the original Scriptures. In this endeavor,
some were influenced by German and Dutch mysticism (see p. 203). To
ascertain Christ's thoughts, they studied the Vulgate version of the Bible and
compared it with older texts, a work resulting eventually in the publication
of several comparative translations (by Erasmus, Lefèvre, and Cisneros).

The humanists were also fascinated by philology. Lorenzo Valla
(1406–1457) sought to purge Latin of all medievalisms and restore the
language to Ciceronian purity. Such attempts actually tended to kill Latin as
a growing, living language. On the other hand, this philological concern
made the humanists aware of the changing meaning and structure of language, an awareness important for the translations of the Bible and of the
classics then being undertaken. Furthermore, philology emerged as a tool for
historiography when Valla used his knowledge of the changes in Latin to
charge that the document containing the Donation of Constantine (see p.
92) could not have been written in the fourth century and presumably was
forged at a later time.

The Italian humanists in particular hoped to reshape education in the ancient tradition of the liberal arts in order to recreate the rational, self-reliant man they so admired. It seems natural that their dedication to Rome reawakened a sense of secular history as it had existed in ancient times. Historiography during the Middle Ages had consisted largely of annals, chronicles, and so-called universal histories that scanned the entire panorama of human history from Noah to medieval times, primarily in order to illustrate divine foresight. These histories had always been teleological, all epochs being treated in essence as necessary steps between the expulsion from Paradise and the Last Judgment. The humanists turned to secular history in which men or political forces were deemed to be historical causes. What could not be readily explained was ascribed to fate rather than to God. Such histories, as for instance Leonardo Bruni's (1369-1444) *History of Florence,* were also more limited in scope, although they usually retained aspects of the chronicles which recounted the founding and long history of the city-state.

Although humanism was an important movement in the transition to the "modern age," it was not scientific by nature. To be sure, there was some haphazard experimentation among doctors, chemists, or alchemists; many technical inventions were made or projected; and the possibility was discussed that neither Aristotle nor the Church might have the ultimate explanation for causation. But essentially, the humanists remained scholastics, albeit critical ones. They might doubt the accuracy of a translation, but they would not question the Bible itself, and most of the arguments among the literati were still settled by quoting Cicero or Plato, rather than by a fresh analysis of the problem.

Moreover, it is worth stressing that the Renaissance was not the equivalent of the Age of Reason (see p. 306). Although praising the dignity of man and the glory of human reason, some humanists pessimistically questioned the power of man's unaided reason. Besides relying on ancient authority and scriptural revelation, many Renaissance thinkers believed in irrational devices and occultism. The versatile Giovanni Pico della Mirandola (1463-1494), for example, a protégé of the Florentine ruler Lorenzo de Medici (1449-1492), was a student of theology, logic, Hebrew, Arabic, mathematics, and a prominent Neoplatonist; nevertheless, he was strongly drawn to cabalistic explanations of Christian mysteries.

Renaissance art

The Renaissance spirit is perhaps most clearly noticeable in the visual arts where the ideals of humanistic individualism could best be expressed. In Italy, this expression differed from that in the North, possibly because the Italians had never experienced a completely Gothic period and had always remained to some extent under the influence of Byzantine art and of the remnants of classical antiquity. Late Gothic painting in fifteenth century Flanders (the Van Eyck brothers and Rogier van der Weyden) also exhibited some interest in individualism and realism, without, however, the same trace of classical influence or the vital concern for the human figure. Similarly, most German Renaissance painters, among them Albrecht Dürer (1471–1528), relied more on lines to mold dimensions, whereas their Italian counterparts rather used strong colors to endow their subjects with form.

Renaissance art was marked by individual artistry. In medieval times, the artist had bowed in anonymity before his work. It is generally not known who designed the Gothic cathedrals or who carved the sculptures that decorated them. Most paintings were anonymous and the uniformity of style makes identification difficult. By the fifteenth century, however, individual styles had become the trade mark of the painter who proudly signed and dated his pictures. We know that Filippo Brunelleschi (1377–1446) designed the famous dome for the cathedral of Florence and that Lorenzo Ghiberti (1378–1455) cast the gilded bronze doors for its baptistry, the so-called Gates of Paradise. Renaissance artists were so proud of their own styles that they established schools to perpetuate them.

The artist himself, who in medieval times had been a craftsman normally associated with a guild, his rank in society rather low, now rose immeasurably in status and became hailed as a genius. Wealthy patrons vied with each other for the retention of renowned artists. The Medici had their Botticelli (1444–1510), Duke Ludovico Sforza had his Leonardo da Vinci (1452–1519), and several popes, among them Julius II and Clement VII (1523–1534), were patrons of Michelangelo (1475–1564). Artists became fit companions of princes and popes and qualified to share their dinner tables. The sculptor Donatello (1386?–1466) requested to be buried by the side of his benefactor, Cosimo de Medici, and was interred in the Medici chapel of the Church of San Lorenzo. The painter Raphael (1483–1520) was buried in the Roman Pantheon amidst pageantry worthy of princes.

Renaissance art was characterized by a greater variety of subject matter. Art in medieval times had been largely connected with religion, with the Church its best patron. Painting had concentrated on the Madonna and on saints, the best architectural efforts had been devoted to the construction of churches, and the function of the sculptor had been to decorate such religious edifices. In the Renaissance, however, secular architecture came to the fore with the erection of luxurious palaces. Painters depicted mythological stories, portraits of individuals or of family life, interior scenes and still lifes; sculptors cast individualistic busts; artists dedicated their talents to the aesthetic design of such utilitarian objects as household furniture and saltcellars.

With new subject matter came new materials. Most medieval painting had been done as fresco on wet plaster, or tempera on wood, or in the form of mosaics and stained glass; sculptures had been carved primarily in limestone or in wood, with an occasional use of marble where it was readily available, as in Italy. In the fifteenth century, oil painting, first developed in Flanders, became the preferred medium, done on canvas or on wood; pen and ink sketches and etchings became popular. In sculpture, the antique art of casting in bronze was revived by Donatello, who also worked with marble, wood, and terra cotta. Michelangelo preferred to carve in marble, while others, such as the della Robbia family, perfected glazed terra cotta sculpture.

Characteristic of Renaissance art was the humanization of its subject matter. Whereas medieval paintings had represented people as types, Renaissance painters portrayed them as individuals, realistically drawn down to the last wart on the nose. The same was true of religious art. The ethereal, symbolic Madonna who held in her stiff arms the figure of Jesus, looking usually like a wise old man in miniature, now gave way to a motherly Mary, cradling or suckling her infant baby. Just as Mary was changed from a symbol of beatitude to a beautiful woman, so the man Jesus was transformed from a flat, linear embodiment of suffering to a muscular, self-confident individual. Renaissance painting and sculpture thus renewed the classical interest in the human anatomy, with its varied representations of the nude body, shown in full, physical perspective.

Renaissance confidence in man was also stressed in the idealized many-sided artist, the *uomo universale,* capable of mastering many forms of creative endeavor. A number of artists came close to embodying this ideal. Leone Battista Alberti (1404–1472), for instance, best known as a Florentine architect and the designer of the Strozzi palace, was also a painter, a philosopher, and an accomplished organist who composed his own music; moreover, he wrote poetry and comedies, and worked as a printer. Better known as "Renaissance men" were Leonardo da Vinci, painter, scientist, engineer, mathematician, architect, and sculptor; and Michelangelo who excelled in sculpture, painting, and architecture, and also wrote beautiful poetry.

At the end of the fifteenth century, Italy entered the period of the high Renaissance, marked by a shift in artistic centers and a change in aesthetic emphasis. Realism gave way to idealism and subjects of classical mythology or of contemporary life assumed more importance over religious representations. Shattered by foreign invasion (see p. 183), Florence and Milan lost their artistic pre-eminence to Rome and Venice. From 1492 to 1549, five of the six incumbents in the papal chair were great patrons of art, dedicated to the embellishment of the city of Rome. St. Peter's Basilica, the Vatican, Castel San Angelo, and parts of Rome were beautified by Raphael, Michelangelo, and other famous artists. Increasingly influenced by classical antiquity, these artists abandoned the realism of the earlier Renaissance and sought to represent the ideal. Raphael's sweet Madonnas, Michelangelo's flawless sculptures or his impressive architectural designs, such as the Campidoglio, embody many characteristics of the high Renaissance: love of formal design, brilliant colors, grandiose use of space, and idealized conceptions of the human anatomy. Stronger classical influence was also seen in other areas. The literary epic and political history were brilliantly conceived by two writers (Ariosto, 1474–1533, and Guicciardini, 1483–1540), both of whom—typical for the Renaissance—were also active in politics.

Finally, the peak of the high Renaissance saw another change: the transition to the Baroque (see p. 229), noticeable particularly in Michelangelo and in the Venetian school of painting. The transition paralleled the changes in classical Greece from the idealistic art of the fifth century B.C. to the more emotional and realistic styles of the fourth century and the Hellenistic period. In his later work, such as the designs for St. Peter's and the frescoes on The Last Judgment in the Vatican's Sistine Chapel, Michelangelo displayed characteristics that foreshadowed the Baroque. Similarly, the Venetian painter Titian (1477–1576) gradually changed his style from formal idealism to a more dramatic, often more sensual, manner.

Economic changes

In Italy, as elsewhere, the Renaissance was accompanied by changes which helped "modernize" society. One might mention such technological changes as the improvement of the compass and the astrolabe, of gunpowder and artillery, and the substitution of movable metal type for wooden blocks in printing (invented about the same time, 1450, in Germany and Korea). Fundamental also were the economic changes wrought by the so-called commercial revolution that had begun in the late thirteenth century.

In a way the commercial revolution initiated mercantile capitalism—to be distinguished from industrial capitalism which arose in most of Europe only during the nineteenth century. Despite ecclesiastical prohibition against usury, there had always been some banking in the Mediterranean, since even the popes needed bankers for their financial affairs. Not only Jews and Moslems, who were unaffected by the Church ban on usury, but Lombards, Genoese, Florentines, and the Knights of the Temple were engaged in loaning money. By the late thirteenth century, financial practices had become quite sophisticated. The introduction of specially minted gold coins, such as the gold florin of Florence, gave some stability to currencies. Bankers and businessmen began to use double entry bookkeeping with Arabic rather than Roman numerals, issued letters of exchange, and developed a system of maritime insurance.

As trade expanded in the fourteenth century, commercial and maritime laws were elaborated to govern interstate commerce. Branch houses of Italian banks began to prosper in Flanders and elsewhere, and banking operations assumed international scope. When, for example, King Edward III of England repudiated his debts to several Italian banking houses, Florence was plunged into a serious financial and political crisis.

By the fifteenth century, capitalism involved the private investment for profit of surplus funds derived from commerce, mining, or banking. The commercial revolution was in full motion. As the term implies, more stress was placed on trade than on manufacture, the growth of the latter still being slowed down by the restrictive practices of the guilds. Commerce, on the other hand, received the active support and protection of most territorial rulers. The Portuguese voyages of exploration along the west coast of Africa, for instance, were in part an attempt to gain a share of the eastern trade that the Italians had monopolized. To carry on this trade, large export-import businesses were formed, such as that of Jacques Coeur in France. Trading partnerships, before usually organized to finance a single maritime expedition, were now often made permanent, the prototype of joint stock companies. Such establishments stimulated investments and speculation by non-merchants, and gradually led to the formation of the great trading companies of the sixteenth century. These were endowed with royal charters and specific monopolies and exercised vast commercial and political power. Such eagerness for trade was a prerequisite for Europe's expansion during the subsequent Age of Discovery.

Geographic expansion

During the fifteenth and early sixteenth centuries, European geographic knowledge expanded vastly more than it had during the thirteenth century (see p. 165). Europe achieved direct sea contact with the coasts of Africa and Asia, discovered a new continent in the West, and found itself in a position to influence these areas.

The initiative for the voyages of exploration came primarily from the Portuguese after they obtained their first foothold in Africa with the conquest of Ceuta in 1415. Portuguese sailors were taught in a special school established and financed by Prince Henry the Navigator (1394–1460). Trained to use the new navigational instruments and to draft accurate charts, they were dispatched on carefully planned expeditions that soon bore ample fruit. The Portuguese obtained the Madeira and Azore islands—the Canaries had been assigned by the papacy to Castile—and then slowly inched their way along the west coast of Africa until Bartholomeu Dias rounded the Cape of Good Hope in 1488.

Once it became clear that discovery of the southern tip of Africa had opened the sea route to the Far East, Portugal's overseas conquests proceeded with speed and aggressiveness. In the years 1497–1499, Vasco da Gama sailed around Africa to India and back. Within a decade, Portugal laid claim to India and established the seat for the governorship of India at Goa. Trading stations were planted along the African and Asian coasts to make sea passage to India more secure. While Portuguese fleets fought and defeated the Arabs in the Indian Ocean and took away their monopoly on trade with the East, other Portuguese pushed on to Siam, the Spice Islands, and China itself where the colony of Macao was founded in 1557.

In 1500, the Portuguese also discovered the coast of Brazil. There, according to the Line of Demarcation set by Pope Alexander VI in 1493 and modified by a treaty between Spain and Portugal, they could claim all land east of a line running some thirteen hundred miles west of the Azores. During the early sixteenth century, they gradually penetrated a portion of Brazil. Unlike the Spaniards, however, they somewhat neglected their interests in America, presumably because so much wealth was already pouring into Lisbon in the form of spices from the East and gold from Africa.

The Portuguese probably sent some probing expeditions west of the Azores and Cape Verde Islands prior to 1492. But historians still debate whether or not any European sailors reached America between the eleventh century and 1492. Christopher Columbus (1451–1506) himself, who made his four voyages to the Caribbean areas between 1492 and 1504—and who, incidentally, might have sailed a decade earlier if the king of Portugal had been willing to finance the venture—was apparently never quite certain whether he had reached Asia or had discovered a new continent. Yet, within a few decades after Columbus' first voyage, Spanish, Portuguese, and English sailors had explored most of the coastlines of the Americas; Ferdinand Magellan (1480–1521) had traversed the breadth of the Pacific Ocean and his companions had completed the circumnavigation of the globe; and the Spaniards had started to conquer a new empire. (See Map 18.)

In the Americas, the Spaniards found diverse Indian civilizations. Because of the lack of draft animals and carts, there was little contact and interchange among the various Indian tribes and hence great cultural differences. On a linguistic basis alone, the native population could be divided into some 125 independent families of languages.

Some peoples were still at a primitive level. They subsisted on hunting, fishing, and collecting wild fruits, depended on wooden or stone implements, and practiced cannibalism. Without cities and with no structured state, their social organization was limited to family ties. Other peoples had reached a high order of culture, with agricultural surpluses permitting large populations to settle in cities and to specialize in their occupations. They used bronze and copper implements, produced exquisite ornaments in gold and silver, built roads and canals, and had elaborated complex governmental structures. Religious practices differed from tribe to tribe, but many tribes worshiped celestial bodies, believed in ghosts and demons, and offered human sacrifices to their highest gods—the Aztecs of Mexico offering still warm human hearts to their god of war. Among the more advanced tribes, society was hierarchically organized. In Mexico slavery existed as punishment for crimes or for debts; as in ancient Greece, people taken as prisoners of war or captured by bandits could also be enslaved. In Peru, land ownership was on a communal basis.

The three largest states which the Spaniards found and soon conquered were the empires of the Aztecs, the Mayas, and the Incas. Each suffered from a flaw which made conquest by Europeans relatively easy. The Aztecs, one of the few Indian tribes to develop a form of writing, had built in Mexico a splendid civilization, which had become politically consolidated only in the early fifteenth century. An effectively centralized, elective monarchy, a large army, and a well-fortified capital should have enabled the estimated five million Aztecs to offer formidable resistance to Hernando Cortes' (1485-1546) little band of some six hundred men—despite the fact that the Europeans had guns and a few horses. But some of the Indian tribes who had been subjected by the Aztecs flocked to Cortes' side. Moreover, the Aztec ruler himself, Montezuma II (1480?-1520), admitted the Spaniards into his capital (Tenochtitlan). He conjectured that Cortes' appearance heralded the prophesied arrival of an invincible priest-king (Quetzalcoatl), who was to appear from the East. Consequently Cortes accomplished the subjugation of the Aztec empire in two and a half years (1519-1521).

South of Mexico, around Guatemala and the Yucatán Peninsula, flourished the older though smaller Mayan civilization. During the fifteenth century, the Mayas had split into various political units and could therefore not offer combined resistance to the Europeans. It was only because the conquest of this area was not pushed with the same vigor as exhibited by Cortes that it took two decades (1527-1546) to turn the Mayan lands into Spanish possessions.

The largest and wealthiest Indian nation, the empire of the Incas, had been created in the fifteenth century, although its cultural development dated back many centuries. From his capital at Cuzco in modern Peru, the lord of the Incas controlled the lands west of the Andes from Colombia to Chile. A system of straight roads—similar to those of ancient Rome, but including steps, since no carts were used—on which armies and messengers could move at great speed, gave cohesion to this vast empire. But when Francisco Pizarro (1470-1541) started his conquest, civil war between the king and his brother weakened the Incas and enabled the Spaniards to break all resistance within four years (1532-1536). In all three conquests, treachery was freely used by the *conquistadores,* who did not feel compelled to observe the customs of war or keep their word when dealing with heathens.

It is interesting to note some of the legal and moral arguments advanced by the Spaniards to justify their conquest of Indian lands. Contrary to what one might expect, there was much discussion of this topic among jurists, churchmen, and government officials. When it was a matter of penetrating into Moslem North Africa or to the Atlantic islands, the Spaniards spoke of the continuation of the anti-Moslem *reconquista,* claiming that these lands had once been held by the Goths, the forefathers of the Christian rulers of Spain. Once the conquest of the Americas had begun, the religious argument tended to predominate. Christians had indubitably more right and more ability to rule than heathens. Many asserted, in fact, that Indians had no soul, were not rational people, and were hence incapable of self-government, until Pope Paul III (1534–1549) in a bull of 1537 solemnly declared Indians to be true human beings.

The role of the *conquistadores* as missionaries was repeatedly stressed in papal bulls adjudicating disputed territories between Portugal and Spain—in Africa as well as America. In these bulls, the conquerors were awarded "full, free, and absolute power, authority, and jurisdiction," including the right to enslave the natives, seize their property, and to exclude other Europeans from the area—provided, of course, that the heathens would be converted to the faith. When Ferdinand's grandson Charles I of Spain (1516–1556) became Holy Roman emperor in 1519 with the title of Charles V, a new argument was advanced, harking back to the Middle Ages. Since an emperor's realm was universal, he was the natural overlord of the newly discovered areas.

Officially, the Indians were protected by the Spanish crown. In practice, they were exploited and many were killed, despite the public remonstrances by some enlightened clergymen. After the Spaniards attained firm control of the land and after imported Negro slaves from Africa had replaced the surviving Indians as the chief labor force, the Spanish attitude began to change. In 1552, Bartolomé de Las Casas (1474–1566), the Dominican missionary, historian, and stanch defender of the Indians, entitled one of his works *Brief Relation of the Destruction of the Indies* (1552). Perhaps it is indicative of the change that two decades later the *conquista* was officially renamed "the pacification of the Indies."

Repercussions in Europe of the voyages of discovery and of the overseas conquests affected every branch of Western civilization, and it would be impossible to analyze all the effects. The Italians and Arabs lost their monopoly on the eastern trade and suffered a commercial recession, while the Atlantic states developed their navies and became wealthy maritime powers. The influx of gold from the New World caused an inflation in Europe that further weakened the landed nobility and gave greater political potential to the middle class. But perhaps most important was a vague feeling of self-satisfaction and superiority which gripped Europeans, since it was they who suddenly had achieved the seemingly impossible: they had burst the medieval confines of their small continent and with a few ships and intrepid sailors and soldiers discovered and conquered the globe. These achievements gave them confidence in progress and change and brought greater variety to their civilization. The Europeans also felt themselves placed in a supposedly hierarchical relationship with the inhabitants of other continents. This legacy of the sixteenth century remains today one of the greatest obstacles to the establishment of truly frank and equal relations between Western states and those of Asia and Africa.

Pre-Reformation currents

It seems fruitless to speculate how much the Renaissance contributed to the Reformation of the sixteenth century. Obviously many of the ideas and changes which accompanied the Renaissance had a profound influence on religious thought: the Christian humanists' preference for a more personal Christianity, or their textual investigations of the Bible, the growth of centralized government, or, in a negative way, the opprobrious behavior of the so-called Renaissance popes. But one can also point to a thread of reforming zeal, often accompanied by waves of mysticism, which ran through the centuries from St. Francis to Luther and which always existed at the periphery of the Renaissance. For contributing factors to the Reformation one must look both at the institutionalized Church and at the actions of individuals and groups within and outside the Church.

Structure and power of the Church

The Church Council of Constance, as we saw (see p. 154), succeeded in healing the papal schism and passed decrees purportedly assuring conciliar superiority over the popes. In certain ways, however, the council divided rather than unified the Church. To avoid giving the Roman pope an advantage over his Avignonese rival, it allowed delegates to vote by nation instead of by head. Moreover, the execution of John Hus (see p. 204) stirred Czech religious nationalism. And the council's concern with the schism did not permit it time to consider questions of Church reform, which the conciliarists also advocated. After Constance, another council, meeting at Basel intermittently between 1431 and 1449, attempted to put conciliar ideas and reforms into practice. At Basel, the conciliarists went so far as to declare it to be heretical to appeal from a Church council to the pope. Despite all efforts, including the election of a new antipope, the Council of Basel also failed, largely because of disunity among the various states. Moreover, the pro-papal forces soon boycotted Basel, enabling the pope to convene his own compliant council at Ferrara and Florence (1438).

Meanwhile, the pope preached unity, called for a general anti-Turkish crusade to prevent the fall of Constantinople, and arranged for reunion with the Orthodox Church, a step that was never carried out (see p. 179). In fact, however, popes as well as lay rulers were contributing to the growing national splintering of the Church. Rather than concede to the combined conciliarist forces, the papacy sought to retain its supremacy by dealing with one ruler at a time. The Pragmatic Sanction of Bourges (see p. 183) is an example of such a bilateral arrangement that was soon imitated in negotiations with the Hapsburgs, with Spain, and others. Each state negotiated the best terms it could for greater ecclesiastical autonomy. The German princes, too, attempted to obtain a Pragmatic Sanction for the Holy Roman Empire, but, unsupported by the emperor who thought only of his own Hapsburg interests, they had to negotiate individually for the separate states within the empire. Without much bargaining power, they could not gain autonomy for their churches and therefore remained more subject to papal control and financial exactions—a condition that caused resentment during the decades approaching the Reformation.

By 1450, the conciliarists clearly had lost, and the papacy celebrated a jubilee in victory over the conciliar movement. Ten years later, Pope Pius II decreed in the bull *Execrabilis* that anyone who should "presume to appeal to a future Council" over the head of the papacy, "of whatever status . . . he may be, even if adorned with imperial . . . dignity, . . . shall *ipso facto* incur sentence of anathema." Freed from the conciliar menace, the popes could devote greater efforts to recentralizing papal institutions, a task begun with great skill by Pius II.

For almost one hundred years after the mid-fifteenth century, most of the incumbents of the Chair of St. Peter were "Renaissance popes," who respected humanism, were great patrons of the arts, and enjoyed the delights which the Renaissance world had to offer. They beautified Rome, established the Vatican library, patronized painters, architects, and scholars, and launched the construction of the new St. Peter's Cathedral, all of which cost vast sums of money. They also devoted their resources to the maintenance of sumptuous riding stables, to the erection and decoration of luxurious palaces, and to the furtherance of the ecclesiastical or political careers of ambitious nephews. Since many a German thought that the money for such enterprises came from his own pockets, the reputation of these Renaissance popes obviously affected the Reformation.

Perhaps most important in this development was the dichotomy between papal recentralization on the one hand and the gradual emergence of national churches on the other. It is probably not a coincidence that where states were strong enough to negotiate a favorable concordat with the papacy, no Reformation occurred.

Search for reform

Throughout the history of the organized Church, there existed individuals and groups who disagreed with some point of dogma or practice of the official Church hierarchy. After 1200, criticism of the Church and demands for reform had become bolder and more organized. Some dissatisfied individuals were primarily concerned with finding a more comforting—and perhaps more secure—path to salvation. Others were filled with missionary zeal to spread their newly found religious convictions. Among the latter arose reform movements that usually went beyond purely spiritual considerations and attacked a whole gamut of social, political, and economic problems. Yet all critics, from St. Francis to Luther, wanted desperately to stay within the Church, and harbored no determination to break from its confines. But some, such as Hus and Wyclif, were expelled from the Church—a decision usually motivated more by politics than by questions of dogma.

Among the critics were many famous mystics who possessed the conviction that close, direct contact with and knowledge of the divine was possible, based on the experience of an emotional, love-filled union with God. Such mysticism was suspect to Church authorities, since it threatened to undermine the sacerdotal functions and sacramental powers of the Church. The Dominican monk and theologian Johannes Eckhart (1260?–1327?) is an example of such a mystic. He was so intoxicated with God that his desire to perceive divine immanence everywhere made his views border on pantheism. Consequently some of his teachings were condemned by the pope. The mystic St. Catherine of Siena (1347–1380), on the other hand, inspired by visions to urge the pope to leave Avignon and to return to Rome, was not condemned but rather canonized, although her attitude inherently assumed that she had more divine knowledge than the pope.

A mystic with a more active missionary zeal was the Augustinian monk from Flanders, Jan van Ruysbroeck (1293–1381). In the Brethren of the Common Life he helped establish a society to propagate his ideal that practical piety should carry more weight than observance of dogma. Ruysbroeck's society became rapidly influential among the poorer classes. Another Augustinian, Thomas à Kempis (1380–1471), the reputed author of *Imitation of Christ,* continued this trend. As the title implies, the book stressed devotion to Christ and emulation of His simple life. It may have influenced a later Augustinian monk, Martin Luther.

Full-fledged protest movements were organized around John Wyclif and John Hus, both of whom were reformers and not simply critics. Wyclif was an Oxford theologian whose teaching and preaching, with its nationalistic and social overtones, stirred wide sections of England. He questioned the validity of transubstantiation, of penance, and of papal indulgences. In general he believed faith to be more important than the sacraments. He saw no value in confession to a priest, since, as he complained, many priests were sinful. Wyclif lashed out at the immorality of the clergy and at the abuses in the Church. Moreover, he advised that every one should interpret the Bible for himself, and to this end he began to translate the Bible into English, a task completed by associates shortly after his death.

In socio-political questions, Wyclif became a champion of the anti-papal forces. He denounced the fiscal demands of the Avignonese papacy and urged that the Church divest itself of its political interests. Like the Spiritual Franciscans, he believed that the Church should practice apostolic poverty. The king, he announced, had the right to confiscate Church lands. It is hence not surprising that the court at first protected Wyclif against papal attempts to silence him. But Wyclif's followers, the Lollards or "poor preachers," who ranged through the land reciting prayers and preaching against the wealth of the Church, stirred up social discontent among the peasants. As was to happen repeatedly, demand for ecclesiastical reforms raised visions of social egalitarianism among the downtrodden and led to uprisings. The peasant revolt of 1381, which actually succeeded in seizing the city of London, was a social, primarily anti-manorial rebellion. But the rebels also embraced some Wyclifian ideas, such as the disendowment of the Church. The frightened upper classes therefore withdrew their protection from the reformer, who died three years later, but whose body was later disinterred and burned and his ashes were scattered. The Lollards were persecuted and within two generations had either disappeared or gone underground.

The reform movement of John Hus (1369–1415), who appropriated many ideas of Wyclif, became even more explosive and revolutionary. As rector of the University of Prague, Hus became the rallying point for Czech national feeling and resentment against German infiltration at the university and in Bohemia in general. Like Wyclif, he accepted only the authority of the Bible, questioned some Church tradition, and fulminated in his sermons against the alleged immorality of the clergy. He even demanded that during communion the laity be given the cup as well as the bread, so as to end the symbolic difference between laymen and ordained priests. Above all Hus attacked the foreign, especially German, clergy and demanded the establishment of a Czech national Church. Called before the Council of Constance to justify his views or to recant, he was condemned and burnt at the stake (1415), despite a prior imperial guarantee of safe-conduct.

Hus' execution unleashed in Bohemia a national rising in support of a curious mixture of demands. The rebels insisted on religious reforms, socio-economic equality, and national autonomy. The resulting Hussite wars (1419–1434) resembled an anti-Czech crusade by the papacy, the emperor, and the German princes, who were more concerned with quelling the social rebellion and suppressing Czech nationalism than with stamping out Hussite heresy. The Bohemians triumphed over all invaders for a decade and a half, until their ranks split under the impact of class strife. The moderates (Ultraquists) agreed to accept a compromise on dogma and they survived as an organized sect (the Moravians). The more radical elements (Taborites) who also insisted on social reform were defeated, persecuted, and exterminated. Yet for two centuries Bohemia remained a stimulus for religious agitation, just as John Hus himself was to have great influence on Martin Luther.

At the end of the fifteenth century, a radical voice for reform was raised even in Italy. In Florence, the Dominican monk Girolamo Savonarola (1452–1498) rose to political and religious prominence through his vehement sermons against sin and Renaissance corruption, against ecclesiastical abuses, and against the Medici rulers and Pope Alexander VI. He hailed the approaching armies of Charles VIII, as if the young French king had been sent by God to scourge the wicked Florentines (see p. 184). After successfully urging the expulsion of the Medici (see p. 224), he helped establish and govern a puritanical republican regime in Florence and continued his attacks on the papacy. Pope Alexander finally excommunicated him, and Savonarola was captured by his enemies, accused of treason, and burnt at the stake. Savonarola's demands, entangled with politics as they were, constituted the last thunderous cry for reform before Luther posted his Ninety-Five Theses in Wittenberg nineteen years later.

SUGGESTED READINGS

General Coverage

Burckhardt, Jacob, *The Civilization of the Renaissance in Italy,* 2 vols. (Harper and Row, 1958). A classic, much debated nineteenth-century interpretation.

Burke, Peter, *The Renaissance* (Barnes and Noble, 1966). A comparison of traditional and revised views.

Dannenfeldt, Karl H., *The Renaissance—Medieval or Modern?* (Heath, 1959).

Gilmore, Myron P., *The World of Humanism, 1453–1517* (Harper, 1962).

Gundersheimer, Werner L., *The Italian Renaissance* (Prentice-Hall, 1965). Collection of contemporary writings.

Helton, Tensley, ed., *The Renaissance: A Reconsideration of the Theories and Interpretations of the Age* (U. of Wisconsin, 1961). A collection of essays.

Mattingly, Garrett, et al., *Renaissance Profiles* (Harper, 1965). From Petrarch to Michelangelo.

Von Martini, Alfred, *Sociology of the Renaissance* (Harper).

Art and Humanism

Bertram, Anthony, *Michelangelo* (Dutton, 1964).

Cellini, Benvenuto, *Autobiography of Benvenuto Cellini* (Simon and Schuster, 1963).

Clark, Kenneth, *Leonardo Da Vinci* (Penguin).

Dolan, John P., ed., *The Essential Erasmus* (New American Library, 1964). Selected readings.

Hartt, Frederick, ed., *Botticelli* (Harry N. Abrams, 1953).

Kristeller, Paul, *Renaissance Thought,* Vol. I, "The Classic, Scholastic and Humanist Strains"; Vol. II, "Papers on Humanism and the Arts" (Harper, 1961).

Stokes, Adrian, *The Quattro Cento: A Different Conception of the Italian Renaissance* (Schocken, 1968). On Italian fifteenth-century architecture and sculpture.

Valsecchi, Marco, *Raphael* (Abrams, 1960).

Vasari, Giorgio, *Lives of the Painters, Sculptors and Architects* (Dell, 1968). Contemporary biographies of Italian Renaissance artists.

Italy

Ady, Cecilia Mary, *Lorenzo dei Medici and Renaissance Italy* (Macmillan, 1962).

Butterfield, Herbert, *The Statescraft of Machiavelli* (Macmillan, 1962).

Jensen, De Lamar, *Machiavelli—Cynic, Patriot, or Political Scientist?* (Heath, 1960).

Plumb, John Harold, *The Italian Renaissance: A Concise Survey of Its History and Culture* (Harper, 1965).

Schevill, Ferdinand, *The Medici* (Harper, 1960).

Vespasiano, *Renaissance Princes, Popes and Prelates: Lives of Illustrious Men of the Fifteenth Century* (Harper, 1963). Memoirs of a contemporary.

Discoveries and Expansion

Cipolla, Carlo M., *Guns, Sails, and Empires: Technological Innovation and the Early Phases of European Expansion 1400–1700* (Funk).

Jensen, De Lamar, *The Expansion of Europe—Motives, Methods and Meanings* (Heath, 1966).

Kirkpatrick, F. A., *Spanish Conquistadores* (World).

Mason, J. A., *Ancient Civilization of Peru* (Penguin).

Morley, Sylvanus Griswold, *The Ancient Maya* (Stanford, 1956).

Parry, J. H., *The Establishment of the European Hegemony: 1415–1715 Trade and Exploration in the Age of the Renaissance* (Harper, 1961).

Penrose, Boies, *Travel and Discovery in the Renaissance, 1420–1620* (Atheneum, 1962).

Von Hagen, Victor W., *The Aztec: Man and Tribe* (New American Library).

Religious Currents

*Petry, Ray C., *Late Medieval Mysticism* (Westminster, 1957).

*Spinka, Matthew, *John Hus and the Czech Reform* (Shoe String, 1966).

*Spitz, Lewis, *The Religious Renaissance of the German Humanists* (Harvard, 1963).

CHAPTER XII

ᚻᚷ *The Age of the Reformation*
(1517-1555)

In European history, the first half of the sixteenth century is usually labeled the Age of the Reformation (or of the Protestant Revolt), since during this period almost half a dozen different sects broke away from the Roman Catholic Church. But one should keep in mind that this was also the age of the high Renaissance in Italy and of the long, indecisive fight between the Hapsburgs and the French. Elsewhere, this period saw the continued expansion of Ottoman Turkey and the consolidation of the Mogul Empire in India. Moreover, it was during this half century that the Spaniards and Portuguese accomplished the conquest of the Americas. Important as the Reformation was in its repercussions on Western civilization, the conquest and development of America in the long run was probably of even greater consequence.

Luther and Germany

The fourteenth and fifteenth centuries had had their share of reformers, just as in Luther's time there were others who advocated ideas like his. But Luther was one of those intelligent, determined, almost obstinate individuals who, when placed in the proper militant environment, become the focal point of a new movement. Hence it seems valid to focus on Luther's actions, while recognizing that the Reformation was in fact the product of countless historical forces.

Background of the Reformation

The early sixteenth century, particularly in Germany, was filled with social and political tension. The territorial princes of the Holy Roman Empire, convinced that the Hapsburgs would act only in their own interest, were determined to grasp more power for themselves in political as well as ecclesiastical affairs, even at the risk of antagonizing pope and emperor. The knights, caught between the growing territorial power of the princes and the mercantile and financial growth of the bourgeoisie, were searching for a way of escaping socio-political extinction. Territorial lords as well as free cities desired more control over the churches in their lands for political as well as financial reasons. The German lands were roused by antiforeign stirrings. Such feelings were hardly assuaged when the Flemish-born King Charles I of Spain, who did not speak German, won the imperial election of 1519 and became German emperor as Charles V.

Besides socio-political tension, there was financial discontent. The Renaissance popes required large sums and much of this money was obtained from Germany, partly through the sale of bishoprics and indulgences. At the same time, inflation caused resentment against all who were rich, including the German banking houses such as the Fuggers of Augsburg who were known as the bankers and creditors of popes and emperors.

Moreover the changed intellectual atmosphere, the writings of reformers and Christian humanists, as well as the greater prosperity of the bourgeois had contributed to creating doubts about some points of Catholic dogma. Partly in view of the financial exactions of unscrupulous priests, the question was raised whether, as Luther was to assert, salvation could be based solely on God's forgiving grace apprehended by faith. In such a case, every man could be his own priest. Some Christian humanists had also begun to question the practice of venerating saints and relics. By Luther's time, the sale of indulgences had become a focal point of debate. Indulgences were based on the doctrine that Christ's sacrifice had stored up infinite grace that lay at the disposal of the Church. If imbued with inner repentance, a penitent believer could purchase an indulgence as a form of penance that would shorten his time in purgatory. In the early sixteenth century, unscrupulous pardon sellers, authorized by popes and bishops who hoped to pay for the construction of St. Peter's Cathedral or pay off personal debts, perverted the practice by making purchasers believe that an indulgence insured salvation for themselves or for someone deceased. Against this background of tension and abuses, Luther entered the controversy.

The course of the revolt

In 1517, Martin Luther (1483–1546), a respected Augustinian monk, priest, and lecturer at the University of Wittenberg, was suddenly drawn into the indulgence controversy when a Dominican monk (John Tetzel) sold pardons at the borders of the electorate of Saxony. It was symptomatic of the period that the duke of Saxony (Frederick the Wise) had refused permission for this particular series of indulgences to be sold in his state. He hoped to stop the drain of gold to Rome and furthermore suspected that the sale would benefit the Archbishop of Mainz, who happened to be a Hohenzollern prince from the dynasty ruling Saxony's neighbor state of Brandenburg. The indulgence sale, organized by the banking house of Fugger, was indeed primarily a financial venture. According to the archbishop's instructions, the sale price of indulgences was to be staggered according to the sinner's ability to pay, from twenty-five guilders for princes to half a guilder for ordinary people.

In anger, Luther drew up Ninety-Five Theses "on penitence and indulgences" and asked for a public disputation of the matter. To the Archbishop of Mainz, he sent a copy, explaining: "I grieve at the very false ideas which the people conceive from them [indulgences]." The sum of his argument, as stated in his first point, was that "the whole life of believers should be penitence." On this basis, he asserted in regard to indulgences, that "the pope has neither the will nor the power to remit any penalties, except those which he had imposed by his own authority."

The Ninety-Five Theses made Luther famous. Spread throughout Germany, they ruined the indulgence business, unfettered other protests, and challenged people to take sides. Luther's rather harmless call for a debate suddenly became a national issue. Humanists, disgruntled knights, nationalistic bourgeois, power-conscious princes, and even poor parish priests suspicious of the wealth of the Church hierarchy applauded the audacious stand of the Wittenberg monk, who soon went beyond the indulgence question to attack other areas of Catholic dogma and practices. Neither Luther's superior, the general of the Augustinian Order, nor the papal legate in Germany was able to persuade Luther to remain silent.

In 1519, a public disputation finally took place in Leipzig between Luther and the theologian John Eck (1486–1543). The debate touched the fundamental question of papal power. Luther had no intention of breaking with the Church, yet in two years his arguments had led him to reject one authority after another. Already, no longer recognizing episcopal or papal authority, he had retained only his willingness to submit his views to a general Church council. But in his debate with Eck, who accused Luther of Hussite heresy, the reformer questioned even the authority of Church councils by asserting that Hus had been unjustly condemned by the Council of Constance. Thereafter, so to speak, Luther was on his own. He claimed to recognize as authority only Holy Scriptures. In essence this meant that man's conscience and faith were to be his sole recourse.

In 1520, Luther elaborated his religious views in three of his most famous tracts. In his *Address to the Christian Nobility* he urged the temporal powers to help reform the Church, since government "has been ordained by God for the punishment of the bad and the protection of the good." He discussed the sacraments in his treatise *On the Babylonian Captivity of the Church*, attacking in particular the concept of transubstantiation in Holy Communion and the clergy's use of sacraments to bolster its own power.

Finally *The Liberty of a Christian Man* stressed what was to be the essence of Lutheranism, that salvation came through God's grace and not through the actions of man, and that justification was solely on the basis of faith. The treatise also analyzed the dual nature of man, whom Luther considered free in spiritual matters even though a subject to established authority in the physical sense. This idea was misunderstood by some of his more radical followers among the lower classes who read into it that all men were to be free and equal.

Pope Leo X (1513–1521) finally issued a bull condemning Luther's teachings and demanding that he recant or be condemned as a heretic. By then sure of his stand, Luther publicly burned the bull to underscore his defiance of the papacy and the pope thereupon excommunicated him. But 1520 was not 1415, when John Hus was burned after condemnation by the Council of Constance. Some of the German princes liked Luther's ideas and insisted that a papal condemnation alone was not binding on the Germans, and that Luther should be examined by an imperial German Diet. Hence Luther appeared before the Diet at Worms in 1521, again refused to retract his pronouncements, and was formally placed under the ban of the Holy Roman Empire. Before any harm could come to him, he had been safely hidden in the Wartburg castle by the elector of Saxony, who sympathized with Luther's views and furthermore was happy to defy the emperor.

Little had been done to check Luther and his growing number of adherents, not only because he had powerful protectors, but also because of political conditions in the empire. After 1515, when he had lost the war to France and with it the territory of Milan, Emperor Maximilian I (see p. 175) concentrated primarily on Hapsburg dynastic problems. The death of Ferdinand of Aragon in 1516 made Maximilian's grandson Charles king of Spain and heir presumptive to the vast Hapsburg holdings, including the entire Burgundian and Austrian hereditary lands. To cap this inheritance and to keep the imperial crown in the Hapsburg family, Maximilian hoped that his grandson could succeed him also as emperor.

When Maximilian died in 1519, the main imperial candidates were his grandson Charles and his archenemy Francis I of France. Rarely had an election been accompanied by so much bribery and so many promises by the candidates, including the assurance to respect the judicial sovereignty of the electoral princes. In the end Charles won the election. Yet the electoral princes, the territorial lords, and the free cities seemed determined to show their new emperor that they intended to retain considerable autonomy. The Lutheran movement served admirably as a vehicle to further these aims.

Emperor Charles V, who was above all interested in his Spanish possessions, visited Germany for the first time in 1521 to attend the Diet of Worms before which Luther appeared. Thereafter Charles' many commitments rarely permitted him to devote his undivided attention to the religious rebellion in Germany. The conquest of the Americas, attempts to acquire islands in the Pacific, four major wars against France, defense against the Turks whose inroads reached as far as the gates of Vienna, war against the Moslems in North Africa as an extension of the *reconquista*—these are only some of the tasks which occupied the emperor. Moreover, his vast territories required different, and often irreconcilable policies. The religious intolerance of the Spaniards was hardly the proper answer for the Lutheran challenge in Germany. Hence Charles V vacillated in his attitude. When he needed the financial or military support of the German princes and cities for his wars against France or Turkey, he offered conciliatory compromises to the Lutherans. When external pressure lessened, he attempted to enforce religious conformity and political obedience.

After his break with Rome, Luther and his friend and colleague at the University of Wittenberg, Philipp Melanchthon (1497–1560), faced the task of defining the dogma for their new church on the basis of their own scriptural interpretation. They retained only two of the sacraments, baptism and communion. Interpretation of the latter was changed, since Luther rejected the doctrine of transubstantiation, which implied the miraculous transformation of bread and wine into the body and blood of Christ; instead he stressed the real presence of Christ in the Sacrament. Luther also abolished monasticism and celibacy of the clergy, and forbade the veneration of saints and relics. Church services were to be conducted in the vernacular. He himself translated the Bible into German and composed many hymns for services.

Ideally Luther would have preferred his church to be independent of the state, but circumstances led him to entrust it into the hands of the princes, upon whom he looked as "emergency bishops." Quite possibly this decision saved his movement. He urged the princes to confiscate the property of the Catholic Church lying within their territories and to use the resulting revenue to maintain church buildings, pay salaries to the clergy, and let the state perform some of the functions formerly handled by the Church, such as running schools, hospitals, and orphanages. The new church would thus become a state church. Such a proposal, involving the prospect of confiscating the vast holdings of the Catholic Church, naturally appealed to the princes and to the magistrates of the free cities. It is impossible to know how many were attracted to Luther's side by this prospect of economic gain rather than by religious convictions.

The tacit understanding between Luther and the princes was also furthered by the uprisings of the 1520's during which Luther sided with the forces of law and order. The first was the rebellion of the knights (1522), who misused Luther's stand on Christian liberty to launch an attack against some princes and against the great archbishops, whom they regarded as symbols of a foreign power and as partly responsible for their own economic plight. The enthusiastic though disorganized bands of knights were quickly crushed by well-aimed volleys of episcopal artillery, and Luther considered their defeat a divine judgment that the sword should not be used to defend the gospel.

Two years later (1524–1525), the peasants of southwestern Germany started an even fiercer insurrection. Basing themselves on Luther's proclamation supposedly implying equality among all Christians, the peasants demanded correction of all social and economic injustices. To prove the urgency of their demands, they burned manor houses, plundered monasteries, and murdered landlords. The horrified Luther, who was asked to support the rebels, reminded the peasant leaders that Christian equality meant spiritual equality in the eyes of God and not socio-economic egalitarianism. He urged all rulers, even those who did "not tolerate the Gospel," to "smite and punish these peasants without offering to submit the case to judgment. For rebellion is not simple murder, but is like a great fire, which attacks and lays waste a whole land." The peasants' rebellion was eventually crushed with much bloodshed and cruelty.

Besides these two major insurrections, there were other disorders in the 1520's. To the horror of Luther, who was no iconoclast, some of his overzealous followers sought to implement his reforms by force. They roamed through churches, smashing statues of saints and desecrating relics, drove monks and nuns out of monasteries and convents, and forced them to marry.

Moreover, almost from the beginning of the Lutheran movement, various reformers in Germany, Switzerland, and elsewhere, diverged from Luther's views in certain fundamentals. Some demanded the complete separation of church and state; some advocated simple church services as found in the primitive church; others believed revelation to be a continuing process; still others preached a social evangelism, hoping that heaven on earth could be attained with the aid of the gospel. Although their doctrines differed on many points, most of these movements shared a common opposition to infant baptism and have often been loosely classed together as "Anabaptists." Most Anabaptists were pacific, in fact, believing in non-resistance. Yet a few radical groups attempted to implement their ideals through the sword. The most violent attempt was made in Münster in northwestern Germany during the 1530's. Here, radical Anabaptists sought to recapture the brotherhood of the early followers of Christ by abolishing social ranks and by sharing possessions, including wives. They plundered and killed the rich in order to provide for the poor and the community. Although the frightened upper classes eventually repressed this movement with bloody vehemence, sporadic uprisings of radical Anabaptists occurred in succeeding decades.

These disorders lost Luther some followers. Many a knight and some of the lower classes were disappointed with the reformer's failure to come to their aid, while some of the moderate members of the middle and upper classes recoiled from a movement that seemed to unleash social revolt. Still, Lutheranism continued to grow in the countryside and became consolidated in certain free cities and in the territories of the princes who had adopted the new faith, such as Saxony and Hesse. Within the Imperial Diet two groups began to form, with an informal league of Lutheran states opposing the emperor, his brother Ferdinand—who ran German affairs during Charles' absences—and such steadfast Catholics as the duke of Bavaria. When the Catholic majority at the Diet (1529) suddenly attempted to enforce the anti-Lutheran Edict of Worms, the Lutheran princes made an official protest, a step which gained them the label "Protestants."

In 1530, the emperor tried to force the opposing sides into a doctrinal compromise. The moderate Philipp Melanchthon drew up the Augsburg Confession for presentation to the Diet. This document eventually became the official creed of the Lutheran Church. Despite its conciliatory tone, the Confession achieved no compromise between Catholics and Lutherans, who faced each other uneasily, both girded in military alliances.

Reactions to Lutheranism

The successful establishment of Lutheranism in many German states represented a serious challenge to pope and emperor. The Catholic Church had to react either by defeating the Protestants or by reforming itself and compromising with the schismatics in order to bring them back into the fold (see p. 239). Lutheranism also threatened the emperor's tenuous hold on the Holy Roman Empire. Confiscation of ecclesiastical lands and wealth made the Lutheran princes particularly powerful; their association in a league made them seem united. Charles V's main enemy, the king of France, had learned to take advantage of this opportunity and supported the Lutheran princes against the emperor, notwithstanding the fact that he persecuted Protestants within France. Such an alliance with the Protestant princes became a customary policy for France until 1648.

Charles V therefore felt compelled to act. After his fourth war against France, he launched an attack upon the Lutheran princes (Schmalkaldic War, 1546–47). Although militarily successful, he was eventually forced into a compromise. By the Peace of Augsburg, 1555, the Lutheran states were granted the same rights as Catholic states, and every ruler was given the privilege of determining the religion of his subjects.

Luther's success also obliged the intellectuals of his day to take a stand. His stress on individualism, as well as his call for reforms in the Church and for a return to the gospel, attracted many writers, pamphleteers, and artists, while his stanch nationalism appealed to others. But most humanists preferred not to be implicated in Luther's activism, and humanism's foremost representatives, Sir Thomas More (1478–1535) and his friend Desiderius Erasmus, remained opposed to the reformer.

The cosmopolitan Erasmus (1466?–1536) is sometimes called the prince of the humanists. His numerous writings made him one of the most influential men of his time. As an ardent admirer of the classics, he translated Greek authors and spent a lifetime perfecting his Latin style. His popular *Adages,* for example, contains selected quotations from Latin classics by which Erasmus hoped to spread the knowledge of good Latin as well as the wisdom of the ancients. Like the Romans, he used satire to make sport of ignorance, pedantry, and human foibles, as in his witty and successful *Praise of Folly.* As many humanists, he stressed personal piety over the traditional theological arguments, a theme expounded in *The Handbook of the Christian Knight* with its emphasis on inner faith and learning rather than on dogmatism and outward observance of forms. His Latin translation of the New Testament, which he published along with the Greek text, differed from the official Vulgate and typified the humanistic hope that a more precise knowledge of the Bible would help man lead a Christian life.

Erasmus at first hailed Luther's attack on Church abuses and began corresponding with the reformer. But Luther's uncompromising stand soon made Erasmus wary of closer association with the reform movement. Although himself suspect in the eyes of conservative Catholics, Erasmus hated violent controversy and was more moderate than Luther and more willing to compromise and retain traditional Church ritual. The two also differed in their concept of man. Influenced by St. Paul and St. Augustine, Luther based man's salvation firmly on the grace of God. Erasmus, on the other hand, nurtured on the classics, believed that man was by nature good. Luther did not reject human reason; on the contrary, he considered it God's greatest gift to man in matters of this world. But he insisted on keeping reason out of theology, where it could easily degenerate into arrogance, blinding man from the word of God. Erasmus, however, believed that human reason was useful even in matters of religion. The gulf between the two men widened into mutual disenchantment.

Another repercussion of Luther's success was that his insistence on the primacy of Scripture opened the gates to religious splintering. Once a believer had rejected the authority of pope and of Church council and was convinced that salvation could be attained outside of the Roman Catholic Church, nothing—except persecution by civil authorities—could prevent him from establishing a new sect with the same validity as had been assumed by Luther. Although most Protestants were to join a relatively small number of religious groups, the resulting multiplication of religious sects, coming on the heels of the national splintering, spelled the final collapse of the dream of universality.

It has been argued that the triumph of the Reformation brought about greater freedom. Of course, Protestantism helped in some countries to undermine political tyranny; and the fight between the churches sometimes provided a freedom of choice, occasioned more intellectual inquiry, and in the very long run even led to religious tolerance. From the beginning, however, Protestantism harbored many conservative elements. Veneration of the

Scripture easily led to literalism, particularly when it was a question of denying the validity of a rival interpretation.

The spread of the Reformation

There are many explanations why Luther succeeded where John Hus had failed: the new climate of the Renaissance, Christian humanism, the improvement of printing, and the political conditions in the Holy Roman Empire all favored the spread of Lutheranism. Perhaps the most significant difference was that the Hussite movement had become embroiled in social upheaval, whereas Luther retained the respect of the propertied classes by dissociating himself from all radical elements. For as Protestantism spread, it usually followed a similar course. Where it became associated with the ruling circles and was actively supported by the government, it triumphed rapidly, as in Scandinavia and Switzerland. Where it entered the country tinged with social demands or connected with minority groups—as in the Low Countries or in Poland-Lithuania—the Protestants faced long struggles before either succeeding or being suppressed.

The initial spread of Protestantism was phenomenal. Within three decades after Luther had published his Ninety-Five Theses, Scandinavia, England, parts of France, of Poland-Lithuania, and of the Holy Roman Empire, including portions of Switzerland and the Low Countries, had turned Protestant.

Lutheranism in Scandinavia

Of the three Scandinavian kingdoms which had been formed in the tenth century, Denmark had generally remained the strongest and most expansionistic, although Norway had acquired overseas interests in Iceland and Greenland. During the thirteenth and fourteenth centuries, when the Hanseatic League practically dominated Denmark for several generations, German commercial and cultural influence had become paramount in Scandinavia. This German penetration later facilitated the spread of Lutheranism, although by the fifteenth century the Hanseatic League had lost its trade monopoly.

In 1387, the regent of Denmark (Margaret) had been elected as queen of Norway and of Sweden, thus uniting the three kingdoms under a single ruler. This Union of Kalmar, which lasted over a century, was dominated by Denmark, although each state retained its own local government. As trade and prosperity increased, a self-conscious bourgeoisie emerged which tended to ally itself with the king against Church and nobility. Such conditions made the country ripe for Lutheranism.

In 1521, Sweden rebelled against Danish overlordship and re-established a separate kingdom under Gustavus Vasa (1523–1560), who founded the

Vasa dynasty which ruled Sweden for two centuries and under which Sweden became one of the major European powers. Gustavus soon recognized the advantages of introducing Lutheranism into Sweden. Between 1527 and 1529, he confiscated the property of the Catholic Church, insisted on Lutheran forms of worship, and set up a state church. Five years later, the king of Denmark, who still controlled Norway, similarly brought the Reformation to his two states by sequestering the lands, buildings, and wealth of the Roman Catholic Church and establishing a state religion.

The introduction of Lutheranism into the three northern kingdoms proceeded very smoothly. It pleased the middle class and greatly strengthened the position of the monarch by giving him access to the wealth of the Church and eliminating the ecclesiastical hierarchy which had opposed the crown by siding with the great nobles. Lutheranism thus became an important ingredient in the establishment of greater monarchical centralism in Scandinavia.

Zwingli and the Swiss cantons

The Swiss Confederacy continued to grow during the fifteenth century through wars and voluntary association. By Luther's day it included thirteen cantons and additional allies. In the course of wars against the Holy Roman Empire, Burgundy, and Milan, the Swiss had developed one of the best mercenary armies in Europe, and their soldiers had become the favorite hired troops in France and Italy. Despite occasional civil war within the confederacy, which retained a loose political framework, the Swiss cities, mostly situated in the northern plain between the Alps and the Rhine, had become highly prosperous. Proud of their independence, which Emperor Maximilian was forced to reconfirm after his defeat in 1499, they became intensely nationalistic and resented all interference from the outside, especially from papal Rome.

In 1519, Ulrich Zwingli (1484–1531) began to preach the Reformation in Zurich. In most essentials his views paralleled those of Luther, but he rejected the latter's teaching on the real presence of Christ in the Eucharist, asserting instead that Holy Communion was meant to be merely a symbolic, memorial service. Friends of the two reformers finally arranged a colloquy at Marburg (1529) in hope that a compromise could be found in their views. But no understanding was possible. Zwingli's and Luther's reformed churches developed into two separate sects, their differences further accentuated by political developments. Luther's state church, controlled by the sovereign, could find no counterpart in the more democratically organized Swiss Cantons, where either the congregation itself or elected city magistrates supervised the church.

By 1529, the northern cantons—the wealthy cities of Zurich, Basel, and Bern—had become Protestant, while the rural cantons remained in the Catholic fold. This split in the confederacy led to war (1529–1531), in the course of which Zwingli himself was killed. For centuries thereafter, despite the further growth of the Swiss Confederacy and a marked transformation of its people, certain cantons remained Catholic and others Protestant, and the two groups continued to distrust each other. The last in a series of many wars over this issue, fought by a majority of the cantons to prevent the secession of the seven Catholic cantons, occurred as late as 1847.

Calvinism

In 1535, Geneva, too, became Protestant (under the guidance of William Farel). A year later, the twenty-seven year old Frenchman John Calvin (1509–1564), who had studied law before turning his attention to theological reforms and who had just published in Basel *The Institutes of the Christian Religion,* settled in Geneva to help consolidate the new Protestant institutions. Alienated by his firm doctrines, the populace drove him out of the city in 1538. Three years later he returned and gradually converted Geneva into the citadel of Calvinism. Although never holding a political office, he eventually acquired unchallenged prestige and dominated Geneva as the seeming interpreter of God's sovereign will.

In his dedication of *The Institutes* to King Francis I, Calvin stated that "where the glory of God is not made the end of government, it is not a legitimate sovereignty, but an usurpation." In fact, distinctions between secular and ecclesiastic jurisdictions in Geneva became blurred; a consistory of clergymen and city elders supervised the public and private morality of the citizens; and Calvin supported disciplinary measures of the church with secular power. Yet, his system was neither the theocracy nor the intolerant tyranny as it has often been presented, and Calvin would actually have preferred a separation of church and state.

Immensely sure of his religious convictions, which he held on the unchallengeable basis of faith, John Calvin wrote: "If our principles be examined by this rule of faith, the victory is ours." Although believing all men to be tainted by original sin, he asserted that God had predestined some to eternal salvation. In the course of long theological debates in which Calvin defended his concept of God's omnipotence, his views on predestination became more rigid, assuming not only the election of some, but also the consignment of others to eternal damnation. Such complete predestination, which to Calvin revealed the power of God in contrast to the baseness of man, inspired his followers to hard work in the hope that those who were allowed to till the Lord's garden might be His elect.

Differences between Lutheranism and Calvinism were considerable, making collaboration between the two impossible and provoking almost a century of mutual antagonism. Although the faith of both reformers was Christocentric and both acknowledged a just but merciful God, many Calvinists came to look upon God as the stern Jehovah of the Old Testament, whereas Lutherans viewed God more as the loving father of the New Testament. Similarly, Calvinism became more insistent on close obedience to the laws, as for instance in observance of the sabbath. Calvin was unbending in his opposition to immorality and in his insistence on discipline. This trait led some followers to advocate puritanical austerity and to suspect all amusements of being immoral or heretical and seek to punish men accordingly. Luther, on the other hand, a family man with wife and children, appeared somewhat less strict in his condemnation of minor lapses from the straight path.

The organizational aspects of the two churches also differed widely. Luther's state church came to be organized hierarchically from the top, and retained much Catholic ritual, including episcopal vestments, elaborate church music, and highly decorated church buildings. In Calvinism, the congregation was theoretically supreme—even though in Geneva a group of ministers assumed all power—and church services were made as plain and ascetic as possible. Strict Calvinism removed itself as far as it could from the fold of the Catholic Church.

From his Genevan stronghold, Calvin directed the dissemination of his faith. He did not succeed in converting other Swiss cantons, which remained either Catholic or Zwinglian. But in other areas he was eminently successful. Calvinist congregations arose all over France and the Low Countries, and after the mid-century the new faith also penetrated into Scotland, England, southwestern Germany, and Brandenburg.

Tudor England to 1553

With Henry VIII (1509–1547), England was to enter both the Renaissance and the Reformation. A strong Renaissance prince, Henry was, according to a Venetian ambassador, "much handsomer than any other sovereign in Christendom," with "a beard which glowed like gold . . . a good musician . . . a superb horseman . . . a fine jouster . . . very religious." Henry was well educated, "not unskilled in letters," as Erasmus put it. He spoke French, Spanish, and Latin, and was keenly interested in tennis, hunting, the arts, and women. He ruled England with a firm hand, though frequently acting in a capricious and tyrannical manner. But by legislating through Parliament and giving its members the illusion of sharing the royal power, he remained popular with the English middle classes.

Under the direction of Thomas Wolsey (1475?–1530), lord chancellor, cardinal, and Henry's favorite advisor, the English assumed an active role in Continental affairs, switching their support back and forth between Charles V and Francis I. Theoretically they always sided with the weaker power so as to prevent the stronger from dominating the Continent. Although fitfully and not always correctly applied, this policy foreshadowed England's subsequent tradition of favoring on the Continent "a balance of power" which would leave England free from binding Continental commitments.

Henry VIII disliked Lutheranism and even wrote a tract against Luther's views on the sacraments. Yet he broke with Rome and launched England on the road to Anglicanism. Although dictated by the king, the separation from Rome was not simply a personal decision by the ruler. It fitted the mood of vast sections of the English population. England had by this time become strongly nationalistic. Thomas Cranmer (1489–1556), for example, who became the first non-Roman Catholic archbishop of Canterbury, stated his conviction that God in heaven was surely an Englishman. The English middle class complained about continued payment of taxes to Rome. For a long time suspicious of the papacy, the English became particularly wary of the Medici Pope Clement VII, who appeared a helpless pawn during the French-Hapsburg struggle for control of Italy, and finally became almost completely dependent on Emperor Charles V.

The king himself had various reasons for his antipapal stand. He was disappointed that Wolsey had not been chosen as pope. He also desired to effect at least a partial expropriation of ecclesiastical property, a practice then becoming common on the Continent. Such a step had been favored by many Englishmen ever since the days of Wyclif.

Finally there was the question of annulling Henry's marriage to Catherine of Aragon (1485–1536), so that he could marry one of the queen's ladies-in-waiting, Anne Boleyn (1507–1536). Only a daughter, Mary, survived from his long union with Catherine, and for the sake of continuing the Tudor dynasty Henry deemed it essential to have a legitimate son. Moreover, as he pointed out, according to the Book of Leviticus, his marriage was "an unclean thing," since Catherine was his brother's widow. In 1527, therefore, the king requested Pope Clement VII to annul the marriage. The latter, however, hesitated in his decision, being afraid to antagonize Catherine's nephew, the Emperor Charles V.

Impatient with the delay, Henry dismissed Cardinal Wolsey in 1529 for having failed to obtain papal approval for the annulment. With the aid of his new favorite, Thomas Cranmer, who was personally inclined toward Lutheranism, the king then proceeded to act on his own. He summoned the so-called Reformation Parliament, which was to sit for seven years and render legal sanction to the king's actions. By working through Parliament, Henry skillfully turned a personal matter into a national affair.

To put pressure on the pope and the English clergy, Henry obtained from Parliament a number of acts curtailing papal prerogatives in England, exacting grants of money from the English church, and threatening to stop the payment of annates to Rome. Meanwhile he dispatched Cranmer to the Continent to consult the universities concerning his proposed unilateral steps. Cranmer returned in 1532, convinced that the question of an annulment was a political rather than a religious issue, since most of those who opposed the emperor seemed little worried about invalidating his aunt's marriage. Henry thereupon decided to withdraw England from all papal authority.

In 1533, Henry and Anne Boleyn were married, seven and a half months before the birth of the future Queen Elizabeth. Parliament then prohibited all appeals to the papacy, so that Henry could act without reference to Rome. As new archbishop of Canterbury, Cranmer then obtained from a convocation of English prelates the pronouncement that the king's first marriage was dissolved and his marriage to Anne Boleyn deemed valid. Instead of yielding, Pope Clement replied by excommunicating the English king.

In the following year, Parliament declared Elizabeth the legitimate heir to the throne, and passed the Act of Supremacy which named the king "Protector and only Supreme Head of the Church and Clergy of England." With these acts, all bonds to Rome were severed, although officially England remained Catholic in dogma. Despite the peaceful aspect of these changes, even here there were martyrs to their faith. After Cardinal Wolsey's dismissal, the humanist Thomas More, the author of *Utopia* (1516) who had so often criticized abuses in the Roman Catholic Church, was made lord chancellor. In 1534, however, More and several others refused to take the oath required to recognize Henry as Head of the Church and were beheaded on charges of treason.

Having acquired control over the church, Henry had Parliament approve the suppression of all monasteries in England and the sequestration of their property. The revenue thus received was used to replenish the royal coffers, to endow some schools and colleges, and to bestow favors on certain nobles, gentry, and burghers, in order to secure their loyalty to the Tudor dynasty. In matters of dogma, however, the king reacted sharply against the introduction of Lutheran ideas into his Church of England. Church services were to be uniform, and nonconformists were punished by death. By the statute of the Six Articles (1539), those who denied the validity of the dogma of transubstantiation were to be burnt as heretics; communion was to be in one kind only (with only bread given to the congregation), celibacy of the clergy enforced, and private masses as well as confession were to be retained.

In 1536, Anne Boleyn was beheaded on charges of adultery. On the following day, Henry married Jane Seymour (1509?–1537), a lady-in-waiting to his last wife. Jane bore him a son, the future Edward VI. After Henry's three further marriages resulted in no royal offspring, Parliament finally settled the succession in 1544 by making Edward the heir presumptive, to be followed by Mary and Elizabeth in case Edward were to die childless.

Since Edward VI (1547–1553) was not quite ten when his father died in 1547, a regency was set up which allowed Cranmer and others to steer the country toward Protestant dogma. Communion in both kinds (both bread and wine) and marriage of priests were authorized, and in 1549 church ritual was "de-Catholicized" by an act which among others forbade the maintenance of "images, relics, lights, holy bells, holy beads, palms, ashes, candles. . . ." At the same time, the First Book of Common Prayer emphasized some Protestant principles. In 1551, Cranmer published his Forty-two Articles which defined the essence of the new English faith and which, reduced in Elizabeth's time to thirty-nine articles, became the basis of the Anglican creed.

Edward's reign was brief and disorderly, with various regents fighting for power over the young ruler. But Tudor popularity did not dim.

The Catholic states

While the Reformation was gaining ground in central and northern Europe, it also appeared in France, but made little impression on Italy, Spain, and Portugal. France, alone among the four major Catholic states, was to suffer a prolonged period of religious turmoil.

France

France during this time was ruled by Francis I, the flamboyant Renaissance king who represented a curious mixture of Greco-Roman revival, medieval chivalry, Catholic orthodoxy, and modern statecraft. When the twenty-year-old Francis ascended the throne, French monarchical institutions had been further consolidated. Although unsuccessful in his claims to Naples and Milan in the face of general foreign opposition, his predecessor (Louis XII, 1498–1515) had been a good administrator of internal affairs. He had been frugal, had encouraged commerce and agriculture, and had left France relatively rich and internally pacified. (See Map 14.)

The ambitious Francis therefore inherited a good basis on which to begin the erection of an absolutistic regime. He confiscated the vast Bourbon estates, the last of the appanages, thus removing the most powerful remaining feudal obstacle to the extension of royal authority. Francis I then helped hasten the transformation of the nobility from quasi-sovereign lords into courtiers. Stripped of their last judicial and territorial powers, rendered "obsolete" through changes in military tactics, impoverished through inflation, and weakened through the commercial revolution that reduced the economic power of agricultural wealth, the nobles began to abandon their strongholds in the country and join the entourage of the king. His love of magnificent spectacles and an opulent life, enhanced by his penchant for lavish disbursement of funds, made Francis I well suited to turning "nobles" into "gentlemen."

With the nobility tamed, bourgeois enrolled in the civil service or were made complacent through prosperity, and the clergy rendered obedient through the Concordat of Bologna (1516) that allowed the king to appoint all bishops, the monarch was indeed supreme. Even the normally obstreperous *parlement de Paris* had to admit to Francis: "To doubt your power would be a sacrilege. We know well that you are above the law." As in the days of Byzantine despotism, the royal will, expressed in the famous motto *le roi le veut* (the king wishes it), became the arbitrary law of the land.

In foreign affairs, Francis I used his power to seek glory for himself and to try to make France the most respected state in Europe. With the Low Countries, Germany, Burgundy, and Spain in the hands of the same Hapsburg ruler, the French king saw as his primary task the need to prevent total Hapsburg encirclement of France. To be sure, the Italian wars were partly motivated by French desire to seize a portion of the rich peninsula. But equally important was Francis' determination to maintain a wedge in Italy in order to keep the Hapsburg ring from closing. For this purpose also he concluded the so-called Perpetual Peace with the Swiss cantons (1516), a tacit alliance which was not broken for almost three centuries. Moreover he concluded an anti-Hapsburg alliance with the Turks and supported the German Protestant princes against the emperor, although both steps had objectionable religious implications for a Catholic ruler.

This anti-Hapsburg policy was continued by King Henry II (1547–1559) with a significant shift in direction. Abandoning the attempt to seize Italy, Henry resumed the practice of the strong medieval French monarchs (Philip II and Philip IV) of expanding France northward and eastward at the expense of the Holy Roman Empire—a policy followed by most French rulers thereafter. Henry was successful in annexing the fortified bishoprics of Metz, Toul, and Verdun, which served as important stepping stones for further eastward expansion.

The reigns of Francis and Henry also saw the blossoming of the French Renaissance, before its vibrancy was stifled by the chaos of the wars of religion that wracked France during the second half of the sixteenth century. Both monarchs used their wealth and influence to convert the court of France into a center of Renaissance elegance. Francis I, in particular, patronized and subsidized scholars and encouraged humanistic studies of Greek, Latin, and Hebrew through creation of the Collège de France, which soon became a rival of the tradition-bound University of Paris. As Erasmus noted, "King Francis . . . invites and entices from all countries men who excel in merit or in learning." He imported samples of Italian art as well as Italian craftsmen and artists (including da Vinci, Benvenuto Cellini, and Andrea del Sarto) and established at Fontainebleau a whole colony of Italian painters and sculptors. A large building program was undertaken. Numerous castles (Amboise, Blois, Chambord, Fontainebleau, and others) were built or remodeled in styles combining French Gothic with Italian Renaissance themes. A chain of castles, such as those in the Loire valley, permitted the ruler to travel in pomp from chateau to chateau, carrying in his entourage not only royal mistresses, courtiers, and attendants, but also furniture, china, and household goods, since he could not afford to furnish all his palaces.

Relatively unspectacular in painting, the French Renaissance was strong in architecture and in humanistic studies. In belles lettres, the foundations were laid for later French classicism. Guillaume Budé (1468–1540), a friend of Erasmus', revived scholarly interest in Greek literature and laid the basis for France's National Library. A typical Renaissance representative was the satirist François Rabelais (1494?–1553), who was a monk, a physician, and an astronomer, as well as a writer. His books on the giant *Pantagruel* and his father *Gargantua* (1532) were satires disguised as adventure stories. In them he ridiculed the practices of the Church and attacked the pedantry of the traditional scholastics. He stressed the importance of education and suggested that one's appetites should be indulged to the fullest. The guiding motto that Gargantua adopted for his model abbey, "Do what thou wilt," typified a major aspect of the Renaissance's revolt against medieval restrictions.

Meanwhile, Protestantism had made its appearance in France. Lutheran ideas were imported by traveling German merchants and spread among the poor, while Calvinism appealed more to the upper classes. There were also indigenous reformers, such as Lefèvre d'Etaples (1450?–1537?), who like Luther was an ardent admirer of St. Paul. He preached a purified religion based on careful study of the Bible and translated the New Testament into French about the time Luther was working on his German version.

Francis I, who controlled the Gallican Church on the basis of the Concordat of Bologna, was at first not particularly worried about the spread of heresy. The king's sister even openly favored the new faith and some Catholic clergy, angered by the king's practice of filling ecclesiastical benefices with courtiers, joined the Protestants. But the iconoclastic zeal of a few ardent Protestants gradually caused alarm. Persecution of Protestants started in the mid-1530's with various provincial *parlements* condemning unrepentant heretics to be burnt alive. Despite such sporadic persecutions, adherents of the reformed faith gained ground, particularly after the militant Calvinists, in France called Huguenots, assumed leadership of the movement.

Under Henry II, proceedings against the Huguenots were systematized and thousands of Protestants were burnt or immured alive like criminals. The new king was perhaps personally not so much stricter than his father had been. But the nature of Protestantism had changed. Lutheranism, as it had evolved in the German and Scandinavian states, represented no threat to monarchical authority. Calvinism, however, with its occasional appeal to republicanism and revolution, embodied a danger to royal absolutism. King Henry's stand against the Huguenots was therefore as political as it may have been religious in motivation. Yet, despite the severe repression, Protestant strength in France continued to grow until the country was plunged into religious and civil wars.

Italy

At the beginning of the sixteenth century, as we saw in the preceding chapter, the Renaissance in Italy reached its most elaborate stage. Yet, this artistic and intellectual flowering occurred against a background of continued turmoil in the Italian Peninsula. After the French invasion of Italy in 1494 (see p. 183), the Italian states continued to be embroiled in almost incessant wars, even more than they had been in the fifteenth century. With masterful duplicity the Italian rulers shifted partners and recast alliances for the sake of minor territorial gains or of an increase in personal power. But if they thought they fought for the benefit of their city-states, they labored under a delusion, for the Italian Peninsula had become a battlefield on which France and the Hapsburgs were engaged in a prolonged test of strength, which ended in 1559 to the advantage of Spain (Peace of Cateau-Cambrésis). France was expelled from the peninsula and all Hapsburg possessions in Italy passed under Spanish overlordship. Only Venice retained a measure of independence, while most of Italy was either directly or indirectly controlled by the new Spanish ruler, Philip II (1556–1598).

In the course of these struggles, some of the states were hopelessly buffeted about between the opposing forces. Milan, for example, was conquered—and lost—by the French three times in three decades, and in 1535 the duchy became Spanish. In Florence, the Medici rulers were expelled by the populace (1494), which had been whipped into action by the harangues of Savonarola and infuriated by their ruler's subservience to the French. Briefly restored with the help of Spain and then again expelled, the Medici were finally installed as grand dukes of Tuscany and ruled over Florence and a large surrounding area until 1737. Naples, on the other hand, which had furnished the original pretext for the French invasion of Italy, was conquered by the Spaniards in 1504 and retained by them until the eighteenth century.

Although attacked alternately not only by the Holy Roman Empire, France, and the papacy, but also by the Ottoman Turks, the Venetian Republic remained wealthy and independent. In the course of two wars with the Turks, she lost all holdings in Greece and retained only some Mediterranean islands and parts of the Dalmatian coast. Unlike Florence and Milan, however, Venice was able to avert foreign invasion and remained for some time at the forefront of Europe's anti-Turkish forces. Her continued independence may explain why she became an important center of art during the high Renaissance.

Protestantism never became a widely organized movement in Italy. Where it appeared, Church authorities and the reorganized Inquisition or Holy Office repressed it severely and effectively. With the propagation of the Counter Reformation in mid-century, Italy was soon purged of heretical doctrines (see p. 240). At the same time, the intolerant domination of Spain and the stern attitude of the post-Renaissance papacy dampened the independent and individualistic atmosphere of the city-states and brought about the gradual transition from the Renaissance to the Baroque period.

The Iberian states

During the first half of the sixteenth century, both Spain and Portugal were deeply occupied with the conquest and consolidation of vast colonial empires, although Spain was at the same time much embroiled in European affairs.

Spanish involvement in European politics was made especially complicated through the Hapsburg-Burgundian inheritance of Charles I (Charles V in the Holy Roman Empire). It is in fact hard to determine in which of his numerous possessions Charles placed his greatest interest. Born and brought up in Flanders, he probably eventually felt his primary allegiance toward Spain. Yet many Spaniards remained suspicious of their Flemish ruler who used Spanish resources for the defense of the Holy Roman Empire, while his German subjects generally viewed him as a foreigner. In his imperial abdication speech at Ghent (1556), he insisted that as emperor he had harbored "no inordinate ambition to rule many kingdoms, but merely tried to ensure the welfare of Germany, to secure the defense of Flanders, to dedicate [his] resources to the protection of Christianity against the Turk, and to work for the propagation of the Christian religion."

As ruler of Spain, he generally continued the policies of his grandfather, Ferdinand of Aragon. He devoted much time to achieving control over the Italian Peninsula, undertook further anti-Moslem crusades in North Africa, and encouraged conquests in the Americas. There was little Protestantism in Spain; only about a hundred prosecutions of Protestants took place during Charles' reign. Yet the firm policies against all possible heretics—converted Jews, converted Moslems, or suspected Protestants—were continued. In the Low Countries Charles ordered the extermination of Protestantism. But political conditions forced him into inconsistency: intolerant in Spain and the Low Countries, he had to be lenient in his German lands.

The influx of gold from the New World made Spain temporarily wealthy but failed to induce a long-term economic reorientation. The precious metals were used to meet current expenses rather than to invest in manufacturing enterprises. Much bullion was drained off to the commercial and textile centers of the Spanish Netherlands or flowed into the hands of German bankers. Unlike their Dutch and English counterparts, the Spanish middle classes on the whole did not become wealthy, independent, or self-confident as a result of the new wealth pouring into Spain from overseas.

Religious thought in Spain was often tinged with mysticism; there was at this time also much theological debate, helping to prepare Spain for the influential role she was to carry in the Counter Reformation. While the great blossoming of Spanish culture, particularly in literature and painting, began only after mid-century, a general awakening took place under Charles. Despite the intolerant climate, much interest was evinced in humanistic studies. Moreover, the tales of the *conquistadores* stimulated the composition of stories of adventure and eventually of picaresque fiction. The problems encountered by Spanish administrators overseas led to an intensified study of international law. The conquest of America also roused the interest of chroniclers and historians (as, for example, the official court historian, Fernandez de Oviedo, 1478–1557, who produced a twenty-one volume history on the West Indies).

In the Americas, the Spaniards rapidly extended their control from their initial military and commercial bases in the Caribbean over a large part of the mainland. Within half a century, their domains reached from the borders of California and from Florida south to Chile and Argentina, except for the portion of the Brazilian coast that had been claimed by Portugal. In theory, this *conquista* was undertaken under the sole auspices of the Castilian crown. In practice, many of the *conquistadores* acted like semi-independent war lords, assuming great power and frequently engaging in jurisdictional disputes with rival conquerors. Within a few decades, however, the government of Madrid achieved more or less direct control over the conquered areas, which were then divided into large vice-royalties and smaller *audiencias,* and coordinated in judicial, financial, and administrative procedures through the publication of laws and regulations applying to all colonial areas.

Considering the difficulty and novelty of the task involved in settling and administering such vast territories, the Spaniards performed miracles. Historians tend to stress their inhuman treatment of the Indians, which was probably no more severe than the customary handling of subject peoples at the time. Perhaps one should rather underscore the Spanish achievement of forging in a relatively short time a new culture, based on a compound of three groups—Indians, Negroes, and Europeans—as well as on a hierarchically organized society divided along social and ethnic lines.

At first, only paid soldier-settlers were allowed on the Caribbean islands; then, starting in 1495, Spaniards willing to serve without pay were allowed to migrate to the colonies to trade, acquire land, or mine gold. Ten per cent of their earnings or one third of the gold they found was to be surrendered to the state. Even the prospect of such lucrative enterprises did not at first entice many to undertake the hazardous task of settling in the New World. Most of those who did migrate came from Castile and only a few from Aragon. By the beginning of the sixteenth century, a special office in Seville (*Casa de Contratación*) was given supervision of commercial and financial relations with the colonies as well as of emigration. All prospective settlers had to receive permits to cross the Atlantic. Jews, Moors, gypsies, and heretics were automatically barred, and it was almost impossible for someone from non-Spanish Hapsburg possessions, such as the Low countries, to obtain such a permit. America was to remain a Castilian preserve. For the sake of morality, married migrants had to be accompanied by their wives. Subject to these and other regulations, a steady flow of Spanish settlers developed. Sometimes the government even paid the costly ocean fare, par ticularly in the case of migrants with critically needed skills.

Soon new cities were founded, with the streets usually laid out in a rectangular pattern, according to an order of the king (1501). Royal approval was officially required for the acquisition of private land. Although the king tried to discourage it, much of the land was acquired by the religious orders, such as the Franciscans, whose power in the colonies closely rivaled that of the royal governors. Besides the mining of gold, the Spaniards also encouraged agriculture and some local industries. To obtain a work force, they enslaved local Indians or imported Negroes from Africa. The Negro trade immediately became immensely profitable, both for the Spanish crown which retained the right to sell permits for the importation of black slaves (the *asiento*) and for the traders who bought the slaves on the coast of Africa and sold them in the New World, mostly in the Caribbean area. Strong, indignant voices were soon raised against the enslavement of Indians, a practice prohibited by royal edict in 1542. But no similar concern was evinced for the Negro slaves.

Although Spain prospered during his reign and gained ascendancy in Italy and the Americas, Charles did not feel satisfied with his accomplishments, for he had neither achieved religious unity in the Holy Roman Empire nor crushed the French monarchy. He gradually transferred the government of his Italian, Burgundian, and finally Spanish possessions to his son Philip II and urged the German electors to choose his brother Ferdinand as the next emperor. Then, "no longer able to attend to . . . affairs without great bodily fatigue," as he complained in his melodramatic abdication speech, the fifty-six-year-old monarch retired from all official duties to spend the remaining two years of his life in a Spanish monastery.

Portugal, during this same period, remained strong and wealthy, with Lisbon one of the major centers of world trade. Notwithstanding the colonial rivalry between Spain and Portugal, the two states adopted essentially similar internal policies, in part perhaps because the two ruling houses were so closely related. Six members of Charles' immediate family married into the Portuguese dynasty to shore up the Hapsburg hope of eventually inheriting Portugal—which they were to do in 1580. Like Spain, Portugal adopted a policy of religious intolerance, expelled the Jews and used the Inquisition to eradicate all traces of religious deviation.

Overseas, the Portuguese were primarily interested in trade, particularly in spices. Acquisition of vast territories held no appeal for them. Hence, except for Brazil, their colonial empire consisted largely of trading posts and naval stations. Although her vast commercial empire placed Portugal among the major European powers, she exerted relatively little influence in European affairs.

SUGGESTED READINGS

General Coverage

Bainton, Roland H., *The Reformation of the Sixteenth Century* (Beacon, 1956). A brief survey.

Dickens, A. G., *Reformation and Society in Sixteenth-Century Europe* (Harcourt, 1966).

Dillenberger, John, *Protestant Thought and Natural Science* (Abingdon).

Elton, G. R., *Reformation Europe: 1517–1559* (World, 1966).

Green, Robert W., *Protestantism and Capitalism, The Weber Thesis and Its Critics* (Heath, 1959).

Huizinga, Johan, *Erasmus and the Age of Reformation* (Harper).

Mosse, George L., *The Reformation* (Holt, 1965).

Spitz, Lewis W., *The Reformation—Material or Spiritual?* (Heath, 1962).

Tawney, Richard H., *Religion and the Rise of Capitalism* (New American Library). On the influence of Protestantism on social and economic developments.

Lutheranism and Germany

Bainton, Roland H., *Here I Stand: A Life of Martin Luther* (New American Library).

Boehmer, Heinrich, *Martin Luther: Road to Reformation* (World).

Brandi, Karl, *Emperor Charles V* (Humanities, 1965).

Erikson, Erik H., *Young Man Luther* (Norton, 1958). A psycho-biography.

Green, Vivian H. H., *Luther and the Reformation* (Putnam, 1964).

*Holborn, Hajo, *History of Modern Germany*, Vol. I, "The Reformation" (Knopf, 1959). The years 1495 to 1648.

*Littell, Franklin H., *The Anabaptist View of the Church* (Beacon, 1958).

Rupp, Gordon, *Luther's Progress to the Diet of Worms* (Harper, 1964).

Sessions, Kyle C., *Reformation and Authority: The Meaning of the Peasants' Revolt* (Heath, 1968).

Calvin and Zwingli

Bainton, Roland H., *Hunted Heretic: The Life and Death of Michael Servetus, 1511–1553* (Beacon, 1960).

Courvoisier, Jacques, *Zwingli: A Reformed Theologian* (John Knox, 1963).

*MacKinnon, James, *Calvin and the Reformation* (Russell, 1962).

Mosse, George L., *Calvinism: Authoritarian or Democratic?* (Holt, 1957).

England and the Reformation

Chambers, Raymond Wilson, *Thomas More* (U. of Michigan, 1958).

Elton, S. R., *Tudor Revolution in Government* (Cambridge).

*Hackett, Francis, *Henry the Eighth* (Liveright).

Hexter, Jack H., *More's Utopia: The Biography of an Idea* (Harper).

Hutchinson, Francis Ernest, *Cranmer and the English Reformation* (Macmillan, 1962).

Mattingly, Garrett, *Catherine of Aragon* (Random, 1960).

Powicke, Frederick M., *The Reformation in England* (Oxford U.P., 1961).

Thompson, Craig R., *The English Church in the Sixteenth Century* (U. of Virginia, 1958).

CHAPTER XIII

≫ऄ *Baroque and*
Counter Reformation
(1555-1610)

On the whole, the second half of the sixteenth century was an intolerant, militant age, plagued by religious struggles. It was the period of the Counter Reformation as well as of the gradual emergence of modern absolutism. The last decades of the century also saw the beginning of the Baroque, a style of art that became predominant in most Catholic lands and influential in many Protestant areas; it lasted throughout the seventeenth century, in some regions even into the eighteenth.

The Baroque

The term Baroque originally meant "contorted" or "grotesque." Strictly speaking, it refers to a style of art that characterized painting, architecture, sculpture, music, and to some extent literature. It was based in part on the classical style of the Renaissance, but was marked by realistic illusionism, an emphasis on movement, force, and tension, and an interest in the emotional and the decorative. Baroque artists liked to fuse various art forms as in the combination of architectural design with painting and sculpture in the interior of churches and palaces. Moreover, there was a strong tendency to subordinate particulars to the whole and to draw attention to a focal point. Whereas Renaissance painters had presented their subject like a tableau, Baroque painters often used dramatic spot lighting to focus the viewer's eyes on a central theme, just as Baroque churches were designed to attract the worshiper's gaze to the heavily decorated high altar.

In Renaissance times, art had often been produced for the sake of beauty or diversion. Much of Baroque art, on the other hand, seemed designed to serve a purpose: to awe the churchgoer into religious reverence, to satisfy the pride of a burgher, to retell a story from mythology, or to enhance the glory of a monarch. As during the Middle Ages, vast funds and efforts were expended on the erection and beautification of splendid churches. Their construction, however, was no longer the community effort which had produced the medieval Gothic cathedrals. Rather, the buildings were commissioned by individual prelates or princes and designed by well-known artists.

The Baroque style, which became fully developed by the first half of the seventeenth century, was highly decorative in church architecture, combining painting and architectural structure in a visually deceptive way to convey a feeling of space. Domes and ceiling windows, some painted and some real, allowed the faithful a glance into heaven or permitted a dramatic ray of light to descend into the church. The transition from walls to ceilings was often blurred by painted decorations, as if to stress the closeness of heaven to earth.

In sculpture, realism was emphasized; suffering, joy, or ecstasy were depicted in faithful detail. Giovanni Bernini (1598–1680), one of the greatest Baroque artists, polished the marble of his statues to look like human flesh. Some stone and wood statues were covered with garments made of cloth. Baroque painting, often emotional in content and cast in strongly contrasting colors, stressed movement through the use of diagonal and curved lines and emphasized depth in spatial relationships. To impress on the viewer the immediacy of the subject, religious or mythological themes were usually rendered in a contemporary setting.

During the Renaissance, there had occasionally been an uneasy compromise between classic and Christian elements. Only rarely, as in Michelangelo's frescoes in the Sistine Chapel, had there been a true fusion of Christian spirituality and classical humanism. Such a combination became characteristic of the Baroque period. Many Baroque painters and sculptors succeeded in depicting Christ's suffering, the visions of saints, or the blessedness of Mary in a physically human, at times even somewhat sensuous manner, without detracting from the spiritual significance of their subject.

Baroque religious fervor notwithstanding, much of the literature of the period was secular. During the Middle Ages, drama had almost died out, except for morality plays performed in churches or on the steps in front of cathedral portals. Revived in the Renaissance, secular drama again dealt with human foibles as it had in ancient times rather than with themes of eternal salvation. The prolific Lope de Vega (1562–1635), the author of well over a thousand plays, who sailed with the Spanish Armada in 1588, often used nationalistic topics to describe the expanding material world around him. At the same time, various literary forms, such as epics, essays, picaresque novels, and madrigals, were revived or newly created (Cervantes, Montaigne, and Spenser). Typical of the Baroque in its fusion of various art forms—music, drama, poetry, ballet, architecture, and painting—was the opera, first devised in Italy at the beginning of the seventeenth century.

The Baroque, however, was more than a style of art. Its characteristics fit the religious, political, and intellectual development of the period so well that one might speak of a baroque spirit that permeated the age. The emotionalism of Baroque art paralleled the newly awakened religious fervor which marked Catholicism as well as Protestantism during the Counter Reformation. Its preference for subordination to a central theme well suited the revived emphasis on hierarchical order. During the Baroque era, unquestioned obedience, be it to the pope, to an absolute lay ruler, or to a Calvinistic consistory, was extolled as it had been in medieval monasteries. Coercion of mind and body, repugnant to a humanist like Erasmus, was again practiced.

Even the new political forms then being elaborated for the consolidation of national states showed this fusion of Christian and secular or classical concepts, so consonant with the Baroque. Medieval kings had derived their power from feudal prerogatives and from their anointed God-given sanctity. Secular concepts of political power, among them a revived Roman *imperium,* had served as a basis for Renaissance rulers. In the Baroque combination, royal power assumed the form of absolutism bolstered by divine right. Most monarchs of the period, whether Catholic or Protestant, were guided by secular considerations and Machiavellian precepts, but acknowledged responsibility for their political actions to God alone.

Although the Baroque was widespread, there were great regional differences in chronology as well as in intensity. England was still in the Elizabethan Renaissance when Italy entered the Baroque period. In France, pure Baroque was rare, and the arts usually showed a strong trace of neo-Gothic or classical strains. Some states, including Russia, had no native Baroque— just as Russia, for that matter, had also bypassed the Renaissance and the Reformation.

Different paths to absolute monarchy

In the realm of politics, the theoretical and practical elements of absolutism were being worked out. One prominent political theorist of the time was the French lawyer Jean Bodin (1530–1596). Disenchanted by the civil and religious wars which were devastating his country, Bodin wrote extensively about the sovereign powers which kings should exercise in order to ensure peace and welfare for their state. He regarded sovereign princes as God's lieutenants on earth. Genuine sovereignty was to allow a ruler "to make peace and war, to appoint all the officers and magistrates . . . to have power of life and death, and in brief to dispose of the whole Commonweal." Such a prince had the "power to give laws to all his subjects . . . without consent of any other greater, equal, or lesser than himself." Bodin's advocacy of sovereignty helped lay the groundwork for seventeenth-century absolutism by suggesting that the ruler was not responsible to his subjects and that, in relations among sovereign princes, none was to recognize a superior power.

To establish absolutism, the monarch had to break the residual strength of the feudal aristocracy, usually with the aid of the middle class, without, however, bestowing effective power upon the latter. The jurisdiction of the estates, where they existed, also had to be reduced, particularly in such essential areas as taxation and legislation. To be truly sovereign, a ruler had to be able to enforce his will at home and abroad. For this purpose he required an efficient and reliable civil service as well as a loyal, and preferably standing army that could act as a police force at home or support the ruler's foreign policy. The maintenance of a civil service and an army, of course, required steady sufficient revenues.

In some cases, as in Russia, the drive for absolutism encountered opposition by the Church; in others, in Spain for example, ecclesiastical authorities cooperated with the ruler. In some lands, such as England, there existed a wealthy bourgeoisie; in others, such as Turkey, the middle class remained small and powerless. Then again, states like France and England possessed relative ethnic homogeneity and national cohesion, enabling the rulers to bolster their regime by appeals to patriotism; whereas in Russia and Turkey, both areas of diverse populations, the monarchs found it more effective to use repressive measures.

This search for absolutistic forms in the sixteenth and seventeenth centuries was perhaps a logical intermediary phase between the feudal monarchy of the late Middle Ages and the bourgeois monarchies of the eighteenth and nineteenth centuries. Types of absolutism that evolved differed widely, of course, from almost unmitigated despotism in the East to tempered absolutism in the West.

Despotism in eastern Europe

The tsars of the fifteenth and sixteenth centuries transformed the small duchy of Moscow into a large Russian state and established the pattern for Russian despotism. Ivan III had assumed the Byzantine title of autocrat, signifying supreme ruler. A Western observer reported of Ivan's son (Basil III), that "he holds unlimited control over the lives and property of all his subjects," and he remarked that the Russian people "openly confess that the will of the prince is the will of God." During Ivan IV's long reign, 1533–1584, despotism became ever more firmly entrenched.

The seven-times married Ivan IV, often called "Ivan the Terrible," was primarily a conqueror. After defeating the Tatars, he seized Kazan and the Volga Valley down to the Caspian Sea, thereby effectively ending Tatar power in Europe except in the Khanate of Crimea, where the Tatars lived under Turkish sovereignty. From the Crimea, the Tatars continued to conduct frequent raids into Muscovite and Polish territory, until Catherine the

Great finally seized the shores of the Black Sea in 1783. As Mongol rule disintegrated, the Russians filtered through the Ural gap into Asia and laid claim to Siberia which they gradually conquered. Just as the Atlantic powers were extending their overseas possessions, so the nascent Russian Empire was expanding beyond the Urals. Besides pushing Moscow's frontiers toward the southeast, Ivan IV also engaged in repeated wars with Poland and Sweden in the hope of gaining land in the west and toward the Baltic, but these wars proved fruitless. (See Map 24.)

Within Russia, Tsar Ivan, considered by many of his subjects to be "God's key-bearer," was determined to impose his authority. During the regency at the beginning of his reign, the great nobles, the boyars, had reacquired much power. Ivan sought to force them into service to the state through "selection," a system resembling compulsory service. He thus hoped to eradicate lingering feudal tendencies. Nobles of doubtful loyalty were "removed" from their estates and given new lands elsewhere—a device for splitting up nuclei of resistance and mixing the population. After an uprising of the boyars which Ivan crushed mercilessly, vast stretches of noble land were confiscated and turned into crown lands in which the tsar would be unquestionably supreme. At the same time, there was a gradual increase in serfdom.

Stalinesque secretiveness surrounded the tsar. Speaking of the Kremlin as "a faire Castle, the walles whereof are of bricke, and very high," an English observer noted that "no stranger may come to view it." Neither Russians nor foreigners were allowed to travel in Russia without the tsar's permission. Higher learning was discouraged, and as in the Orient, women remained secluded.

It has been said that Ivan sought to imitate the ruthlessness of the Tatars and the efficient despotism of the Turks. Actually his power never equaled that of the earlier khans. To be sure, the peoples he conquered were accustomed to Tatar despotism, and his position in Moscow was strengthened by the lack of distinction among legislative, administrative, and judicial functions, so that the tsar in fact could exercise all three. Yet, he depended on the cooperation of the landed and military classes, no matter how much he awed certain nobles into servility.

Five years after Ivan IV's death, the metropolitan of Moscow broke the last ties with Constantinople and assumed the title of Patriarch of the Russian Orthodox Church. Nationalistic Russians were pleased, for they had come to suspect the envoys of the patriarch of Constantinople of being disguised Turkish agents. On the other hand, a new problem arose. The tsars claimed not only temporal control but also the guardianship over the spiritual power of the church. The Muscovite patriarchate, for its part, hoped to safeguard its newly acquired independence. A prolonged struggle between tsar and patriarch developed, ending only in 1721 when Tsar Peter I (1689–1725) abolished the patriarchate.

During the sixteenth century, the Ottoman Empire continued its phenomenal expansion. Numerous successful wars led to extensive Turkish conquests in the Middle East and North Africa. In Europe, the Turks seized Belgrade and large parts of Hungary, including Budapest, as well as Transylvania and Moldavia. (See Map 22.) They besieged the city of Vienna (1529), and sent raiding expeditions along the coasts of Italy and as far away as India.

Centered in Constantinople, the sultanate benefited from more or less regular hereditary succession, marred only by frequent civil wars among contending brothers. The height of Turkish power was attained under Sultan Suleiman I, the Magnificent (1520–1566). Like Ivan the Terrible, Suleiman was a ruthless sovereign. Both Ivan and Suleiman in fact have been accused of personally strangling one of their sons, or at least of causing him to be put to death. Suleiman enjoyed the advantages of a well-trained professional army of Janissaries (see p. 178), of an adequate revenue, and of good advisers. The civil service, based largely on Byzantine customs and staffed to a great extent by Greeks, was reorganized and made even more efficient.

Like most sultans, Suleiman I ruled despotically but was tolerant in religious matters. He sent ships (1533) to evacuate expelled Moors from Spain and permitted Jews driven from Spain and Italy to settle in Greece, on the Aegean Islands, or in Constantinople itself. As the territory under Turkish control increased, it was no longer possible to put Turks in charge everywhere. Hence the sultans retained local rulers subject to Turkish control and employed many Christians in high administrative positions.

Toward the end of the sixteenth century, the Turkish Empire entered a period of gradual decline. At the Battle of Lepanto, 1571, one of the largest naval battles fought by grappling and boarding, the combined Spanish and Venetian fleets destroyed the Turkish navy, thereby eliminating Turkish naval domination of most of the Mediterranean. The empire ceased to expand and the Janissaries, who at first had not been allowed to marry, tended to become a corrupt hereditary caste. The sultan's harem and the eunuchs who served him assumed increasing power through political intrigues, and local districts began to gain greater autonomy. Turkish despotism and arbitrary rule continued, but by the seventeenth century it was becoming inefficient and often ineffective.

Autocracy in Spain

With Philip II's accession to the Spanish throne in 1556, the Hapsburg dynasty split into two houses: that of Spain and that of Austria. The division of territory, however, was impolitic, for in an age of religious militancy it included within Philip's share a large number of Protestants in the Low Countries. Since the Netherlands were a part of the Holy Roman Empire, they should have gone to the Austrian Hapsburgs. Such an arrangement would have made Philip's European lands religiously and linguistically more homogeneous by containing only Catholics speaking Romance languages. But when assigning his inheritance, Charles V was largely concerned with preserving the encirclement of France by keeping the Low Countries, Luxemburg, Burgundy, Milan, and Spain in the hands of the same monarch. (See Map 14.)

As a ruler, Philip II was exceedingly industrious and methodical. After 1559, he remained in Spain and never again traveled to any of his numerous possessions. Distrustful of others, he tried to direct everything personally, first from Madrid and later from the Escorial, the gigantic, austere palace he ordered constructed nearby. A devout Catholic and a powerful advocate of Spanish hegemony, Philip identified the interests of Spain with those of the Catholic Church. At times he seemed to use the power of the state to pursue religious aims, such as fighting Protestants and infidels; at others, he used the Church to gain political ends. Thus he employed the Inquisition to insure his absolute authority. Heresy, insubordination, and treason, in his eyes, were all similar crimes, and it would be hard to determine whether he hated Calvinism more for its unorthodox dogmas or for its politically subversive views. Bolstered by the Church, Philip repressed local privileges in Aragon and Castile in order to eliminate internal opposition and nonconformity. If one overlooks his failure to heed the economic decline that was beginning to undermine Spanish power despite the inflow of wealth from the colonies, Philip must be judged an effective autocrat.

In foreign policy, Philip II was less successful, perhaps because he engaged his forces on too many fronts and refused to compromise short of total victory. Each of his four marriages had important political implications. At age sixteen (1543) he married his cousin Mary of Portugal—a highly profitable alliance through which he gained the Portuguese throne in 1580 and joined the crowns of Spain and Portugal in a personal union. Until the Portuguese broke from Spain in 1640, the Spaniards retained indirect control of the Portuguese colonial empire and thus were for a few decades the only large colonial power in the world.

Philip's second marriage (1554) to another cousin, Mary Tudor (1553–1558), who was eleven years his senior and had just become queen of England, raised politically explosive issues. Although he did not become king of England, he exerted considerable influence on his wife and reinforced her determination to restore Catholicism in England. But the English distrusted Philip, particularly after he became king of Spain in 1556, for they feared—with considerable justification—that he might subordinate English interests to those of Spain. After Mary's early death (1558) and the accession of Elizabeth I, who turned England back onto the Protestant path, Philip retained a dogged determination to attain influence over England or at least to smother its heretical beliefs. His resolve to subdue England was not motivated solely by religious considerations. He also sought to end the ever increasing piratical raids of English privateers on Spain's colonial shipping and, after rebellion broke out in the Netherlands, he hoped to frustrate English aid to the rebels.

Unsuccessful in his quest for the hand of Queen Elizabeth, Philip next hoped to derive advantage from the eventual succession of the Catholic queen of Scotland, Mary Stuart (born 1542), who, as the great-granddaughter of Henry VII, was the heir to the English throne. After Mary Stuart's execution in 1587 (see p. 238), he had to abandon this expectation and decided to use force to tame the English, who were then aiding the Dutch in their rebellion against Spain. While the so-called Invincible Armada was being readied for an invasion of England, Sir Francis Drake (1545?–1596) sailed into the Bay of Cadiz and destroyed a part of the Spanish fleet in a surprise raid similar to the Japanese attack on Pearl Harbor in 1941. In the following year (1588), the Armada sailed for England, but several storms and the skillful maneuvers of the English fleet routed it and dampened the pride of the master of the Escorial. Despite this setback, the war with England continued until 1604.

Philip's third marriage (1560) to the fifteen-year-old fiancée (Elizabeth of Valois) of his fifteen-year-old son (Don Carlos) was to have cemented friendly relations between France and Spain after the long period of Hapsburg-Valois wars. But Philip frequently interfered in French affairs during the French religious wars (1562-1598), furnishing aid to the Catholic Guise family. His aim was to keep France Catholic but weak. Despite his French wife's premature death in 1568, Philip used this marriage connection to claim the French throne in 1589, after the extinction of the house of Valois. He tried to enforce his claim by invading France and launching a long war against the new king of France, Henry IV (1589-1610). At the time of his death in 1598, it had become evident that Philip had failed in his French policy. He had neither gained the throne of France nor prevented the ex-Protestant Henry IV from ascending it. In the peace treaty (Peace of Vervins, 1598), he was obliged to return all conquests of French territory. The intolerant Philip must have been particularly vexed when Henry IV promulgated the Edict of Nantes, granting toleration to the French Protestants (see p. 244).

Finally, in 1570, King Philip took as his fourth wife his niece (Anne of Austria). This marriage was the first in a series of intermarriages between the Austrian and Spanish Hapsburgs that were designed to bolster Spanish influence at the court of Vienna.

Unsuccessful against England and France, Philip was even less fortunate in his attempt to retain the loyalty of his Dutch subjects whose revolt (see p. 248) he was unable to quell. The success of his navy against the Turks at the Battle of Lepanto (see p. 241) was spectacular, but not of long-range consequences for Spain. The temporary acquisition of Portugal united the Iberian peninsula under a single ruler, but it also enabled Spain's enemies, particularly the Dutch, to encroach upon the Portuguese colonies. Meanwhile Spain's colonial empire in the Americas and in the Philippines was further expanded and consolidated. Her naval power, however, and her overseas trade continued to be challenged by English, Dutch, and French privateers raiding the Spanish trade routes and by navigators searching for new routes to Asia. Seeking a northeast passage, the English discovered the White Sea and established direct trade with Russia; after discovering the St. Lawrence River in 1535, the French continued their search for a northwest passage and in the course established their claim to Canada. Yet, all these reverses and potential threats to Spanish hegemony did not dim Spain's reputation as Europe's greatest and wealthiest military power.

Despite the repressive atmosphere surrounding Philip's autocracy, his reign paralleled a brilliant period in Spanish art and literature. The Italian-trained painter El Greco (1541–1614), residing most of his mature life at Toledo, became one of Europe's foremost exponents of mystic expressionism. Among the writers, Lope de Vega and Miguel de Cervantes (1547–1616), the author of the satirical *Don Quixote* (1605), earned renown and influence among the great figures of Western literature.

Tudor absolutism

Absolutism in England differed considerably from autocracy in Spain. The Tudors, as we saw (see pp. 185 and 218), had to reckon with a strong parliamentary tradition and even had to heed to some extent what one might call public opinion. They were strong and sometimes capricious, but they could hardly afford to be recklessly arbitrary.

When Mary Tudor, "thin and delicate, and moderately pretty," as she was described by a contemporary, ascended the throne, she informed the crown council that, while herself a Roman Catholic, she would not "compel or constrain other men's consciences." Yet, within two years, Mary Tudor reestablished Catholicism as the official religion and again acknowledged papal supremacy over the English Church, although she did not restore the confiscated ecclesiastical lands. This return to Catholicism was partly motivated by pressure from papal authorities and from Mary's husband, Philip II of Spain. Moreover, Archbishop Thomas Cranmer and other ardent Protestants had perhaps proceeded too fast in doctrinal changes and many Englishmen welcomed a respite. But Mary stepped back farther and more rapidly than was politic. Although the papal legate proclaimed that he had come "to reconcile, and not to condemn," and that what happened in the past "shall be as things cast into the sea of forgetfulness," the Protestant leaders soon were persecuted. Several hundred were burnt at the stake, while others fled to the Continent.

Mary Tudor's half-sister, Elizabeth I, "the most English woman in England," according to one historian, ascended the throne in 1558. The new queen, whose mother had been beheaded and who herself had once been declared illegitimate by Parliament, had learned the art of survival and dissimulation during her troubled youth and was thus well prepared to face difficult tasks.

After the country had been shuttled between Protestantism and Catholicism, the so-called Elizabethan compromise was attempted. With the promulgation of the Thirty-Nine Articles in 1563 (based on Thomas Cranmer's Forty-Two Articles), the Anglican Church remained traditional in ecclesiastical organization and rites, but Protestant in its formal theology. The Articles stipulated specifically that "the bishop of Rome has no jurisdiction in this realm of England." Naturally not all Englishmen were happy with this compromise. The queen herself was fairly tolerant. Not much concerned with what people believed in private, she insisted on outward conformity for the sake of public order. Only extremists were persecuted. Some ardent Puritans, nurtured on ideas brought from Switzerland to England by returning Protestants who had fled during the Marian persecutions, objected to Anglican rites and vestments; a few Calvinists opposed the Anglican hierarchy; while the Catholics would not recognize the queen as "Supreme Governor" of the church, nor renounce their allegiance to the pope. Despite this opposition, Elizabeth's religious policy was a success.

A second problem involved the security of Elizabeth's life and with it the continuance and stability of the Tudor regime. Since she refused to marry, despite repeated entreaties by Parliament, there were no direct heirs, and Mary Stuart was the next in line to the throne. Succession by the Catholic queen of Scotland, who through her mother belonged to the Guises (see p. 242)—one of the strongest and most devoted supporters of the Counter Reformation movement—would have imperiled the religious settlement in England and opened the kingdom to Spanish influence. Numerous plots against Elizabeth were hatched by ambitious nobles, by Jesuits, or by foreign agents, some with the connivance of Philip II of Spain. Many of these plots implicated Mary Stuart, who in 1568 had fled from a rebellion in Scotland and had been placed in confinement by Queen Elizabeth (see p. 245). Mary Stuart was kept imprisoned for nineteen years, while demands mounted to have her eliminated as a possible rallying point for anti-Tudor, Catholic elements in England and abroad. For Elizabeth, it would have been easier to have her rival murdered rather than to permit the trial and public execution of a crowned head. Yet, in the end, Mary Stuart was tried and found guilty of "incitement to insurrection . . . against the life and person of her sacred Majesty," and decapitated in 1587.

Notwithstanding these internal problems, Elizabeth pursued an active foreign policy. Even though she was averse to Presbyterianism, she aided the Scottish Protestants in order to prevent the French from gaining a permanent foothold in Scotland. During the French religious wars, Elizabeth dispatched occasional aid to the French Huguenots, not for religious reasons, but because Spain was supporting the Catholic forces, because she hoped to prevent a victory of the Guise family, and because a disunited, weakened France would be advantageous to England. Similarly, she helped the Dutch in their rebellion against Philip II (see p. 248) and ultimately (1585) even dispatched an expeditionary force to weaken the Spanish hold on the Low Countries. In these foreign ventures, England was essentially successful and emerged from Elizabeth's reign as a powerful and respected nation.

England's new power depended largely on her commercial wealth and on her fleet, both of which were greatly developed in Elizabeth's reign. The royal navy, which had been established under Henry VIII, was increased and numerous heavily armed merchant ships were constructed. The queen urged explorers to sail the oceans, and encouraged buccaneers to intercept Spanish and Portuguese ships—provided the royal treasury received a part of the booty. Overseas trade, carried on by chartered bodies like the Muscovy Company, also helped furnish revenue for the government and made the English middle classes prosperous and content.

The Elizabethan age as a whole was marked by harmonious relations between the popular queen and most of her subjects. Although an absolute ruler, she followed the Tudor tradition of working *with* Parliament. Social legislation during her reign, including the Poor Laws, showed that the government had at least some concern for the lower classes and that the queen recognized that secular authorities had to assume some of the social functions previously fulfilled by the church. Not only were the lower nobility and middle class happy with their prosperity, but most Englishmen thrived in the nationalistic atmosphere surrounding the queen's court. Self-assurance and pride in England also marked some of the work of the writers of the Elizabethan Renaissance, as for instance William Shakespeare's (1564-1616) historical dramas and Edmund Spenser's (1552?-1599) call for English subjection of Ireland.

Papal supremacy and the Counter Reformation

Renaissance secularism and Protestant beliefs had both presented serious challenges to Roman Catholicism. These challenges were met in the Counter Reformation. The term Counter Reformation has become customary, especially in Protestant circles. Particularly among Catholics, the movement is also known as the Catholic Reformation or Catholic Reform. Although we will use the more conventional term, the distinction is important, for the word Counter Reformation seems to imply that the movement was primarily a reaction to the challenges of the Protestant reformers. Actually, the Counter Reformation was significantly more than that. It represented a strong religious revival within the Church, a time when sainthood and inner devotion were again stressed, when the Catholics redoubled their efforts to regain those who had strayed over to Protestantism, and when they launched concerted missionary drives to convert the peoples of America and Asia. The revitalization of old monastic orders, for example, or the formation of new ones—some fifteen new orders were created between 1524 and 1641—certainly met a spiritual need of the time and can hardly be attributed solely to "anti-Protestantism."

An important aspect of the Counter Reformation was the popes' successful endeavor to reassert their power within the Church and to establish firm absolutism in the government of the Papal States. Only such centralization would permit the popes to exert control over the Counter Reformation movement.

Initial guidance for the Counter Reformation came from Pope Paul III. Soon after his accession in 1534, Pope Paul authorized a commission to check on ecclesiastical abuses and to suggest needed reforms. In 1540, he approved the constitution for the newly founded Society of Jesus and two years later inaugurated the revitalized and more centralized Holy Office of the Inquisition at Rome. Finally, he convened the Council of Trent (1545), one of the most important church councils in the history of Roman Catholicism.

Much of the Catholics' success in stemming the spread of Protestantism can be ascribed to the labors of the Jesuits, for, within a few years after its formation, the Society of Jesus became the militant backbone of the Counter Reformation and a vital support for papal supremacy. It was founded by St. Ignatius of Loyola (1491–1556), who had been severely wounded in service in the Spanish armies and whom spiritual visions and great suffering had led to redirect his life toward the greater glorification of God. A man of perseverance and a compelling leader, Loyola became a stanch advocate of papal absolutism and organized his followers along military lines. According to the constitution of the Jesuits, "whoever desires to fight under the sacred banner of the Cross, and to serve only God and the Roman pontiff" might be eligible to join the Society. Actually admission was highly selective, and those accepted had to pass rigorous training and a long apprenticeship. In addition to the usual monastic vows, Jesuits in the higher ranks took a special vow of obedience to the pope. For the training of members, Loyola wrote *The Spiritual Exercises* (1548), designed to render the reader obedient by forcing him to contemplate the suffering of Christ and the glories of the resurrection.

The Society was dedicated to "perfecting souls in life and in Christian doctrine" and to the "propagation of the faith . . . especially through the teaching of the young and uninstructed in the Christian precepts." Working under the direction of their general and under direct supervision of the papacy, they became ardent missionaries among the Protestants north of the Alps. Among the heathens overseas, not only in America, but also in India, Japan, and China, they acquired considerable influence and power. In Europe, the Jesuits established schools or took over existing institutions, and soon exercised a quasi-monopoly over education in some areas. As advisers and confessors to kings and princes, they also exerted great influence in the realm of politics.

The popes had hesitated convoking a church council for several reasons: for fear that it might reawaken conciliarist ideas inimical to papal absolutism; second, in case the council voted for compromise with the Protestants, conservative Catholics would be alienated and the ecclesiastical hierarchy endangered; third, if, on the other hand, the council reaffirmed traditional dogma, the religious split would be widened; and finally, membership in the council would have to be determined in some arbitrary way that in itself would influence the outcome of its deliberations, and the Protestants refused to recognize the jurisdiction of a council unless they were fully represented.

In the end, Pope Paul III decided that a clear restatement of Catholic dogma was vital in order to end the erosion of the Church. He convened the Council of Trent, which held three long and stormy sessions between 1545 and 1563. To minimize the dangers for the papacy, he saw to it that membership consisted largely of Italian and Spanish ecclesiastics and ordered all decisions of the council to be submitted for papal approval. In the later sessions, the council's deliberations were more or less dominated by the Jesuits, and hence hardly endangered papal absolutism.

Convened officially to discuss statements of Catholic dogma, to propose necessary reforms, and to organize a crusade against the Turks—the order of the agenda itself was heatedly debated at the first session—the council in essence reaffirmed and clarified existing Catholic dogma. The seven sacraments, transubstantiation, justification by faith *and* works, the need for priests and for an ecclesiastical hierarchy, the practice of monasticism, all were reconfirmed. Indulgences—the original point of dissension—were reapproved, although moderation was suggested in granting them, "lest, by excessive facility, ecclesiastical discipline be enervated." To strengthen clerical discipline and prevent abuses, important reforms were decreed, including the establishment of Cathedral schools for the education of the priesthood and the composition of a catechism for instruction of the laity. The Index of Prohibited Books, which the pope had set up in 1559, was endorsed by the council. Only the third item on the agenda, that of a crusade, was neglected, though a few years later the papacy helped organize and finance the Spanish-Venetian naval expedition that led to the Turkish defeat at Lepanto.

The conclusions of the Council of Trent were promulgated by the pope as the *Tridentine Profession of Faith* (1564), which became the standard of Catholic dogma. Catholicism was immensely strengthened by having a clearly defined creed, whereas the Protestants, without recourse to an absolute authority such as the pope, continued to splinter on the basis of differing interpretations of the Scripture. Not all the Catholic rulers, however, accepted the decisions of the council, fearing that the increased papal powers over the church hierarchy might dim their control of the clergy in their own states.

Failure to achieve absolutism

Whereas absolutism triumphed in many countries, attempts to institute it in others failed, either temporarily or permanently. This failure stemmed from a variety of causes, differing from state to state.

France

Strong centralized rule had been established in France under Francis I and Henry II (see p. 221). Yet, within three years of Henry's accidental death in a tournament (1559), France was plunged into religious and civil chaos that prevented all royal absolutism for over thirty years and threatened to shatter the body politic.

During much of this period, the French state was nominally in the charge of Henry II's widow, Catherine de Medici (1519–1589). Married to Henry when both were only fourteen years of age, Catherine had wielded no authority at all during the lifetime of her husband, who himself had remained for twenty-three years under the influence of his mistress (Diane de Poitiers), his senior by twenty years. After a barren marriage for ten years, Catherine had borne ten children in thirteen years—three of whom became kings of France, and two respectively queens of France and of Spain. When she became regent of France, she suddenly faced the grave task of safeguarding the French monarchy and her sons' legacy. In the process, the astute and determined regent and queen-mother gained a reputation for intrigues and political assassination—yet her behavior was hardly unusual for the period.

Turmoil began in 1559, when various noble families vied for influence over Catherine's oldest son, the fifteen-year-old new king (Francis II, 1559–1560). The Guise family emerged victorious. Duke Francis of Guise (1519–1563), a successful general, victor over Emperor Charles V and over the English, controlled the French armies; his brother (Charles, cardinal of Lorraine, 1524–1574), a stanch supporter of the Counter Reformation, dominated the Inquisition in France; their niece, Mary Stuart, was married to the young king. The princes of the house of Bourbon and other great nobles resented being shunted aside by the Guises and plotted unsuccessfully to kidnap Duke Francis in 1560.

The failure of this conspiracy and the succession of the ten-year old Charles IX (1560–1574) resulted in a sharing of power between the Guises and Catherine de Medici, who continued to dominate her son even after he was officially declared of age. Meanwhile the leaders of the disappointed opposition drifted toward Protestantism, for religious or for political reasons. Despite persecution, the Huguenots had become numerous and well-organized. The rivalry between great noble families thus became enmeshed with the Huguenot-Catholic controversy.

Afraid of losing power to the Guises, Catherine sought to steer a middle course, balancing Protestant against Catholic nobles. She also hoped to find a religious compromise. Hence, the secular-minded queen presided over a theological disputation in 1561 at which Theodore Beza (1519–1608)—who was to become Calvin's successor—debated with the Guise cardinal of Lorraine. But theological accommodation between the two protagonists of their faith proved impossible. Still seeking a compromise, Catherine then issued the Edict of St. Germain, 1562, granting Huguenots the right to worship in the countryside, but not in cities. Ardent Catholics resented this concession to the Protestants, whereas Huguenots deemed the edict insufficient. Thereafter religious antagonism became entwined with political jealousies until it was impossible to separate the two.

Open warfare erupted in 1562, initiating a series of nine civil wars interspersed by truces. The wars entailed much cruelty and slaughter, and gradually led to international involvement, the Huguenots receiving aid from Germany, Geneva, Holland, and England, and the Catholics obtaining assistance from Spain, Italy, the papacy, and Savoy.

During the first eight years of the wars, most of the older leaders of both camps were either killed in battle or assassinated. Catherine de Medici for her part continued her attempts at conciliation. She induced the young king to conclude the third civil war by a treaty (St. Germain, 1570) that granted to the Huguenots four fortified cities as strongholds for their armies. Moreover, she arranged the marriage of her daughter (Marguerite of Valois) to the nineteen-year old Henry of Bourbon, the potential heir to the throne of France, who had become the leader of the Huguenots.

During this period of rapprochement, the young Charles IX fell under the influence of Admiral Gaspard de Coligny (1519–1572), the forceful head of the Huguenot armies. Ironic as it seems, Coligny had been converted to Protestantism while a prisoner of war in Spain. In the 1560's, Coligny had unsuccessfully tried to establish Huguenot colonies in South Carolina to help his coreligionists escape persecution and to improve French ability to prey on Spanish shipping. He now urged the king to rally the French behind a renewed anti-Hapsburg policy.

Disturbed by the growing power of Coligny and of the Huguenot party, the Catholic forces arranged for the murder of the admiral, an event that entailed a general massacre of Protestants throughout France (Massacre of St. Bartholomew, 1572) and a resumption of the civil wars. But after two further campaigns and the accession of Catherine's twenty-three-year-old son Henry III (1574–1589)—who had briefly been the elected king of Poland (see p. 246)—the government again made wide concessions. The Huguenots were reconfirmed in their possession of the four fortified cities and granted freedom of worship anywhere except in the city of Paris. At the same time, some of the great nobles, Protestant and Catholic alike, were awarded vast appanages. Absolute monarchy was sinking toward its nadir and an era of neo-feudalism seemed to be dawning.

With the support of Philip II, the Guises then organized the Holy

League, aimed at eradicating French Protestantism and at preventing the succession to the throne of the Huguenot Henry of Bourbon. At the same time another group emerged, the so-called *Politiques*, patriotic and moderate Catholics who were tired of the senseless slaughter and regarded the survival of the state and the resumption of order and economic stability more important than adherence to a particular faith or advancement of a particular noble family. The complex struggle among four groups—the government under King Henry III, the Huguenots under Henry of Bourbon, the Holy League under Henry of Guise (1550–1588), son of the assassinated Duke Francis, and the *Politiques*—then became hopelessly intertwined with the Spanish fight against England and the rebellious Netherlands. After the Holy League seized Paris with the help of Spanish forces, King Henry III in desperation ordered the murder of the Guise leader. In retaliation, the king himself was mortally stabbed by a monk.

The death of Henry III (1589) left the French crown to the Huguenot Henry of Bourbon, the great-nephew of King Francis I, who had to fight for several years against the Holy League and the Spaniards before gaining control of his kingdom. The Parisians and the *Politiques* soon became weary of Spanish domination, and Henry of Bourbon, for his part, took the diplomatic step of abjuring Protestantism (1593). In the following year he was crowned at Chartres as King Henry IV, and Paris thereupon opened its gates to the first king of the Bourbon dynasty. After bribing the principal members of the Holy League into submission and obtaining papal absolution for his embracement of Protestantism, Henry rallied the French around a patriotic campaign to oust the Spanish troops from French soil.

By 1598, the Spaniards were expelled and a peace treaty signed with Philip II. To ensure internal calm, Henry issued the Edict of Nantes that granted religious toleration but not equality to his former comrades-in-arms. Huguenots were allowed to reside anywhere in the realm and hold any office, but *public* worship by Protestants was strictly limited by numerous clauses in the Edict, in order to prevent open clashes with Catholics. As a guarantee of their security, the Huguenots were permitted to retain certain fortified cities, and thus continued to form an armed political party within the state.

With peace established abroad and at home, Henry IV could devote his full attention to reconstructing France and could resume the building of royal absolutism. "France and I must catch our breath," he supposedly said as he undertook the vast task before him (see p. 253).

Scotland

In Scotland, the trend toward absolutism was hampered by the presence of a strong, independence-loving nobility and by frequent minority reigns *

---

* At their accession, James I was twelve years of age, James II seven years, James III nine years, James IV fifteen years, James V one year, Mary Stuart six days old, and James VI one year.

during which the nobles gained even more power. The strong Calvinist ministry, the bitter religious cleavage, and the Scots' ready recourse to political murder and civil war were added impediments to absolutism.

For a long time, the Scots had maintained close relations with France to obtain help for their constant wars against England. For this reason, James V (1513–1542) had married into the Guise family (Mary Guise), and his daughter Mary Stuart had become the bride of the king of France (Francis II). But as Protestantism grew, the alliance with France lost its popularity.

Protestantism spread rapidly during the 1550's while Scotland was as usual under a regency (Mary of Guise). When John Knox (1505–1572), the fiery Calvinist minister, who had spent several years of exile with Calvin in Geneva, returned to Scotland in 1559, he at once began his crusade to turn Scotland into a Presbyterian stronghold. In 1560, the Scottish Parliament voted to break with the pope; bishoprics were abolished, and local churches were given self-government under the supervision of church elders who began to meet in regular synods. At the same time, Queen Elizabeth dispatched troops to help expel the French forces that had supported the Catholic regent.

When the eighteen-year-old, widowed Mary Stuart, who had been brought up at the French court, returned to Scotland in 1561 hoping to reestablish Catholicism and strong royal government, she faced the hostility of the greater part of her subjects. John Knox had just published his *First Blast of the Trumpet Against the Monstrous Regiment of Women* (1558). He now fulminated against the supposed immorality of Mary Stuart and lashed out against French frivolity. He urged his countrymen to resist rulers if they demanded something "expressly repugnant to God's commandment and plain will." Significantly, most Continental rulers were then beginning to assert that they themselves were answerable only to God, whereas Knox's theory of resistance allowed the people to determine whether a ruler's action contravened God's wishes.

Mary Stuart's brief reign as Queen of Scotland from 1561 until her forced abdication in 1567 is so replete with romance, intrigue, and murder that it has attracted the attention of many dramatists. Historians debated for a long time about the exact occurrences during these six years. Mary married her cousin (Lord Darnley) by whom she had a son, James, who later became king of England. After her husband's murder and a precipitate third marriage (with her lover Bothwell), Mary was imprisoned by rebellious nobles and compelled to abdicate in favor of her one-year-old son. Escaping from prison after a year, she rallied an army, was again defeated, and fled to England where Queen Elizabeth had her put into confinement (see p. 238).

Thereafter Scotland was ruled by a series of regents who were frequently embroiled in intrigues against one another. When at the age of fifteen James assumed personal rule in 1581, he found himself buffeted between Protestant and Catholic nobles. By trying to curb the influence of the Presbyterians, who opposed all hierarchical order, and of the Roman Catholics, who sought new ties with Spain and Rome, he hoped to re-establish greater monarchical centralization. To promote his views, he published *The True Law of Free Monarchies* (1598), a classic statement of government by divine right. His policy for increased royal control was beginning to show some success in Scotland when, in 1603, he inherited the throne of England and henceforth had to balance his Scottish and English interests.

Poland

During the sixteenth century, the kingdom of Poland, then still united with Lithuania, experienced a socio-political development contrary to that in most of Europe. While serfdom was declining in the West, it was established in Poland and enforced by new legislation. The lower nobility, fiercely independent in spirit, grew in power and came to dominate the Polish Diet. Since the middle class remained weak, no fruitful cooperation between bourgeoisie and monarchy developed.

The religious split in Poland was particularly complicated. A strong Protestant movement was countered by a tenacious group of Jesuits. Among the Orthodox some agreed to recognize Rome, most remained loyal to Constantinople, and a few looked for guidance to the patriarch of Moscow. Frequently Protestants and Orthodox banded together against the Jesuits.

Although the kings were strong enough to engage in repeated wars with Russia and Sweden as well as in several clashes with the Turks, the monarchy was losing strength. As in the Holy Roman Empire, the rulers could not command a standing army and were always dependent on the good will of the nobility for armed support. The crown was further weakened in 1572 when it became completely elective and therefore subject to bribery and foreign interference. Subsequent elections demonstrated the complications such elections could produce. In 1573 the vote fell to the French Henry of Valois, who a year later discarded the Polish crown to become king of France. In 1575, the ballots favored a Hungarian (Stephen Bathory), and in 1587 the nobles elected a Swede (Sigismund III), who for a while also served as king of Sweden.

The Holy Roman Empire

In the Holy Roman Empire, the emperors had never succeeded in establishing a strong centralized government. The Peace of Augsburg of 1555 (see p. 213) doomed whatever chances there had been to establish absolutism. It further weakened the emperor by increasing the territorial sovereignty of the princes, since control over religious matters gave Protestant as well as Catholic rulers more power over their subjects. At the same time, the territorial lords such as the dukes of Saxony, Bavaria, and Brandenburg acted like sovereign lords not subject to any emperor, and freely contracted alliances with foreign powers. As absolutism grew in the separate states, the possibility of establishing absolutism for the empire as a whole lessened.

Although the Treaty of Augsburg was called a peace, it turned out to be a long truce. It satisfied neither the Jesuits nor the militant Calvinists—the latter were not even granted legal recognition in the treaty. It is in fact surprising that the tenuous peace between Catholics and Protestants as well as between emperor and princes lasted over three generations, until 1618.

The Hapsburg emperors during this period were relatively weak. Nominally separated from Spain, the Austrian Hapsburgs still remained under the influence, if not control, of their more wealthy Spanish relatives. Many Austrian princes were educated at the Spanish court and married to Spanish infantas. As lords of Burgundy and of the Netherlands, the Spanish kings were also princes of the empire and felt justified in interfering in German affairs, even to the extent of using Spanish troops against German Protestants. And when the Austrian emperors contemplated leniency toward Protestantism, their Spanish cousins usually frustrated such intentions.

During the first decade after the Peace of Augsburg, Protestantism continued to grow, even in Austria and Hungary. In some regions, Catholicism was simply diluted with Lutheran ideas, as when communion of both kinds was authorized or priests were allowed to marry. Kept busy by repeated Turkish onslaughts, the emperors seemed relatively unconcerned with the religious problem. However, under strong pressure from Philip II of Spain, they became more militantly anti-Protestant in the 1570's. Concessions to Lutherans were rescinded where possible, and in some areas Catholicism was re-established by force of arms. The spread of the Counter Reformation was facilitated by disunity among the Protestants, caused particularly by the enmity between Lutherans and Calvinists.

By the early seventeenth century, tension in the Holy Roman Empire reached such intensity that compromise became impossible. In preparation for outright war, the Catholics organized the Catholic League and, despite mutual suspicion between Calvinists and Lutherans, the Protestants formed the Protestant Union. The point at issue between the League and the Union was not simply the religious question but also whether the emperors could use the thrust of the Counter Reformation to gain greater power over the princes.

The emergence of new forces

So far, we have discussed the Baroque, the success and failure of absolutism, and the Counter Reformation, all developments which still had strong roots in the past. But the second half of the sixteenth century also saw the emergence of new forces—political, economic, social, and intellectual—that accelerated the approach of modern times. A gradual change in people's interests evoked a new scientific curiosity that ultimately led to the Age of

Reason (see p. 302), during which Western man began to emancipate himself from the past. The growing wealth and rising power of the middle class in Western Europe unleashed potential strength which not only was to transform the political structure of states—at first in England and eventually in all of Western society—but also led to the creation of new states, such as Holland. Finally, during this period, the development of navies helped transform European history into world history.

The United Provinces (Holland)*

The establishment of the United Provinces (Holland) was not a dynastic creation but the result of such "new" factors as bourgeois wealth and determination, Calvinistic militancy, and naval power, aided, to be sure, by aristocratic, military, and political experience.

The revolt of the seventeen provinces of the Low Countries against their Spanish overlords in the 1560's had many causes. The Netherlanders resented Spanish autocracy, which was depriving the local estates and nobility of their accustomed voice in government. They objected to remaining second-class citizens, heavily taxed to pay for Spanish enterprises, but not allowed to participate in the rich American trade. The Protestants naturally abhorred the persecutions ordered by Spain. King Philip II himself was despised by most Netherlanders as an absentee foreign ruler who seemed disinterested in their problems. Discontent was increased by Philip's refusal to compromise, by his recourse to ruthless regents, and by the behavior of the Spanish soldiers, who acted like troops of occupation. Resistance to Spain was also encouraged by German, French, and English Protestants.

In 1562, a group of nobles, contemptuously labeled "beggars" by their opponents, petitioned the Spanish regent for restoration of their rights. Soon thereafter Calvinistic mobs launched iconoclastic raids, destroying images, statues, and paintings in churches, while sailors, the so-called beggars of the sea, began to intercept Spanish shipping off the coasts of the Netherlands. To quell the disorders, King Philip dispatched a large army under the Duke of Alva (1508–1583?). In five years of merciless repression—executing hundreds of nobles and burning thousands of heretics—and defeating the rebels in open battle, Alva succeeded only in rendering the Netherlanders more determined to overthrow Spanish domination.

By this time, the revolt had spread to wide sections of the population, both Protestant and Catholic. Its direction had been assumed by William of Orange (1533–1584) who in his youth had been a favorite of Emperor Charles and who had been made governor of the northern provinces and been given command of an army at the age of twenty-two. William henceforth devoted his life and resources to the fight against Philip II.

Exasperated by the cruelty of the Spanish occupation troops, the leaders

---

* Holland was actually the name of one of the seven provinces; but being the most influential, its name was gradually applied to all the "united provinces."

of the seventeen provinces concluded a pact (Pacification of Ghent, 1576) to assist one another in expelling the Spaniards. This solidarity, however, did not last long. Starting in 1578, a new Spanish governor (Alexander Farnese) resorted to a skillful mixture of force and diplomacy in order to divide the rebels. By political concessions and an appeal to Catholic sympathies, he gained a solid foothold in the south while fighting the northern rebels. As a result, many Protestants from the southern provinces fled to the north. To unite in opposition to Spain, the seven northern provinces formed the Union of Utrecht (1579), the embryo of a new state which at first was called the United Provinces and later Holland or the Netherlands. William of Orange was then made the first stadholder general of this new state. Not much interested in religion, William hoped that all faiths would be tolerated in the United Provinces. Actually, as the war against Spain progressed, Holland became more and more Calvinistic.

In 1581, the United Provinces abjured their allegiance to Philip II, accusing him of being "not a prince, but a tyrant," and of having failed to "fulfill his duty as protector." The enraged king of Spain replied to this declaration of independence by putting a price of twenty-five gold crowns on the head of William of Orange, "dead or alive." Three years later William fell victim to an assassin. The stadholdership of Holland was then assumed by William's seventeen-year-old son (Maurice of Nassau, 1567–1625) who became an excellent general and who succeeded, in the course of continued fighting against the Spaniards, in slightly enlarging the territory held by the United Provinces.

After four decades of war, Spain finally agreed to a truce in 1609, although still refusing to grant *de jure* recognition to the new state. The ten southern provinces—usually called the Spanish Netherlands and later Belgium—remained under Spanish control and were made thoroughly safe for Catholicism. The dividing line between the United Provinces and the Spanish Netherlands was based neither on language nor on religion but followed the truce line of 1609. Although largely Protestant, the northern state included many Catholics; the French-speaking southern provinces contained many who spoke Flemish, a language related to Dutch. Whereas the Spanish Netherlands experienced some commercial stagnation under continued Spanish domination, the United Provinces throve economically and almost overnight became a political, naval, and financial world power.

The importance of navies

Medieval Europe had been land oriented. To be sure, much inland commerce had been transported on navigable rivers, and by the fourteenth century, the ships of the Hanseatic League, the Genoese, Venetians, and others were ranging along the coasts of Europe. Moreover, navies, such as those of the Byzantines, Venetians, and Arabs had been vital in determining domination of the Mediterranean. Yet, in shaping European history, ships had been relatively unimportant.

After the voyages of discovery of the fifteenth and sixteenth centuries and the emergence of great Atlantic powers—Spain, Portugal, France, Holland, and England—merchant marines and navies became important. It was not simply that more ships were being built and that the size of men-of-war and merchantmen greatly increased; the existence of large fleets, commercial as well as military, fundamentally affected the development of Europe.

Navies changed the nature of wars. Land warfare had formerly consisted of campaigns with rather specific and limited aims. In the sixteenth century, however, the conduct of wars became more diffused and complex, as wars were fought also "overseas." The English raided Spanish shipping, the Dutch extended their struggle against Spain by seizing Portuguese-Spanish colonial possessions, and the fight against the Ottoman Empire was conducted by land as well as by sea. As domination of the high seas became more important for commercial and strategic reasons, European wars began to have global repercussions. As in the days of ancient Greece, two types of powers emerged: those dominating the land with their armies and those controlling the seas with their navies. Until the advent of long-range bombers and missiles in our own day, most conflicts in the long run tended to be won by naval powers.

The importance of merchant marines in the development of Europe's economy is obvious. Less obvious are the social and political repercussions of this naval build-up. Armies were generally led by the nobility, which had a long-established monopoly on the officer corps. Navies, however, required technicians, who were more likely to come from the middle class. Moreover, individual enterprising generals could still gather a mercenary army with relatively little expenditure of funds, since most mercenaries furnished their own meager equipment. Fitting out ships, however, was costly and required support from wealthy merchants or from the coffers of the state. The growth of navies, therefore, represented another facet of the gradual shift in power from nobility to king and middle class.

Finally, the spread of Western civilization and the domination of the world by Europe depended, of course, on this spectacular development of navies and merchant fleets. After the sixteenth century, as stated before, European history turned into world history.

SUGGESTED READINGS

Counter Reformation and Baroque

Burnes, Edward McNall, *The Counter Reformation* (Van Nostrand, 1964).
*Busch, Harald, and Lohse, Bernd, *Baroque Europe: Buildings of Europe* (Macmillan, 1962).
*Daniel-Rops, Henri, *Catholic Reformation* (Dutton, 1961).
Tapié, Victor L., *The Age of Grandeur: Baroque Art and Architecture* (Praeger, 1966). On Baroque art and manners.
*Van Dyke, Paul, *Ignatius Loyola, The Founder of the Jesuits* (Kennikat, 1926).

Political Theory

Allen, John W., *History of Political Thought in the Sixteenth Century* (Barnes and Noble, 1960).
Figgis, John Neville, *The Divine Right of Kings* (Harper, 1965).
*———, *Political Thought from Gérson to Grotius, 1414–1625* (Cambridge U.P., 1960).

Spain

Davies, Trevor R., *The Golden Century of Spain, 1501–1621* (Harper, 1965).
Elliott, J. H., *Imperial Spain, 1469–1716* (New American Library, 1963).
Geyl, Pieter, *The Revolt of the Netherlands, 1555–1609* (Barnes and Noble, 1958).
Mattingly, Garrett, *The Armada* (Houghton, 1962).
Rule, John C., and TePaske, John J., eds., *The Character of Philip II, The Problem of Moral Judgment in History* (Heath, 1963).

England and Scotland

Bindoff, Stanley Thomas, *Tudor England* (Penguin, 1950).
Bryne, M. St. Clare, *Elizabethan Life in Town and Country* (Barnes and Noble, 1961).
Knappen, Marshall M., *Tudor Puritanism, A Chapter in the History of Idealism* (U. of Chicago, 1939).
McCollum, John I., Jr., ed., *The Age of Elizabeth* (Houghton Mifflin, 1960). Documents on social and literary history.
*MacNalty, Arthur S., *Mary, Queen of Scots* (Ungar, 1961).
Neale, John E., *Elizabeth I and Her Parliaments, 1559–1581* (Norton, 1966).
———, *Queen Elizabeth I* (Doubleday, 1957).
*Percy, Eustace, *John Knox* (John Knox, 1965).
Prescott, Hilda F. M., *Mary Tudor* (Macmillan, 1962).
Quinn, David B., *Raleigh and the British Empire* (Macmillan, 1962).
Rowse, Alfred L., *England of Elizabeth* (Macmillan, 1953).
Williamson, James A., *Sir Francis Drake* (Macmillan, 1962).

Other States

*Kurbsky, A. M., *History of Ivan IV* (Cambridge U.P., 1965).
*Merriman, Roger B., *Suleiman the Magnificent 1520–1566* (Cooper, 1966).
Neale, John E., *The Age of Catherine de Medici* (Harper, 1957).
*Thompson, James Westfall, *The Wars of Religion in France, 1559–1576: The Huguenots, Catherine de Medici, Philip II* (Ungar).

CHAPTER XIV

❧❧ *Toward Absolutism*
(1610-1648)

The seventeenth century is often called the age of absolutism; yet, diverse political developments marked the period. England, for instance, rejected absolutism which had been successful under the Tudors and was plunged into civil and religious strife for much of the century. France took the opposite path. After the long civil wars, the French rulers gradually reasserted royal power until France emerged as a model of absolutism by the second half of the century. For much of Europe, in effect, the first half of the century was marked by wars and disorders, in the course of which many states declined in power.

Yet, it should be stressed that there was no necessary correlation between political trends on the one hand, and the economic prosperity or artistic development of a state on the other. England, for example, thrived economically despite internal disorder; Spain flourished culturally, especially in painting, although her power was on the wane; Holland became powerful and prospered both materially and artistically without experiencing absolutism; the Holy Roman Empire, on the other hand, became a cultural as well as an economic wasteland in the course of the Thirty Years' War.

Success of royal consolidation

During this period, royal authority was greatly strengthened in France, Sweden, and Denmark. This was done at the expense of the power of the Estates General and the *parlements* in France. In the Scandinavian monarchies, absolutism was started initially with the cooperation of the estates, although ultimately here, too, the latter lost their power. In all three monarchies, royal consolidation seemed to entail a more active and aggressive foreign policy.

France

After arranging peace and granting toleration to the Huguenots in 1598 (see p. 244), King Henry IV became one of France's most popular rulers, known affectionately as "father of the fatherland." Much of the necessary work of reconstruction was supervised by his friend, the Duke of Sully (1560–1641), a Huguenot who from the age of eleven had served Henry. Officially in charge of finances, public works, and defense, Sully directed most of the nation's economy. He sought to increase agricultural production by encouraging peasants to plant more crops, ordering soldiers to cease pillaging farms, and admonishing nobles not to take their hunting parties across plowed fields. Together with the king, he urged the nobles, albeit with little success, to leave the court and return to the country to tend to their estates.

Henry and Sully also fostered industry—primarily the production of luxury goods such as tapestries, silk, and velvet—and hoped to improve trade by building roads and canals and by encouraging overseas expansion. Quebec was founded in 1608 (by Samuel de Champlain, 1567?–1635). Above all, Sully sought to make the state solvent. By lowering some taxes but tightening the system of collection and reducing expenditures, he achieved a surplus for the royal treasury. But his introduction of a new tax, later called *paulette,* created problems. Intended as an emergency levy, the *paulette* became a permanent annual tax, payment of which gave certain judicial and financial officials the right to transmit their offices to their children. By guaranteeing the inheritable nature of these offices, the *paulette* undermined the king's control over appointments and laid the basis for a new nobility. These nobles of the robe, as they came to be called, soon vied for prestige with the traditional nobles of the sword and constituted a potential new obstacle to royal absolutism.

By 1609, Henry IV deemed France sufficiently recuperated to allow him to resume a more active foreign policy. He made preparations to intervene in behalf of several German Protestant princes in their struggle against the emperor and Spain. Two days before leaving Paris to take charge of his army and the march into the empire (1610), he was stabbed to death—the second consecutive French ruler to be assassinated.

Henry's eldest son, Louis XIII (1610–1643), was then not quite nine years old. Hence a regency was established, resulting in a new, prolonged period of disorders. The regency of his mother, Marie de Medici (1573–1642), and most of his personal reign, was laced with spectacular court intrigues which made this period good subject matter for later historical fiction and romantic plays (Dumas' *The Three Musketeers* and Rostand's *Cyrano de Bergerac,* for example). Even after the resourceful Cardinal Richelieu (1585–1642) became chief of the council of ministers in 1624, intrigues continued to abound, some centering on the king's wife (Anne). Many of the plots were directed against Richelieu, who counterplotted assiduously with an efficient spy system and ruthlessly repressed all machinations, not hesitating to have members of the highest nobility decapitated.

Richelieu, bishop at the age of twenty-two, had made his political debut as spokesman for the clergy at the meeting of the Estates General of 1614, where he caught the attention of Marie de Medici. The suave bishop and nobleman then became an adviser to the regent and worked for her for ten years. In 1622, he was made a cardinal, though his interests always remained more political and military than ecclesiastical. Two years later, the proud and subtle cardinal gained primary influence over the king and hence became the virtual ruler of the land until his death in 1642. Richelieu's power resulted as much from his own determination and skill as from unflinching royal support. Louis XIII himself enjoyed tending to military affairs, but in politics he ordinarily deferred to the judgment of Richelieu, whom he stanchly defended against all intriguers.

In his *Political Testament,* Richelieu stated that when assuming office, he promised Louis to do everything possible "to ruin the Huguenot party, to abase the pride of the nobles, to bring back all your subjects to their duty, and to raise your name among foreign nations to the point where it belongs." He implemented this program with considerable success.

Among the complex problems faced by Marie de Medici in 1610 and later by Richelieu was the relationship of the crown to the *parlements.* The twelve provincial *parlements* performed judicial functions, whereas the *parlement de Paris* acted also as the keeper although not initiator of royal legislation. Within hours after her husband's murder, Marie asked the *parlement de Paris* to confirm her regency, thereby inadvertently encouraging the ambitions of the parliamentary groups. Richelieu later engaged in frequent disputes with the *parlement de Paris* which sought to assume more power than that of merely registering royal decrees. It seems surprising that he waited until 1641 to prohibit remonstrances by the *parlement* and that he did not simply abolish all *parlements,* which during the next century developed into annoying thorns in the side of French absolutism.

More serious was the threat presented by ambitious nobles who bled the government by extorting bribes, intrigued with Spain, and resorted repeatedly to armed revolt. Although Richelieu razed many noble fortresses and had some rebellious lords executed, he could not completely eradicate the independent spirit of the nobles who had regained status during the religious wars and were to rebel again after the Cardinal's death.

Richelieu was more successful in his handling of the Protestants. During the regency, Protestant uprisings had resumed, some motivated by fear of resurgent Catholicism in southern France, others stirred up by ambitious nobles seeking to use Protestant troops for their own purposes. Although a three-year anti-Protestant war (1619–1622) ended with a victory for the government, the Huguenots continued to gain strength. The city of La Rochelle became the quasi-capital of a French Protestant state, with Huguenots again collecting their own taxes and raising their own troops.

Intent on eliminating all possible impediments to royal authority, Richelieu took up the anti-Huguenot struggle in 1625 and soon laid siege to La Rochelle. Wearing a helmet and armor instead of his cardinal's cap, he for a time personally directed the siege, which lasted fourteen months. Richelieu had the city surrounded with a seven-mile-long trench and had the entrance to the port blocked by a stone jetty extending some five thousand feet in order to prevent English supply ships from reaching the beleaguered enemy. After fifteen thousand had died of famine, the city surrendered, and by the following year Huguenot resistance was broken. The government then issued the Grace of Alais (1629), a peace treaty called "grace" to denote that the Huguenots were not a power with whom the king would deign to negotiate but subjects who obtained concessions through the grace of his majesty. Freedom of worship was reconfirmed, but the Huguenots had to relinquish their fortified towns, disband their armies, and dissolve their political organization. Richelieu, who was no religious fanatic, tolerated religious deviation but not the existence of any political force that might challenge the king's authority.

To render France obedient to the royal will, Richelieu resumed the centralizing work of Francis I and Henry IV. Although not much of an innovator, he was skilled at improving existing institutions. The ministers of the government were assigned greater specialization in their functions and thus gained more control in their fields, with Richelieu himself supervising all important transactions. The Estates General, always a potential menace to absolutism, were no longer convened after 1614. On the other hand, Richelieu continued the practice of selling government offices, a financial expedient ill suited to improving administrative efficiency.

Richelieu also gained better control over the provincial governors. The intendants, established by Francis I as inspectors, were now used more extensively and systematically. Endowed with wide judicial, financial, and police powers, the intendants became dreaded itinerant agents for Richelieu. Under Louis XIV (1643–1715), they were given long-term assignments to specific regions and constituted the backbone of the administrative system of the central government.

The cardinal's love of order and thirst for control also reached into social and cultural affairs. He prohibited dueling as harmful to public order. In 1635, he encouraged the founding of the Académie Française "to purify the language and fix its proper use" through development of a dictionary which, he hoped, would also "achieve and maintain the unity of the language." The Académie Française eventually completed its dictionary and for centuries remained influential in setting standards for French literature. Like the Royal Academy of Painting founded under Louis XIV, Richelieu's Académie Française helped further classicism in France (already begun with Ronsard and Malherbe in the preceding century). The classical trend with its stylistic rules and its appeal to reason suited the cardinal's political ideals, just as it was to fit the absolutistic regime of Louis XIV. Richelieu was delighted with classical French drama as it was then emerging with Pierre Corneille's (1606–1684) *Le Cid* (1636).

To make France again respected abroad, he enlarged the army from about ten thousand men in 1610 to about 142,000 infantry and 22,000 cavalry by 1640, increased armaments, devised a more regular pay system, and improved logistics. At Brest and Toulon, he developed naval bases for two sizable fleets, one for the Atlantic, the other for the Mediterranean. He also relied on diplomacy and, where needed, French gold. Reversing Marie de Medici's policy of friendship with Spain, Richelieu resumed the anti-Hapsburg stand of Francis I. So long as France herself remained internally insecure, he contented himself with supporting those who fought the Hapsburgs in the Thirty Years' War. Once he felt firmly in control of France, he threw French forces actively into the war from which the French eventually acquired important territorial acquisitions (see p. 277).

Cardinal Richelieu died in 1642, a year before the death of Louis XIII. During the subsequent decade, France once again suffered from internal disorder, including rebellion by obstreperous nobles and by the *parlements* (see p. 276). Yet Richelieu had built well. He had laid down the blueprints for the absolutistic state that enabled Louis XIV to become the glorious Sun King, powerful at home and feared throughout Europe.

Sweden and Denmark

Also growing in royal power, at home as well as abroad, were the two Scandinavian monarchies. Gustavus II Adolphus of Sweden (1611–1632), nicknamed the "Golden King" because of his blond hair, governed, like the Tudors of England, in agreement with his Senate—a small group of dignitaries and ministers—and with the concurrence of the Diet (Estates). Gradually the well-educated, intelligent, and forceful Gustavus Adolphus and his chief minister after 1612, Axel Oxenstierna (1583–1654), acted more independently of all controls. After the King's death, Chancellor Oxenstierna continued to govern Sweden with a firm hand as guardian for the young queen (Christina, 1632–1654), even after she had become ruler in her own right. Despite disorders during the queen's reign and despite the scandals attendant on her abdication and her departure with an Italian nobleman, royal absolutism continued to grow, and by the 1680's (under Charles XI) the Senate and Diet had lost most of their power.

To bolster royal power and to gain for Sweden dominance over the Baltic littoral, Gustavus Adolphus made significant changes in the army.

Instead of employing a motley group of mercenaries and volunteers, he tried to recruit only Swedes, in part through forced service. Through strict discipline and thorough training, the king, himself a good general, fashioned a formidable army. He increased its mobility through better tactics in the field and through such technical innovations as the construction of lighter cannons and the preassemblage of cartridges—giving his soldiers a fourfold advantage in fire power over those who still had to mix powder and ball between each shot.

Sweden had grown during the sixteenth century by acquiring Estonia—Finland had been annexed as early as the twelfth century—and by taking over some of the Baltic trade formerly monopolized by the Hanseatic League. To further increase Swedish possessions, Gustavus Adolphus in succession fought Denmark, Russia, and Poland. As a result, Sweden obtained several areas along the southern and eastern shores of the Baltic (see map 15). He also encouraged the Swedes to seek colonies overseas, an endeavor leading to the establishment of New Sweden in Delaware—a colony which fell to the Dutch in 1655.

In 1630, Sweden entered the Thirty Years' War (see p. 265) on the side of the anti-Hapsburg forces, supposedly, as Gustavus Adolphus asserted, in order to save the Germans "from terrible tyranny and oppression" and to safeguard Protestantism. Actually he was primarily worried that the Hapsburgs might succeed in creating a strong, centralized, Catholic empire that would nullify Sweden's chance for dominating Northern Europe. When the war ended in 1648, Sweden—by then a first-rate power—received Western Pomerania, Bremen, and Verden, all three territories within the Holy Roman Empire. In the course of further wars during the rest of the seventeenth century, Sweden continued to expand, but lost almost all her gains again at the beginning of the eighteenth century. Sweden's rise to power was spectacular but short-lived, for she lacked the resources and manpower that would have enabled her on the long run to compete with the major powers. Also, with Denmark in control of the entrance to the Baltic, Sweden could not participate in world trade and colonial expansion as easily as the naval powers.

As in Sweden, the monarchy in Denmark had been strengthened through the Reformation. Hence the Danish rulers could hardly look calmly upon the progress of the Counter Reformation. Denmark was a large state, stretching south to the outskirts of Hamburg, and including Norway, Iceland, Greenland as well as the southern coast of present-day Sweden. King Christian IV (1588–1648), a strong ruler who impressed his power on the nobility and expanded the army and navy to support a more active foreign policy, repeatedly fought with Sweden over domination of the Baltic. He also found it expedient to help and encourage the German Protestants. As duke of Holstein, Christian was an important prince of the Holy Roman Empire and was quickly drawn into the Thirty Years' War. But unlike

Sweden, the Danes were defeated by the imperial forces, gained nothing from the war, and began to decline in international power. Yet internally, after a short period of disorders (1648), the absolute power of the monarch became firmly entrenched during the second half of the century.

Failure of royal consolidation

While royalty gained greater power in France, Sweden, and Denmark, similar attempts failed in England and Holland, where the Stuart and Orange dynasties—after 1641 related by marriage—would have liked to set up absolutistic regimes.

England

English history from James I (1603–1625) to the Glorious Revolution (1688) encompassed a prolonged struggle between Parliament and the Stuart dynasty. Before his accession to the English throne—he had been king of Scotland since his mother Mary Stuart's forced abdication in 1567—James had published his *The True Law of Free Monarchies*, a clear statement of his belief in divine right monarchy. James admired the absolutism that was then emerging on the Continent, and he asserted that "kings are not only God's lieutenants upon earth and sit upon God's throne, but even by God himself are called gods." Claiming absolute sovereignty for his office, he admonished Parliament not to "meddle with the main points of government." Specifically, for example, he insisted that Parliament had no right to discuss foreign policy.

Parliament, on the other hand, while not claiming sovereign rights for itself alone, wanted assurance that it shared with the king in the process of government. The House of Commons sought to guide its own deliberations rather than remain controlled by the Speaker, who acted like a royal agent. Since foreign relations normally entailed expenditures, Commons considered itself entitled to debate questions of foreign policy. The "privileges and jurisdictions of Parliament," so its members protested to the king, "are the ancient and undoubted birthrights and inheritance of the subjects of England." As proper subjects of debate they considered "the arduous and urgent affairs concerning the king, state and defense of the realm and of the Church of England. . . ."

If James I was inflexible in his views, his son, Charles I (1625–1649), proved even more intractable, so that tension between king and Parliament mounted until both sides resorted to arms and threw England into a prolonged civil war. During the reigns of the first two Stuart rulers, the confrontation between parliamentary and royal prerogatives focused on several specific issues, among them religion, foreign policy, and taxation.

As under Queen Elizabeth, there was a tendency among many Englishmen to equate Protestantism with patriotism and to look upon "papism" as subversive. With Parliament on the whole favoring Protestantism and the Stuarts being suspected of pro-Catholic leanings, an atmosphere of distrust enveloped their reigns. Actually, James I preferred Anglicanism, presumably because it ensured more power for the crown, and he tried to reintroduce the Anglican episcopal system into Scotland. But his policy to enforce religious conformity aroused opposition from many groups. The Scottish Presbyterians strongly resented episcopacy. The Catholics were heartened by the Stuarts' foreign policy, but frightened by the strict enforcement of the recusancy laws. The Puritans, for their part, called for the separation of church and state, and for the abolition of bishops; they emphasized preaching rather than ceremonial services, and insisted on strict observance of the sabbath while disregarding official saints' days. Worried that their demands would undermine the established order, James vowed to "harry them out of the land," unless they conformed. A number of harassed Puritans fled to Holland whence they later sailed for America and founded a colony at Plymouth (1620). Religious dissension grew even more under Charles I, whose marriage to a stanch Catholic (Henrietta Maria of France) aroused further suspicion.

Questions of foreign policy also produced irritation. The English merchant and gentry classes as well as a majority in Parliament favored an anti-Spanish and anti-French stance, for economic as well as religious reasons. The Puritans, in particular, wanted England to take a more active part on the Continent to prevent the triumph of the Counter Reformation. James I, however, wanted peace, in part because he lacked the financial resources to conduct a successful war. He concluded peace with Spain (1604) and forbade his subjects to raid the lucrative Spanish trade. England's role in the Thirty Years' War also embittered Parliament, which was more eager to support the Protestant forces in Germany than was James, although his son-in-law was the leader of the Protestant army during the first years of the war (see p. 264). And when Charles I reluctantly made war on France (1626–1630) and attempted to aid the Huguenots of La Rochelle, he was unsuccessful. The war merely required increased funds, which made him more dependent on Parliament. Finally, relations with Scotland were also clouded. The Stuarts desired a legislative union of Scotland and England, but differences in religious preference frustrated all attempts, and such plans merely antagonized Parliament and the Scottish leaders.

Regarding taxation, the Stuarts and Parliament were in fundamental disagreement. The cost of government was rising sharply at a time when the wealth of those represented in Commons was also increasing. But Parliament asserted that tradition entitled it to control over financial levies, whereas the Stuarts, perennially short of funds and unwilling to make political concessions to Parliament in return for financial grants, resorted to various devices for raising revenue without parliamentary approval. Despite objections by Parliament, James insisted on the right of the crown to raise customs rates. Charles had recourse to forced loans and had those who refused to contribute arrested, or had troops billeted in their homes. Such questionable use of military and judicial power in part led Parliament to draw up the Petition of Right (1628). The Petition asserted the right of Parliament to approve all taxes and government loans, prohibited martial law in time of peace as well as the arbitrary quartering of soldiers in private homes, and stipulated that no Englishman should be imprisoned except on a specific charge. Although Charles accepted the Petition in return for a parliamentary grant of money, he did not observe its conditions and simply ruled without convening Parliament for eleven years (1629–1640).

When the Scots rebelled in 1639 against Charles' insistence on episcopacy, he lacked funds to raise sufficient troops against them and was forced to seek parliamentary support. The Short Parliament, however, refused to vote him moneys, and the king dissolved it within three weeks. Faced with new revolts in Scotland and large-scale discontent in England, Charles finally convened what turned out to be the Long Parliament, which theoretically lasted for twenty years. The Long Parliament attempted a veritable political revolution. It stipulated that the king could not dissolve the Parliament then in session, an act of defiance similar to that taken by the Estates General of France (the Tennis Court Oath) which was to initiate the French Revolution of 1789. Parliament further insisted that future Parliaments convene at least every three years without waiting for a royal summons (Triennial Act), abolished the dreaded Court of Star Chamber and attempted to suppress episcopacy.

The first Civil War began in the wake of a rebellion in Ireland (1641). Parliament was unwilling to trust Charles with an army to suppress the rebellion and rather sought to control its own militia. Soon after it drew up the Grand Remonstrance, a list of objections to royal policy, Charles left the hostile environment of London. When, by the summer of 1642, further negotiations between king and Parliament proved fruitless, verbal acrimony gave way to military confrontation.

In the ensuing war, the supporters of the king, the so-called Cavaliers, drew their strength mainly from the North and West of England, from Catholics, Anglicans, the landed nobility, and in general the conservative, agricultural interests. The Roundheads, for their part, supporters of Parliament, represented the merchant and middle classes mostly from southern and eastern England, including the city of London, in general Presbyterians, Puritans, Independents, and some great nobles. But neither party alignments nor issues remained constant throughout the war. The Roundheads fought not only to impose parliamentary supremacy on a would-be absolute monarch, but also to abrogate the power of the entrenched Anglican Church. Yet they were hardly united themselves. Army leaders vied for power with members of Parliament; conservative Roundheads wanted continued domination of Parliament by the propertied classes, whereas some groups, such as the Levelers, wanted the composition of Parliament to be more "demo-cratic." Moderate Puritans were content to keep episcopacy, Presbyterians insisted on abolishing it, while Independents called for free churches, inde-pendent of state control. King Charles himself, while trying to divide the members of Parliament by taking advantage of their differences, was forced to change partners. Although an Anglican who thoroughly disliked Presby-terianism, he had to rely at first for support on the Scottish army. Later he enlisted the aid of Irish Catholics, and toward the end of the war, he found himself ranged on the side of English Presbyterians against the more radical Independents.

The first Civil War (1642–1646) consisted of various skirmishes and battles in the course of which Oliver Cromwell (1599–1658) emerged as a powerful general and potential political leader. His army, the "Ironsides," shaped by strict discipline and inspired by religious fervor, was so successful that it soon became the mainstay of the parliamentary forces. For three years, the war appeared to be in a deadlock, until the royalists were decisively defeated in 1645, and the vanquished Charles surrendered himself to the Scots. After a further defeat of royalist forces, the first Civil War was terminated in the following year.

During the truce that followed, the Roundheads bought the royal prisoner from the Scots in exchange for paying arrears in Scottish army sal-aries, and attempted to negotiate a settlement with the king. But hesitation on Charles' part and disagreements within the Roundhead camp made an understanding impossible. Parliament by then had become dominated by Presbyterians, who distrusted the parliamentary army that was controlled by Cromwell and the Independents. Taking advantage of this division, Charles eventually escaped (1647) and arranged for military aid from the Scots, who feared that the growing strength of the Independent army might lead to a defeat of the Presbyterians in Parliament.

Consequently, a second, even more complex, civil war erupted in 1648. Roundheads resumed their fight against Cavaliers; Scottish Presbyterians clashed with Cromwell's army; and English Independents fought against English Presbyterians. In this second Civil War, Cromwell carried the day. He defeated the Scots, purged Parliament of its Presbyterian members, and arranged for Charles to be indicted for exercising "unlimited and tyrannical power" and trying to "overthrow the rights and liberties of the people." Convicted of treason, the Stuart king was executed in 1649. Cromwell and his army, together with the unpurged parliamentarians who constituted the Rump Parliament, then proceeded to inaugurate a republican regime in England, the Commonwealth.

The United Provinces

The newly created United Provinces was a loose confederation of seven autonomous provinces, each run by provincial estates, a pensionary (prime minister), and a stadholder, formerly chosen by the king to act as governor and after independence named by the Estates. The central government of the United Provinces consisted of the Estates General (the representatives of the seven provinces meeting at The Hague) and the grand pensionary. The latter post was usually filled by the pensionary of the province of Holland, the richest and most populous of the provinces, which contributed 58 per cent of all tax payments and tended to dominate the confederation.

During the rebellion, the United Provinces had almost become a monarchy when the Dutch had offered the crown in turn to French and English princes in order to secure foreign support for their struggle against Spain. With the ascendance of the house of Orange, however, the state became instead a monarchical republic. As elected stadholder of six of the seven provinces, William of Orange's son acted as stadholder general, a prestigious office which the Orange princes eventually made hereditary. Since they were also heads of the army and navy, only the political power retained by the grand pensionary prevented them from assuming royal prerogatives.

These conditions led to a bitter struggle between the house of Orange and the grand pensionaries. The pro-monarchists, calling themselves the "democratic" party, found support among the peasants of the five agricultural provinces and the sailors of Zeeland and Holland. They demanded a tighter union of the provinces, with more centralized control in the hands of a ruling prince. They also favored continuation of the war against Spain to enable the sailors to prey on Spanish trade and to ensure continued military power for the house of Orange. Opposed to these "democrats" were the "republicans," supported mainly by the middle class of the province of Holland. Led by the grand pensionary, this group wanted to preserve the existing loose federation and favored peace, which would be better for trade and less costly in taxes.

The struggle between "democrats" and "republicans" first erupted during the truce with Spain (1609–1621), when the powerful Jan van Olden Barneveldt (1547–1619) was grand pensionary. Religious issues also entered into the conflict. The "republicans" sided with a liberal branch of Calvinists (Arminians), who believed in conditional predestination and asserted that God forgives repentant sinners. The "democrats," on the other hand, supported those (Gomarists) who defended Calvin's stricter view of predestination. The Orangists emerged victorious from this first clash. A national synod condemned the liberal interpretation (Arminian), and in 1619 Olden Barneveldt was executed on fabricated charges of treason.

The quarrel reopened after the termination of the Thirty Years' War (1648). While the heir to the Orange dynasty was still a minor, the post of stadholder general was abolished, and the United Provinces fell under the domination of the grand pensionary Jan de Witt (1625–1672), a skillful diplomat and governor. Then once again, war brought a reversal. In 1672, the twenty-one-year-old William III (1672–1702) was made stadholder general and entrusted with command of the armies to face the onslaught of Louis XIV, and de Witt was murdered. With the re-establishment of Orange power, the United Provinces again became a monarchical republic.

Despite internal friction, the Dutch achieved power and wealth. During the Thirty Years' War, they fought on the anti-Hapsburg side and gained land south of the Meuse and Schelde rivers from the Spanish Netherlands. Their wealth was based in part on local production of cloth, velvet, tapestries, lenses, and china, as well as on fishing, agriculture, and the growing of tulips. With a large merchant marine, protected by a sizable navy, the Dutch also captured first place in the carrying trade. Dutch traders roamed the seas from the Baltic to the East Indies, with trade contacts in Japan, Formosa, Canton, India, Africa, and the Americas. They even resorted to a naval blockade to close the rival port of Antwerp in the Spanish Netherlands. Profit from trade and shipping, and tolls collected in ports turned Amsterdam into the banking center of the seventeenth century world.

In addition, the Dutch developed a large colonial empire. Taking advantage of Spain's acquisition of Portugal and the consequent neglect of Portuguese colonial interests, the Dutch gradually seized some of Portugal's colonies. The Dutch East India Company, founded in 1602 and awarded a monopoly for trade with India, established outposts in Malaya and Indonesia, with headquarters at Batavia (modern Djakarta), and took Ceylon and the colony at the Cape of Good Hope from the Portuguese. The company's profits were so immense that dividends rose at times as high as 75 per cent. For trade with the West, the Dutch West India Company was founded in 1621 and proceeded to establish colonies in the West Indies, Guiana, and at New Amsterdam, and to seize a part of Brazil.

Independence and wealth encouraged the rich burghers to beautify their homes and patronize the arts. Dutch painting—in particular of portraits, landscapes, and genre pictures—attained the forefront of European art with such painters as Rembrandt (1606-1669), Franz Hals (1580?-1666), and Jan Vermeer (1632-1675). Despite occasional stodgy intolerance in matters of religion—the famous historian and political scientist Hugo Grotius (1583-1645), for instance, had to flee from Holland because he had been a leader of the condemned liberal Calvinists (Arminians)—the United Provinces furnished an atmosphere conducive to relatively free intellectual inquiry. Amsterdam became a publishers' haven, where books were printed which their authors could not get approved by the censors in the absolutistic kingdoms. Dutch universities, too, assumed an important role in the scientific and intellectual revolution that was beginning to permeate Europe.

An era of wars and decline

Unlike France, England, and Holland, most of Europe underwent an economic decline and political disorder during the first half of the seventeenth century. Most seriously affected was the Holy Roman Empire, which for thirty years was torn apart by a devastating war.

The Thirty Years' War

Essentially the Thirty Years' War (1618–1648) started as a struggle between the emperor and the German princes. Dissatisfied with his titular sovereignty, the emperor sought to gain more control over the empire, whereas the princes wanted to consolidate their autonomous princedoms. Another issue involved Catholic and Lutheran attempts to secure and extend their religious rights and the Calvinists' endeavor to attain recognition of their faith. Moreover, dynastic connections as well as political and religious involvement turned the struggle into a general European war involving a majority of the European states.

Lutherans and Catholics, German principalities, imperial free cities, and Hapsburg emperors had for several decades confronted one another in a precarious truce. Fighting erupted in 1618 when Bohemia, heavily Protestant and mindful of its autonomy within the Austrian realm, was placed under the rule of the Hapsburg Archduke Ferdinand, an implacable Catholic who was soon to be elected emperor as Ferdinand II (1619–1637). After rejecting allegiance to their new king—an act symbolized by throwing the Hapsburg envoys out of a palace window (the defenestration of Prague)—the Bohemians sought aid from the Protestant Union of German states and elected as new ruler the Calvinist Elector of the Palatinate (Frederick V), son-in-law of James I of England.

During the first phase of the long war, most of the Lutheran princes, distrustful of the Calvinists and intent on preserving their own freedom of action, remained on the side lines, whereas the emperor received the aid of Bavaria, the Catholic League, and Spain. Within two years, the Catholic and imperial forces crushed Bohemia and the Palatinate, and proceeded to extirpate all visible traces of Protestantism in these regions.

After the defeat of Bohemia, the armies of the emperor and of the Catholic League, superbly led by generals Wallenstein (1583–1634) and Tilly (1559–1632), continued their successful fight against the minor German princes still struggling to preserve Protestantism and princely independence. At the same time they defeated the Danish forces of Christian IV, that had entered the struggle to prevent a Catholic victory.

Upon the conclusion of this second phase of the war, Emperor Ferdinand II issued the Edict of Restitution (1629), which stipulated that all ecclesiastical territories secularized after 1552 were to be restored to the Catholic Church. Such a demand not merely antagonized those who had come into possession of former church lands but also alarmed other Protestant princes. In addition, the edict reiterated that only Lutherans would be allowed to practice their religion, notwithstanding the considerable growth of Calvinism.

The third phase of the war opened with the landing of Swedish forces on the Continent (1630). Gustavus Adolphus soon forced the electors of Brandenburg and of Saxony out of their lethargic neutrality. Like many Americans during the cold war after 1945, the Swedish king regarded neutrality as immoral. "God is struggling with the devil," he wrote to his brother-in-law, the elector of Brandenburg. "If the Elector wants to side with God, let him join me; if with the devil, he will have to fight me; no third course will be permitted." Gustavus Adolphus' well-trained forces scored several victories during the next two years and even occupied Bavaria, before the Swedish king was killed in battle (1632). Under the guidance of Chancellor Oxenstierna, Swedish forces remained actively in the field, but greater importance was again assumed by predatory mercenary generals who, like the *condottieri* of the Renaissance, fought largely for personal gain. Two years later, the imperials for their part lost their foremost general with the assassination of Wallenstein, who had grown too powerful to suit the emperor.

By 1635, imperial success seemed again imminent, when Ferdinand II concluded peace with Saxony. To gain the support of the Lutheran princes for driving the Swedes out of Germany, he suspended execution of the Edict of Restitution. But he outlawed alliances among the princes of the empire and ordered the disbanding of all private armies. If successful in this program, the emperor would have triumphed politically over the states of the empire, although the religious issue would have remained unsolved.

At this point Richelieu opened the fourth and last phase of the war by initiating hostilities against Spain and dispatching French armies to help Sweden and those German princes still fighting the emperor. In the course of numerous battles, fought mainly between Swedish-French and Bavarian-imperial armies, the new emperor (Ferdinand III, 1637-1657) lost the strong imperial position gained in the first three phases of the war and gradually abandoned the hope of turning the empire into a centralized Hapsburg state. Peace discussions began in 1644, and fighting gradually ceased after conclusion of the Peace of Westphalia in 1648.

Although the battles against the emperor and the Catholic League took place primarily in Germany, Bohemia, Hungary, and Austria, fighting associated with the Thirty Years' War occurred in many areas of Europe. The United Provinces fought Spain at sea and in the Spanish Netherlands. Swiss, Spaniards, Austrians, and French battled over the vital Valtellina Pass leading from Spanish Milan into Austria. French and Spanish troops were engaged in the Spanish Netherlands, Alsace, Burgundy, and along the Pyrenees until the Franco-Spanish war ended in 1659 (see p. 277). Finally, Denmark fought Sweden (1643-1645), the former supported by the emperor, the latter by France.

The Peace of Westphalia not only ended the Thirty Years' War but also terminated the period of the Counter Reformation. Actually religious strug-

gles within states did not cease altogether, but international politics henceforth were secular. The peace treaty also took all vestiges of political power
from the Holy Roman Empire and sealed the splintering of Germany until
Bismarck unified the German states in the nineteenth century.

The religious clauses of the Treaties of Westphalia embodied a compromise favorable to Protestantism and revealed a slight trend toward greater
toleration. Calvinism was awarded the same legal status as Catholicism and
Lutheranism, but no other faiths were given such recognition. Church
lands secularized prior to 1624 could remain the possession of their new
owners. The political settlement represented a victory for the German territorial lords, who were given complete control over their lands, secure from
interference by the emperor. *De facto* sovereignty was to allow the territories
and free cities to raise their own armies, conduct their own foreign policy,
and conclude alliances with other princes or foreign powers, provided such
pacts were not directed against the emperor himself. Among others, Sweden,
France, Bavaria, Saxony, and Brandenburg-Prussia obtained territorial accre-
tions. In addition, the *de jure* sovereignty of Holland and of Switzerland
was internationally recognized.

Central Europe emerged considerably changed from the long struggle.
Ravaged by armies living off the land and by vagabonds pillaging villages,
Germany was weakened economically, culturally, and politically. The
mouths of its main rivers were in the hands of Holland, Sweden, and
Denmark, so that the Germans were cut off from the lucrative sea trade.
With France and Sweden acting as the official guarantors of the status quo
in Germany, and both states occupying seats in the German Diet, foreign
influence, political as well as cultural, became preponderant in German
affairs. Austria, on the other hand, still in control of Bohemia and parts of
Hungary, emerged strengthened from the war. Bohemian Protestantism and
Czech nationalism had been crushed, the latter to emerge once again in the
nineteenth century. More or less deprived of influence over the Holy Roman
Empire, the Hapsburgs could concentrate on making Austria a thoroughly
Catholic and more consolidated power. Finally, France gained in territory
and as a result of the war passed Spain as Europe's foremost military
power. (See Map 15.)

Disorders in Poland and Russia

During the late sixteenth century, as we saw (see p. 246), the monarchy in Poland had become elective, and, although the kingship was retained, government came to resemble an aristocratic republic, ultimately
deteriorating into legally sanctioned anarchy. Royal authority was continually sapped through the *pacta conventa,* pre-election promises candidates had
to make to the nobility in order to be elected. By 1652, the *liberum veto* had
become institutionalized: in both houses of the Diet, the upper house of
great nobles and the lower for the lesser nobility—bourgeoisie and peasantry

not being represented—unanimity was required for all legislative acts. The veto of a single member could dissolve the Diet and annul all decisions taken during the current session. Such insistence on individual prerogatives made a travesty of governmental processes.

From 1587 to 1668, relatives of the Swedish Vasa dynasty ruled over Poland and frequently involved her in Swedish affairs. Meanwhile Poland's middle class could not profit from the commercial revolution as much as its counterpart in the West, and the peasantry fared worse as serfdom increased. In the Southwest, there were frequent Cossack revolts.

Although still a large country, Poland also began to shrink through territorial losses to Sweden, Russia, and the Ottoman Empire. Late in the century, King John Sobieski (1674–1696), one of the few Poles on the Polish throne during this period, undertook a more active and successful foreign policy. Together with the Austrians, with whom he helped free Vienna from a Turkish siege in 1683, he stemmed the Turkish menace. With the election of the elector of Saxony as king of Poland in 1697, however, Poland resumed her internal and external decline and lost her remaining independence of action.

Russia also began a time of disorder and civil wars at the end of the sixteenth century. Since the dynasty of Rurik had died out, one of the powerful *boyars* (Boris Godunov, 1598–1606) was elected tsar, an act that kindled jealousy among the great nobles. The "time of troubles" that followed was filled with intrigues and bloodshed. Tsars were deposed and murdered, and pretenders fought one another with the support of Swedish and Polish armies. The disorders demonstrated how much power remained with the *boyar* families and proved that tsarist despotism was as yet more personal than institutionalized. The frequent peasant uprising, often backed by the Cossacks, also revealed the unhappiness of the peasantry which was sinking into serfdom.

A semblance of order gradually reappeared after the election of Michael Romanov (1613–1645), the founder of the dynasty that was to rule Russia until 1917. With the guidance of Michael's father, the patriarch of Moscow, external and internal peace was re-established, but attempts to bring the army, government, and commercial activity up to Western standards failed. Under the next tsar (Alexis, 1645–1676), Cossack troops helped Russia gain a part of the Ukraine from Poland, but only with Peter I (1682–1725) was tsarist power fully re-established, permitting resumption of a more aggressive foreign policy.

Decline of Spain, Portugal, and Italy

The son and grandson of King Philip II (Philip III, 1598–1621, and Philip IV, 1621–1665) differed considerably from their stern forebear. Whereas Philip II had personally supervised all phases of government, his successors devoted themselves to religion or entertainment and left governmental affairs in the hands of favorites. Hence, the great nobles regained power, and court intrigues abounded. At the same time, the church wielded great influence, and religious intolerance left its mark on internal and foreign affairs. The remaining Jews and Moriscoes were expelled, with detrimental consequences for the Spanish economy. Her inflexibly anti-Protestant stance plunged Spain into the Thirty Years' War in Germany, a struggle which sapped her resources without benefiting the Spanish state. The French monarchy, although Catholic, could ally itself with Protestants or Moslems when such a step seemed advisable; Spanish policy, however, permitted no such flexibility.

While Spain spent large sums on wars, her industry, commerce, agriculture, and even her population declined. Bullionism—the theory that wealth lay in gold and silver rather than in trade and industry—continued to predominate, and a sales tax of 10 per cent tended to discourage commerce. Nor did Spain reap worthwhile benefits from her many European possessions. Portuguese prosperity waned under Spanish rule, until its people, encouraged by France, successfully rebelled in 1640 and re-established their independence under the Braganza dynasty. Even the Spanish Netherlands, formerly among the richest regions of Europe, suffered economically, in part because of Dutch competition.

Also encouraged by France, then at war with Spain, the Catalonians revolted in 1640 to press for greater autonomy. The government of Madrid required two decades to crush this Catalan rebellion and could not obliterate the Catalan spirit of independence. Similar revolts were to occur down to recent times. Moreover Spain was worsted in the long war against France (1635–1659) and forced to make large territorial cessions (see p. 277).

Spanish art, however, particularly painting (Ribera, Velázquez, Murillo, and others) retained its brilliance, just as Flemish art flourished in the Spanish Netherlands. Yet it is perhaps symptomatic that the two greatest Flemish painters of the period, Peter Rubens (1577–1640) and Anthony van Dyck (1599–1641) spent much of their time abroad, the former in Italy and France, the latter in London.

Most of Italy remained under the direct or indirect control of Spain, and only three important states retained their independence: the papacy, Venice, and Piedmont-Savoy. Although weakened by a series of brief incumbencies, the popes further expanded the papal states and improved the efficiency of papal government. With the aid of such Baroque artists as the sculptor and architect Giovanni Bernini, they also beautified the city of Rome. Yet they could not stem the decline of their influence over secular powers abroad. The pope, for instance, strongly disapproved of the religious clauses of the Treaties of Westphalia, but his protests proved to no avail.

Despite increasing economic stagnation, Venice remained fairly powerful. With the Ottoman Empire in momentary decline and occupied in Persia, the Venetians fought a prolonged successful war against the Turks in the middle of the sixteenth century; yet in the end, they had to cede the island of Crete.

In northwestern Italy meanwhile, the dukes of Savoy and Piedmont increased their holdings, expanded their armies, and developed an effective governmental system. Possessing lands on both sides of the Alps, they gained political advantages from siding alternately with one of their two powerful neighbors, the Spaniards in Milan and the French to their west. Meanwhile their sons and daughters married into the great royal families of Europe. Thus the rulers of Savoy slowly prepared the path that ultimately led them to pre-eminence in Italy.

Although exerting less influence than in the sixteenth century, the Italians remained prominent through their achievements in Baroque art and in music—with the development of string instruments and of the opera (Monteverdi). In science, Galileo's (1564–1642) discoveries in astronomy and dynamics made him a European luminary, and his condemnation by the Inquisition became a *cause célèbre* that helped popularize Copernicus' heliocentric theory (see p. 303).

Europe overseas

The seventeenth and eighteenth centuries saw a breathing spell in overseas expansion after the expansive burst of the sixteenth century. Except in the Caribbean and in North America, there was a slowing down of European conquests, a lull which lasted until the second great wave of colonial growth in Asia and Africa during the nineteenth century. After 1600, the Dutch, English, and French supplanted the Spaniards and Portuguese as principal colonizers. Most of the work of founding settlements and developing trade nets was done by great trading companies that were chartered in the three countries. These companies were usually endowed with monopolies for a particular region or for specified commodities and empowered to exclude rival nations from interloping.

On a world-wide scale, the Dutch were unquestionably the most active traders during the first half of the seventeenth century (see p. 263). But in the West, France and England became the most dynamic colonizers. France established herself along the St. Lawrence River and in the region of the Great Lakes. Fur trade and missionary work among the Indians were at first the main occupations of the French settlers in New France. Administration of the French colonies was closely supervised from Paris, and emigration to the new settlements was not encouraged. Hence the French population of New France remained small. Only the rich French possessions in the West Indies attracted relatively more colonists.

The English meanwhile seized some Caribbean islands, including Jamaica, and began the colonization of North America. The colonies of Virginia, Massachusetts, Connecticut, Rhode Island, and Maryland were founded in the first half of the century. Despite frequent interference by London, such as the revocation of Virginia's charter by James I (1624), the settlers in these colonies enjoyed more local rights than settlers in New France. The English colonies also became more populous and more heterogeneous in religion than New France, where only Catholics were allowed to settle.

During this period, there was little further exploration of sub-Saharan Africa. The Europeans seemed content to consolidate their trading posts along the west coast of Africa, where slaves, gold, and other commodities could be obtained. In India, the English East India Company (chartered in 1600) established posts at Surat, Madras, and Bombay, and together with the Dutch, and later the French, began to supplant the Portuguese traders. Here, too, the Europeans stayed along the coast and presented no challenge to the Mogul Empire (see p. 181) in the interior. The French were to encroach on India only in the second half of the century.

In the Far East, England and France were less active than the Dutch, or even than the Spaniards and Portuguese. In Japan, for instance, English, Spanish, and Portuguese traders were expelled in 1637, while the Dutch were allowed to keep some trade contacts—although in the course of the seventeenth century Japan gradually made itself impervious to European penetration.

SUGGESTED READINGS

General Works on the Seventeenth Century

Ashley, Maurice, *England in the Seventeenth Century* (Penguin).
Clark, George N., *The Seventeenth Century* (Oxford U.P., 1961).
Friedrich, Carl Joachim, *The Age of the Baroque, 1610–1660* (Harper, 1962).
Lisk, Jill, *The Struggle for Supremacy in the Baltic—1600–1725* (Funk, 1967).
Willey, Basil, *The Seventeenth Century Background* (Doubleday, 1953).

France

Boulenger, Jacques, *The Seventeenth Century in France* (Putnam, 1963).
Nef, John U., *Industry and Government in France and England, 1540–1640* (Cornell, 1957).
Richelieu, Cardinal, tr. by Henry B. Hill, *The Political Testament of Cardinal Richelieu: The Significant Chapters and Supporting Selections* (U. of Wisconsin, 1961).
Wedgwood, Cicely V., *Richelieu and the French Monarchy* (Macmillan, 1966).

England

Akrigg, G. P. V., *Jacobean Pageant: The Court of King James I* (Atheneum, 1967).
Haller, William, *Liberty and Reformation in the Puritan Revolution* (Columbia, 1963).
Hill, Christopher, *The Century of Revolution, 1603–1714* (Norton, 1966).
———, *Puritanism and Revolution* (Schocken, 1964).

Pocock, J. G. A., *The Ancient Constitution and the Feudal Law: English Historical Thought in the Seventeenth Century* (Norton, 1967).

Stone, Lawrence, *Social Change and Revolution in England 1540–1640* (Barnes and Noble, 1966). Extracts of different historical views.

Tanner, Joseph R., *Constitutional Documents of the Reign of James I, 1603–1625* (Cambridge U.P., 1960).

———, *English Constitutional Conflicts* (Cambridge U.P., 1960).

Taylor, Philip A. M., ed., *Origins of the English Civil War: Conspiracy, Crusade, or Class Conflict?* (Heath, 1960).

*Wedgwood, Cicely V., *The King's War, 1641–1647* (Macmillan, 1959).

The United Provinces and Spain

Barbour, Violet, *Capitalism in Amsterdam in the Seventeenth Century* (U. of Michigan, 1963).

Davies, R. Trevor, *Spain in Decline* (St. Martins, 1957).

Elliott, John Huxtable, *Revolt of the Catalans: A Study in the Decline of Spain, 1598–1640* (Cambridge U.P., 1963).

*Geyl, Pieter, *The Netherlands in the Seventeenth Century,* Vol. I, "1609–1648"; Vol. II, "1648–1715" (Barnes and Noble, 1961, 1964).

Koehler, Wilhelm, ed., *Rembrandt* (Abrams, 1953).

The Thirty Years' War

Fletcher, C. R. L., *Gustavus Adolphus and the Thirty Years' War* (Putnam, 1963).

Grimmelshausen, Johann, *Simplicius Simplicissimus* (Bobbs, 1964). A fictional account of the horrors of the Thirty Years' War by a contemporary.

Rabb, Theodore K., *The Thirty Years' War—Problems of Motive, Extent, and Effect* (Heath, 1964).

Wedgwood, Cicely, V., *The Thirty Years' War* (Doubleday).

Europe Overseas

Cheyney, Edward Potts, *European Background of American History: 1300–1600* (Macmillan, 1962).

Notestein, Wallace, *English People on the Eve of Colonization: 1603–1630* (Harper, 1962).

Nowell, Charles E., *Great Discoveries and the First Colonial Empires* (Cornell, 1954).

CHAPTER XV

❧ *The Age of Louis XIV*
(1648-1688)

In the middle of the seventeenth century—particularly between 1647 and 1651—Europe experienced an epidemic of revolts, affecting some ten states. Although they occurred more or less simultaneously, no noticeable ties or common purposes marked these rebellions. England at the time was plagued by civil war and by the disorders preceding her first experiment with a republican government. In Holland, the Estates General abolished the stadholdership by a *coup d'état* and made themselves supreme (see p. 262). In Turkey, the Janissaries revolted and overthrew the sultan (1648). Aristocratic rebellions against centralized monarchical power rocked Russia (1647), Denmark (1648), and France (see p. 277). Peasants staged uprisings in the Swiss Cantons (1653), and various revolts of serfs struck Poland. Finally, there were antiforeign insurrections among Ukrainian cossacks, and in Catalonia and Naples the population rebelled against Spanish taxes and the harsh rule by the government of Madrid.

Conceivably, the recollection of this period of unrest led many people on the Continent to welcome growing royal absolutism, if only as a safeguard for internal tranquility.

Political aspects of the period

During the third quarter of the seventeenth century, England and France, although following different methods, became Europe's two most powerful states, prepared to challenge each other for supremacy in the known world. Within the Holy Roman Empire, meanwhile, several states rose to considerable importance and independence.

England's transition to constitutional monarchy

After the execution of Charles I in 1649 and the formal abolition of the kingship and the House of Lords, the army still had to suppress rebellious Irish and Scots who refused to recognize the Commonwealth and instead supported the nineteen-year-old Charles Stuart as his father's legitimate heir. The future Charles II eventually fled to France, and Cromwell savagely crushed the rebellions. Cromwell used the occasion to try to extirpate Irish longing for autonomy, to stamp out Irish Catholicism—by transferring Catholic lands to Protestants—and to weld Scotland, Ireland, and England into a single state.

But there was no consensus as to the kind of republic to establish. Radicals, such as the Levelers, demanded a written constitution based on a contractual theory of government, a concept that was to become an accepted political rallying cry by the end of the seventeenth century. They also demanded that all male citizens, not only property holders, should be given full political rights. Cromwell however was paternalistic and did not trust the people. Government, he thought, should do "what's for their good, not what pleases them."

In 1653, he disbanded the Rump of the Long Parliament and called a new assembly selected by leaders of the army. When disagreements within this body made it ineffective, army leaders wrote the conservative *Instrument of Government,* England's first and so far only written constitution. This document redistributed the franchise by granting representation to new areas that had grown wealthy and populous. Although Parliament was to meet every three years, decisive control rested with Cromwell, who was proclaimed Protector for life, and with an executive council consisting mostly of generals. Dissension between Parliament and Protector, however, continued, and Cromwell's regime became more and more a military dictatorship. "Authorities and powers are the ordinance of God," he asserted and acted as though God had sent him to remake England, although he refused the kingship when it was offered to him in 1657. He conceived of his mission as transcending the purely political and attempted to impose morality by force —closing theaters, establishing strict censorship, and compelling Sunday worship.

Cromwell's foreign and commercial policies were popular with the middle class. Foreshadowing the mercantilism of Colbert (see p. 280), Parliament enacted the First Navigation Act to help English trade and shipping by undermining the Dutch monopoly on the carrying trade. The act stipulated that only English ships, or vessels from the producing country, could carry goods to English ports. This step became the opening salvo in a twelve-year struggle between Dutch and English commercial interests, and led to the first (1652–1654) of three Anglo-Dutch wars. The war consisted mostly of naval engagements in which the English carried the day. In 1656, Cromwell pleased the anti-Spanish factions in England by joining France in her war against Spain, a war from which the English gained Dunkirk which they soon thereafter sold to France.

In 1658, Richard Cromwell succeeded as Lord Protector upon the death of his father. Lacking in determination, the younger Cromwell could not prevent new struggles between Parliament and the army, which within a year brought the Rump Parliament back to power. After Richard Cromwell's resignation in 1659, England fell into near anarchy, with generals rivaling for power and royalist uprisings in various areas. Most Englishmen grew tired of military tyranny and the failure of the Commonwealth regime to ensure internal peace. With the help of General George Monck (1608–1670), the commander of the army in Scotland, the Long Parliament at last voted to dissolve itself after issuing writs for a new Parliament. The latter promptly arranged for the restoration of the Stuart monarchy.

After the exiled Charles II (1660–1685) issued the Declaration of Breda in which he promised to grant "a free and general pardon," and declared "a liberty to tender consciences" in matters of religion, the new Parliament welcomed him back to England. Although some legislation from the revolutionary period was retained, Parliament promptly re-established the House of Lords and the Anglican episcopate, abolished Puritan austerity, and reduced the standing army to a small force of five thousand.

Charles II was courageous and intelligent, yet filled with a good measure of duplicity and debauchery. At heart he remained an absolutist. "A king who can be contradicted," he averred, "is king in name only." In practice, he frequently compromised with his opponents and with public opinion in order to save his throne and avoid a second exile. His first Parliament, which he kept for eighteen years, was heavily royalist in sentiment, in part out of antipathy for the Puritan regime of the 1650's. Royal prerogatives were restored intact. The king could still call and dismiss Parliament at will and was even voted a yearly income from state funds for the duration of his reign—the first English sovereign to receive such a regular allotment. Combined with the secret funds he received from Louis XIV of France, this money gave him relative independence from Parliament.

Parliament was determined to exclude non-Anglicans from the conduct of governmental affairs. It adopted measures to punish nonconformists, to enforce Anglicanism, and to ensure unflinching support for the monarchy and the Anglican Church. Government officials not only had to swear allegiance to the crown but be practicing Anglicans (Test Act). Attempts were also made to suppress the Scottish Presbyterians, who staged two unsuccessful revolts in defense of their faith.

Tension between king and Parliament again increased in the late 1670's, when the king and his Catholic brother James acted more friendly to Catholicism despite increased anti-Catholic feeling among the English. Alleged "popish" plots and fear of the growing power of Louis XIV—France having replaced Spain as the champion of Catholicism—led to persecution of "papists" and stirred Parliament into passing the Disabling Act (1678), barring Catholics from parliamentary membership.

The new Parliament that convened in 1679 was no longer so amenable to Charles II. It passed the *Habeas Corpus* Act, a landmark in the history of civil rights. The act stipulated that a prisoner had to be given the specific reason for his detainment, should be tried promptly, and, once acquitted, could not be recommitted for the same offense. Conceivably the members of Parliament thought of their own security under Charles II when passing this act. Disagreement on the advisability of permitting the Catholic James to succeed his brother helped coalesce two groups that eventually developed into political parties. Although displeased by the prospect of a Catholic sovereign, the pro-Anglican Tories favored the principle of hereditary monarchy and the undiminished retention of the royal prerogative. The Whigs, on the other hand, advocated parliamentary supremacy and favored more toleration for dissenters, albeit not for Catholics.

Charles II's foreign policy followed the lines initiated by Cromwell but was more vacillating. In the course of two more wars against Holland, England acquired supremacy of the seas. The Second Dutch War (1665–1667), in which Holland received French aid, ended in a tie, although England seized New Amsterdam—soon renamed New York—to which she received official title in 1674. During the Third Dutch War (1672–1674), Charles joined the French attack on Holland; but under pressure from the English merchant class less worried about the remaining Dutch competition than about the growing power of Catholic France, England withdrew from the war, and in its last year (1677–1678) even aided the Dutch against France.

Charles' conduct of foreign affairs was in part guided by his clandestine connections with Louis XIV. The French court had supported Charles during his exile and thereafter supplied him with funds. In the Treaty of Dover (1670), an official Anglo-French agreement directed against Holland, Charles had signed secret clauses, promising to join France in contemplated wars against Holland and Spain in return for French subsidies, and to restore Catholicism in England as soon as feasible. One cannot tell whether Charles entered into this agreement primarily to obtain more funds for his court—Louis' offer amounted to one-sixth of Charles' normal yearly income—or whether religious convictions influenced his decision.

Despite Whig opposition, the Catholic James II (1685–1688) succeeded his brother and soon began to relax the laws against Roman Catholics. He enlarged the royal army, defeated uprisings by Protestant pretenders to the throne, and proceeded to impose his rule on the country with little regard for tactful diplomacy. Louis XIV's revocation of the Edict of Nantes in 1685 (see p. 282) increased the apprehensions of the English Protestants. Although even the pope urged caution, James appeared determined to return

England to Catholicism. When his second wife, a Catholic princess (Mary of Modena), gave birth to a son in 1688, even the Tories became alarmed by the prospect of continued Catholic rule. Hence, a secret invitation was sent to James' oldest daughter Mary and her husband, William III of Orange, stadholder of Holland, to "rescue England from Catholicism." William accepted the offer, but first had to ascertain the intentions of Louis XIV, who was threatening to reinvade Holland. When the French king instead invaded the Palatinate (see p. 280)—thereby unleashing the War of the League of Augsburg—William felt safe to take his troops to England. Six weeks after he landed, James II fled to France. Although returning to Ireland in 1689 to raise an unsuccessful rebellion for his cause, James spent the remainder of his life in France.

After James' flight, Parliament declared the throne vacant and offered the crown to Mary. When William insisted on being king in his own right, and not merely a prince consort, Parliament consented to making William and Mary joint sovereigns. The accession of the new rulers embodied a revolution, known in England as the Glorious Revolution, since Parliament had enthroned the new sovereigns. The settlement of 1689 was to make this abundantly clear (see p. 298).

The apogee of French absolutism

The long reign of Louis XIV (1643–1715) can be divided into three periods. During the years of turbulence and subsequent consolidation, 1643–1661, France was ruled by Cardinal Mazarin. The first three decades of Louis XIV's personal reign, 1661 to the late 1680's, were an age of glory and success. The last period, from the 1680's until the king's death in 1715, was marked by overextension and gradual decline.

As Marie de Medici had done in 1610, Louis XIII's widow (Anne), immediately after her husband's death in 1643, asked the *parlement de Paris* to nullify his testament and make her the sole regent for the five-year-old Louis XIV. The new regent then reappointed as chief minister her favorite (and possibly her secret husband), Cardinal Mazarin (1602–1661), an Italian who had served for four years under Richelieu and had succeeded him in his post. Mazarin was an excellent diplomat and tactician. Like his predecessor, he was interested in politics rather than in religion. Although a cardinal, he had not even been ordained as a priest. Moreover he had been skilled at amassing an enormous personal fortune.

Two main tasks faced Mazarin and he handled both successfully. One was to protect the monarchical structure during the minority of Louis XIV. The second was the successful conclusion of the Thirty Years' War and the war with Spain.

In the 1640's the country was restless. Peasants were suffering from economic misery; the state's finances were depleted by the war; some nobles were hoping to regain power by plotting against Mazarin; the *parlement de*

Paris became more obstreperous over questions of taxes and royal prerogatives; and fiscal expedients used to raise money for the war antagonized the
Parisians. The mood of discontent gave rise to a series of insurrections
(1648–1653) which the French called *Frondes.*

The parliamentary *Fronde* began when the *parlement de Paris* suddenly
imitated England's Parliament by demanding control over all taxation, a law
of *habeas corpus,* and the abolition of the intendants. The *frondeurs*
claimed the right to act as "mediators between the king and the people," although essentially they represented the interests of the nobility of the robe.
When Mazarin and the regent used troops returning from the Thirty Years'
War to arrest some members of the *parlements,* Paris rose in revolt, forcing
the royal family and Mazarin to flee. The young Prince of Condé (1621–
1686), twice victor over the Spanish, then besieged Paris, which surrendered
after a civil war of three months.

A new *Fronde,* that of the nobles, erupted in 1650. It was provoked by
friction between the regent and the ambitious and proud Condé who demanded exorbitant compensation for his war services. A fierce civil war developed between some of the nobles from the provinces, supported by the
parlement and the city of Paris, and the small armies remaining loyal to the
regent. Mazarin, against whom most of the hatred was directed, fled to
Cologne. Condé then made the political blunder of negotiating for help
from Spain, then at war with France. Fearful of a new Spanish occupation
of their city, as had occurred when the Guises invited the aid of Philip II in
1589, the Parisians abandoned Condé, who finally fled to Spain. Condé's
flight ended the second *Fronde.* In late 1652, the regent and the young monarch re-entered Paris, soon followed by Mazarin.

The *Frondes* devastated the countryside and added to the ruination of
the nobility of the sword. The experience may also have left a lasting impression on Louis XIV, who at the age of ten had to flee from Paris and spend
almost four years as an itinerant refugee in army camps. Conceivably, it re-
enforced his determination to make himself an absolute ruler and live in
luxurious splendor.

In foreign affairs, Mazarin was eminently successful. In the Treaties of
Westphalia, France gained parts of Alsace, an important stepping stone for
further expansion toward the Rhine. Victory over Spain (Treaty of the
Pyrenees, 1659) brought France acquisitions in the south (Roussillon) and
north (Artois, and parts of Flanders and of Luxembourg). Condé, who
for six years had fought with the Spaniards against France, was pardoned,
readmitted to France, and served again as a trusted general during the early
wars of Louis XIV. With the empire and Spain weakened, France emerged
from the wars with added prestige and power. Moreover Mazarin's policy toward England furthered his Continental designs. He promptly extended
diplomatic recognition to Cromwell's republican regime, although he disliked dealing with regicides at a time when France herself was torn by anti-

royalist rebellions. As justification, he explained that the English revolution had not altered the geographic fact that England was still close to the shores of France. At the same time, he extended welcome and subsidies to the exiled Charles II. Both policies bore fruit. Except for a brief period (1666–1668), England remained France's tacit or open ally until 1677, and became determinedly anti-French only when William III ascended the throne of England. England's friendship or neutrality made it easier for Louis XIV to start his "reign of glory."

In 1661, Louis XIV began his personal reign of fifty-four years, determined to act as chief minister himself and not govern in the shadow of a new Richelieu or Mazarin. Well schooled in governmental and military affairs, he was prepared for the task. Despite his pride and vanity, he was a hard and meticulous worker, obsessed by the notion that everything—work, amusement, eating, even retiring to bed—had to be performed according to rigid schedules and rules. His belief in absolute kingship by divine right was inflexible. He felt himself to be truly "king by the Grace of God," a concept he underscored grandiosely in all outward appearance. The king was deemed to be wiser than other humans, since he seemed "to share in divine knowledge." His son's tutor (Bishop Bossuet) eloquently justified these assertions by biblical citations. Louis himself wrote that the king has "full and inherent right to dispose of all property, lay and ecclesiastical," but admitted that such unlimited power should be used "for the benefit of the state."

The name "Sun King" under which he became known was not a nickname, for he had chosen the sun as his emblem; all was to radiate from him. The cult of majesty based on court etiquette resembled church ritual. During the ceremony attending his arising in the morning, for instance—one is tempted to call it the sunrise service—an honored courtier of the highest nobility was required to present the king his shirt, much as an acolyte helps a bishop into his vestments. Considerable time and money was spent on the observance of proper etiquette, at official functions, on hunting parties, during meals, and even on the battlefield. His court contained some fourteen thousand military and civilian attendants, supervised by hundreds of great nobles. Besides bringing glory to the king, this system kept the nobles at court—when they were not on military service—and thus more amenable to the royal will. To run the government and the civil service, Louis relied mostly on members of the bourgeoisie, to some of whom he awarded minor titles of nobility.

Louis devoted his primary attention to developing an active and aggressive foreign policy. Like Richelieu, he hoped to expand France to her "natural frontiers" or those of ancient Gaul—the Pyrenees, the Alps, and the Rhine. In view of Spain's inherited possessions, such a policy called in fact for the dismemberment of the Spanish empire in Europe. But aggrandizement alone was not Louis' objective. He also insisted on French pre-eminence on the Continent. When, for example, the French and Spanish ambassadors in London quarreled over which one was to be the first to enter a room, Louis threatened Spain with war until the Spaniards agreed that French envoys everywhere were to be accorded precedence. In his foreign policy and the wars that resulted, the king was aided by excellent generals (Condé, Turenne), skilled diplomats, well-trained armies, and a new system of effective siege warfare.

Under Louis, France fought four major wars extending for over half his reign. The first two were fought during the period of glory and success. In 1667, Louis claimed the Spanish Netherlands as inheritance through his first wife (Maria Theresa), daughter of the king of Spain. Without declaring war, French troops invaded the disputed area and for added pressure on Spain also seized Burgundy. The resulting war (War of Devolution, 1667–1668) was short. The Dutch did not cherish the prospect of a strong France as their new neighbor across the Rhine. The grand pensionary Jan de Witt established an anti-French alliance with Sweden and England, although Holland had barely terminated a war with the latter. As a result, Louis XIV negotiated a peace with Spain, in which France acquired some border areas in the north, but not the entire Spanish Netherlands.

Louis' second war (Dutch War, 1672–1678) was directed against Holland, which he now regarded as a stumbling block to his planned annexation of all the Spanish Netherlands. Moreover he intensely disliked Dutch Calvinism and republicanism. There were also economic motivations. His financial and economic planner, Colbert, was convinced that neither Europe's population nor its consumption of goods would increase; hence the volume of trade and shipping required to satisfy economic needs would remain constant. He further calculated that all European trade "is carried on with about 20,000 ships, and . . . this cannot be increased." Estimating that of this number, the Dutch had fifteen thousand or more ships and the English over three thousand, he advised his king that the French could not hope to "increase their commerce without decreasing the . . . ships controlled by the Dutch."

To thwart a new anti-French coalition, Louis used gold and diplomacy to convert possible opponents into client states of France. The king's "pensioners" soon included Sweden, England (Treaty of Dover, see p. 275), a number of German states, and for a while the emperor himself. In 1672, French troops crossed the Rhine and rapidly invaded Holland. Alone and unprepared for war, the Dutch saved their major cities from French occupation by breaking the dikes and flooding large portions of the country. They then proposed to negotiate peace with France on the basis of some territorial cessions, but Louis rejected their offer as insufficient. Hence the war lasted six years and turned into a general European conflict. After the murder of Jan de Witt (see p. 262), William III assumed control of Holland and inspired the formation of a new anti-French coalition, which soon included

Spain, the emperor, and several German states. Campaigns were fought in the Spanish Netherlands and in western Germany, and Dutch and French navies even fought in the Mediterranean. In many battles and sieges, the Sun King personally supervised the functioning of his superb war machine. When peace was concluded in 1678 (at Nimwegen), France was awarded Burgundy and another strip of the Spanish Netherlands.

Flushed with success and taking advantage of the weakness of the Holy Roman Empire and its preoccupation with war against the Ottoman Empire (1682–1699), Louis promptly launched his "peaceful" expansion. He annexed areas in the Spanish Netherlands, in Lorraine, and in Alsace, including the major city of Strasbourg. To justify his actions, he asserted that the lands he seized had at some time in history formed a part of territories allotted to France in the four peace treaties since 1648. For several years, the imperial princes and Spain contented themselves with protests against this piecemeal aggression. But when Louis also presented claims to the Palatinate, France's apparent insatiableness aroused the apprehensions of most European rulers. Protestant princes also became worried about possible implications entailed by Louis' revocation of the Edict of Nantes (see p. 282).

As a result, William III of England found it easier to fashion another anti-French coalition (League of Augsburg) that ultimately included Austria, Sweden, Spain, Bavaria, Saxony, the Palatinate, Holland, Savoy, and England. Nonetheless, Louis XIV ordered the invasion of the Palatinate (1688), thereby opening the War of the League of Augsburg (1688–1697), which belongs to the third period of his long reign (see p. 289).

French internal affairs, under close supervision by the monarch, were run by six ministers and four administrative councils, staffed for the most part by highly skilled men. The royal intendants were made permanent agents of the king, responsible only to him, and placed in charge of military, judicial, and financial affairs as well as public works. In view of the many wars, the army reforms undertaken by the Marquis de Louvois (1641–1691), secretary of war from 1666 to 1691, were of fundamental importance. He professionalized the army and almost quadrupled the number of available regiments. The introduction of uniforms, regular military ranks, standardized weapons, improved artillery and logistics greatly enhanced French military capabilities. One of Louvois' colleagues, a military engineer (Vauban, 1633–1707), was the period's foremost designer of fortifications and siege tactics.

The French economy was supervised by Jean-Baptiste Colbert (1619–1683), who acted as Controller General of Finances from 1662 until his death. An ambitious bourgeois, Colbert was said to love work so much that he felt unhappy when he could not spend sixteen hours a day at his desk. The tasks entrusted to him probably required such herculean efforts, for within his supervision lay the finances of state and court, commerce, industry, agriculture, public works, the merchant marine, colonial development, and to some extent French culture in general. Colbert was hardly the first mercantilist, but he tried to apply the theories so assiduously, that mercantilism is often associated with Colbertism.

The aim of mercantilism was to make the state solvent and strong. Colbert believed that the strength of a state depended primarily on its "abundance of money," by which he meant specie. According to him, the government should prevent the outflow of gold and silver by restricting imports and insisting on payment in specie for all exports. Yet, unlike the bullionists of the sixteenth century, Colbert recognized the need for developing the internal economy. He intervened in industry and commerce on a far larger scale than had been attempted by Sully (see p. 253). State funds were used to expand existing industries and establish new ones (steel, lace, porcelain, and glass). The government assisted in importing skilled workers, supervised labor conditions, and encouraged concentration of shops into larger, more economical factories. In addition, Colbert sought to control the quality of production, so that French goods could better compete in European markets.

Colbert also tried to increase agricultural production and the raising of livestock, and passed regulations for the conservation of natural resources. To further trade, he abolished internal tariffs in parts of northern France, but was unable to extend this free market to all of France. On the other hand, he placed high protective tariffs on imports, a favored mercantilistic measure. Canals and roads in France were improved, and the merchant marine and navy expanded.

Attempts to set up trading companies to exploit world trade proved less profitable than similar efforts in Holland and England. Colbert was probably least successful in budgetary matters. As treasurer, he attempted to chart state receipts and expenditures and even make a yearly forecast. But royal expenses—for war, subsidies, pensions, and maintenance of the court—were so enormous that he could not balance the budget and barely improved the royal credit for further borrowing.

Colbert also acted like a minister of culture. With his help, the government supported writers (Racine, Molière, Boileau), established academies (for science, painting, and sculpture), and assisted in founding the influential periodical, *Le Journal des Savants*. Although he deplored the extravagance, Colbert had to help Louis in his enormous building program, which included the Hotel des Invalides, additions to the Louvre, and the vast complex of Versailles, which took thirty-one years to build.

Architecture, as well as painting and sculpture, revealed strong Italian influence and reverence for the antique. Columns, geometric triangles, domes, flat roofs, and large symmetrical spaces bore traces of ancient Rome rather than of northern France. This reversion to classicism, equally noticeable in drama, sculpture, and painting, admirably fitted the regime of the Sun King. It was orderly, appealed to reason, and frequently bordered on the pompous.

Absolutism confronted Louis with several religious issues: the position of the Gallican Church and the fate of religious dissidents. His desire to exert more control over the French Church, especially the bishoprics of southern France, led to a twenty-year struggle with the papacy. Aided by a number of French ecclesiastics (including Bishop Bossuet), the king reopened the question of conciliar supremacy over the papacy in spiritual matters, in order to put greater pressure on the pope. A compromise of 1693 finally gave the king more authority over the Gallican Church, in return for French abandonment of the conciliar cause.

In regard to dissident groups, Louis became increasingly intolerant as his reign progressed. The notion of one king, one country, one faith fitted his concept of absolutism. It seemed to him absurd that if the little princes of Germany had the legal right to force religious conformity on their subjects, the Sun King should lack such power. Moreover, one should recall that intolerance was still the norm in Europe, and that France had in a way been an exception since 1598. The king's tendency toward intolerance became even more confirmed after his secret marriage—upon the death of his first wife—to the devout Madame de Maintenon (1635-1719), who successfully weaned him from his mistresses and attempted to guide him toward greater religious devotion.

One religious group with whom Louis clashed were the Jansenists, a Catholic sect, ardent disciples of St. Augustine, believing in predestination. They had been attacked by the Jesuits and condemned by the pope as early as 1653, and vigorously defended by one of France's foremost writers (Pascal). Persecution of Jansenists started in the 1660's. Louis disliked the emotional aspects of Jansenism as well as the fact that many Jansenists belonged to the nobility of the robe, a growing class whom he had not completely succeeded in taming. The anti-Jansenist campaign lasted throughout Louis' reign. Two further papal condemnations were pronounced in 1702 and 1713, and Louis had the Jansenists' monastic school and headquarters (Port Royal) razed in 1709, but Jansenism was to re-emerge under Louis XV.

His second religious campaign was aimed at the Huguenots, numbering perhaps 1,200,000 at the beginning of his reign. As early as 1668, Louis had decided "little by little to subdue the Huguenots." First, he ordered their harassment by enforcement of the Edict of Nantes to the point of absurdity, such as prohibiting Protestant burials during day time, on the grounds that the edict did not specifically grant such permission. Then followed discrimination in opportunities for employment, intimidation, and finally forced conversion to Catholicism. It is impossible to tell how many practicing Protestants were left in France when Louis revoked the Edict of Nantes in 1685, although he was presumably convinced that very few Protestants remained.

The decree of revocation enjoined "all ministers of the so-called reformed religion . . . to leave our kingdom . . . within fifteen days." Their
churches were to be "demolished without delay," emigration of lay Huguenots was forbidden, and their children were to be raised as Catholics.
While persecution increased, perhaps more than 300,000 Huguenots secretly
crossed the border to find ultimate refuge in Holland, Brandenburg, Switzerland, England, or overseas.

The states of the Holy Roman Empire

After 1648, the Imperial Diet continued to meet and at times the empire
operated as a unit. Most of the time, however, the more than three hundred
political entities comprising the empire tended each to act autonomously.

Politically, the German states were becoming increasingly entangled
with foreign nations. Sometimes this involvement stemmed from dynastic
inheritance, as when one of the counts of the Palatinate also became king of
Sweden, when the Duchy of Oldenburg was inherited by the king of Denmark, or when the elector of Hanover acquired the crown of England. More
often the connections resulted from political alliances—for example between Prussia and Holland or Bavaria and France—which usually subordinated the weaker German states to stronger foreign powers, or from subsidy
payments which tended to turn the German states into mercenaries of other
nations. French cultural influence was also increasing. French became the
court language of the empire, and the German princes tried to emulate the
Sun King, building their little Versailles and lavishly entertaining their mistresses in the French manner.

At the same time, most German rulers attempted to make themselves
absolute in their lands by suppressing the estates, enforcing serfdom, and
creating an efficient army and civil service. In many states they succeeded.
Unlike the French nobility, however, the German nobility generally retained
its importance and power.

Among the many imperial states, Hapsburg Austria, less devastated
than most of the Holy Roman Empire by the ravages of the Thirty Years'
War, remained the largest and strongest. Like other rulers, the emperor
(Leopold I, 1658–1705) sought to cement his inherited lands into a uniform, centralized state. His task was complicated by differences in language
and political customs among his subjects. In the absence of a strong bourgeoisie, the Hapsburgs tried to impose their rule with the aid of the nobility
and the Catholic Church at the expense of the peasantry, which remained in
serfdom. Hence, perhaps even more than in other German states, the nobility
retained its prerogatives. Hapsburg control also relied on domination of its
numerous Slavic and Hungarian subjects by the German-speaking Austrians. Finally, the emperor sought to consolidate his realm by eradicating
remaining traces of Protestantism.

Although Austria entered every war against Louis XIV in the West, her main concern lay in the Balkans. In the East, the emperors faced not only the Ottoman Empire but also the Hungarian nobles—many of them Protestants—who resented rule by Vienna and the Jesuits' attempt to convert them to Catholicism. A brief Turkish-Austrian war in the 1660's remained indecisive. But when Hungarian rebels appealed for aid to the Turks in 1682, a major war developed (1682–1699). The Turks, still holding the greater portion of Hungary, laid a three months' siege to Vienna (1683), which was finally rescued by a combined force of Austrian, Polish, Bavarian, and Saxon troops. Thereafter the Hapsburgs continued the campaign with the aid of German troops, seized most of Hungary from the Turks, and forced the Hungarians to grant to the Hapsburgs the hereditary rights to the Hungarian crown. Austria was thus successfully launched in her role as the dominant power in southeastern Europe.

Next to Austria, Bavaria, Saxony, and Brandenburg-Prussia were the most important states in the empire. Bavaria had emerged strengthened and enlarged from the Thirty Years' War. In conjunction with the Catholic Church in Bavaria, its dukes wielded wide power over their subjects. The extensive family connections of its ruling house (Wittelsbach), as well as a deft policy of alternating alignment between France and Austria, made Bavaria more influential than expected on the basis of her size and resources. Saxony, too, had gained land from the Thirty Years' War, and its local prosperity enabled a fairly rapid recovery from wartime devastation. Mining, manufacture, and trade turned Saxony into one of the richest areas of Central Europe. Its Protestant middle class was relatively large, and no real absolutism developed.

The fourth state of consequence within the empire was Brandenburg-Prussia, which in 1648 consisted of territories scattered over northern Europe from the Rhine to the Niemen. In the East, it included Lutheran East Prussia, the former lands of the Teutonic Order, which Brandenburg had inherited in 1618. In the West, it comprised several wealthy but small areas, mostly Catholic, between the Rhine and the Weser, inherited in 1614. Between the two lay the Electorate of Brandenburg itself, Lutheran and Calvinist in population, held by the Hohenzollern dynasty since 1411. After the acquisition of East Prussia, it was often called Brandenburg-Prussia. Finally after 1660, the electors preferred to apply the name Prussia to all their holdings, since in Prussia they were absolute sovereigns, whereas in their other lands they still owed theoretical allegiance to the emperor.

Brandenburg-Prussia emerged as an important power under Duke Frederick William (1640–1688), later known as "the Great Elector." A good administrator and military leader, Frederick William, who had been educated partly in Holland, was ready to adopt any device successfully tried in other countries, in order to make his realm prosperous and his dynasty strong. Like most of his contemporaries, he took the road toward absolutism

by reducing the powers of the local estates. He built up a highly efficient civil
service and increased the standing army from two thousand to thirty thousand men, in part to bolster his control over his subjects. Instead of turning
the nobles into social parasites as was being done by Louis XIV, Frederick
William granted wide political and economic concessions to the *Junkers,* the
noble landlords of the large estates in Prussia and Brandenburg. In fact,
Hohenzollern absolutism was to rely to a large degree on army, civil service,
and support of the *Junker* class.

The Great Elector also attempted to infuse the peoples of his diverse
lands with a sense of unity. By improving transport and communications—
including the postal service—by assigning officials to areas other than their
native provinces, and by seeking to lessen the distrust between the nobles of
his eastern lands and the bourgeois of the Rhineland, he hoped to bridge
internal differences. Himself a Calvinist, he adopted a policy of religious
toleration that was to remain characteristic for Prussian history. In view of
the three different faiths held by his subjects, only a tolerant policy could help
keep his divergent lands united. When Louis XIV revoked the Edict of
Nantes, Frederick William countered with his Edict of Potsdam and invited
the French Huguenots to Brandenburg-Prussia—despite the Sun King's ex-
press prohibition of emigration for Huguenots. Since his lands were as yet
underpopulated and economically underdeveloped, the Prussian ruler favored immigration. He even offered to help defray travel costs and to sub-
sidize new businesses established by the Huguenots.

Frederick William applied mercantilism to rebuild the economy, which
had suffered heavily from the Thirty Years' War. Unlike most contemporary
rulers, he was frugal and ran his state with austerity. A new system of taxation soon yielded a full treasury. Improvement in agriculture and in manufacture was considerable, but attempts at emulating Holland with trading
companies for overseas failed.

In foreign affairs, the Great Elector was equally energetic. Numerous
powerful states bordered on his scattered territories: Holland, Spain (in the
Spanish Netherlands), Sweden, Poland, and Hapsburg Austria (in Silesia). Since Brandenburg-Prussia was as yet weak, Frederick William developed a judicious skill for shifting alliances to suit the contingency of the
moment. He switched back and forth between the pro-imperial and pro-
French camps, alternately sided with Poland or with Sweden, and changed
between alliance and benevolent neutrality in his relations with Holland. At
opportune moments, he used his small but effective army to evoke greater
respect among his neighbors. But he was unable to achieve the two objectives that were to occupy subsequent Hohenzollern rulers. He could not acquire the land bridges between his eastern, central, and western territories
needed to fashion a single contiguous state, nor was he able to drive the
Swedes out of Pomerania in order to acquire better seaports.

During the First Northern War (1655–1660), involving Sweden, Poland, and others, he was able to force the king of Poland to renounce his feudal suzerainty over East Prussia—an act which allowed Frederick William to consider himself sole sovereign in Prussia. He also achieved some spectacular military victories over Poles and Swedes, thus adding to Prussia's prestige; yet in the end, French opposition prevented him from keeping any of the lands he had conquered. During the French war against Holland, he once again successfully attacked Sweden but again was forced by Sweden's ally, Louis XIV, to restore his gains. Thus Brandenburg-Prussia did not grow during the reign of the Great Elector after the initial gains at the end of the Thirty Years' War. Yet at his death in 1688, Frederick William left Prussia economically and financially prosperous, and respected—if not yet feared—as a new, rising power in northern Europe.

Europeans overseas

The history of the Europeans overseas reflected changes on the Continent. Spain continued to lose power, and hence slowed down in her overseas expansion. English, Dutch, and French freebooters preyed profitably on Spanish shipping and on South American coastal settlements, and their three countries extended their control in the Caribbean, an area lying within the heartland of the Spanish colonial empire. Meanwhile England and Holland accompanied their three European wars by a commercial and colonial duel in which England gradually gained the upper hand. Although France rose to pre-eminence in Europe and pursued an active policy of overseas expansion, Louis XIV was inclined to concentrate his efforts on Europe. Hence the French lagged behind England and Holland in the world at large. Yet after Holland had been relegated to a secondary place, France was ready to be the new challenger. The ensuing Anglo-French colonial duel was to last almost a hundred years, from 1689 to 1763.

In the Western Hemisphere, the French expanded in the Caribbean and explored and claimed the upper and lower Mississippi Valley (Marquette, Joliet, and La Salle). To their north and east, the English extended their claims around Hudson Bay and organized new colonies in New York, New Jersey, Pennsylvania, and the two Carolinas. In the South, the Portuguese, after regaining their independence from Spain (1640), succeeded in driving the Dutch out of Brazil and reacquiring control over that vast colony.

The Dutch, British, and French at the same time showed increased interest in gaining trading posts and privileges in Africa. And whereas the Dutch concentrated their efforts on the Indonesian Archipelago, the French East Indies Company established outposts in India (Pondichery, 1674), from which it hoped eventually to encroach on the English trade with India.

Intellectual trends

The Age of Reason brought about greater changes in Western history than the Renaissance or the Reformation. In theory as well as in application, the new age came to full fruition only after 1688 and will therefore be discussed in the three subsequent chapters. But it was during the third quarter of the seventeenth century that much of the basis for the Age of Reason was laid.

The new view on life and science is well illustrated in a letter written in 1662 by the Secretary of the Royal Society in London to the Dutch philosopher Baruch Spinoza (1632-1677): "Come, excellent Sir, banish all fear of stirring up the pygmies of our times; too long have sacrifices been made to ignorance and absurdity; let us spread our sails to the wind of true knowledge and search out the innermost secrets of nature more thoroughly than has been done hitherto." A comparison of this passage with St. Augustine's view that the primary value of knowledge was its use as an aid to salvation reveals the revolution that was taking place in men's thought.

Already before the mid-century, Galileo had made his discoveries in astronomy and physics, and René Descartes (1596-1650) had completed his mathematical and scientific speculations. The work of both men helped prepare the ground for the mechanistic explanation of the material universe, a notion that profoundly affected the philosophical thought of the Age of Reason. Thereafter new theories in the natural and social sciences multiplied. Thomas Hobbes (1588-1679) published his *Leviathan* (1651) containing his ideas of a social contract which regulates secular states in a materialistic universe. Pascal (1623-1662), Newton (1642-1727), and Leibniz (1646-1716) vastly expanded mathematical knowledge—including differential calculus—making mathematics the *sine qua non* of science and philosophy. Robert Boyle (1627-1691) at the same time laid the basis for modern chemistry, including speculation on the atomic composition of matter. Meanwhile scientific journals and societies were founded to spread the new discoveries and create a new international community of scholars.

Toward the end of the period, John Locke (1632-1704) was beginning his writings on toleration, contractual political theories, philosophic empiricism, and education, all fundamental to the speculations of succeeding generations; Pierre Bayle (1647-1706) was preparing his *Historical and Critical Dictionary* (1697), a skeptical analysis of seventeenth century thought and a guide to the rationalists of the following century; and in 1687 appeared Newton's *Principia Mathematica,* which included his theories of universal gravitation and became a cornerstone of the Age of Reason.

Cultural trends of the period 1648-1688 continued to be heavily influenced by the Baroque spirit, especially in architecture and music. Italian opera and contrasting polyphonic styles showed Baroque characteristics as did the ballets and operas of Jean-Baptiste Lully (1632–1687), who rose from kitchen scullion to become the musical arbiter of France. The Baroque also marked the work of England's Henry Purcell (1659–1695), the composer of odes, church music, songs, and the opera *Dido*.

At the same time, there was a greater variety in literary output. Next to the serious writings of John Milton (1608–1674) and the allegorical *Pilgrim's Progress* (1678) by the Baptist preacher John Bunyan (1628–1688), other English works displayed a strong reaction to Puritan austerity. The poems of Samuel Butler (1612–1680), the plays of John Dryden (1631–1700), as well as the diary of Samuel Pepys (1633–1703) were full of wit and ridicule, frequently licentious in tone, and frankly aimed at evoking gaiety. While Spain was entering the end of its golden age of literature with the serious dramas of Calderon de la Barca (1600–1681), France was then at the height of its classical period with a great variety of literary forms: emotional tragedies by Jean Racine (1639–1699), satirical comedies by Molière (1622–1673), and allegorical fables by La Fontaine (1621–1695).

SUGGESTED READINGS

England

Ashley, Maurice, *The Greatness of Oliver Cromwell* (Macmillan, 1962).
*Clark, George N., *The Later Stuarts, 1660–1714* (Oxford U.P., 1955).
Haller, William, *The Rise of Puritanism* (Harper, 1957).
Krutch, Joseph Wood, *Comedy and Conscience After the Restoration* (Columbia, 1961).
Straka, Gerald M., *The Revolution of 1688—Whig Triumph or Palace Revolution?* (Heath, 1963).

France and Prussia

Church, William F., *The Greatness of Louis XIV, Myth or Reality?* (Heath, 1959).
*Doolin, Paul Rice, *Fronde* (Harvard, 1935).
*Guérard, Albert, *France in the Classical Age, The Life and Death of an Ideal* (Harper).
Lewis, Warren Hamilton, *Splendid Century: Life in the France of Louis XIV* (Doubleday, 1957).
Minchinton, Walter E., *Mercantilism: System or Expediency?* (Heath, 1968).
Saint-Simon, Louis Duc de, *The Age of Magnificence: Memoirs of the Court of Louis XIV* (Putnam, 1964). Extracts from the memoirs of a disgruntled contemporary of Louis XIV.
Schevill, Ferdinand, *The Great Elector* (Shoe String, 1965).
Wolf, John B., *Louis Fourteenth* (Norton, 1968).

CHAPTER XVI

✻ *Absolutism in Action*
(1689-1715)

For several decades after the 1660's, France had been an example to European rulers of the potential power of an absolute monarch. Hence, more and more rulers sought to imitate Louis XIV or construct absolutistic regimes of their own. Yet, during this same period when absolutism became so prevalent, some philosophers and political theorists, writing during the early stages of the Age of Reason, were laying the foundations for modern democracy. This was a striking antithesis to the governmental concepts of Louis XIV.

The spread of absolutism

Despite the example of France during Louis XIV's period of glory, it appears that there was no necessary correlation between the absolutistic structure of a state and its power. Absolutism probably strengthened Prussia, Russia, and Sweden during this period, whereas it could not stem the decline of Spain. In France itself, it began to weaken the state, while across the Channel England rose to pre-eminence after having rejected absolutism.

The last decades of Louis XIV

The third period of the long reign of Louis XIV, from 1688 to 1715, was marked by overextension, even greater extravagance, and decline. Outwardly France remained the most powerful state in Europe and its court the most brilliant. More than ever before, French became the language of Europe's upper society. French culture and etiquette set the tone, and the Sun King, although disliked for continually disturbing the peace, was still admired as the heroic monarch par excellence.

289

Yet signs of trouble, unheeded by the king himself, were beginning to herald an end to the reign of glory. The formation of the League of Augsburg (see p. 280) resulted in a formidable anti-French coalition that fought France for over two decades. Such European alliances against an actual or potential aggressor were to become common in succeeding centuries, when Europeans united to prevent a single state from dominating the Continent—as for example the anti-French coalitions during the revolutionary and Napoleonic periods, or the anti-German and anti-Russian alliances during the twentieth century.

In addition, France was approaching bankruptcy. Despite various expedients to raise revenue—increasing taxes, devaluating coins, issuing paper vouchers, selling offices, and securing forced loans—income never caught up with expenditures. Louis, whom some historians call the "gravedigger" of the French monarchy since the country's finances never recovered completely until after the French Revolution, seemed unconcerned about spending more and more on war, on the upkeep of Versailles, and on favors to his courtiers. Only on his deathbed did he confide to his heir his unhappiness with his failure to cut expenses and thereby "relieve the burden on his people."

Several contemporary writers saw as the core of the problem Louis' excessive, arbitrary power. By this time Louis had lost some of his best advisers and some of his best generals. He seemed to surround himself with mediocre people, so that by comparison he could shine all the more, a practice not uncommon with modern dictators. In foreign policy, in particular, he became more stubborn and refused to change course even when most signs augured against success.

The Palace of Versailles became a nemesis for French absolutism much as the existence of the Escorial had affected the reign of Philip II (see p. 235). The French court moved there in 1682, although construction was not completed until 1695. Withdrawal to the artificial atmosphere of Versailles had serious political, social, and financial consequences. The king became even more isolated from his subjects, probably ignorant of the discontent and misery among many segments of the population. Only those considered "presentable" were admitted to court, and Louis was beset by flatterers and those seeking royal favors. Cabals began to interfere with the process of government, a condition that was to mark French politics until the Revolution. The nobles retained their social and financial privileges as well as a disproportionate share of the landed wealth, while degenerating into a parasitic class, content to warm themselves in the rays of a setting sun.

During this last period of his reign, Louis XIV was primarily occupied with the conduct of two major wars that lasted a total of twenty-two years. In the War of the League of Augsburg (1688–1697), France faced a majority of the European powers. Skirmishes and campaigns, some of them terribly destructive, were fought in the Rhineland, Pyrenees, Spanish Netherlands, Alps, Ireland, India, North America (King William's War), and on the high seas. In view of its extent, this war is sometimes called the first of a series of four world wars fought between England and France between 1689 and 1763. Early in the war, Louis supported an invasion of Ireland by the dethroned James II of England in the hope of toppling William III from his newly gained throne. James secured much of Ireland but a year later was defeated by William. When peace was concluded in 1697 (Ryswick), the powers restored to each other almost all the conquests made during the campaigns. France even handed back many areas seized during the period of "peaceful" expansion (see p. 280), except for Alsace and Strasbourg. Dutch troops were allowed to secure certain fortresses in the Spanish Netherlands as protection against renewed French aggression, and Louis consented to recognize William III as legitimate ruler of England.

The fourth and longest of the wars of Louis XIV was fought over the inheritance and division of Spanish possessions (War of the Spanish Succession, 1701–1714). There is no need to dwell on the intricate dynastic relations which gave the rulers of France, Austria, Bavaria, and Savoy the hope of inheriting all or a part of the lands of the Spanish Hapsburgs upon the death of the king of Spain (Charles II, 1665–1700). The stakes involved were tremendous, since Spain still owned Sardinia, Naples, Milan, the Spanish Netherlands, the Philippines, and a large part of the Western Hemisphere.

For almost four decades, Louis XIV had hoped to inherit at least the Spanish Netherlands and some Italian areas which he could then exchange for Lorraine and Savoy in order to attain for France her "natural frontiers." England and Holland, however, did not want France in the Spanish Netherlands. From 1668 on, frequent diplomatic discussions among the powers produced a number of treaties dividing the Spanish inheritance. The moribund king of Spain himself changed his testament several times. In the last moment, he willed his entire realm to the grandson of Louis XIV, in the belief that France alone had the strength to maintain the integrity of the Spanish inheritance. England, Holland, and Austria were alarmed by the thought that France and Spain and their two colonial empires might be united under one crown. Hence, when Louis XIV accepted the Spanish offer in the name of his grandson, Europe was promptly plunged into another war, with both sides blaming the other for unleashing hostilities.

Again France faced an overwhelming alliance of England, Holland, the Holy Roman Empire, Austria, Prussia, and Portugal, although this time she was supported by Spain under Louis' grandson, Philip V (1700–1746), the founder of the Spanish Bourbon dynasty that ruled Spain until 1931. Two of the other hopeful heirs, Bavaria and Savoy, also sided with France, although the latter soon switched to the anti-French camp, a desertion later rewarded by his allies with permission for the duke of Savoy to turn his duchy into a kingdom. The campaigns of this war were fought in many parts of Europe and the world, including North America (Queen Anne's War). This time the allies were served by two superior generals: Prince Eugene of Savoy

(1663–1736) who, in the service of Austria, had just vanquished the Turks, and the English Duke of Marlborough (1650–1722).

France lost most of the major battles. By 1708, she appeared utterly exhausted, but the war continued because of the tenacity, if not obstinacy, of the Sun King, and because of the overbearing demands of the allies, who insisted that Louis send French armies to Spain to overthrow his grandson. The French king supposedly replied that he would rather "fight his enemies than his children." In the end the coalition broke up after Charles VI (1711–1740), the Austrian pretender to the Spanish throne, succeeded as emperor and ruler of Austria and announced his intention to combine the Spanish and Austrian lands. Since the other powers had no interest in seeing the revival of such a gigantic Hapsburg monarchy, they now preferred to see Spain in the hands of Philip V. Hence, they initiated negotiations with Louis XIV.

In the settlements of the Treaty of Utrecht (1713), England emerged as the victor. France abandoned to her all claims to Newfoundland, Nova Scotia, and Hudson Bay territory. Moreover, England obtained Gibraltar and rights to the lucrative *asiento* from Spain (see p. 227). Holland was again allowed to garrison fortresses along the French border to add to her own security. Savoy was awarded a royal crown and received the Island of Sicily, which she exchanged with Austria for Sardinia in 1720. Thereafter her rulers called themselves kings of Sardinia. The young Philip V was recognized as legitimate king of Spain and ruler of the Spanish colonies. Although Austria received the Spanish Netherlands, Emperor Charles VI was not satisfied, fought one more year against France, and then quarreled with Spain over the Italian possessions until 1720, when Austria was awarded Milan, Naples, and Sardinia. Finally, the French had to promise that the two Bourbon dynasties of France and Spain would never be united.

As a consequence of this last war, first place among the powers shifted from France to England. Despite Louis' earlier success, England and Austria in the end had gained more land. France, to be sure, had secured a potentially valuable ally in the new Bourbon dynasty south of the Pyrenees, but Spain's friendship proved to be of dubious value during the eighteenth century. Moreover, the reign of Louis XIV had worn out the energies of France. With the nobility rendered idle, the bourgeois had assumed greater importance, but they were beginning to chafe under the restrictions of absolutism. When Louis XIV was lowered into his grave in 1715, it is said that many Frenchmen cursed his name and breathed a sigh of relief.

Austria and Prussia

Within the Holy Roman Empire, most rulers followed the same policies as before 1688: they continued to imitate everything French and attempted to acquire more absolutistic power. Bavaria rose briefly to greater importance through its alliance with France and the prospects of sharing in the Spanish inheritance. But the War of the Spanish Succession, some of it fought on Bavarian soil, weakened the country and again relegated it to a secondary place among the German states. Meanwhile, Saxony was diverted from its normal development when its duke accepted election to the throne of Poland (1697). The combination of Catholic Poland and Lutheran Saxony under a single ruler (King Augustus II) turned Saxony toward greater religious tolerance, made absolutism less feasible, and provided a freer intellectual climate than existed in most German states. But the Saxons also became involved in the turmoil of Polish politics and in frequent Polish wars, both of which weakened their state. The decline of Bavaria and Saxony brought to the foreground the two other contenders for pre-eminence within the empire, Austria and Prussia.

Although obliged for eight years to fight a two-front war, against the Turks in the East and against Louis XIV in the West, Austria emerged successful from the long Turkish War (see p. 284). In 1699, she annexed most of Hungary and the northern part of present day Yugoslavia, including the city of Belgrade. During the War of the Spanish Succession that followed, her armies performed well in battle, and, as we saw, Austria made large territorial gains. Immediately thereafter, a new war with the Ottoman Empire erupted (1716–1718), and once again Prince Eugene of Savoy carried the day. From this conflict, the Austrians acquired the rest of Hungary, another slice of Yugoslavia, and a part of present day Rumania.

As a result of these three wars, Austria became larger and stronger than ever. However, the addition of Belgians, Italians, and Rumanians to the polyglot realm of the Hapsburgs complicated even further the governmental problems of Vienna.

In Prussia, the successor to the Great Elector (Duke Frederick III, 1688–1713, who later became King Frederick I) was a mediocre ruler. Yet Prussia's power increased even during his reign. In both major wars against France, the Prussians sided with the Hapsburgs. At the outbreak of the second war, the Prussian elector struck a bargain with the emperor: in return for recognition of a royal title for himself, the elector agreed to support the Hapsburg claim to the Spanish throne. The elector promptly crowned himself king of Prussia (1701), a title which the powers later recognized in the Treaty of Utrecht. In an age stressing etiquette and precedence, acquisition of the royal title greatly added to the prestige of Prussia.

The new king, a lavish spender, soon depleted the savings of his predecessor. Some of his disbursements, however, added to the renown of Prussia. He embellished the city of Berlin with Baroque palaces, patronized the arts, established academies for the arts and for the sciences, and thus helped Prussia's capital to emerge as a new center of culture.

One challenge to Prussia's increasing domination of northern Germany arose during this period. The neighboring dukes of Brunswick proved highly successful during the seventeenth century in enlarging their holdings, which in 1692 were given the rank of Electorate of Hanover. Since the wife of the elector of Hanover was the granddaughter of James I of England, her son became the heir apparent to the English throne in 1701 (see p. 300). When George of Hanover became king of England in 1714, Prussia had to face the possibility of losing pre-eminence in northern Germany to the new Anglo-Hanoverian combination.

Russia's emergence in Europe

After a new period of disorders, which ended when the young Peter I overthrew the regent (his sister, whom he banished to a convent), the new tsar began his personal rule in 1689. Tall, strong, and full of vitality, as well as ruthless and uncouth, Peter was immensely ambitious for Russia and for himself. At home, he sought to make the monarchy safe and absolute and to bring Russia up-to-date with the West. Abroad, he hoped to break through the ring of Poland, Sweden, and the Ottoman Empire in order to give Russia direct contact with the West. Considering the size of his task, Peter, later called the Great, was surprisingly successful.

His projected reforms touched on almost all phases of Russian life. He freely adopted or adapted ideas and practices from other countries, particularly from Holland and Sweden. Where no models existed or fitted, he improvised with feverish impatience. Like Lenin, two centuries later, he welcomed foreign experts and technicians to help him modernize Russia. Supposedly he stated prophetically: "For a few score years only shall we need Europe. Then shall we be able to turn our back on her." Peter was not the first Russian "modernizer." Westernization had begun during the seventeenth century. A sizeable colony of Western Europeans had been established in Moscow, and Peter's father had undertaken some governmental reforms to secure better tsarist control. But it was Peter who in a few decades tried to whip his countrymen out of their lethargic provinciality and force them into the eighteenth century.

To better acquaint himself with the West, particularly with the Dutch technique of shipbuilding, he visited Königsberg, Holland, England, and Vienna (1697–1698). With a voracious curiosity, he observed all he could and even worked in shipyards and other enterprises so that he could personally teach his countrymen. Upon his return to Russia, he launched his reforms, remaining continually on the move, traveling, inspecting, ordering, and trying to dominate all phases of government, while at the same time fighting a long series of wars.

Modernization to him meant attacking actual or symbolic strongholds of conservatism as well as introducing new ideas and procedures. He ordered that Western dress be substituted for the traditional long robes, that men cut their beards—long beards being a religious as well as social custom —and that women be emancipated from their purdah-like seclusion. He also abolished the patriarchate of the Orthodox Church as it represented a focus of conservatism. The tsar then assumed greater control of the church through an appointed board, the Holy Synod. Such administrative changes at the top, however, hardly altered the traditional outlook of most parish priests and peasant believers.

On the other hand, Peter the Great arranged for the opening of schools and institutions of higher learning and had books published at state expense, first in Holland, later in Russia. Constantly he stressed the need for education, technical as well as liberal, as a basic step in Russia's advancement. Yet, he was not always consistent, for while he hoped that the lower classes would become literate in Russian, he urged the nobility to adopt French or German as the language of polite society.

To centralize the government and ensure more absolute power for the tsar, he deprived the *boyars* of their last political power. Rather than convert the nobles into an idle class, as in France, he tried to press them into governmental or military service. The central administration was streamlined into functional governmental boards, each entrusted with a specific jurisdiction. To control newly organized provincial districts, he instituted royal governors who, in many respects, resembled the intendants of Louis XIV. Moreover, he built a sizeable fleet and a large army.

His wars, his reforms, and his building program naturally required vast sums, and Peter I never succeeded in making his state solvent, no matter what fiscal expedients were devised. Nor was he very successful in his mercantilistic efforts to improve the economy. Agriculture was stimulated, some new industries established—particularly shipbuilding—and trade increased, but the middle class remained small. In spite of her vast potential resources, Russia stayed economically far behind the West.

In foreign affairs, Peter the Great succeeded in his aim of making Russia a respected European power, even though he could not achieve all of his specific objectives. During his reign of thirty-six years, Russia was at war for a total of twenty-eight years. On several occasions, the tsar's military exploits were unsuccessful at first, but he learned from his mistakes and often succeeded during a second attempt.

In a war against the Turks (1695–1700), the Russians finally captured Azov at the mouth of the Don River, thus gaining an outlet to the Black Sea. But they were forced to return the area in a subsequent unsuccessful war with the Turks (1710–1711). In the Far East, where Russians had continued their penetration during the seventeenth century, the Chinese obliged Peter to abandon the region north of the Amur River, an event which hardly dimmed Russia's continued interest in that area. In the South, Russia fought Persia and was able to increase her holdings along the western shore of the Caspian Sea.

The most important of Peter's military engagements was the drawn-out Great Northern War (1700–1721) with Sweden, which started disastrously for Russia (see p. 296). Undaunted by defeats, Peter built up a new and larger army and eventually routed the Swedes, who had penetrated as far as the Ukraine (Battle of Poltava, 1709). Russia's ultimate victory was not due merely to the tsar's military skill. Peter's cause was aided by good luck, by his allies, Denmark, Poland-Saxony, and Prussia, and by the fact that the Swedes had foolhardily overextended themselves. Russia profited immensely from this war, acquiring Livonia, Estonia, a part of Karelia, and Ingria, where Peter had already confidently started to build his new capital, St. Petersburg. Thus Russia had gained an outlet to the Baltic and sufficient coastal land to make her a potential mistress of this inland sea.

The apogee and decline of Sweden

Following her expansion during the seventeenth century, Sweden briefly reached the apogee of her power during the reign of the "Lion of the North," the adventure-loving Charles XII (1697–1718), who ascended his throne at the age of fifteen. Under his father (Charles XI), absolutism had been firmly enforced and the nobility rendered submissive to the wishes of the monarch (see p. 256), so that the young ruler felt confident enough of his power at home to spend the greater part of his reign campaigning abroad. Moreover, toward the end of his father's reign, Sweden had severed the strings which had tied her policies to the influence of Louis XIV. She had joined the League of Augsburg against France, but played no major role in the subsequent war. Her policy was becoming more independent, and her position more isolated.

Almost the entire reign of the impetuous Charles XII was spent on one long war, which ultimately cost Sweden her primacy in northern Europe and undermined the absolute role of her monarchs. The initial pretext for the Great Northern War was the conclusion of an anti-Swedish alliance among Denmark, Poland, and Russia for the purpose of dismembering Sweden's Baltic empire. In fact, Poland initiated hostilities by invading Swedish Livonia. Supported by a well-trained army and a full treasury, Charles promptly seized the offensive with supreme self-confidence. In the span of a year and a half, he forced the Danes to sue for peace, sailed up the Baltic and defeated the Russians (at Narva), expelled the Poles from Livonia, and conquered Poland. Once launched with such spectacular success, his military ambitions stood no bridling.

As master of Poland, he forced the Poles to elect a puppet ruler (Stanislas Leszczynski, a Polish nobleman whose daughter later married King Louis XV of France), and then conquered Saxony and compelled the elector to acknowledge his loss of the Polish throne (1706). Since Peter the Great had meanwhile seized some Swedish coastal lands along the eastern Baltic, the Swedish king launched an offensive into Russia proper. Hoping to obtain adequate support from rebellious Cossacks in the Ukraine, Charles marched southeast until his army was 1100 miles from his nearest supply base at Riga in Livonia. At Poltava (1709), he was overwhelmed by Peter the Great's reorganized forces, lost his army, and fled for refuge in Turkey. Despite such patent foolhardiness as Charles' dash into the heart of Russia, his exploits evoked admiration and hero-worship.

After Poltava, Charles' behavior became puzzling. With his encouragement, the Turks attacked and defeated Russia and took back Azov. Thereafter, for some inexplicable reason, Charles remained in the Ottoman Empire for three additional years, while Sweden had to face the onslaughts of a growing coalition. The Saxon elector dethroned Charles' Polish puppet king and resumed control over Poland. Russian, Polish, Danish, and Prussian armies seized most of the Swedish possessions south and east of the Baltic from Bremen in the West to Karelia in the Northeast. Even Hanover joined the anti-Swedish alliance. When Charles finally dashed back north in 1714, it was too late. He attacked the Prussians and Danes with limited success and finally was killed in battle in 1718.

After his death, the peace party came to power in Sweden and sought an end to the war, even at the cost of Sweden's domination of the Baltic. To curtail the power of future ambitious rulers, they forced the new queen, Charles' sister, to endorse a constitution. The Diet—consisting of four estates, nobles, clergy, burghers, and peasants—was again granted legislative powers, and a strong royal council was to supervise the actions of the monarch. As a result, the nobles regained influence and even the other classes attained some prerogatives. For some decades, absolutism remained discredited in Sweden.

Conclusion of peace treaties with Sweden's various enemies took three years (1718–1721). In the end, Hanover gained Bremen and Verden, and thereby access to the North Sea and better communications with England. Prussia obtained a part of western Pomerania, including the valuable harbor of Stettin. Russia took the greatest spoils (see p. 296), and only Poland-Saxony acquired nothing. By 1721, Sweden retained only Finland and two small enclaves on the coast of Germany. The impetuosity of the "Lion of the North" had accelerated the process of dissolution of her Baltic empire.

Dismemberment of the Spanish empire

During the seventeenth century, Spain had been at war for more years than she had been at peace. With her government increasingly inefficient under the imbecile Hapsburg king (Charles II, 1665–1700), Spain had become even less able to resist Louis XIV's encroachment on her European possessions north of the Pyrenees. Finally, the War of the Spanish Succession seemed like the death knell for the Spanish monarchy. Austrian, English, French, and Portuguese armies, supported by Catalonian rebels, fighting on behalf of the Austrian claimant Charles, battled the French and Spanish armies of the Bourbon Philip V. Although Philip was ousted twice from

Madrid, he returned both times to reconquer it. Wherever the armies passed, the countryside was devastated.

In the end, Philip V retained the Spanish throne, but, as we saw (see p. 292), was forced to surrender all of Spain's European possessions except for a few Mediterranean islands. Yet, largely through the skillful intrigues and diplomatic maneuvers of the king's ambitious second wife (Elizabeth Farnese), Spanish princes were eventually placed on the thrones of Naples, Sicily, and several north Italian principalities. Although these areas remained politically separated from Spain, their possession by Spaniards helped maintain Spanish influence and prestige.

King Philip himself was not very competent. Nevertheless some of his ministers tried to institute absolutism of the French type. Government became more centralized, the large landholders lost some of their power, and Catalonia was further deprived of privileges and more tightly controlled by Madrid. Some mercantilistic measures and a better fiscal policy brought a slight economic improvement. At the same time, more interest was again shown in America. A ministry of the Indies was established in Madrid, and additional vice-royalties were created in the Americas for better administrative control. Missionaries were encouraged to extend Spanish and Christian influence into Texas and California. Furthermore, several trading companies were chartered for trade with America, but they proved generally unsuccessful, and trade with the colonies continued to decline. From 1721 to 1735, an insurrection occurred in Paraguay, in which creoles and mestizos rebelled against the Spanish, a foretaste of the Latin American revolutions that were to occur a century later.

Despite the family relationships with the French Bourbons, Franco-Spanish relations were marked by frequent discord until 1733. Thereafter, Spain sided with France in every war until the outbreak of the French Revolution. Notwithstanding continuing decline, Spain was still a relatively important European and a formidable colonial power.

Toward the emergence of democratic institutions

The Glorious Revolution of 1688 not only changed England from a government by divine right into a constitutional monarchy, but indirectly gave new impetus to the development of democratic institutions in Holland and in England's North American colonies. The Revolution allowed Parliament and the Estates General of Holland to assume greater power, and helped to restore government by charter in some of the colonies. Moreover, in all three regions, the changes of 1688 favored the upper middle class and opened an era of greater religious toleration. It must be understood, though, that 1688 did not herald the triumph of "democracy" nor the advent of religious equality.

Constitutional monarchy in England

William and Mary had been called to the throne by Parliament in order to deliver England "from popery and arbitrary power." Establishment of government under law and the settlement of religious problems were therefore foremost in the minds of the members of Parliament. The Declaration of Rights they drew up and later enacted as the Bill of Rights (1689) embodied the basis for curtailing the power of the monarch through the will of Parliament. The bill stipulated the need for Parliament's consent to the making or suspending of laws, the levying of money, and the retention of a standing army. It guaranteed free elections to Parliament, which was to be allowed to convene frequently and debate openly. The bill also safeguarded certain civil rights: it legalized petitions to the king, prohibited excessive bail, and ordered trial by jury.

In the same year, Parliament passed the Toleration Act, granting freedom of worship to all Protestant dissenters who believed in the Trinity, provided they met behind unlocked doors, and their preachers gave an oath of allegiance to the king. Discrimination against Catholics continued, however, and soon even the teaching of Catholicism was prohibited.

The new and freer atmosphere, coupled with growing self-confidence of the middle class, was felt in politics as well as in economics. Most censorship laws against the press were abolished. Political life became more active as the two great parties grew in cohesion. The Whigs, composed largely of members of the merchant class, favored greater religious toleration—except for Catholics—and supported the government in its anti-French policy. They dominated Parliament from 1689 to 1701 and again from 1705 to 1710. The Tories, more Anglican in outlook and made up largely of the gentry class, were more wary of foreign entanglements. They grew tired of the interminable anti-French wars and helped the government take England out of the war after their return to power in 1710. Gradually the rulers recognized the advantage of choosing their ministers among members of the party which predominated in the House of Commons. Under the Hanoverians, this practice was to develop into a tradition and finally into the modern structure of parliamentary government.

Like the Tudors, William and Mary were well disposed toward the commercial interests of the middle class, with the result that new financial practices and institutions were introduced, which later helped England's entrance into the age of industrialism and capitalism. Yearly budgets for governmental revenue and disbursements were set up. The practice of financing the state in part through haphazard borrowing by the king was replaced by the sale of government debentures with a specific interest payment, thus making the national debt a permanent institution and a safe place for investment. Chartering of the Bank of England also facilitated governmental borrowing and investment credit, while the opening of the London Stock Exchange stimulated commercial enterprise, although it also led to occasional excessive financial speculation as during the reign of George I (1714–1727).

Besides the task of conducting the war against Louis XIV (see p. 290), William III faced three major problems. One was the question of his succession, since he had no heir. Parliament had made it explicit that no Catholic could rule over England. Yet, even after James II's failure to seize Ireland and invade England with the help of French forces (1689–1690), the danger of a return of the Catholic Stuarts remained alive. After the death of James II (1701), the Jacobite cause—the followers of James and of later Stuart pretenders were called Jacobites—was taken up by his son, the "Old Pretender" (James Edward, 1688–1766), who twice attempted to invade England (1708 and 1715) with the aid of French troops and Scottish rebels. As late as 1745, the "Young Pretender" (Charles Edward, 1720–1788), again aided by French and Scots, was to make a last attempt at a Stuart restoration. Meanwhile, in 1701, Parliament passed the Act of Settlement, stipulating that after first passing to James II's daughter, Anne of Denmark (1702–1714), the crown would go to the house of Hanover, as direct descendants of James I.

A second problem concerned William's relations with his native Holland. Some Englishmen complained that the king was using English resources and manpower to fight Holland's war against France. Because of his obsession with bringing Louis XIV to his knees, William was suspected of having accepted the English crown largely for the purpose of launching England's forces against France. Moreover, there was resentment against the king's Dutch favorites at the court in London. Hence Parliament decreed that foreigners were not to occupy public offices in England and that England was not to go to war for the benefit of the ruler's foreign interests. Officially directed at the house of Hanover, which was to furnish future rulers for England, this stipulation also represented an indirect warning to William III.

Finally, William faced the perennial problem of Scottish love of independence. Several prominent Scottish leaders hesitated to take the required oath of allegiance to the new king, and some seemed ever ready to support a return of the Stuart pretenders. The framework for Anglo-Scottish cooperation was constructed by Parliament in the Act of Union, 1707. The two states were to be joined in the Kingdom of Great Britain, with a single Parliament; but the Scots and English respectively were to retain their existing legal systems and their separate churches, Presbyterian in the North and Anglican in the South. The Act of Union helped bridge the gap between the two peoples but did not mollify resentment among all Scotsmen, some of whom continued to join occasional anti-English uprisings during the eighteenth century.

Much of William's time during his thirteen years as king of England was taken up by the War of the League of Augsburg, especially since he frequently led his own troops into battle. Under his successor, Queen Anne, England's main concern continued to be war—the War of the Spanish Succession with its accompanying colonial struggles. As we saw, England emerged from these two world wars as the strongest and wealthiest of the powers, with naval supremacy—an advantage which was to turn subsequent colonial competition ever more in her favor.

The Estates General of Holland

In 1672, the house of Orange had reassumed control of Dutch affairs with the leadership of William III (see p. 262). After William became king of England, he could no longer devote primary attention to Holland, although he remained its stadholder. Hence, the grand pensionary of Holland, Antonius Heinsius (1641-1720), conducted the actual administration of the Dutch Republic, a task he performed with great skill until his death in 1720. Heinsius helped keep Holland in the forefront of European diplomacy. He also retained his state in the pro-English and anti-French camp during the two great wars, which in the end, however, brought Holland no tangible benefits. On the contrary, the wars proved a serious drain on Dutch resources.

When William III died without offspring in 1702, his landholdings in Holland were inherited by a related branch of the house of Orange (usually known as Orange-Nassau). But the Dutch did not appoint a new stadholder. Since 1688, the Estates General, working with Heinsius, had enjoyed a constant increase in power and prestige, and they were not eager to risk falling again into the shadow of a new stadholder. Moreover, for many, the stadholdership had become associated with war, and the Dutch wanted peace.

During this period, Holland remained a great colonial power with extensive world trade from Japan to the Caribbean. But three wars against England and three against France in the span of half a century began to demonstrate that in the long run tiny Holland could not successfully maintain her power status in competition with the larger countries. Within the state, freedom of expression gained further ground, as it had in England, so that the two countries became the refuge for victims of political persecution and centers for the dissemination of ideas inimical to conservative monarchs.

Meanwhile the house of Orange-Nassau gradually consolidated its new possessions in Holland. In 1747, once again during a time of war (War of the Austrian Succession, 1740-1748) and of imminent danger to Holland, when the French had conquered the Austrian Netherlands and stood at the Dutch borders, a new stadholder was appointed. This time the stadholdership remained hereditary in the house of Orange-Nassau. Although the Estates General did not wield such wide powers as the English Parliament

after 1689, it retained effective checks on the stadholders, who acted like limited, uncrowned monarchs.

The twelve American colonies

Before 1688, the Stuart kings of England had repeatedly shown irritation
at the growing tendency of the settlers in the twelve North American colonies—Georgia was to be founded only in 1733—to assert wider powers of
self-government. Virginia had lost its charter of home rule as early as 1624;
that of Massachusetts was revoked in 1684; and New York was deprived of
hers soon thereafter. Parliament's victory in England, however, led to the re-
establishment of government by charter in various colonies and permitted
the settlers to reassume greater political independence from the crown.

Although all colonies possessed some type of legislative assembly with
the right to control local taxation, no common type of governmental system
was developed because of differences between the colonies in economic interests as well as in social structure. In fact, differences tended to become
greater as more immigrants from outside of England—French Huguenots,
Scottish Presbyterians, German political refugees, and others—moved to the
colonies.

These pragmatic experiments in governmental structures, conducted in
the less restrictive climate of the colonies, formed even better guidelines for
later political developments in Western society than England's constitutional
monarchy, even though many ideas implemented in America had their
origin in English tradition. Parliament's victory of 1688, which at first helped
secure more local freedom for the colonists, in the end turned out to be a
major cause for the American Revolution. For, as Parliament grew in power
and self-esteem, it tried to increase its jurisdiction. After 1707, it was empowered to legislate also for Scotland. Some decades later, especially after 1763, it
sought to extend its tax legislation (Stamp Act and others) over the colonies. The colonists, by tradition empowered to determine their own taxation, replied that they were subject to the crown of England, but outside the
jurisdiction of Britain's Parliament and prepared to resist against this encroachment on their traditional rights.

The theoretical basis of the Age of Reason

By the end of the seventeenth century, Western civilization was entering
the Age of Reason. Of course, no precise dates can be assigned to such an
age. Rationalism took root earlier in England and Holland, for instance,
than in Germany. There was also a time lag between the theoretical speculations of the English philosophers and the practical applications suggested by
the French *philosophes* or attempted by various enlightened rulers. Some
historians designate the entire span from the middle of the seventeenth to
the end of the eighteenth century as the Age of Reason. Others attempt to

distinguish between theoretical propositions and actual implementation, and they use the term "Enlightenment" for the middle of the eighteenth century (about 1730 to 1780), when rationalism began to affect politics, economics, and the outlook on life among the educated classes, a period when man had presumably become "enlightened."

Even in the eighteenth century, of course, rationalism was not to be universally accepted. In France, the new thought became widely entrenched in most of the noble and upper middle classes; in Russia, however, it remained the preserve of only a small segment of the nobility. On this basis, some observers assert that Russia never really experienced an "Age of Reason."

Here we shall briefly discuss the precursors of the Age of Reason, whose work, by its very nature, was mostly theoretical and speculative. Subsequent chapters will deal with the more practical effects of these theories.

The Age of Reason was based on a revolution in science which had begun with Nicholas Copernicus (1473-1543) in the early sixteenth century and was to culminate with Isaac Newton in the early eighteenth. Since this scientific revolution was a slow, cumulative process, the word "revolution" characterizes the nature of the change in man's scientific and mathematical thinking rather than its speed.

Copernicus' rejection of the Ptolemaic earth-centered universe in favor of a sun-centered system undermined many cherished ideals of the Middle Ages. According to churchmen and most laymen, such a notion contradicted the Bible as well as Aristotle; moreover it was considered contrary to common sense. Copernicus, as well as influential philosophers and scientists after him—such as Francis Bacon (1561-1626), Johann Kepler (1571-1630), Galileo Galilei, and Newton—abandoned unquestioned acceptance of biblical or Aristotelian pronouncements on science in favor of reliance on a new scientific method of investigation combining empirical data and mathematics. This scientific method, with its emphasis on empirical observations, was made more accurate with the application of newly discovered mathematical devices and through the use of better scientific instruments of observation and measurement. Logarithms, analytical geometry, and calculus were all discovered in the seventeenth century. When properly applied, the new method became a formidable tool for discovering scientific principles and permitting verifiable scientific predictions.

Discovering the principles or laws of the universe was particularly important for the scientists of the seventeenth century who were no longer interested in searching for divine purposes as the scholastic philosophers had been. The scientists rather wished to discover *how* things worked than *why* they happened, a change marking the transition from philosophy to science. As new scientific principles or laws were discovered—for example Kepler's laws of planetary motion and Galileo's law of acceleration—the notion that ascertainable laws underlie all observable phenomena gained acceptance. Finally, Newton's law of universal gravitation, which not only applied to gravity on earth but also explained the motion of celestial bodies, filled the scientists with boundless faith in natural laws and seemingly opened the entire universe to man's investigation, perhaps even to his domination.

These discoveries and speculations affected Western society and culture in numerous ways, only a few of which can be taken up here. In the fields of religion and philosophy, the new ideas called for fundamental re-evaluations. Besides contradicting the assumption that man was at the center of the universe, they tended to undermine the concept that the universe was relatively small and finite. Hence some philosophers began to re-examine the relationship of God to man, the place of God in the universe, in fact, the entire connection between mind and matter.

The monk and teacher Giordano Bruno (1548?–1600) deduced from the assumption of an infinite universe that God could not possibly be outside of infinity and must therefore be a part of the universe, manifest everywhere. Pantheism, which had been almost eradicated during the Middle Ages, was thus reborn. The ethical philosopher Spinoza agreed with this conception of a pantheistic universe but was also influenced by the growing mechanistic interpretation of the world and identified God with universal order. Descartes, on the other hand, could not accept such a monistic theory that combined mind and matter into one. Instead he adhered to a strict dualism of mind and matter. The material universe, he thought, could be explained in purely mechanical and geometric terms, on the basis of motion and form or extension. Although he believed in an immaterial soul, he found no satisfactory explanation for the relationship between this soul and the world of matter. Thomas Hobbes (1588–1679), for his part, asserted that "the mysteries of religion are like the pills prescribed by physicians for the sick." He decried Descartes' dualism as well as Spinoza's spiritual monism. To him, the world, even the soul and God, if He existed, were material.

Discussion of the relationship between mind and matter naturally led to renewed interest in epistemology—the study of how man arrives at knowledge. Most philosophers began to reject the notion of innate ideas in the mind of man and relegated revelation to a place of lesser importance. In essence, two main theories were developed: rationalism and empiricism. Descartes doubted the certainty of sense experience and retained as the only valid assumption the fact that he himself existed. From this basis, he proceeded to reconstruct all knowledge through reasoning. Mathematical, especially geometric, conclusions he considered as invariably valid. Hence, he believed that truth could be discovered by a process of ratiocination, and Cartesian philosophy came to be called "rationalism." John Locke, on the other hand, considered "the mind to be, as we saw, white paper, void of all characters, without any ideas." Hence he looked upon sense experience as the primary source of knowledge. Since observation of "external sensible objects" or "the internal operations of our minds" furnished "all the materials of thinking," Locke's theory is sometimes called environmentalism, although usually empiricism. Whereas Descartes had rejected empirical data as untrustworthy, Locke's empiricism did not deny the need for reason to develop sense experience from simple perceptions into more complex thought. In most respects, the Age of Reason was to be based upon a combination of Descartes' pure rationalism and Locke's empiricism.

SUGGESTED READINGS

Intellectual Revolution

Anthony, H. D., *Sir Isaac Newton* (Macmillan, 1961).

*Farrington, Benjamin, *Francis Bacon, Pioneer of Planned Science* (Dufour, 1963).

Geymonat, Ludovico, *Galileo Galilei: A Biography and Inquiry Into His Philosophy of Science* (McGraw, 1965).

*Hall, A. Rupert, *From Galileo to Newton; 1630–1720* (Harper, 1963).

Hazard, Paul, *The European Mind, 1680–1715* (World).

Kearney, Hugh F., *Origins of the Scientific Revolution* (Barnes and Noble, 1966).

Koyré, Alexandre, *From the Closed World to the Infinite Universe: The Intellectual Roofs of the Satellite Age* (Harper, 1958).

Nussbaum, Frederick Louis, *The Triumph of Science and Reason: 1660–1685* (Harper, 1962).

Wolf, Abraham, *A History of Science, Technology and Philosophy in the Sixteenth and Seventeenth Centuries* (Harper, 1961).

Political Developments

Klyuchevsky, Vasili, *Peter the Great* (Random, 1959).

Raeff, Marc, *Peter the Great—Reformer or Revolutionary?* (Heath, 1963).

Sumner, B. H., *Peter the Great and the Emergence of Russia* (Macmillan, 1962).

———, *Peter the Great and the Ottoman Empire* (Shoe String, 1965).

Wolf, John B., *The Emergence of the Great Powers, 1685–1715* (Harper, 1951).

American Colonies

Colbourn, Trevor, *The Colonial Experience: Readings in Early American History* (Houghton, 1966). Collection of primary and secondary sources.

Eggleston, Edward, *The Transit of Civilization: From England to America in the Seventeenth Century* (Beacon, 1959).

Hawke, David, ed., *U.S. Colonial History: Readings and Documents* (Bobbs, 1966).

Miller, John C., *The First Frontier: Life in Colonial America* (Dell, 1966).

Nye, Russel B., and Grabo, Norman S., eds., *American Thought and Writing*, Vol. I, "The Colonial Period" (Houghton). Documents.

Wright, Louis B., *The Cultural Life of the American Colonies: 1607–1763* (Harper, 1962).

CHAPTER XVII

❧❧ *The Enthronement of Natural Law*
(1715-1763)

The Age of Reason reached its bloom during the middle of the eighteenth century. Among the educated classes of most areas of Europe, it was assumed that all relationships in nature that are discernible by human reason were governed by natural law. This trust in natural law in turn led to the conviction that nothing in the universe is arbitrary. Since human reason was capable of discovering laws, man should be able to comprehend natural law. Through study and observation, through scientific discoveries and better education, man could constantly increase his knowledge of the world without the aid of divine revelation. The rationalists of the age thus became confident of man's ability to achieve progress. They looked upon past centuries, in particular the Middle Ages, as "dark ages," when man was confused by irrational superstitions and had underestimated the potentially enlightening power of his own reason. As a result, the eighteenth century became an age of general optimism.

This confidence in the existence of natural law and in man's ability to discover it affected philosophy, political theory, religious thought, and Western cultural development in general. It also induced changes in governmental practices in most of Europe.

The Age of Reason in action

Among the bases for this change in attitude was the theory of environmentalism. John Locke, one of its chief proponents, denied the existence of innate ideas in man. At birth, man was neither good nor bad, but endowed with the potential for rational thought. If later in his life man became bad or unhappy, the fault lay in his environment. Imperfect political institutions, religious superstitions, or corrupt social customs restricted man's natural behavior. To improve society and render people happy, one had to change the environment. This preoccupation with man's environment hastened the emergence of the social sciences. Many eighteenth century *philosophes*—those searching for practical applications of the new ideas are usually called by the French term *philosophes* rather than philosophers—became convinced that by finding better and more rational political and economic institutions, by improving education, by developing social welfare, in short by "rationalizing" society, it would be possible to create a heaven on earth. Naturally, not all *philosophes* agreed on the means needed to achieve this end. Voltaire (1694–1778), for instance, argued that science—the flower of man's intellect—and "rational" social behavior would lead man to a happier life. Jean-Jacques Rousseau (1712–1778), on the other hand, asserted that artificial social codes and even science and technology had corrupted man, and that the solution lay in man's returning to a more simple, natural life.

The conviction that there is nothing arbitrary in nature, coupled with the new interest in political science, led political theorists to devise governmental systems designed to substitute the rule of law for the arbitrary powers of absolute monarchs. Most of the theories involved some type of contract between the people and their government, either an unwritten, self-understood agreement or a written constitution.

Writing in the middle of the seventeenth century, Thomas Hobbes believed man to be primarily motivated by an instinct of self-preservation and a desire for power. In the state of nature, with no government to control human behavior, there is "war of every man against every man." But, Hobbes asserted, man's reason had helped him make the transition from the savage state to civilized society, in which the government was given absolute power to control those incapable of governing themselves. Such sovereign power was based on the natural order of things, not on divine sanction. If the government did not fulfill its duty of protecting all subjects, it lost its rights to absolute power and should be replaced by a more effective ruling body.

Not sharing Hobbes' opinion of the selfish and predatory nature of man, John Locke developed a contractual theory which stressed the inherent rights of individuals. Subjects surrendered to the government—which could be a constitutional monarch or a group of elected representatives—only limited rights, such as the power to judge and punish. In return, the government had to safeguard the subjects' rights to life, liberty, and property, the latter being anything that man "hath mixed his labor with." Locke's second of his *Two Treatises of Civil Government* (1679?) included the people's prerogative to change their government by revolution. People had the "right to resume their original liberty" and establish a new government, if the former one attempted to "destroy the property of the people, or to reduce them to slavery under arbitrary power." Locke's contract between ruler and ruled placed responsibility on both, but active participation in government was reserved to the property-owning classes.

In his *Social Contract* (1762), Rousseau, on the other hand, stressed not merely the inherent rights of the individual but also the theoretical ability of the masses to decide issues for themselves. In theory, the state was to be governed in accordance with the "general will." This "general will" was to determine what was best for society as a whole and not just for a majority or for a ruling clique. As a native of Geneva, Rousseau himself preferred direct democracy as best suited to ascertain and implement the "general will." In practice, however, his theories were to bolster not only the growth of radical, direct democracy during the French Revolution, but also the Jacobin concept of total dictatorship in which the dictator was deemed best qualified to fulfill the "general will."

Meanwhile another influential *philosophe,* Montesquieu (1689–1755), attacked the problem of arbitrary government not by proposing a contractual theory but by advocating a system of checks and balances which he thought he detected emerging in contemporary England. In his *The Spirit of the Laws* (1748), he proposed that tyranny could best be avoided if the functions of government were divided among executive, legislative, and judicial branches. His proposals later influenced American constitutional theory.

The rejection of innate ideas also raised new questions concerning equality among men. If children at birth were essentially alike, then one could not be born to one's station in life; nor could there be nobility by birth. All men were in essence equal. Such undermining of the existing class structure at first perturbed some of the *philosophes,* for even a Voltaire, the son of a lawyer, preferred to hobnob with the more refined aristocracy and basically disdained the lower classes. Rousseau and others during the second half of the eighteenth century, on the other hand, became emotionally enamored with the concept of equality among all people, a notion that was to find its echo in the revolutionary slogan of liberty, equality, and fraternity.

With men considered equal at birth, education assumed greater importance. Locke, Rousseau, Bishop Fénélon (1651–1715), and others wrote treatises on moral and intellectual education and helped spread the concept that education should not be limited to the ruling class. Rousseau's advocacy of permissive education, in which the child was to be allowed to follow its natural development, without social restraints and without unnatural inhibitions, was to lay the groundwork for entirely new educational theories.

Although discounting the existence of innate qualities, most *philosophes,* in particular Rousseau, believed that man by nature was good. Like nature itself, man's nature was deemed initially uncorrupted. Hence there existed no original sin and no sinfulness transferred from generation to generation. The "noble savage," popularized by Daniel Defoe (1659?–1731) in his *Robinson Crusoe* (1719), became an ideal in literary and philosophical circles. As part of the natural order of things, the "noble savage" was presumed to lead a pure, moral life. Just as Alexander Pope (1688–1744) wrote, "whatever is, is right," so the eighteenth century *philosophes* inferred that whatever is natural is right. Such a concept, of course, endangered existing values of morality and in time led to new standards of utilitarianism, which became popular during the nineteenth century.

The mechanistic interpretation of the universe, faith in natural law, and the concept of the "noble savage" also led to the formulation of a natural or rational religion. Many variations notwithstanding, the basic tenets of natural religion were similar. In his book *The Age of Reason* (1794), Thomas Paine (1737–1809) explained them succinctly: "I believe in one God, and no more; and I hope for happiness beyond this life. I believe in the equality of man, and I believe that religious duties consist in doing justice, loving mercy, and endeavoring to make our fellow creatures happy." The main concern of those who believed in natural religion was that man should lead a moral life. They were convinced that such a religion could be discovered and practiced by all men, Europeans and "noble savages" alike, without the benefit of revelation or of an organized church.

The relationship between God and man in such a natural religion was conceived of differently by various groups. John Locke, sometimes called a supernatural rationalist, saw no reason for rejecting revelation in its entirety. He asserted that revelation, although not proved by empirical knowledge and not verifiable *according* to reason, might conceivably be *above* reason. Moreover he inferred that revelation was useful as a stimulus to morality. The most widespread type of natural religion during the eighteenth century was Deism. Although believing in a God-created universe, Deists asserted that after creating this world machine and setting up its activating laws, God retreated from the universe, His further interference not necessary. Prayer, mysticism, and revelation had no function in such a world. The new ideas sometimes led to skepticism, as with the English philosopher David Hume (1711–1776), who could not be sure even of the existence of an original creator; or they ended in atheism such as that of Baron d'Holbach (1723–1789), who insisted on a mechanistic, materialistic interpretation of both mind and matter.

The *philosophes* of the Age of Reason were above all interested in accumulating critically and rationally analyzed knowledge. Inspired by Bayle's *Dictionary,* most of them contributed articles to the *Encyclopaedia* edited by Denis Diderot (1713–1784), himself a formidable exponent of rational thought. Rather than a mere record of knowledge, the *Encyclopaedia* was an exposition of the creed of the Enlightenment and served as an indictment of whatever the *philosophes* considered wrong with their own age. Similarly, Voltaire, Hume, Montesquieu, and Edward Gibbon (1737–1794) wrote historical works not merely to develop a more rational interpretation of the past, but also to indict their contemporaries. Meanwhile scientists continued the remarkable progress of the seventeenth century in astronomy, medicine, zoology, and botany. Others devoted themselves to technological inventions, using applied science to make life more comfortable. As a result, the basis for the approaching industrial revolution was created.

The aim of life during the Age of Reason was considered to be happiness. An abundance of didactic literature, social satire in painting, and pseudo-philosophic moralizing was aimed at helping man avoid the pitfalls of misjudgment and enabling him to lead a happy life. Like the Rococo style in architecture, the gentle music of the minuet, and the swaying of the crinoline, all seemed designed to amuse and to please. Furniture was made more comfortable, the boudoir was adapted for intimate gatherings, and painters—Watteau (1684–1721) and Fragonard (1732–1806), for example—produced canvasses that pleased the senses without provoking deeper thoughts. Despite the *philosophes'* call for a return to a more natural environment, the Age of Reason among the upper classes became the epitome of refined, artificial elegance. On the other hand, the growing importance of the middle classes entailed the diffusion of culture from its more restricted aristocratic circles. For instance, the founding of the British Museum (1753), the proliferation of public theaters and opera houses, the spread of magazines and the growth of popular literature involved increasingly greater segments of the population in the cultural processes of the period.

Government under natural law

The search for "rational" government, for secular, non-arbitrary ways of securing happiness for the people and strength for the state, underlay most reform movements of the eighteenth century. Most ideas naturally remained mere theoretical topics for heated debates in fashionable drawing rooms and for correspondence among *philosophes*. Yet a surprising number of attempts were made in Europe and North America to implement some of the theories and to reform social, political, and economic institutions. In general, two different approaches developed. One was based on the notion that only an enlightened ruler, a philosopher king, could know what is best for state and people, and that whatever this ruler could achieve for the state would ultimately benefit the people. The other approach rested on the assumption that the people themselves know best what would secure their happiness, and that whatever is good for the people will help strengthen the state. The first theory led to the development of enlightened despotism; the second to limited, constitutional monarchy or to republican forms of government.

Enlightened despotism in Prussia

From 1740 to 1786, Prussia was ruled by Frederick II, the Great, hailed by many contemporaries as a philosopher king. Frederick was indeed an extraordinary individual. An intellectual as well as a man of action, he was interested and gifted in music, science, the arts, philosophy, military strategy, diplomacy, and of course statecraft. He surrounded himself or corresponded with the best minds of his day and was himself a voluminous writer. Besides devoting much time to intellectual and artistic pursuits, he supervised all phases of Prussian government, conducted the state's foreign affairs, and commanded his own armies during eleven years of war, in which he distinguished himself as one of the best generals of the century.

From the *philosophes* he adapted a motley array of ideas. Like Hobbes, he assumed the power of the ruler to be absolute. In accord with Locke's environmental theories, he believed that the improvement of institutions would make people happy. He made the judicial branch relatively independent of the crown, perhaps influenced by Montesquieu's theories of the separation of powers; legislative and executive control however remained firmly lodged in the hands of the king. His concept of freedom resembled that of Rousseau in that he considered subjects free who obediently worked for the good of the state. In matters of religion, his personal beliefs might be called skeptical Deism and his official attitude favored toleration for all faiths, although he was not fond of Catholics or Jews.

The paternalistic Frederick II followed the *philosophes* in his conviction that rulers should act according to the principles of reason and that government should be rule under law. "Let the laws speak and the ruler be silent," was an ideal he attempted to implement. He reformed the legal system to ensure uniform procedures and speedier trials. Judges henceforth had to pass bar examinations and were given salaries by the state, thereby ending their development into an independent class as was the case in France. The composition of a law code was begun, although not completed during Frederick's reign, and an attempt was made to abolish torture and needlessly cruel punishments.

Even more important than law was the state itself, and Frederick regarded service to the state as the king's primary duty. Although believing in equality before the law, he considered equality among the people impossible. In fact, he insisted that each class perform a particular function in society, with only nobles permitted to staff the upper ranks of army and government. Despite the pleas of the *philosophes,* serfdom was retained in Prussia, except on the royal domain itself.

Economic practices were generally mercantilistic, with state subsidies to industry, the creation of royal factories, and the introduction of state monopolies in tobacco and coffee. Agriculture and forestry received particular attention from the king. He also permitted the state to grant mortgage credit to

impecunious nobles so that they would not have to sell their estates. Moreover he arranged for the sale and purchase of grain by the state in order to
keep prices relatively low and stable.

Frederick's success in turning Prussia into a first-rate power owed much
to his own skill and good fortune, and was also based on the legacy of his
frugal, austere father (Frederick William I, 1713–1740). Nicknamed the
"garrison king" because of his infatuation with drilling his soldiers, his
father had not been interested in intellectual pursuits, but had been an efficient administrator. Government under him had become strongly centralized, the provincial estates rendered powerless, and even the cities deprived
of home rule. Loyalty to crown and state as well as efficiency and strict discipline in army and civil service had been his primary concern. In addition, he
had recognized the need for basic education and initiated compulsory elementary schooling. When he died, his son inherited a well-governed state, a
full treasury, and a large, well-trained army.

Frederick II had a rather clear conception of what he hoped to accomplish in foreign affairs. He surmised that in the long run only the Hohenzollerns or the Hapsburgs would remain as serious contenders for pre-
eminence in the Holy Roman Empire. To be free to act in this contest, he
discontinued the pro-Hapsburg policy of his two predecessors and returned
to the independent position of the Great Elector. Recognizing that Prussia
was as yet small and poor in comparison with such giants as France, Austria,
and Russia, he was determined to increase Prussia's size, population, and resources. This task he accomplished successfully by doubling Prussian territory and even acquiring a land bridge between East Prussia and Brandenburg.

Shortly after his accession (1740), conditions seemed opportune for
Frederick's first move. England and Spain were at war in the Americas
(War of Jenkins' Ear, 1739–1748) and Anglo-French colonial rivalry in
India and America was at such a pitch that renewed fighting seemed imminent. Above all, Austria appeared weakened after her unsuccessful war
against France (War of Polish Succession, 1733–1738) and her defeat by
the Turks (1736–1739). In addition, Austria's future was clouded by a
question of succession rights. Since Emperor Charles VI had no male heirs,
he decreed that all Austrian holdings should be inherited by his eldest
daughter, Maria Theresa. In the course of some twenty years of diplomatic
maneuvers he had obtained written agreements from most of the powers
that they would respect his inheritance decree (the Pragmatic Sanction).
Frederick II surmised that such paper guarantees would not be respected by
those who laid claim to a part of the Austrian inheritance—Bavaria, Saxony,
and Spain—and that even France would try to acquire her share by seizing
the Austrian Netherlands. Hence, when Charles VI died in 1740 and was
succeeded by the young Maria Theresa (1740–1780), Frederick immedi-

ately dispatched troops to seize the province of Silesia as Prussia's portion of the inheritance.

Frederick's move initiated three Austro-Prussian wars over Silesia (1740–1742, 1744–1745, and 1756–1763). During these wars, the Prussian king developed a pattern of action which gained him a reputation for aggressive unscrupulousness. He showed little regard for treaties or agreements, or even for his allies, and followed only the principle of *raison d'état*. Three times he attacked without declaring war. He preferred making a quick military move to gain an advantage in the field and then offering peace terms favorable to Prussia. Conscious of diplomatic opinion, he always tried to justify his moves by a barrage of propaganda distributed in the capitals of Europe.

His first two wars against Maria Theresa became parts of a world war (War of Austrian Succession in Europe, King George's War, and War of Jenkin's Ear in America), in which Prussia, France, Spain, Naples, Bavaria, and Saxony, all hoping to snatch parts of the Austrian inheritance, fought against Austria and England. Constant distrust and disagreement marked the camp of the allies, whereas Austria demonstrated surprising strength and eventually received some aid not only from England, but also from Hanover, Holland, Hesse, Sardinia, and finally Russia. During the campaigns, not all of which turned in favor of Prussia, Frederick was sometimes quite despondent, but never willing to give up. Almost like Hitler two centuries later, he once wrote: ". . . either I will assert my power, or else . . . everything Prussian shall be buried with me." Since Prussian resources were insufficient for a long war, he twice concluded a unilateral peace with Austria, without consulting his allies. Each time Maria Theresa was obliged to confirm cession of Silesia to Prussia.

Between 1748 and 1755, the European states, in particular the colonial powers, enjoyed a respite in fighting, a truce before the final, great Anglo-French duel. The Prussian king, distrusted and diplomatically isolated, used the period for strengthening his army and training it in peacetime maneuvers—an innovation in military practice. But Prussia's position seemed precarious. In view of Frederick's general distaste for women, it seemed ironic that he should have to worry most about the intentions of three ladies—the tsarina of Russia (Elizabeth), Maria Theresa of Austria, and the Marquise de Pompadour (1721–1764), the real power at the court of France. The three women seemed determined to destroy Frederick, and together with the rulers of Saxony and Sweden concocted vague plans for a possible partitioning of Prussia. When renewed fighting broke out between the French and English in the Ohio Valley (1755) and, when soon thereafter France and Austria—traditional enemies for two and a half centuries—concluded an alliance, Frederick decided to strike.

In 1756, he launched his third war against Austria, which became a part

of the Seven Years' War (1756–1763) in Europe—called French and Indian War in the colonies. For the first part of the war, England and Hanover sided with Prussia, but British support was largely financial, since her
main efforts were concentrated overseas against France. Opposed to Prussia
was a gigantic coalition of Austria, Russia, Sweden, Saxony, France, and
most of the German states. Repeatedly invaded from all sides, Prussia was
several times at the edge of collapse. Since his opponents rarely moved in
cooperation, Frederick was able to rush his forces from one front to another,
fighting the allies one by one. Despite the king's prodigious efforts, Prussia
seemed lost by 1761. Berlin itself had twice been raided by Russian and Austrian troops, most of Prussia's territory was in enemy hands, and Frederick's
only ally, England, had discontinued its subsidies after the accession of King
George III (1760).

In the end, Prussia was saved by good fortune. A change of rulers in
1762 turned Russia from an enemy into an ally and then into benevolent
neutrality; Sweden left the coalition; and England and France seemed ready
to terminate hostilities. Hence, peace was made among all belligerents in
1763, and Prussia was allowed to retain Silesia. Although exhausted, Prussia
emerged as one of the strongest powers in Europe.

After these wars of the mid-century, Frederick the Great ruled Prussia
for another twenty-three years. The experience of the wars led him to a fundamental decision concerning Prussian international alignment that remained a maxim in German history. In view of the Franco-Austrian rapprochement, Prussia could no longer moderate Hapsburg ambitions by relying on friendship with France. Instead, Prussia needed the friendship of
Russia, which had become a major power. With Russia as an enemy, Prussia
always faced the fateful possibility of a two-front war against a Russo-
French combination, as had occurred during the Seven Years' War. With
Russia as a benevolent neutral or an ally, however, Prussia might be strong
enough to stand up to most European powers. Frederick's advice was to
guide most Prussian and German statesmen until 1914.

During the remainder of Frederick's long reign, he was primarily engaged
in internal reforms and reconstruction, and hence interested in remaining at
peace. Nonetheless, as a result of highly complex diplomatic maneuvers, he
obtained a sizable chunk of agricultural land from the first partition of
Poland in 1772 (see p. 334). Six years later, he engaged in a brief flourish of
hostilities to prevent Austria from buying a part of Bavaria from its impecunious elector.

Tension between arbitrary rule and enlightenment in France

Under Louis XV (1715–1774), increasing tension marked French society. Discontent stemmed from many factors: the attitude of the nobility of
the robe as represented by the *parlements;* the selfishness of the nobility of
the sword; the myopic favoritism practiced by the court; politico-religious

quarrels; and the threat of governmental bankruptcy, despite the fact that France was the wealthiest state on the Continent. Essentially the tension derived from a dichotomy of views: some nobles and clergymen and most of the upper middle class embraced the new ideas of "government under law." The insouciant royal regime, on the other hand, attempted to perpetuate the arbitrary rule that had existed under the Sun King.

Louis XV, the great-grandson of the Sun King, was five when he succeeded to the throne. Legally, the government remained a regency only until 1723; actually, Louis paid only perfunctory attention to governmental matters until the death of his tutor and chief minister, Cardinal Fleury (1653–1743). Even thereafter, the royal roué dabbled in affairs of state only intermittently when he was bored with other amusements. The state was run by royal favorites, one of whom, the astute Marquise de Pompadour, dominated the government as well as the king from 1745 to 1764. When Louis showed a sudden interest in politics, the results were sometimes harmful. For instance, he liked to amuse himself in foreign affairs with the so-called King's Secret by dispatching secret agents to promote a policy different from that pursued by the official French ambassadors, who received their instructions from the ministry of foreign affairs.

At age fifteen, Louis was persuaded to marry the twenty-two year old, penniless daughter of the dethroned Polish king (Maria Leszczynska, see p. 296). Although the queen bore him ten children, the king spent much of his life flitting from one royal mistress to another.

The official regent from 1715 to 1723 was a grandson of Louis XIII, the intelligent and indulgent Philip of Orléans (1674–1723). Since Louis XV was a sickly child, the regent hoped to become the founder of a new dynasty in case the young prince died. For this purpose he contracted an understanding with the newly enthroned Hanoverian king of England for mutual support between the houses of Hanover and of Orléans. Philip also reversed Louis XIV's practice of relying on bourgeois administrators. For the existing ministries he substituted government by councils in which the upper nobility dominated. Although his council system was later abandoned because it proved impractical, the trend toward allowing the nobility a greater voice in government continued. In the course of Louis XV's reign, the upper ranks of army, church, and government became increasingly reserved for nobles—at a time when the wealthy bourgeois were being nourished with ideas of enlightenment and equality.

During Orléans' regency, the Scottish speculator John Law (1671–1729) was allowed to undertake an interesting experiment, similar to one tried in contemporary England. He founded a bank, endowed by the government with power to issue paper money, which was to help the state redeem its public debts. For better exploitation of the advertised riches of Louisiana, he then created a trading company which quickly prospered on the basis of monopolies awarded by the government. Those receiving paper money in settlement for previous loans to the state were encouraged to invest in shares of the Louisiana company. Within two years, the Paris stock exchange had become the scene of run-away financial speculation. Shares rose to forty times their value, without being backed by commensurable company profits. The crash came in 1720, shortly after similar speculation had burst the "South Sea Bubble" in England. A few who sold in time made huge fortunes, most others were ruined financially. John Law fled from France, suicides abounded, and the French remained for a long time wary of paper currency. Despite its failure, John Law's scheme helped stimulate the French economy and in retrospect seems to foreshadow the age of capitalism.

Under the administration of Cardinal Fleury, 1726–1743, France enjoyed relative financial stability. To reduce state expenses, the cardinal favored peace; yet France went to war twice during his regime. Despite Fleury's accommodation, there was almost continuous political tension, which further increased under his numerous successors. Struggles between the *parlement de Paris* and the government reappeared. The *parlement,* which had been kept in submission by Louis XIV, assumed more power to remonstrate against royal edicts, at times refusing to register them or failing to enforce them. The government reacted fitfully to such challenges. The king occasionally commanded the *parlement* to obey his order or even condemned its members to temporary exile from Paris; at other times he did little to enforce the royal will. The *parlement* enjoyed wide popular support, as it pretended to resist an arbitrary ruler in favor of a limited monarchy under law. Actually, the members of the *parlement,* fearful of losing their hereditary jobs, were primarily defending the interests of their own class, the nobles of the robe. In 1771, the *parlement de Paris* was abolished (by the reforming Chancellor Maupeou) and an entirely new judiciary created. This momentary victory of the government was short-lived; when Louis died three years later, the *parlements* were re-established with their former obstructionist prerogatives.

Tension also resulted from politico-religious quarrels between the Jansenists (see p. 282) and the Jesuits. The two groups disagreed on doctrinal matters—such as the question of predestination—on control of education, which was largely in the hands of the Jesuits, and on the ideal amount of papal power over the French Church. The *parlements* generally supported the Jansenist cause, whereas the government at first sided with the Jesuits. In the end, the government itself grew suspicious of the independent power and wealth of the Jesuits and expelled them from France in 1764.

Throughout, Louis XV condoned an arbitrary policy that seemed ill-suited to the Age of Reason and that contrasted sharply with government under law as it was developing in England and Prussia. Political arrests could still be made by *lettres de cachet,* a sealed royal order from the king sending victims to prison for unlimited periods. Civil service examinations, as developed in Prussia and China, did not exist. Candidates obtained their positions regardless of their qualifications, either by inheritance, by purchase, or by connections with an influential courtier.

In foreign affairs, the reign of Louis XV began with a complete disregard for the advice left by his dying great-grandfather. Toward the end of his reign, Louis XIV had recognized that England had supplanted the Hapsburgs as France's principal rival, and he had urged that French policy henceforth be directed at preventing further British growth. Yet, as we saw, Philip of Orléans immediately initiated a pro-British policy, and before the so-called Diplomatic Revolution of 1756, France fought two more wars against Austria. Consequently, the French continued to concentrate their attention on Continental affairs, whereas England devoted increasing energies to consolidating and enlarging her overseas empire.

In the War of the Polish Succession, France, Spain, and Sardinia fought against Austria and Russia, ostensibly to help restore Louis' father-in-law (Stanislas Leszczynski) to the Polish throne which he had briefly occupied under the protection of Charles XII of Sweden (see p. 296). Such an endeavor seemed hardly vital to French interests. Unexpectedly, however, France gained from the war the rights to Lorraine, which she formally annexed in 1766.

During both wars of the mid-century, Spain sided with France against England. In the War of the Austrian Succession, France was allied with Prussia against Austria, whereas in the Seven Years' War she was Austria's ally against Prussia. Fighting occurred in Europe, North America, India, and on the high seas. The English captured Louisburg in North America, while the French took Madras in India and conquered the Austrian Netherlands. Despite some spectacular French victories on the Continent, England and France arranged for a reciprocal restoration of all conquests at the end of the first war (Peace of Aix-la-Chapelle).

In the interval between the two wars, both England and France prepared for renewed fighting. In America, the French sought to fortify their possessions by constructing a series of forts and concluding new alliances with Indian tribes against the English who began to press into the Ohio Valley. In India, the French were at first successful in expanding their influence under the skilled Joseph-Francis Dupleix (1697–1763), governor general at Pondichéry for the French East India Company. Paris, however, was more interested in trade than in seeing Dupleix conquer Indian land and recalled him in 1754. Meanwhile, the initiative was assumed by Dupleix' rival, the intrepid Robert Clive (1725–1774), who worked for England's East India Company. In a series of brilliant victories, Clive eventually drove out the French and Dutch and gained control over large areas of India, including Bengal. He thus helped found what was to become Britain's Indian empire.

On the Continent, France prepared for the next war through the Diplomatic Revolution which gained her the alliance of Austria. This new Austro-

French friendship, sealed in 1770 by the marriage of Maria Theresa's daughter Marie Antoinette to the future Louis XVI (1774–1792), was to last until 1792; yet, the alliance hardly benefited France against England during the Seven Years' War.

During the initial fighting, France gained some victories on the Continent and in America. But on the long run, she was soundly defeated overseas. In the Peace of Paris (1763) that ended the war, France lost all her North American holdings, except for two off-shore islands and some fishing rights. In India, she retained only Pondichéry and a few trading stations. Thus ended the Anglo-French colonial duel that had begun in 1689. What was left of the French overseas empire consisted largely of islands and trading posts—some of the islands, especially those in the Caribbean, still furnishing a rich source of trade. In 1768, France acquired another island by purchasing Corsica from the Republic of Genoa—a sale made one year before the birth of the Corsican Napoleon.

Limited monarchy in England

While enlightened Frenchmen remained under an arbitrary government, and Prussians experimented with enlightened despotism, the British gradually worked out the practical implementation of limited monarchy as theoretically framed in the Bill of Rights of 1689. The growth of rule by law and the consolidation of parliamentary government were facilitated by the fact that the early Hanoverian kings were neither astute rulers nor overly concerned with English government. The first Hanoverian king (George I, 1714–1727) was kept busy by his German mistresses and did not even learn the English language. The Whigs saw in his accession a chance to return to power and supported him more out of fear of a Jacobite and Catholic restoration (see p. 300) than out of respect for the new monarch. The second Hanoverian ruler (George II, 1727–1760) also remained much interested in his native Hanover and in Continental affairs. Both monarchs, however, carefully abided by the limitations which English tradition had placed upon the king. Hence, Parliament could further consolidate its position.

Eighteenth century England was of course no democracy in the contemporary sense of the word. The governmental process was still dominated by the crown and by the "establishment," that is, the commercial and landed interests who were represented in Parliament. The king could still appoint and dismiss ministers at will, without parliamentary approval; he could create new lords and thus influence the deliberations of the upper house; and he could declare war, sign treaties, and veto legislation—although the Hanoverians no longer made use of the latter prerogative. Through bribery and dispensation of royal favors, he could also influence elections.

Still, the trend toward parliamentary government continued. The House of Commons, containing representatives from the boroughs, counties, and the universities, controlled financial matters and exercised a dominant voice in legislation. Vital for the development of an executive body relatively independent of the crown was the emergence of the cabinet. With the ministers usually chosen from one party, the one that predominated in the House of Commons, the cabinet acquired greater solidarity, and, indirectly, more dependence on Parliament than on the king. The power of the cabinet was also enhanced by the development of the prime ministership. Since the first Hanoverian king (George I) rarely attended the deliberations of his ministers—in part because they knew no German and discussion had to be conducted in French or Latin—the "prime minister" gradually replaced the monarch as chairman of the meetings of the cabinet. Sir Robert Walpole's long tenure of the office of "prime minister" further consolidated the relatively independent position of the cabinet.

The two political parties, the Whigs and Tories, were still only loosely organized, with allegiances often more personal than ideological. Yet party cohesion continued to grow. Although their ranks were not always united, the Whigs remained in power from 1714 until 1761. When George III, the first "British" Hanoverian truly concerned with English politics, ascended the throne in 1760, he used his influence to help the Tories attain control of Parliament in the hope of gaining more power over his ministers and thereby acquiring more sway over Parliament.

From 1721 to 1742, Parliament was dominated by the remarkable Sir Robert Walpole (1676–1745), whose power was based on skillful political maneuvers and well-placed bribes. Walpole helped re-establish government credit after the bursting of the South Sea Bubble, and his policies in general contributed to England's growing prosperity. In the end he was toppled from power by the many jealous enemies he had made through his rather unscrupulous machinations.

Meanwhile another formidable politician, William Pitt, the Elder, later the Earl of Chatham (1708–1778), had risen to prominence in the House of Commons through his persuasive oratory and his fierce opposition to the king's preoccupation with Hanoverian affairs at the expense of the overseas empire. At the crucial point in the French and Indian War, Pitt was entrusted with the conduct of diplomatic and military matters and helped organize England's victories over France. Although partly responsible for the spectacular growth of the British empire, he was dismissed in 1761 by George III, who wanted a quick peace and did not wish to be outshadowed by a powerful prime minister.

With her government relatively stable, England experienced great economic progress during the eighteenth century. More land was placed under cultivation and agricultural methods and the breeding of livestock were improved, providing more available food. The enclosure movement, which had begun in the fifteenth century, reached its high point during the eighteenth. The open fields and common lands of the medieval manors were abolished, and landed estates were surrounded by fences, ditches, or hedges. Enclosures permitted increased raising of sheep and thus more production of wool. They also furthered the growth of larger estates, while hurting the smaller peasant holdings and driving small landholders into becoming agricultural workers or moving to the city in search of work. Thus, the enclosure movement contributed to the availability of cheap labor for the development of industry. On the other hand, the larger, prospering estate owners gained surplus capital for commercial investments.

Despite the bursting of the South Sea Bubble, trade and manufacture also expanded. Aided by new technical inventions and by improved transport, production soared in wool, cotton weaving, silk, coal, iron, pottery, and glass. More banks and even some insurance companies—among them the famous Lloyds of London—were organized to further this expansion. Thus, while becoming the foremost imperial power through her successful wars against France, England was also laying the economic and financial basis for the Industrial Revolution.

Even more than the French, Englishmen began to engage in social criticism. Churchmen, writers, painters—Jonathan Swift (1667-1745) and William Hogarth (1697-1764), for example—criticized social conditions, and an occasional politician called for social reform. Although little was actually done to ameliorate conditions among the poor, a secular social conscience seemed to emerge. In 1750, the English gave up the *asiento* for the Negro slave trade, but slavery was not yet outlawed. There was also somewhat greater toleration for religious dissenters, and the statute against witchcraft was abolished, ending the nefarious practice of executing people on charges of sorcery.

Non-rationalist tendencies

Despite the pervasiveness of rational thought among the upper classes in most of Europe, the period was not one of unadulterated rationalism. One must keep in mind that the bulk of the people—the lower middle classes, the workers, and the peasants—were basically untouched by the new thought. Also among the educated segment of society, the Enlightenment did not completely obscure earlier tendencies. This was particularly true in some areas of the arts. Johann S. Bach (1685-1750) and George F. Handel (1685-1759) continued to compose polyphonic, Baroque church music at a time when Christopher W. Gluck (1714-1787) was about to "rationalize" opera with a new way of combining music and drama. Also, Baroque architecture and sculpture with its appeal to the emotions continued to dominate in most of Germany, Austria, and Italy.

A new antirational trend also arose, less a continuation of the past—such as Baroque art—than a protest against the Age of Reason. Such a trend was particularly noticeable in religion. Many took exception to the cold, impersonal rationalism of natural religion as well as to the frequently perfunctory services of the established Protestant and Catholic churches. The Quakers, or Society of Friends, with their stress on personal faith, had launched their movement in England during the seventeenth century. During the Age of Reason, groups in various countries—the Convulsionaries and Quietists in France, the Pietists and Moravians in Germany—advocated a more personalized, emotional religion than the God-created world machine of the Deists. In England, John Wesley (1703–1791), who had begun his missionary work in Georgia and Pennsylvania, together with his brother Charles (1707–1788) organized the Wesleyan societies, the basis for later Methodism. Insisting that faith, love, and practiced Christianity were more important than church ritual, they preached outdoors to the lower classes, when pulpits of the established churches were not made available to them. Their fervent appeals, supported by the singing of hymns, turned their sermons into moving religious experiences. A measure of mysticism characterized early Methodism, Quietism, and Pietism.

In areas other than religion, a gradual reaction against the Age of Reason gained momentum after the mid-century and pointed the way toward the Romantic era that was to follow. In his later canvasses, the English painter Thomas Gainsborough (1727–1788), for instance, used an impressionistic style to exalt nature and the exceptional individual. English gardens, with their twisted, tree-shrouded paths and mysterious by-ways, began to supplant the formal, classical French parks.

The reaction was particularly noticeable in literature. Samuel Richardson's (1689–1761) novels—such as *Pamela* (1740) and *Clarissa Harlowe* (1747)—were didactic in consonance with the Age of Reason but also sentimental and emotional. Romantic epics and poetry of the Middle Ages were being revived (James McPherson, 1736–1796), and even the rational Diderot wrote plays apt to produce tears rather than logical thought. Jean-Jacques Rousseau, although a representative of the Age of Reason, was at the same time an influential advocate of antirational thought. He believed in natural religion, not because he perceived the marvels of nature by rational deduction, but because he felt them through emotional perception, since intuition rather than reason was his guide. The beauties of mountains and valleys he worshiped with a sense of abandoned emotion. From his *Confessions* (1781) and his treatise on education, *Emile* (1762), one surmises that if man would but lead a natural life, following his instinctive impulses, he would be happy. Thus Rousseau was not only an important forerunner of revolutionary political thought (see p. 308), but also a precursor of the Romantic movement.

SUGGESTED READINGS

General Works on the Eighteenth Century

Anderson, Matthew Smith, *Eighteenth-Century Europe, 1713–1789* (Oxford U.P., 1966).

Barber, Elinor G., *The Bourgeoisie in Eighteenth Century France* (Princeton, 1955).

Beloff, Max, *The Age of Absolutism 1660–1815* (Harper, 1962).

Bruun, Geoffrey, *The Enlightened Despots* (Holt, 1967).

*Green, Frederick C., *Eighteenth-Century France* (Ungar, 1964).

Humphreys, Arthur Raleigh, *The Augustan World; Society, Thought and Letters in Eighteenth Century England* (Harper, 1963).

Manuel, Frank E., *The Age of Reason* (Cornell, 1951).

Palmer, Robert R., *Catholics and Unbelievers in Eighteenth Century France* (Princeton, 1966).

Robbins, Caroline, *The Eighteenth-Century Commonwealthman* (Atheneum, 1968). On English political thought, 1688 to 1776.

Stephen, Leslie, *History of English Thought in the Eighteenth Century,* 2 vols. (Harcourt, 1902).

White, Reginald James, *Europe in the Eighteenth Century* (St. Martins, 1965).

Enlightenment

Becker, Carl L., *Heavenly City of the Eighteenth Century Philosophers* (Yale, 1959).

Cassirer, Ernst, *The Philosophy of the Enlightenment* (Beacon, 1955).

Gay, Peter, *The Party of Humanity, Essays in the French Enlightenment* (Knopf, 1964).

Havens, George R., *The Age of Ideas: From Reaction to Revolution in Eighteenth Century France* (Macmillan, 1965).

Manuel, Frank E., *The Eighteenth Century Confronts the Gods* (Atheneum, 1967).

———, *The Enlightenment* (Prentice-Hall, 1965). Excerpts from the writings of the *philosophes.*

Martin, Kingsley, *French Liberal Thought in the Eighteenth Century: A Study of Political Ideas from Bayle to Condorcet* (Harper, 1963).

Willey, Basil, *The Eighteenth Century Background: Studies in the Idea of Nature in the Thought of the Period* (Beacon, 1961).

Wolf, A., *A History of Science, Technology and Philosophy in the Eighteenth Century* (Harper, 1952).

Political Developments

*Dodwell, Henry, *Dupleix and Clive: The Beginning of Empire* (Verry, 1962).

Dorn, Walter L., *Competition for Empire 1740–1763* (Harper, 1962).

Ford, Franklin L., *Robe and Sword: The Regrouping of the French Aristocracy after Louis XIV* (Harper, 1953).

Gooch, George Peabody, *Frederick the Great: The Ruler, the Writer, the Man* (Shoe String, 1962).

*Priestley, Herbert I., *France Overseas Through the Old Régime* (Octagon, 1966). History of the French colonies to 1815.

Robert, Penfield, *The Quest for Security; 1715–1740* (Harper, 1963).

Robertson, Charles Grant, *Chatham and the British Empire* (Macmillan, 1962).

CHAPTER XVIII

✿✿ *From Reform to Revolution*
(1763-1789)

During the second half of the eighteenth century, implementation of enlightened theories gained momentum. Many rulers became captivated by the proposals of the *philosophes* and attempted to institute enlightened reforms. Even the revolt of the thirteen colonies in America resulted in many respects from the practical application of the new political and philosophical thought of the century. In France and Poland, where attempts at reform failed, the consequences were disastrous.

Continued attempts at enlightened reform

In Russia and Austria, as well as in the Iberian and Scandinavian monarchies, the governments during this period were concerned with legal, social, and economic reforms. Unlike in England, however, no political reforms were undertaken that might limit the power of the ruler. On the contrary, the monarchs of all six states sought to establish a more or less enlightened despotism.

Russia under Catherine II

Russia had emerged as a major factor in European diplomacy during the reign of Peter the Great (see p. 294) whose defeat of Sweden had only partially broken the ring around his state. He had gained no influence over Poland nor weakened the Turkish hold on the Black Sea. Hence, Poland and Turkey remained among the main concerns of Russia's rulers during the eighteenth century. Peter left another legacy because of his inability to establish an orderly system of succession to the throne. After the death of his son, whom he had condemned on charges of treason, Peter had decided that the ruler should have the right to name his own successor, although he himself did not avail himself of this prerogative. Such an arrangement left ample room for palace intrigues. During the century after Peter's death, four of the nine rulers of Russia (among them three women) achieved their position through violence. As in ancient Rome, palace guards or dissident army groups assumed the role of king-makers.

The period 1725-1741 was one of internal chaos, with four short reigns, during which adventuresome German nobles gained paramount influence at the Russian court. Nonetheless Russia was successful in her foreign undertakings. In the War of the Polish Succession, her armies prevented the French from establishing their candidate on the Polish throne. Although another Saxon elector (Augustus III, 1734-1763) became king of Poland, Russian influence over Polish affairs was sharply increased through this intervention. In the South, the Russians succeeded in retaking Azov from the Turks.

During the mid-century (under the strong-willed Tsarina Elizabeth, 1741-1762), Russian foreign policy continued to be relatively successful. The Tsarina acquired a portion of Finland from Sweden and established close ties with Austria to support further Russian designs on Poland and Turkey. In the Seven Years' War, Russian victories over Frederick the Great introduced Russia as a major military power into Central European affairs. At the time she experienced an intellectual awakening, the Tsarina encouraged the introduction of enlightened ideas, founded the University of Moscow and an Academy of Fine Arts, patronized Italian and French Rococo art, and imbued her court with her own admiration of the French language, literature and customs.

Catherine II (1762-1796), a German princess who had married a grandson of Peter the Great, came to power through a military coup in which her husband was murdered. According to Catherine herself, "the cause of [her husband's] death was established as inflammation of the bowels and apoplexy"; and she added, "he had an inordinately small heart, quite withered." Intelligent, ruthless, and rather uncomely, endowed—according to the British ambassador—with "a propensity to voluptuousness," Catherine faced a dilemma in her policies. In her ideals, she shared the aspirations of the *philosophes*. In practice, she soon became convinced that the ideals of the Enlightenment could not be applied to Russia.

Catherine engaged in a lively correspondence with Voltaire, Diderot, Rousseau, and other *philosophes*. From an exchange of letters with a famed Italian professor of law (Beccaria, 1738-1794), she gathered suggestions for her planned legal reforms. Early in her reign, she convoked a large assembly of nobles, burghers, and even some peasants to discuss needs for reform, especially in legislation. The lengthy *Instructions* which she issued to this assembly sounded like a credo of her enlightened ideas. Although insisting that "the sovereign is absolute," she enunciated such new concepts as that "it is better to prevent crimes than to punish them," and that the purpose of government should not be "to deprive people of their natural liberty; but to correct their actions, in order to attain the supreme good." Although copies of the *Instructions* in four languages were distributed all over Europe, few concrete reforms resulted in Russia.

In 1775, Tsarina Catherine undertook some governmental reforms that divided Russia into smaller administrative units, providing on the one hand more efficient centralized control and on the other a slight amount of participation in government on the part of locally elected officials. Ten years later, she awarded some self-rule and economic privileges to the inhabitants of towns. In religious matters, she was tolerant like her contemporary, Frederick II of Prussia, but she assumed even tighter control over the Orthodox Church than had been done by Peter the Great. In economic affairs, she was less mercantilistic than Frederick and more influenced by the physiocrats (see p. 330), trying to free trade and manufacture from unnecessary restrictions, tariffs, and monopolies. During her reign, Russia's manufacture and foreign trade expanded significantly. Like her predecessor, she loved everything French, and under her, St. Petersburg came to resemble Paris.

Despite her flirtations with the Enlightenment, Catherine was conservative in practice. Upon the nobility she lavishly bestowed increased prerogatives, economic and tax privileges, more jurisdiction over their estates, and greater power over their serfs—whom the nobles could treat as they wished, provided they did not kill them. Even more than Frederick the Great, she tried to turn Russia into a nation of estates, dividing nobles, burghers, peasants, and serfs into four distinct groups, each endowed with—or deprived of—specific privileges. The nobles and burghers were given stated rights. The peasants were left to shift for themselves, and serfdom was more strictly enforced than ever, especially after a violent peasant and serf uprising (Pugachev rebellion, 1773-1774) frightened the government. Catherine's reign thus added to the cleavage between the small, upper social crust, living in an atmosphere of privilege and French culture, and the vast masses of peasants and serfs, who remained untouched by the Enlightenment.

When the French Revolution broke out in 1789, the tsarina became terrified by the spectre of popular violence. "Equality is a monster," she commented, "it wishes to be king." She tried to shield Russia from the revolutionary fever by a curtain of censorship, persecuted outspoken Russian liberals, and expelled French nationals who were not willing to sign an anti-Jacobin loyalty oath. Thus the era of Enlightenment came to an abrupt end in Russia.

In foreign affairs, Catherine the Great was highly successful, adding more territory to Russia than any ruler except Ivan IV, who had laid claim to all of Siberia but had not obtained it. In two successful wars against

Turkey and in three partitions of Poland (see p. 334), Catherine broke the ring around Russia, advanced the Russian frontier over three hundred miles westward, and seized the shores of the Black Sea from the Dniester River to east of the Crimea. Russia thus gained warm water ports in the South and common frontiers with Prussia and Austria in the West, a change which drew her even more into European affairs.

Catherine's reign also saw the beginning of the Near Eastern and Balkan questions: the rivalry between Russia and Austria—later also France and England—for control over the declining Ottoman Empire. As an initial step, Russia obtained treaty rights to intervene in Moldavia and Wallachia (modern Rumania) and to protect Greek Orthodox believers in Turkey. In 1781, Catherine concluded an alliance with Austria, and suggested that Russia and Austria partition the Balkan Peninsula between themselves. But this Russo-Austrian understanding was short-lived, and the two states soon became contenders for paramount influence in the Balkans, a rivalry that was to last until the outbreak of World War I in 1914.

Austria under Maria Theresa and Joseph

Maria Theresa was a devout Catholic, with a motherly devotion to her large family and to her numerous subjects. Although she regarded the French *philosophes* with suspicion, she introduced some reforms consonant with their ideas. A state budget was instituted, the penal system improved, and more humane treatment of serfs ordered. The local estates were deprived of their remaining functions and governmental controls were concentrated more directly under Vienna. To futher Hapsburg power, German was decreed as the only official language throughout her multilingual possessions. As under her father, Charles VI, economic progress remained slow and uneven, with the government showing more interest in furthering trade than in stimulating production.

In view of Austrian failures in the 1730's, Maria Theresa's success in war and diplomacy seems all the more remarkable. Despite her piety, she furthered Austrian interests by practicing Machiavellianism in the manner of Frederick II and Catherine II. Yet she always retained some religious scruples. "God grant," she once remarked, "that I be not held accountable for it in the next world." Immediately after her accession, she rallied her peoples to tremendous sacrifices to weather the onslaught of the War of the Austrian Succession when Austria was attacked by six powers. In the peace treaty (1748), she had to cede some small Italian lands to the Spanish Bourbons and confirm the loss of Silesia to Prussia. Thereafter, Austria grew in strength, supported by her new friendship with Russia and France. Her attempt to gain part or all of Bavaria was thwarted by Prussia, yet she obtained a small enclave along the Inn River. Finally, Austria seized a large slice of Polish territory in the First Partition of Poland in 1772 (see p. 334), an event which arose partly from Maria Theresa's fear that Russia was gaining too much land from Turkey and that Austria needed compensation in Poland to balance Russian gains.

Maria Theresa's idealistic son Joseph II became emperor of the Holy Roman Empire in 1765, but in Austria his mother retained power until her death in 1780, so that his personal reign over the Hapsburg possessions lasted only a decade (1780–1790). Joseph was a doctrinaire reformer, intent on implementing the theories of the *philosophes,* regardless of whether they fitted local requirements. "I have made philosophy the legislator of my empire," he proclaimed, and his letters and official acts reveal the impatience with which he sought to overhaul his state. With "his life of perpetual motion," as one observer noted, he urged one of his ministers in a typical letter: "Hasten everything that brings me more to the accomplishment of my plans for the happiness of my people."

During his brief personal reign, he issued some six thousand reform decrees and over eleven thousand new laws. He emancipated the serfs, without making workable provisions for their economic livelihood. Although theoretically free, most ex-serfs were unable to pay the indemnities owed to their former lords and hence remained under serf-like obligations. He attempted to make the legal systems of all the Hapsburg possessions uniform, irrespective of local needs. He ordered compulsory school attendance for seven years, without finding the funds to provide the necessary schools and teachers.

Sharing the *philosophes'* antipathy to the Catholic Church, Joseph tried to subordinate the church to the state by confiscating a part of its wealth, including some monasteries, and by having the state supervise clerical activities, including the education of the clergy. Stating his "contempt" for "fanaticism" in Voltairian fashion, he ordered freedom of worship, "since it is not the business of the sovereign to watch over individual consciences but only over the general good." In line with the humanitarianism of the Enlightenment, state hospitals, insane asylums, and public institutions for the deaf, for orphans, and for wayward children were established. Joseph also suggested the need for a more equitable distribution of tax assessments among the various social classes and tried to undermine the power of the nobility in order to gain more control for the centralized state machinery. In the area of economics, he prohibited the importation of foreign goods, as he explained, "for the encouragement of home production, and in order to check the progress of luxury," which he considered economically detrimental and morally harmful.

Joseph's reforming whirlwind, particularly his program for turning Austria's polyglot possessions into a unitary state, excited much opposition. When the emperor had the crown of St. Stephen shipped to Vienna for storage in a museum, in order to symbolize an end to Hungary's separate status as a kingdom, a revolt by Hungarians forced him to have it sent back to Budapest. Similarly, there was a rebellion in the Austrian Netherlands, when he ordered the province to be governed directly from Vienna. The clergy and nobility naturally resented his interference with their privileges. In the end most of his reforms either were abandoned or fell short of their intended goals, and Joseph died in disillusionment. As an experiment in implementing theory, his reign presents a fascinating epoch; historians still disagree, however, whether his attempts revitalized or disarrayed the state.

Reform in the Iberian kingdoms

Trends in the two Iberian kingdoms were similar. In both states, enlightened reforms were attempted to arrest continuing decline. The astute King Charles III of Spain (1759–1788), who had been king of Naples since 1734, was an enlightened despot in his own right. Although the Catholic Church in Spain wielded much power, Charles was thoroughly anticlerical, since he regarded the church as an obstacle to reform. In 1767, he followed the example of Portugal and France, expelled the Jesuits from his possessions, and sent several thousand of them to Italy. When six years later, Austria, too, banished the Jesuits, the pope abolished the order.

With the help of a number of skilled ministers, Charles III worked for greater governmental centralization and attempted to reduce the power of the Spanish grandees, nobles who owned vast estates and exerted strong economic, social, and political influence. Peasants were to be aided by the division of common lands. The king also took interest in cleaning up and beautifying the city of Madrid. The first Spanish ruler in some time to devote himself to economic matters, he used mercantilistic practices to encourage industry, build roads, improve communications, and effect a monetary reform. To increase trade, he adopted some physiocratic ideas (see p. 330). The tax on grain was abolished, and a freer flow of trade was achieved in Spain and in the colonies. More Spanish ports were opened to the American trade—hitherto restricted to Cadiz and Seville. As a result of Charles' measures, Spanish economic life quickened, but the power of church and landed aristocracy was hardly broken.

Unspectacular in Europe, Spain's role overseas remained impressive. Because of family compacts between the Spanish and French Bourbons as well as continuing Anglo-Spanish colonial rivalry, Spain sided with France in her wars against England. Although this pro-French policy did not benefit Spain on the continent, it entailed potential advantages overseas. Despite losing Florida to England at the end of the French and Indian War (1763), she was compensated by France with the vast Louisiana territory, which she retained until 1801. As a result, the North American continent came to be divided between Spain and England, in addition to the Russian settlements in Alaska. Hence Spain sided with the colonists during the American Revolutionary War in order to weaken England's colonial position rather than for the sake of helping the colonists gain independence.

King Charles also instituted reforms in his overseas possessions. The

Americas were divided into intendancies to ensure greater administrative, judicial, military, and financial control from Madrid. The king encouraged the spread of higher education, as well as artistic and literary development, with the Franciscans assuming the work previously done by the Jesuits. At the same time there was constant rivalry and occasional fighting between Spain and Portugal over the delimitation of Portuguese Brazil.

Portugal herself was at the time in the hands of a reforming government. In these reforms, the king (Joseph I), who later became insane, played a secondary role to his dictatorial minister, the Marquis de Pombal (1699–1782), who ran the state from 1750 to 1777. After the disastrous earthquake of 1755 that destroyed much of Lisbon, Pombal rebuilt the city and helped the surviving population in the philanthropic and paternalistic manner characteristic of the Enlightenment. He fought the privileged positions of church and nobility, and attempted to strengthen Portugal by building up the army, stimulating manufacture and education, and increasing trade, particularly with Brazil. Unlike her Spanish neighbor, Portugal practiced a pro-British policy, partly to perpetuate her traditional economic ties, but primarily to gain support for her continued quarrel with Spain over territories in South America. Among Pombal's suggested reforms was his advocacy of racial equality and intermarriage between whites and Indians in Brazil, ideas sharply at variance with practices in the neighboring Spanish and English colonies. On the whole, Pombal's regime gave Portugal a measure of prosperity without being able to stay the decline of the kingdom.

The Enlightenment in Scandinavia and the minor German states

Like the king of Portugal, the king of Norway-Denmark (Christian VII, 1766–1808) lacked influence and suffered from insanity. Ideas of reform struck Denmark during the brief ascendancy of Count Struensee (1737–1772), a German physician and enlightened *philosophe,* who in the two years before he fell victim to a conspiracy of nobles attempted to reshape Denmark. Besides trying to deprive the nobility of their regained powers and privileges and attain more centralized control for the state, Struensee worked for the abolition of serfdom and of torture, and for more equitable judicial processes. Despite the brevity of his career and the failure of his reforms, his ideas left an imprint on the Danish monarchy.

In Sweden, it was the king himself (Gustavus III, 1771–1792) who reversed the trend toward government by the Diet, which had regained power after the death of Charles XII. Like his contemporaries on the Continent, the Swedish king advocated legal reforms, religious toleration, and sought to stimulate trade. In 1792, he fell victim to a murder plot by disgruntled Swedish nobles.

Similar enlightened tendencies appeared in a number of German and Italian states, particularly in some of the lesser principalities of Saxony and Thuringia. Most notable because of their influence on German cultural and political development were the duchies of Baden and of Weimar. The former became a center of progressive, quasi-republican thought for the next century; the latter developed into the home of Germany's intellectual re-awakening, by attracting such writers as Johann Gottfried von Herder (1744–1803), Johann Wolfgang von Goethe (1749–1832), and Friedrich von Schiller (1759–1805).

Changes in political economy

The concept of natural law gradually affected economic theories. The physiocrats, a group of French political economists (inspired by François Quesnay, 1694–1774), many of whom contributed to Diderot's *Encyclopaedia*, advocated the removal of all artificial economic restrictions such as tariffs, monopolies, indirect taxes, and tolls. They looked upon mercantilism as a futile and even harmful attempt by man to interfere in nature's domain. As one of them wrote, "it is the demand which regulates production." If left alone, they thought, production and trade would flourish. Hence their by-word: *laissez-faire*.

The physiocrats rejected bullionism as well as mercantilism. Not specie but "the earth is the only source of wealth," they argued, since only agriculture and mining truly add to man's property. Manufacture they regarded as less important, as it merely transformed a product from one form into another. Hence they advocated that taxes "should be assessed upon the immediate net product of lands," and all other direct or indirect taxation should be abolished.

The Scotsman Adam Smith (1723–1790), a student of the physiocrats, also thought that economics was by nature self-regulating. Like the physiocrats, he believed that mercantilistic practices interfered adversely with the natural laws imbedded in economic life. His book, *An Inquiry into the Nature and Causes of the Wealth of Nations* (1776), a study of contemporary economic conditions, made him the founder of the so-called school of classical economics that dominated most nineteenth-century economic thought with its belief in inexorable economic laws.

Adam Smith rejected the physiocratic notion that land was the only truly productive source. To him, the wealth of nations lay rather in labor, for only work could transform raw materials into something useful and valuable. He thus became the first in a series of economists before Karl Marx who concentrated on the role of labor in economic life. To make labor more productive and efficient, he saw the need for increased specialization, which to him, again, was the result of a natural law. "Division of labor," he wrote, "is the necessary . . . consequence of a certain propensity in human nature." Whereas the medieval guild worker had fabricated an entire product, such as a suit of armor, Smith saw greater efficiency if a number of workers each specialized in producing only a part. Such an arrangement required the concentration of greater work forces in factories as well as the widest possi-

LIST OF MAPS

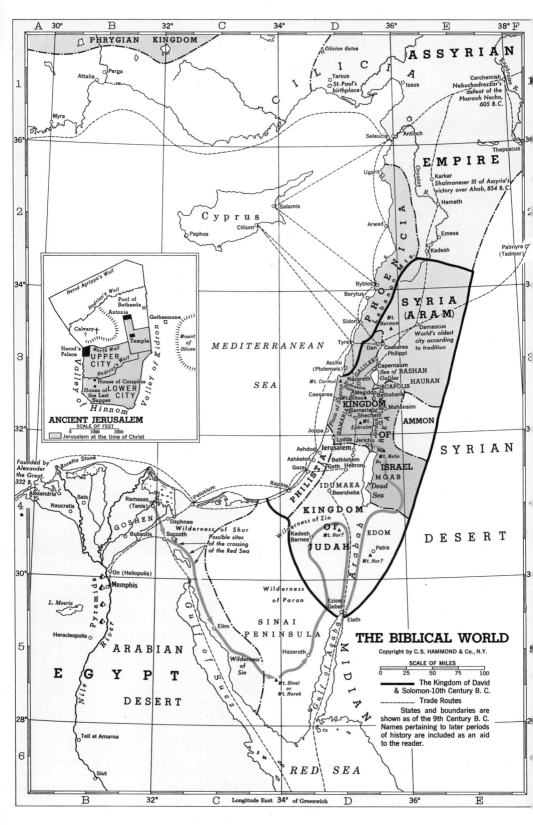

THE BIBLICAL WORLD

Copyright by C.S. Hammond & Co., N.Y.

SCALE OF MILES
0   25   50   75   100

—— The Kingdom of David & Solomon-10th Century B. C.

---- Trade Routes

States and boundaries are shown as of the 9th Century B. C. Names pertaining to later periods of history are included as an aid to the reader.

ANCIENT JERUSALEM
SCALE OF FEET
0   1000   2000
Jerusalem at the time of Christ

MAP 1

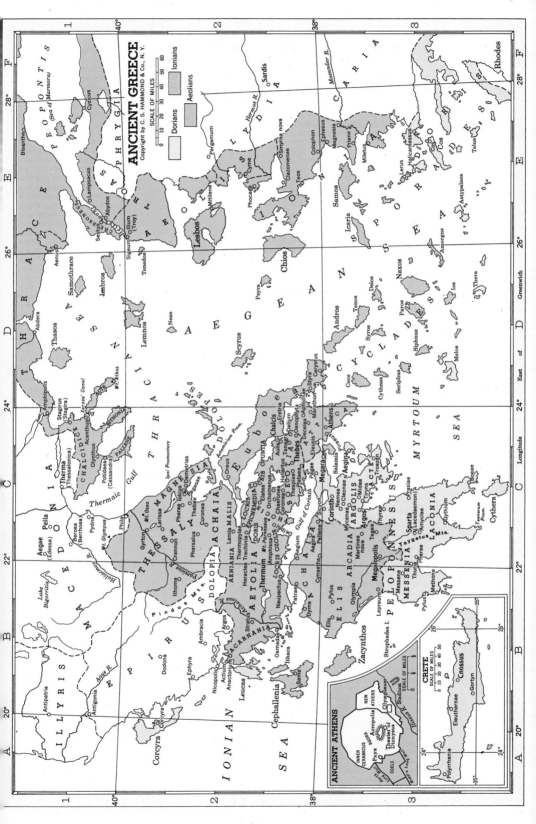

ANCIENT GREECE

Copyright by C. S. HAMMOND & CO., N. Y.

SCALE OF MILES

0 10 20 30 40 50 60

Ionians
Aeolians
Dorians

MAP 2

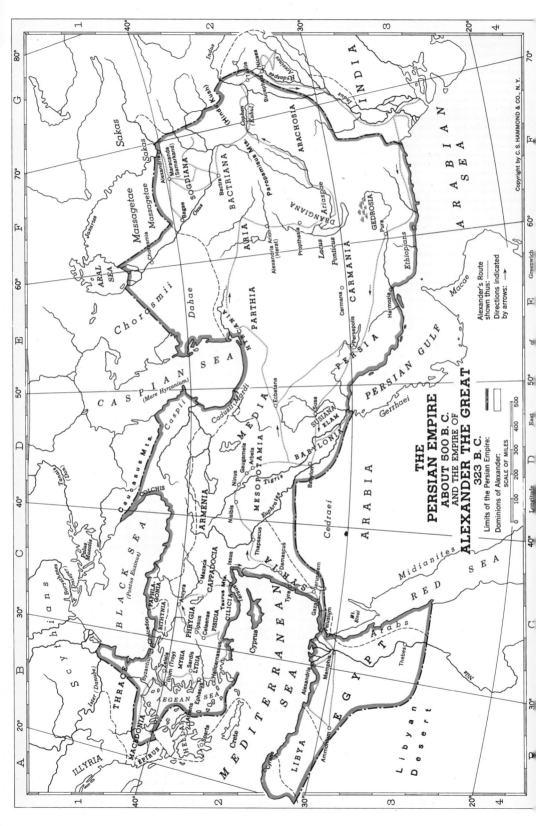

THE
PERSIAN EMPIRE
ABOUT 500 B.C.
AND THE EMPIRE OF
ALEXANDER THE GREAT
323 B.C.

Limits of the Persian Empire: ──────
Dominions of Alexander:
SCALE OF MILES
0 100 200 300 400 500

Alexander's Route
shown thus: ·········
Directions indicated
by arrows: ─→

Copyright by C. S. HAMMOND & CO., N.Y.

MAP 3

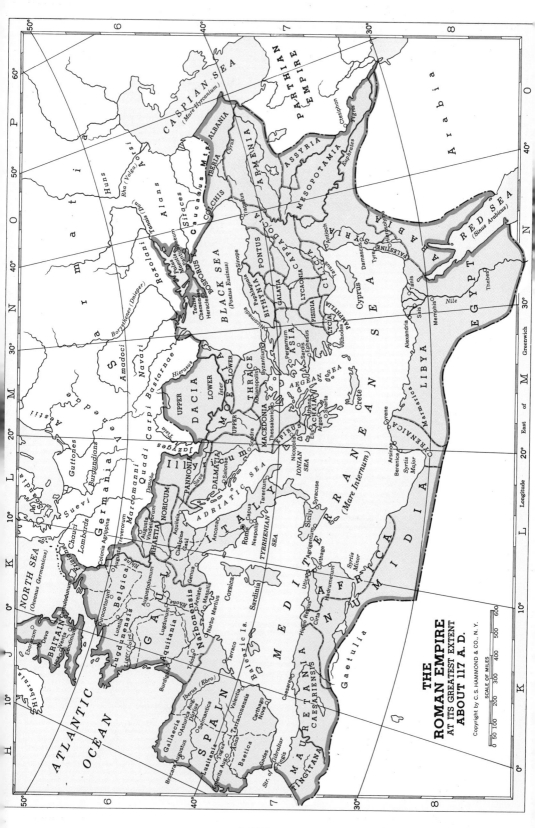

THE
ROMAN EMPIRE
AT ITS GREATEST EXTENT
ABOUT 117 A.D.

Copyright by C. S. Hammond & Co., N.Y.

SCALE OF MILES

0 50 100 200 300 400 500 600

MAP 4

MAP 5

EUROPE
SHOWING BARBARIC MIGRATIONS
IN THE
FOURTH AND FIFTH CENTURIES

Copyright by C. S. HAMMOND & CO., N. Y.

SCALE OF MILES

0   50 100   200   300   400   500

→ Goths
→ Huns
→ Alans, Suevi, Vandals
⋯← Angles, Saxons, Jutes

☐ Western Roman Empire
☐ Eastern Roman Empire

TIC SEA

Esthonians

Goths

cirians
dians

Vandals

Pistula R.

Goths sometime after 150

W e n d s
(Northern Slavs)

Antes
(Southern Slavs)

H u n s

A l a n s

Roxolani

Sea of
Azov

Panticapaeum

Huns 373

Pityus   Dioscurias

Quadi

408

about 160

Attila's Capital ?   433

Huns (Rugilas)

Gepids

East Goths   380 to 454

152

Sarmatae

H u n s

East Goths
(Greutungs)

Goths
350

Tanais

Hypanis

Kuban R.

Phasis

BLACK   SEA

Chersonesus
Heracleotica

Quadi

East Goths

Jazyges

Attila

Sirmium

Singidunum

Viminacium

MOESIA
(UPPER)

DACIA

440

Ratiaria

Naissus

West Goths

West Goths
(Thervings)

West
Goths
376

Ister (Danube)

MOESIA
(LOWER)
Beroea
351

Marcianopolis

Anchialus

Tomi

West R.

Goths

377

THRACE

Philippopolis   Attila 447

Adrianople
378

Perinthus

MACEDONIA   Attila 446

Alaric 398

Thessalonica

Constantinople

Nicaea

Cyzicus

Alexandria Troas

Lesbos

BITHYNIA

Nicomedia

Paphlagonia

Ancyra

Kizil Irmak R.

GALATIA

Sinope

Amasia

PONTUS

Polemonium

Trapezus

Theodosiopolis

ARMENIA

Caesarea

Halys

CAPPADOCIA

Melitene

Euphrates R.

Amida   Nisibis

Edessa

MESOPOTAMIA

ICUM

Alaric
400

Dyrrhachium

sentia
ric died, 410)

EPIRUS

Alaric 399

Thessaly

Thermopylae

Corinth

Peloponnesus   Sparta

Athens

Euboea

Chios

Ephesus

Miletus

MYSIA

Sardis

LYDIA

CARIA

PHRYGIA

Apamea

Iconium

PISIDIA

PAMPHYLIA

LYCIA

LYCAONIA

Tarsus

CILICIA

Rhodes

Cyprus

Salamis

Apamea

Antioch

Circesium

SYRIA

Damascus

Tyre

Caesarea

O R I E N S

Scythopolis

AN

SEA

Apollonia

Cyrene

Berenice

Crete

Alexandria

Hierosolyma
(Jerusalem)

Gaza

E G Y P T

Pelusium

Greenwich   20°   G   25°   H   30°   J   35°   K

50°

45°

4

40°

5

35°

6

30°

Rha Volga R.

1

2

3

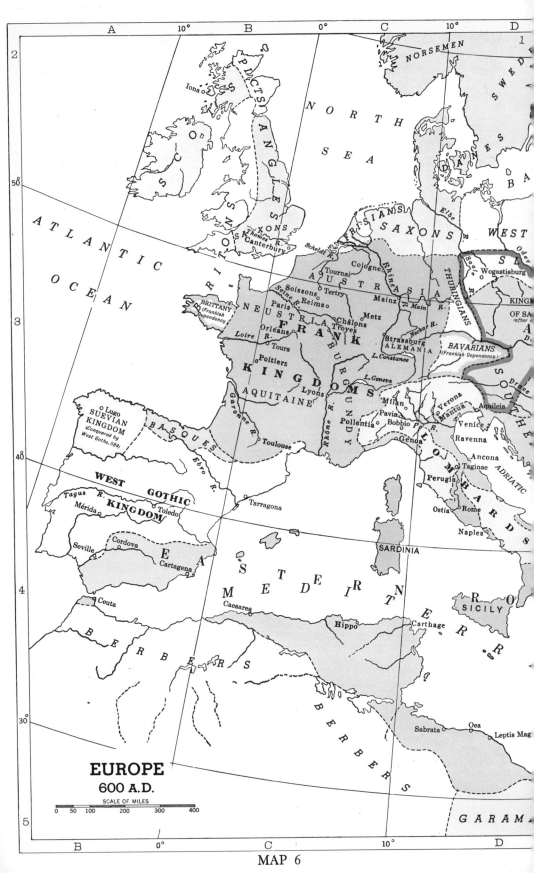

MAP 6

EUROPE
600 A.D.

SCALE OF MILES

0 50 100   200   300   400

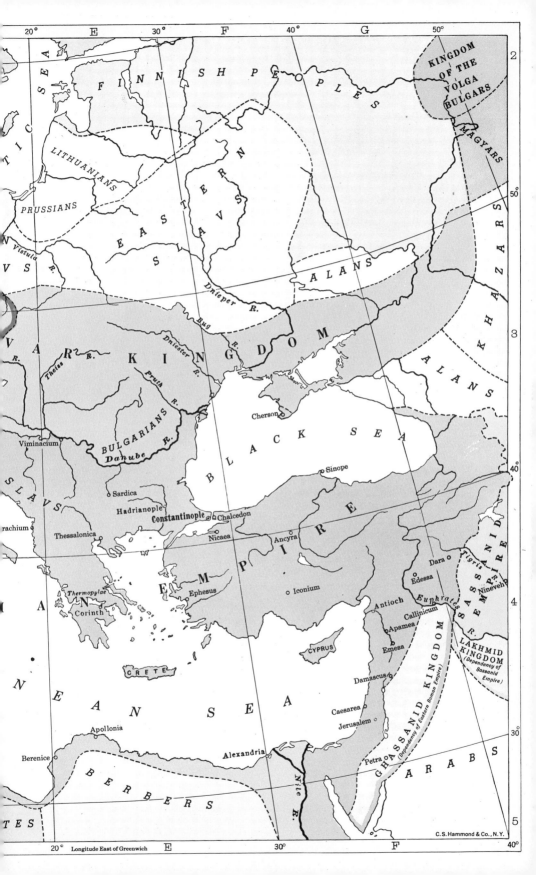

2

KINGDOM OF THE VOLGA BULGARS

FINNISH PEOPLES

MAGYARS

LITHUANIANS

PRUSSIANS

EASTERN SLAVS

50°

N Vistula R.

VS

ALANS

KHAZARS

Dnieper R.

3

Bug R.

VAR

KINGDOM

ALANS

Theiss R.

Dniester R.

Prut R.

Cherson

BLACK SEA

40°

Viminacium

BULGARIANS

Danube R.

Sinope

SLAVS

Sardica

Hadrianople

Constantinople   Chalcedon

rachium

Thessalonica

Nicaea

Ancyra

EMPIRE

Dara

Edessa

SASSANID EMPIRE

Nineveh

Tigris R.

E M P I R E

Ephesus

Iconium

Antioch

Euphrates R.

Callinicum

A

Thermopylae

Corinth

N

Apamea

Emesa

LAKHMID KINGDOM (Dependency of Sassanid Empire)

CYPRUS

Damascus

CRETE

N

EAN

SEA

Caesarea

Jerusalem

GHASSANID KINGDOM (Dependency of Eastern Roman Empire)

Apollonia

30°

Berenice

Alexandria

Petra

ARABS

BERBERS

Nile R.

TES

C.S. Hammond & Co., N.Y.

5

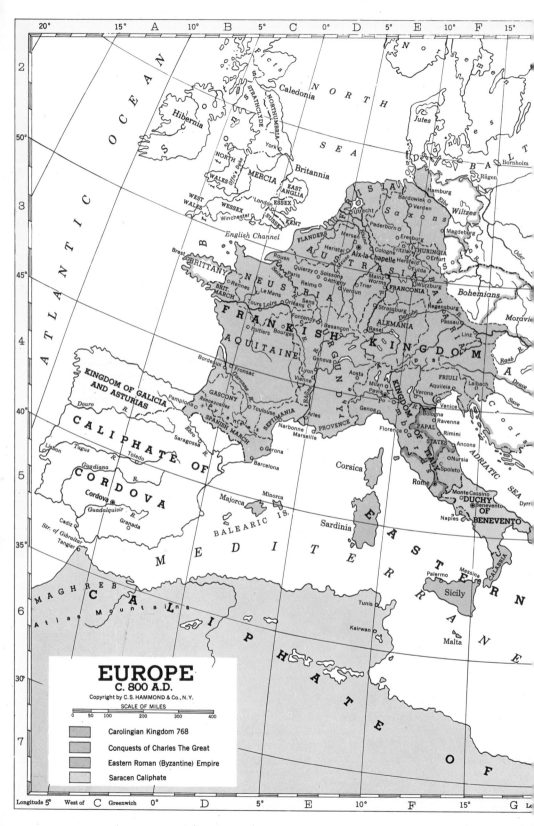

EUROPE
C. 800 A.D.

Copyright by C. S. HAMMOND & Co., N.Y.

SCALE OF MILES

Carolingian Kingdom 768
Conquests of Charles The Great
Eastern Roman (Byzantine) Empire
Saracen Caliphate

MAP 7

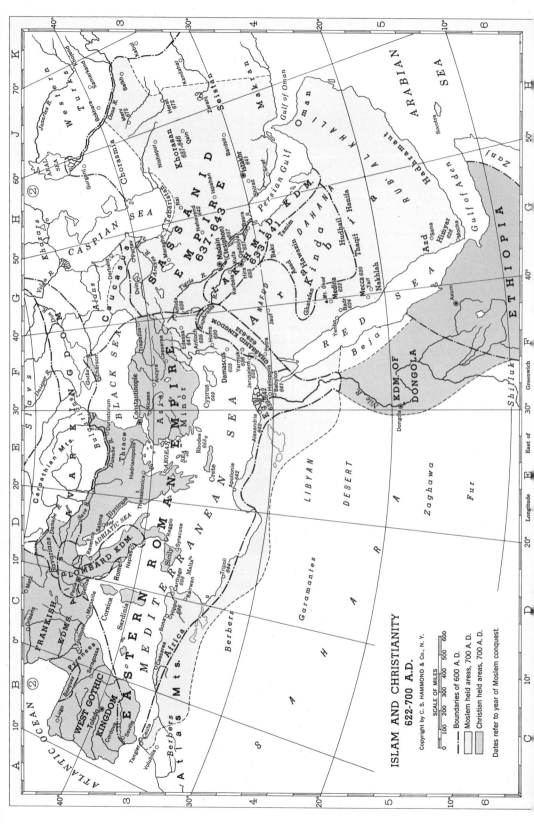

ISLAM AND CHRISTIANITY
622-700 A.D.

Copyright by C. S. Hammond & Co., N. Y.

SCALE OF MILES

0 100 200 300 400 500 600

- - - Boundaries of 600 A.D.
Moslem held areas, 700 A.D.
Christian held areas, 700 A.D.

Dates refer to year of Moslem conquest.

MAP 8

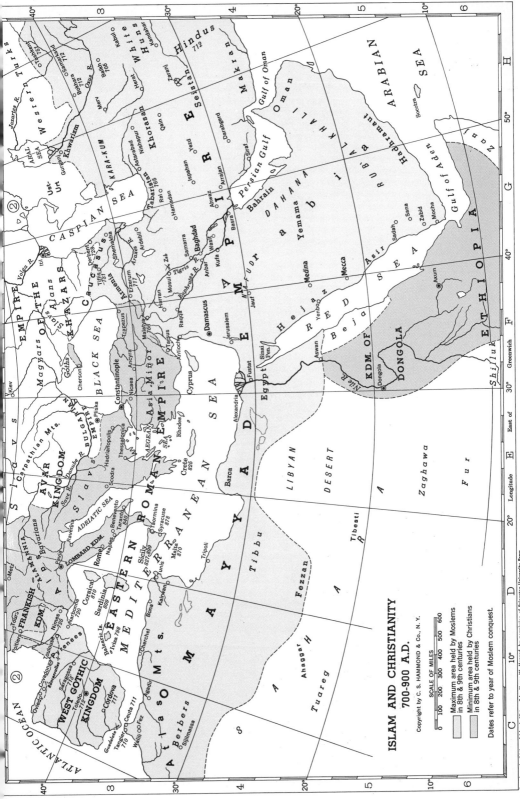

ISLAM AND CHRISTIANITY
700-900 A.D.

Copyright by C. S. HAMMOND & Co., N.Y.

SCALE OF MILES

0 100 200 300 400 500 600

Maximum area held by Moslems
in 8th & 9th centuries

Minimum area held by Christians
in 8th & 9th centuries

Dates refer to year of Moslem conquest.

Based on the "Atlas of Islamic History," by Harry W. Hazard, by permission of Princeton University Press.

MAP 9

EUROPE
and the
BYZANTINE EMPIRE
ABOUT 1000

Copyright by C.S. HAMMOND & CO., N.Y.

SCALE OF MILES

0   50   100   200   300   400

——— Boundary of the Holy Roman Empire
········· Route of the Varangians

Co. = County   Kdm. = Kingdom
D. = Duchy   Th. = Theme

Longitude East of Greenwich

MAP 10

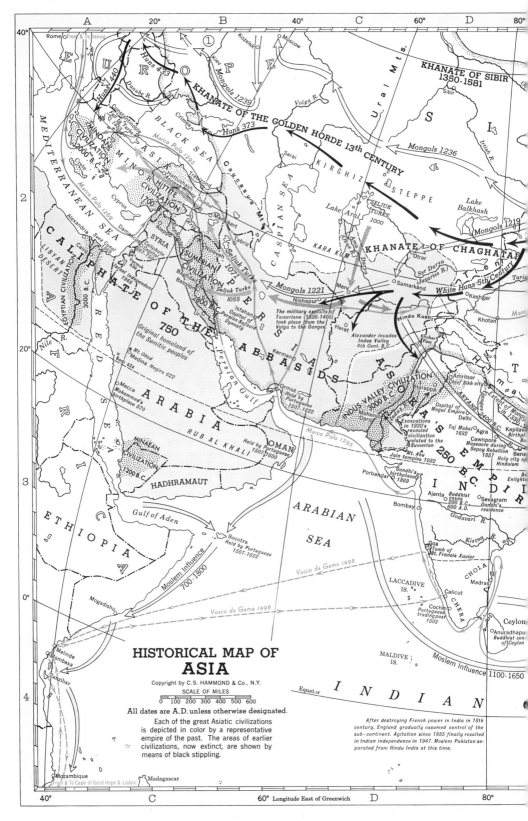

HISTORICAL MAP OF
ASIA

Copyright by C.S. Hammond & Co., N.Y.

SCALE OF MILES

0 100 200 300 400 500 600

All dates are A.D. unless otherwise designated.

Each of the great Asiatic civilizations
is depicted in color by a representative
empire of the past. The areas of earlier
civilizations, now extinct, are shown by
means of black stippling.

After destroying French power in India in 18th
century, England gradually assumed control of the
sub-continent. Agitation since 1885 finally resulted
in Indian independence in 1947. Moslem Pakistan separated from Hindu India at this time.

MAP 11

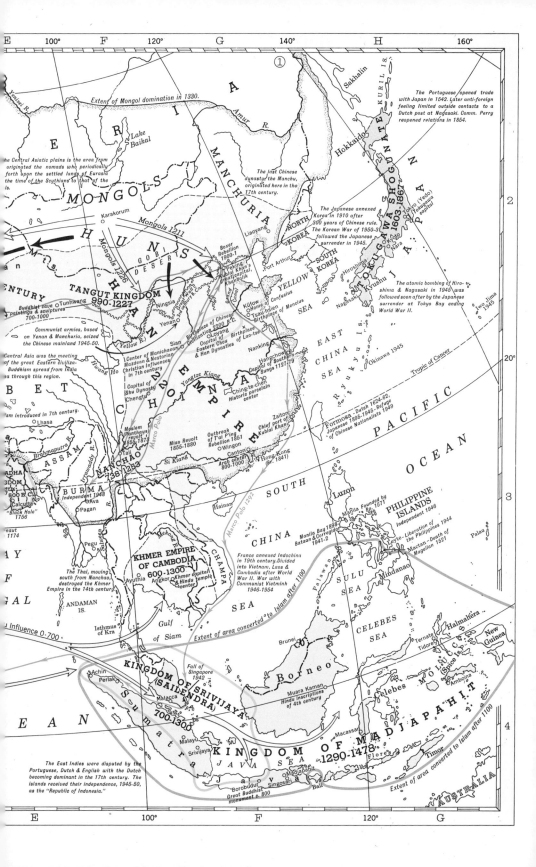

EUROPE
c. 1200 A.D.

Copyright by C. S. HAMMOND & Co., N. Y.

SCALE OF MILES

0 50 100   200   300   400   500   600

▬▬▬ Boundary of the Empire

• Cities of the Lombard League

English Possessions in France in 1200

English Possessions in France in 1223

English Possessions in France in 1328

ICELAND
Reykjavik
Holar
Skalholt

Arctic Circle

NORWAY
SWEDEN
Bergen
Opslo
Upsala
Visby
Kalmar

ATLANTIC OCEAN

NORTH SEA

BALTIC

DENMARK
Viborg
Roskilde
Lund

SCOTLAND
Aberdeen
Perth
Stirling
Glasgow
Edinburgh
Dumfries

IRELAND
Armagh
Dublin
Carlisle
York
Waterford
Wexford
Cork

ENGLAND
WALES
Aberfraw
Chester
Lincoln
Albans
Ely
Oxford
Cambridge
Norwich
Winchester
London
Bristol
Hastings

FRIESLAND
Hamburg
SLAVINIA
Rügen
Kammin
Danzig
POMERANIA

Bremen
SAXONY
Brunswick
Brandenburg
Magdeburg
Dresden
POSEN
PO...

FLANDERS
Bruges
Antwerp
BRABANT
LOWER
Liege
LORRAINE
Cologne
THURINGIA
Frankfurt
BOHEMIA
Prague
SILESIA
Oder
MORAVIA

NORMANDY
Rouen
VERMANDOIS
Paris
Laon
Rheims
Trier
Mainz
Speyer
FRANCONIA
Ratisbon
Press...

BRITTANY
MAINE
Nantes
Melun
Orleans
CHAMPAGNE
Metz
UPPER LORRAINE
Strassburg
SWABIA
Augsburg
BAVARIA
Salzburg
Vienna
AUSTRIA
Stuh...

Tours
Loire
POITOU
Poitiers
D. OF
BURGUNDY
Auxerre
Nevers
Basel
Constance
Innsbruck
CARINTHIA
Kalo...

FRANCE
Limoges
Clermont
AUVERGNE
Lyons
Vienne
Trent
M. OF
VERONA
FRIULI
Aquileia
CARNIOLA

Angouleme
Bordeaux
GUIENNE
ARELATE
Vercelli
Brescia
Milan
Venice
Zara
Spalato
GASCONY
Bayonne
TOULOUSE
Avignon
Rhone
Alessandria
Pavia
Genoa
Parma
Verona
ROMAGNA
Bologna
Ravenna
Ancona
REP. OF RAGUSA

Pamplona
NAVARRE
Foix
Toulouse
Arles
Lucca
TUSCANY
Pisa
Florence
Siena
PATRIMONY
Corsica
(To Pisa)

LEON
Oviedo
Leon
Oporto
SANTIAGO DE COMPOSTELA

ARAGON
Saragossa
Lerida
Barcelona

CASTILE
Toledo
Tagus R.

PORTUGAL
Coimbra
Lisbon
Silves

DOMINIONS
Cordova
Granada

PAPAL STATES
Rome
OF ST. PETER
Aquila
Tagliacozzo
Monte Cassino
APULIA
Naples
KINGDOM O...

Sardinia
(To Pisa)

MEDITERRANEAN

THE TWO SICILIES
Palermo
Sicily

DOMINIONS OF THE ALMOHADES
Fez
Marrakesh

HOLY ROMAN EMPIRE

Longitude West of Greenwich   0°   Longitude 10° East of Greenwich

MAP 12

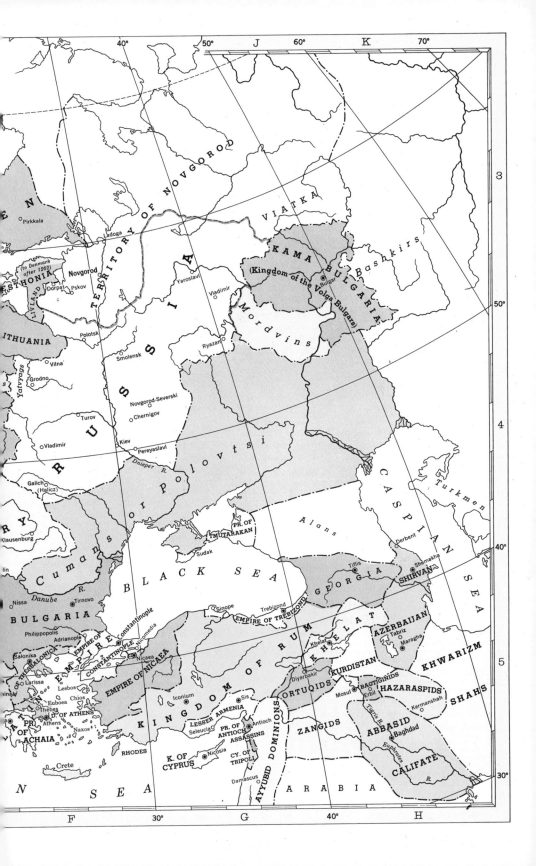

40°   50°   60°   70°

o Pirkkala

TERRITORY OF NOVGOROD

V I A T K A

K A M A

KAMA

Bashkirs

(to Denmark
after 1202)

LIVLAND
ESTHONIA

Ladoga

BULGARIA

Novgorod
o Dorpat
Pskov

o Yaroslavl

(Kingdom of the Volga Bulgars)
o Bulgar

ITHUANIA

R
U
S
S
I
A

o Vladimir

Polotsk

M o r d v i n s

Vilna

o Smolensk

o Ryazan

Yatvyaga
Grodno

Novgorod-Severski

o Turov

o Chernigov

C A S P I A N

o Vladimir

Kiev
Pereyaslavl

Dnieper R.

Galich
(Halicz)

C u m a n s o r P o l o v t s i

T u r k m e n

RY

Klausenburg

PR. OF
TMUTARAKAN

A l a n s

o Sudak

Derbent

S E A

o Tiflis

o Shemakha

lin

B L A C K   S E A

G E O R G I A

SHIRVAN

Nissa

Danube R.

o Tirnovo

o Sinope

Trebizond

EMPIRE OF TREBIZOND

AZERBAIJAN

BULGARIA

Philippopolis

o Constantinople

K H E L A T

Tabriz
o Maragha

Adrianople

o Nicomedia

Khelat

KURDISTAN

KHWARIZM

Salonika
THESSALONICA

EMPIRE OF
Constantinople

o Nicaea

Diyarbakir

BAGTIGINIDS

o Larissa

CONSTANTINOPLE

Mosul

Erbil

HAZARASPIDS

Lesbos
Euboea

Chios

EMPIRE OF NICAEA

K I N G D O M   O F   R U M

o Iconium

o Sis

Kermanshah

SHAHS

Thebes

LESSER ARMENIA

Tigris R.

Athens
PR. OF
ACHAIA

D. OF ATHENS

o Naxos

Seleucia

PR. OF
ANTIOCH

o Antioch

ZANGIDS

ABBASID

o Baghdad

ASSASSINS

AYYUBID DOMINIONS

ORTUQIDS

CALIFATE

Euphrates R.

RHODES

K. OF
CYPRUS

o Nicosia

CY. OF
TRIPOLI

o Crete

Damascus

A R A B I A

N   S E A

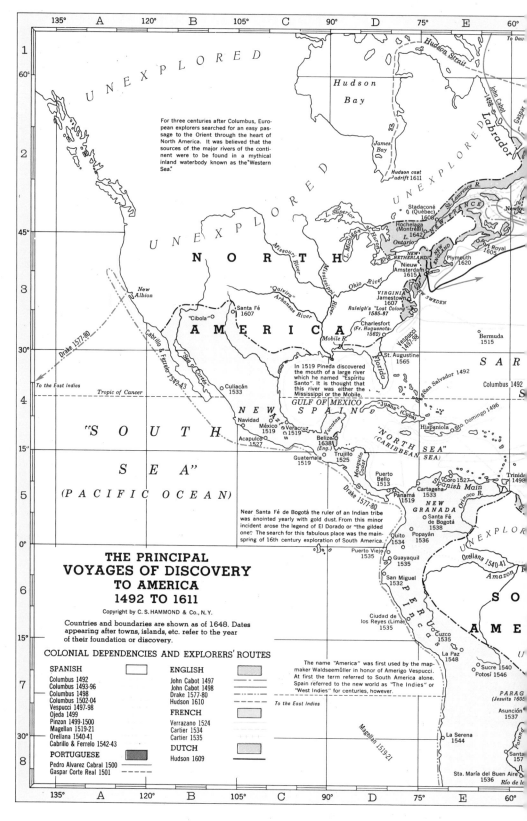

THE PRINCIPAL
VOYAGES OF DISCOVERY
TO AMERICA
1492 TO 1611

Copyright by C. S. HAMMOND & Co., N.Y.

Countries and boundaries are shown as of 1648. Dates
appearing after towns, islands, etc. refer to the year
of their foundation or discovery.

COLONIAL DEPENDENCIES AND EXPLORERS' ROUTES

SPANISH
Columbus 1492
Columbus 1493-96
Columbus 1498
Columbus 1502-04
Vespucci 1497-98
Ojeda 1499
Pinzon 1499-1500
Magellan 1519-21
Orellana 1540-41
Cabrillo & Ferrelo 1542-43

PORTUGUESE
Pedro Alvarez Cabral 1500
Gaspar Corte Real 1501

ENGLISH
John Cabot 1497
John Cabot 1498
Drake 1577-80
Hudson 1610

FRENCH
Verrazano 1524
Cartier 1534
Cartier 1535

DUTCH
Hudson 1609

To the East Indies

The name "America" was first used by the map-
maker Waldseemüller in honor of Amerigo Vespucci.
At first the term referred to South America alone.
Spain referred to the new world as "The Indies" or
"West Indies" for centuries, however.

For three centuries after Columbus, European explorers searched for an easy passage to the Orient through the heart of
North America. It was believed that the
sources of the major rivers of the continent were to be found in a mythical
inland waterbody known as the "Western
Sea."

In 1519 Pineda discovered
the mouth of a large river
which he named "Espíritu
Santo". It is thought that
this river was either the
Mississippi or the Mobile.

Near Santa Fé de Bogotá the ruler of an Indian tribe
was anointed yearly with gold dust. From this minor
incident arose the legend of El Dorado or "the gilded
one". The search for this fabulous place was the main-
spring of 16th century exploration of South America.

MAP 13

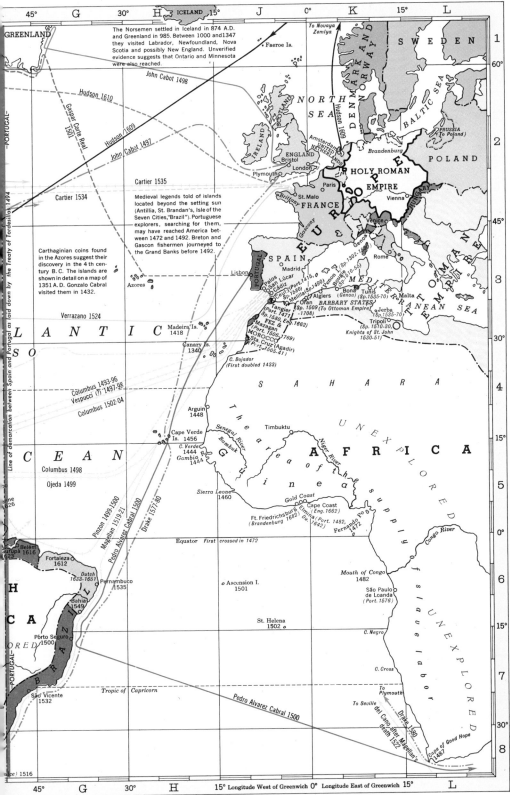

EUROPE IN 1559

Copyright by C.S. HAMMOND & CO., N.Y.

SCALE OF MILES

0   50   100   200   300   400

DOMINIONS OF THE HABSBURGS

Spanish branch

Austrian branch

Boundary of the Holy Roman Empire, about 1526

POSSESSIONS OF THE BOURBONS

Hereditary lands of Henry of Navarre

Lands of Charles of Bourbon - Montpensier

KINGDOM OF DENMARK

Bergen

Stavanger

SHETLAND IS.

ORKNEY IS.

NORTH SEA

HEBRIDES

OCEAN

SCOTLAND

Inverness   Aberdeen

Scone

Perth   St. Andrews

Stirling   Lochleven

Glasgow   Dunbar

Douglas   Berwick

Edinburgh   Flodden

Solway Firth   Solway Moor

Carlisle

Ulster

Armagh

Connaught

IRELAND

Galway   Leinster

Limerick

Munster

Waterford

Cork

I. of Man

Dublin

York

ENGLAND

Shrewsbury   Leicester   Peterborough

Montgomery   Tutbury   Norwich

Coventry   Fotheringham

Wales   Oxford   Cambridge

Gloucester

Severn R.

London   Thames R.   Canterbury

Portsmouth   Dover   Calais (to France, 1559)

Plymouth

Amsterdam   Groningen   Oldenb

Utrecht   The Hague   Münster

Bruges   Ghent   Antwerp

NETHERLANDS   Cologne

Flanders   Brussels   Aachen

Artois   Liège

Cambrai   Château-Cambrésis   Rhine R.

Cherbourg

Guernsey   Jersey

Brest

Rohan

Rennes

Mayenne

Alençon

Vaucelles   Noyon   Guise   Luxemburg

Rouen   Soissons   Vervins   Verdun

St. Germain   Crépy   Mainz

Ivry   Meaux   Metz   Speyer

Dreux   Paris   Châlons   Lorraine   Toul   Stra

Verneuil   Fontainebleau   Vassy   Joinville

Vendôme   Orléans   Langres   Besançon

FRANCE   Blois   Amboise   Romorantin   La Charité   Bern

Nantes   Tours   Bourges   Chalon   Basel

Loire R.   Poitiers   SWISS CONFEDER

La Rochelle   Charolais   Geneva

Montpensier   Beaujeu   SAVOY

Jarnac   Limoges   Lyons   Gattinara

Cognac   Clermont   Turin R.

Garonne R.   Coutras   Grenoble   Pinerolo   Po

Bordeaux   Bergerac   PR. OF ORANGE   Saluzzo

Montauban   Languedoc   Avignon   Nice

Albret   Toulouse   Aiguesmortes   Provence

Bayonne   Bearn   Foix   Narbonne   Marseilles   Toulon

Corunna   Santiago   León   Santander   Bilbao   Loyola   Perpignan   Roussillon

Bragança   Zamora   Valladolid   Pamplona   Saragossa   Corsica (to Genoa)

Oporto   Burgos   Lérida

Coimbra   Douro R.   Salamanca   Segovia   Tortosa   Barcelona

PORTUGAL   Yuste   Madrid   Escorial   Alcalá   Tarragona   SAR

SPAIN   Aranjuez   Valencia   BALEARIC ISLANDS   Minorca   Ca

Santarém   Alcántara   Toledo   Jàtiva   Majorca

Lisbon   Tagus R.   Castile   MEDIT

Setúbal   Guadiana R.   Badajoz   Calatrava   Iviza

Beja   Murcia   Cartagena

Algarve   Cordova   Galera

Faro   Palos   Seville   Santa Fé   Granada

S. Lúcar   Ronda   Granada   Almería

Cádiz   Málaga

Gibraltar   C. Matifu

Tangier   Ceuta   Algiers   Bona (to Spain)

Algarve   Oran (to Spain)

El Araish   Melilla (to Spain)

El Ksar el Kebir   ALGERIA   BARBARY STATE

FEZ AND MOROCCO   Tlemcen

Fez

MAP 14

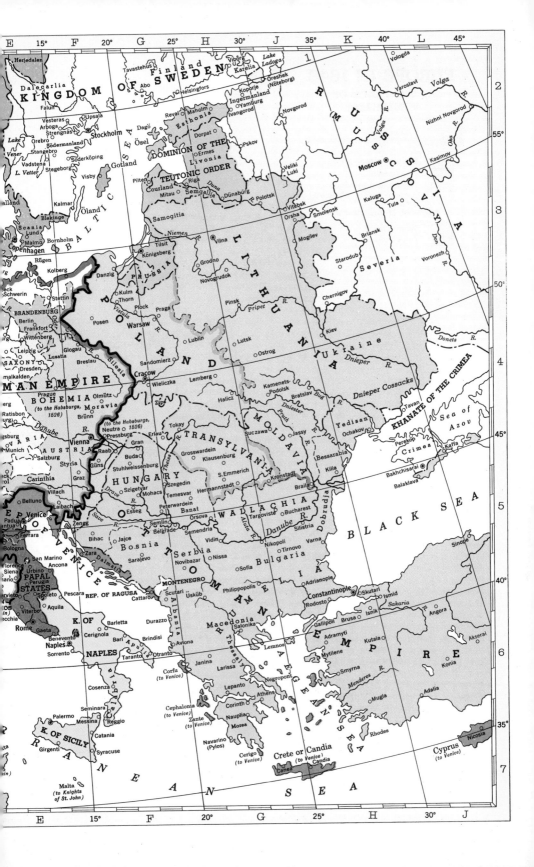

EUROPE IN 1648

AT THE PEACE OF WESTPHALIA

Copyright by C. S. HAMMOND & CO., N.Y.

SCALE OF MILES

0   50   100   200   300   400

— Boundary of the Empire

Church Lands

Transylvania, independent of
Hungarian Kingdom with Turkish
Backing.

DOMINIONS OF THE HABSBURGS

Spanish Branch

Austrian Branch

MAP 15

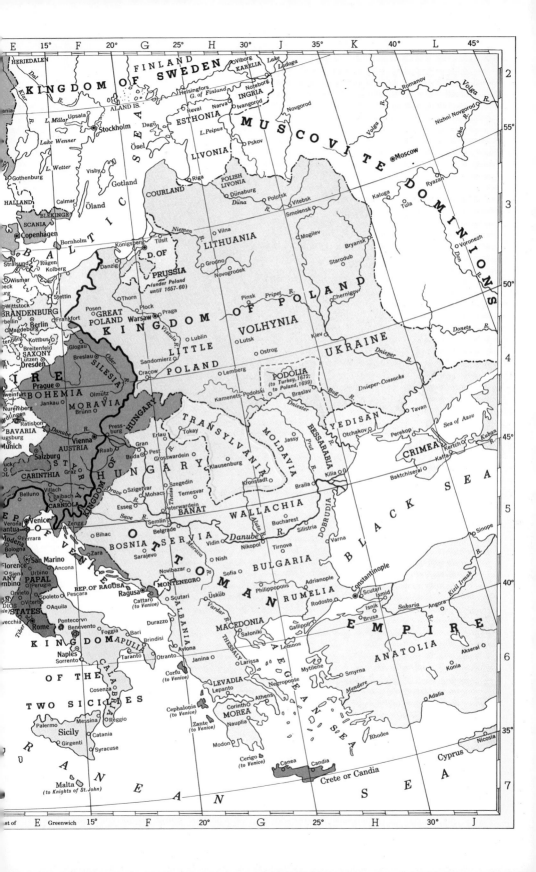

EUROPE IN 1812

AT THE HEIGHT OF NAPOLEON'S POWER

©C. S. HAMMOND & Co., Maplewood, N. J.

SCALE OF MILES

| 0 | 50 | 100 | 200 | 300 | 400 |

French Empire

States under control of Napoleon

AUSTRIAN EMPIRE — States allied with Napoleon in 1812

Napoleon's campaign in Russia

MAP 16

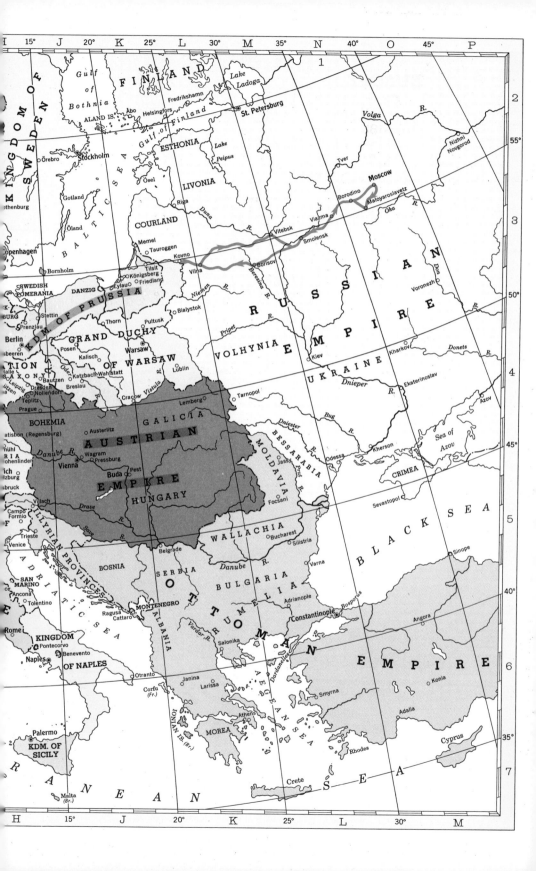

EUROPE

after the

Congress of Vienna
1815-1839

Copyright by C. S. HAMMOND & Co., N. Y.

SCALE OF MILES

0   50   100   200   300   400

Boundary of the Germanic Confederation, 1815 ▬▬▬▬

MAP 17

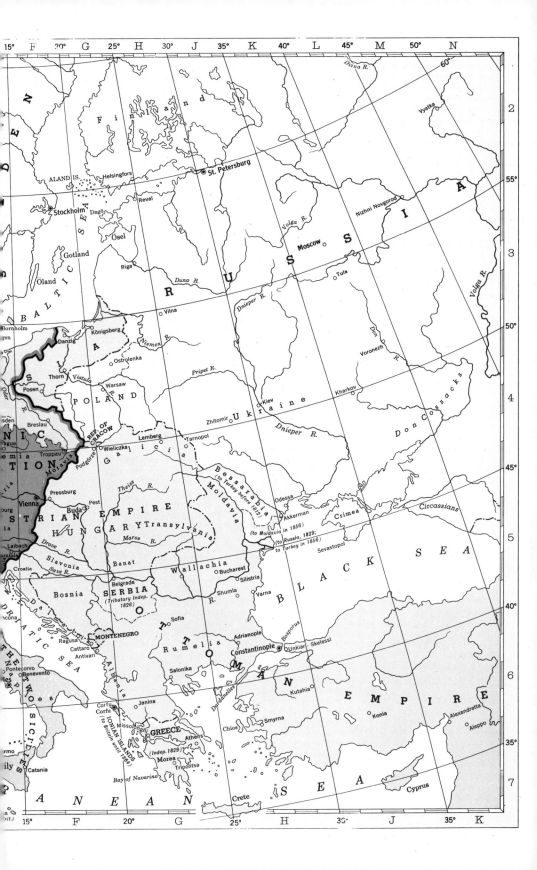

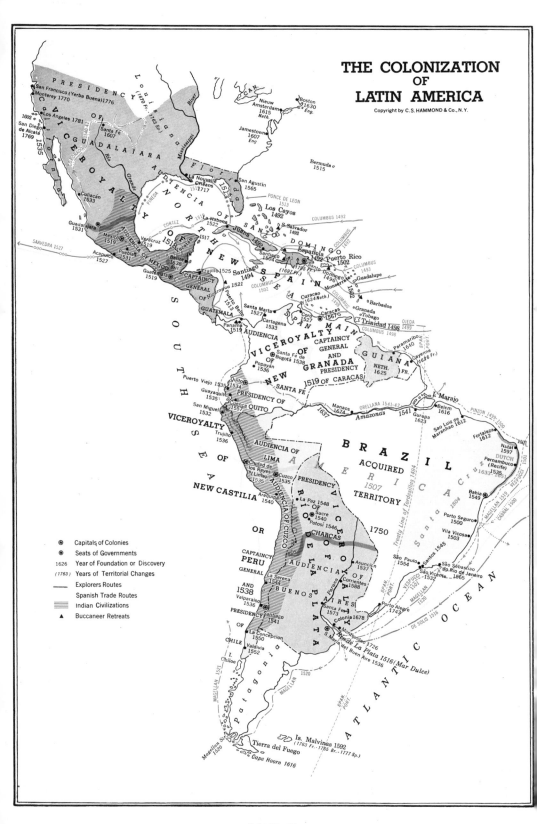

THE COLONIZATION
OF
LATIN AMERICA

Copyright by C.S. HAMMOND & Co., N.Y.

MAP 18

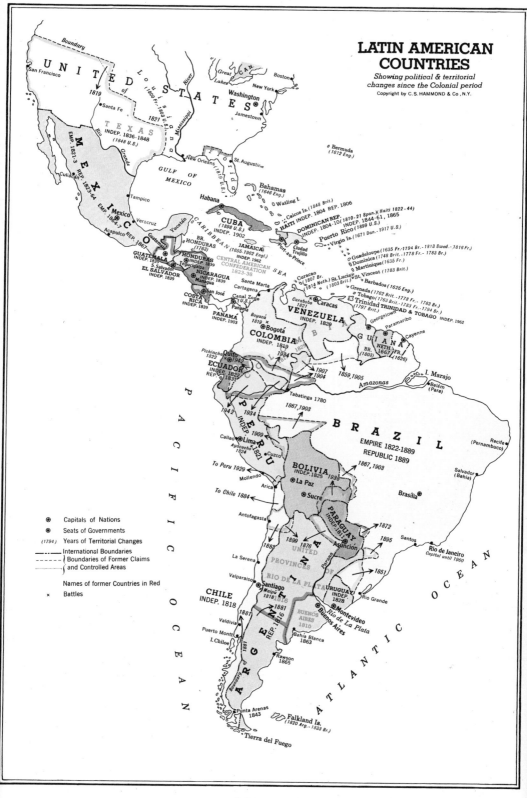

LATIN AMERICAN COUNTRIES

Showing political & territorial changes since the Colonial period

Copyright by C.S. HAMMOND & Co., N.Y.

UNITED STATES

Boundary 1819

San Francisco

Santa Fe

Louisiana (1800 Fr.-1803 U.S.)

Great Lakes

CAN.

Boston

New York

Washington

Jamestown

M E X I C O
EMP. 1821-3
REP. 1823-64
EMP. 1864-7
REP. 1867

T E X A S
INDEP. 1836-1848
(1848 U.S.)

1891

Mississippi River

New Orleans

St. Augustine

Culiacán

Rio Grande

Tampico

Veracruz

Mexico

Acapulco

Yucatán

Guatemala

GULF OF MEXICO

FLORIDA (1819 U.S.)

Habana

Bahamas (1646 Eng.)

Watling I.

CUBA (1898 U.S.) INDEP. 1902

Caicos Is. (1848 Brit.)

HAITI INDEP. 1804

DOMINICAN REP. 1806
INDEP. 1804-10 (1810-21 Span.)(Haiti 1822-44)
INDEP. 1844-61, 1865

Puerto Rico (1899 U.S.)

Port-au-Prince

Ciudad Trujillo

Virgin Is. (1671 Dan.-1917 U.S.)

Bermuda (1612 Eng.)

BR. HONDURAS (1768)

GUATEMALA INDEP. 1839

HONDURAS INDEP. 1839
Tegucigalpa

S. Salvador
EL SALVADOR INDEP. 1839

NICARAGUA INDEP. 1839
Managua

CENTRAL AMERICAN CONFEDERATION 1823-38

JAMAICA (1655-1962 Engl.) INDEP. 1962

Guadeloupe (1635 Fr.-1794 Br.-1813 Swed.-1816 Fr.)
Dominica (1748 Br.-1778 Fr.-1783 Br.)
Martinique (1635 Fr.)

COSTA RICA INDEP. 1839
San José

PANAMA INDEP. 1903

Canal Zone (U.S.)
Panamá

Santa Marta

Cartagena

Curaçao (1807 Br.) (1814 Neth.)

St. Lucia (1803 Brit.)

St. Vincent (1783 Brit.)

Barbados (1625 Eng.)

Grenada (1762 Brit.-1778 Fr.-1783 Br.)
Tobago (1763 Brit.-1783 Fr.-1794 Br.)
TRINIDAD & TOBAGO INDEP. 1962
Trinidad (1797 Brit.)

Carabobo 1821

Caracas

VENEZUELA INDEP. 1830

Georgetown

Paramaribo

Cayenne

BR. (1803)
NETH. (1667)
FR. (1626)
G U I A N A

Boyacá 1819

Bogotá

COLOMBIA INDEP. 1819

Pichincha 1822

Quito 1942

ECUADOR INDEP. 1822
REP. 1831

1934

1907
1904

1859, 1905

Amazonas

I. Marajó

Belém (Pará)

Tabatinga 1780

1867, 1903

B R A Z I L

EMPIRE 1822-1889
REPUBLIC 1889

Recife (Pernambuco)

1942

1934

P E R U INDEP. 1821

Callao

Lima

Ayacucho 1824

Cuzco

1909

To Peru 1929

Mollendo

Arica

BOLIVIA INDEP. 1825

La Paz

Sucre

1930

1867, 1903

Brasília

Salvador (Bahia)

To Chile 1884

Antofagasta

PARAGUAY INDEP. 1811

Asunción

1872

1899 1876

1895

Santos

La Serena

UNITED PROVINCES OF RIO DE LA PLATA

1889

1851

Rio de Janeiro
Capital until 1960

Valparaíso

Santiago

Maipú 1818

1816

URUGUAY INDEP. 1828

Rio Grande

CHILE INDEP. 1818

1881

1881

Montevideo

BUENOS AIRES 1810

Buenos Aires

Rio de La Plata

Valdivia

Puerto Montt

I. Chiloé

A R G E N T I N A REP. 1816

Bahía Blanca 1863

Rawson 1865

Boundary 1881

Punta Arenas 1843

Falkland Is. (1820 Arg.-1833 Br.)

Tierra del Fuego

PACIFIC OCEAN

ATLANTIC OCEAN

CARIBBEAN SEA

Legend

⊛ Capitals of Nations
◉ Seats of Governments
(1794) Years of Territorial Changes
—·—·— International Boundaries
— — — Boundaries of Former Claims and Controlled Areas
Names of former Countries in Red
× Battles

MAP 19

ITALY
AT THE CLOSE
OF THE
XV CENTURY

SCALE OF MILES
0 20 40 60 80 100

A 6° **B** 8° **C** 10° **D** 12° **E** 14° **F** 16° **G** 18° **H**

BURGUNDY

SWISS
CONFEDERATION

TYROL

SALZBURG AUSTRIA

Salzburg

STYRIA

HUNGARY

Rhine R.

Lucerne

Lausanne

Geneva

VALAIS

Aosta

Bellinzona

Como

Bergamo

Monza

MILAN

Novara

Vercelli

Susa

Turin

Pinerolo

MONT FERRAT

M. OF

SALUZZO

Saluzzo

Alessandria

Pavia

Cava

Lodi

Crema

Brescia

VENETIAN

Verona

Vicenza

Padua

Treviso

Feltre

Belluno

Trent

B. OF
TRENT

Brixen

Bozen

CARINTHIA

Isonzo

FRIULI

Drave

CARNIOLA

Save

CROATIA

SLAVONIA

Drave

Save

OTTOMAN

EMPIRE

BOSNIA

HERZEGOVINA

ISTRIA
(to Venice)

Pola

DALMATIA
(to Venice)

Zara

Spalato

Ragusa

Cattaro

REP. OF
GENOA

Genoa

Savona

Nice

Po

Piacenza

Parma

Fornovo

Reggio

D. OF MODENA

Modena

D. OF FERRARA
(ESTE)

MANTUA

Mirandola

Guastalla

Bologna

Imola

Faenza

EMILIA

ROMAGNA

Ravenna

Rimini

REP. OF
LUCCA

Lucca

Pistoja

Prato

Pisa

Arno R.

Fiesole

REP. OF FLORENCE

Florence

REP. OF SAN MARINO

Pesaro

D. OF URBINO

Urbino

Ancona

Volterra

Siena

Arezzo

Cortona

REP. OF
SIENA

ELBA

Piombino

D. OF
PIOMBINO

Perugia

UMBRIA

Assisi

Spoleto

STATES

OF THE

CHURCH

Orvieto

Viterbo

SABINA

Civitella

Aquila

PATRIMONY OF ST. PETER

Civita Vecchia

Tivoli

Rome

Anagni

Ostia

Fondi

ABRUZZI

Pescara

MOLISE

CAPITANATA

KINGDOM

Traietto

Gaeta

Capua

Benevento

CAMPANIA

OF

Naples

ISCHIA

CAPRI

Sorrento

Amalfi

Salerno

TERRA DI LAVORO

NAPLES

APULIA

Bari

Mola

Brindisi

Taranto

Lecce

Otranto

Gallipoli

BASILICATA

CORSICA
(to Genoa)

SARDINIA
(to Naples)

TYRRHENIAN

SEA

ADRIATIC SEA

LIPARI OR
AEOLIAN IS.

Cosenza

Castiglione

CALABRIA

Cotrone

Squillace

Geraco

Palermo

Messina

Reggio

SICILY

Catania

Syracuse

Girgenti

Avola

Ragusa

MEDITERRANEAN

SEA

MEDITERRANEAN

SEA

AFRICA

MALTA

FERMO
THE MARCHES

C. S. HAMMOND & CO., N.Y.

A 6° **B** 8° **C** Longitude 10° **D** 12° East **E** of 14° Greenwich **F** 16° **G** 18° **H**

MAP 20

UNIFICATION OF
ITALY
1859-1924

SCALE OF MILES

0   20   40   60   80   100

The dates are those of the Union with the Kingdom of Sardinia and of Italy. Bracketed dates indicate year of loss to the Kingdom of Sardinia.

GERMANY

FRANCE

AUSTRIA

SWITZERLAND

Neutral Ter.

SAVOY
To France (1860)

KINGDOM

PIEDMONT

Novara
Vercelli

Magenta
1859

T·Y·R·O·L
1919

A·U·S·T·R·I·A·N   E·M·P·I·R·E

VENETIA
1866

Custozza

Verona

Turin

Milan

Susa
Cavour

Solferino
Villafranca

Trieste

Venice

1919

ISTRIA

To France (1860)

Monaco
(Indep.)

Nice

LIGURIA

Genoa

(DUCHY)
Parma
1860

Reggio
(DUCHY)

Finale

Ferrara

Modena
1860

Bologna

ROMAGNA
1860

Ravenna

San Marino
(Indep. Rep.)

Zara   DALMATIA

JUGO·SLAVIA

Save R.

Drave R.

Lucca
To Tuscany

Pisa

Leghorn

Florence

Pesaro

THE MARCHES
1860

Ancona
Castelfidardo

Spalato

OF   SARDINIA

CORSICA
(To France)

ELBA

GRAND DUCHY

Siena

OF TUSCANY

1860

PAPAL

STATES

UMBRIA
1860

THE PATRIMONY
1870

Chieti

Rieti

Mentana

Civitavecchia

Rome
1870

LISSA

LAGOSTA

Ragusa

A·D·R·I·A·T·I·C

CAPRERA

SARDINIA

Cagliari

TYRRHENIAN

SEA

Gaeta

1860

Foggia

Benevento

Capua

Naples

Castellamare

BASILICATA

Bari

Taranto

Brindisi

KINGDOM

OF   THE

Otranto

Gulf of Taranto

S·E·A

MEDITERRANEAN

TWO   SICILIES

Palermo
Termini

Milazzo

Aspromonte

Messina

Reggio

CALABRIA

Marsala   Calatafimi

SICILY
1860

Catania

SEA

AFRICA

C. S. HAMMOND & Co., N.Y.

Longitude   12°   East   of   14°   Greenwich

MAP 21

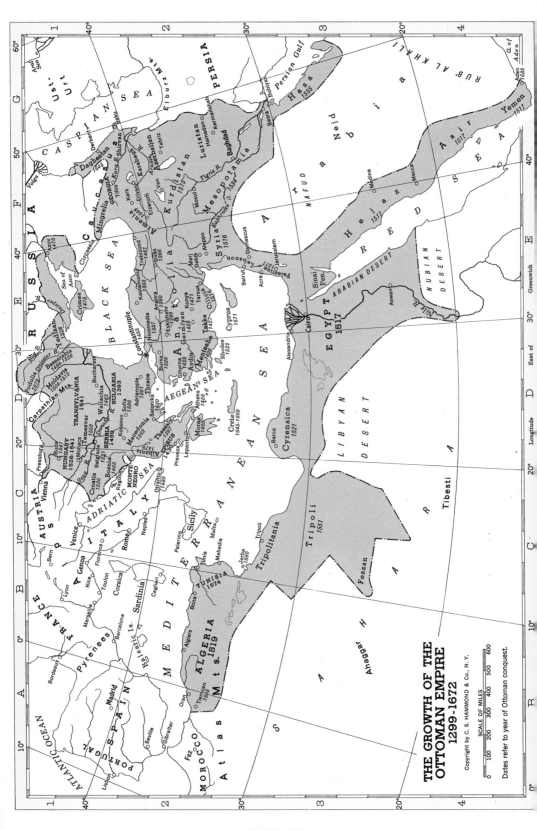

THE GROWTH OF THE OTTOMAN EMPIRE
1299-1672

Copyright by C. S. HAMMOND & Co., N.Y.

SCALE OF MILES

0 100 200 300 400 500 600

Dates refer to year of Ottoman conquest.

MAP 22

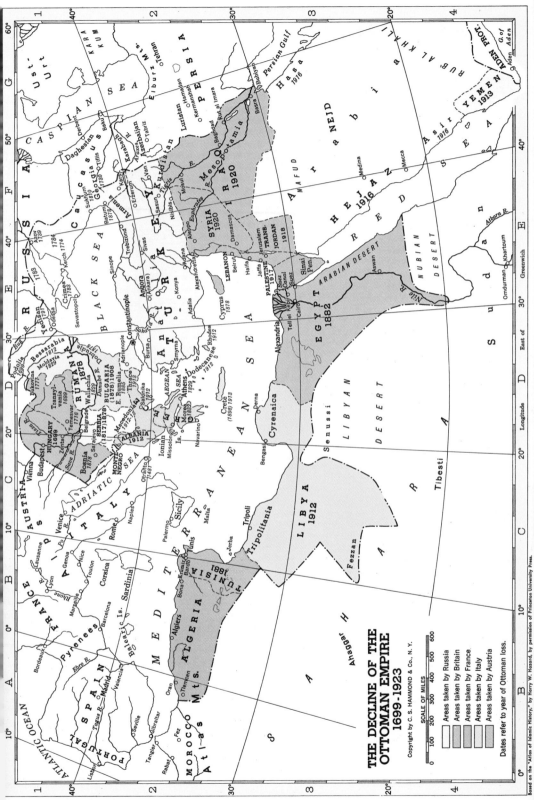

THE DECLINE OF THE
OTTOMAN EMPIRE
1699-1923

Copyright by C. S. HAMMOND & Co., N.Y.

SCALE OF MILES

0   100 200 300 400 500 600

☐ Areas taken by Russia
▨ Areas taken by Britain
▨ Areas taken by France
☐ Areas taken by Italy
☐ Areas taken by Austria

Dates refer to year of Ottoman loss.

Based on the "Atlas of Islamic History," by Harry W. Hazard, by permission of Princeton University Press.

MAP 23

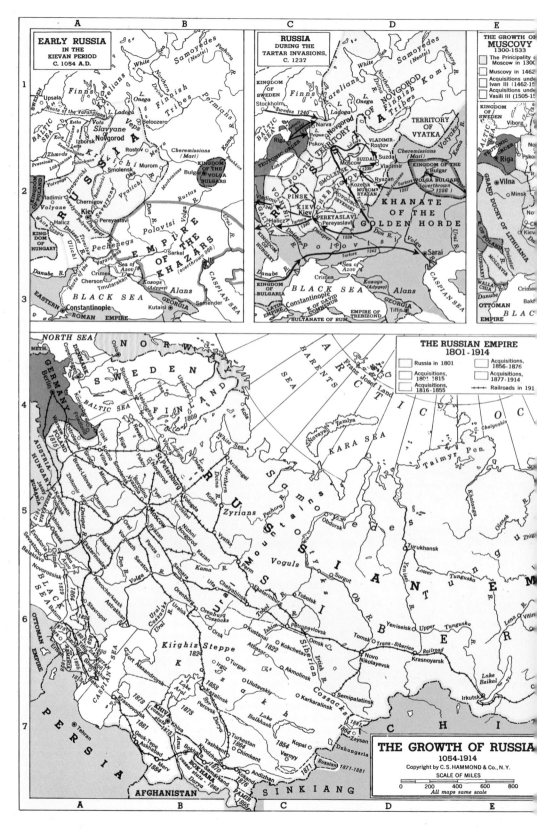

MAP 24

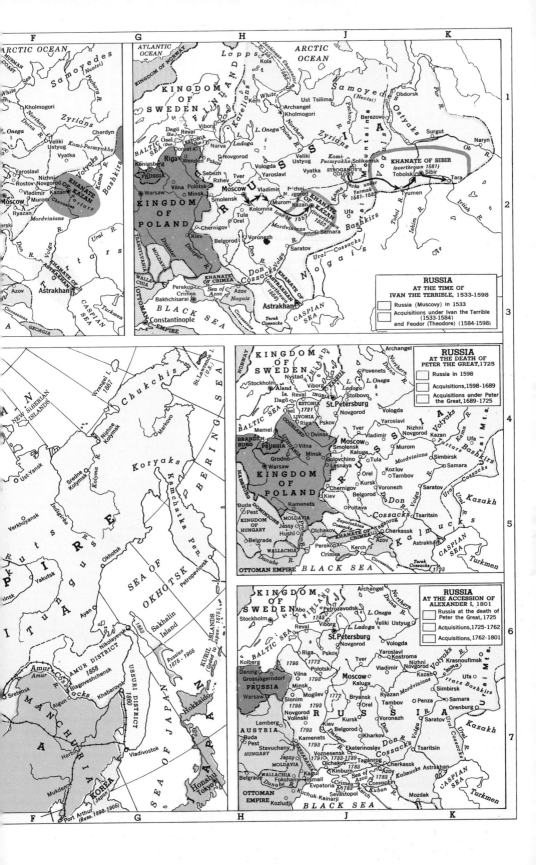

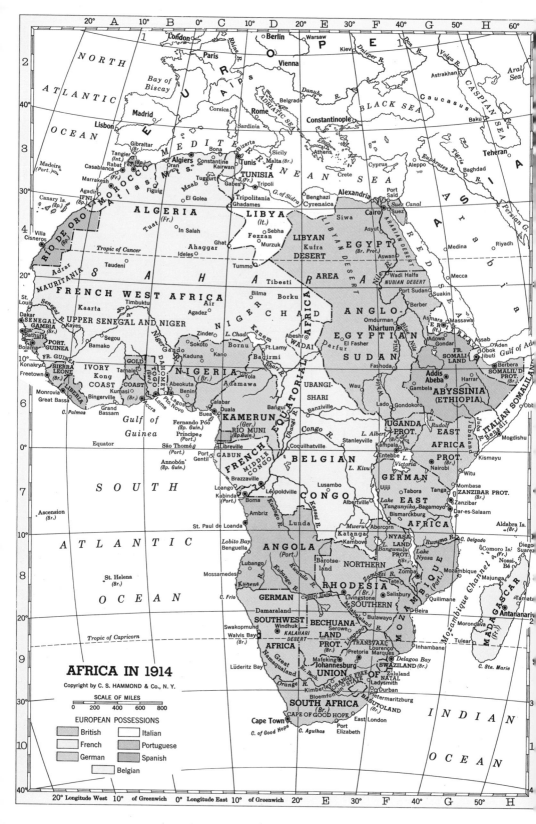

AFRICA IN 1914

Copyright by C. S. Hammond & Co., N.Y.

SCALE OF MILES

0   200   400   600   800

EUROPEAN POSSESSIONS

British	Italian
French	Portuguese
German	Spanish
Belgian	

MAP 25

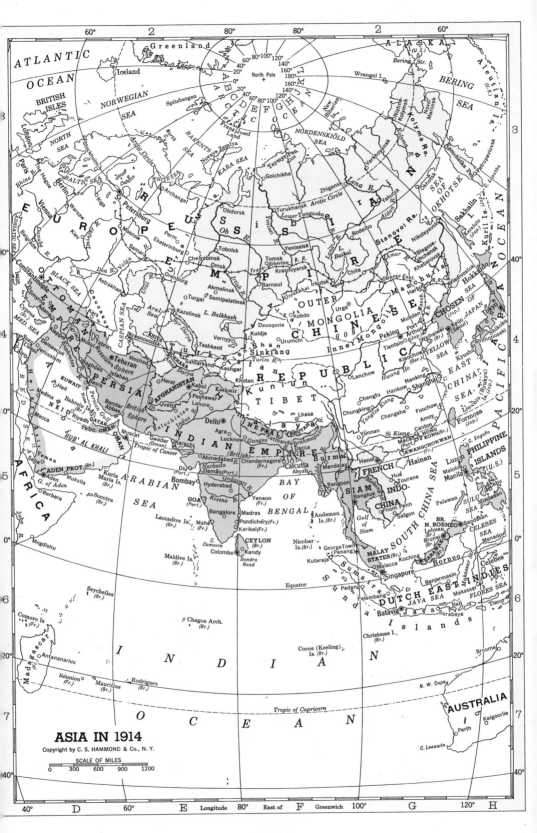

ASIA IN 1914

Copyright by C. S. HAMMOND & Co., N. Y.

SCALE OF MILES
0   300   600   900   1200

MAP 26

MAP 27

MAP 28

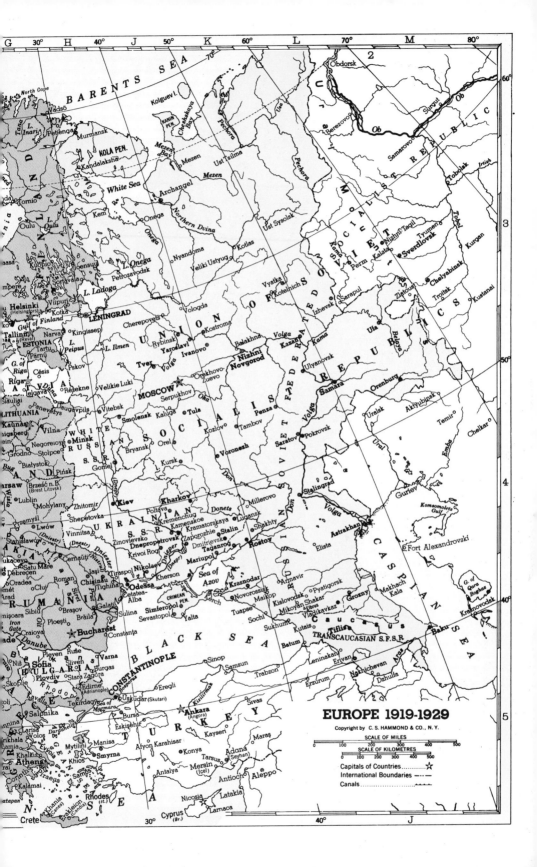

EUROPE 1919-1929

Copyright by C. S. HAMMOND & CO., N. Y.

SCALE OF MILES

SCALE OF KILOMETRES

Capitals of Countries............☆
International Boundaries —·—·—
Canals.................................

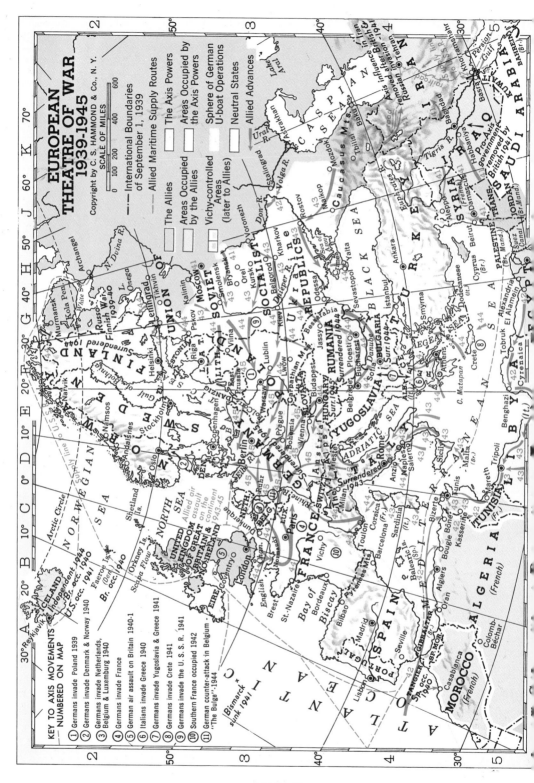

EUROPEAN THEATRE OF WAR 1939-1945

Copyright by C. S. HAMMOND & Co., N. Y.

SCALE OF MILES

0 100 200 400 600

- - - International Boundaries of September 1, 1939
——— Allied Maritime Supply Routes

The Allies
The Axis Powers
Areas Occupied by the Allies
Areas Occupied by the Axis Powers
Vichy-controlled Areas (later to Allies)
Sphere of German U-boat Operations
Neutral States
Allied Advances

KEY TO AXIS MOVEMENTS NUMBERED ON MAP

① Germans invade Poland 1939
② Germans invade Denmark & Norway 1940
③ Germans invade Netherlands, Belgium & Luxemburg 1940
④ Germans invade France
⑤ German air assault on Britain 1940-1
⑥ Italians invade Greece 1940
⑦ Germans invade Yugoslavia & Greece 1941
⑧ Germans invade Crete 1941
⑨ Germans invade the U. S. S. R. 1941
⑩ Southern France occupied 1942
⑪ German counter-attack in Belgium - "The Bulge" 1944

MAP 29

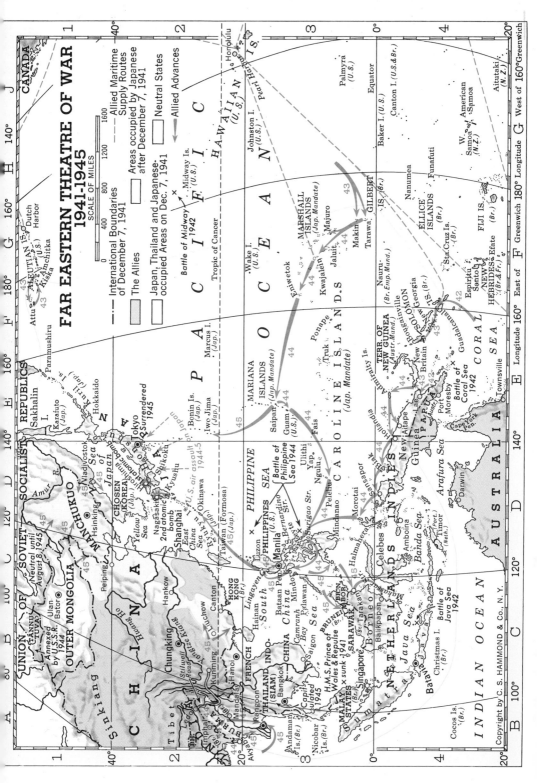

FAR EASTERN THEATRE OF WAR
1941-1945

SCALE OF MILES

Legend:
- International Boundaries of December 7, 1941
- The Allies
- Japan, Thailand and Japanese-occupied Areas on Dec. 7, 1941
- Allied Maritime Supply Routes
- Areas occupied by Japanese after December 7, 1941
- Neutral States
- Allied Advances

MAP 30

Copyright by C. S. HAMMOND & Co., N.Y.

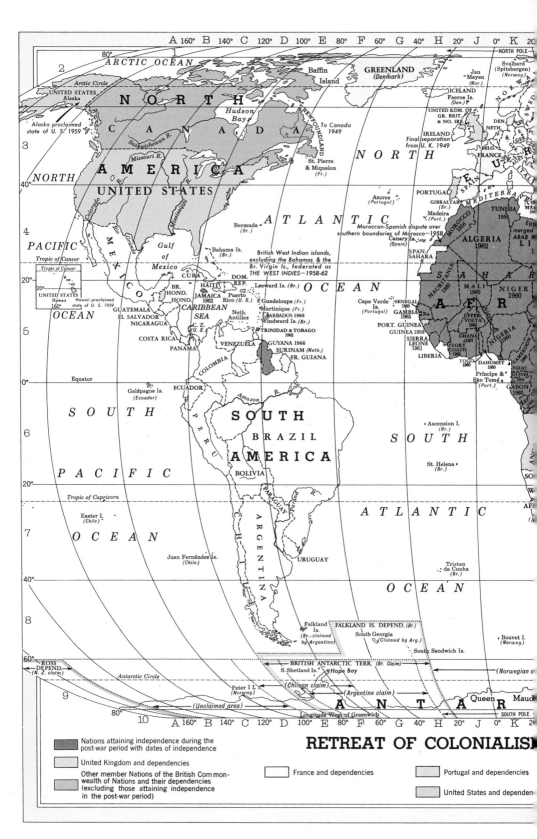

RETREAT OF COLONIALISM

Legend:

Nations attaining independence during the post-war period with dates of independence

United Kingdom and dependencies

Other member Nations of the British Commonwealth of Nations and their dependencies (excluding those attaining independence in the post-war period)

France and dependencies

Portugal and dependencies

United States and dependencies

MAP 31

THE POST-WAR PERIOD

Netherlands and dependencies

Spain and dependencies

Norway and dependencies

Denmark and dependency

Other countries

Areas of the Soviet Union in which Great Russians constitute a majority of the population. Names of other peoples are underlined.

ECKERT PROJECTION
SCALE OF MILES ALONG EQUATOR
0   500   1000   1500   2000   2500

Copyright by C. S. HAMMOND & Co., N. Y.

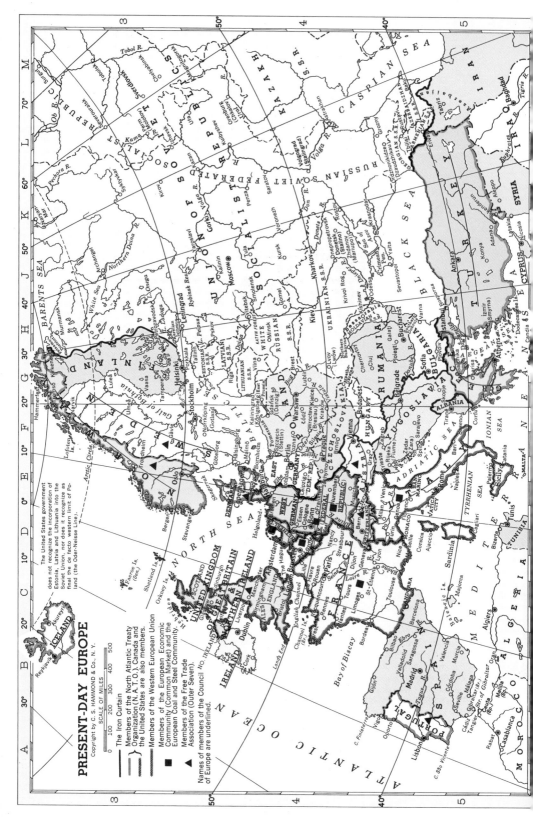

PRESENT-DAY EUROPE

Copyright by C. S. HAMMOND & Co. N.Y.

SCALE OF MILES

0   100   200   300   400   500

The United States government does not recognize the incorporation of Estonia, Latvia and Lithuania into the Soviet Union, nor does it recognize as final the de facto western limit of Poland (the Oder-Neisse Line).

———— The Iron Curtain

Members of the North Atlantic Treaty Organization (N.A.T.O.) Canada and the United States are also members.

Members of the Western European Union

■ Members of the European Economic Community (Common Market) and the European Coal and Steel Community.

◀ Members of the Free Trade Association (Outer Seven)

Names of members of the Council of Europe are underlined.

MAP 32

ble markets. Hence, contrary to the mercantilists, he advocated free competition and free trade, so that each area and state could produce and distribute its specialized products most cheaply and efficiently. Adam Smith's observations thus played an important role in the Industrial Revolution which was then beginning.

While economists talked of freeing trade, production, and agriculture from medieval restrictions and mercantilistic regulations, industrialization gradually assumed the proportions of an industrial revolution. New inventions began to multiply, at first particularly in England's textile industry. The harnessing of new sources of power through the invention of the steam engine and the water turbine not only increased production but also called for greater concentration of labor in a single factory, in order to utilize the costly new machines to the fullest extent. This process of industrialization and the accompanying creation of an industrial proletariat gathered momentum toward the end of the eighteenth century.

Failure to reform

By the time reforms of the political system were belatedly attempted in France and Poland, it proved impossible to implement them. As a result, France became engulfed in revolution, and Poland disappeared as an independent state. In Britain's North American colonies, the question of reform was more complicated. The colonists, on the one hand, believed in the contractual political theories of the *philosophes*. The English government, on the other hand, sought to gain greater financial and administrative control over the colonists. These differences led to the war for independence.

The last decades of the ancien régime

At the accession of Louis XVI in 1774, France was in serious financial trouble and filled with social discontent. The twenty-year-old grandson of Louis XV was kind and pious, but irresolute and incapable of imposing himself on his own court or on the government. At the age of sixteen, he had married the vivacious fifteen-year-old Marie Antoinette (1755–1793), who had been delighted to exchange the strict supervision of her mother, Maria Theresa of Austria, for the free and gay atmosphere of Versailles. The new queen, according to one observer, a girl "without depth of feeling," was not popular among the French and became carelessly involved in several scandals that helped arouse Parisian feeling against her. Moreover she freely lent herself to court intrigues, which were usually directed against those favoring reform. Nonetheless the carefree Marie Antoinette was hardly a villain, as she has sometimes been pictured.

Louis XVI's first controller general of finances—the most important minister in a state facing bankruptcy—was Anne Robert Jacques Turgot (1727–1781), a physiocrat who had served as a successful intendant for over a decade. Turgot at once launched an impressive reform program that might possibly have saved French finances, if he had been steadfastly supported by the king, as Louis had promised him. After his appointment, he informed the monarch of his aims: "No bankruptcy. No increase of taxes. No loans." His physiocratic measures included the abolition of medieval guilds and a decree ordering the free circulation of grain, so that supply and demand might determine its market price. Turgot also envisioned tax reforms and started by tightening the collection system so that more of the money collected from the people might reach the royal treasury. Such a move naturally infuriated the tax farmers, private financiers who paid the government specified sums in return for the privilege of collecting certain taxes in a given area. Finally, Turgot proposed to attack the tax exempt status of the privileged classes—nobles and clergy—and began to reduce feudal privileges by abolishing the *corvée,* a surviving medieval custom whereby tenant farmers and certain peasants owed forced labor to noble lords or to the state.

Turgot's actual and proposed reforms aroused such alarm among the privileged classes that a court clique soon persuaded Louis XVI to dismiss his reforming minister. On leaving office, Turgot supposedly told the king: "Never forget, Sir, that it was weakness which brought the head of Charles I to the block"—an incorrect judgment of the English monarch, but a valid prophecy for Louis XVI.

Turgot was succeeded by Jacques Necker (1732–1804), a native of Geneva and a wealthy banker, who was made only minister of finance and not controller general, since he was a Protestant. Necker tried further tax reforms and attempted to reduce government expenses. But in the face of the war against England (American War of Independence) and the refusal of the court to curtail its vast expenses, even the adroit Necker could not balance the budget. Despite fierce opposition by the court cabal, he stayed in office five years (1776–1781), a remarkable achievement under the fickle Louis XVI. After his dismissal, he published his controversial *compte rendu,* an open accounting of the state budget, showing the vast expenses of Versailles and the cost of keeping royal favorites. It is uncertain whether he hoped to alarm the nation to the danger of financial collapse or wanted to take vengeance upon those who brought about his dismissal. Necker remained an influential politician, was recalled to office seven years later, and played a vital role in the early days of the French Revolution.

After 1781, the hapless king switched from one minister to another in the hope of bolstering the dwindling royal resources. Some ministers borrowed money and spent lavishly in the expectation that it would improve the credit rating of the French government; others tried retrenchment and attempted to devise new taxes. But all contemplated reforms were frustrated by the entrenched interests—the nobility, the upper clergy, and a majority of the courtiers. In addition, the *parlement de Paris* again became a focal point of resistance to royal authority. Ironically, the only successsful reforms accomplished during the dying years of the *ancien régime* were improvements in the military establishment—reforms that no longer benefited the monarchy but were to help the revolutionary regime, and later Napoleon, win their spectacular victories after 1792.

Criticism of the regime became increasingly strong. The American War of Independence, which France entered on the side of the colonists in the hope of regaining some lands lost to England in 1763, created further dissatisfaction. French forces, particularly the navy, performed well during the war, and France regained some former territory at the peace treaty (1783), but the undertaking hardly restored the prestige of the monarchy. On the contrary, the cost of the war and of the loans to the colonists aggravated French financial problems, and reports of returning French soldiers about the social equality and political rights in America stirred up further dissatisfaction.

Discontent with the failure to reform grew particularly among the Third Estate, which comprised the vast majority of Frenchmen who were neither noble nor ecclesiastics. Theses "commoners" paid most of the taxes but shared few social and political privileges. They did not seek to overthrow the monarchy but rather to free the king from domination by the privileged minority, so that he could act for the benefit of the majority. Despite censorship, pamphlets were circulated echoing Rousseau's ideas on equality and the *philosophes'* distaste for arbitrary rule. Even publicly staged plays, such as Pierre Beaumarchais' (1732–1799) *The Marriage of Figaro* (1784), contained open indictments of the social uselessness of the nobility.

Finally, with no further financial expedients in sight, Louis XVI was persuaded to convoke the Estates General against the advice of his wife and his brother, the future Charles X. Although the Estates General was a medieval institution that had been dormant since 1614, it was to become the nucleus of the revolutionary government which destroyed the monarchy and the *ancien régime*.

The decline and end of Poland

Polish territory had begun to shrink in the seventeenth century through losses to Russia, Turkey, and Sweden (see p. 267). During the eighteenth century, Poland declined further until its ultimate dissolution at the end of the century.

For almost seven decades, with the exception of two brief interludes (under Stanislas Leszczynski), Poland was ruled by Saxon electors. The first Saxon king (Augustus II) tried to strengthen the Polish monarchy. He was, however, an ineffective ruler and his plans for an absolutistic regime failed in the face of determined opposition by the Polish nobility and interference by Russia, which preferred to see a weak and anarchic Poland. The second king of the house of Saxony (Augustus III, 1734–1763) was so involved with Saxon and German affairs and occupied by two wars with Frederick the Great that he devoted little time to Poland. Nonetheless various reforms to consolidate the monarchy were proposed during his reign. However, the reformers could not agree whether to look to France or to Russia for protection, or whether the nobility should be allowed to retain some of its power.

After the death of the last Saxon ruler, Russian influence over Poland became paramount with the election of Stanislas Poniatowski (1764–1795), a Polish nobleman who had been a favorite of Catherine the Great and was to be Poland's last king. In consonance with their alliance of 1763, Catherine of Russia and Frederick of Prussia had agreed to cooperate on Polish affairs and stipulated that Protestants and Greek Orthodox in Poland should be granted equal rights with Roman Catholics. Such a measure was adopted by King Stanislas, but it was unpopular with the Polish nobility. Eventually the nobles rebelled against subservience to Russia, thereby unleashing a train of events that culminated in the First Partition of Poland. With French encouragement, the Polish rebels appealed for Turkish aid, whereas Catherine II dispatched Russian troops to crush the rebellion. The result was a Russo-Turkish war, won by Russia. Russian successes in turn prompted Austria to seek territorial compensations. Since it was easier to seize Polish rather than Turkish land, Austrian and Prussian forces occupied a part of Poland in 1770 as a bargaining point in negotiations with Russia. Ultimately Frederick the Great and Maria Theresa persuaded Catherine to take less Turkish territory and rather participate in a reduction of Poland. Consequently Poland was forced to surrender almost one third of her territory to Austria, Russia, and Prussia in this First Partition of Poland (1772).

After the shock of the First Partition, some Poles, again encouraged by France, worked for reforms to consolidate their truncated state, a movement which resulted in the adoption of a new constitution in 1791, designed to strengthen the monarchy by making it hereditary and by abolishing the *liberum veto* (see p. 266). But Catherine II hardly cherished the prospect of a strengthened Poland under her former favorite. Hence, she sent troops to support those conservatives who opposed the new constitution. Although Prussia was then engaged in the initial stages of the war against revolutionary France (see p. 346), Prussian troops also entered Poland. These maneuvers resulted in the Second Partition of Poland (1793), in which Austria did not participate. Soon the Poles staged another uprising (under Thaddeus Kosciusko, 1746–1817) in order to regain their independence, but the revolt was crushed by Russian and Prussian troops, and the remainder of the state was divided among Russia, Prussia, and Austria in the third and final Partition of Poland. Until her resurrection at the end of World War I, Poland thus ceased to exist as a state.

The revolt of the thirteen colonies

The professional and upper-middle classes in the British colonies of North America were strongly affected by the widespread dissemination of enlightened principles. By the second half of the eighteenth century, the American colonists had gathered considerable practical experience in self-government. Although the more immediate occasion for the American Revolution was imbedded in financial and economic grievances, the colonists' practical and theoretical knowledge of the new political thought directed the course of the rebellion and helped ensure its success and create a new political order, unique in history.

The American scene must be regarded against the background of British politics under George III (1760–1820). Unlike his two Hanoverian predecessors, he wished to rule to the fullest extent permissible under the settlement of 1688. Through legal means and through lavish dispensation of favors, he succeeded in gaining influence over the House of Commons and depriving the Whigs of their strong position.

George's ascendancy as a strong monarch lasted for two decades after his accession, years that represent the crucial period of restlessness and revolt in the American colonies. Finally, the failure of his North American policy encouraged Parliament to reverse the trend toward increased monarchical power. Under the eloquent William Pitt, the Younger (1759–1806), who dominated English politics intermittently from 1783 until shortly before his death, the House of Commons gradually reasserted its influence—a task facilitated by the recurring madness and physical debility of the king. With the monarch in eclipse, rule by the cabinet ministers—rather than by the king—became an established fact in British government.

George also extended his policy of tighter control to the colonies, which caused increasing friction between the thirteen colonies and their home government. After 1765, repeated riots and clashes with British troops occurred, and the colonists sent petitions to the king, stressing their "rights and liberties." George, for his part, asserted that king and Parliament could legislate for the colonies, without granting the colonists the same rights as those of the British subjects in Great Britain.

The American colonists found ample causes for friction. They were dissatisfied by George's proclamation of 1763, closing the western lands (beyond the Alleghenies) to the colonists, but leaving them open for commercial penetration by British subjects from newly acquired Canada. They resented not being treated as equals with English citizens, while having to pay taxes to help pay for the French and Indian War and for the general defense of England's possessions in North America. They especially objected to the tightening of mercantilistic restrictions on their trade, limitations they had hitherto been able to evade rather easily. Finally, a series of British commercial acts—such as the Sugar Act and the Stamp Act—designed to raise revenue and to afford Britain greater control over colonial affairs, together with several British punitive and discriminatory measures, brought the colonists' resentment to a head.

As friction with Britain grew, closer cooperation among the colonists developed. This movement was aided by committees of correspondence (after 1772), whose appeals borrowed freely from the ideas of the eighteenth-century *philosophes*. The Declaration of Rights, for example, issued by the First Continental Congress in 1774, seemed inspired by Lockian principles of the social contract. Moreover the Congress emphasized that the inhabitants of the thirteen colonies, while possessing the same natural rights as all men, had different needs from those of the British and hence were entitled to the greatest possible amount of self-rule. To press their stand against England, the Congress called for an economic boycott of British goods. Soon thereafter, fighting between British and colonials erupted (1775), a civil war at first, which after 1776 turned into a war for independence in which the colonists eventually received aid from France, Spain, and Holland.

As a result of the war, England lost not only the thirteen colonies, but also Florida (to Spain). It was England's first major defeat in over a century. But as the Napoleonic wars were to demonstrate, she remained a formidable European and imperial power, despite her small population.

Incipient Romanticism

The non-rationalist trend (see p. 320) that had become accentuated after the mid-century gradually became a torrent leading toward the Romantic era. Ever more it became a protest against the artificiality and cold logic of the Age of Reason.

With its roots in Rousseau's stress on passion rather than reason, the new trend became particularly powerful in the Germanies in the 1770's. The philosopher and philologist Herder exalted folk tales and national languages as expressive of a people's true spirit or "folksoul." Such an idea stimulated national feelings, despite the irrational nature of this concept. The young poet Goethe, who in his later years became an exponent of classicism, also contributed to this rebellious literary explosion, often called the German Storm and Stress movement. Goethe attacked all rules as then evidenced in neoclassical architecture and instead praised the mysterious, more emotional Gothic style, which had been despised by the rationalists. In his widely popular novel *The Sorrows of Young Werther* (1774) and his drama *Goetz von Berlichingen* (1773), he not only shunned all rules of classical literature but indulged in a veritable outpouring of emotions. His friend Schiller filled his dramas, such as *The Robbers* (1781) and *Don Carlos* (1787) with impassioned calls for political freedom. To all these writers, artistic creation motivated by man's soul seemed more important than mathematical rules or concepts of a mechanically perfect universe. This reawakening of the human soul was to be important during the era of the French Revolution, for although the revolution was largely based on the theoretical thought of the *philosophes,* its impetus came in part from men's irrational passions.

In philosophy, too, a new trend emerged. The influential German philosopher Immanuel Kant (1724–1804) was not an antirationalist, but he cautioned that the vaunted empiricism of the Enlightenment did not embody the final answer in epistemology. In his *Critique of Pure Reason* (1781), he argued for the existence of *a priori* knowledge, which he called "that with which no empirical element is mingled." On this basis, he reopened the whole question of innate knowledge apart from human experience, a concept which was to dominate much of the Romantic era.

The new trend became noticeable in many areas. Marie Antoinette ordered a replica of a little peasant village (Le Hameau) constructed on the grounds of Versailles, so that she could play shepherdess with her friends and commune with nature. The Order of the Freemasons, with its mysterious and occult ceremonies and its emphasis on fraternity, gained an increasing number of adherents. Even Wolfgang Amadeus Mozart's (1756–1791) last opera, *The Magic Flute,* extols the magical powers of supernatural beings and is filled with the spells of secret rites.

Growth of European influence overseas

During the eighteenth century, particularly the latter half, Europeans continued to explore, colonize, and extend their domination in all parts of the world. The search for better and shorter trade routes, the desire for raw materials and increased trade, hope for more land for colonial settlements, scientific curiosity, as well as missionary zeal motivated this movement which was facilitated by improved shipping and more accurate navigational instruments.

The Russians investigated the northern coastlands of Siberia. Dispatched by Peter the Great, the Dane Vitus Bering (1680–1741) explored the Asiatic and American coasts of the North Pacific, discovered the Bering Straits between Alaska and Siberia, and paved the way for the penetration of Russian fur traders into Alaska. While the Danes established some colonies on Greenland, the British expanded in many areas of the globe. They increased their control over India, pushed westward in Canada, and began their commercial penetration of southern Persia. Most successful from the point of view of geographic exploration were Captain James Cook's (1728–1779) three voyages to the South Pacific—between 1768 and 1779—during which he finally disproved the suspected existence of a vast Antarctic continent and charted the coasts of Australia, New Zealand, New Guinea, and other Pacific islands. Cook also went north to rediscover the Hawaiian Islands and explore the coast of Alaska before his eventual death in

Hawaii. As a result, Great Britain acquired New Zealand and Australia, with the first community founded at Sydney in 1788.

In the Americas, there was also a great increase in European settlements. Spanish missionaries penetrated into upper California, established missions along the coast, and founded San Francisco in 1776. In the South, Spanish colonization concentrated on areas south of the Rio de la Plata, in what was to become Argentina. Meanwhile, the former thirteen colonies organized the so-called Northwest Territory and began to penetrate into the region between the Alleghenies and the Mississippi River.

Expansion in Africa and Asia was less spectacular. The Dutch moved slowly inland from their colony at Cape Town. Persia, alternating between periods of power and decline, became more open to foreign penetration— particularly by Russia and England. Commercial contact with China continued to be limited, since only the port of Canton was opened to European traders. Yet, there was a significant cultural exchange between China under the Manchu Dynasty and Europe. Before the dissolution of their order, Jesuit missionaries and scholars were particularly active in China, introducing European scientific and technological ideas. On the other hand, through returning missionaries and merchants, Chinese thought and Chinese administrative and educational practices became better known in Europe and fascinated the imagination of the intellectuals. The *philosophes,* Voltaire in particular, praised the teachings of Confucius and asserted that the concept of government by an intellectual élite was being successfully carried out in China. Rococo art, too, had been affected by Chinese aesthetic patterns. The rich Parisian and Londoner decorated his home with Chinese porcelain, lacquer-covered furniture, silks, and painted scrolls. Chinese pagodas and gardens were copied, and Chinese shadow plays became popular. China thus played a significant role in Europe's Enlightenment.

SUGGESTED READINGS

General Works

Behrens, C. B., *The Ancien Régime* (Harcourt, 1967).
Gershoy, Leo, *From Despotism to Revolution 1763–1789* (Harper, 1963).
Sorel, Albert, *Europe Under the Old Regime* (Harper, 1964).

Eastern Europe

*Gooch, George P., *Catherine the Great, and Other Studies* (Shoe String, 1966).
*———, *Maria Theresa and Other Studies* (Shoe String, 1951).
*Kaplan, Herbert H., *The First Partition of Poland* (Columbia, 1962).
*Padover, Saul K., *The Revolutionary Emperor: Joseph the Second, 1741–1790* (Shoe String, 1967).

Raeff, Marc, *Plans for Political Reform in Imperial Russia, 1730–1905* (Prentice-Hall, 1966). Documents.

Thomson, Gladys S., *Catherine the Great and the Expansion of Russia* (Macmillan, 1962).

Economics

Mantoux, Paul Joseph, *The Industrial Revolution in the Eighteenth Century; The Beginnings of the Modern Factory System in England* (Harper).

Pike, E. Royston, *Adam Smith: Father of Economics* (Hawthorn, 1966).

Taylor, Philip A. M., *The Industrial Revolution in Britain—Triumph or Disaster?* (Heath, 1958).

England

Namier, Lewis, *England in the Age of the American Revolution* (St. Martins, 1961).

——, *The Structure of Politics at the Accession of George III* (St. Martins, 1957).

Reitan, E. A., *George III—Tyrant or Constitutional Monarch?* (Heath, 1964).

The Americas

Adams, Randolph G., *Political Ideas of the American Revolution* (Barnes and Noble, 1958).

Alden, John Richard, *The American Revolution 1775–1783* (Harper, 1954).

Beard, Charles A., *An Economic Interpretation of the Constitution of the United States* (Macmillan, 1965).

Burnett, Edmund Cody, *Continental Congress* (Norton, 1964).

Gipson, Lawrence H., *The Coming of the Revolution: 1763–1775* (Harper, 1962).

Haring, C. H., *The Spanish Empire in America* (Harcourt, 1963).

Jameson, J. Franklin, *The American Revolution Considered as a Social Movement* (Beacon, 1956),

Jensen, Merrill, *The New Nation* (Random, 1950).

Knollenberg, Bernhard, *Origin of the American Revolution: 1759–1776* (Macmillan, 1961).

McDonald, Forrest, *We The People: The Economic Origins of the Constitution* (U. of Chicago, 1963).

Nye, Russel B., and Grabo, Norman S., eds., *American Thought and Writings,* Vol. II, "The Revolution and the Early Republic" (Houghton). Documents.

Whitaker, Arthur P., ed., *Latin America and the Enlightenment* (Cornell, 1961).

CHAPTER XIX

✼ *The French Revolution*
(1789-1799)

During the last decade of the eighteenth century, the history of Europe, and to some degree even that of the Americas, was dominated by the French Revolution. To be sure, in some areas life went on as usual, with hardly a ripple felt from the revolutionary waves emanating from France. Yet in its total impact, it is hard to exaggerate the effect of the French Revolution on Western civilization. Peoples and rulers of other states had to take a stand, either in favor or in opposition to the revolutionary ideals. Ideological neutrality seemed impossible.

The revolutionary basis

Political scientists have long debated whether revolutions occur spontaneously or whether they result from well-prepared plots. With an event as complex and prolonged as the French Revolution of 1789, which changed in color, direction, and participants during its tortuous course, there is room for both interpretations. One can detect instances of plots in preparation for some of the famous "revolutionary days," and yet concede the role played by spontaneity in sudden mob action and other unpredictable events.

Whether or not accepting the theory of premeditation, all observers agree that by 1789 the political barometer in France was falling. The changed climate resulted in part from the new ideas permeating the middle class professionals who were to be the main movers of the revolution. The enlightened ideas had become widespread among the middle class through the writings of the *philosophes*, through discussion in the Parisian *salons*, and through dissemination by the *sociétés de pensées,* groups that resembled the American committees of correspondence.

Fundamental among these ideas (see p. 307) was the notion that institutions can be altered in order to make people happy, for the revolution did not stem from utter despair but from the conviction that a few socio-political corrections would right all wrongs. The specific concepts guiding the revolutionaries were compounded from the writings of Locke, Montesquieu, Voltaire, Rousseau, and others. They included the demand for government under law, for a written constitution to limit arbitrary rule, for separating at least the legislative and executive branches of the government, safeguarding the rights of private property, securing social equality, and reducing the power of the clergy. Many of these demands were included in the Declaration of the Rights of Man and the Citizen, issued early in the revolution as an intended preamble to France's first constitution.

Besides these ideas that bolstered the hope for a new order, there were countless grievances. The peasants, comprising about four-fifths of the population, resented the tax structure, which affected them most heavily without securing them visible benefits. They were also irritated by the outworn manorial obligations which the landed nobility attempted to re-enforce in order to remedy their own growing financial distress. Furthermore, the peasants sought to end the nobles' hunting privileges, which often wrought havoc with crops. The Parisian and agricultural proletariat suffered from the inflation and from several economic depressions.

The middle class objected to its continued social and political inequality in comparison with the nobility. It deplored the financial chaos and impending bankruptcy, derided occasional abuses by the privileged classes, and made much ado about court scandals, real or imagined. In the mind of the educated middle class, such conditions contrasted sharply with what was known about England and what was being reported about the American states. According to some pamphleteers, even distant China seemed better equipped to solve its socio-political problems than France. The presence of the much admired Benjamin Franklin (1706–1790) in Paris from 1776–1785, and the publication of Crèvecoeur's (1735–1813) *Letters from an American Farmer* (1782) contributed to the unrealistic notion that the American experiment could be duplicated in France. Thus the French middle class seemed prepared to attempt drastic changes when Louis XVI decided to convoke the Estates General in the hope of finding a remedy to French financial problems.

The French Revolution

For the sake of clarity, the revolutionary period can be subdivided into smaller segments. The first three years, 1789–1792, were filled with attempts to create a viable constitutional monarchy. Two distinct governmental frameworks were used. The first of these was the Constituent Assembly (1789–1791), the former Estates General which had endowed itself with constituent powers. The Constituent Assembly dismantled the *ancien régime* and built the theoretical foundations for a constitutional monarchy. Except for some outbursts of violence, it was on the whole a moderate period. Almost from the beginning, the Parisians gained great influence over the king and the Assembly, thus in fact turning the French Revolution into a Paris-dominated event. The second governmental framework was that of the Legislative Assembly, instituted in accordance with the constitution of 1791. It lasted for a year, was marked by more vociferous disagreement among political parties, plunged France into the revolutionary wars against Europe, and ended by terminating the monarchy.

The next three revolutionary years, 1792–1795, were dominated by the National Convention, a new constituent and executive body which governed France while attempting to frame a republican constitution. This period saw the height of terroristic violence, the growth of radicalism, and its ultimate defeat. With the final adoption of yet another constitution in 1795, and the establishment of a new government, the Directory—which lasted from 1795–1799—the revolution was officially terminated. In many respects, however, the period of the Directory as well as the early years of Napoleonic rule remained essentially revolutionary.

The Constituent Assembly

When the Estates General convened at Versailles in May, 1789, representation of the Third Estate had been doubled at the suggestion of Necker, so that its numbers equaled those of the combined two other estates, the clergy and the nobility. It had, however, not been stipulated whether the three estates were to deliberate in common and vote by head, thus giving an advantage to the middle class; or whether, as was traditional, the three orders would meet separately and vote by estate, thereby preserving the two-to-one advantage of the two upper estates. Moreover, from the start there was tension between the king and a majority of the delegates. The instructions to the representatives as contained in the *cahiers* drawn up in each electoral district called for the redress of various grievances; yet Louis XVI admonished the delegates to confine their discussions to the financial problems.

For over a month, the delegates of the Third Estate waited for those of the other two to join them. Finally they took steps which amounted to a political revolution. Asserting that they represented the will of the "nation," they called themselves the National Constituent Assembly, implying that they had a mandate to write a constitution for France. They took a pledge not to disband until they had completed their constituent task (Tennis Court Oath), and defied the king's orders to deliberate by separate estates. Informed of the delegates' refusal to obey the royal command, the vacillating

Louis XVI turned about face and ordered the three estates to meet jointly. He had thus tacitly condoned the political aspirations of the Third Estate.

After this peaceful, political transformation, mob action in Paris and peasant uprisings in many parts of France led the Constituent Assembly to undertake a social revolution. Early in July, the court cabal persuaded the king once again to dismiss the reform-minded Necker and to assemble troops for possible use against the Assembly. News of these events, wild rumors of impending reprisals, and incitement by agitators stirred the mobs of Paris' working-class quarters into seizing the arsenal and then storming the Bastille which had served as a political prison. With this action of July 14—a day which became France's national holiday—Paris came under the mixed control of street mobs and a new, insurrectional provisional government established in Paris' city hall, as well as a newly created National Guard commanded by General Lafayette (1757–1834). Once again the king bowed to the *fait accompli* and on a visit to Paris even accepted the new revolutionary tricolor emblem. The king's brothers, however, together with some great nobles, ill at ease about events in Paris, left France in what was to be the beginning of a large-scale emigration of nobles.

Meanwhile peasants rioted, burned manor houses, killed landlords, and roamed the countryside in a movement which the French called "the great fear." On August 4, in the course of an emotional session lasting all night, the Assembly tried to pacify the peasants by abolishing all feudal and manorial privileges and even prohibiting titles showing social rank. This social revolution with its Rousseau-like appeal to equality was soon supplemented by legal guarantees embodied in the Declaration of the Rights of Man. Thus, by the end of August, France had seemingly been transformed into a limited monarchy with social and legal equality, its people had been changed from subjects to citizens, and only the writing of a constitution remained to be done.

While the Constituent Assembly discussed constitutional clauses, in particular the question of whether or not to accord the king veto power over legislation, the Parisian mob once again took matters in hand. In the aftermath of bread riots, thousands of Parisian women marched to Versailles and forced Louis XVI and his family, guarded only half-heartedly by Lafayette and his National Guard, to return to Paris. With the king, as it were, an honorary but closely watched guest of Paris, the Assembly also moved to the city. Thereafter both king and Assembly became increasingly subject to radical pressure by revolutionary mobs.

In the course of the next year, the Assembly continued its political recasting of France by replacing the old, tradition-bound provinces with new administrative divisions (departments), by abolishing the *parlements,* and by many other measures. The legislators also launched a religious and agrarian revolution, and tackled the problem of government deficits. The vast lands of the Church were confiscated by the state and converted into national property. Currency notes, called assignats, were then issued, backed not by specie but by the value of the new state lands—a financial expedient which worked relatively well until over-issue of assignats and devaluation of land made this paper currency almost worthless. The sale of this available land spread land ownership among more people, although much of it eventually came into the possession of bourgeois investors rather than peasant owners. Deprived of its independent wealth, the church was turned into a national institution. The Civil Constitution of the Clergy (1790) stipulated that clergymen were to be elected by the voters, salaried from state funds, and obliged to give a "solemn oath . . . to be loyal to the Nation, the Law, and the King and to support . . . the constitution decreed by the National Assembly." The so-called non-juring priests, those refusing to take the oath, were expelled from their parishes and soon persecuted. This attempted nationalization of religion raised profound discontent among believers and fortified many Frenchmen in their instinctive opposition to the revolutionary movement.

To commemorate the first anniversary of the fall of the Bastille, the revolutionists staged a gigantic festival of national union in Paris on July 14, 1790. Revolutionary clubs and communes from all corners of France sent delegates to attend this celebration which demonstrated the new nationalistic flavor that was to characterize the revolutionary and Napoleonic eras—and for that matter most of French history thereafter. Reforms, terror, and war, almost all actions were soon to be justified on the basis of the nation's needs. With this substitution of the "national will" for arbitrary royal rule, France, one might say, inaugurated the contemporary age. One wonders what Rousseau might have said at this perversion of his ideals.

By early 1791, Louis XVI had become increasingly antipathetic to the new religious policy, particularly after the nationalized church was condemned by a papal bull (April 1791), and the pope had threatened those who abided by the Civil Constitution of the Clergy with "the anathema of the Universal Church." Probably more disturbed by the anti-Catholic trend of the new regime than by its political implications, the king decided to flee from Paris. Some 130 miles east of the city he was captured and ignominiously returned to the capital. The king's flight evoked the first outbreak of determined republicanism, which in turn stirred the moderate forces into action. The latter bloodily suppressed the republican uprising and finally persuaded the king to accept the constitution of 1791, which reserved primary power to a single-chamber legislature, based on limited, indirect voting.

The Legislative Assembly

As constituted in October of 1791, the new government of France was theoretically a moderate constitutional monarchy with a Legislative Assembly dominated by the propertied middle class. Yet from its beginning, the regime was subjected to pressure and tension, which within less than a year toppled the monarchy and exploded all pretension of fraternal harmony within France. The tension resulted primarily from four factors: the attitude of the court; street risings in Paris; dissension among political groups; and the threat of intervention from abroad.

After the added humiliation of his unsuccessful flight, Louis XVI looked with increasing distaste upon the revolution, although he had accepted the new constitution. His wife's secret correspondence with her brother, the emperor of Austria, and the open intrigues of the royal princes who had fled abroad jeopardized his position even further.

Tension and chaos were heightened by the frequent interference of the Parisian mob during the so-called revolutionary days. Moreover, neither the king—as executive—nor the Legislative Assembly really controlled France. Grass-roots control had slipped into the hands of local revolutionary communes or had come under the supervision of the powerful Jacobin clubs which had well-organized branches throughout most of France.

Among the political groups themselves, both inside and outside of the Legislative Assembly, there was growing dissension. Political parties had started to form in 1789, when in the Assembly those with similar opinions sat together—the more conservative on the right, the more liberal on the left, a circumstance from which we derived our political designation of *left* and *right*. With revolutionary action between 1789 and 1794 steadily moving to the left, toward greater political participation by the masses and more socio-economic equality, the same leftward movement occurred among the parties. Conservative groups—true royalists and constitutional monarchists, for example—gradually disappeared as republicanism grew. On the other hand, those championing a conservative republic with limited popular sovereignty, who were considered extreme leftists at the beginning of the revolution, found themselves on the right by 1792.

Among the various clubs and parties, only a few can be mentioned. The moderate monarchists (*Feuillants*), with Lafayette among their leaders, who hoped the constitution of 1791 would prove workable, were gradually suppressed under the avalanche of republicanism. The Jacobin club, which gave birth to a number of splinter groups, stood for radical republicanism. Dominated at first by Maximilien Robespierre (1758–1794) and briefly by Georges Danton (1759–1794), the Jacobins included in their ranks many of the best-known revolutionary leaders, including Jean Marat (1743–1793). Within the Legislative Assembly, there was mounting bitterness between the Girondists, who sought to establish a federal republic with wide powers reserved to the provinces or departments, and the *Mountain,* a group of dedicated Jacobins who favored a tightly organized, highly centralized republic based in Paris. The various clubs and political groups issued their own inflammatory newssheets, had their own network of communications, and in many cases commanded their own shock troops to support political action by force.

Tension within France was further heightened by pressure from abroad. French noble émigrés were trying to get the powers to intervene in their behalf, German princes were demanding compensation for losses in Alsace, and the Austrian court became interested in helping Marie Antoinette. Most European monarchs, as yet more or less absolute in their realms, naturally looked with trepidation upon what was happening to monarchical institutions in France. Already in July 1791, the emperor publicly urged the powers to help "restore the liberty and honor" of the French rulers. A month later, Prussia and Austria (in the Declaration of Pillnitz) suggested joint action by all powers and vaguely threatened to send armed help to Louis XVI "in harmony with the rights of sovereigns." Such threats merely heightened republicanism in France and incited further distrust of Louis XVI.

In the spring of 1792, France declared war on Austria, which was soon joined by Prussia, and later by England, Spain, and Holland. This action opened a period of twenty-three years of almost uninterrupted revolutionary and Napoleonic wars. The French Girondists, then in control of the government, contended that France's revolutionary gains were not safe while absolute monarchs sat on neighboring thrones. They also hoped that a foreign war would unite the French people. Moreover missionary zeal inspired in them the desire to export the revolutionary accomplishments. The Austrians and Prussians, for their part, favored war, believing that the disorganized revolutionary regime of France would be quickly defeated and that it would be best to nip the revolutionary blossom in the bud.

The war soon changed conditions in France. News of initial French reverses in the field helped incite an invasion of Louis' Tuileries Palace by a Parisian mob shouting "Down with Mr. Veto," since the king had availed himself of his veto power to obstruct the Legislative's bill against non-juring priests and émigrés. Soon thereafter, the French were further infuriated by a tactless manifesto issued by the commander of the Austro-Prussian forces (Brunswick Manifesto), ordering all Parisians "to submit at once and without delay to the king [Louis XVI]" and threatening to condemn the city of Paris "to a military execution and to complete ruin," if the French would not comply with his orders. The result in France was a nationalistic outburst and a rallying behind the war effort. A month later, the republicans staged another uprising in Paris, seized and imprisoned the royal family (August 1792), and transferred *de facto* power to the revolutionary commune of Paris. This event marked the end of the monarchy in France and the beginning of the violent phase of the revolution. During September 1792, the Jacobins organized *ad hoc* criminal tribunals in Paris and in the provinces and entrusted them with the task of condemning political suspects and overseeing their summary execution. The revolutionary fever demanded that internal enemies be eliminated before the nation could face the external foe. While the people elected a new assembly, since the constitutional monarchy had become inoperative with the imprisonment of the king, the improvised

French armies stopped the Prussians at Valmy (September 1792), thereby saving France from invasion and launching a period of almost continuous successes for the French revolutionary forces.

The National Convention

The new assembly, the National Convention, theoretically elected by universal male suffrage (actually only 10 per cent of the qualified voters cast their ballots), faced the tasks of deciding the fate of Louis XVI, writing a new constitution, prosecuting the War of the First Coalition, creating order at home, and consolidating the republic. The real executive power lay most of the time with the Jacobins, the Commune of Paris, and several revolutionary committees.

Even before half the delegates had arrived, the Convention proclaimed France a republic, "one and indivisible." To herald their zeal for building a new era, the delegates devised a new revolutionary calendar and made September 22, 1792, the start of Year I of the revolution. Later, as the anti-Christian trend mounted, they even abolished the customary days, months, and holidays. They divided the year into twelve even periods of thirty days, each given a "natural" designation such as fog-period, snow-period, heat-period; each period was subdivided into three "decades" of ten days each, and once a year there was to be a revolutionary festival of five days, in order to complete the calendar year.

A few months later, the Convention embarked on a lengthy and stormy trial of Louis XVI. Found guilty of conspiracy "against the liberty of the nation," condemned to death by a small majority, the king was guillotined in January 1793. Most radicals seemed to agree with Danton who asserted that "the head of a king" might serve as proper challenge and warning to the tyrannical rulers of Europe. During the heightened terror later in the year, Marie Antoinette was also tried and executed.

The war soon affected many European countries and had wide repercussions in France itself. After Valmy, the French successfully took the offensive and invaded the Austrian Netherlands, Germany, and Italy. Success stimulated revolutionary zeal and boldness. The Convention proclaimed its readiness to aid "all who wish to throw off tyranny," and laid down policy for the treatment of occupied territory, in which they promised to establish "the sovereignty and independence of the people," and to "treat as enemies whoever, refusing liberty and equality . . . tried to . . . collaborate with the prince and the privileged castes." The revolutionaries thus launched full-scale ideological warfare.

When in the spring of 1793 the anti-French coalition gained several victories, some prominent French generals deserted to the enemy, and uprisings of peasants and royalists erupted in France, the worried revolutionaries resorted to terror and total war. A life and death struggle ensued between the moderate republicans, such as the Girondists, and the radical Jacobins, who dominated the *Mountain* in the Convention and preached that only a total revolution, backed by the proletariat, could safeguard revolutionary gains. Marat, who advocated a total dictatorship "in the name of the people," was assassinated; but the Jacobins under Robespierre triumphed with the arrest and eventual execution of the Girondist leaders.

The task of defending the revolution against foreign invaders and counterrevolution at home was entrusted to the Committee of Public Safety, dominated by Danton and Robespierre. A Revolutionary Tribunal was created to ferret out and eliminate suspected subversives. In an atmosphere of increasing fanaticism, the Jacobins justified all actions in the name of the nation and the revolution. To prosecute the war, they undertook a total mobilization of human and material resources. All single men were drafted, married men and women had to work in war industries, and old men were ordered to make themselves useful by preaching "the hatred of kings and the unity of the republic." A forced loan was levied on the rich, new assignats were issued based on confiscated estates of emigrated nobles, and maximum prices were decreed to check inflation.

To purify the country of real and imagined counterrevolutionaries, Robespierre instituted what the French called the Reign of Terror, which increased in intensity and horror from September 1793 to July 1794. A new "suspect law" defined as traitors "those who though having done nothing against liberty, have done nothing for her either." Agents dispatched from Paris and local Jacobins sought out royalists, nobles, foreign agents, Catholics not accepting the Civil Constitution, Girondists, or anyone suspected of the slightest misgivings about Jacobinism. When the guillotine could not work fast enough, eager executioners resorted to mass drownings and shootings. At the height of the Terror, a new law gave the Revolutionary Tribunal power to convict people without a hearing and without evidence, and over 1300 persons were guillotined in Paris during the last forty-seven days before the fall of Robespierre.

During the Terror, radical revolutionaries also sought to exterminate Christianity. For the worship of God they tried to substitute the cult of Reason. Many churches were closed and during the Festival of Reason in 1793, a pretty dancer stood on the altar of Notre Dame in Paris as a symbol of Reason. Atheistic extremists deemed that the belief in God should be supplanted by the revolutionary, patriotic creed, with its symbols, festivals, and slogans. During his last months in power, Robespierre sought to counter this materialistic trend. Insisting that the human soul was immortal, he organized a gigantic festival in honor of the Supreme Being, during which he set fire to a statue symbolizing Atheism. Robespierre also hoped to establish a so-called Republic of Virtue, in which citizens, uncorrupted and utterly dedicated, would practice pure, republican behavior.

By the winter of 1793, terror and total mobilization had turned the tide of war. The revolutionaries had reassumed the offensive against the allied

XIX · THE FRENCH REVOLUTION

coalition and crushed the uprisings inside France. But Robespierre and his colleagues on the Committee of Public Safety refused to relinquish their power and proceeded to eliminate possible rivals and ideological deviationists. First exterminated were the left-wing radicals, the Hébertists, who wanted to push the revolution toward further atheism, and the "enraged ones," who preached egalitarianism. With their execution (March 1794), the leftward movement of the revolution was ended, and France was launched on a gradual return to conservatism. Next Robespierre struck at Danton and his supporters, the so-called indulgents, who demanded an end to the Terror in the belief that the revolution had been saved and that further bloodshed was unnecessary.

After these massacres, Robespierre reigned supreme for three months until he and his close supporters were overthrown and executed by a motley group of disgruntled revolutionaries, intriguers, and moderates. The fall of Robespierre (July 1794) in turn unleashed a reaction by the moderates. The Terror was gradually discontinued, and the Jacobins and revolutionary committees were stripped of their power. Meanwhile the French continued to win victories, forced Holland to transform herself into the French-sponsored Batavian Republic, and concluded a favorable peace with Prussia (Peace of Basel, 1795), whereby France expected to gain permanent possession of the left bank of the Rhine. This was followed by peace with Spain. But it was not easy to find a middle-of-the-road settlement for French political problems. Bread riots and revolts from the left alternated with the "White Terror" of royalist reaction. Finally the Convention drew up another constitution and then dissolved itself to give way to the new government, the Directory, in October 1795.

The work of the Convention was not all destructive. Besides successfully organizing resistance to foreign invasion, many hard-working committees labored on internal reforms, some of which were completed under the Napoleonic regime. The Convention initiated the codification of the French law, funded the public debt, and, in cooperation with the Academy of Sciences, established throughout France uniform weights and measures based on the decimal system. It created the National Library and the National Archives, and turned a part of the Louvre into a public museum. Besides founding new schools for higher education, it proclaimed the principle of "free and compulsory primary education," albeit lacking funds and teachers for implementing the systems. For the sake of unifying France, the Convention also attempted to replace local dialects with a single French language.

The Directory

Government under the Directory (1795-1799) consisted of a bicameral legislature, elected by restricted, indirect suffrage, and an executive of five directors with a rotating presidency, designed to make dictatorship by a single director impossible. The new regime faced serious financial problems with the continuing decline of the assignats as well as mounting expenses for the war. Moreover there were determined attempts by neo-royalists on the right and Jacobins and "egalitarians" on the left to draw the regime from its tenuous political equilibrium. Among the latter activists was the colorful Gracchus Babeuf (1760-1797) with his Society of Equals, advocating "an equal share in all property" for all. Although Babeuf's poorly planned conspiracy failed, he became a nostalgic symbol for later socialism.

Despite internal instability, the Directory conducted a successful and highly aggressive foreign policy. In the peace treaty with Austria (1797), France gained the Austrian Netherlands and some territories in Italy, and received confirmation of French rights to most of the left bank of the Rhine, subject to negotiation with the princes of the empire. In the Italian Peninsula France thus expanded even beyond her "natural frontiers." She also acquired influence in the Mediterranean through seizure of Malta and the Ionian Islands, and through Napoleon's campaigns in Egypt and Syria, although the success of the latter was frustrated through the destruction of the French fleet by Horatio Nelson's (1758-1805) ships.

The seemingly insatiable expansive drive of the French provoked a new, second coalition against France, including Russia, England, Austria, Turkey, and many other states. In 1799, France suddenly suffered defeats on most fronts, including several battles with the Russians who were campaigning in Switzerland and northern Italy. One by one, France's client republics fell to allied occupation or were restored to their former rulers.

The unstable financial and political conditions of the Directory, coupled with these foreign defeats in 1799, furnished the background for Napoleon's *coup d'état* and his rise to power. The middle class was longing for economic stability and the nation feared a new threat of foreign invasions. Napoleon had already established his fame as a "savior of the republic" by defending the Convention against an attempted royalist coup (1795), and had gained a brilliant military reputation through his successful campaigns in Italy (1796-1797) and his daring, though unsuccessful, foray into Egypt (1798-1799). Having made himself acceptable to the higher Parisian circles through his marriage to the widowed Josephine de Beauharnais (1763-1814) and through opportune friendships with several of the directors, he found it relatively easy to topple the Directory by a *coup d'état* in November 1799. One might debate whether the ensuing Napoleonic regime was a continuation and fulfillment of the revolutionary promises, or a reaction and an undoing of the revolutionary achievements.

Repercussions from the revolution

News about the happenings in France spread rapidly through newspapers, pamphlets, and verbal reports by émigrés and travelers. After 1792, accounts of revolutionary ideals as well as atrocities were also disseminated by the conquering French armies and by soldiers who had met the new French forces in battle.

Favorable reception of the revolution

William Wordsworth's line, "bliss was it in that dawn to be alive . . . ," echoed the enthusiasm of many people in England, the Continent, and the Americas as they heard about the early accomplishments of the French revolutionaries. Intellectuals, historians, poets, journalists, the middle classes in general, and even some peasants hailed the events as the inauguration of a new era. As a Prussian observer noted later, "revolution is like a deep cultivation of the soil when everything seems buried," and there seemed to be a conviction that the changes in France would bring forth new life and growth. In many countries, particularly in the urban areas of the Rhineland, the Low Countries, and parts of Italy, a strong desire was manifested to imitate the French example.

Schiller in Germany hailed the vision of freedom and brotherhood evoked by the revolution. Tom Paine defended the French experiment in his book *The Rights of Man*—in part against the attacks of the English statesman and brilliant orator, Edmund Burke (1729–1797), who, although no extreme conservative, believed in the guidelines of tradition and deplored the passion-dominated upheaval of the revolution. Paine then went to France, became a French citizen, and even a member of the Convention; but like many revolutionaries, he was imprisoned during the Terror. Charles James Fox (1749–1806), one of the most powerful and eloquent members of Parliament and the foremost antagonist of the younger Pitt, was convinced that the French experiment had much to offer to the progress of liberalism and hence steadfastly opposed British intervention against France.

The degree of desire to imitate the French revolutionary example depended largely on the amount of political power the middle classes had already attained in a given state. In Holland, for instance, friction had erupted in 1785 between the stadholder (William V, 1766–1795) and liberal groups who cherished the ideals of the French *philosophes*. This tension increased during the early years of the revolution, particularly after France declared war on Holland in 1793. After the French armies overran Holland in the spring of 1795, they found it easy to turn Holland's quasi-monarchical regime into the Batavian Republic and place the Dutch liberals in power, backed by French armed and political support.

Pro-French sentiment was particularly strong in the German Rhineland, where the people demanded constitutions and even union with France in order to benefit from the "blessings of liberty, equality, and fraternity." But as in other areas of Europe, feelings were ambivalent when French armies actually approached with the purported aim of liberating the people from tyranny. It was sometimes hard to distinguish whether the revolutionary zealots came as liberators or as conquerors. Similar experiences occurred in the papal states and the Swiss cantons. There was strong republican and pro-French pressure in Rome, which was occupied by French troops in 1796 and then converted into the Roman Republic (1798). Yet with the French as their new masters, many Italian liberals began to wonder about the advantages of liberty imposed from the outside. Within most Swiss cantons, popular unrest spread rapidly after the outbreak of revolution in Paris. But only in Geneva were the people successful in overthrowing the oligarchic administration (1792). Later, as French military power spread, France forced the Swiss to organize the Helvetian Republic, still based on cantonal government but more centralized than Switzerland had been before.

The attitude abroad toward the French Revolution naturally changed in the course of the revolution itself and the subsequent expansion of France. Many who hailed the new era at first recoiled in revulsion because of the Terror. During the nineteenth and twentieth centuries, the French Revolution—with its slogans and Jacobin methods as well as its application of ruthless terror—was to serve as the "classical" pattern for radical revolutions. In the 1790's, however, most observers, lacking perspective on revolutionary techniques, were simply shocked by the violence. They wondered whether to attribute the bloody excesses to the perversity of certain revolutionary leaders like Danton, Marat, and Robespierre, to a peculiarly ferocious characteristic in Frenchmen, or to the unleashed wrath of suppressed peoples, a fury which might well explode in other lands.

After 1795, when the French—under the Directory and later under Napoleon—overran ever larger portions of the Continent, the attitude toward the revolution changed with local circumstances. At first, the French organized most conquered areas into semi-autonomous republics, with constitutions, more centralized governments, and lip service paid to social, political, and legal equality for all citizens—all of it modeled on France. Soon, however, the French began their frequent redrawing of the political map of Europe, casting peoples into new republican units—such as Italy's Cisalpine Republic—assuming more and more direct control, and ultimately resorting to outright annexation of conquered lands (particularly after 1806). Moreover, parallel to Napoleon's transformation of France, the French changed the republics they had just created back into kingdoms, most of them ruled by Napoleon's relatives. Consequently, most liberals had second thoughts about French intentions.

Distrust and fear of the revolution

Initially, some rulers, such as the stargazing king of Prussia (Frederick William III, 1786-1797), surmised that the revolution would disorganize and weaken France and topple her from among the first rank powers. Soon, however, most rulers and the privileged classes recognized that this "strange, nameless, wild, enthusiastic thing," as Edmund Burke called the revolution, represented a dangerous threat to feudal and princely privileges. This fear increased when the middle classes began to demand constitutional limitations on the monarchs, and when liberal groups seemed eager to accept the French offer to help them overthrow tyranny. The landed bishops of the empire and most high ecclesiastics throughout Europe were naturally alarmed by the nationalization of the French church and by the growing anti-Christian trend.

After the execution of Louis XVI, most European governments assumed a determined antirevolutionary stand and joined the growing allied coalitions that were to fight revolutionary and Napoleonic France for over two decades. Since these wars against France were in part ideological, they required a new type of surveillance at home. Under the younger Pitt, who guided England's government from 1783 to 1801, Britain reacted sharply against suspected revolutionary sympathizers at home. Similar repercussions were felt in the newly created United States. The French envoy (Edmund Genêt) tried to take advantage of American liberal feeling to persuade the United States to join France against the anti-French coalition. His failure perhaps illustrates how conservative the American Revolution had been in contrast to the revolution in France. The conservative federalists who controlled the United States government from 1789 to 1801 were profoundly suspicious of all Jacobinism emanating from France. Hamilton, Jay, and other federalists favored the English cause, although many Jeffersonians contemplated intervention on the French side. President Washington, for his part, insisted on neutrality and non-involvement in the Anglo-French struggle. By 1797, hostilities occurred on the high seas between France and the United States, and the administration of John Adams passed various acts similar to those in England to counteract possible subversion by revolutionaries contaminated by the French example.

When France rose to unprecedented power under Napoleon, even normally conservative politicians in some countries became convinced that French strength was based on a release of popular energy, and that to become strong, nations would have to unleash this latent vitality. To avoid the excesses experienced in France, however, they hoped popular enthusiasm could be roused by limited governmental steps rather than by popular action as in France.

Thus the French Revolution came to symbolize different concepts even during its own time: the dawning of a fraternal heaven on earth, the monstrous specter of popular passion run amuck, or the sad lesson from which others could learn to institute timely, measured reforms.

SUGGESTED READINGS

General Treatment of the Revolutionary Period

Hobsbawn, Eric J., *The Age of Revolution; 1789-1848* (New American Library).
*Palmer, R. R., *The Age of the Democratic Revolution: A Political History of Europe and America, 1760-1800* (Princeton, 1964).
Postgate, Raymond W., ed., *Revolution from 1789-1906* (Harper, 1961). A collection of documents.

Background of the French Revolution

Church, William F., *The Influence of the Enlightenment on the French Revolution— Creative, Disastrous, or Non-Existent?* (Heath, 1964).
Greenlaw, Ralph W., *The Economic Origins of the French Revolution—Poverty or Prosperity?* (Heath, 1958).
Lefebvre, Georges, *The Coming of the French Revolution* (Knopf, 1957).
Tocqueville, Alexis de, *Old Regime and the French Revolution* (Doubleday, 1955).

The Course of the French Revolution

Bienvenu, Richard T., ed., *The Ninth of Thermidor: The Fall of Robespierre* (Oxford, U.P., 1968). Source readings.
Brinton, Crane, *A Decade of Revolution: 1789-1799* (Harper, 1964).
——, *The Lives of Talleyrand* (Norton, 1963).
Dawson, Philip, *The French Revolution* (Prentice-Hall, 1967). Source readings.
Hampson, Norman, *A Social History of the French Revolution* (U. of Toronto, 1963).
Palmer, Robert, *Twelve Who Ruled, The Year of the Terror in the French Revolution* (Atheneum, 1965).
Rudé, George, *The Crowd in the French Revolution* (Oxford U.P., 1967).
——, *Robespierre* (Prentice-Hall, 1967). Source readings.
Salvemini, Gaetano, *The French Revolution: 1788-1792* (Norton, 1962).
Thompson, J. M., *Robespierre and the French Revolution* (Macmillan, 1962).

Interpretations of the French Revolution

Amann, Peter, *The Eighteenth-Century Revolution—French or Western?* (Heath, 1963).
Cobban, Alfred, *The Social Interpretation of the French Revolution* (Gordian, 1968).
Kafker, Frank A., and Laux, James, M., eds., *The French Revolution: Conflicting Interpretations* (Random, 1968). Readings.
Gershoy, Leo, *The Era of the French Revolution, 1789-1799: Ten Years That Shook the World* (Van Nostrand, 1957). Impact of the revolution on other nations.

CHAPTER XX

⚘ *Napoleon and the Western Hemisphere* (1799-1815)

Napoleon's ascendancy in France started with his spectacular victories in Italy. After his *coup d'état* of 1799, he rapidly consolidated his control over France; and through foreign conquests and ruthless use of military, diplomatic, and economic pressure, he soon dominated almost two thirds of the European Continent. The Napoleonic era as such lasted from 1799 to 1815, but the Napoleonic legend cast its shadow over many later decades of French and European history. In Latin America, the revolutionary and Napoleonic periods enabled the colonists, by inspiration and opportunity, to initiate their independence movements. At the same time, a revolution of sorts occurred in the United States when the conservatives were defeated by Thomas Jefferson in the election of 1800.

The Napoleonic era

After the overthrow of the Directory, Napoleon established the consulate and became the new executive of France as the first among three consuls. In 1802, he assumed life tenure, with the right to appoint his successor, and two years later he changed France from a republic to an empire. In their search for socio-economic solutions and political stability, the French thus passed within a decade and a half from absolute to constitutional monarchy. to republic, and then to absolute empire.

Napoleonic rule of France

Born in Corsica and hence an outsider to France, Napoleon Bonaparte (1769–1821) attended French military schools, quickly proved his mettle as a daring military tactician, became a brigadier general at age twenty-four, and three years later was given command of the armies for the conquest of Italy. Exotic looking with his long hair and penetrating eyes, he was soon lionized by Parisian society. Endowed with sharp political acumen, he knew how to win useful friends and how to gain political support by making promises to divergent groups. Adept at uttering striking phrases at opportune moments and vastly self-assured—except in his romantic attachments to women—Napoleon was immensely successful in imposing his will and image on the French nation at a time when there existed few of the media of mass communication available to today's dictators.

In 1799, Napoleon promulgated a new constitution, instituting powers, as he proclaimed, that were "strong and stable, as they must be in order to guarantee the rights of citizens and the interests of the state." In 1802 and again in 1804, he modified his own constitution, just as he constantly reorganized the French political and economic structure and adapted the revolutionary changes to his own needs. Many of his administrative, judicial, and financial reforms, most of which were undertaken during the four years of his consulship, remained permanent in France. Besides serving to consolidate his own power, his reforms were motivated by a desire for "order and stability," catchwords that were replacing the revolutionary "liberty, equality, fraternity." In essence, popular sovereignty gave way to control by the state and to almost unlimited power of the first consul and later emperor. Occasional plebiscites, a device imitated by later dictators, were used to pacify public opinion. The plebiscites consisted of a question to which eligible voters could reply with a "yes" or "no." In 1802, for example, the voters were asked: "Should the first consul be nominated for life?" Over three and a half million people replied in the affirmative and fewer than nine thousand voted "nay."

Order and stability, in Napoleon's view, depended on absolute centralization of power—even more than had existed under the *ancien régime*. Local self-government, an ideal of non-Jacobin revolutionaries, was again abolished. Instead, prefects (similar to the former intendants) and other magistrates, chosen by Napoleon, acted as agents of the central government in the departments. Judicial institutions and the tax collection system were equally centralized. Legal changes, most of them initiated during the revolutionary period—such as equality before the law, secularization of marriage and divorce, greater distinction among types of crimes, and extended guarantees of property rights—were coordinated and included in the French Civil Code. Begun in 1790 and completed in 1804, this compilation became known as the Napoleonic Code, which was later imitated in many parts of Europe, Asia, and the Americas.

Napoleon also tried to heal relations with the Roman Catholic Church, not because of strong religious feelings on his part, but because, as he said, "religion gives the state firm and lasting support." He insisted on freedom of worship, but in his Concordat (1801) with the papacy, which remained in effect until 1905, he agreed to recognize Catholicism as "the religion of the great majority of Frenchmen." By the Concordat, the pope accepted the loss of the church property sequestered during the revolution. The state continued to pay the salaries of the clergy. But instead of being elected by the people, bishops were to be appointed by the government, confirmed by the pope, and were required to tender an oath of allegiance to the head of the French state. Although there were to be sharp disagreements between Napoleon and the papacy over political and economic matters, the Concordat proved relatively effective in soothing ruffled religious feelings in France.

In addition to his mercantilistic preoccupation with industry, commerce, and public works, Napoleon also revised the educational system. Primary, secondary, and higher education were all placed under the supervision of the so-called imperial university (1808), a state controlled system of education aimed at indoctrination as much as pragmatic instruction. The schools were to teach "loyalty to the emperor," and their purpose was "to create citizens devoted to their religion, their prince, their fatherland, and their family." In order to permit poor youngsters to get advanced training and thus fill Napoleon's needs for competent military and civilian personnel, the emperor also set up a system of scholarships.

The switch from consulate to empire in 1804 entailed many changes that further removed France from the republican dream of the revolutionaries. Although Napoleon tried to assuage republican opinion by calling himself "Emperor of the French" rather than Emperor of France, the imperial regime soon became ever more arbitrary and despotic. Strict censorship was enforced on all publications, an efficient police and spy system was developed to ferret out opposition, and like the kings of the *ancien régime,* the emperor freely resorted to using political imprisonment without due process.

Like the revolutionists, Napoleon was fond of ancient Rome. The revolutionary credos had been laced with Roman political ideas and Latin names. The very notion of "citizen" instead of "subject," for example, was derived from the Roman ideal of *civis romanus,* and their revolutionary calendar used Latin designations such as *Fructidor,* the fruit-bringing month (August–September). With Napoleon, this imitation of Rome became almost an obsession. Roman titles and symbols—among them "consuls," "tribunes," and "Senate"—neoclassical art with its Roman arches of triumph, its temple-like Church of the Madeleine in Paris, its idealized sculpture (Canova), and form-conscious painting (David), all fitted the Napoleonic design for an orderly state. The similarity between Napoleon and Augustus is remarkable. Like the thirty-two-year-old Octavius, the thirty-year-old Napoleon transformed a republic into an empire within the span of four years, while retaining certain republican trimmings. Both acted ostensibly in the name of order and stability.

In their quest for equality, the revolutionists had abolished all titles, ranks, and privileges, had forbidden the sale of offices, and launched a system of advance by merit. Napoleon continued to promote those in the army and in public employment on the basis of proved ability, but his custom of rewarding service with financial grants and new dignities led to the formation of a new élite. In 1802, he founded the Legion of Honor, in which membership was bestowed in recompense for service to the state. After his own imperial coronation, he proceeded to create an entire "imperial nobility." Generals, ministers, and civil functionaries were given the titles of princes, dukes, and barons, and the imperial court became enveloped in pomp and ceremonies reminiscent of the age of Louis XIV. Gone were the days of republican frugality and austerity.

Napoleon and war

The history of Napoleonic France is essentially one of a nation at war. Many explanations have been advanced for this prolonged state of war. From the revolutionary wars, Napoleon inherited a France enlarged to her "natural frontiers." Since the European powers would not accept such French aggrandizement, the Napoleonic wars have been interpreted as attempts to defend these revolutionary gains. Napoleon's offensives, it is said, were defensive in purpose, designed to force England and Russia into accepting French absorption of Belgium, the Rhineland, and parts of Savoy. Some nineteenth-century historians saw in the wars Napoleon's genuine desire to export the ideals of the French Revolution and the benefits of his rule. Finally there are those who insist that the war continued for decades because, on the one hand, Great Britain refused to give up the struggle, and because on the other, Napoleon's overbearance and seemingly unquenchable thirst for glory and conquests constantly roused those whom he came to "liberate" to new pitches of resistance.

Perhaps the simplest explanation for the long duration of the wars was that Napoleon was going against the stream of his time. In an age of rising nationalism, inflamed in part by the French themselves, he sought to create a new European empire under French hegemony. Such a notion had died with the waning Middle Ages and hardly fitted the temper of Napoleon's age.

There is no need to give details of the many spectacular campaigns of these wars, which in the eyes of most Frenchmen and military enthusiasts everywhere brought so much glory to the emperor. The wars required vast contributions in manpower and material resources, sacrifices which Napoleon imposed on the French peasantry, while inspiring them with patriotic enthusiasm. Moreover, Napoleon's own military genius was powerfully supplemented by the devoted service of a great number of superbly qualified young generals.

In the fall of 1799, the war of the second coalition turned in favor of

France. Russia withdrew from the fighting, England abandoned her attempt to wrest Holland from the French, and, after inflicting several defeats on Austria in 1800, Napoleon made peace with all belligerents except Britain. The Italian states were again reorganized to suit Napoleon's designs, Louisiana was taken from Spain and two years later sold to the United States, and a major territorial reorganization of the Holy Roman Empire was initiated under French auspices. The number of states within the empire was reduced by more than two thirds, ecclesiastical lands were decreased in number and size, and territories were reassigned and bartered between princes, subject to Napoleon's approval. As a result of this transformation of the empire, completed in 1803, Napoleon gained considerable influence over the German states. Those, like Bavaria and Württemberg, which increased in size, thanks to French intervention, tended to become client states of France.

In 1802, Britain and France concluded a peace treaty (Amiens), after the resignation of the stanchly anti-French prime minister of England, Pitt the Younger. England agreed to restore to France all colonial conquests. Thus, for the first time since 1792, Europe was at peace; but it proved to be no more than a short truce. War with England resumed in 1803, and thereafter Great Britain remained France's constant and most determined foe until the overthrow of the Napoleonic regime. England organized one anti-French coalition after another and used her fleet for an economic blockade of France and for ferrying troops to Portugal and Spain. The only concerted challenge by France to British naval supremacy ended with Admiral Nelson's destruction of the French and Spanish fleets at Trafalgar (1805).

On the Continent, however, French military might reigned supreme. In 1805, Napoleon crushed the anti-French third coalition by defeating the combined Russo-Austrian forces at Austerlitz on the first anniversary of his imperial coronation. The tactics used in this battle of the three emperors have been widely acclaimed by military historians. Austria once again sued for peace and was further crippled through territorial losses. After Austerlitz, Napoleon accelerated his revamping of the map of Europe and annexed more and more lands to France, extending the French boundaries far beyond her natural frontiers. He freely dispensed lands and crowns, turning the recently created republics into kingdoms, placing his brothers on the thrones of Naples, Spain, Holland, and the newly formed Kingdom of Westphalia in northwestern Germany. He also awarded royal titles to the dukes of Bavaria, Württemberg, and Saxony, in order to make them more loyal to France.

In 1806, he combined most of the German states, except Prussia and Austria, into the Confederation of the Rhine under his personal protection. He then convinced the Hapsburg Emperor, Francis (1792–1835), to dissolve the fiction of the Holy Roman Empire. Francis retained the title of emperor, but his imperial rule was to be limited to the Hapsburg hereditary possessions. The dissolution of the Holy Roman Empire after its thousand-year existence spurred Napoleon's ambition to resurrect the empire of Charlemagne under French auspices. Control over Germany, Italy, and Spain also terminated French isolation, since in his further wars, Napoleon could usually count on support from the growing number of French client states.

Late in 1806, the French emperor decided to push his domination further east and to attempt to bring England to her knees through economic pressure. In a lightning campaign he completely crushed Prussia, which had maintained an equivocal neutrality since 1795. Prussia was shorn of all her lands west of the Elbe and put under French military occupation. Napoleon then defeated the Russians, who had aided Prussia, and concluded with Tsar Alexander I (1801–1825) the Treaty of Tilsit (1807), which permitted the extension of French hegemony as far east as the newly constituted Duchy of Warsaw. The treaty also included a tentative Russian offer of aid against England, if the latter refused to make peace. As a result of these arrangements, domination of the European continent was divided between the French emperor and the Russian tsar. (See Map 16.)

Meanwhile, Napoleon had proclaimed the so-called Continental System, an injunction which prohibited all European states from trading with England. Such an economic blockade of the British Isles could be effective only if France could control and police the entire shoreline of the European continent. The attempt to implement this ambitious design forced the French to overextend their diminishing forces, even though Napoleon induced a number of states voluntarily to close their ports to British goods. To tighten the Continental System, Napoleon annexed Holland, the German coast as far north as Hamburg, and western Italy to south of Rome. French troops were sent to guard the coasts of Spain and to occupy Portugal, which initially refused to stop trading with its traditional British ally. Napoleon even annexed Rome and the papal states. Like Hitler a century and a half later, Napoleon averred that he hoped to "conquer the oceans with land forces."

By 1808, Napoleon had reached the pinnacle of his power over Europe. Yet, British resistance had not been broken, and there was increasing evidence that many Europeans resented French hegemony. During the early years of the wars, resistance to France had been inspired largely by the princes who were afraid of losing their power and prerogatives to the Jacobin cause. The mass of the people, on the other hand, had at first rather welcomed the constitutional guarantees, the benefits of the Napoleonic Code, and the feeling of self-importance brought by the French invaders. In the long run, however, the French invasions aroused nationalistic passions. Nineteenth-century European nationalism was thus inaugurated by a series of popular uprisings against the French. In Spain, local patriots organized anti-French guerrilla warfare, which lasted until the downfall of Napoleon. Prussia launched a reform of its military and social structure which, although directed by the government, appealed to popular emotions for its success. Anti-French outbreaks erupted in various regions of occupied Europe. In 1809, Archduke Charles of Austria, the brother of the emperor, appealed to the Germans for a war of liberation against the French and reopened hostilities against Napoleon. Although Austria was once again defeated and forced to relinquish more territory (Treaty of Schönbrunn, 1809), the spark of the liberation movement was to remain alive in much of Europe until the final downfall of the French emperor.

After this fourth war against Austria, Napoleon decided on a more conciliatory attitude toward his Hapsburg foes. In 1810, he surprised the courts of Europe by marrying Marie Louise of Austria (1791–1847), the daughter of Emperor Francis. His marriage to Josephine, contracted in 1796 for love as well as for her political connections, had on the whole been a happy one, but it had produced no heir to perpetuate the Napoleonic dynasty. Moreover, the ambitious Napoleon must have considered it a crowning achievement to marry into the house of Hapsburg, one of Europe's oldest reigning families. The Austrians, for their part, hoped that the marriage might ensure their survival. Since Austrian armies seemed unable to defeat the French, Prince Metternich (1773-1859), Austrian ambassador to Paris and after 1809 in charge of foreign affairs, resorted to the old Hapsburg device of a diplomatic marriage—notwithstanding Emperor Francis' dislike for the Corsican upstart. In 1811, Marie Louise gave birth to a boy whom Napoleon promptly made "King of Rome." The continuation of the Napoleonic dynasty seemed ensured.

Despite this success, signs of trouble were multiplying. Most Europeans were becoming increasingly restive under French domination and under the economic restrictions of the Continental System. Many Catholics were shocked by the imprisonment of the pope—an action taken by Napoleon in 1809 in answer to papal excommunication after he had annexed the papal states. The rebellion in Spain, supported by British troops under the Duke of Wellington (1769-1852), had turned into outright war in which the French suffered many defeats and severe losses. Finally, there was increasing friction with Russia.

Alexander I had reopened Russia to British imports and had become aroused by Napoleon's marriage and his alliance with Austria. He was also alarmed by French interference in areas that Russia considered to be within her own sphere of influence. The French had encouraged Turkey to make war on Russia and England, had annexed Illyria (northern Yugoslavia), expanded the French-dominated Duchy of Warsaw, and installed a French marshal (Bernadotte) as crown prince of Sweden. Alexander keenly resented this French "encirclement" of Russia. The French emperor, for his part, had lost confidence in his erstwhile ally Alexander; moreover he was at heart loath to share power over Europe with the tsar, or, for that matter, with anyone else.

In June of 1812, the emperor launched his invasion of Russia. The composition of the Napoleonic forces made the campaign resemble a united European war effort. Accompanied by contingents of his Austrian and Prussian allies, the French "Grand Army" itself included recruits from most European countries—Italians, Swiss, Poles, Danes, Croats, Dutch, Germans, and others. Napoleon's initial success was as spectacular as the subsequent debacle. In less than three months, the Grand Army covered six hundred miles and captured Moscow, but failed to destroy Alexander's armies. To deprive the invaders of supplies and shelter, the Russians burned their crops and fired their villages and cities, including Smolensk and Moscow. Lack of logistical support and the approach of an early, severe winter determined Napoleon to order a westward retreat after four weeks in Moscow. The withdrawal from Russia turned into a disaster, with five-sixths of the French forces either killed by frost or famine, or captured by pursuing Russian units.

News of the débacle in Russia provoked an attempted coup d'état in Paris against the absent emperor and ultimately served as signal for the Wars of Liberation (1813–1814). An enthusiastic popular uprising in Prussia forced the hesitant Prussian king to abandon the French cause and conclude an anti-French alliance with Russia. During the next half year, a gigantic new anti-Napoleonic coalition took shape, financed largely by English subsidies. To entice Napoleon's allies into deserting him and joining the coalition, diplomats offered lavish territorial promises—a fact which greatly complicated the task of reshaping the map of Europe after termination of the war. Russia, for instance, promised British Hanover to Prussia, and England offered Norway to Sweden. Unwilling at first to fight against his son-in-law, Emperor Francis hoped Austria could serve as mediator between Napoleon and the coalition. But the French emperor, winning one minor engagement after another against the poorly coordinated coalition forces, was in no mood for a compromise peace, even if France were allowed to retain her natural frontiers. After Austria finally joined England, Russia, Prussia, and Sweden, Napoleon's German client states gradually abandoned the French cause and switched to the side of the coalition.

In October 1813, Austrian, Prussian, and Russian forces at last coordinated their movements and defeated Napoleon in the so-called Battle of the Nations near Leipzig. Thereupon Napoleon withdrew his armies across the Rhine. Having cleared Spain, English forces meanwhile invaded France across the Pyrenees. During the winter and spring, Austrian, Russian, and Prussian armies invaded France from the East, while Napoleon's dwindling forces raced from one field of battle to the next in a prodigious effort to save France from foreign occupation.

After the allies had captured Paris at the end of March, the French Senate, led by the opportunistic Talleyrand (1754–1838), proclaimed the deposition of the Napoleonic dynasty. When Napoleon abdicated a week later in favor of his three-year-old son, the allies rejected this proposed continuation of a Bonaparte dynasty since they had decided on a Bourbon restoration. Hence the emperor was forced to abdicate unconditionally and to accept the allies' offer of sovereignty over the tiny island of Elba, situated between Italy and Corsica. His wife was allotted three Italian duchies. While the allies installed Louis XVI's brother, Louis XVIII (1814-1824), on the French throne and prepared to write a peace treaty for France, Napoleon departed for his first exile on Elba.

The first Treaty of Paris (1814) was a lenient peace, designed not to antagonize the French against their restored Bourbon ruler. It left France with some minor territorial gains and called for no indemnity payments. The powers then gathered at Vienna (September 1814 to June 1815) for a conference to determine the geographic and political recasting of Europe. While the brilliant Congress of Vienna was dancing and debating, Napoleon suddenly returned to power. After landing in southern France with a small force, he marched triumphantly toward Paris. Most Frenchmen promptly abandoned Louis XVIII and again rallied behind their emperor. This return from exile in the face of the combined opposition of all of Europe greatly enhanced the glory and legend of the Corsican. Within three weeks, he had re-entered Paris which Louis XVIII had abandoned. For a hundred days he once again ruled France and faced the re-established coalition of European powers, until his armies were routed by Anglo-Prussian forces at Waterloo. For a second time, Napoleon then abdicated and the allies reoccupied Paris to restore Louis XVIII. This time the French emperor was treated more like a prisoner and sent to permanent exile on the island of St. Helena in the South Atlantic. Moreover the allies imposed a more severe second Treaty of Paris (1815), by which France lost almost all revolutionary gains and was obliged to pay a war indemnity. (See Map 17.)

The Napoleonic legacy

The legacy of the Napoleonic era is almost incalculable in its extent. In the regions occupied by the Napoleonic armies, particularly Germany, Italy, Spain, and Poland, French constitutionalism, egalitarianism, and nationalism left a profound impression. Military occupation by France evoked a long-standing fear of French aggressiveness. It also convinced people that nationalism on their own part would strengthen their states and enable them to resist future foreign encroachment. Moreover, as a result of the Napoleonic wars, the concept of "empire" came to signify expansionism. This apprehension was seen later in the century when the French (1852) and then the German (1871) rulers revived the titles of emperor—much to the alarm of many Europeans.

Within France, the Napoleonic legend, carefully nursed by the emperor's memoirs dictated during his exile on St. Helena, left a lasting impression. On the one hand, there was the devoted hero worship of his veterans which furnished romantic inspiration to generations of French adolescents. During the more prosaic days of the nineteenth century, the French looked with nostalgia on the days of glory under their emperor, when despite wars, high taxes, and sacrifices, France had been blessed with political stability. The feeling that a strong leader, a "man on horseback," could save the nation from chaos remained a permanent feature of French political life, down to the acclamation of Charles de Gaulle in 1958.

On the other hand, French liberals developed a permanent fear of Bonapartism. They associated Napoleon with war and dictatorship and remained reluctant to entrust strong powers to any single executive.

Thus Bonapartism bequeathed a serious dilemma to France. Moreover, the long period of wars had thoroughly exhausted the French nation. French political, intellectual, and artistic influence continued undiminished during the nineteenth century; French power, however, began to decline after 1815.

The Western Hemisphere

During and soon after the Napoleonic era, the Western Hemisphere underwent profound changes with the creation of the Latin-American republics and the consolidation of democratic institutions in the new United States. The changed climate in the Americas in turn altered the relationship between Europe and the transatlantic states.

Beginning of a transatlantic dialogue

Before this period, especially before 1783, Europeans had not looked upon the Americas as "entities" in themselves. Two views had prevailed. Politicians and economists in Europe had tended to regard the Americas as mere European appendices, useful as sources of raw materials and valuable for the expansion of trade and naval power. Colonial wars—not those against local Indian tribes—had been mere extensions of the European power play. One might say that the lands beyond the Atlantic had lacked identity. European intellectuals, on the other hand, had viewed the Americas as the distant abodes of noble savages, as strange to Western eyes as the peoples of Cathay. Those who had moved overseas were considered to be "Europeans" living abroad.

Among the peoples of the Americas, only the settlers in the thirteen colonies of North America had developed a feeling of being distinct from Europeans. Perhaps this attitude derived from the fact that the colonists, being more concentrated in numbers than those in Latin America, could participate in local government and acquire a sense of running their own affairs. In the Spanish and Portuguese colonies, however, the wealthy and politically active people—the government officials and high-born creoles— generally felt like Europeans; whereas the rest of the population, Indians,

Negroes, and mestizos, remaining in political obscurity, were hardly extended the opportunity of developing a particular identity.

New attitudes developed during the revolutionary and Napoleonic periods. With the acquisition of independence and the creation of separate political units, the former colonial peoples developed their own individuality and assumed a voice of their own within Western society. As a result, a transatlantic dialogue began, despite political and other differences. To grasp the full import of this development, one might contrast the self-assurance of the American states with the subordinate status that marked most European colonies in Asia and Africa until the mid-twentieth century.

To many Europeans, America, especially the United States, suddenly became an inspiration, the proverbial land of freedom, opportunity, and equality. Romantic poets like René de Chateaubriand (1768–1848) extolled the charms of the American wilderness; political observers, among them Alexis de Tocqueville (1805–1859), admired its model political structure. Tired of Europe, some saw the future of Western civilization in America. Others, like the conservative French writer Joseph de Maistre (1753–1821), deemed it too early to judge "this child in arms," the United States, and remarked: "Let it first grow up."

Since Europe was growing more conservative at a time when the United States was becoming more liberal under the Jeffersonian Democratic-Republicans, political views on America differed. European liberals were enchanted by Jeffersonian and later Jacksonian policies. Harassed by strict censorship, police surveillance, and political oppression during the Metternich era, they marveled at Jefferson's proclamation in his First Inaugural Address, "that the minority possess their equal rights, which equal law must protect." Moreover, they cheered when during the 1820s the Americans generally discarded wigs from official American functions, the wig being considered symbolic of the *ancien régime*. European conservatives, on the other hand, were alarmed at the progress of American democratization and looked with apprehension upon America's industrial and territorial growth.

The inhabitants of the Americas, for their part, began to develop a sense of political separateness from Europe. In Latin America, this national awakening was not quickly accomplished. Simon Bolívar (1783–1830), the famous liberator of South America, was hard pressed to persuade some of the colonists to consider themselves Latin Americans rather than Spaniards. Similarly, some Tories in the United States retained for a long time a strong affinity for Great Britain. Soon, however, Americans north and south asserted themselves as equal and separate in relation to Europeans. This feeling was reflected in President Monroe's declaration of 1823: "The political system of all the allied [European] powers is essentially different . . . from that of America." Monroe moreover dissociated the United States from "the wars of the European powers," and, in reference to the new Latin-American republics, asserted that no one could "believe that our southern brethren, if left to themselves, would adopt it [the political system of conservative Europe] of their own accord."

America's withdrawal from Europe was only political. In most other aspects, such as education, inventions, the arts, letters, law, as well as industrial and economic development, the Americas worked with Europe. Constant interaction between the two continents permitted each to learn from the other. The transatlantic dialogue had started.

The United States

Events in Europe, such as the French revolutionary upheaval and the Napoleonic campaigns, were spectacular, but in the long run the gradual legal, constitutional, socio-political, and economic changes in the United States were to be of greater importance for Western civilization. The Europeans, one might say, were debating ideas, while the more pragmatic Americans were implementing them. The inspiring French Declaration of the Rights of Man, for instance, remained a paper creed, violated by the revolutionists themselves and trampled upon by Napoleon and the restored Bourbon rulers. In America, on the other hand, the Bill of Rights, adopted in the same year, became the backbone for the legal rights of individual citizens. Or again, the French, whose *philosophes* had clamored so loudly for constitutional limitations on arbitrary government, produced five different constitutions between 1791 and 1815, none of which ended arbitrary rule or ensured stability. In the United States, however, constitutional amendments and reinterpretations, based on Justice Marshall's enunciated principle of judicial review, gradually turned the constitution into a workable instrument for imposing checks on federal and state governments.

While Europe floundered in war and in the painful post-revolutionary and post-Napoleonic readjustments, the young United States underwent profound changes. Its territorial growth was phenomenal. The purchase of the Louisiana Territory and acquisition of Florida almost doubled the size of the Union. Europeans fought costly wars over a few square miles, whereas the Americans were able to purchase vast areas with seemingly infinite possibilities for economic and demographic expansion. Moreover, they quickly developed a method for admitting into the Union new states on a basis which generally safeguarded local rights. The new states, in fact, tended to be more democratic, granting more suffrage to their citizens, a trend which in turn influenced the more conservative original thirteen states.

Equally rapid was America's economic growth. Cut off from European manufactured products because of the turmoil of the wars and the economic blockade of Europe, America had to industrialize quickly in order to produce the goods formerly imported. American technological inventiveness helped industry, and industrial concentration in turn brought forth a city proletariat with concomitant political pressure for increased democratization.

The defeat of the Federalists in the election of 1800 perhaps removed the young nation further from the mainstream of English conservative political traditions than had the secession from Great Britain in 1776. Jefferson and his Democratic-Republicans tried to advance the interests of the agricultural classes and the western frontiersmen in opposition to the financial and commercial groups that had dominated political life in the early years after independence. He encouraged the sale of public land in the West to less affluent farmers and tried to expand public education. Where possible he sought to democratize institutions, while reducing the expenditures of the federal government. Like the French *philosophes,* of whom he was an ardent admirer, Jefferson believed that a nation should be governed by an aristocracy of intellect rather than one of birth and wealth. Although no egalitarian in the sense of Rousseau, he favored advancement by merit and had considerable faith in the common sense of the people.

Finally, during this period most Americans developed antiforeign feelings as well as a greater sense of national cohesion. Nationalism was sharply roused by the British invasion of the United States in 1812 and the burning of the new capital of Washington—the first and last time that the United States experienced a foreign invasion. National feelings were also nurtured by pride in American growth and accomplishments. Nationalism in turn advanced the gradual conviction that the federal government had to be strengthened, if the new state were to function effectively. Despite strong sectionalism and insistence on states rights among the commercial interests of New England, the power of the federal government grew. The Second Bank of the United States, chartered in 1816, was empowered to issue a national currency, Congress made provision for federal roads and canals, and the national military and naval forces were considerably increased. Most telling was the acceptance of Justice Marshall's insistence on the supremacy of the Supreme Court over state courts and his conviction "that the government of the Union, though limited in its powers, is supreme within its sphere of action."

The Latin-American revolutions

The revolutionary spirit in Latin America was nurtured by the writings of the eighteenth century *philosophes* and by the example set by the United States. Economic discontent with continued Spanish trade restrictions added a measure of rebelliousness. Furthermore, the creoles and mestizos resented the dominating class representing wealth, Spain, and the Church. The impetus for action stemmed from the turmoil and confusion accompanying Napoleon's seizure of Spain. In 1808, French troops ousted the new Bourbon King Ferdinand VII (1808–1833) from Madrid and installed Napoleon's brother Joseph as king of Spain. This action resulted in prolonged Anglo-French fighting over the Iberian peninsula.

With Spain a French satellite, the colonists were left largely to themselves. When patriots in Spain formed anti-French juntas, the Latin Americans promptly imitated their action with encouragement by the British, who did not wish South America to fall under French control and who were keen on gaining for themselves economic privileges in the colonies. The patriotic rebels in Spain, fighting against the French-imposed Joseph Bonaparte, in fact urged the colonists to consider themselves equal to Spaniards and to resist any attempts at French encroachment in the colonies. Thus, the initial uprisings in Latin America—in some cases supported by British military assistance—were in favor of the legitimate ruler, Ferdinand VII, with the colonists undertaking special celebrations to proclaim Ferdinand king in Mexico, Bogotá, Buenos Aires, and other American centers.

Latin-American solidarity with Ferdinand VII and with the Spanish anti-French patriots soon disappeared. Starting in 1810, the Latins one by one proclaimed their independence from Spain and accepted volunteers from England, Ireland, the United States, and even France to help them fight the Spanish royalist armies dispatched to suppress the secession movements. The colonists' anti-Spanish stance became even more confirmed after Ferdinand VII was restored to the Spanish throne in 1814 and attempted to eradicate all liberalism in Spain.

In the South of Latin America, the liberation movement was guided by the idealistic General José de San Martín (1778–1850), aided by the Irish-Chilean Bernardo O'Higgins (1778–1842). After defeating the Spaniards in Argentina (1813), San Martín crossed the Andes to help liberate Chile and then sailed up the coast to expel the Spanish royalists from Peru (1821). In Lima, he was soon supplanted by the more ambitious Simon Bolívar, the *libertador* of the North. With the aid of British sailors and native troops, Bolívar had freed Greater Colombia (the future Venezuela, Colombia, and Ecuador) and had then marched south to liberate Bolivia and Peru. Somewhat later, Mexico and Central America also achieved independence from Spain.

Events in the more populous area of Brazil took a different course. Prince John of Portugal (1769–1826), who acted as regent for his insane mother, fled to Brazil in 1807 to gain safety from the approaching French armies. In Brazil, Prince John instituted various liberal reforms and cooperated with his British allies. Hence, England did not attempt to stir up a Brazilian independence movement, and Brazil remained attached to Portugal. John remained in Brazil even after he became king of Portugal (1816), and returned to Lisbon only in 1821, leaving his son Dom Pedro as viceroy in charge of Brazil. When the Portuguese attempted to subordinate Brazil once again to dictates from Lisbon, Dom Pedro was pressured into rebelling against his father and declared Brazil's independence (1822). Brazil thus became a separate state, with Dom Pedro as emperor. The monarchical structure in Brazil was to last until 1889. Meanwhile the new Brazilian state constantly grew by seizing and annexing lands from its neighbors, Venezuela, Colombia, Ecuador, Bolivia, Paraguay, Argentina, and Uruguay.

The independence movement as a whole faced certain fundamental problems. The former colonists had to decide whether to follow the example of Europe, where princes were being restored everywhere after 1815, and adopt monarchical forms of government, or whether to imitate the United States and establish republics. San Martín hesitatingly advocated a monarchy as best suited for political stability, whereas Bolívar remained a convinced republican. The lower classes generally expected to gain more rights under a republic. In the end, all but Brazil adopted republican regimes.

A second question concerned the size of the state to establish: one gigantic nation, a federation of semiautonomous entities, or numerous smaller divisions. Almost until his death, Simon Bolívar hoped for a union, if not of all Latin America, then at least of the northern part of South America. Yet in the end, twenty separate states arose with Cuba added as a twenty-first in 1898. This splintering of Spain's and Portugal's former colonial empire resulted from numerous causes: poor communications, disagreement among its revolutionary leaders, and geographic barriers, such as the high Andes separating Chile and Argentina. Moreover, there were ethnic differences between various regions, the South being heavily Spanish in population, Peru largely Indian, and Central America largely Negro. Finally, Great Britain used her influence in favor of political splintering, since she did not care to see the creation of a new giant power in Latin America. (See Map 19.)

After the post-Napoleonic settlements had been completed in Europe and the princes had been restored to their thrones, some Europeans were tempted to aid Spain in reconquering her rebellious colonies. Great Britain thereupon made it clear that she would not tolerate such intervention and was prepared to use her fleet to enforce her determination. President Monroe's doctrine concerning non-intervention was an affirmation of this British decision. Hence, the former colonies were allowed to take their separate course.

Unlike the United States, whose people had previous experience in self-government, the Latin-American republics found it difficult to make their republican regimes function smoothly. Besides frequent wars with neighbors over territorial adjudications, civil strife interspersed with military coups and periods of despotic government characterized their histories from the beginning. With high illiteracy and little industrialization, the middle class in the Latin American republics was to remain weak, and social discontent usually ran at a high pitch. The new Latin-American states, therefore, were not able to exert a major role in nineteenth-century world politics.

SUGGESTED READINGS

Napoleon

Bruun, Geoffrey, *Europe and the French Imperium: 1799–1814* (Harper, 1957).

Butterfield, Herbert, *Napoleon* (Macmillan, 1966).

Dowd, David L., *Napoleon: Was He the Heir of the Revolution?* (Holt, 1957).

Ferrero, Guglielmo, *The Gamble* (Walker, 1961). Napoleon's Italian campaign of 1796–97.

Friedlaender, Walter, *David to Delacroix* (Schocken, 1968). On French Neoclassic and Romantic art.

Geyl, Pieter, *Napoleon: For and Against* (Yale, 1963).

Herold, J. Christopher, *The Horizon Book of the Age of Napoleon* (Dell).

———, ed., *The Mind of Napoleon: A Selection of His Written and Spoken Words* (Columbia, 1955).

Kohn, Hans, *Prelude to Nation States: The French and German Experience, 1789–1815* (Van Nostrand, 1967).

Markham, Felix, *Napoleon* (New American Library).

The Americas

Charles, Joseph, *The Origins of the American Party System* (Harper, 1961).

Humphreys, Robert A., and Lynch, John, eds., *The Origins of the Latin American Revolutions, 1808–1826* (Knopf, 1965). Collection of essays.

Johnson, John J., and Ladd, Doris M., *Simon Bolívar and Spanish American Independence, 1783–1830* (Van Nostrand, 1968).

Perkins, Bradford, ed., *The Causes of the War of 1812: National Honor or National Interest?* (Holt, 1962). Collection of essays.

Potter, David M., and Manning, Thomas G., *Nationalism and Sectionalism in America, 1775–1877* (Holt, 1949).

CHAPTER XXI

❧ *The Emergence of the Modern State*
(1815-1848)

Rather than calling the period after 1815 the "age of reaction," as is often done, or a period of conservatism, liberalism, romanticism, and revolt, one should perhaps stress the gradual emerging of the modern state which occurred after 1815 and which profoundly altered Western civilization and distinguished it even further from non-Western cultures.

The new era after 1815

The years of relative peace in Europe after the fall of Napoleon inaugurated the participation of the masses in the national processes on a scale never before known in history. At the same time, Romanticism was then entering its most pervasive stage. With its antecedents reaching back to the mid-eighteenth century (see pp. 320 and 336), the Romantic movement in literature took root in Germany and England in the late eighteenth century and came to the fore in France after the Napoleonic era. After the turn of the century, the Romantic style also characterized music and painting. Idealistic in philosophy, the Romantics stressed imagination and extolled individualism. To escape the mechanization of urban life, they reveled in the delights of primitive nature, indulged in passion for passion's sake, and longed for the exotic, the mysterious, the distant in time or space, particularly the Middle Ages and the Orient. Historical romances, popular ballads, melancholic poetry, and Gothic novels dealing with the bizarre were among the favorite literary products of the period.

The growing importance of the masses

The modern state was essentially based on the emergence of the masses. The nineteenth century was not, as was to be the twentieth after 1914, the "century of the common men," but it witnessed the participation and finally the domination of the middle classes in most phases of life as well as the awakening of the proletariat and the peasantry. The nation-state ceased to be a dynastic entity and became a state of people. Even in regions where the middle and lower classes did not yet exercise any voice in government, their economic and emotional influence on the state was becoming pronounced.

This transformation had begun with the American and French revolutions. National uprisings during the Wars of Liberation had further awakened enthusiasm among the masses which could no longer be overlooked. Moreover, improvements in transportation and communications, new inventions for mass consumption, and urbanization, as well as the further secularization of society began to draw more and more of the population into the social processes.

Evidence of the growth of this "mass civilization" was visible almost everywhere, although in the western states of Europe it was far more pronounced than in the eastern countries, such as Russia. Industrialization itself was of course based on mass markets. The proliferation of cheap newspapers stimulated public debate of social and political issues and created tides of popular opinion, which in some states became influential enough to affect the conduct of domestic and foreign policy. Romanticism, with its revival of medieval legends and its glorification of national heroes, accompanied by a sudden interest in national histories, awakened national consciousness among the masses.

There was also more concern for the populace among the ruling circles. Social legislation and the beginning of socialistic thought pointed to a slowly growing awareness of social responsibility. The civic spirit of communities, which had been fairly strong in the Middle Ages and had then waned during the absolutistic era, now again quickened in pulse. Municipal authorities developed public utilities, opened museums, and built theaters. A great number of popular movements were organized for political or socioeconomic aims, as for example, the Chartists in England who worked for political reform, the secret *Carbonari* in Italy who sought Italian unification, or various mutual benefit associations which sometimes operated like early trade unions at a time when labor unions as such were still prohibited by law.

New impulses

Western civilization also changed significantly after 1815 as a result of new impulses and endeavors, most of which were initiated by the middle classes, with repercussions filtering down to the lower classes. Interest in applied science stimulated a host of new inventions that profoundly altered the systems of transportation and communications in the West. The development of steamboats (by Robert Fulton and others) around the turn of the century ensured faster and more dependable transportation of goods and people and helped tie the continents closer together. Steam-powered warships soon became a vital factor in Europe's new colonial expansion. Successfully tested in 1814, George Stephenson's (1781–1848) steam locomotive not only revolutionized land transport but began to lessen the traditional cleavage between country and city. With the extension of railroad systems during the 1830's, the isolation of the peasants gradually waned. When they could afford it, peasants could visit a nearby town, and those with surplus crops could more easily ship them to the cities, thereby making it possible for urban populations to grow faster.

Communication was markedly improved by more extended postal services and the invention of the telegraph. Invented around the turn of the century, the electro-magnetic telegraph was perfected and made commercially useful by Samuel B. Morse (1791–1872) in New York in 1837. At first reserved for government use, telegraphy, like steamships and railroads, gave governments more power over their citizens and brought the people within a nation into greater contact with one another.

Educational facilities were expanded for the masses—an area neglected during the eighteenth century because the Enlightenment had been concerned mostly with the élite. Although churches retained their importance in education, the state took an ever more active part through aid and regulations. The Factory Act of 1833 in England stipulated that children aged nine or ten who work in textile mills "attend some school." In the same year, François Guizot (1787–1874), then French Minister of Public Instruction, sponsored a far-reaching education law, establishing free but not yet compulsory primary education to be conducted by lay or clerical teachers. The United Kingdom of Sweden and Norway adopted an elementary school statute that provided for at least one elementary school in each parish. At the same time, there was a considerable increase in secondary institutions and technical and trade schools, as well as in university attendance. Despite these efforts, which were more pronounced in the countries of western and northern Europe, school attendance was not always enforced, and illiteracy remained high.

Moreover, new views arose on the role of the state. In spite of the great differences between the ideas of conservatives and liberals, it was generally recognized that the machinery of the state could be used for the attainment of specific social purposes. Thus, the influence of the state grew particularly in socio-economic matters, the plea of the liberals for a hands-off policy notwithstanding (see p. 385). Until the eighteenth century, trade had been more important than production. With industrialization, however, mass production required a new system of distribution, more reliable monetary policies, and new economic regulations. Since old-fashioned mercantilism no longer sufficed, a mixture of laissez-faire and government involvement arose to take its place. The new manufacturing class that had superseded the merchants as the dominant element among the bourgeoisie wished to develop their budding industries at their own discretion. Yet, they required ever increasing help from the government: improved transportation, tariffs against foreign competition, naval protection to obtain raw materials from overseas, enforcement of industrial patent rights, and police support against labor unrest.

France, for example, passed a law (1830) permitting the government to expropriate private property needed to serve public utility. Such right of eminent domain, contained implicitly in the Fifth Amendment of the American Constitution, was vital for the building of railroads. To speed up railroad construction, the French government decided in 1842 to acquire rights of way and build road beds, tunnels, bridges, and stations, but let the railways themselves be constructed and operated by private enterprise.

In England, the government sought to counteract the postwar depression by various economic measures that helped the agricultural and industrial interests. The Corn Laws of 1815 prohibited the importation of foreign wheat so long as the domestic price remained below a certain level. Moreover, the income tax (10 per cent) was abolished, and money was deflated by a return to the gold standard. As a consequence of these measures, however, social unrest increased among the poorer classes, which suffered from higher food prices and lower wages.

Spurred by religious and social reformers and fearful of increasing outbreaks of social violence, governments hesitatingly stepped up social legislation. In 1809, the British government ruled against employment of children under nine. After royal commissions investigated the inhumane working conditions prevailing in factories and mines in the 1830's, the government passed a series of factory acts for the protection of female and child labor. Children aged nine and ten were to work no more than nine hours a day in textile mills, and special inspectors were empowered to check on the "condition, employment, and education" of child workers (1833). The Act of 1840 prohibited the use of children as chimney sweeps, and by the Mines Act of 1842, boys under thirteen and all women were barred from working in the mines. England generally led the way in such social legislation. In France, for instance, child labor under the age of eight was prohibited only in 1841.

How extensively central and local governments should intervene in social and economic areas—a question sharply brought out during the French Revolution and raised in the controversy between Jeffersonians and Hamiltonians—became a serious issue of debate in most Western countries during this period. In fact, the urgency of the question became a characteristic of modern times. Answers ranged over a wide gamut of opinions. Typical of those believing in complete laissez-faire was the statement of the owner of several coal mines before a British parliamentary committee of investigation (1842): "I object on general principles to government interference in the conduct of any trade." According to this principle, he also denied the government the right to try to "secure education" for children working in his coal mines. The English philosopher John Stuart Mill (1806–1873), on the other hand, propounded a modified liberalism. Although a strong believer in complete freedom for individual citizens, a condition which would lead to their greatest happiness, Mill recognized the need for the state to supervise the requirements of society as a whole.

For their part, most of the early Socialists, such as François Charles Fourier (1772–1837), were highly idealistic in their concept of human nature and utopian in their views on reorganizing society. Fourier thought that the establishment of independent rural communities (so-called phalansteries), based on cooperation and vocational specialization, would bring happiness to mankind. There was no need for a state as such in his system. But after 1830 Socialists began to look more and more to the state for the attainment of social justice. Louis Blanc (1811–1882), historian, journalist, and social reformer, believed that the state should guarantee the right to work and that the government should finance business enterprises organized by workers, establish national workshops to relieve unemployment, and generally supervise production and distribution, in order to eliminate competition and ensure that the poor get their share of the goods produced.

Conservatism

After the decades of revolution and war, the conservatives called for order and stability. There were many types of conservatism. A few reactionaries hoped to return to conditions as they had existed before 1789. Most conservatives, however, rather heeded Edmund Burke's advice that social change should follow the guidance of tradition. One might conveniently label the two groups ultra-conservatives and preventive conservatives.

Ultra-conservatives

Ultra-conservatism became particularly pronounced in the Roman Catholic Church. Understandably, the ecclesiastical hierarchy was animated by fierce resentment against rationalism and Jacobinism, both of which had tried to eradicate organized Catholicism. The pope himself (Pius VII), condemned to years of exile by Napoleon, was intent on restoring the *ancien régime* upon his return to Rome. He reopened the Society of Jesus, reinstituted the Inquisition and the Index, and urged churchmen everywhere to fight against the dangers of liberalism and rationalism. Clerical-political groups were formed in many countries to help the Catholic Church regain its former influence in government and education. In France, the church secured compensation for the lands confiscated during the revolution and obtained passage of a much debated Law of Sacrilege (1826), which made profanation of the Host a criminal offense and the theft of holy objects from a church punishable by death. In general, the church retained its ultra-conservative character until the latter nineteenth century.

Ultra-conservatism was also bolstered by the revived interest in religion which characterized the Romantic era. In contrast to rationalism with its speculation and experimentation, traditional Christianity seemed to offer reassuring certainty and was more attuned to the emotional and mystic needs of the Romantics. Many poets, journalists, historians, and statesmen, initially supporters of liberalism and nominally Protestants or Deists, became converted to Catholicism and conservatism. Among many of the rulers there existed a solidarity of religious conservatism. Thus, Catholic Austria, Orthodox Russia, and Protestant Prussia cooperated to restore the pope to power in Rome. Characteristic of this "profound conviction that the policy of the powers, in their mutual relations, ought to be guided by the sublime truths taught by the eternal religion of God our Saviour" was the Holy Alliance, initiated by Tsar Alexander I in 1815. Signed initially by the rulers of Russia, Prussia, and Austria, this idealistic document was later subscribed to by all European rulers, except the king of England, the sultan of Turkey, and the pope. In terms of practical politics, the Holy Alliance was meaningless; but its pious pronouncements that the conduct of government should be guided by "holy religion," that all the rulers should consider themselves "as members of one great Christian nation," and that "justice, charity, and peace" would prevail if the people would "fortify themselves each day in the principles and practice of those duties which the Divine Saviour has taught to men," reflected the views of many contemporary conservatives.

Ultra-conservatism also guided some of the rulers restored to their thrones after the collapse of the Napoleonic regimes. This was particularly true in the Italian peninsula, where the French had introduced far-reaching political, social, and economic reforms and had imposed a measure of unification on the diverse states. Despite promises to maintain constitutionalism, the restored monarchs turned back the clock to despotism. Civil rights were suppressed, the pre-revolutionary nobility was restored to its prerogatives, and a "white terror" was unleashed against all suspected of Jacobinism. The restoration of Ferdinand VII in Spain (1814) entailed a similar reaction. The stubborn king abolished the constitution of 1812 which had become a symbol of progress to Spanish liberals, restored the Jesuits to control of education, re-established the Inquisition, and permitted the ascendancy of court favorites. Even Charles X of France (1824–1830) attempted to restore greater absolutism based on the old concept of "throne and altar," although his power was limited by a constitution and by the heritage of the revolutionary legacy among his subjects.

Such ultra-conservatism provoked widespread unrest and stimulated the growth of secret societies, like the *Carbonari*. In 1820, Spanish troops mutinied in Cadiz as they were about to be sent to South America to reconquer the rebellious colonies. A general revolution then shook Spain and forced Ferdinand VII to restore the constitution of 1812. Soon thereafter, revolutions erupted in Naples and Piedmont-Sardinia, forcing their monarchs to grant constitutions. The conservative powers, particularly Austria and Russia, were alarmed by these revolutionary successes. In 1815, England, Prussia, Russia, and Austria had concluded the Quadruple Alliance for the purpose of maintaining the peace settlement with France and guarding Europe against renewed French aggression. The alliance also stipulated that the powers meet periodically to discuss common problems and "employ all their means to prevent the general tranquility . . . from being again disturbed." By 1818, France was considered safely restored to Bourbon rule and allowed to join this "Concert of Europe." Despite British protests, Russia, Prussia, and Austria adopted a protocol at the Congress of Troppau (1820) which declared that a state forfeited its membership in the European Alliance when it was taken over by revolutionary elements, and that the powers had the right to force such a state "back into the Great Alliance." On the basis of this protocol, Austrian troops invaded Naples and Piedmont and restored the absolutistic regimes; a few years later, France sent troops to Spain to re-establish Ferdinand VII in his full powers.

Ultra-conservative political theorists and philosophers developed new concepts of the state to fit the Romantic era. Just as the Romantics relied on intuition and emotion rather than on reason and etiquette, so they distrusted the artificial political constructions of the eighteenth-century rationalists. Seeking their inspiration in the Middle Ages rather than in classical times or in the Age of Reason, they looked upon the state as an entity in itself. This organic state was not the aggregate of its citizens but a living myth, a fictitious construct endowed with presumed real existence. According to the German philosopher Friedrich Hegel (1770–1831), the most influential conservative political thinker of the period, each state or nation possessed its own *Volksgeist* (national or folk spirit), which guides its development and sets it apart from other nations. The state was deemed to be all-powerful in relation to its members, and its function was not, as the rationalists had asserted, to serve the individual. On the contrary, the citizen could not exist apart from the state and found his true identity as a member of his nation.

Although widely discussed, the theories of Hegel and other conservative political thinkers found little application at first. Yet, with the rise of totalitarianism in the twentieth century, dictators were to reinterpret Hegel to bolster their own construction of an all-powerful state.

Preventive conservatives

Only a few conservatives attempted to turn the clock back. Most rulers and theorists were willing to make some compromises between their own ideals and the changes brought by the revolution and Napoleon. Yet once in power, these rulers were determined to prevent further liberalization. An example of this type of conservative was the corpulent Louis XVIII of France (1814–1824), who, after twenty-three years in exile and a second flight from Paris upon Napoleon's return from Elba, resolved to avoid the risk of another dethronement.

Louis' role was by no means easy. France was occupied by the armies of the Quadruple Alliance. Returned émigrés and ultra-royalists unleashed a "white terror" against Bonapartists, Jacobins, and liberals in general, and demanded restitution of the properties and prerogatives which they or their fathers had lost a quarter of a century before. To please the middle class and rally support to his cause, Louis granted a constitution which set up a bicameral legislature, with the upper house (Peers) nominated by the king and the lower house (Deputies) elected by a highly restricted suffrage. Civil and legal equality, the inviolability of property, and freedom of religion were guaranteed. Eventually there was even a relaxation of censorship laws and more freedom of speech.

On the other hand, Louis made it clear that he ruled by divine right, and that his ministers were responsible to him alone. Moreover, he insisted on readoption of the white flag of the Bourbons to underline his contempt for the revolutionary and Napoleonic tricolor, which symbolized all that he personally detested. After 1820, discouraged and beset with gout, the king lost power to the ultra-royalists who gained control of parliament. They further restricted suffrage in favor of the conservative landed interests, instituted new censorship laws, and granted more power to the Catholic Church. This reactionary trend characterized the brief reign of Charles X, Louis' stubborn brother. Under Charles, the French middle class, accustomed to enjoying a fair measure of importance, grew increasingly restive and finally overthrew the Bourbon ruler in the Revolution of 1830.

The Tories in England, who had organized the anti-Napoleonic struggle, also practiced preventive conservatism after 1815 in face of rising discontent among the lower classes. Harried by the postwar depression, workers and agricultural laborers were pressing demands for an extension of suffrage and redress of social grievances. Although most of this pressure took the form of peaceful petitions, riots occurred and a band of radicals even hatched a fantastic plot to blow up the entire Cabinet, seize the Bank of England and the Tower of London, and set fire to the city—a conspiracy which was betrayed by one of its members and quelled by the government. The Tories suppressed all riots by military force and passed a series of acts designed to curb subversion. Habeas corpus was suspended, stricter supervision of newspapers was instituted, and the right of search was extended.

This period of repression was violent but short. After 1822, liberal Tories and some Whigs gained more power and steered England toward the path of compromise and gradual reform. Trade unions were permitted to organize, the criminal code was revised in the interest of humanitarianism, and

Catholics were given political rights, though not yet absolute equality with Anglicans. As radicalism faded, the conservatives shed some of their fears of change, thus paving the way for the first period of major reforms which began in 1830.

During the Wars of Liberation, the future of Germany had been at stake (see p. 362). The demise of the Holy Roman Empire and Napoleon's frequent territorial reshuffling had raised the question of Germany's permanent political configuration. The petty princes naturally hoped to regain their principalities; the larger states, such as Bavaria, sought to retain the aggrandizement granted by Napoleon; and nationalists and liberals wished to seize the opportunity for creating a united Germany. The diplomat Baron Karl von Stein (1757–1831), hesitantly supported by the king of Prussia, attempted to unify the German states at the time Prussian and Russian armies liberated them from French occupation. Austria's Metternich, on the other hand, fearing that centralization might breed liberalism, insisted on restoring the legitimate rulers to their thrones, where possible. By keeping the German states disunited, he hoped to ensure Austrian influence over the secondary states.

In the end, Metternich's policy prevailed, and the First Peace of Paris (1814) called for the re-establishment of independent German states and their association in a federal league. As formed in 1815, the new German Confederation of thirty-five principalities and four free cities was a loose union with a central diet under the permanent presidency of Austria. The diet lacked all executive powers, so that the sovereign powers of the component states remained unimpaired. For the ensuing several decades, Metternich succeeded in exercising paramount influence over most of them.

Within the Austrian realm, which now included Lombardy, Venetia, and the Dalmatian coast—obtained as compensation for the loss of Belgium —Metternich's rule was rather autocratic and static. Army, police, and the influence of the Catholic Church were used to extirpate liberalism and repress the demands for autonomy voiced by restless ethnic groups, such as Italians, Czechs, and Hungarians. With Metternich interested primarily in politics, the Viennese government paid little attention to economic and industrial development. As a result, the middle class and proletariat remained relatively small and weak, except in the centers of Prague, Vienna, and Milan.

In foreign policy, Metternich tried his best to further Austrian hegemony in Central Europe through his personal influence over the rulers of Germany and even of Russia. Often called a reactionary, he was really more a traditionalist, desirous of maintaining the status quo and of avoiding changes "while agitated by passion." Fearful of the possible resurgence of Jacobinism, he considered the maintenance of the legitimate dynasties in Europe a requisite for political stability. Although the German Articles of Confederation provided that each member state should grant a constitution,

Metternich urged the rulers to disregard this provision. In the end, only a handful of secondary states adopted conservative constitutions. Despite his promises during the Wars of Liberation, the Prussian king steadfastly refused to limit his powers by constitutional restrictions.

Soon after 1815, liberal and nationalistic demands were pressed by some segments of the middle class, particularly by intellectuals and university students organized in fraternities. At a boisterous festival in 1817 to commemorate Napoleon's defeat at Leipzig and the three-hundredth anniversary of Luther's posting of his Ninety-five Theses, students and professors delivered impassioned speeches against conservative princes and in favor of German unification. The Austrian and Prussian governments soon reacted to this challenge, ordered the arrest of extreme liberals and nationalists, and placed suspects under police surveillance. Metternich then persuaded the federal diet to adopt the Carlsbad Decrees (1819) which outlawed fraternities and political clubs and called for government agents to monitor all university lectures. Subversive students were to be dismissed, and disloyal professors fired and denied the right of finding government employment in any other German state. Furthermore, the diet set up an all-German investigating committee to stamp out subversive publications.

Metternich's influence was felt even in Russia. The ambitious and visionary Alexander I had always been an anomalous mixture of autocrat and idealistic liberal. Early in his reign, he had made some liberalizing reforms, surrounded himself with innovators, and spoke repeatedly about his intention of granting a constitution. Although advocating the creation of a peaceful league of European states, he engaged in numerous wars and continued Russian expansion by acquiring Finland, Bessarabia, Georgia, and an additional slice of Poland—upon which he bestowed some autonomous rights—and enlarging Russian holdings in Alaska and northern California. Impatient with the tsar's procrastination in the matter of serious reforms, activists, particularly among the officer corps, organized secret societies, some pressing for constitutionalism and an end to serfdom, others even advocating land reform and republicanism. After a plot on his life in 1818, Alexander abandoned his pseudo-liberalism and slipped more under the influence of Metternich. "The limits of liberty," he now asserted, "are the principles of order," and he therefore supported European intervention against the disorders in Italy and Spain (see p. 377). Yet Alexander faced a dilemma when the Greeks revolted against their Turkish overlords in 1821 (see p. 389). Despite Metternich's advice against siding with the rebels, the tsar wanted to support the Christian Greeks against the Islamic Turks and not forfeit Russia's long-standing anti-Turkish stance and her general interest in penetrating the Balkans.

Under Alexander's successor, his brother Nicholas I (1825-1855), Russia was returned to undisguised conservative autocracy. The accession of the "Iron Tsar" was accompanied by an abortive uprising in the army. After executing its leaders and exiling their accomplices to Siberia, Nicholas imposed harsh discipline on his troops, regimented his growing bureaucracy, developed an efficient and dreaded secret police, and attempted to minimize the spread of liberal ideas by discouraging all but technical education, resorting to strict censorship, and isolating Russia by a sort of "iron curtain." Distrustful of others, he tried to supervise everything himself in the manner of King Philip II of Spain. There naturally remained strong currents of discontent among the intelligentsia, but Nicholas' iron rule was firm enough so that Russia was one of the few European states that experienced no revolts in the revolutionary year 1848.

Abroad, Nicholas acted as champion of antirevolutionary repression. He crushed the Polish rebellion of 1830 and was even ready to send an army into France when the July Revolution toppled King Charles X. Only in the case of Greece was his distaste for revolution outweighed by diplomatic and anti-Turkish considerations. Jointly with Great Britain and France, Russia fought against the Turks and helped the Greeks obtain their independence.

Liberalism

Liberalism at this time found its roots either in Romanticism or in eighteenth-century rationalism, or in an amalgamation of the two. Romantic liberalism was essentially an emotional call for the bursting of all chains that bind man, be they those of political tyranny, of literary and artistic rules, or of social conventions. Poets and politicians launched fervent appeals for individual freedom. Those following the rational *philosophes,* on the other hand, asserted that the guidelines of tradition could never solve the new problems of mankind, and that man instead had to devise new institutions to emancipate himself from arbitrary government and ensure his basic freedoms.

National aspirations (see p. 386) in many cases were also a form of liberalism. Greeks rising against their Turkish overlords, Czechs demanding freedom from Viennese rule, or Belgians breaking away from Holland (1830) all emanated from a spirit of liberalism. Yet, not all nationalism was liberal, for some nation-states, such as Germany, were created under the aegis of conservatism.

Finally, one can distinguish between political, economic, and social liberalism, depending largely on the class involved in the movement.

Political liberalism

Political liberalism, largely a middle-class phenomenon, preached the ideal of participation in government. Besides calling for strict limitation of the powers of the government, the liberals demanded an extension of suffrage and eligibility, as well as guarantees for basic civil rights, such as freedom of press, of religion, of assembly, and of speech. A significant quandary for these liberals was their uncertainty as to how far "left" they dared go without helping the cause of Jacobins and Socialists whom they distrusted. Liberalism made noticeable gains during the 1830's in England, the United States, France, Belgium, and Denmark.

In England, the Whigs, soon called the Liberal Party, came to power in 1830 and launched an era of reform in conjunction with reform-minded Tories like Sir Robert Peel (1788–1850). Despite strong objection by the Tories in the House of Lords, the Whigs under the leadership of Lord John Russell (1792–1878) passed the parliamentary Reform Bill of 1832 amidst much popular agitation and rioting. The bill made representation in Commons somewhat more equitable by allotting more seats to the populous areas as well as to Scotland and Ireland, and by lowering suffrage requirements. The Reform Bill did not institute manhood suffrage nor truly democratic representation, but it pleased the middle class and encouraged Commons to embark on further political, social, and economic reforms.

Among the measures passed between 1833 and 1847 were the prohibition of slavery in the British colonies—the slave trade had already been more or less effectively outlawed by 1811; the Factory Act of 1833, an initial attempt at regulating working conditions; an Education Grant, allotting government funds to elementary schools; the New Poor Law, forcing the impoverished to enter workshops; the reorganization of municipal governments; and the legalization of civil marriages. The period also witnessed a curious application of the spoils system which was becoming popular in the United States during the contemporary Jacksonian era. In 1839, shortly after accession of the eighteen-year-old Queen Victoria (1837–1901), Peel refused to form a new cabinet unless the queen dismissed a number of ladies of the bedchamber, appointed by the preceding Whig cabinet. Since the headstrong queen rejected Peel's request, a compromise was later effected, designating certain positions in the queen's entourage as non-political.

Despite the reforms, the lower classes remained unhappy. Frequently accompanied by violence, pressure for further parliamentary reform increased during the late 1830's. The so-called Chartists petitioned Parliament for the granting of six points: manhood suffrage, vote by ballot, payment for members' attendance at Parliament, annual meetings of Parliament, eligibility for membership in Parliament regardless of wealth, and electoral districting on the basis of population. The Chartists' demands were steadfastly rejected by Parliament, whose middle-class members had no intention of opening the flood gates of political power to the lower classes.

English liberalism was never completely laissez faire. While inching toward freer trade, the government became more involved in the regulation of social problems, a gradual change that pointed toward the day during the late nineteenth and early twentieth century when liberalism came to stand for more, rather than less, government intervention for the protection of the interests of the underprivileged.

England's first era of reform coincided with the Jacksonian revolt of the lower classes and of the West against domination by the aristocratic eastern seaboard in the United States (1829–1837). There were considerable parallels between the two countries, although America was ahead of England on the path toward political democracy, whereas the English were more advanced in social concern. Most American states were then following the example of the more democratic Western states in granting white manhood suffrage, and the election of 1828 had shown a vast increase in popular participation. Moreover, in almost all states the presidential electors came to be chosen by popular vote rather than by state legislators. President Jackson's attitude was typically expressed in the campaign he waged against the Bank of the United States, which he considered an undemocratic institution dominated by a financial elite. As in England during the 1830's, labor began to organize to obtain better working conditions, and the abolitionist movement (started by William Lloyd Garrison in 1831) began with the establishment of several antislavery societies.

The year 1830 was marked by several revolutions in Europe. The Bourbons were overthrown in France, and revolts erupted in Poland and Belgium, as well as in several Italian and German states, all generally inspired by the uprising in Paris. Led by the middle class and in part instigated by clandestine and semisecret societies, the revolutionaries called for moderate constitutional reforms, guarantees of civil liberties, and, where applicable (as in Poland, Belgium, and Italy), national autonomy or independence. Although the lower classes helped man the barricades, their demands for social and economic gains were not yet vociferous, and hence were easily shunted aside by the middle class.

In France, Charles X's attempt to further disenfranchise the upper middle class, his preference for ultra-conservative ministers, his dissolution of the national guard, and his attempts to muzzle the press brought Parisian revolutionary temper to a boil. In late July 1830, motley groups of insurgents erected barricades, seized control of the city, and forced Charles X into renewed exile. Afraid that the republicans, led by the aged Lafayette, might attain power and open the doors to radicalism, moderate liberals quickly proclaimed as king Louis Philippe (1830–1848), a descendant of Louis XIII and the head of the House of Orléans.

The new regime, usually called the July or Bourgeois Monarchy, was a plutocracy rather than a truly liberal, democratic system. To be sure, Louis Philippe agreed to substitute the revolutionary tricolor for the white flag and the fleur-de-lis of the Bourbons, accepted the title of "King of the French" in lieu of the former "King of France," and concurred superficially with the concept of popular sovereignty. Censorship laws were relaxed, the national guard reformed, and the constitution revised to deprive the king of the power to suspend laws or to initiate legislation on his own. Moreover, suffrage was extended by reducing financial electoral qualifications. Even so, as late as 1846, only 2.8 per cent of the male population was eligible to vote. Since one had to be affluent to vote, it was no wonder that the July Monarchy enhanced the worship of prosperity and provoked much financial speculation.

King Louis Philippe tried to make himself popular by simulating bourgeois habits and taking leisurely, unattended strolls through Paris. Yet his basis of support was small. On the Right, his reign was resented by most clericals, by the Legitimists who looked upon Louis Philippe as a usurper on the Bourbon throne, and by ultra-conservatives in general. On the Left, his regime was opposed by the lower-middle class which had not received the vote, and by Republicans and workers who felt cheated out of the fruits of their revolution. There was even a revival of Bonapartism among those bored with the stodgy, inglorious atmosphere of the July Monarchy. The king tried to placate this group by permitting the return of the ashes of Napoleon and having them ceremoniously interred in the Dome des Invalides in Paris amidst the frenzied acclamations of the populace.

Among Louis Philippe's most important ministers were two historians: Louis Adolphe Thiers (1797–1877), a liberal monarchist who advocated further democratization and an active foreign policy, and François Guizot, a conservative who favored peace and the status quo. During the 1840's, Guizot became the dominant figure in the government and, despite increasing pressure for liberal and social reforms, refused all accommodation with the opposition.

Although Louis Philippe promised to the powers (Russia, Great Britain, Prussia and Austria) in 1830 that France would not attempt to export her revolution as she had done in the eighteenth century, the events in France precipitated uprisings in many areas. With few exceptions, these European revolts were unsuccessful because of the weakness of the middle class in most areas.

The Belgians in the former Austrian Netherlands, however, who had been placed under Dutch control in 1815, were successful in their revolt. Resentful of what they considered exploitation by the Dutch, they declared their independence in 1830, obtained Anglo-French aid to resist Dutch efforts to reconquer them, devised a liberal constitution, and offered the crown to a new royal house (Saxe-Coburg). Although the Dutch refused for almost a decade to concede their loss, Belgium consolidated her independence and relative liberalism. In 1839, the new frontiers between Belgium and Holland were finally settled and the powers guaranteed Belgium's perpetual neutrality. For centuries a major battlefield among France, England, Holland, and Germany, Belgium was to enjoy peace until the outbreak of World War I.

Spurred by the Revolution in France, the Danes, who had lost Norway to Sweden in the settlement of 1815 and had gradually recovered from the effects of the Napoleonic wars, also embarked on a period of liberalization after 1830, with the gradual introduction of political representation and self-government for municipalities. Liberalism and nationalistic fervor also increased in the twenty-two Swiss cantons which had been loosely reunited in a federal pact in 1815. Several Protestant cantons had granted universal male suffrage and guarantees of basic civil liberties in the late 1820's, a trend that was accelerated after 1830. After two decades of struggles between Liberals and Conservatives, Protestants and Catholics—including a brief intercantonal war in 1847—the Liberals carried the day and wrote a new constitution for Switzerland, with a much strengthened central government based on universal male suffrage and proportional representation.

Economic and social liberalism

During this period, classical economists, social philosophers, merchants, financiers, and the growing group of industrial entrepreneurs waged a concerted campaign against mercantilism (see p. 281). Laissez faire was given a further theoretical basis by several English classical economists who followed Adam Smith and were firm believers in the eighteenth-century concept of natural law. Thomas Malthus (1766–1834), for instance, asserted that the human population increases at a geometric rate, whereas man's food supply grows only arithmetically. He believed that this natural law, which in effect condemned the surplus population among the poor to death by starvation, could not be circumvented by charity, or socialistic policies, or government intervention. Similarly, the economist David Ricardo (1772–1823) proclaimed an inexorable law of wages, which in the long run kept wages at subsistence level. "The natural price of labor," he wrote, "is that price which is necessary to enable the laborers . . . to subsist and to perpetuate their race." There was, therefore, no reason for the state to interfere with any attempt at setting a minimum wage structure and no sense to pay higher wages for humanitarian reasons.

The Utilitarian philosophers also added their reasons for laissez faire. Jeremy Bentham (1748–1832) believed that society should ensure the happiness of the greatest number and that every individual knows best what is conducive to his own happiness. Whatever restricts such happiness is bad and should be eliminated.

Implementation of economic liberalism was advocated with particular fervor in England's industrial center of Manchester, and so is sometimes called Manchester liberalism. To Richard Cobden (1804–1865), pamphleteer, member of Parliament, and a leader of the Manchester group, laissez faire meant not only free trade but also freedom of contract between individuals, hampered neither by unions nor by industrial monopolies. Cobden, who became an active leader in the Anti-Corn Law League which succeeded in having the Corn Laws repealed in 1846, saw in free trade a safeguard for England's prosperity as well as international peace. Opposing government restrictions not only at home but also abroad, he proposed an end to imperialism and advocated self-rule for the colonies. At the same time, Robert Peel secured the lowering of tariffs and an end to export duties.

The theory of unbridled economic liberalism in foreign trade became a peculiarly British ideal, probably because British industry was more developed than that of other nations and hence less worried about harmful competition. More typical of Continental liberals were the ideas of the German economist Friedrich List (1789–1846), who believed that economic freedom benefited the individual, but was harmful to a state with young industries, such as the United States and the German states. Hence he proposed laissez faire in domestic economies and protective tariffs in foreign trade.

In questions of social reform, the term "liberalism" began to assume a different meaning in the course of the nineteenth century. Most of the Utopian Socialists saw no need for state intervention in behalf of the downtrodden. To alleviate poverty, they advocated collectivism (collective control of production and distribution) rather than the individualism extolled by the middle-class economic liberals. This type of socialism, which rejected state aid, was perpetuated by the anarchists of the later nineteenth century.

However, as the power of the entrepreneurs grew while labor conditions worsened, Socialism became mixed with Jacobinism and turned from utopian to so-called "scientific" solutions. To overcome the entrenched interests of the upper middle class, Socialists in the 1840's began to look upon the state as a means of curbing the unbridled powers of employers and ensuring social justice. The workers were to gain control of the state either by revolution or by democratic practices such as universal suffrage. Karl Marx (1818–1883), whose journalistic activity began in the 1840's, used theories of economic law to make the transition from utopian to scientific Socialism. Where the classical economists had tried to show that natural law made subsistence wages inevitable, Marx attempted to prove that economic and historic inevitability entailed the eventual self-destruction of capitalism and the ultimate triumph of the proletariat (see p. 426).

National aspirations

Nationalism was a by-product of the American and French revolutions and the Romantic era. Influenced by Rousseau's enthusiasm for popular sovereignty and by Herder's stress on ethnic peculiarities among peoples, nationalism drew strength from an emphasis on vernacular languages and on a people's history and literature. Although nurtured on patriotic mass emotions, nationalistic drives were often motivated by economic considerations and the desire for political power on the part of some would-be ruling group or class. In practice, nationalism expressed itself in many ways, from purely cultural manifestations to political conspiracies among small groups and popular uprisings on a massive scale.

Cultural nationalism

Cultural nationalism was first most noticeable in the arts and literature during the Napoleonic period, particularly the Wars of Liberation. The Spanish painter Francisco Goya (1746–1828), for instance, excelled in painting Spanish customs and depicting the sufferings of Spanish peasants during the war. Somewhat later, one of the most notable French Romantic painters, Eugène Delacroix (1798–1863), fanned nationalistic passions by symbolically casting nations in the shape of beautiful women.

In Germany, anti-French sentiments excited by the French military occupation led poets, dramatists, and journalists to produce intensely nationalistic works. These writers extolled the beauty of the German landscape and the German language, praised the heroic deeds of German medieval folk heroes, inveighed against all foreigners, and called for German unity. In response to Napoleon's Imperial Catechism, a *Catechism of Patriotic Love* (by Heinrich von Kleist, 1777–1811) was composed to imbue children with devotion to the fatherland. Soon most countries produced their share of nationalistic writers and poets, exalting the virtues of their own people.

Historians, too, were caught up in the nationalistic trend. The Germans and French, in particular, began to assemble vast collections of documents on the past of their respective countries. The romantic French professor Jules Michelet (1798–1874) wrote an emotional seventeen-volume *History of France* to enhance the glory of the French people. Prussian historians (such as Johann Droysen, 1808–1884, and Heinrich von Treitschke, 1834–1896) conceived German history in terms of the destined leadership of the Hohenzollern dynasty and proclaimed that the historian's duty was to educate the people in nationalism. Among the nationalities of eastern and southeastern Europe that were trying to gain or regain statehood during the nineteenth century—Greeks, Poles, Czechs, Hungarians, South Slavs, and others—historians, philologists, and collectors of folklore played a significant role in stimulating a national awakening and in rousing the desire for unity and independence.

The same trend affected musicians of the Romantic era. The use of folk tunes and a frank appeal to national emotions—as in some works of Frédéric Chopin (1810–1849) and Franz Liszt (1811–1886)—characterized many compositions. Musicians were called upon to produce stirring national anthems or often felt moved to celebrate national victories in musical scores. *The Ring of the Nibelung* by the nationalistic German composer Richard Wagner (1813–1883) was a veritable apotheosis of Germanism.

Conspiratorial and idealistic nationalism

Early in the century, small clandestine groups were organized in various areas of Europe, especially those under alien domination, for the purpose of fighting for greater political liberties and self-government. Most of them were part of a wide network of conspiratorial cells. The Italians generally showed the greatest interest in such revolutionary activities, and their organizations served as models in other countries. Most famous among the secret societies of Italy was the *Carbonari,* initially organized in Naples toward the end of the Napoleonic wars. The *Carbonari* set up branches all over Italy, even in France and Belgium, and attracted to its membership activists and idealists from all walks of life, including such visionary foreigners as the English poet Lord Byron (1788–1824). With a heavy emphasis on brotherhood, despite the hierarchical organization of its members, the conspirators used a wide array of secret symbols and oaths and practiced an elaborate ritual, which suited the love of the occult in the Romantic era. Generally republican in outlook, the *Carbonari* were primarily interested in driving the Austrians out of Italy and working for national unity. None of the various uprisings they staged was successful.

In 1832, the young ex-*Carbonaro* Giuseppe Mazzini (1805–1872), an idealistic writer from Genoa, organized a new movement, Young Italy, based more on idealism than on conspiracy. From exile in France, Switzerland, and England, Mazzini urged Italian enthusiasts to strive for Italian independence and unity, as well as for freedom and republicanism. He believed that success would depend in part on the political education of the masses, since the small groups of *Carbonari* had patently failed to get mass support. Force, he thought, should be used only rarely; nevertheless, his followers hatched a number of unsuccessful plots.

In his enthusiasm for freedom and brotherhood, Mazzini also founded Young Europe (1834), a loose organization designed to lend guidance to similar idealistic movements which were being formed in other countries, such as Young Switzerland, Young Ireland, Young Poland, and Young Norway.

Besides the *Carbonari* and Mazzinians, many other conspiratorial or idealistic groups espoused nationalistic causes. Thousands of Polish exiles plotted in Paris, awaiting the day when they could help free Poland from Russian domination. The German poet Heinrich Heine (1797–1856) and many of his exiled compatriots, also residing in Paris, sought to stir German liberalism and nationalism with their impassioned writings. Pan-Slavs secretly urged the Serbs to rise against the Turkish Janissaries. Greek merchants helped finance clubs throughout Europe to attract volunteers and support for the struggle for Greek independence. And Czech nationalists, among them the historian František Palacký (1798–1876), worked on refining the Czech language as an instrument for national cohesion, while directing their attacks against the hegemony of the German-speaking Austrians within the Austrian empire.

Successful national uprisings

Several years after the small, mountainous principality of Montenegro had been granted quasi-independence from Turkey (1799), the Serbs around Belgrade also arose against their Turkish overlords. After several insurrections, they were granted some autonomy in 1817. By 1830, Serbia had become semi-independent, although Turkish garrisons remained on its territory until 1867 and complete sovereignty was not obtained until 1878. Belgium, as we saw (see p. 384), staged a successful national revolt and obtained *de jure* sovereignty in 1839.

The Latin-American revolutions (see p. 367) were at first not nationalistic in the same sense as similar uprisings in Europe, since the various groups generally lacked national cohesion and traditions. The different states resulted rather from political and economic developments. There were no particular ethnic reasons, for instance, for dividing the provinces south and east of the Paraná River into the three separate states of Argentina, Paraguay, and Uruguay. Yet, national feeling soon developed. In 1830, splinter movements broke Colombia into three states, with the separation of Ecuador and Venezuela. Ten years later, the United Provinces of Central America dissolved into the four states of Honduras, El Salvador, Costa Rica, and Nicaragua. (See Map 19.)

The national uprising that most inflamed the enthusiasm of the Western world was that of the Greeks. Middle-class Europeans hailed this Greek renaissance, formed philhellenic societies, and gathered contributions for the Greek cause. Poets addressed odes to the Greeks, and volunteers, including Lord Byron, joined the insurrectionists. "We are all Greeks," exclaimed the English Romantic poet Shelley (1792–1822). "Our laws, our literature, our religion, our arts have their roots in Greece." Even President Monroe praised the Greek revolutionists, asked Congress to pass an aid-to-Greece bill, and sent a naval detachment to cruise off Greece, despite the professed American ideal of non-intervention.

Launched in 1821, the Greek revolt against Turkey was one of the most bloody in modern times, with Greeks and Turks massacring each other by the tens of thousands. Disagreeing among themselves as they had in ancient times, the Greeks also fought two civil wars and murdered some of their own leaders, while at the same time battling the Turks and the Egyptians. Despite the daring of the insurrectionists and the relative weakness of the Turkish armies, the Greek cause seemed hopeless by 1825, with the mainland reconquered by the Turks and most of the Peloponnesus occupied by the Egyptians.

The powers decided to intervene actively on the side of the revolution when Russia, after Nicholas I's accession in 1825, prepared for war against Turkey. In expectation of territorial gains in the Balkans, Russia had long been tempted to aid the Orthodox Greeks against the Moslem Turks, especially after the patriarch of Constantinople had been hanged by the Turks in reprisal for the massacre of Turkish garrisons in Greece. Fearful lest the Russians alone bear the fruits of victory and pressed by philhellenic public opinion, England and France eventually joined the struggle. In 1827, a Russian, French, and British squadron blockaded Greece to keep supplies from reaching Turkish troops in Greece and, without declaring war, sank the bulk of the Turko-Egyptian fleet in a brief naval engagement (Battle of Navarino). In the following year, Russian troops invaded the Balkans and a French expeditionary corps landed in Greece. Within less than two years, Turkey succumbed and accepted the solution imposed by the allies. Finally, in 1832, Greece emerged as an independent state, having chosen as king a prince from the Bavarian royal house. The frontiers of the new state were highly restricted, however, and the best grain-producing areas as well as many Greek nationals living in northern Greece and on many islands, including Crete, were left outside of the new state. Hence the Greek question was to be reopened several times during the next century and, as seen in the problem of Cyprus, is even yet not closed.

The national revolts that succeeded during this period were all of the centrifugal type in which a people broke away from domination by an alien nationality or by an estranged mother country, as in the case of the Latin-American colonies. However, the national movements in Italy and Germany, which failed to make significant progress during this period, were centripetal in that they sought to unify diverse states into a single nation.

Modern multilateral involvement of nations

Before 1815, international congresses had usually convened to negotiate settlements at the end of a war. After the Napoleonic period, however, consultation among the nations in time of peace became more frequent, as did exchange visits by heads of governments and ranking diplomats. With economic and ideological considerations supplanting dynastic questions and European wars changing from conflicts between two professional armies to struggles between two peoples—as they had been in ancient times—foreign policy was becoming more complicated. More and more issues were assuming multilateral interest and demanding closer international collaboration. Hence, even after the "Concert of Europe" (see p. 377) disintegrated in the early 1820's, following Britain's withdrawal to protest Metternich's insistence on the right of interference in the internal affairs of other states, the powers met often in consultation. They held these meetings when the equilibrium of Europe appeared threatened.

When the four main victorious powers, Russia, Prussia, Austria, and England met with representatives of France and others at Vienna in 1815 to recast the map of Europe, they based their considerations on the twin principles of legitimacy and compensation. Wherever feasible, the former legitimate dynasties were restored to their thrones, and the more important states that had lost territories were compensated with other lands, regardless of the wishes of the populations involved. Thus Russia received a major share of Prussian Poland and was allowed to retain Finland. In compensation for the loss of Finland, Sweden gained Norway from Denmark. The latter in turn received a small German duchy (Lauenburg). Prussia had to cede territory to Russia, Bavaria, and Hanover but was allowed to annex a large part of Saxony and areas in the Rhineland. In exchange for her loss of Belgium— which was turned over to Holland—Austria acquired, among others, Lombardy, Venetia, and Salzburg and emerged with an enlarged and consolidated realm. (See Map 17.)

These settlements seem strangely at odds with the nascent feeling of nationalism of the period. Yet, following the peace of 1815, there was no major war in Europe until the outbreak of the Crimean conflict in 1854. Some historians have ascribed the relative peacefulness of these decades to the success of the Vienna settlements. It seems more likely that the ordeal of twenty-three years of revolutionary and Napoleonic wars induced the powers to adopt a more cooperative attitude.

Europe's influence overseas expanded during this period through new colonization as well as through the spread of Western ideas. After obtaining South Africa from the Dutch who were then under French occupation (1806), the British seized Singapore (1819), penetrated into Burma (1824), and obtained Aden (1839) and Hongkong (1842), while continually increasing their holdings in India. The French meanwhile began their conquest of Algeria (1830), and obtained Madagascar and Guinea. Equally significant was the fact that non-Europeans started to emulate European governmental systems. Egypt, under its ambitious ruler Mehemet Ali (1805–1849), who tried to expand his power by entering the Greco-Turkish war (see p. 389) and succeeded in making Egypt semi-independent from Turkey, was "modernized" by adopting the French administrative system. Algeria was gradually Europeanized after its conquest by France. Even Persia, under the impact of Russian and English rivalry over spheres of influence, embarked on a measure of Westernization. Thus the trends were set for the second half of the nineteenth century, during which European imperialism attempted to Westernize the world.

SUGGESTED READINGS

General Works on the Period 1815–1914

Albrecht-Carrié, René, ed., *The Concert of Europe* (Harper, 1968). Source materials for the period 1815–1914.

Anderson Eugene N., Pinceti, Stanley J., and Ziegler, Donald J., *Europe in the Nine-*

teenth Cenutry: A Documentary Analysis of Change and Conflict, Vol. I, "1815–
1870"; Vol. II, "1870–1914" (Bobbs, 1961).

*Bell, John F., *A History of Economic Thought* (Ronald, 1967).

Carr, Edward Hallett, *The Romantic Exiles: A Nineteenth Century Portrait Gallery, Russian Revolutionaries in the Meccas of European Radicalism* (Beacon, 1961).

Caute, David, *The Left in Europe Since 1789* (McGraw).

*Gewehr, Wesley M., *The Rise of Nationalism in the Balkans, 1800–1930* (Shoe String, 1931).

Henderson, W. O., *The Industrial Revolution in Europe, Germany, France, Russia, 1815–1914* (Quadrangle, 1968).

Kohn, Hans, *Prophets and Peoples: Studies in Nineteenth Century Nationalism* (Macmillan, 1961).

Marcuse, Herbert, *Reason and Revolution: Hegel and the Rise of Social Theory* (Beacon, 1960).

Merz, John Theodore, *A History of European Thought in the Nineteenth Century*, 4 vols., (Dover, 1904).

Perkins, Dexter, *A History of the Monroe Doctrine* (Little, 1955).

Seaman, Lewis Charles Bernard, *From Vienna to Versailles* (Harper, 1963).

Snyder, Louis L., *Fifty Major Documents of the Nineteenth Century* (Van Nostrand, 1955).

Somervell, David C., *English Thought in the Nineteenth Century* (McKay, 1966).

Stavrianos, L. S., *The Balkans, 1815–1914* (Holt, 1963).

Taylor, A. J. P., *The Hapsburg Monarchy, 1809–1918: A History of the Austrian Empire and Austria-Hungary* (Harper, 1965).

Political Developments: International

Artz, Frederick B., *Reaction and Revolution, 1814–1832* (Harper, 1961).

Ferrero, Guglielmo, *The Reconstruction of Europe* (Norton, 1963). On the post-Napoleonic period.

Gulick, Edward Vose, *Europe's Classical Balance of Power* (Norton, 1967).

May, Arthur J., ed., *The Age of Metternich, 1815–1848* (Holt, 1963).

Nicolson, Harold, *The Congress of Vienna: A Study of Allied Unity: 1812–1822* (Viking, 1961).

Teng, Ssu-Yü, and Fairbank, John K., *China's Response to the West. A Documentary Survey 1839–1923* (Atheneum, 1963).

Webster, Charles, *Congress of Vienna 1814–1815* (Barnes and Noble, 1966).

Political Developments: National

*Almadingen, E. M., *Alexander I* (Vanguard, 1966).

Beik, Paul H., *Louis Philippe and the July Monarchy* (Van Nostrand, 1965).

Black, Eugene C., ed., *European Political History, 1815–1870. Aspects of Liberalism* (Harper, 1967). Collection of essays.

*Ford, Guy S., *Stein and the Era of Reform in Prussia, 1807–1815* (Peter Smith, 1922).

Halévy, Elie, *The History of the English People in the Nineteenth Century*, Vol. I, "The Liberal Awakening"; Vol. II, "The Triumph of Reform, 1830–1841" (Barnes and Noble, 1961).

Hamerow, Theodore S., *Restoration, Revolution, Reaction: Economics and Politics in Germany, 1815–1871* (Princeton, 1958).

*Kolokotronis, T., *Greek War of Independence, 1821–1833* (Argonaut, 1965).

*Leslie, R. F., *Polish Politics and the Revolution of November 1830* (Oxford U.P., 1956).

*Resnick, Daniel P., *White Terror and the Political Reaction After Waterloo* (Harvard, 1966).

*Riasanovsky, Nicholas V., *Nicholas I and Official Nationality in Russia, 1825–1855* (U. of California, 1959).

Southgate, Donald, *The Passing of the Whigs: 1832–1866* (St. Martins, 1962).

Van Deusen, Glyndon G., *The Jacksonian Era: 1828–1848* (Harper, 1959).

Socio-Economic and Cultural

Altholz, Josef L., *The Churches in the Nineteenth Century* (Bobbs, 1967).

Ashton, Thomas S., *The Industrial Revolution: 1760–1830* (Oxford, 1964).

Briggs, Asa, ed., *Chartist Studies* (St. Martins, 1960). Collection of essays.

Filler, Louis, *The Crusade Against Slavery, 1830–1860* (Harper, 1960).

Halévy, Elie, *The Growth of Philosophic Radicalism* (Beacon, 1955).

Halsted, John B., ed., *Romanticism: A Collection of Documents* (Harper, 1968).

———, *Romanticism—Problems of Definition, Explanation, and Evaluation* (Heath, 1965).

Kohn, Hans, *The Mind of Germany: The Education of a Nation* (Harper, 1965).

Raeff, Marc, *The Decembrist Movement* (Prentice-Hall, 1966). On the Russian revolution of 1825).

Talmon, J. L., *Romanticism and Revolt: Europe 1815–1848* (Harcourt, 1967).

Thorlby, Anthony, *The Romantic Movement* (Barnes and Noble, 1967).

CHAPTER XXII

❦ *Unification by Force*
(1848-1870)

In the middle of the nineteenth century, the era of relatively peaceful solutions and idealistic harmony gave way to a period of violence and realism. The change was noticeable in many areas of Western civilization, in politics and economics, as well as in artistic and intellectual concepts. Slow colonial penetration turned into imperialism and gunboat diplomacy. In Italy and Germany, idealists and romantic conspirators lost control of the nationalistic movements to men of action who did not shrink from war to achieve their aims. Instead of continued compromises on the issues of slavery and states rights, Americans resorted to civil war. With the demise of mercantilism in its old form and the triumph of economic liberalism, open competition was extolled in all industrial countries.

Romanticism was replaced by Realism in literature, Idealism was followed by Positivism and the enthronement of science in philosophy, and the strong religious and spiritual feelings of the post-Napoleonic period ebbed into increasing materialism and even atheism. The belief in the goodness of human nature had to battle with Darwin's evolutionary theory and its implication that man, in his fight for survival, was in fact selfish. And in the struggles of the growing proletariat, utopian solutions were abandoned in favor of Marxian Socialism.

The revolutions of 1848–1849 with their miscarried idealistic solutions represented a significant transition from one period to the next.

The revolutions of 1848–1849

Starting in Sicily in January of 1848, revolutionary outbreaks rocketed through much of Europe. Major revolutions that were temporarily successful occurred in most Italian and German states, France, the Austrian Empire, Hungary, and the Rumanian provinces of Turkey. Ireland, England, Spain, Poland, and Switzerland experienced minor unrest and uprisings; while in Belgium, Holland, and Denmark only timely political concessions by the rulers averted open flare-ups.

Considerable parallelism marked the sequence of revolutionary events in the various areas of Europe. The initial outbreaks occurred during the first five months of the year, followed after June by the gradual triumph of the conservative forces over the revolutionary elements. In the spring of 1849, a second wave of uprisings took place in many regions, which in turn were crushed within a few months.

Three distinct aims drove the various revolutionary groups into action. The middle classes, fighting against conservative governments and residual aristocratic power, sought political changes—extended suffrage, civil rights, and in some cases a people's militia in lieu of a royal army. The degree of political changes desired naturally varied with the extent of democratization already achieved and the strength of the middle class. In France, there was a strong demand for universal male suffrage, and even the establishment of a republic. In Prussia, which as yet lacked a constitution, the bourgeois were happy with the prospect of limited constitutional safeguards and a more equitable representation in an all-Prussian diet.

A second aim was nationalistic: to achieve independence from foreign domination, as in the case of the revolts in Milan, Budapest, and Prague against their Austrian masters; or to unite into a single national state, as in the case of the movements in Germany and Italy.

Finally, a third aim, on the part of the lower classes, was social and economic gain. Serfs and peasants insisted on an end to manorial restrictions, and the city proletariat called for shorter working hours, lower food prices, higher wages, and a guarantee of employment. Communists demanded the abolition of private ownership of the means of production and preached egalitarianism.

These three sets of aims were not always mutually compatible, and friction between them in some respects explains the failure of the revolutions. Liberal bourgeois, fighting on the barricades with the proletariat to topple a conservative government, were quickly frightened by the idea of social egalitarianism and, in most cases, soon joined the conservatives to repress social revolt, even at the sacrifice of the greater political freedom for which they had originally taken up arms. Similarly, many German and Italian nationalistic liberals were faced with the question of whether democracy or a strong, conservative monarchy was better equipped to unify their nation. In the end, many were driven to the conclusion that national unification was more important than liberal institutions.

Revolutions in Italy and France

In Italy, revolts from Sicily in the South to Piedmont in the North forced the rulers, including Pope Pius IX (1846–1878), to grant mildly liberal constitutions; thus, the liberal movement seemed to gain some rapid successes. The task of expelling the Austrians from northern Italy and uniting the entire peninsula, however, was more complicated. Three proposed solutions divided the Italians among themselves. Inspired by Mazzini, republicans favored the overthrow of all local dynasties and the creation of a united, liberal Italian republic. The so-called Neo-Guelfs—a name harking back to the medieval struggles over Italy between popes and emperors— sought a federation of the existing kingdoms and duchies under the presidency of the pope. The moderate bourgeois who feared the radicalism of the Mazzinians preferred such a solution, especially since Pius IX at his accession had appeared to be a champion of limited liberalism and of stanch resistance to Austria. Monarchists, restrained anti-clericals, and other liberals, however, looked to Piedmont and its king, Charles Albert (1831–1849), who had granted some liberal reforms in 1847, as the only force strong enough to defeat the Austrians, unite Italy, and ensure stability.

After news of the overthrow of Metternich in Vienna had reached Lombardy, the Milanese expelled the Austrian garrisons, the Venetians proclaimed their independence and established the Republic of St. Mark, and Charles Albert of Piedmont declared war on Austria. In a brief moment of nationalist ecstasy, Neapolitan, papal, and Lombard forces were readied to help the Piedmontese drive the Austrians from northern Italy. But Pius IX reversed his decision, reluctant to place the papacy at war with Catholic Austria, and when the revolution collapsed in Naples (May 15), Neapolitan troops also were recalled. Thus, the Piedmontese faced the Austrians almost alone. The weakened Viennese government, facing revolutions in all the corners of its empire, was willing to grant independence to Lombardy for the sake of peace in Italy, but the eighty-two-year-old Austrian commander, Field Marshal Joseph Radetzky (1766–1858), continued the war and completely defeated the Piedmontese (Battle of Custozza). The first stage of the Italian war for liberation and unification was lost.

Unhappy with the slow pace of reforms, the Romans revolted again late in the year, forcing Pope Pius to flee from the city. The liberals then converted Rome into a republic (February 1849), which soon came under the leadership of Mazzini. With this reawakening of revolutionary sentiment in the spring of 1849, Charles Albert reopened the war against Austria; but once again the Piedmontese forces were defeated by Marshal Radetzky (Battle of Novara), and Piedmont was forced to conclude peace and pay an indemnity to Vienna.

The second Austrian victory allowed the conservative forces gradually to regain control over the Italian states. At Pope Pius' appeal for help, a

French expeditionary corps was dispatched to seize Rome in order to restore him to his see—notwithstanding the fact that France, herself, had become a republic. Led by Mazzini and the adventure-loving Giuseppe Garibaldi (1807–1882), the Romans endured a siege of two months before surrendering to French occupation and readmitting the pope. Soon thereafter, the Austrians laid siege to Venice and finally bombarded the Venetians into submission. By the end of August 1849, Italy was calm again, with the liberal forces crushed everywhere and only the Piedmontese retaining the constitution that had been granted at the beginning of the revolutionary conflagration.

In 1848, just as in 1789, the revolution in France was, in fact, a Parisian revolution. The February uprisings which led to the flight of King Louis Philippe and the proclamation of the Second French Republic were instigated by two distinct groups. On the one hand were constitutional monarchists, tired of the corruption of the Guizot regime, and moderate republicans and reformers, demanding extension of the suffrage and a more imaginative foreign policy. On the other were radical republicans, Socialists, and workers; hurt by the depression of 1846–1847, they mounted the barricades in the vain hope of improving their miserable lot. Even the Catholic clergy sided initially against Louis Philippe and his Protestant minister Guizot. The atmosphere of revolutionary fervor was intensified by rousing speeches of opposition leaders, by the activities of clandestine societies, and by the publication, shortly before the revolution, of histories of the Great Revolution of 1789 by Michelet, Louis Blanc, and the poet Alphonse de Lamartine (1790–1869).

Under the leadership of Lamartine, the provisional republican government which succeeded the monarchy was dominated by moderates. Only two Socialists belonged to the cabinet, of whom one was Louis Blanc. Nevertheless, pressure from Parisian mobs forced the provisional government to initiate a social revolution. Among others, decrees were promulgated establishing direct universal suffrage, abolishing all titles of nobility, shortening the work day from eleven to ten hours, prohibiting the "exploitation of the workers by the subcontractors," engaging the government "to guarantee work to all citizens," and creating national workshops—a relief measure rather than Blanc's idea of workers setting up their own shops with government loans.

Alarmed by the radicalism of the populace, the moderates strained to regain full control of the revolutionary movement. This task was complicated by the presence in Paris of thousands of Polish and German exiles who appealed to the radicals for revolutionary solidarity and urged the French to launch a crusade in the style of 1792 (see p. 346) to bring freedom to Germany, Poland, and Russia. In late April, the elections for a National Assembly resulted in a better than eight to one majority for moderates and conservatives over radical republicans and socialists. The middle class had become frightened by the red danger, and the peasants voted conservative on the advice of parish priests who had turned against the revolution. When the moderates put the brakes on the social revolution and finally even closed down the national workshops, considered to be a hotbed of radicalism, the workers made a desperate attempt to topple the government. Deprived of their dole and fearful of having mounted the February barricades in vain, they resorted to new violence in late June. This time the moderates were prepared to react with overwhelming military force, and they crushed the uprising in four days of bloody street fighting.

The "June Days" ushered in a period of reaction. Thousands of radicals were imprisoned or deported, stringent antisubversive legislation was adopted, and a new constitution was promulgated which, although retaining universal male suffrage, accorded wide powers to a president—a device expected to render stability to the new republican regime. While workers and radicals licked their wounds, bourgeois and peasants streamed to the polls in December 1848, to elect as their first president Louis Napoleon Bonaparte, the nephew of Napoleon I, whose name—though hardly his character—evoked visions of glory and of deliverance from radical disturbances. With Louis Napoleon's election, the French political merry-go-round of monarchy to republic to empire was once again in full swing (see p. 407).

Revolutions in the German Confederation

All three types of revolution—political, socio-economic, and national—were working at cross-purposes in the Austrian Empire, making events more complex. In the larger cities, the middle class rose against the aristocracy and the imperial bureaucracy, while the proletariat sought to prevent exclusive domination by the bourgeoisie. At the same time, the ten or more national groups that made up the empire fought for independence from Vienna, for local autonomy, or for a share in dominating other nationalities.

Under the impact of the uprisings of mid-March 1848, the Austrian emperor compromised on all sides. The seventy-five-year-old Metternich, who had influenced Austrian affairs and European politics for four decades, was allowed to depart into exile. Vienna itself was left under control of a bourgeois national guard and revolutionary student committees. The emperor acknowledged the constitution which the Hungarians had adopted under the leadership of the fiery, though politically moderate, Louis Kossuth (1802–1894) and recognized Hungary's semi-independence; he gave Austria itself a constitution, promised one to the Czechs, and agreed to consider autonomous rights for Bohemia and Croatia. But radical agitation in Vienna continued, and the emperor finally fled to Innsbruck in the more conservative province of Tyrol. By late May, the central government—or what was left of it—had lost control over the empire.

At this point, two Austrian generals and their armies stepped in to save the empire and the imperial regime and to destroy the revolution. In June, Prince Alfred zu Windisch-Graetz (1787–1862) conquered revolutionary Prague and put all of Bohemia under military control. A month later, as we saw before, Marshal Radetzky won a similar success in northern Italy. Thereupon, the Austrian government urged the more conservative Croatians to invade Hungary and suppress the liberal and separatist movement in Budapest. The Hungarians, however, not only repelled the Croatian army, but also invaded Austria and incited the radicals in Vienna to new outbreaks. Finally, Windisch-Graetz and his Croatian allies bombarded and stormed Vienna (October 31), ruthlessly putting down all revolutionary elements.

Imperial and conservative authority was thus re-established throughout the empire, with the exception of Hungary, and a new ministry was installed under Prince Felix von Schwarzenberg (1800–1852), who completely dominated the new eighteen-year-old Emperor Francis Joseph (1848–1916). Early in 1849, Prince Windisch-Graetz succeeded in conquering Budapest; within a few months, however, his forces were again driven out by the supporters of Kossuth, who then declared Hungary to be an independent republic. With Austrian forces again occupied in subduing northern Italy, Tsar Nicholas I, fearful that republicanism in Hungary might endanger his own autocratic regime, offered his assistance to Vienna and dispatched a Russian army to crush Kossuth's Hungarian Republic. By August 1849, all was once again calm in the Austrian Empire. Despite the clamors of the various national groups for autonomy, Schwarzenberg had meanwhile produced a constitution which recentralized most power in Vienna and paid only lip service to the liberals' demand for a representative diet and a responsible ministry. The revolutionary years had achieved a few lasting reforms, such as the final extirpation of serfdom; but the failure of the revolution to satisfy the aspirations of the middle class and of the component nationalities contributed much to sapping the strength of the Austrian Empire and causing its ultimate dissolution.

In Germany, liberal revolutions, sometimes accompanied by social demands, erupted in most states soon after news of the overthrow of the monarchy in France had reached across the Rhine. Most of these upheavals involved little bloodshed and resulted in liberal concessions by the governments in power, which at the same time rejected the more radical and republican demands.

In Prussia, growing tension between the restless middle class and the king as well as serious economic discontent among the workers had made the ground fertile for revolution. King Frederick William IV (1840–1861), kindhearted but politically inept and vacillating, had at first roused the enthusiasm of the liberals through his vague talk of reforms; yet disillusionment was soon to come. Although Frederick William had felt compelled to convene a United Diet for all of Prussia in 1847 to obtain approval of new taxes, the diet had been granted neither power nor permanence. Before dismissing it, the king had made it clear that he would never "transform the natural . . . relationship between prince and people into a contractual and constitutional one."

When fighting erupted between Berlin crowds and the Prussian army (March 18, 1848), Frederick William quickly compromised with the populace. He ordered his army out of the capital—thereby leaving himself at the mercy of bourgeois and student volunteer guards—took a liberal ministry, and promised to reconvene the United Diet and to grant Prussia a constitution. The ruler, at heart a believer in divine-right monarchy, even rode through the city displaying a black-red-gold cockade, the symbol of German unity, which had been outlawed during the height of the Metternich days. Moreover, the Prussian king spoke promisingly of planning to remake Germany.

This honeymoon between the conservative king and his liberal Berliners was short-lived. Within a few weeks he left his capital to rejoin his loyal army and bide his time, while a constituent assembly met in Berlin to discuss a constitution that never saw the light of day. After the triumph of reaction had been ensured in Austria by the capture of Vienna, Frederick William returned to Berlin with his army, dismissed the assembly, and reinstalled a conservative regime; thereafter he issued his own, highly conservative constitution. By 1849, Frederick William felt confident enough not merely to crush new, social rebellions in his own Rhineland provinces, but also to assist other German princes in suppressing renewed uprisings in their states.

Concurrently with the revolutions in the German states, various groups were working assiduously to unify Germany. There was no agreement as to what peoples and lands to include in such a state nor what type of government to devise for it. Some deemed that Austria, the center of the defunct Holy Roman Empire, should constitute an integral part of a united Germany. Others wanted to limit Germany to German-speaking regions, thereby raising a question as to the inclusion of Prussia's Polish subjects. Concerning the political frame and leadership for such a state, four serious proposals were entertained: a united German monarchy could be led by the Hapsburgs, by the Hohenzollerns, or by a royal directorate including all or most of the six ruling monarchs, with a rotating chairmanship; or else Germany could be turned into a republic, a solution advocated not only by radicals but also by those who were convinced that Germany could never be unified so long as the thirty-five ruling princes were not forced to forfeit their sovereign powers and prerogatives.

After much preparation, a German National Assembly, elected by universal male suffrage, convened at Frankfurt and began to deliberate on the draft of a constitution for a united Germany. While debating constitutional issues, this Frankfurt Parliament, as it was called, attempted to assume executive powers by appointing a provisional German government which temporarily supplanted the German federal diet. The provisional German government actually received some diplomatic recognition abroad, but never acquired a military force or other powers with which to implement its decisions. For all intents and purposes it remained a paper government.

Although the majority of the delegates at Frankfurt were liberals or constitutional monarchists, they were also intensely nationalistic. Hence they applauded proudly when Windisch-Graetz's army crushed the Czech independence movement and when Frederick William's troops subdued the rebellious Poles in Prussian Poland. The delegates appeared unwilling to concede to other nationalities the same right to shape their own destiny that the Germans claimed for themselves. The Frankfurt Parliament also approved of Prussia's war against Denmark (April to August 1848) in behalf of the provinces of Schleswig and Holstein, which were largely peopled by German-speaking inhabitants who sought more autonomy from the Danish crown. In all three cases, the delegates at Frankfurt were in fact cheering the victories of troops belonging to those rulers who soon were to use their armies to crush the liberal movement and obstruct the cause of German unification.

Instead of acting speedily while the German princes were reeling from the revolutionary assault, the idealistic and legal-minded orators in the Frankfurt Parliament debated for almost a year before concluding their constitutional draft which called for a federal state, guided by an "Emperor of the Germans." Schwarzenberg, meanwhile, had provided the Austrian Empire with a highly centralizing constitution which tied the subject nationalities more than ever to Vienna. Hence, the plans for a German state which would exclude the Italian, Slavic, and Magyar peoples and would be led by the Hapsburg emperor had to be abandoned. At the end of March 1849, the Parliament, therefore, offered the German crown to Frederick William, who haughtily refused it. The Prussian king was afraid of provoking Hapsburg retaliation; moreover he disliked the liberal provisions in the proposed constitution and complained that "the crown you mean dishonors one inexpressibly, stinking as it does of the Revolution."

With Frederick William's refusal of the crown, the unitary movement collapsed. Some radicals and even some princes still proposed other schemes to salvage a spark of unity, but it became obvious that Frederick William was not the man to lead a united Germany, that Schwarzenberg would not permit the creation of a German state that might prove to Austria's disadvantage, and that, of the two contenders for pre-eminence in Germany, Austria still outweighed Prussia.

An era of forced unification

After the disruptive episodes of the revolutions of 1848–1849, the state—based on industrial power, moral persuasion, improved transportation and communications, as well as on better organized military and police contingents—tended to become increasingly powerful. The central authorities of the state henceforth appeared less hesitant to resort to force for the attainment of foreign and domestic aims.

Creation of the Italian Kingdom

The experiences of 1848–1849 had discredited the Mazzinian and Neo-Guelf proposals for Italian unification, and the twice defeated Piedmontese learned that they had to strengthen their state and their military forces if they wished to try once again to challenge Austria. While the governments of the other Italian states returned to phlegmatic conservatism, Piedmont prepared for its task through internal reform and diplomatic activity abroad. Credit for successfully accomplishing this work goes largely to Count Camillo di Cavour (1810–1861), the enlightened, moderate liberal and methodical planner who became Piedmontese Prime Minister in 1852. (See Map 21.)

Cavour strengthened the kingdom's economy and finances, improved its army, and weakened the power of the Catholic Church. By carefully respecting Sardinia's constitution, he attracted the approval of most liberal Italians as well as the sympathy of Great Britain. To gain prestige and allies among the powers and provide realistic training for his army, Cavour arranged for Piedmont-Sardinia to enter the Crimean War (1854–1856) on the side of England, France, and Turkey against Russia, at a time when Austria's ambivalent neutrality was antagonizing both sides in the conflict. This step earned Cavour the support of Emperor Napoleon III (see p. 408), himself an ex-*Carbonaro* and an idealistic champion of national rights. In a secret agreement with Cavour (1858), the French emperor promised French military aid against Austria, provided the latter was made to look like the aggressor. Piedmont was to obtain Lombardy and Venetia, in return for which France was to get Nice and Savoy, the original home of the Piedmontese dynasty. But to safeguard Napoleon's good relations with the Catholic Church, it was stipulated that the sovereignty of papal Rome should not be disturbed.

In 1859, Austria, suitably provoked by the Piedmontese, attacked Piedmont and, true to his agreement, Napoleon's armies rushed to the aid of Cavour. While the Franco-Sardinian forces defeated the Austrians in two rapid battles, liberals in the central Italian states overthrew their rulers and asked for union with Piedmont. At this point, Napoleon suddenly concluded an armistice and peace with Austria, even though the task of liberating Italy had not been completed. Napoleon's unilateral action, which infuriated Cavour and the Italian patriots, was motivated by Prussia's decision to mobilize her forces along the Rhine, as well as by the revolutionary moves in Central Italy which were affecting Napoleon's protégé, the pope, and by the emperor's customary tergiversation. According to the Franco-Austrian terms,

Lombardy was ceded to Piedmont—a gesture toward Italian nationalism; but the rulers of central Italy were to be restored to their principalities, Venice was to remain Austrian, and Italy was to be made into a confederation "under the honorary presidency of the Holy Father."

After Napoleon's desertion of their cause, the Italians had to act for themselves. Plebiscites held in central Italy in early 1860 opted in favor of union with Sardinia, while Napoleon was kept satisfied by the cession of Nice and Savoy—also after consultation of the population. Thereupon, the intrepid Garibaldi and a small army of volunteers conquered Sicily and Naples, while Sardinian forces occupied the papal states, except for Rome itself, which was still protected by French troops. By the spring of 1861, all of Italy with the exception of Rome and Venetia had been incorporated with Sardinia, and shortly before Cavour's death the king of Sardinia, Victor Emmanuel II, changed his title to King of Italy.

Five years later, Italy made an alliance with Prussia, which was about to attack Austria in the course of its own wars of unification. During the resulting Austro-Prussian War, Italy was defeated by the Austrians on land and at sea, but since Prussia won the war in the north, the Austrians were obliged to cede Venetia to the Italians. Only Rome now remained out of the grasp of the Italian Kingdom, and despite several bold attempts by Garibaldi to seize the city, Napoleon's French forces persisted in upholding the pope's sovereignty. Finally, Prussian action once again brought an indirect solution to the problem. At the outbreak of the Franco-Prussian War in 1870, Napoleon recalled his troops from Rome, and the Italians stormed the city after a brief bombardment. The pope's sovereignty was then restricted to the few square miles of Vatican City, while Rome itself was annexed to Italy and turned into its capital.

In the course of twenty-two years and five wars, Italy thus became unified through a mixture of military force and plebiscites. Immediately, however, irredentist voices were raised, claiming that unification was not complete so long as Italian-speaking peoples in Nice, Savoy, Corsica, the Dalmatian coast, and southern Tyrol lived under alien domination. This irredentist movement was to remain a major factor in Italian politics.

Establishment of the German Empire

The creation of a united Germany in many ways paralleled the formation of the Italian Kingdom. In both cases, one state imposed itself on the others after successfully excluding Austrian hegemony. But, while Italy became a relatively liberal, unitary state, the German Empire was based on conservatism and federalism.

Starting in the 1840's, the German states began to grow constantly closer together. Intra-German ties were fortified by growing railroad nets, by industrial and banking establishments which had branches in various states, and by increased trade, which was facilitated through a customs union (Zoll-

verein), created by Prussia and including, by 1853, all German states except Austria. The experiences of 1848, however, had shown not only the difficulty of forming a political union, but also the urgency of settling the Austro-Prussian rivalry.

During the 1850's, the political atmosphere in Prussia was repressive. Its constitution was a highly conservative document, leaving most power in the hands of the king. Voting for the Lower House was based on an indirect, three-class system of suffrage, heavily weighted in favor of the wealthy. At the same time Prussia enjoyed a tremendous industrial development with a concomitant increase in its military potential. Austria, however, continued to decline. Ruled by the same clique of nobility, army, and clergy, nothing effective was done to reconcile the subject nationalities, and there was little industrial progress. During the Crimean War, the Austrians mobilized without entering the conflict, thereby antagonizing their erstwhile ally, Russia, without achieving any diplomatic gains.

The German unification movement resumed its pace after 1858, when William I of Prussia (1861–1888) became regent for his insane brother, Frederick William IV. The new ruler, somewhat more liberal than his brother but also more interested in military matters than in politics, was determined to reform and increase the Prussian army. This decision led to a prolonged conflict between the ruler and the Prussian parliament which refused to grant the requested funds for army reforms unless the king agreed to liberalize the constitution and to allow some parliamentary control over the military. While Prussia was thus entering a new era, events in Italy exerted a profound influence on Germany. Austria's defeat in the war with France and her loss of Lombardy was a patent indication of her growing weakness, while the creation of the Italian Kingdom furnished an example which German nationalists were eager to emulate.

Unable to overcome parliamentary obstruction to his army reforms, William I turned to Otto von Bismarck (1815–1898), an intelligent, irascible Prussian, already known for his loyal devotion to the Hohenzollern dynasty, who had been in the diplomatic service since 1850. The new prime minister, who all his life remained more interested in foreign than in domestic affairs, rode roughshod over the liberal opposition in parliament, announcing that Prussia should be ruled "monarchically like a great power," and not by "professors, judges, and small-town politicians." He had some obstreperous liberals imprisoned and used force to collect unauthorized taxes so that the army reforms could proceed.

In preparation for the inevitable confrontation with Austria, Bismarck then effected a rapprochement with Tsar Alexander II (1855–1881) by cooperating with Russia in the crushing of yet another Polish uprising. When, a year later (1864), the Schleswig-Holstein question was reopened through Denmark's renewed attempt to incorporate the duchies more closely into the Danish Kingdom, Bismarck found his first opportunity to test the rejuvenated Prussian army. While the German federal diet made a clumsy attempt to aid the duchies by dispatching Hanoverian and Saxon troops, Bismarck persuaded the Austrians to join Prussia in a war against Denmark. After Denmark's defeat, the duchies were placed under Austro-Prussian military occupation, although Bismarck would have preferred to annex them so that Prussia would at last gain direct access to the North Sea.

As Austro-Prussian tension grew over various proposals for the reorganization of the German Confederation, Bismarck assured himself of Napoleon III's benevolent neutrality by hinting at possible compensations for France in the Rhineland, if Prussia were to make gains in Germany. By 1866, both Austria and Prussia were ready for war. The government of Vienna resented Prussia's growing strength in Germany, and the Prussian general staff felt confident of its ability to deal Austria a crushing blow.

Although almost all the states of the German Confederation sided with Austria, Prussia won a lightning victory in the Austro-Prussian War of 1866. The army reforms, which included the introduction of a breech-loading needle gun, as well as the skillful use of railroads and telegraphs, made the Prussian army vastly superior to that of its opponents. Despite the overwhelming success and William I's desire for "punishing the opponent," Bismarck negotiated a lenient peace with Austria to avoid antagonizing her and throwing her into the arms of France. In Germany, however, Prussia reaped great advantages: Schleswig, Holstein, Hanover, and three minor states were annexed; the German Confederation was dissolved; and Prussia was given the right to reorganize the states north of the Main River.

The results of the Prussian victory were far-reaching. Austria henceforth was excluded from Germany, and her regime was so shaken that Vienna was compelled to compromise with Budapest. In 1867, the Austro-Hungarian Dual Monarchy was created, giving the Hungarians quasi-equal rights with the German-speaking Austrians; the Hungarians ran their own affairs and controlled their own subject nationalities, but foreign, military, and financial affairs were administered jointly under the aegis of a common emperor.

Prussia at last gained a land bridge between Brandenburg and her Rhineland possessions, thus completing the work of unification begun by the Great Elector in the seventeenth century (see p. 285). Within Prussia, the war brought the triumph of Bismarckian authoritarianism and the demise of the liberals. The parliament retroactively legalized Bismarck's illegal collection of taxes, thereby conceding that the ruler and his minister knew how to handle Prussia's affairs better than a parliamentary majority.

Bismarck then organized the twenty-one states of northern Germany into the North German Confederation, which was completely dominated by giant Prussia. The federal structure of this new state left some dignity, though little power, to the princes of the small states and was to facilitate the later accession of the southern states. By the end of 1866, only the four states south of the Main remained outside of a united Germany. The Bavarians, in particular, felt little inclination to subordinate themselves to Prussia. In the end, final unification came in the course of war with France, a war which Napoleon III desired to bolster his lagging prestige and which Bismarck welcomed on the theory that "a common national war against our aggressive neighbor would serve better than anything else to bridge the historical gulf which dynastic and ethnic feelings and modes of life [have] created between the south and the north of our fatherland." Between 1867 and 1870, Bismarck played skillfully with Napoleon's desire for compensation in the Rhineland, so as to underscore Napoleon's aggressive designs before the eyes of Europe and to frighten the southern German states into joining a common anti-French front with Prussia and her North German Confederation. With German national feeling thus inflamed and with Napoleon maneuvered into declaring war on Prussia, Bismarck's war with France took on the aspect of a united German war effort.

During the Franco-Prussian War (1870–1871), Prussia's armies once again achieved lightning successes. Within six weeks, the Prussians had surrounded a large French army (Battle of Sedan) and captured Emperor Napoleon himself. Three weeks later, they laid siege to Paris. Although the capital and a few units in the field continued their resistance for some time and the war was not officially concluded until the spring of 1871, France had been effectively defeated in the first two months of the campaign. Even before the end of hostilities, King William of Prussia, surrounded by the German princes and ranking officers of the army, journeyed to the Palace of Versailles to proclaim the transformation of the German states, including those south of the Main, into the German Empire. It was as if the imperial crown, which Napoleon III had been forced to relinquish, was being picked up by the Germans, just as Napoleon I had taken the crown away from the Hapsburgs. Germany thus became unified in the course of three wars and as a result of Bismarck's coercive measures at home.

Internal unification

Force was used not only to forge separate states into unified nations, but also to cement closer internal bonds in existing states. When, for instance, the seven Catholic cantons of Switzerland united (1845) and threatened secession in protest against the centralizing and anti-Catholic tendencies of the liberal majority, the latter resorted to war, defeated the "extraordinary league" of the Catholic cantons (1847), and reorganized Switzerland with a greater centralization of power in the federal government.

Similarly in the United States, the Compromise of 1850 represented the last attempt at a peaceful solution to the questions of slavery and states rights. When Kansas and Nebraska were organized in accordance with the Act of 1854, violence dominated relations between pro- and antislavery settlers. Finally, the Americans resorted to civil war to determine whether the

Union or the rights of the separate states should prevail, and the federal government emerged from the conflict immensely strengthened.

In India, too, violence brought about major changes. In 1857, a majority of the natives in British military service rebelled, in part because of rumors that the new greased cartridges issued to them contained the fat of cows and pigs—the former considered sacred by Hindus, the latter repugnant to Moslems. After crushing this "Great Mutiny," the British government took away all political power from the East India Company and proceeded to destroy the remnants of the Mogul Empire. Although publicly renouncing further annexations in India, the British in effect began to enforce their rule on the entire peninsula; in 1877, Queen Victoria (1837–1901) was officially proclaimed "Empress of India."

Napoleon III, too, used force to impose political unity on France and to harvest external glory. Elected in December 1848, the ambitious Louis Napoleon began at once to assert his power. His political method made him in some ways a prototype for twentieth-century dictators: he slowly, but effectively, clamped down on all opposition, while seeking popularity by trying to please a wide variety of groups: clergy and workers, peasants and bourgeois. During his long exile in Germany, Switzerland, Italy, America, and England, he had written socialistic tracts, had twice attempted to "conquer" France with a small band of conspirators, and had grown accustomed to surrounding himself with unsavory intriguers. He was thus well prepared for political adventures. Three years after his election (December 1851), he used the army to stage a *coup d'état* and to destroy the republican regime. Many were killed and thousands imprisoned or exiled during clean-up operations. He then proceeded to give France a new constitution which, in fact, gave him dictatorial powers. Like Hitler, Napoleon liked to ratify the force he used through plebiscites, and the French, eager for stability, cast more than 95 per cent affirmative votes to approve his changes.

A year later, after a campaign tour through the provinces, he felt confident enough to transform the republic into an empire and have himself crowned as Emperor Napoleon III (another step ratified by plebiscite). In a campaign speech to promote his imperial designs, Napoleon tried to appease those who feared that "the empire means war." He insisted that he only wished "to conquer for conciliating the hostile parties." "I wish to conquer for religion, morality, and comfortable living." And he promised help to those who, "in the midst of the most fertile land in the world, can scarcely enjoy products of the first necessity." Actually, the Second French Empire came to stand for imperialistic wars abroad as well as war on poverty at home.

Like Charles de Gaulle a hundred years later, Napoleon III assumed that an active foreign policy would restore French prestige in the world. To this effect, French diplomacy made itself felt on a world-wide scale. A dispute with Russia over the protection of Christians in Turkey led to the Crimean

War, in which Anglo-French forces fought a costly campaign in the Crimea and ultimately forced the Russians to surrender the city of Sebastopol. From the Congress of Paris (1856) which concluded the war, France gained no tangible benefits, but Napoleon was proud to act as arbiter among the powers of Europe. Posing—probably quite genuinely—as champion of the oppressed nationalities, he interfered in favor of an independent Rumanian principality, which was ultimately created in 1878. His desire to aid nationalistic movements also brought France into the war against Austria in behalf of Piedmont (see p. 402). The annexation of Savoy and Nice, resulting from this war, constituted a new step toward French attainment of her "natural frontiers." But the war also presented the emperor with a dilemma: he permitted the Italians to incorporate the bulk of the papal states into the newly created Italian Kingdom, an event which displeased many Catholics. On the other hand, Napoleon sought to attract Catholic support at home— and please his wife, the beauteous and devout Empress Eugénie—by defending the pope against the Italian nationalists, who wanted to deprive the papacy of the city of Rome itself. His actions, unfortunately, alienated the Catholics and his erstwhile Italian friends alike.

During the same period, France joined England in carving out spheres of commercial influence in China. The French also initiated the religious, commercial, and military penetration of Indo-China, eventually leading to complete French control of the area.

Generally successful during the 1850's, Napoleon's foreign policy during the 1860's was an almost unbroken chain of failures. The Mexican adventure (1861–1867) revealed Napoleon's misjudgment of political realities. British, Spanish, and French use of naval and military forces to compel the Mexican government to honor its debts in 1861 was typical of the gunboat diplomacy of the period; but Napoleon's subsequent attempt to establish a French-sponsored empire in Mexico under Emperor Francis Joseph's brother Maximilian was clearly chimerical. His protégé's ignominious death before a Mexican firing squad (1867) did much to damage Napoleon's prestige.

Napoleon fared little better in Europe. Although he had posed as a friend of Poland, he stood by idly as Russian and Prussian troops suppressed the Polish rising of 1863. At every turn, he was outwitted by Bismarck's superior diplomatic maneuvers. In a series of badly calculated moves, he permitted the crushing of Austria, a potential ally, and failed to gain compensation in the Rhineland to keep step with Prussia's growth. Finally, he blundered poorly prepared into the debacle of the Franco-Prussian War.

At home, Napoleon was paternalistic, seeking to promote industry and to help the workers through charitable institutions and public works. Among the latter was the beautification of Paris, which included the construction of large boulevards, making the city a worthy capital of imperial splendor and at the same time facilitating military control against possible future uprisings and barricades. On the whole, France prospered economically under the Napoleonic regime.

Nevertheless, beginning in 1860, anti-Napoleonic opposition gathered momentum, inducing the harassed emperor to grant one concession after another and slowly to change his authoritarian administration toward greater liberalism in order to safeguard his dynasty. Industrialists were displeased by the sudden conclusion of a trade agreement with England (1860), sharply reducing tariffs; the clergy was alienated from the regime by Napoleon's Italian policy; labor, despite the emperor's paternalism, was irritated by legislation which still outlawed unions; liberals resented his authoritarianism; and Frenchmen as a whole rapidly became disillusioned by the lack of glory in foreign affairs. Seeing his support dwindle, Napoleon embarked on a cautious policy of dismantling his dictatorship. Debates in parliament were allowed to be published, budgetary controls were established, and labor was accorded the right to strike. Soon, more freedom was granted to the press and the holding of public meetings was authorized. In the end, Napoleon even made the cabinet in some measure responsible to parliament.

Despite these and other concessions, the emperor's popularity continued to wane while republicanism gained adherents. In the elections of 1869, Napoleon's parliamentary support obtained only a four to three majority over the combined opposition. When, in the next year, Napoleon was captured by the invading Prussians and a Parisian revolutionary mob forced the legislature to declare the downfall of the empire and the re-establishment of the republic, few Frenchmen regretted the loss of their emperor, although the middle class feared the vehemence of renascent Jacobinism. As the civil war of 1871 (see p. 416) was to show, France was socially and politically as disunified as ever, despite all of Napoleon's efforts at forced unification.

Expansion of Europe overseas

After a lull of several decades—caused possibly by the revolutionary wars in America and Europe—colonial expansion experienced a new burst of activity about the middle of the nineteenth century. Improvements in transportation and communications (through the invention of steamships and telegraphy), an increase in industrial needs for raw materials as a result of developments in technology and applied science, a sudden growth of population, and a revived missionary zeal may partly account for this new spurt in colonization. The change also involved a measure of power politics, as European nations began to gauge their international prestige in terms of colonial acreage. As the governments themselves began to take over control of colonial activities from the earlier, private companies, eighteenth-century colonialism turned into nineteenth-century imperialism, and national pride and prestige became intertwined with economic and political motives. (See Maps 25 and 26.)

There were many different types of expansion during this period. The French in Algeria, for example, attempted complete Europeanization by encouraging French settlements in the conquered area and by converting the newly acquired territory into three departments of continental France. In Egypt, on the other hand, the khedive was ostensibly allowed to retain his sovereign independence, while in fact Franco-British financiers gradually assumed control over the country. In India, the British slowly incorporated conquered areas into a wider political union, ultimately creating the British-controlled Empire of India. In Indo-China, the French found it preferable to retain the local emperor and the subordinate rulers and to establish a protectorate over the existing kingdoms, reserving all vital controls to the government of Paris. Finally, in sub-Saharan Africa, Europeans established outright colonies, in which the natives enjoyed no self-government and European officials exerted all local power. In addition, some states, such as Ethiopia, retained complete sovereignty while experiencing strong European penetration, just as Japan and China were opened to trade and missionary activities, but remained essentially independent powers.

European imperialism advanced through many paths. Great Britain found it useful to encourage local wars of national liberation, as, for instance, inciting the Egyptians against Turkey and the Indians against the Mogul dynasty, in order to bolster British power. Napoleon III liked to follow up a vanguard of missionaries with political and military infiltration; and the great powers in general, including America, used the pretext of commercial relations as an opening wedge for further penetration.

As a result, the world increasingly came under the direct impact of Western civilization, bringing material advantages, but also creating considerable friction and problems of adjustment.

SUGGESTED READINGS

General Works and the Revolutions of 1848

Binkley, Robert C., *Realism and Nationalism, 1852–1871* (Harper, 1963).

Bruun, Geoffrey, *Revolution and Reaction—1848–1852, A Mid-Century Watershed* (Van Nostrand, 1958).

Engles, Friedrich, *The German Revolutions, The Peasant War in Germany* and *Germany: Revolution and Counter-Revolution* (U. of Chicago, 1967). Socialist interpretation of 1848.

Kranzberg, Melvin, *1848—A Turning Point?* (Heath, 1959).

Namier, Lewis B., *1848: The Revolution of the Intellectuals* (Harper, 1964).

Robertson, Priscilla, *Revolutions of 1848: A Social History* (Harper, 1960).

Unification of Germany and Italy

Delzell, Charles F., *The Unification of Italy, 1859–1861: Cavour, Mazzini, or Garibaldi?* (Holt, 1965).
Eyck, Erich, *Bismarck and the German Empire* (Norton, 1964).
* Pflanze, Otto, *Bismarck and the Unification of Germany*, Vol. I, "Period of Unification, 1815–1871" (Princeton, 1963).
———, ed., *The Unification of Germany, 1848–1871* (Holt, 1968). Collection of essays.
Salvadori, Massimo, *Cavour and the Unification of Italy* (Van Nostrand, 1961).
Smith, Denis Mack, ed., *The Making of Italy, 1796–1866* (Harper, 1968). Collection of documents.
Taylor, Alan J. P., *Bismarck: The Man and the Statesman* (Random, 1967).

United States Civil War

Catton, Bruce, *The Coming Fury; Glory Road; Mr. Lincoln's Army; Never Call Retreat; A Stillness at Appomattox; Terrible Swift Sword; This Hallowed Ground: The Story of the Union Side of the Civil War* (Simon and Schuster, 1951–1967).
Commager, Henry Steele, *Fifty Basic Civil War Documents* (Van Nostrand, 1965).
*Randall, James G., and Donald, David, *The Civil War and Reconstruction* (Heath, 1961).
*Rolle, Andrew F., *The Lost Cause, The Confederate Exodus to Mexico* (U. of Oklahoma, 1965).
Stampp, Kenneth M., *The Era of Reconstruction, 1865–1877* (Knopf, 1965).
*Thomas, Benjamin P., *Abraham Lincoln,* (Knopf, 1952).

Second French Empire

Gooch, Brison D., *Napoleon III, Man of Destiny, Enlightened Statesman, or Proto-Fascist?* (Holt, 1963).
*Guérard, Albert Léon, *Napoleon III: A Great Life in Brief* (Knopf, 1955).
Osgood, Samuel M., *Napoleon III—Buffoon, Modern Dictator, or Sphinx?* (Heath, 1963).
Thompson, J. M., *Louis Napoleon and the Second Empire* (Norton, 1967).

Russia

Gooch, Brison D., *The Origins of the Crimean War* (Heath, 1968).
Mosse, Werner E., *Alexander II and the Modernization of Russia* (Macmillan, 1958).
Page, Stanley, W., ed., *Russia in Revolution: Selected Readings in Russian Domestic History Since 1855* (Van Nostrand, 1965).
Seton-Watson, Hugh, *The Decline of Imperial Russia 1855–1914* (Praeger, 1956).

CHAPTER XXIII

❧❧ *Final Consolidation of the Modern State* (1870-1914)

The modern state which had gradually emerged became firmly consolidated during the last part of the nineteenth century. It was essentially an industrial state controlled by a self-confident middle class, strongly influenced by Darwinism and Marxism.

The "power state"

During this period, the five great powers—England, Germany, the United States, France, and Russia—were all expansionist. Four of them were racing to industrialize, with only Russia lagging behind in this respect. In all five, there was intensified concentration of power in the hands of the central government, despite purported economic liberalism and growing democratization.

The United States

In the course of three generations, the United States rose from a minor state to the rank of a first-rate power. All indices during the second half of the nineteenth century point to America's phenomenal growth and concomitantly to the strengthening of the federal government. With some twenty-three million inhabitants in 1850, America had been less populous than Great Britain; yet by 1910, its population of ninety-two million was more than twice that of the former mother country. Similarly, the creation of new states from Minnesota and Kansas to the Pacific Coast between 1850 and 1912 more than doubled the size of the United States.

Industry, business, agriculture, transportation, and communications developed spectacularly, especially after the end of the depression of the 1870's. The basic industries thrived. Steel production rose from less than four million tons in 1870 to almost twenty-six million by 1910. During the same period, coal mining increased by seven thousand per cent, while lucrative new industries, such as the extraction of petroleum (1859), were started. The railroad nets in the East were vastly expanded and the transcontinental tracks were constructed with federal subsidies in order to tap the agricultural and mining wealth of the West. As industries grew, some of them combined into monopolistic trusts, and labor unions consolidated in the American Federation of Labor (1881).

Industrial growth as well as the Civil War greatly influenced the role of the federal government. Military occupation of the southern states and federal authority to "reconstruct" the ex-confederates enhanced the political, financial, and economic powers of Washington. During Grant's administration, the federal government even used legal and military measures in an effort to suppress conspiracies by the Ku Klux Klan and other secret, terrorist organizations in various states. With the establishment of the Interstate Commerce Commission (1887), the passage of the Sherman Anti-Trust Act (1890), and the adoption of almost prohibitive tariffs on industrial goods (1890), federal power made itself increasingly felt within the United States. At the same time, America's external might began to intrude into world affairs through her industrial and commercial growth and her expanding military potential.

Imperial Germany

The constitution which Bismarck devised for the united German states made the king of Prussia hereditary German emperor, with power over the military forces and foreign affairs, and ensured Prussian domination of the German Empire. The states were represented in the Upper House, which was endowed with considerable power. The Lower House, the Reichstag, elected by direct, universal suffrage, was given control over the budget and shared in the legislative process with the Upper House. There was, however, no ministerial responsibility, and the constitution contained no fundamental bill of rights. As planned by Bismarck, the German Empire was to be authoritarian, with just enough democratic trimmings to assuage public opinion.

United at last and self-confident after having won three wars in seven years and having seized from France the rich provinces of Alsace and Lorraine, the Germans embarked on a phenomenal industrial and material expansion. Within four decades, they came to rank among the first three nations in the world in the production of coal and iron, in volume of international trade, and in the size of their merchant marine. By 1910, they had constructed a railroad net of some 38,000 miles; Italy, by contrast, had completed only 10,000 miles of track. With industry and government working in close cooperation, the German government provided much financial and protective assistance to spur industrial growth. A large increase in population and a massive shift from agricultural to industrial employment turned Germany rapidly into a highly urbanized society.

Until 1890, Bismarck remained imperial chancellor and effectively directed the internal and external affairs of Germany. Political parties, a new phenomenon in German political life, were noisily active, yet exercised no substantial power. Their influence was diffused by division into six major and over a dozen minor parties, and the chancellor could deftly shift from one voting coalition to another in order to have his legislative and financial measures approved by the Reichstag.

Since essential political power was concentrated at the top—in the emperor and his chancellor, both supported by a large and loyal bureaucracy—Bismarck assumed that he could eradicate all opposition to the imperial regime. During the 1870's, he engaged in a protracted struggle with the Roman Catholic Church which was reasserting considerable power and influence under the conservative leadership of Pope Pius IX. It was as if the medieval struggle between emperors and popes had been resurrected with the recreation of the German Empire. Many who opposed Bismarck's centralizing policies and demanded more rights for minorities and for the federal states—Bavarians, Poles, Alsace-Lorrainers, for instance—rallied to the Catholic cause. Bismarck was successful in some of his measures: civil marriage was made compulsory and the jurisdiction of ecclesiastical courts was curtailed. But he failed in his over-all aims and finally gave up the struggle in 1878, a decision facilitated by the accession to the papal throne of the more conciliatory Pope Leo XIII (1878–1903).

The chancellor next turned his attention to the suppression of socialism. Anti-socialist measures were enacted, outlawing socialist organizations and publications and forbidding as "subversive" financial contributions to socialist causes. For the sake of upholding democratic principles, however, the Reichstag insisted that socialists as individuals be allowed to stand for election. Bismarck then sought to steal the thunder from workers' agitation by enacting a series of highly advanced social laws, covering health, accidents, old age, and invalidism. Although these measures placed Germany in the forefront for social security legislation, they did not slow down the growth of German socialism. By 1912, the Socialists constituted the largest party in Germany.

Two years after the impetuous William II (1888–1918) became emperor, he dismissed Bismarck and replaced him by a series of less capable chancellors. Economic and political pressure groups from among the large landholders of the eastern provinces, the Rhineland industrialists, and those with colonial and naval interests began to dominate the Reichstag and chart the political course of Germany. William II preferred sailing on his pleasure yacht to tending the day-to-day tasks of government. Spasmodically interfering in political affairs, he neither gave concise direction to German affairs nor permitted greater democratization of his regime, a step which might have disarmed the growing opposition. Industrial and commercial expansion continued unabated; educational facilities were vastly expanded; municipal services—including not merely public utilities but also cultural enterprises such as theaters, opera houses, and museums—were greatly extended; newspapers, magazines, and cheap paperbacked books helped engender ever more of a mass culture; and organized labor developed large unions. Yet there was restlessness among the masses, who resented their inability to acquire their share of political and socio-economic power.

While much of the middle class basked in prosperity and success in international endeavors, discontent mounted and provided a base for the ultimate overthrow of the imperial regime in 1918. Liberals and democrats, particularly in Prussia, resented the electoral and political restrictions which still deprived the lower middle class of effective political power. Although Bismarck had instituted universal suffrage for federal elections, the three-class vote still persisted in Prussia, and no reapportionment was effected, neither in Prussian nor in federal electoral districts, despite the tremendous urbanization that occurred after 1871. Socialists and proletarians were rebelling against disenfranchisement, miserable housing, low wages, militarism, and clericalism. Alsace-Lorrainers and Poles sought greater autonomy; and many Germans, while otherwise content, simply grew tired of the anachronistic, aristocratic pretensions of the imperial regime.

The Third French Republic

After the capitulation and capture of Napoleon III in September 1870 (see p. 409), control over France once again became divided between Paris and the provinces. Parisian socialists and republicans hoped to rouse the nation to revolutionary fervor in order to hurl back the Prussian invaders as had been done in 1792. However, most of the generals, as well as the bulk of Frenchmen in the provinces, were soon ready to accept the consequences of defeat and to negotiate peace with the Germans. Soon after the surrender of Paris, which had bravely endured a siege of over four months, a national assembly was elected to ratify peace terms and decide on a new political frame for France. Highly conservative in membership and eager to terminate the war, the assembly accepted Bismarck's proffered terms of peace, including the cession of Alsace and Lorraine, the payment of a war indemnity, and German military occupation of northern France, including the city of Paris, "in order to assure the execution of the contracted engagements by France."

Disgruntled by the humiliating conditions of peace and wary of the conservative character of the national assembly, Parisian radicals thereupon organized a revolutionary commune which seized control of Paris (March to May 1871). The *communards,* a motley group of Jacobins, socialists, communists, patriots, republicans, and national guardsmen heaped defiance on the "capitulators" of the national assembly and proceeded to carry out a social revolution in Paris. With the permission of Bismarck, who hardly cherished the possibility of triumphant radicalism, Adolphe Thiers, the assembly's provisional chief of state, launched the French army against the Paris Commune. The resulting civil war, one of the bloodiest and most vengeful in French history, ended with the annihilation of the *communards* and the execution, imprisonment, or deportation of thousands of radicals.

France thus entered the Third Republic in shattering confusion. The shock of the crushing defeat by Prussia engendered fear and hatred of the new German Empire and stirred French nationalistic passions, while the violent civil war produced a bitter gulf between the middle class and the proletariat. Moreover the Bonapartist regime left Frenchmen once again attracted to as well as repelled by the vision of "a strong man on horseback," a leader who might save France from internal chaos but might also plunge her again into destruction.

While Thiers arranged for payment of the indemnity to Germany so that German occupation forces would be withdrawn, the national assembly struggled to decide on a new regime for France. Had the monarchists been able to agree among themselves, royalism might well have been re-established in France. However, Bonapartists, Legitimists favoring the Bourbons and the white flag, and Orleanists opting for the grandson of Louis Philippe worked at cross-purposes, so that Thiers' compromise solution of a "monarchical republic" finally prevailed. Distrustful of constitutions, of which the French by then had had more than their share, the assembly adopted three organic laws which created a presidency with a term of seven years. The president was to be elected by a joint session of the two houses of parliament rather than by direct popular vote. Although members of the lower house (the Chamber of Deputies) were to be chosen by universal, direct manhood suffrage, the monarchists hoped that the new structure was sufficiently conservative to permit the eventual restoration of royalty.

During the next three decades, France vacillated between monarchism and republicanism. The usually more conservative Senate tilted with the more liberal and republican Chamber of Deputies, while several unsuccessful rightist coups were staged to undermine the republic. In 1877, President MacMahon (1808–1893), a marshal of France and veteran of many wars, acting as a shield for a monarchical restoration, dissolved the Chamber of Deputies and made an unsuccessful bid for dictatorial powers. A decade later, another ambitious "strong man on horseback," General Georges Boulanger (1837–1891), used the vengeful emotions of a war scare with Germany and the blotch of a financial scandal on the republican regime, involving the son-in-law of the president, in order to gather popularity among radicals as well as clericals and monarchists. On the point of staging a coup d'état that might have achieved its aim, he suddenly lost nerve in front of a dubious crowd and fled to Brussels.

As republicans, liberals, and socialists continued to gain ground, the conservatives made a final attempt to discredit the existing regime during the famous Dreyfus affair. In 1894, Captain Alfred Dreyfus (1859–1935) was arrested on charges of treason and sentenced to degradation and imprisonment in a penal colony. Although increasing evidence was soon brought to light to prove that Dreyfus had been convicted on the basis of forged documents, the Dreyfus case quickly ceased to be judicial matter and became a national issue pitting liberals, republicans, socialists, and anticlericals against conservatives, royalists, churchmen, and army officers. After the novelist Émile Zola (1840–1902) published his famous letter *I Accuse* to pinpoint the malfeasance of certain army officers—an act for which he was promptly convicted of libel—the Dreyfus affair almost precipitated a civil war. Liberals defending the republic and fighting anti-Semitism were ranged against the conservatives shielding the honor of the army, appealing to national patriotism, and hoping once again to restore the monarchy. In 1899, five years after the original trial, a conciliatory ministry came to power and marked the triumph of the republican elements by having Dreyfus pardoned —it was to be another seven years before he was exonerated of all charges, reinstated in the army, and promoted to major. Together with Dreyfus' rehabilitation (1906), the government ordered the transfer of Zola's ashes to the Pantheon. After this victory, the republican regime seemed firmly entrenched, although a new form of nationalistic royalism arose in the last decade before World War I when repeated international crises led the conservatives to call for a military, political, and moral regeneration of France.

Apart from the consolidation of the political system, other problems faced the Third Republic. The close ties between Napoleon III and the Roman Catholic Church had increased the anticlerical attitude of most republicans. After achieving control over the legislature (1880's), the liberals and Socialists launched their campaign to disestablish the Catholic Church. The Jesuit Order was redissolved, religious education forbidden in public primary schools, and divorce again permitted. Despite a *rapprochement* between the church and the republicans under Pope Leo XIII, the Napoleonic Concordat of 1801 was abolished in 1905. Complete separation of Church and state was enacted, with Protestants and Jews given the same legal standing as Catholics. Thus the republicans carried the day, although the role of the Church within the French state reappeared as a major political issue in the 1920's.

A second problem plaguing the republic concerned the position of the proletariat and the growth of socialism. Crushed by the defeat of the Commune in 1871, labor regained some confidence after an amnesty was proclaimed for all *communards* in 1880. Unions, which had existed for almost two decades, were given legal status in 1884, and, with the rapid growth of labor as a result of industrialization, groups of unions began to merge and finally organized the General Confederation of Labor (1895). Despite growing pressure, however, the government passed no social legislation, and the gulf between the proletariat and the middle class became more bitter and was marked by frequent violence and clashes between workers and the army.

The socialists, however, were not united. Four main groups and many splinters were developing their own political organizations: the revolutionary or Marxian socialists rejected all accommodation with the bourgeoisie; the evolutionary socialists showed more interest in using the ballot box, education, and the political machinery of the republic to further their ends; the anarchists, inspired by the Russian exile Michael Bakunin (1814–1876), who sought to terrorize and destroy the existing state through bombs and assassination, hoped that a new, more equitable society would arise from the ashes of the old; and finally the syndicalists, whose spokesman became Georges Sorel (1847–1922), believed that labor could attain power and social justice only by sabotaging industry and organizing strikes, including a general strike to paralyze the machinery of the state.

During the last prewar decade, as the conservatives were regaining strength and socialist power was growing, the moderates in the middle of the political spectrum lost influence. This phenomenon, presaging political instability, was to become characteristic not only of France but of many continental states during the twentieth century.

Russia

When Alexander II became tsar during the Crimean War, he soon recognized the shortcomings of his father's inflexible regime. Russia's poor showing in the war demonstrated how far she was lagging behind the Western powers. Her army, composed largely of illiterate serfs, proved worthless; lack of education and of industrial development made Russia weak in transportation and supplies; and the nation as a whole needed revitalization if she hoped to remain a first-rate power. Although no liberal, the tsar recognized the need for change and therefore embarked on a cautious program of reforms.

The government liberalized access to the universities, relaxed censorship laws, and rescinded restrictions on foreign travel, measures which helped breed a new generation of liberals and form a new climate of public opinion highly critical of tsarist autocracy. In 1861, he abolished serfdom, granting personal freedom to the peasants and transferring about 50 per cent of the cultivated land from the gentry to the village communities which were to parcel it out among the freed serfs. The expropriated landlords were to be compensated by the state, while the peasants, collectively responsible through the village community, were to reimburse the government over a period of forty-nine years. Although this act was an essential first step in turning the vast masses of serfs into citizens, little was done to give the free peasants economic security or civil equality. Soon thereafter, the reforming tsar granted a measure of self-government to provinces and municipalities, modernized the court system, introduced trial by jury, and attempted to revamp the army by introducing universal military service.

Alexander II's reforms raised the feeling of "participation" among the masses, gave hope to the intelligentsia, and spurred nationalistic fervor, including the Pan-Slav movement which aimed at incorporating all Slavic peoples into a single nation. Yet the reform program embodied no fundamental political changes, and tsarism remained autocratic. As a result, opposition groups acquired more boldness and organizational skill. Idealistic *narodniks* went among the peasants to propagate literacy and socialism; populists spread revolutionary terror and propaganda; nihilists and anarchists looked for a regeneration of Russia through bold, imaginative measures and terroristic violence to destroy the tsarist regime; and Pan-Slavs pressed for a more aggressive policy in the Balkans. Caught midway between his sympathies for reform and his attempt to suppress increasing terror and anarchy, Tsar Alexander finally fell victim to a terrorist bomb in 1881.

His successor, Alexander III (1881–1894), incensed by the murder of his father, became frankly reactionary. He attempted to enforce religious unity, repress all revolutionary activity, and eliminate Western influence. Yet, at the same time, Russia began to industrialize at an accelerated rate. As a result, her proletariat increased and became an important oppositional group to the antiquated tsarist regime.

The year 1894 saw the succession of the religious, well-meaning, but incapable Tsar Nicholas II (1894–1917), who was dominated to a great extent by his spiritualistic wife. During Nicholas' reign, accelerated industrialization and railroad building as well as an increase in trade and financial resources stimulated urbanization and gave confidence to the growing middle class. The hapless tsar found it difficult to adjust to such new conditions. While political parties opposing his regime began to organize, Nicholas sat obliviously on his throne or went sailing with his cousin, the emperor of Germany. Organized secretly in 1898 and directed by exiles from abroad, the Social Democrats soon split into two groups: the moderate Mensheviks who favored a massive, popular party devoted to gradual and, if possible, peaceful social change, and the radical Marxist Bolsheviks, led by Nicholas Lenin (1870–1924), who preferred a small, tightly organized, well-disciplined group of revolutionaries, ready to take instant action at an opportune moment. In 1901, the former *narodniks* and the populists organized the Social Revolutionary party which was more interested in the peasants than in the less numerous city proletariat. Working for the nationalization of the land, the Social Revolutionaries at first used terrorism but soon became more moderate. The bulk of the middle class, for their part, belonged to a fourth group, a liberal party that favored constitutionalism for Russia.

A revolution erupted in 1905 after Russian forces had been defeated in the initial stages of the Russo-Japanese War. Workers' riots in January induced the tsar to grant some concessions that were considered insufficient by liberals and socialists. New unrests, strikes, and mutinies in the army and navy during the summer persuaded Nicholas to agree to the establishment of a duma, or parliament, although not yet granting it any worthwhile powers. Thereupon the disgruntled opposition resorted to further pressure. In late October, a general strike threatened to paralyze the country, while in St. Petersburg a soviet, or council of workers, was organized to assume control of the revolutionary movement, a step soon imitated in other cities. The frightened tsar now made another round of concessions and took as prime minister the moderately liberal Count Sergei Witte (1849–1915), who had held various ministerial posts before and had actively furthered Russia's industrial expansion. While Witte took advantage of the conclusion of peace with Japan to rush back troops from Siberia in order to suppress the social rebellion, Nicholas issued his October Manifesto granting a constitution, a truly legislative duma, and guarantees for civil liberties.

The October Manifesto marked the high point in the government's yielding. Scared by the social demands of the lower classes, the middle class began to rally to the tsarist regime which thus felt more confident to use government troops for the suppression of the soviets and other revolutionary elements. By the time the first Duma met in the spring of 1906, Nicholas was reassured of his power. In a series of laws he made it clear that the jurisdiction of the Duma was to be strictly limited and that Russia was in fact to remain an autocracy, even more so than Bismarck's German Empire. Count Witte was dismissed and the more conservative elements gradually gained ground. Within the Duma, the liberals themselves split into Octobrists, those willing to abide by the October Manifesto, and the Constitutional Democrats, those who wanted parliamentary government and a limited tsardom in the style of Great Britain.

Little was accomplished by the first two Dumas, and in 1907, the tsar restricted suffrage in favor of the propertied classes, so as to ensure a more conservative membership for the third Duma. Although clamping down on all revolutionary activity, Nicholas permitted his new prime minister, Peter Stolypin (1863–1911), to institute a series of social and agrarian reforms, designed to bring Russia more in line with Western practices. Yet Stolypin's reforms, handed down from above in Bismarckian fashion, failed to satisfy the masses and the limitations placed on the Duma robbed the middle class of a true feeling of participation in government, so that dissatisfaction with the tsarist regime persisted. In 1911, Stolypin was assassinated, and, notwithstanding the tsar's efficient police, unrest increased as Russia was plunged into World War I.

Victorian England

During the reign of Queen Victoria, England, probably the most powerful nation in the world, acquired unprecedented, although unevenly distributed, prosperity through industrialization and financial growth. Her political life, punctuated with acrimonious debate, was nonetheless guided by compromise and the willingness to embark on slow, but steady reforms. Although there existed a number of smaller parties and splinter groups, such as the Radicals who favored absolute free trade and the Irish party battling for Irish Home Rule, the two major parties of Conservatives and Liberals developed an effective two-party system that was rare in European politics. Of twenty cabinets between 1835 and 1902, eleven were dominated by Liberals and nine by Conservatives, with the two parties trading off in power with almost clock-like regularity. The Liberals generally favored free trade, a greater concentration on developing internal prosperity, and more Home Rule for Ireland, whereas the Conservatives believed in protective tariffs, greater devotion to imperialist ventures, and rejected Home Rule for Ireland. Yet, as in the United States, principles were less important in determining party actions than were individual leaders. On some issues, the Conservative Benjamin Disraeli (1804-1881), for example, was more liberal than the Liberal William Gladstone (1809-1898).

The Victorian era was characterized by the emergence of a great number of famous and talented parliamentarians who dominated Britain's political life and nearly overshadowed the popular queen. Among them was Lord Russell, a leader of the Liberal party, an author of the Reform Bill of 1832 and sponsor of other reforms, who became prime minister twice during the mid-century. Influential, also, was Lord Palmerston (1784-1865), an ex-Tory turned Liberal, who served in the House of Commons for fifty-eight years and devoted his attention mostly to foreign affairs. At first sympathetic to the national aspirations of other states, such as Belgium and Switzerland, he later became stridently pro-English and served as prime minister for most of the last decade of his life. Another ex-Conservative who turned into a democratic Liberal was the powerful William Gladstone, four times prime minister between 1868 and 1894. Although successful in enacting various reforms—in education, army reorganization, and parliamentary elections through the introduction of the secret ballot—he failed in his Irish policy. Gladstone's political rival, whom he twice succeeded in the prime ministership, was the Conservative Disraeli, novelist by avocation and politician by inclination. Disraeli favored protectionism and vigorous colonial expansion, while seeking to modernize his party by sponsoring the second suffrage Reform Bill (1867) and undertaking needed social reforms.

Despite the imperialism which marked Victoria's long reign—Great Britain fought twenty-six colonial wars in six decades—internal democratization continued. The two Reform Bills (1867 and 1884) further extended suffrage and redistributed parliamentary seats, however, without establishing universal manhood suffrage. Property qualifications for members of Parliament were abolished, and the House of Lords, whose members were hereditary or appointed by the crown and were therefore not subject to the popular will, was gradually shorn of its power. In 1911, the Lords were deprived of all jurisdiction over financial measures and retained only a suspensive veto for other bills. Meanwhile municipal affairs were placed directly under local control, primary education was widely extended with attendance made free and compulsory, and the governmental and administrative powers of the Church of England were gradually reduced.

Despite the growth of unionism, the government was slow to undertake widescale social legislation until after the turn of the century, when many measures were passed, including workmen's compensation, old age pension, national insurance, and a minimum wage. Most of these bills were the work of Liberals, spurred by the entrance of labor into politics. Starting in the 1880's, the Fabian Society, guided by the playwright and novelist G. B. Shaw (1856–1950) and by Sidney and Beatrice Webb (1859–1947; 1858–1943), had actively advocated municipal socialism and the use of peaceful, political pressure to improve labor conditions. In 1900, various socialist groups joined the Fabians to create the nucleus of the Labor party, a separate group in Parliament dedicated to peaceful social reform.

The Victorian penchant for compromise, however, did not solve the Irish question. Hurt by famines and tired of the lack of progress in their nationalistic movement, the Young Irish party switched from peaceful means to revolutionary tactics in the 1840's. By the 1860's, terror and armed rebellion became the main weapons of the Fenian Brotherhood, a revolutionary group receiving most of its financial and moral support from Irish immigrants in the United States. Despite Gladstone's attempt to improve agrarian conditions by granting more rights to Irish tenant farmers working on land owned by English landlords, terrorism and murder continued. Neither was the Irish nationalist Charles Stewart Parnell (1846–1891), a member of Parliament after 1875, successful when he called for passive resistance by the Irish and used obstructionist and filibustering techniques in Parliament to force its members to vote for Home Rule. While the government used increasingly coercive measures to suppress the Irish revolutionaries, Gladstone made two unsuccessful attempts to secure passage of a Home Rule Bill. In the end, it was only in 1921 that southern Ireland gained dominion status within the British Empire, a first step in the ultimate emergence of an independent Republic of Ireland (1948).

The secondary powers

As was seen among the five great powers, no clear-cut relationship existed between democratic participation and the power of the state. The same was true of the lesser states. During the last decades of the nineteenth century, Japan rose to almost first-rate-power status through rapid industrialization and the adoption of Western institutions, but with very little democratization of the government. In the Scandinavian and Low Countries, on the other hand, popular participation was constantly expanded and social welfare improved with an aim of strengthening the population; but the five states—Norway separated from Sweden in 1905—did not reattain great international power.

Despite a seemingly propitious beginning, the Italian Kingdom floundered in internal troubles, economic problems, and social unrest. Through industrialization, including the construction of a large navy and merchant marine, and an adventuresome colonial policy, the new state gradually forced its way into the ranks of the great powers. Yet, as World War I was to show, Italian strength lacked a viable basis—a condition Mussolini vainly tried to alter in the 1930's.

Among the problems facing Italy were relations with the Catholic Church. After the annexation of Rome, the Italians passed the Law of Guaranties, granting sovereign and inviolable rights to the pope in his Vatican territory and assigning him an annual payment as compensation for loss of the Papal States. Pope Pius IX, however, refused to accept this offer which, he felt, would have made the papacy dependent on Italy. As a result, there was constant friction between ecclesiastical and governmental authorities about questions of education, the taxation of church lands, and the political life of Italian Catholics in general. Pius' successor, Leo XIII, urged Catholics in other states to support democratic movements, to establish their own Catholic political parties, and to switch their solicitude from conservative peasants to liberal workers, but he instructed the clergy to advise Italian Catholics to boycott political activities. With many Catholics abstaining from politics, Italian radicalism gained greater influence, a development hardly favorable to Catholicism. Hence, the next pope (Pius X, 1903–1914) relaxed the prohibition against Catholic participation in political life, a step that eventually led to the formation of the Popular Catholic party in Italy. Still, papal-Italian relations remained tense until the advent of Mussolini.

The political life of the Italian Kingdom was characterized by considerable corruption among ministers and parliamentary delegates. The Piedmontese constitution, which had been extended to all of Italy, was based on rather limited suffrage. Although the franchise was extended in 1881 and again shortly before World War I, lack of literacy and political experience among the voters made popular sovereignty difficult. Large groups—unreconciled republicans, conservative landowners, Catholics, poverty-stricken peasants in the South, and a growing number of socialists and syndicalists— were basically inimical to the royal regime. Moreover groups of nationalistic irredentists continued to agitate against Austria and sometimes against France for the "liberation" of Italian-speaking peoples in the Alps, in Dalmatia, Nice, Savoy, and Corsica.

In Spain, the reign of Ferdinand VII, who had been twice restored by foreign troops without learning to mellow his antiliberal stand, was followed by a fierce civil war and decades of unrest. The king had left the throne to his three-year-old daughter, Isabella II (1833–1868). Her cause was supported by the liberals against the conservatives and regionalists—Basques, Catalonians, and others who sought greater autonomy—who sided with the royal pretender, Ferdinand's ambitious brother, Don Carlos (1788–1855). Like the Spanish Civil War a century later, the Carlist War aroused much foreign interest. The English and French, in particular, were rooting for Isabella, since the regents had granted a constitution in her name. A British corps of volunteers was even dispatched to fight on her side.

Don Carlos' eventual defeat and exile brought no internal peace to Spain. New constitutions were devised—five in less than four decades—or existing ones rewritten to suit whatever group was momentarily in power. Governmental policy alternated between liberal and repressive legislation as well as between pro- and anticlericalism. Eight major insurrections occurred between 1840 and 1868, ending with the overthrow of Queen Isabella and the temporary establishment of a republic (1873–1874). The various uprisings were staged by many diverse groups: conservatives, Catalonians, supporters of the queen mother (Christina), and liberals who demanded the strict limitations of royal power embodied in the constitution of 1812.

After the renewal of civil war and the suppression of the republic by the army, a conservative constitution (1876) brought a semblance of order to Spanish politics. It left the new king in effective control while satisfying most moderate constitutionalists. A measure of industrialization, especially around Barcelona, and the development of mining in the former province of Navarre provided some economic development. Yet antagonism between liberals and conservatives soon reassumed its fierceness and the government lacked the strength to enforce conciliation, particularly after it had been discredited by the debacle of the Spanish-American War. Nor was the well-intentioned King Alphonso XIII (1886–1931) capable of imposing himself on his torn nation after he was declared of age in 1902. While army officers, clergy, and landlords remained strongly conservative, extremism grew on the left. Spain proved a fruitful recruiting ground for anarchists, some of whom made repeated attempts to assassinate the monarch. Agrarian socialists demanding land reform, Catalonian separatists seeking autonomy, industrial syndicalists, and anticlerical republicans were all becoming increasingly disenchanted with the existing socio-political regime. Hence it is surprising that the monarchy was not overthrown before World War I, as it was in neighboring Portugal (1910).

The apotheosis of materialism

During the last decades of the nineteenth century, materialism became enthroned in the realm of Western ideas as well as in the practices of Western society. Its growth during this period was accelerated by the phenomenal industrial production, by the seeming triumph of science, by the growing belief in evolution and progress, and by the spread of Marxism. Materialism also went hand in hand with capitalism which reached its high point after the enactment of limited liability laws (starting in the 1850's) had unleashed vast amounts of investment capital.

Immense strides were made in applied science, technology, and inventions bearing directly on the enhancement of material comforts in Western society. Perhaps even more important were the advances made in pure science which infused in Western man an almost infallible belief in science, gave him even greater self-confidence, and imbued him with a strong conviction in the inevitability of progress. Studies in thermodynamics, in astrophysics, in atomic values, and in microbiology seemed to reveal that all was ultimately matter and measurable and hence ultimately understandable to human beings.

The new god, science, and the reverence for the scientific method soon affected most disciplines. Earlier in the century, the Frenchman Auguste Comte (1798–1857), with his philosophy of Positivism, had already urged reliance on the scientific method in philosophy, history, and even religion. He regarded the social sciences, especially sociology, as the most important of the sciences inasmuch as their contributions to the solution of social problems were a vital step in human progress. Although in his later writings Comte deviated from his scientific views by propounding a social religion that was somewhat mystical, his Positivism remained highly influential. Scientific-minded scholars also undertook analytical studies of the Bible, questioning the feasibility of miracles and, in some instances, transforming Jesus from a god into a socially conscious, altruistic man. The social scientist Herbert Spencer (1820–1903), a voluminous writer, insisted that ethics, too, should have a scientific rather than a moral basis.

Spencer was not alone in proclaiming his belief in evolution and progress before the publication of Charles Darwin's (1809–1882) *On the Origin of Species by Means of Natural Selection* (1859). Geological studies —a new science in the nineteenth century—had already revealed that the earth had changed in the course of its long existence; evolution had also been suggested by research in biology and by the discovery of fossils of extinct animals. But the naturalist Darwin attempted to make evolution into a coherent theory, and, although parts of his hypotheses were later disproved,

Darwinism became one of the most influential forces in the later nineteenth century. His theory of natural selection, whereby higher species develop from lower forms through the survival and propagation of the fittest, strongly reinforced the current belief in progress and admirably suited the socio-economic thought of the day. Darwin's writings, including *The Descent of Man* (1871), in which he declared that man, too, had evolved from lower forms of animal life, naturally provoked much public outrage, particularly among strongly religious people. The theory of evolution seemed at first sight to contradict the concept of divine creation; it raised doubts concerning man's special place in the universe; and led to painful questions such as the difference between an animal soul and a human soul in an evolutionary development.

The combination of classical economics, economic liberalism, Bentham's utilitarianism, and Darwin's theory of natural selection resulted in Social Darwinism, sometimes called "rugged individualism" in America. Insisting that the individual knows best how to satisfy his own self-interest, Jeremy Bentham had suggested that the happiness of society as a whole consisted of the sum total of individual self-interest. Spencer, a firm believer in the rights of private property, added that "the poverty of the incapable . . . the starvation of the idle, and those shoulderings aside of the weak by the strong . . . are the decrees of a large, far-seeing benevolence." In view of nature's example, pity for the weak was considered unnatural and unprogressive, and advocates of social reform were deemed misguided. If evolution were left to take its natural course, the weak would fall by the wayside, in business as well as in ordinary life. As the American steel magnate Andrew Carnegie (1835–1919), later one of the greatest philanthropists, wrote in his essay "The Gospel of Wealth": ". . . while the law [of competition] may be sometimes hard for the individual, it is best for the race, because it insures the survival of the fittest in every department."

A different type of materialism was propagated by the militant Karl Marx. Living in exile and poverty in London, Marx studied voraciously and produced articles and books—some in collaboration with his friend and benefactor Friedrich Engels (1820–1895)—to spread his theories of scientific socialism. In his *Communist Manifesto* (1848), he outlined his economic and materialistic interpretation of history which explained the socio-political structure of society on the basis of how people, at a given time, earn their living, or, more technically speaking, of who owns the means of production. The analysis of economic life was thus made the basis for understanding historic developments. Moreover, Marx saw the moving force in history as an inevitable dialectic of material forces, the dialectic being the struggle between two opposing elements which is resolved in a synthesis of the two. In the social struggle, this dialectic, according to Marx, was most clearly evident in the class struggle which had dominated all history. The class struggle, itself a form of evolution, leads inexorably to the triumph of the proletariat. Just as the bourgeoisie had gradually supplanted the aristocracy in the acquisition of economic, and hence fundamental, power, so the workers now would "expropriate" the bourgeoisie. Marx and Engels saw as the role of the Communists the duty to guide the proletariat into becoming more class conscious and acquiring greater unity for the final struggle, in which the productive property would be taken away from the dominant bourgeoisie. Thereafter, a classless society would presumably arise, exploitation of man by man would cease, and universal peace would be achieved.

In the lengthy *Das Kapital,* an analysis of capitalism as implied in the title, Marx set up various economic laws from which he made deductions for the future. He insisted that the "surplus value" or profit—the differential between the cost of production and the actual sales price—should be distributed among the workers, since labor alone creates the "surplus value." So long as capitalists retained this profit, Marx declared, workers would be unjustly exploited and the capitalist system would ruin itself through recurrent industrial crises. A second law proving the inevitable doom of capitalism was that of the concentration of capital. More productive machines, new techniques, and wider international markets would lead to ever larger industrial complexes, while fierce competition would eliminate the smaller firms or end with their absorption by the trusts. The inevitable trend was obvious. An ever smaller number of big capitalists would be facing an ever growing number of expropriated proletarians, ready to overthrow capitalism. The capitalists were thus digging their own grave.

Marx's involvement in actual socialist organizations was not particularly productive. The First International, a loose organization of socialists from various countries which he helped found in 1864, was wracked with bitter internal disagreement. Marx conducted a vehement struggle against Michael Bakunin and his proposals for anarchistic decentralization. As a result, the anarchists left the International which was eventually dissolved in 1876. There were equally violent disagreements between so-called orthodox Marxists and evolutionary socialists. But despite these differences, Marx left an indelible imprint on the various socialist movements as well as on social thought in general.

Attacks on materialism

The middle classes naturally welcomed the material progress engendered by science and industry, with its greater comforts in everyday life, opportunities for wealth and luxuries, and prospects for better education and new careers. Despite slums and wretched working conditions, the benefits of progress also "trickled down" to the lower classes in the form of rising standards of living, better sanitation, and improved health services. Nonetheless, many bourgeois objected to the prevalent materialistic attitude, while the lower classes multiplied their attacks against the rugged individualists' lack of compassion.

Religious bodies felt compelled to take a stand on "modern" developments. Pope Pius IX issued numerous pronouncements against the dangers of unqualified rationalism, liberalism, secular concepts of ethics, and materialistic thought which were summarized in an encyclical of 1864, the so-called Syllabus of Errors. More important in the long run than such negative advice were the efforts of churchmen to use Christianity as a political weapon against materialism and Social Darwinism. An inspired French priest, F. R. de Lamennais (1782–1854), had already attempted during the Restoration period to bring the Church to the side of reform, but his efforts had been rejected by the papacy. In England, Charles Kingsley (1819–1875), an Anglican priest, denounced economic liberalism as un-Christian, since it stressed self-interest rather than love; on the other hand, he predicted the failure of socialism without the aid of Christian morality. From suggestions such as those of Lamennais and Kingsley eventually emerged the Christian Social movement. This trend gathered momentum in the wake of Leo XIII's encyclical *Rerum Novarum* (1891), which attacked materialistic socialism while trying to gain the confidence of the growing proletariat by placing the Church on the side of the weak and the downtrodden and by proclaiming that every human being deserves a decent living. In most Catholic countries this movement led to the formation, early in the twentieth century, of Christian Socialist or Christian Democratic political parties, dedicated to achieving a measure of social justice while stanchly fighting against social revolution.

Similarly, there was a strong revival among various Protestant groups determined to combat materialistic thought and religious indifference. Some preferred direct action, inspired by the highly successful Salvation Army (founded in 1878) with its dedication to social reform and active engagement in relief work in the slums of industrial cities.

Dismay with social conditions was voiced not only by reform-minded political groups but also by writers and journalists. Like the muckrakers during the presidency of Theodore Roosevelt who denounced predatory businessmen in popular magazines, Continental journalists and cartoonists attacked the prevalent system when censorship laws permitted such criticism. In literature, the Realism of the mid-century which had tried to depict things as they really were, without romantic embellishments or spiritual undertones, gave way to Naturalism. Émile Zola, one of the founders of French Naturalism, attempted to be scientifically accurate in his descriptions of life among the lower classes but at the same time sought to evoke human compassion. The German playwright Gerhart Hauptmann (1862–1946) tried to shock the audience in his early naturalistic dramas depicting contemporary social conditions.

Others in the arts and literature countered the materialistic realism of the period by evading it. Impressionist painters, symbolist poets, and neo-Romantic dramatists who rejected what one might call "obvious" reality looked for deeper meanings or escaped into a world of art for art's sake. In philosophy, where the Idealists were fighting a desperate rearguard action against growing Positivism, the German Friedrich Nietzsche (1844-1900), more a perspicacious commentator on the ills of his time than the formulator of a philosophic system, led the attack in a different direction. Highly contemptuous of the humility and "slave morality" he saw imbedded in Christianity, Nietzsche was equally repelled by the materialism of his age and called for the reassertion of intellectual and civilized values in a society guided by amoral, self-confident, rational supermen.

Although the dominant middle class slipped confidently into the twentieth century, comfortable in its possession of political power, economic wealth, and optimistic faith in progress, more and more portents appeared, presaging an end to the period of certainty. Psychologists began to suggest that man was not motivated solely by rational considerations; demagogues intimated that new ways might be found to change society; and recurring international crises made it doubtful that peace could forever be guaranteed by the existing military and diplomatic countervailing pressures.

SUGGESTED READINGS

United States and England

Brandes, Georg, *Lord Beaconsfield* (Crowell, 1967). On Disraeli.

Clark, G. Kitson, *The Making of Victorian England* (Atheneum, 1967).

Fine, Sidney, *Laissez Faire and the General-Welfare State, A Study of Conflict in American Thought, 1865-1901* (U. of Michigan, 1964).

Halévy, Elie, *The History of the English People in the Nineteenth Century,* Vol. I, "Victorian Years, 1841-1895"; Vol. II, "The Rule of Democracy, 1905-1914" (Barnes and Noble, 1961).

Magnus, Philip, *Gladstone, A Biography* (Dutton, 1964).

Mann, Arthur, ed., *The Progressive Era: Liberal Renaissance or Liberal Failure?* (Holt, 1963).

Young, George M., *Victorian England: Portrait of an Age* (Oxford U.P., 1964).

France and Italy

*Curtis, M. R., *Three Against the Third Republic: Sorel, Barrè, and Maurras* (Princeton, 1959).

Derfler, Leslie, ed., *The Dreyfus Affair—Tragedy of Errors?* (Heath, 1963).

———, *The Third French Republic 1870-1940* (Van Nostrand, 1966).

Jellinek, Frank, *Paris Commune of 1871* (Grosset).

Kedward, Roderick, *The Dreyfus Affair* (Barnes and Noble, 1966).

*Mack Smith, Denis, *Italy: A Modern History* (U. of Michigan, 1959).

Germany and Russia

*Bismarck, Otto von, *Memoirs* (Fertig, 1966).

Hamerow, Theodore S., *Otto Von Bismarck—A Historical Assessment* (Heath, 1962).

*Medlicott, William N., *Bismarck and Modern Germany* (Verry, 1965).

Pares, Bernard, *Russia—Between Reform and Revolution, Fundamentals of Russian History and Character* (Schocken, 1962).

Rosenberg, Arthur, *Imperial Germany: The Birth of the German Republic 1871–1918* (Beacon, 1964).

Yarmolinsky, Avrahm, *Road to Revolution: A Century of Russian Radicalism* (Macmillan, 1962).

Socialism, Darwinism, and other concepts

Barzun, Jacques, *Darwin, Marx, Wagner: Critique of a Heritage* (Doubleday, 1958).

Berlin, Isaiah, *Karl Marx: His Life and Environment* (Oxford U.P., 1963).

Dewey, John, *The Influence of Darwin on Philosophy* (Indiana, 1965).

Fremantle, Anne, *This Little Band of Prophets: The British Fabians* (New American Library, 1959).

Hayes, Carlton, *A Generation of Materialism, 1871–1900* (Harper, 1963).

Hofstadter, Richard, *Social Darwinism in American Thought* (Beacon, 1955).

Hook, Sidney, *From Hegel to Marx, Studies in the Intellectual Development of Karl Marx* (U. of Michigan, 1962).

Infeld, Leopold, *Albert Einstein: His Work and Its Influence on Our World* (Scribner, 1950).

Irvine, William, *Apes, Angels, and Victorians* (World). On Darwin and Huxley.

Kautsky, Karl, *The Dictatorship of the Proletariat* (U. of Michigan, 1964).

Mehring, Franz, *Karl Marx: The Story of His Life* (U. of Michigan, 1962).

Mills, C. Wright, *The Marxists* (Dell). Collection of documents from Marx to Mao.

Morgan, George A., *What Nietzsche Means* (Harper, 1965).

Rumney, Jay, *Herbert Spencer's Sociology* (Atherton, 1966).

Wolfe, Bertram D., *Marxism: One Hundred Years in the Life of a Doctrine* (Dell, 1967).

CHAPTER XXIV

❧ *The International Scene* (1870-1914)

Rugged individualism marked the international behavior of the powers during the four decades preceding World War I. In their drive for power, prestige, and economic advantages, many nations entangled themselves in ever more complicated nets of alliances for the supposed purpose of establishing or maintaining a balance of power. It was of course always hoped by the statesmen that the "balance" was in favor of their own nation. At the same time, as the world grew smaller through better transportation and communication and as international friction increased in intensity, there were more efforts at improving international cooperation and finding new ways of curbing the selfish individualism of the powers.

Rivalry and solidarity in imperialism

European overseas expansion reached its zenith during this period. Although Asia and Africa were to reject European domination less than a century later and throw off colonialism, world civilization after 1870 became essentially "European." This Westernization applied especially to material fields—industry, commerce, transportation, communication, and to a large extent even to dress, social ideals, and political theories. Although many Asians and Africans might hesitate to admit it, progress came to be measured by European standards. Westernization outside of Europe was much less evident in art, religion, literature, and modes of thought. Hence, many Asians and Africans were faced by a painful dichotomy between spiritual and material conditions of life.

Clashes of imperial interests

The race for the acquisition of colonies and spheres of influence led to many clashes among the powers. In most cases, the conflicts were eventually settled by bilateral agreements, although they usually left a residue of bitterness and suspicion between the contestants. A few examples must suffice to show the nature of these confrontations. (See Map 25.)

During the 1880's, Great Britain became increasingly interested in East Africa, an area hitherto left vaguely within the sphere of Portugal. When the Germans began their penetration of Tanganyika, the British became worried about the future status of Lake Victoria, one of the important sources of the Nile River. Moreover, the British hoped to obtain access to a contiguous strip of territory from Egypt to their expanding holdings in South Africa, perhaps eventually to build a Cape to Cairo railroad. After several years of Anglo-German tension (1885–1890), the two states settled their differences by treaty. Germany retained Tanganyika and received the island of Heligoland in the North Sea, which Britain had obtained from Denmark in 1815. Great Britain, by then firmly entrenched in Kenya, was allowed to take Uganda.

To the North, Britain's determination to control the Lower Nile and safeguard her strategic position at Suez almost led to war with France. Starting in the 1820's, the Egyptians had gradually penetrated into the Sudan and expanded their dominion up the Nile and along the Red Sea coast. Meanwhile, Britain and France had clashed over control of Egypt herself, especially after the vital Suez Canal was opened to traffic in 1869. Despite joint Anglo-French financial supervision over Egypt, officially confirmed in 1876, England gradually attained the dominant voice in Egyptian affairs and assumed military and financial control of the state in 1882. Hence, Egyptian penetration into the Sudan gradually involved Great Britain. In 1883, however, the Sudanese rebelled, massacred a small British force, and made themselves quasi-independent. The British did not contemplate the reconquest of the Sudan until the French suddenly showed interest in the area. During the mid 1890's the French entered the Sudan from West Africa in order to reach the upper Nile and perhaps conquer a strip across central Africa from the Atlantic to the Red Sea, while the Ethiopians planned to expand to the Nile from the southeast. Hence, British and Egyptian forces were again sent into the Sudan. In 1896, they defeated the Sudanese but found a French contingent already in possession of Fashoda, a small town on the upper Nile. Under threat of war (1898), the British forced the French to withdraw their forces from Fashoda and France agreed in 1899 not to extend her African possessions to the Nile and to leave the Sudan in Anglo-Egyptian hands.

Dispute over possession of Tunisia for years embittered Franco-Italian relations. Nominally under Turkish suzerainty but relatively independent under its own bey, Tunisia had been placed under joint Anglo-French-

Italian financial control in 1869. In 1878, however, when Great Britain acquired the island of Cyprus, France was compensated by receiving tacit approval for her conquest of Tunisia. With the possession of Algeria the French had become Tunisia's next-door neighbor. On the other hand, the Italians, with many nationals residing in Tunis which lay not far off from Sicily across the narrow point of the Mediterranean, felt an equal justification for colonial penetration. To thwart Italian designs, the French invaded Tunisia in 1881 and forced the bey to accept a French protectorate, much to the dismay of Italy. Almost two decades of tension between the two nations ensued, until they finally reached an agreement (1900) recognizing the *fait accompli* in Tunisia. At the same time, the Italians agreed to give France a free hand in Morocco, and the French consented to Italy's conquest of Tripolitania, which the Italians undertook successfully in the course of a war against Turkey in 1911.

Persia was the object of a different type of European encroachment, involving deep-seated rivalry between Great Britain and Russia. British interest in Persia dated from the early nineteenth century. Persia's proximity to India, her geographic location along the trade route to the East, prospects of commercial advantages, and fear of Russian penetration were all factors of British concern. Russia, on the other hand, in her constant search for warm water ports with free access to the high seas had begun to penetrate beyond the Caucasus during the Napoleonic period and had started to expand southward on both sides of the Caspian Sea, while the British advanced eastward from Afghanistan. Toward the end of the nineteenth century, Russia and Great Britain engaged in open competition for control of the Persian army, for concessions to exploit mineral and commercial rights, and for the collection of Persian customs duties in return for financial loans to the tottering Persian government. The discovery of oil in Persia in 1901 and the repeated revolutions within the Persian government after 1905, combined with a growing fear of German penetration into the Near East, finally induced Russia and England to settle their differences. Within the framework of the Anglo-Russian Entente of 1907 they agreed to reserve northern Persia to Russian penetration, while assigning southern Persia as Britain's sphere of influence. (See Map 26.)

A final example of colonial confrontation involved Germany's commercial interests in the Near East. In 1888, with the railroad from Budapest to Constantinople just completed, the sultan of Turkey requested a consortium of German financiers and construction companies to extend the rail system to Ankara in central Turkey. This request delighted Emperor William II who soon thereafter proclaimed during an official visit to Turkish Palestine that the Germans were "the friendly protector of the three hundred million Moslems in the world," a prospect which alarmed Russia and Great Britain. After completing the railroad to Ankara (1892), the German firms were given further contracts to extend the system ultimately to Baghdad, an area quite close to Persia which was then being infiltrated by Russia and England. This so-called Berlin to Baghdad Railroad became a considerable irritant in international relations until shortly before World War I, when Germany assured Great Britain that it would not attempt to extend the railroad to the Persian Gulf.

International solidarity in imperialism

Despite frequent clashes of imperial interests, the Western powers also displayed occasional flashes of solidarity in their colonial enterprises. Relative cooperation was particularly noticeable. vis-à-vis China, where Great Britain had acquired Hongkong in 1842 and had forced the opening of certain coastal cities to British trade. During the 1840's, other powers, including the United States, embarked on the commercial invasion of China, aided by the growing influx of Catholic and Protestant missionaries. After the midcentury, joint intervention by two or more Western powers became customary. An Anglo-French expedition seized several Chinese cities during the T'ai P'ing Rebellion, forcing the Chinese to grant further commercial privileges to England, France, Russia, and the United States.

At the end of the century, Japan joined the powers in penetrating China. As a result of victory in the Sino-Japanese War of 1894–1895, she obliged China to cede Formosa and to abandon her claims to Korea, which fell first to joint Russian and Japanese control, ultimately to sole Japanese control. Thereupon Russia, France, and Germany intervened together to prevent a further crippling of China by Japan, while France, Russia, Germany, and Great Britain helped one another gain further commercial concessions from a weakened China.

In the course of partitioning Africa, many agreements were made concerning colonial frontiers. In 1884, a fifteen nation conference that included the United States convened in Berlin to discuss trade and slavery in the Congo and to define the extent of the Congo territories which the king of the Belgians claimed as his personal possession. The convention agreed to suppress slavery in the Congo and enacted regulations concerning trade in the area. Three years later (1887), England, Italy, Spain, and Austria-Hungary concluded the Mediterranean Agreements stipulating no alteration of the *status quo* in the Mediterranean and Black Sea areas without prior joint consultation. The agreements were designed to bolster the Ottoman Empire against further encroachment by Russia or France in the Near East as well as in North Africa. The question of Morocco also received the attention of the powers. In 1880, most of the European nations and the United States signed a convention at Madrid, promising to uphold Moroccan independence and an open door policy for trades. When the Germans objected to French penetration of Morocco in 1905 and Franco-German relations reached a point of crisis, an international conference met at Algeciras which reaffirmed Moroccan independence but awarded Spain and France the right to police Morocco, an opening wedge which led to gradual French and Spanish control of the country. International agreement thus helped avert a Franco-German clash. (See Map 23.)

The changing balance of power

Industrial and population changes caused a significant shift in the balance of power between 1870 and 1914, requiring readjustments in international alignments. Britain, France, Russia, and even Italy recognized the need to reappraise their foreign policies, especially during the last decade and a half before World War I. Germany and the United States, however, failed to perceive this need, perhaps because both had only recently become world powers and were overconfident with the blissful exuberance of youth. Germany stuck tenaciously to the Triple Alliance (see p. 436) which Bismarck had designed for the protection of the Continental German Empire he had created; yet this alliance with two other land powers possessing only insignificant navies could hardly satisfy Germany's needs after she had herself become a colonial world power. Similarly, the United States remained isolationist in spite of having obtained colonies in the Far East (the Philippines, Guam, and other islands) and having developed world-wide commercial interests. Germany's and America's failure to reassess their foreign policies was to become one of the dilemmas in international relations during the pre-World War I era.

The growing nations

The shift in the balance of power derived largely from the growing power of Germany, the United States, and Japan, as well as from the continued strengthening of Great Britain and her empire. To some extent, the changes were demographic. At the time of the Franco-Prussian War, Germany had forty-one million inhabitants (of whom 4.7 million males were between the ages of twenty and thirty-four and therefore considered as military manpower) as compared to thirty-six million for France (with 4.4 million in military manpower). Yet by the outbreak of World War I, Germany had increased in number to sixty-four million (with 7.7 million of military manpower), whereas France had grown to only thirty-eight million (with 4.5 million of military manpower). Industrial indices reveal similar changes. In 1890, Germany produced 2 million metric tons of steel and England 3.5 million tons; by 1910, Germany's production had risen to 13.5 million tons and England's to only 6.5 million.

After the creation of the German Empire in 1871, Bismarck sought to maintain peace in Europe out of fear that any war might provoke a European coalition against Germany and endanger the fruits of unification and of the Franco-Prussian war. To ensure peace for Germany and safeguard Germany's paramount position in Central Europe, Bismarck aimed at keeping France isolated to prevent a possible French war of revenge. He encouraged French expansion overseas, particularly in areas where France might clash with Great Britain. At the same time, the German chancellor contracted alliances designed to keep Austria and Russia from allying themselves with France, so that Germany would be spared a possible two-front war.

As the focal point of his system, Bismarck chose Austria-Hungary as a partner in the Dual Alliance of 1879, a defensive agreement aimed primarily at protecting both countries against a possible Russian attack. His choice of Austria, motivated in part by his concept of solidarity among German-speaking peoples and his desire to prevent Austrian support for the anti-Prussian Catholic forces inside Germany, also helped prevent a Franco-Austrian *rapprochement.* Moreover, such a pact facilitated German commercial penetration of the Balkans. Furthermore, the pact may have resulted from Bismarck's overestimation of Austro-Hungarian power. The Dual Alliance, which lasted until the end of World War I, proved at first useful to Germany, but in the long run it embroiled Germany needlessly in the troubled Balkan affairs, forced her to choose between either Russia or Austria as an ally, and finally turned into a liability during World War I when Austrian weakness hampered Germany's war effort.

In 1882, Bismarck concluded with Italy and Austria the Triple Alliance which was periodically renewed until World War I. During the first two decades of its life, this alliance served Germany as added protection against France. It also strengthened Italy in her dispute with France over Tunisia and in the Franco-Italian trade war and reduced Italian fears of renewed French intervention in support of the papacy. But once Italo-French differences had been adjusted and Italian irredentist demands on Austria increased, Italy became a lukewarm partner in this alliance. Moreover, the Italians realized that in order to acquire colonies they needed the friendship of a large naval power, such as England or France, rather than a land power like Germany. As a result of Italy's change of policy, the Triple Alliance was of no value to Germany in 1914.

Crucial for Germany, as Bismarck saw it, were her relations with Russia. In view of Germany's past experience and the nightmare of a possible Franco-Russian alignment, he deemed it essential to maintain friendly relations with Russia. Yet constant Austro-Russian clashes over expansion in the Balkans complicated Bismarck's task. After Russia had defeated Turkey in 1878 and forced the Turks to cede territory to Serbia and to permit the creation of a large Bulgarian state, Bismarck had to decide whether to support such Russian expansion or to support Austria and Britain. Both of them were opposed to Russian growth through the establishment of satellite Slav states. At the congress of Berlin (1878), where the powers persuaded Russia to reduce her demands, Bismarck sided against Russia. In the following year, he concluded his Dual Alliance with Vienna. In 1881, he succeeded in repairing Russo-German relations by forming the Three Emperors' League among Germany, Austria, and Russia. When this league broke apart during the next Balkan crisis (1885–1888), Bismarck negotiated a bilateral pact with Russia, the so-called Reinsurance Treaty (1887), which stipulated benevolent neutrality in case either state became involved in war. On the basis of these treaties, Bismarck considered Germany relatively safe along her eastern and southern borders. Since relations with England remained fairly friendly, except for some colonial friction during the 1880's, Bismarck thus felt confident that he could deal with France from a position of strength.

Although there was much German commercial invasion of Africa during the 1870's, Bismarck was Continental-minded and saw no particular need for a German colonial empire. Yet pressure by merchants, industrialists, shipbuilders, missionaries, and nationalists forced Bismarck to go along with colonial adventures. During the mid-1880's, Germany suddenly seized vast areas in Africa and the Pacific islands and became, within the span of two and a half years, the third largest colonial nation following England and France. This propulsion into imperialism turned Germany into a world power.

After Bismarck's dismissal in 1890, German foreign policy changed significantly. William II was eager to demonstrate Germany's standing as a world power and to prove, as he explained, that "on the seas and in distant lands, no great decisions should be made without Germany and without the German Emperor." Consequently, to the consternation of the older powers, Germany made herself felt on a global scale—in China and the Pacific, in Africa, the Near East, and Latin America. The Germans exchanged industrial exports for agricultural imports and thereby achieved considerable influence over other countries through commercial infiltration, particularly in the Balkans and Turkey. After 1898, they began to enter the naval arena with the construction of a large fleet which soon led to an acute naval rivalry with Great Britain. Meanwhile Germany gradually increased her army and perfected her armaments in a growing military race with France.

William II's conduct of foreign affairs, however, lacked the perspicacity of Bismarck's. He failed to renew the Reinsurance Treaty with Russia when it expired in 1890, and, although Russo-German relations remained intermittently friendly, especially after William's cousin and friend Nicholas II ascended the Russian throne, William permitted Russia to drift into the arms of France, with disastrous consequences for Germany's military security. Relations with England followed a similar course. Despite attempts at friendship, William's tactless behavior frustrated all attempts at a *rapprochement*. Anglo-German relations were further clouded by increasing commercial and naval rivalry and by King Edward VII's (1901–1910) distaste for his German nephew who, according to the British king, "must always strut about like a peacock." In the end, England, too, drifted into the anti-German camp. As a result, Germany felt increasingly isolated and feared encirclement by hostile powers, a condition which in turn led the Germans to increase their armaments. A vicious circle of international suspicions thus developed into one of the causes for World War I.

Great Britain, meanwhile, attempted to stay clear of Continental involvements except when her trade or the freedom of the seas seemed threatened. She championed the independence of Denmark, the Low Countries, and Turkey, since all three commanded control over important international waterways. Her insistence on keeping open the Turkish Straits and on preventing Russia from gaining a foothold in the Mediterranean entangled her in every Balkan crisis between 1875 and World War I, but she steadfastly refused to enter into a formal alliance with any Continental power.

Britain's strength was based not only on her navy, her industrial production, and her financial wealth, but also on her colonial empire. The English learned how to develop considerable imperial solidarity among their subject peoples, so that they could rely on colonial armies in time of emergencies to supplement their own insufficient resources in manpower.

Relations with the Boers in South Africa differed somewhat from this usual pattern, since the Boers were themselves Europeans, the descendants of Dutch settlers who had colonized the area in the seventeenth century, and were accustomed to a measure of self-government. After Great Britain had obtained Cape Colony from Holland in 1815, English immigrants began to expand the colony and attempted to impose English law and culture on the local population. Resentful of the British, many Boers moved inland and northward and eventually founded the Orange Free State and the Transvaal. Starting in the 1840's, disagreements between British and Boers led to occasional violence. The Boers objected to Britain's lenient policy toward the black population and to the importation of labor from India; they also wanted free access to the sea, which the English denied them; and they feared losing their independence through the constant expansion of British power and influence. Tension increased after rich diamond deposits, discovered near the Orange Free State (1867), were taken over by the British mining interests. The great gold strikes of 1886 in the Transvaal merely added to the friction. (See Map 25.)

After Paul Kruger (1825–1904) became president of Transvaal, Boer resistance against the British hardened. At the same time, British economic and political expansion in South Africa came under the influence of the aggressive Cecil Rhodes (1853–1902), whose De Beers Company absorbed most competing mining companies to gain control of the diamond industry in 1888. As leader of the British South Africa Company, founded in 1889 to develop the area north of the Transvaal (which later became Rhodesia), and as prime minister of Cape Colony (1890–1896), Rhodes hoped to force the Boers into cooperation and federation with the British. Furthermore, since Kruger and the Boers refused to extend voting rights to non-Boers, although the latter comprised a majority of the European population, the British finally decided to try to oust the Boer minority before it became too powerful as a result of profits from its gold mines. Hence, Rhodes secretly encouraged an armed raid by members of the British South Africa Company and others into the Transvaal to foster a revolution against the Kruger government. The raid proved unsuccessful, but four years later full-scale war erupted between the British and the Boers. In this Boer War (1899–1902) the British eventually defeated the forces of the Transvaal and the Orange Free State, a victory leading to the creation of the Union of South Africa (1909). Despite a generous peace settlement, the Boers remained embittered. Nonetheless, the new Union of South Africa sided faithfully with England during World War I.

Until the turn of the century, England remained comfortable in her "splendid isolation." She used her powerful fleet to exert diplomatic pressure wherever and whenever she deemed it advantageous. In accordance with the Naval Defense Act of 1889, naval construction was to keep the British fleet at least as strong as the combined strength of the next two strongest naval powers. So long as the new German Empire served as a welcome counterbalance to France on the Continent, British diplomats did not object to German growth. However, once Germany entered the naval arena while at the same time overshadowing French land power, British distrust of German intentions began to color her foreign policy. In addition, frequent friction with France about colonial acquisitions and apprehension because of Russian expansion—in Turkey, Persia, Afghanistan, India, and the Far East —dominated the considerations of the British Foreign Office.

Britain's policy changed markedly after Victoria's death and the accession of the Francophile King Edward VII. Recognizing the rising power of Japan in the Far East, the British concluded the Anglo-Japanese Alliance of 1902, in part to bolster Japanese determination to thwart Russian encroachment on China. Two years later came the conclusion of the Anglo-French Entente (1904). After decades of friction, the two nations decided to settle their colonial differences and to cooperate henceforth in international affairs (see p. 443). In 1907, Russia and England, too, agreed to come to terms in the Anglo-Russian Entente by setting limits to their respective spheres of influence in Asia. Within the brief span of five years, Great Britain thus acquired an ally in the Far East and partners, if not formal allies, among two of the five great powers in order to ensure her continued hegemony—an arrangement many German diplomats failed to appreciate during the years approaching World War I.

After the Civil War, the United States began to expand beyond her continental borders, even before the process of "filling in" between the Atlantic and the Pacific had been completed. The purchase of Alaska from Russia (1867) stimulated American interest in the Pacific. Americans infiltrated the Samoan Islands in the 1870's and intervened in Hawaii. After prolonged congressional debate over the wisdom of such a move, the Hawaiian Islands were annexed in 1898. To Latin America the United States pledged inter-American cooperation in the Pan-American Union formed in 1889, but she soon began to interfere more actively in Latin-American affairs. Proclaiming its intention of preventing violation of the Monroe Doctrine, Washington proposed itself as arbitrator between Venezuela and Great Britain in a border dispute of 1895. Thereafter, with the Spanish-American War and Theodore Roosevelt's aggressive Latin-American policy, United States' intervention in Central America and the Caribbean became more and more frequent.

The Spanish-American War of 1898 was probably the most significant event in America's swing into imperialism. Spain's prolonged attempt to suppress revolution in Cuba irritated those Americans who sought to uphold the gospel of the Monroe Doctrine. The sinking of an American battleship at Havana and the machinations of the warhawk press eventually induced President McKinley to declare war on Spain. In their first war against a major European state in almost a century, the Americans defeated the Spanish on land and at sea in the brief span of three and a half months. As a result, United States forces occupied Cuba until the island was deemed ready for self-government. Moreover, the United States annexed Guam, the Philippines, and Puerto Rico and had to develop an imperial policy for overseas possessions which had not been foreseen in the United States Constitution.

Thus launched into territorial expansion, the United States awoke to find herself a world power at the beginning of the twentieth century. In 1900, she intervened in China, and under Theodore Roosevelt, American presence became felt in many areas. In order to build the Panama Canal, a project long discussed and planned, Roosevelt encouraged the Panamanians to secede from Colombia (1903), to establish an independent republic and grant America the right to the Canal Zone for building the canal. Roosevelt also used United States troops to occupy Santo Domingo for the ostensible purpose of collecting customs to pay foreign creditors; he acted as mediator between Russia and Japan to terminate the Russo-Japanese War, and helped convoke the Algeciras Conference to avoid a Franco-German confrontation over Morocco.

While American military and diplomatic power thus appeared upon the world stage, American business expanded into the markets of the world and turned the United States into one of the foremost commercial nations. Yet, despite this change in military, diplomatic, and commercial status, America clung to a policy of isolation and refused to join alliances or make commitments that might impair her absolute freedom of decision.

During the first half of the nineteenth century, the Western nations had attempted to establish trade relations with Japan, but the Japanese had remained unreceptive and on the whole hostile to Western ideas. After the

United States had broken through this barrier (Commodore Perry's mission in 1853), trade relations were gradually set up with other nations. This "opening of Japan" evoked serious internal dissension, for many Japanese resented the subsequent influx of Western influence. Certain clans from southern Japan used the apparent inability of the shogunate to deal effectively with the foreigners as rationale for demanding the downfall of the Tokugawa family that dominated Japan. To achieve their aim, they called for the re-establishment of imperial authority. This movement led to a radical change in Japanese institutions which opened a new era for Japan in 1868.

In that year, the shogunate was destroyed and the emperorship restored to its traditional role as the ultimate symbol of political power. With the imperial capital moved to Tokyo, Japan was launched on a course toward modern nationhood. The leaders of the same clans who had at first objected to foreign intrusion now began to replace the old, neo-Confucian, feudal order with Western patterns of social, economic, and political organization. A period of almost frantic Westernization ensued. Industrialization, partly subsidized by the state, was pushed with great vigor. The navy and army were "modernized," based on universal military service rather than on reliance upon the former warrior class. Western legal and financial practices were adopted, the Western calendar was introduced, and Western governmental institutions gradually evolved. In 1889, the emperor proclaimed a constitution, based on a modified version of the German imperial constitution of 1871. It set up a diet of two houses, the lower house being elected by a restricted suffrage which permitted about one per cent of the population to vote. Despite such nods toward democracy, essential political power was retained by power-cliques operating behind the throne.

Westernization, industrialization, and the expansion of trade greatly strengthened Japan and catapulted her into the maelstrom of world politics. During the 1890's, she terminated the extraterritorial rights of foreigners in Japan; thus she completed her transformation from a semicolonial to a sovereign state. After a successful war against China (1894–1895), from which the Japanese gained Formosa, they began to challenge the Russians over spheres of influence in Korea. In 1900, Japan assumed the role of a world power by joining Britain, France, Germany, Russia, and America in suppressing the Boxer Rebellion in China. The alliance with England in 1902 not only increased her international stature but also strengthened her determination to check Russian expansion in the Far East. Two years later, the Japanese fought and defeated Russian land and naval forces. This astonishing victory over Russia gave Japan a green light for taking over Korea, which she annexed in 1910. Moreover, Russia ceded to Japan the southern half of Sakhalin Island, an area which the Russians took back in 1945. With her appetite whetted through her successful rise to the status of a world power, Japan then continued her imperialistic ventures with the gradual penetration of Manchuria—a step that caused anxiety on the part of some Americans but tacitly delighted the British Foreign Office which did not wish to see Manchuria fall into Russian hands.

The static nations

France and Russia both remained first-rate powers but failed to gain significantly in strength and therefore experienced a relative decline, particularly vis-à-vis Germany. Yet neither state fully grasped the significance of this change. In the seventeenth and eighteenth centuries, France had successfully fought against coalitions including most of the European states. Yet by 1900, she was no longer strong enough to stand up to Germany alone. In Napoleon's day, the French had accounted for 16 per cent of Europe's population; by 1914, barely 10 per cent of Europeans were Frenchmen. Despite active industrialization, France lagged significantly behind Great Britain and Germany in the production of coal and pig iron, in volume of trade as well as in the construction of railways.

Two main themes dominated French foreign policy: the attainment of security against Germany and the expansion of the French colonial empire. Several serious crises in Franco-German relations provoked among French nationalists frequent calls for a war of revenge against those who had deprived France of Alsace-Lorraine. Similarly, some Germans urged another campaign against France before the French might recuperate sufficiently from the defeat of 1871. Despite occasional attempts at a *rapprochement,* mutual suspicion between the two powers grew after the turn of the century and led to an unhealthy race in armaments.

On the other hand, once Russo-German relations had cooled with the dismissal of Bismarck, France eagerly courted Russian friendship in order to break out of her isolation and to gain protection against Germany. French loans to Russia, reciprocal visits by the fleets of the two nations, and drawn-out negotiations led to the conclusion of a pact (1894) which stipulated mutual military aid in case of attack by the Triple Alliance. Revised and strengthened several times during the next two decades, this treaty—the first step toward dividing Europe into two hostile camps—embodied the only firm continental alliance contracted by the Allies in the prewar period. Its importance was fundamental. Based on France's long-standing preference for allies in eastern Europe who might put pressure on Germany from the East at opportune moments, this alliance forced the German General Staff to make contingency plans for a two-front war. The Russo-French combination also made it more likely that any Austro-Russian conflict over the Balkans would lead to a general European war.

A *rapprochement* with Italy was the next step in securing French security (see p. 436). Although Italy remained officially in the Triple Alliance, the Italian government made it increasingly clear after 1902 that it would remain neutral in the case of a Franco-German conflict. In 1904 came the

most surprising international realignment when France and England concluded the so-called Entente Cordiale. Since the days of William the Conqueror, the two states had rarely been friends; they had engaged in more
than two hundred years of war against each other. At the time of the
conclusion of the Entente, their respective allies, Russia and Japan, were at
war, further complicating Franco-British relations. Although the Entente
was no alliance, the two nations began to cooperate at times of international
crisis and even engaged in military conversations to determine the assign-
ment of forces in case of war. The Entente thus was of great benefit to
France by removing Anglo-French friction over colonial matters and by
serving as a backstop in the various pre-war crises with Germany. Nonetheless, until Germany invaded Belgium at the outbreak of World War I, the
French could never be absolutely sure that England would be her full-
fledged ally in a war with Germany.

Outwardly, Russia seemed to be growing more powerful during the late
nineteenth century. Her population increased from 58 million at the time of
the Crimean War to 144 million by World War I. Industrialization, the
opening of vast resources in southern Russia and Siberia through the construction of railroads (including the Trans-Siberian Railway), and the
maintenance of three fleets (in the Far East, the Baltic, and the Black Sea)
seemed to make Russia formidable. Her boundaries and influence were
constantly expanding. After defeating Turkey (1877–1878), Russia obtained southern Bessarabia and the Black Sea shore beyond the Caucasus,
while her role as protector of the southern Slavs gave her an increasing voice
in Serbian and Bulgarian affairs. During the 1880's, she extended her boundaries east of the Caspian Sea toward Afghanistan, gained more influence in
Persia, and during the following decade penetrated into Manchuria and
Korea and acquired extensive rights in northern China. While expanding in
Asia, Russia felt relatively secure in Europe, bolstered at first by her friendship with Germany and later by her alliance with France.

Russia's economic development and territorial gains overshadowed most
signs of debility until after the turn of the century, when her disastrous
defeat by Japan, coupled with a year of revolutionary upheavals (1905),
suddenly revealed a serious weakness. Austria sensed this change and took
advantage of it during the Balkan crisis of 1908. Russia's foreign minister
Alexander Izvolski (1856–1919) had previously reached bilateral agreements with each of the powers for altering the international convention on
the Turkish Straits (concluded in 1841) so as to permit the passage of
Russian warships to the Mediterranean. Great Britain had given her consent
within the frame of the Anglo-Russian Entente of 1907. Germany and Italy
had withdrawn their objections; the former in return for a freer hand over
the Berlin to Baghdad railroad and the latter for Russian acquiescence to
Italian acquisition of Tripoli. Austria's bargain in these negotiations involved the annexation of Bosnia and Herzegovina, two Turkish provinces

she had administered since 1878, but which still remained under Turkish sovereignty.

The Balkan crisis of 1908 erupted when Austria suddenly annexed Bosnia and Herzegovina, without however being willing to help Russia gain the compensation the latter expected. In fact, despite the bilateral agreements, none of the powers was ready to pressure Turkey into satisfying Russian demands. The landlocked Serbs, who had hoped to obtain an outlet to the Adriatic Sea via Bosnia or Herzegovina, promptly threatened war on Austria. Izvolski, furious at what he considered an Austrian double-cross, offered to aid Serbia and called for Russian military preparations. In accordance with the Dual Alliance, the Germans stood by Austria and warned Russia against helping the Serbs. Unprepared for war, the Russians eventually backed down, despite assurances of Anglo-French sympathy. Austria-Hungary retained her unilateral gains.

This Russian diplomatic retreat in 1909, coupled with Russia's relatively minor role in the succeeding pre-war crises, gave the Austrians and Germans an unwarranted confidence in the effectiveness of the Dual Alliance vis-à-vis their eastern neighbor. When an almost identical confrontation to that of 1908–1909 occurred in the summer of 1914 between Serbia, backed by Russia, and Austria, supported by Germany, the governments of Berlin and Vienna expected Russia again to back down. Yet Russia had meanwhile rearmed and recuperated from the defeat by Japan and this miscalculation thus represented a factor in the outbreak of World War I.

After Italy's consolidation in 1870, followed by a rapid increase in her army, navy, and merchant marine and the conclusion of the Triple Alliance, there was speculation whether the new state would become a significant world power like Germany. In Bismarck's considerations, Italy did not count among the five great continental powers; yet during the 1880's, she appeared to be a growing, powerful nation. Enjoying relatively cordial relations with Spain and England, she took the first steps toward acquiring a colonial empire by obtaining a foothold in Eritrea at the southern end of the Red Sea and soon thereafter obtaining Somaliland along the Indian Ocean. Italy's primary antagonist at the time was France which obstructed Italian growth both in the Mediterranean and in Ethiopia. Meanwhile Italian nationalists agitated against Austria and France for the cession of Dalmatia, Trieste, the Trentino, Nice, Savoy, and Corsica, and urged the government to seize a share of the Balkan spoils from the weakening Turkish Empire.

During the 1890's, Italy's prestige lessened. Trying to implement a claim to Ethiopia, an Italian army was disastrously mauled by the Ethiopians in 1896, forcing Italy to abandon all hope of acquiring Ethiopia and to recognize the latter's independence. When three years later, the Italians attempted to obtain concessions in China as had been done by the other great powers, they were peremptorily and successfully rebuffed by the Chinese. With

Italian strength less than what it had seemed to be, the Roman government decided to adjust its differences with France (see p. 442).

In 1911, Italy had another and this time successful fling at imperialism by making war on Turkey for the acquisition of Tripoli, an enterprise to which the powers had given their agreement in advance. Italian forces conquered Tripoli and seized the Dodecanese Islands off the shores of Turkey in order to force the Turks into a settlement. In view of the outbreak of the First Balkan War in 1912, in which Turkey faced an alliance of Greece, Serbia, Montenegro, and Bulgaria, the Turks finally submitted to Italian demands for the session of Tripoli.

Despite this victory over Turkey, Italy's strength in 1914 looked doubtful. She lacked strategic raw materials and was therefore vulnerable to possible blockade; internally she was disunified by bitter quarrels between socialists and conservatives as well as between nationalists and pacificists. Although still a member of the Triple Alliance, Italians saw little purpose in fighting for Austria or Germany, unless they were assured of obtaining the Trentino, Trieste, and Dalmatia from Austria and a sphere in the Balkans. Hence, the Italian government took advantage of the fact that Germany declared war on France instead of vice versa, and decided that Germany's action relieved Italy of her treaty obligations to aid the Germans. On the day Germany declared war on France, Italy announced her neutrality.

The declining nations

The decline of Turkey and Spain appeared most obvious. Once the dread of Europe, the Ottoman Empire had been slowly declining since the middle of the eighteenth century and had become the so-called "Sick Man of Europe," a ready prey for whoever wished to seize a chunk of its vast possessions. While not reluctant to grab Ottoman possessions in North Africa, the Western powers repeatedly tried to shore up Turkish internal power and induce her to modernize her government, largely from fear that Russia might inherit Turkey's Balkan possessions and thereby become a Mediterranean power. But reforms and modernization of sorts did not suffice to reconcile the numerous subject nationalities under Constantinople's rule, nor did they prevent continued partitioning of the empire. Even the revolutionary Young Turk movement, which desperately sought to press the sultan toward constitutionalism and decentralization, and which obtained the establishment of parliamentary government in 1908, could not stay the decline of the Ottoman Empire. In the First Balkan War (1912–1913), Turkey lost almost her entire Balkan possessions. Finally, as a result of World War I, in which they were allies of Germany, the Turks had to cede all lands in the Middle East and retained only Asia Minor and a small enclave around Constantinople. (See Map. 23.)

Although Spain still featured in many international agreements regarding the Mediterranean and received a small slice of Moroccan territory in 1912, largely through the good offices of France, she had ceased to be a major power. After her defeat in the Spanish-American War, only a coastal strip in West Africa and a few scattered possessions remained of her once immense colonial empire. At the outbreak of World War I, although favoring France, the Spanish government declared its neutrality, fully cognizant that the country lacked the resources to engage in a major war.

The decline of Austria-Hungary was much less obvious. Next to Russia, Austria-Hungary was still the largest European state and even continued to grow through the acquisition of Bosnia and Herzegovina. With the powerful backing of Germany through the Dual Alliance, she often engaged in skillful diplomacy which gave her a strong voice in European affairs. Although her industrial growth lagged behind that of the great powers and her navy was small, Austria controlled a large army, buoyed by presumed loyalty to the emperor. In view of her determined stand in the various Balkan crises, especially that of 1908, and her forceful attitude in July 1914, Austria still loomed as a world power.

Yet, as World War I was to show, Austria had become a shell without inner coherence. None of the numerous compromises that had been essayed to placate the aspirations of the subject nationalities had obliterated their nationalistic aspirations. Czechs, Slovenes, Croats, Poles, and others showed little will to fight for a Hapsburg emperor who refused to grant them equality with his German- and Hungarian-speaking subjects. Moreover, the war was to show that Austria's industrial basis was insufficient for the fighting of a modern war. Austria, in fact, had ceased to be a world power long before 1914, but few diplomats had fully recognized this change.

The web of alliances

Never before in history had governments fashioned such intricate nets of alliances and ententes as during the four decades preceding World War I. Many of the pacts were secret or contained secret clauses, giving some statesmen the confidence of holding a trump, while relegating others to a dangerous guessing game. Designed ostensibly for the maintenance of peace, the alliances actually made it more difficult to keep conflicts localized.

As the alliance system developed, its center of gravity shifted gradually from Berlin and Vienna to Paris and London. During the 1880's, largely as a result of Bismarck's work, Germany and Austria-Hungary represented the hub of the alliance net. In addition to the Dual and Triple alliances and the Three Emperors' League (succeeded by the Reinsurance Treaty), Austria had special pacts with Serbia and Rumania. In return for their promise not to incite nationalistic feelings among the southern Slavs residing within the Austro-Hungarian Empire, the Serbs received Austrian support against Bulgaria at a time when both Serbia and Bulgaria were hoping to acquire

Turkish-held Macedonia. Austria's alliance with Rumania, besides further-ing her commercial interests in the lower Danube basin, was more clearly directed against Russia. The Rumanians welcomed the alliance as insurance against further Russian encroachment, after Russia had taken from them southern Bessarabia in 1878. The Austrians, for their part, looked upon the alliance with Bucharest as a useful east-west block thrown across the north-ern Balkans to prevent Russian penetration to the South. Rumania was to remain in the Austro-German camp until the outbreak of World War I.

Thus, Germany, Austria-Hungary, Italy, Russia, Serbia, and Rumania formed a political block until Bismarck's dismissal in 1890, while Paris and London remained isolated. Two weak links threatened the viability of this pattern of alliances: Austro-Russian competition in the Balkans and Austro-Italian friction over Italy's irredentist aspirations.

After 1907, the European powers became divided more clearly into two separate camps, with few links between the two. The Central Powers—Germany, Austria-Hungary, and Italy—were left with only the Dual and Triple alliances and the extension to Bucharest. The alliance with Serbia had expired in 1895, and Serbia had slipped under the protectorship of Russia. No formal bonds remained between Berlin and St. Petersburg, except for the friendship of its two rulers. Moreover Italy had become a less valuable ally in view of her *rapprochement* with France, so that the only firm and secure alliance among the Central Powers was the Berlin-Vienna axis.

London and Paris, on the other hand, had become the nuclei of alliances and ententes among the so-called Allied Powers, which included Russia, France, England, Japan, and Portugal, with Spain as an added neutral friend and Serbia as a restless protégé. Except for the fairly specific military conventions between St. Petersburg and Paris, which stipulated mutual con-tributions in case of war, and the Anglo-Japanese alliance, the agreements between the Allied Powers were rather vague. Yet, during the crisis of 1914, the major Allies, notwithstanding some hesitation on the part of England, were to act in surprising agreement.

International cooperation

Despite jingoism, imperialistic rivalries, armaments races, and industrial competition, an increasing sense of unity permeated the Western world. Literary and artistic movements retained their international character. Not-withstanding the emphasis placed on folk themes in the various nationalistic schools of music, Western music (composers, performers, orchestras, and all that make up the musical world) became more and more an integral part of Western civilization. Similarly science and scholarship, although employed frequently to increase a nation's military posture or to bolster its national ego, as in the writing of nationalistic textbooks for the schools, engaged increasingly in international cooperation.

Faster transportation and communications, the tripling of world trade, and the consequent increase in contacts between peoples led governments and private groups to conclude countless international agreements, some essential for the functioning of a particular enterprise, others designed to make life more comfortable or interesting. Industrial expansion led to the establishment of corporations on a world-wide basis: an international agreement for the protection of trade-marks (1883); regulations concerning civil law suits in different countries (1896); and agreements on the exchange of currencies and bank checks (1910). World trade fairs became more and more common, and there were occasional congresses to discuss measures for the protection of labor on an international scale. Changes in transportation and communications required innumerable international agreements such as the creation of the Universal Postal Union (1875), accords on the placement of telephone and telegraph cables, and an international motor car treaty (1910). For the convenience of travelers, Thomas Cook, probably the first travel agent, organized the first "Cook's Tour" of Europe in 1856 and soon established a wide net of travel offices. In 1876, the International Wagons-Lits Company was formed to manage sleeping and dining cars and the running of luxury trains on a Europe-wide basis. And in the realm of sports, one might mention the establishment of the International Olympic Committee in Lausanne in 1894.

Many attempts were also made to bridge the gap between nations in political, social, and humanitarian matters, and to elaborate international law. The Paris Convention of 1856, for example, defined rules for naval blockades and for the protection of neutral shipping in time of war. The International Red Cross, established in Geneva in 1864 after the carnage of the Crimean and Franco-Austrian wars had aroused public opinion, gradually became a vital link between states, even when they were officially at war. To make a concerted effort for women's suffrage, the International Women's League was founded in Washington in 1888.

By the turn of the century, certain governments and organized groups became concerned about the growing armaments race, not only because of a possible war but also for financial and economic reasons. In 1899, delegates from twenty-six nations met at the invitation of Tsar Nicholas II at The Hague in Holland to discuss limitations on armaments. No agreement on disarmament was reached at this First Hague Peace Conference, but the powers subscribed to certain regulations designed to make warfare more "humane." They agreed not to use poisonous gas or so-called dumdum bullets (blunt projectiles causing wide-open wounds), not to drop bombs from balloons, or to mistreat prisoners of war. In addition, they set up a Permanent Court of Arbitration at The Hague, in the hope that nations would resort to arbitration rather than war. In 1907, a Second Hague Peace Conference convened at the Peace Palace built by Andrew Carnegie. Meeting at the suggestion of President Theodore Roosevelt, who enjoyed his role as international mediator, delegates from forty-four states again failed to achieve accord on disarmament, but they elaborated further rules of warfare, particularly in regard to the treatment of neutrals.

Meanwhile the Second Socialist International, founded in 1889, also concerned itself with the problem of war. Many Marxists saw in war the inevitable by-product of capitalism and imperialism; others considered it a possible tool for the toppling of reactionary governments and for paving the way to a socialist victory. The question of whether workers should and could prevent wars was discussed at various congresses, most of which were marked by profound disagreements, with moderates and revolutionaries bombarding each other with invectives rather than agreeing on solutions. A theoretical answer was finally adopted by many moderate socialists. In case of impending war, the workers of all countries should refuse to fight, should strike and engage in sabotage rather than kill fellow-workers "on the other side," and thus make war impossible. In the summer of 1914, however, the workers' patriotism and their distrust of foreigners proved generally stronger than international socialist solidarity, and the efforts of the Second International proved as ineffective in preventing World War I as did the efforts of the statesmen.

SUGGESTED READINGS

Imperialism

Betts, Raymond F., ed., *The Scramble for Africa, Causes and Dimensions of Empire* (Heath, 1966). Collection of readings.

Caldwell, Theodore C., ed., *Anglo-Boer War* (Heath, 1965).

*Chapman, Maybelle K., *Great Britain and the Bagdad Railway, 1888–1914* (Peter Smith, 1948).

Hobson, John A., *Imperialism* (U. of Michigan, 1965).

Huttenback, Robert A., *The British Imperial Experience* (Harper, 1966). From the eighteenth to the mid-twentieth century.

*Langer, William L., *The Diplomacy of Imperialism, 1890–1902* (Knopf, 1935).

Morgan, Howard W., *America's Road to Empire* (Wiley, 1965).

Remak, Joachim, *The Origins of World War I* (Holt, 1967).

Wright, Harrison, *The New Imperialism, Analysis of Late Nineteenth Century Expansion* (Heath, 1961).

The European International Scene

Fainsod, Merle, *International Socialism and the World War* (Octagon, 1967).

Langer, William L., *European Alliances and Alignments 1871–1890* (Knopf, 1950).

*Schmitt, Bernadotte E., *England and Germany, 1740–1914* (Fertig, 1967).

Stavrianos, Leften S., *The Ottoman Empire: Was It the Sick Man of Europe?* (Holt, 1957).

Asia

*Hutchins, Francis G., *Illusion of Permanence: British Imperialism in India* (Princeton, 1967).

*MacNair, Harley F., and Lach, Donald F., *Modern Far Eastern International Relations* (Van Nostrand, 1955).

*Miller, William, *The Ottoman Empire and Its Successors, 1801–1927* (Octagon, 1967).

Rowe, David Nelson, *Modern China, A Brief History* (Van Nostrand, 1959).

*Sansom, George B., *The Western World and Japan: A Study in the Interaction of European and Asiatic Cultures* (Knopf, 1950).

Smith, Thomas C., *The Agrarian Origins of Modern Japan* (Atheneum, 1966).

Tiedemann, Arthur, *Modern Japan, A Brief History* (Van Nostrand, 1962).

Upton, Joseph M., *History of Modern Iran* (Harvard, 1960).

Wright, Mary Clabaugh, *The Last Stand of Chinese Conservatism, The T'ung-Chih Restoration 1862–1874* (Atheneum, 1966).

CHAPTER XXV

The War of 1914 and Its Consequences (1914-1919)

The four great wars between 1689 and 1763 as well as the revolutionary and Napoleonic wars shared some characteristics of world wars; the conflicts had involved most European nations, and fighting had occurred not only in Europe but also in parts of Asia and America. The war of 1914–1918, however, was the first real world war, eventually involving a majority of the world's states. Its campaigns were fought in Europe, the Near East, Africa, on the oceans, and in the air. World War I was a total war, in the manner attempted by the French in 1793. It was not simply a struggle between two contending armies, but, at least in Europe, a battle involving the economic resources and the entire population of the countries engaged. Finally, World War I, even more than the wars of 1792–1815, completely altered the political, social, and economic face of Europe and strikingly affected the psychological configuration of Western civilization.

The course of World War I

By a chain reaction through the alliance system, Austria's declaration of war on Serbia in the summer of 1914 immediately embroiled all the major powers, except Italy and the United States. In the resulting conflict, Germany and Austria-Hungary, later joined by Turkey and Bulgaria, were arrayed against the Allied powers, Russia, France, and England, and their numerous partners. The Allied states were joined by Italy in 1915 and by the United States in 1917, although they lost Russia's support in the same year. The four Central Powers, however, gained no further adherents. On the contrary, Germany's allies, Turkey, Bulgaria, and Austria-Hungary, gradually collapsed in the fall of 1918, leaving Germany alone to surrender in November 1918.

The outbreak of the conflict

Six major crises during the period 1905–1914 had each brought the powers perilously close to a general war. The last two crises provoked acute tension between Austria and Russia over the Balkans. Taking advantage of Turkey's defeat by the Italians, Greece, Montenegro, Serbia, and Bulgaria launched a successful campaign against the Turks in 1912. In the following year, in the Second Balkan War, Greeks, Serbs, Turks, and Rumanians fought against the Bulgarians over the division of spoils from the first war. In the course of these struggles, the Serbs and Montenegrins, with Russian blessing, gained a foothold on the Adriatic, a step still opposed by Austria. With Vienna threatening war on Serbia, the tension eased only when Russia withdrew its support from the Serbs, who then felt compelled to yield to Austria's ultimatum. The powers thereupon created an independent Albanian state as a buffer between Serbia-Montenegro and the Adriatic Sea.

The crisis in the summer of 1914 was not much different from previous Balkan crises. The murder at Sarajevo of the heir to the Hapsburg throne by Serbian nationalists was not an unusual event, since several assassinations of rulers and statesmen had occurred in Europe and America in the prewar decades. Nor did the resulting confrontation between Austria and Serbia, backed respectively by Germany and Russia, depart from the usual pattern of Balkan tensions. The difference was that this time none of the powers backed down.

As tension deepened over Serbia's refusal to bow unconditionally before Austria's demands of satisfaction, Germany's strategic plans for a possible two-front war added urgency to the last few days of peace. The German General Staff had decided that in the event of war against both Russia and France, the bulk of German forces should at once rush through Belgium into northern France, seize Paris, and fall upon the rear of the French armies, which would presumably be concentrated along the upper Rhine. After such a lightning defeat of France, the German troops could then be transferred to the eastern front to face the Russians who, it was believed, would take longer to mobilize. The success of this plan (the Schlieffen Plan) depended on Germany's speedy initiative, since once Russia had begun mobilization German troops had to attack France within the shortest possible time.

The decision to resort to arms was facilitated by the climate of the period. A measure of Social Darwinism had come to characterize the calculations of statesmen not only in the treatment of colonial areas but also in dealings with other powers—be that of the United States against Spain, or the British against the Boers, Italy against Turkey, or all the powers against

China. This confidence in war as a guarantee for the survival of the fittest had been accompanied by a steady increase in tension, the result of chauvinistic nationalism, imperialistic and commercial rivalry, and uneasiness engendered by the growing arms race. Thus the nations plunged into battle with confidence and an anomalous sense of relief that the period of ill-defined tension had given way to the certainty of a military encounter.

A month after the assassination at Sarajevo, Austria declared war on Serbia and began the bombardment of Belgrade, followed a day later by Russia's mobilization. Ready to support their Austrian ally and expecting France to side with Russia, the German military urged rapid action. After frantic exchanges of telegrams between the capitals of Europe, France and Germany began to mobilize, and the Germans declared war on Russia. Two days later, Germany declared war also on France and invaded Belgium, whereupon England declared war on Germany. A week later, Austria joined the struggle against Russia, England, and France. (See Map 27.)

The campaigns

World War I, in which the Allied powers eventually mobilized forty-two million men against twenty-nine million for the Central powers, was fought in western and eastern Europe, in the Balkans and northeastern Italy, along Turkey's farflung borders and in the German colonies, as well as in the air and on the seas.

In the West, the German armies overran southern Belgium and plunged to within sight of Paris before being pushed back beyond the River Marne. After this loss of Germany's momentum, the front became more or less stabilized along endless trenches from Alsace to the North Sea. Repeatedly, the opponents threw millions of men into gigantic battles resulting in hundreds of thousands of casualties without succeeding in shifting the trench lines more than a few miles. Neither the use of poison gas, the employment of new weapons such as tanks, nor the increased utilization of war planes could alter the bloody stalemate of the western front.

In the East, meanwhile, where the Russians initially invaded East Prussia and Austrian Galicia, the Germans quickly reversed the trend and gradually rolled back the Russians along a vast front from the Baltic to the Black Sea. Despite several Russian counteroffensives, Russia's war effort began to slacken with increasing shortages of war materiel and the breakdown of morale. After two revolutions in 1917 had completely disrupted her war machine and German troops had advanced to the gates of Petrograd (formerly St. Petersburg) and deep into the Ukraine, Russia's new Bolshevik government headed by Nicolai Lenin agreed to accept German peace terms. The resulting Treaty of Brest Litovsk (1918) forced the Russians to cede Finland, Estonia, Latvia, Lithuania, Poland, the Ukraine, and Transcaucasia and to deliver vital raw materials to Germany.

Austria's campaigns in south-eastern Europe were at first unsuccessful.

She failed in two attempts to conquer Serbia and was unable to invade northeastern Italy, after the latter had joined the Allied camp in 1915. The Allies, for their part, were equally unsuccessful in their efforts to conquer the Turkish Straits and to invade the central Balkans from a beachhead at Saloniki. After Bulgaria joined the Central Powers in 1915 and German troops were dispatched to the Balkans, Serbia was rapidly defeated, giving the Austro-Germans direct land access to their Turkish ally. In 1917, German forces also aided the Austrians in breaking through the Italian front and bringing Italy close to collapse. It was not until September 1918 that the Allied armies in the Balkans broke through Bulgarian, Austrian, and German defenses, forced Bulgaria to sue for peace, and proceeded to liberate Serbia. A month later, the Italians launched a successful offensive with Allied aid and forced Austria to agree to an armistice.

Despite little aid from the Central Powers, Turkey organized stiff resistance to Russian and British invasions and successfully maintained her position until late 1916, when the Arabs, with British encouragement, began to rise against their Turkish overlords. After the loss of southern Mesopotamia and parts of Palestine in 1917, there was a relative lull in the fighting, while the Allies concentrated their efforts on France. When the British and Arabs resumed their offensive in September 1918, Turkey collapsed within six weeks and demanded an armistice.

Whereas the British and French colonial empires were of invaluable aid to the Allied war effort, Germany was in no position to profit from her colonies since she did not control the high seas. Except for German East Africa, where German forces held out until the end of the war, Germany's colonies were quickly seized by English, French, Japanese, Australian, New Zealand, South African, and Indian forces.

Like her colonies, Germany's High Seas Fleet proved of little value. Soon after the outbreak of the war, the British navy established a relatively effective blockade in the North Sea, designed to pen in the German navy and to strangle Germany's economy. An occasional German surface raider—light cruisers or armed merchant ships—slipped through the British blockade to attack Allied shipping or mine British ports, but Germany's only real hope for challenging Britain's naval supremacy lay in the use of submarines, since Emperor William was reluctant to test his High Seas Fleet against the British Grand Fleet. In February 1915, the Germans opened a first period of unrestricted submarine warfare, declared a blockade of Britain, and began to attack neutral ships carrying goods to the British Isles. When the loss of American lives and ships almost brought the United States into the war, the Germans for a while limited their underseas attacks to British shipping. By January 1917, however, the Germans concluded that unrestricted submarine warfare might after all starve Britain into submission, even if its application might provoke American hostility. Hence, they resumed all-out underseas attacks, inflicting vast damage to Allied shipping. Yet, by the winter of 1917 it became evident that the war could not be won at sea.

Despite the failure of the submarine campaign and the weakening of Austria and Turkey and despite increasing shortages at home, the German General Staff felt confident in the spring of 1918. With Russia defeated, Rumania about to surrender, and Italian strength dwindling, the Germans launched a giant offensive against the Anglo-French lines in the West in the hope of gaining a victory before the Americans, who had entered the war in April 1917, could shore up the Allies with the full resources of their man-power and industry. Successful at first, the German offensive was finally stopped just short of Paris. Aided by newly arrived American reinforce-ments, the Allies then rolled back the German lines. After her three allies had surrendered and a revolution had overthrown the German emperor, the new government of Berlin finally accepted the armistice terms of the Allies (November 11, 1918), which demanded the withdrawal of German forces to the east of the Rhine and the surrender of sufficient war matériel to make Germany's resumption of hostilities impossible.

The home fronts

There were, of course, differences in the way the course of the war affected various nations. Serbia suffered enormous physical destruction, while England was only occasionally exposed to explosives dropped from German planes or dirigibles. The economies of Russia and Germany were hurt more than those of France, England, and the United States. Austria-Hungary and Turkey disintegrated during the later phase of the war, while Italy and Germany merely experienced revolutionary discontent. Yet, despite such different conditions, the problems of conducting a total war led to similar developments in most participating states.

Most governments soon found it essential to assume control over indus-trial production and distribution, the use of raw materials and labor, trans-portation, exports, imports, prices, and wages—in short, over the entire eco-nomic life of their peoples. Censorship became common, martial law was used to curb possible disorders, and the governments resorted to extensive propaganda to buoy up morale, particularly in Germany where official gov-ernment releases hinted at imminent victory until almost the day of the German collapse. In France, President Raymond Poincaré (1860–1934) usually ruled by decree rather than through the parliamentary process. In all belligerent states, the military High Command naturally gained vast powers, but in France and England the civilian ministry retained its ultimate su-premacy, whereas a military dictatorship was established in Germany in 1917. After the war, this new power structure of the central governments in the democratic as well as the non-democratic nations proved to be difficult to dismantle.

At the onset of the war, political disagreements in most countries gave way to patriotic harmony. A coalition government in France called for a "sacred union" of all Frenchmen for the defense of the fatherland. The Russian Duma and the German Reichstag voted war credits and then desisted for a while from further criticism of the government. In Great Britain, too, a coalition cabinet directed the war effort under the energetic leadership of David Lloyd George (1863–1945). Despite such initial political harmony, there was occasional friction in most states between the military hierarchy and the civilian authorities, between conservatives insisting on the status quo and liberals seeking to rouse the people to greater enthusiasm through political reforms, and between industrialists and the workers who thought their vital contribution to the war effort should earn them greater social benefits. Changes in the course of the war also affected the political peace on the home front. In France, for instance, the closing of ranks lessened sharply with the reappearance of self-confidence in 1915. Similarly criticism of the government resumed in Russia in 1916 after the failure of two Russian offensives, and in Germany in 1917, when opposition leaders became convinced that total victory was not possible.

Total war produced hitherto unknown shortages, which complicated the war efforts and gravely affected all civilians among Europe's belligerents. Losses in manpower and lack of skilled workers made it difficult to increase industrial production while keeping the armies replenished with recruits. The war was to cost 13,500,000 men in dead and missing and 21,000,000 in casualties of whom about 12,000,000 became permanently disabled. Such horrendous losses forced most countries to resort to labor conscription and to encourage female labor in industry and even in the army. England created its WAAC (Women's Auxiliary Army Corps) in 1917, thereby providing a powerful boost to the suffragette movement. Strict rationing was used to counteract severe shortages in food which reached critical proportions in Germany, England, and Russia in 1917. England was also short on munitions until 1916, and Russia's ordnance supply worsened steadily after 1915. To counter industrial shortages, chemists devised substitutes: clay was turned into aluminum to replace copper; woodpulp was converted into artificial yarn; oil was obtained from animal tissues and seeds; and sugar was fermented into glycerine for use in explosives.

In 1914, morale on the homefronts and in the armies was generally high, enveloped in "romantic heroism." Thereafter morale sank or rose with the outcome of campaigns or the war-weariness of the population. A large segment of the Italians had opposed Italy's entry into the war from the beginning, and the government used lavish promises of glory and material rewards to counteract their pacifism. Civilian and military morale in Russia sank very low in late 1916 and never recovered, and in the spring of 1917, a mutiny erupted in some French armies until discipline was restored by the newly appointed commander in chief, General Henri Pétain (1856–1951).

The question of morale was more complicated in the Austro-Hungarian Empire. Many among the subject peoples—Poles, Czechs, Slovenes, and others—were hoping for a defeat of the Hapsburg monarchy, so as to improve their chances for gaining national autonomy or independence; hence their spirits were lifted when the Austrian Empire began to disintegrate.

War aims

At the beginning of the war, the nations found it difficult to ascertain what they were fighting for. Russia hoped at last to seize the Turkish Straits, France expected to recover Alsace-Lorraine, and Germany sought an end to her encirclement. But these were not aims for which the three states had actually gone to war. In ordering mobilization and initiating hostilities, the governments generally spoke of a defensive war. Austria alone, it seems, entered the conflict with a fairly concrete aim: the humiliation of Serbia in order to keep her from continuing to serve as an anti-Hapsburg rallying point for the South Slavs inside her empire.

Various statesmen soon added ideological motives to the conflict, largely to justify their actions and rouse their citizens to fighting fervor. Woodrow Wilson's statement to Congress (April 1917) that "our object . . . is to vindicate the principles of peace and justice . . . as against selfish and autocratic power," and that the United States was fighting "for the rights of nations great and small and the privilege of men everywhere to choose their way of life and of obedience," eloquently summarized similar pronouncements made by Allied statesmen from the beginning of the war. Yet, although ideology figured in the aspirations of many peoples, it was not contained in the calculations of governments. Ideology had been infinitely more important during the early phases of the French revolutionary wars and was to play an even greater role in World War II and in contemporary conflicts than it did in World War I.

In a true war "against autocratic power" British democracy could hardly have allied itself with Russian autocracy. Moreover the announced aim of self-determination for all peoples was repeatedly violated during and after the war. To obtain Rumania's adherence to the Allied side (1916), the Western powers promised her a large slice of Hungarian territory. In the secret Treaty of London (1915), designed to entice Italy into the war, England, France, and Russia awarded her lands inhabited in part by Germans, Slovenes, Croatians, Greeks, and Turks. And the Treaty of Versailles (1919), for example, expressly prohibited a union between Austria and Germany, regardless of the wishes of the inhabitants.

The real war aims of the nations were formulated only gradually in the course of the war, and it remained difficult to arrive at a consensus within the various states, not to mention the problem of reaching agreement among the victorious Allies. Generally speaking, conservatives tended to expect greater external gains from the war than liberals and socialists.

In Russia, the tsarist government anticipated territorial gains to compensate for the sacrifices of the war. In 1915, Russia received the consent of England and France—later joined by the United States—for the acquisition of Constantinople, parts of the Turkish Straits, and Thrace. A year later, England and France also gave their assent to Russian annexation of Armenia and eastern Turkey. But after the tsarist regime had been overthrown in the revolution of March 1917, the liberal Provisional Government (see p. 459) issued a manifesto declaring that "the aim of free Russia is not domination over other peoples, deprivation of their national possessions, violent acquisition of alien territory, but the establishment of a stable peace on the basis of self-determination." In accordance with these precepts, the Provisional Government abandoned all expectations of territorial gains from Turkey and even recognized the independence of Poland, after the Poles— then under German military occupation—had announced their separation from Russia. After the November 1917 revolution, the Bolshevik government, seeking to facilitate peace negotiations and at the same time weaken Austria-Hungary by inspiring anti-Hapsburg independence movements, adopted a similar policy by proposing an immediate "just, democratic peace without annexations and indemnities." A week later, Russia's Commissar for Nationalities, Joseph Stalin (1879–1953), issued a decree acknowledging "the right of the peoples of Russia to free self-determination, even to the point of separation and the formation of an independent state," a permission promptly heeded by the Ukrainians, Estonians, Finns, and others.

Within Germany, ideas on war aims diverged sharply. In 1915, a group of conservatives published a statement of war aims. In it they demanded the annexation of a part of northern France, a protectorate over Belgium, territorial acquisitions in eastern Europe for colonization by Germans and military security against Russia, more colonies, and a large war indemnity. These demands were to secure for Germany "a stronger position in the world." Opposed to these advocates of a "strong peace" were liberals and socialists more interested in gains at home in the form of political reform and socioeconomic improvements. In 1917, the liberal opposition in the Reichstag united to pass a Peace Resolution, calling for a peace of reconciliation without territorial annexations and for true constitutionalism at home. The conservatives saw in this resolution the blueprint for a "peace of hunger" and labeled its proponents traitors to the soldiers dying at the front.

During the early part of the war, the expectations of the Allied Powers were frankly imperialistic. Japan claimed the German colonies in the Pacific as compensation for her war effort. The French foreign office called for "the destruction of the German Empire" through dismemberment, and English and French statesmen devised plans for the acquisition of Turkish possessions in the Near East. Gradually the horrors of war induced the Allied governments to accept a victory that might not satisfy all of their grandiose hopes. They became somewhat less vociferous in their imperialistic claims, without, however, ever accepting Wilson's dictum that "we desire no conquest, no dominion."

Revolutions

The states that had developed fairly democratic institutions before 1914 appeared better equipped to withstand the strains of total war than those with autocratic regimes. In Russia, Austria-Hungary, Germany, and the Ottoman Empire, the defeats of World War I produced the conditions that enabled discontented groups to stage successful revolutions.

Revolution in Russia

Despite the revolution of 1905 and the establishment of the Duma, Russia entered the war with a highly conservative government, dominated by an autocratic tsar, a cumbersome, aristocratic, and somewhat indolent bureaucracy, and a caste-conscious officer corps. The inelasticity of the system proved a serious handicap for meeting the demands of a total war and for satisfying the growing aspirations of the middle class. When disasters at the front multiplied and casualties mounted (by December 1916, 300,000 replacements a month were needed to take the place of those killed, wounded, or taken prisoner), when soldiers had to launch night assaults with bayonets to conserve sparse ammunition, and when food and fuel shortages brought famine and frost to the lower classes, revolutionary fervor and anti-tsarist sentiment increased. Nicholas II hardly helped matters. He stayed in his military headquarters near the front and left the direction of affairs in the hands of the unpopular tsarina, who was dominated by various court favorites, including the monk Gregory Rasputin (1871?–1916).

After a winter of occasional strikes and riots (1916–1917) and open discontent among some officers who murdered Rasputin, outright revolution erupted in March 1917. This first revolution started without particular planning or leadership with a series of bread riots, demonstrations, strikes, and mutinies among sailors, soldiers, and the police. After a fruitless attempt at restoring order, Tsar Nicholas abdicated. Although unprepared and untrained to act, the Duma sought to govern the country and hoped to guide Russia toward constitutional government. It appointed a Provisional Government (headed by Prince Georgi Lvov, an advocate of constitutional monarchy) and passed legislation to enhance the civil rights of Russian citizens: Political prisoners were amnestied, freedom of the press and of assembly was granted, and distinctions between castes, races, and religions abolished. In the mistaken belief that an accelerated war effort against the authoritarian Central Powers would unite the Russians behind a common aim and would keep the soldiers from deserting to the Socialists, the Provisional Government announced at once that Russia would continue the war and prepared for a summer offensive. Delighted by the prospect of a democratized and perhaps more effective ally, the Allied Powers promptly extended diplomatic recognition to the Provisional Government. Despite strong undertones of lower-class participation, the March Revolution appeared to be the type of liberal, middle-class revolution favored by the United States in particular.

Actually, the new liberal government, based on a small middle class, failed to gain wide popular support, was unable to prevent a successful German counter-offensive, and faced the growing strength of socialistic groups seeking to supplement the liberal reforms of the March Revolution with a social revolution. Favoring legal and democratic processes, the Provisional Government deferred decisions on all fundamental reforms until a constitutional convention could be convened to decide on a political frame for Russia and to establish a permanent government with a popular mandate. Such procrastination did not satisfy the peasants who were agitating for land reform, nor the workers seeking better labor conditions and possible control over the management of factories. Hence, despite occasional weeks of apparent tranquility, the period between the March and November revolutions represented a prolonged struggle between the middle and the lower classes, ending with the triumph of the Bolsheviks.

The soviets, which were councils of workers, soldiers, and sailors first used in the revolution of 1905 and resembling the committees of public safety during the French Revolution, were the organizations through which the lower classes gained power. With a network of local councils in many parts of Russia, the soviets organized fighting units of soldiers and workers, tried to undermine the legalistic policies of the Provisional Government, and agitated for an end to the war. The executive committee of the Petrograd Soviet even gained control of some local army and navy units by establishing elected committees among soldiers and sailors who were to take orders from the soviet, keep officers from having access to weapons without permission of the soviet, and report officers guilty of "rude treatment of soldiers."

At first, the Mensheviks and Social Revolutionaries dominated the soviets. But after the return of their exiled leaders, the Bolsheviks directed their all-out effort to gaining control of the soviets. Once in command of the soviets, Nicolai Lenin intended to await an opportune moment when a brief burst of violence could topple the Provisional Government, transfer power over Russia to the soviets, and thereby ensure the triumph of his Bolsheviks. As he wrote in the Bolshevik paper *Pravda:* "we . . . wish to convince the majority of the people that power must reside solely in the Soviets of Workers', Soldiers', Peasants' and other Deputies."

Riots by supporters of the soviets on Labor Day (May 1) and again in July were quelled in sanguinary streetfighting by troops loyal to the Provisional Government. The Social Revolutionary Alexander Kerensky (1881–) then assumed the prime ministership and had Russia declared a republic in order to end the uncertainty concerning Russia's political structure. On the other hand, he sought to placate the worried middle class by attempting to weaken Bolshevism. *Pravda* was suppressed; Lenin fled to Finland; and the fiery revolutionary, Leon Trotsky (1879–1940), who had only recently joined the Bolsheviks, was arrested. For a brief moment, Kerensky's Provisional Government seemed to have gained the upper hand. Yet, by September, Kerensky found himself attacked from almost all directions. The Germans were overrunning Russia's armies in the field; the soviets increased their agitation for fundamental reforms; the conservatives, including high ranking army officers, distrusted the socialistic prime minister's ability to withstand pressure from the radical left. Faced with a counterrevolution by the Right, Kerensky amnestied the Bolsheviks in order to get the backing of the soviets.

Having helped the Provisional Government foil the attempted counter-revolution, the Bolsheviks reassumed their plans for overthrowing Kerensky himself. Released from prison, Trotsky became the head of the vital soviet of Petrograd and organized the shock troops needed for the final assault. Upon his return from Finland, Lenin urged workers to strike, peasants to seize the land, and soldiers to desert in order to stop the war. Kerensky's authority thus dwindled rapidly.

At the first All-Russian Congress of Soviets in June, the Bolsheviks had been too weak to impose their plans on the majority of Social Revolutionaries and Mensheviks. Lenin now decided to seize control of the second All-Russian Congress called for November 7, even though the Bolsheviks were still in a minority. On the eve of its meeting, Bolshevik shock troops in Petrograd seized government buildings and arrested most of the members of the Provisional Government (Kerensky succeeded in escaping and eventually fleeing to the United States). When the All-Russian Congress met, the Bolsheviks forced it to approve the dissolution of the Provisional Government and its replacement by a Council of Peoples' Commissars, acting presumably in the name of the soviets.

The new Bolshevik government, guided by Lenin as President, Trotsky as Commissar for Foreign Affairs and organizer of the new Red Army, and Stalin as Commissar for Nationalities, immediately attempted to convert Russia into a communist state. It decreed the abolishment of "all private ownership of land . . . without compensation," in order to secure the confidence of Russia's vast landless peasantry. It encouraged workers to seize factories, confiscated the property of the Orthodox Church, and nationalized all banks. While organizing police forces to suppress all possible anti-communist forces, Lenin and Trotsky arranged for an armistice with Germany, much to the consternation of the Allied Powers. When the Russians rejected Germany's exorbitant demands, the German armies resumed their advance into Russia until Lenin decided that safeguarding the Bolshevik cause was more important than attempting to save a few hundred square miles of Russian territory. In March 1918, the Bolsheviks signed the humiliating Treaty of Brest Litovsk (see p. 453) and thereafter concentrated on achieving total power over Russia by defeating the counterrevolutionary forces which were then gathering in the provinces (see p. 484).

The German revolution

In view of the growing restlessness of the opposition groups in the Reichstag in 1917, Emperor William II made several public promises concerning intended political reforms, including the granting of universal suffrage in Prussia. Mere promises however did not alleviate the discontent. The majority in the Reichstag consisted of the Center party (mostly Catholic in composition and middle-of-the-road in political views), the Progressive (advocates of democratic institutions), and the Social Democratic party (socialists). These groups not only disputed the war aims of the conservatives (see p. 458), but also objected to the military dictatorship exercised by Generals Paul von Hindenburg (1847–1934) and Erich F. W. Ludendorff (1865–1937). They believed that a peace of understanding could not be achieved without internal political reforms which would give the Reichstag control over the military, since on their own the latter would never consent to peace except on the basis of a total victory. In the course of 1917, the socialists split over the issue of how best to end the war. Inspired by Russia's Bolsheviks, left-wing socialists formed the Spartacus League, the forerunner of the German Communist party, which attempted to convince workers, soldiers, and sailors of the futility of continuing an "imperialistic war." A second splinter group set up the Independent Social Democratic party. The Independents objected to the socialists' cooperation with the bourgeois parties and insisted that the war had lost its purpose with the overthrow of tsarism in Russia.

With the collapse of the Balkan front at the end of September 1918, and the successful Allied offensive against the German armies in the West, Hindenburg and particularly Ludendorff urged the Berlin government to seek an armistice while Germany still held a slice of northeastern France as a bargaining point at the peace table. To get popular backing for the task of facing his nation with the admission of defeat, William II installed a new chancellor (the liberal Prince Max of Baden) and permitted the Reichstag to make constitutional reforms to insure parliamentary supremacy. The cabinet was made responsible to the majority in the Reichstag, consisting at that time of the Center, Progressive, and Social Democratic parties. This move shifted the onus of approving an armistice to the opposition.

Despite incipient constitutionalism in the German governmental structure, the Allies refused to negotiate with what President Wilson called "monarchical autocrats" and suggested that either the emperor abdicate or that Germany surrender. Hence increasing pressure was exerted from all sides on William II to relinquish his throne. The emperor however demurred even after revolutionary outbreaks erupted in various cities and after the Bavarian monarchy was overthrown. Finally, the chancellor simply announced William's abdication without consulting him and turned over his office to Friedrich Ebert (1871–1925), the leader of the Social Democrats; another socialist leader meanwhile proclaimed the establishment of a German republic. While the remaining German princes abdicated their thrones, ex-Emperor William slipped into permanent exile in Holland. Two days later (November 11), the Germans and the Allied Powers signed the armistice that terminated World War I.

Despite some disorder and violence and the establishment of soviets of workers and soldiers in various areas of Germany, the revolution of 1918 involved few radical changes. Like Russia's Provisional Government after the March Revolution of 1917, the German Provisional Government, consisting of Social Democrats and Independent Socialists, undertook no major social reforms, such as nationalizing the land or the means of industrial production. All fundamental changes, President Ebert insisted, had to await the establishment of a regularly elected government. For this purpose a constituent assembly was elected on the basis of universal suffrage and entrusted with the task of writing a new constitution for Germany. The Social Democrats, in particular, feared that radical steps might play into the hands of the Communists or even might provoke an Allied invasion in order to prevent a social revolution in Germany. Hence, nothing was done to lessen the power and prestige of the conservative groups that had supported the defunct empire: the officer corps, the nobility, the industrialists, the large landlords, and the imperial bureaucracy and judiciary. The failure to weaken these antidemocratic elements was to handicap Germany's first experiment with a republican system during the subsequent Weimar Republic.

Revolutions in Austria-Hungary and Turkey

The Hapsburg Empire was destroyed by the centrifugal force of the nationalistic movements rather than by liberal and social upheavals. During the war, Polish, Czech, Serb, Croat, Slovene, and Montenegrin exiles propagandized their cause in the Allied capitals and obtained particular sympathy from President Wilson. In 1918, they even formed a Congress of Oppressed Austrian Nationalities and many of them organized volunteer units to fight on the Allied side. The Allies gladly encouraged the aspirations of these national groups in order to weaken the Austro-Hungarian Empire, and they even recognized the independence of Czechoslovakia and Yugoslavia before these states were actually created.

In the fall of 1918, the Austro-Hungarian Empire disintegrated. Decimated by desertions, its armies collapsed on the Balkan and Italian fronts, while riots in the cities made it impossible for the Viennese government to retain control over the provinces. A week after Austria signed an armistice (November 3), the emperor abdicated and a provisional government of

German-speaking Austrians proclaimed Austria a republic. In the face of bitter antagonism among communists, socialists, and Catholic conservatives, a constituent assembly convened in early 1919 and voted in favor of joining Austria to the newly created German republic. Since this decision was promptly vetoed by the Allies, the Austrians then wrote a constitution for a federalized Austrian republic.

Meanwhile the Czech Provisional Government in exile in Paris, guided by the philosopher Thomas Masaryk (1850–1937) as president and the sociologist Eduard Beneš (1884–1948) as foreign minister, prepared for the establishment of a Czechoslovakian state, completely independent of Vienna. The new nation adopted a democratic constitution, undertook some moderate land reforms, and slowly attempted, not always successfully, to weld its numerous national minorities into a coherent nation. Meanwhile south of the Alps, Serbs, Slovenes, Croats, and Montenegrins in exile had agreed to work for a union of their four peoples. A month after the armistice they established what was to become the Kingdom of Yugoslavia.

Hungary, too, seceded from Vienna, but its case was different from that of Czechoslovakia and Yugoslavia. The Hungarian Kingdom had existed for almost a thousand years, and its Magyar people had become accustomed to dominating other nationalities. Moreover, as a co-equal with Austria in the Dual Monarchy, Hungary was considered an enemy country by the Allies, whereas Czechoslovakia was treated as a "liberated" territory and Serbia as a partner of the Allies. In November 1918, the Hungarians decided on a republican form of government and attempted a moderate program of land reform in order to weaken the small but powerful class of Magyar nobles who owned most of the agricultural land. But social discontent and furor over the harsh peace terms proposed by the Allies enabled the Bolshevik journalist Bela Kun (1885–1937?) to establish a communist dictatorship in the spring of 1919. As a result, Hungary was plunged into a civil war, in which conservative Magyars, aided by Rumanians and French, eventually stormed Budapest and ousted the communist regime. When order was restored in 1920, Admiral Nicolas Horthy (1868–1957), the conservative commander of the armed forces, re-established the monarchy to prepare for a possible Hapsburg restoration but had himself declared regent. Since the Allies refused to permit a return to Hapsburg rule, Horthy's conservative and nationalistic regency for a non-existent king continued until Hungary's second communist take-over in 1944.

Similar to Austria-Hungary, the Ottoman Empire was torn apart by nationalistic movements aided by the Allied Powers. The Turkish monarchy, however, did not fall immediately at the end of the war. The new sultan dismissed his nationalistic ministry and sought to save his throne by cooperating with the British, French, Italians, and Greeks who occupied portions of Turkish territory. In opposition to the pliable sultan, a new nationalist movement was organized by Mustapha Kemal Pasha (1881–1938)—later known as Atatürk—an energetic general who sought to prevent Turkey's further dismemberment. Kemal installed his revolutionary government at Ankara (1920), obtained aid from Soviet Russia, and successfully resisted Greek attempts to seize further Turkish territory. Whereas the sultan was willing to accept the harsh terms of peace proposed by the Allies (Treaty of Sèvres), Kemal's nationalists refused to bow to the Allies. They rapidly gained in popularity, increased their army, instituted a provisional constitutional government of the Western type, and succeeded not only in defying the hapless sultan but also in driving out Greek and Italian occupation forces. Finally, in 1922, Kemal had the sultan deposed, concluded a new and more favorable peace treaty with the Allies (Treaty of Lausanne), and transformed Turkey into a republic. As Turkey's first president, Kemal then undertook a slow revolution aimed at Westernizing and strengthening the new Turkish republic. (See Map 28.)

The peace settlements

In 1919, representatives of twenty-seven Allied nations gathered in Paris to discuss peace terms for the four defeated Central Powers. Almost from the start, the proceedings were dominated by Clemenceau, Lloyd George, Wilson, and, to a lesser degree, by the representatives of Italy and Japan. Although the Treaty of Brest Litovsk had been declared invalid in the Allied armistice with Germany, Soviet Russia, then in the midst of civil war, was not invited to the peace conference.

Woodrow Wilson had hoped that the peace discussions would be guided by the idealistic principles he had enunciated in his Fourteen Points (January 1918), which the Allies had tacitly accepted subject to specific reservations. Among others, Wilson had called for an end to secret treaties, "absolute freedom of navigation upon the seas," removal of trade barriers, reduction of armaments, "absolutely impartial adjustment of all colonial claims," territorial settlements based on self-determination of peoples, and a "general association of nations." Yet, the Fourteen Points were conspicuously disregarded and acid disagreements marked the deliberations of the Big Five. The five treaties—separate treaties being presented to Austria and to Hungary—that were finally drafted were the results of compromises that left unhappy scars among the Allies, particularly with the Italians. Moreover, the treaties were drafted by the victors and then submitted to the vanquished for signature rather than being elaborated in joint conferences between the Allied and Central Powers. This procedure caused particular resentment with the Germans, who insisted that they had not surrendered unconditionally and therefore should not be subjected to a "dictated" peace.

The treaties

By the Treaty of Versailles, which the Germans signed after deep hesitation, Germany returned Alsace-Lorraine to France, surrendered territory to Poland, Denmark, and Belgium, and relinquished Memel, a territory later annexed by Lithuania. Germany's loss amounted to about 13 per cent of her territory and 10 per cent of her population, as well as a good share of raw materials. Her colonies were awarded as mandates to various Allied Powers. Her army was limited to 100,000 men, based on long-term enlistments; the General Staff, submarines, military aircraft, tanks, and heavy artillery were outlawed; and the navy was limited to a few ships. The left bank of the Rhine was demilitarized, part of the Rhineland remained under Allied military occupation, and an Allied commission was to reside in Berlin to supervise continued German disarmament. Germany was to pay reparations "for all damage done to the civilian population of the Allied and Associated Powers and to their property," the exact amount to be determined by an Allied commission. To aid reconstruction in Allied countries specified manufactured and raw materials were to be delivered and German foreign assets transferred to Allied accounts. Finally, among many other clauses the treaty proposed the trial of Emperor William "for a supreme offense against international morality and the sanctity of treaties"—a trial never held since Holland refused to extradite the emperor. Moreover, the Germans were required to accept "the responsibility of Germany and her allies for causing all the loss and damage to which the Allied and Associated Governments and their nationals have been subjected as a consequence of the war imposed upon them by the aggression of Germany and her allies." This so-called war guilt clause, coupled with the demand for reparations, angered the Germans even more than the loss of territory and colonies.

Although Austria-Hungary had surrendered unconditionally, the Austrian delegates were allowed more leeway for negotiations than those of Germany, in part, perhaps, because the Austrians insisted that they had created a new state which deserved as good a treatment as Czechoslovakia. Yet the final treaty for Austria (Peace of St. Germain) closely paralleled the Treaty of Versailles, even to the point of outlawing Austrian submarines —an ironic clause since Austria had become landlocked. Austria's territorial losses to Czechoslovakia, Poland, Yugoslavia, and Italy were confirmed (see Map 28), her armaments were strictly limited, and she was to pay reparations and deliver to the Allies industrial equipment, foodstuffs and livestock, even though she was on the verge of bankruptcy and starvation. Union with Germany was expressly forbidden by the treaty.

The peace with Hungary (Treaty of Trianon) was delayed by the civil war between communists and conservatives. When the treaty was finally presented (1920)—again similar in tenor to that of Versailles—the Hungarians protested against the cession of over three million Magyars to

Czechoslovakia, Rumania, and Yugoslavia on the grounds that it violated the principle of self-determination. Nonetheless, the Hungarians signed the peace treaty, with its clauses on territorial cessions, disarmament, war guilt, and reparations.

Bulgaria, too, was shorn of some territory, limited in its military establishment, and requested to pay reparations (Treaty of Neuilly). The initial settlement with Turkey (Treaty of Sèvres) was foiled, as we saw, by the nationalist uprising of Kemal Pasha. When a final peace treaty was negotiated with Turkey in 1923 (Treaty of Lausanne), the Turks retained considerably more territory than initially contemplated by the Allies, paid no reparations, and emerged relatively stronger than anyone might have expected in 1918.

Consequences of the settlements

As Italy's prime minister remarked in 1918, World War I represented "the greatest political and social revolution in history, surpassing even the French Revolution." The accompanying suffering, losses, and disillusionment, and the peace settlements wrought untold changes in Europe. Much of the history between World War I and World War II, in fact, can be explained on the basis of repercussions from the great war.

The postwar settlements resulted in a multiplication of states in eastern Europe and the Near East. Some states, such as Poland, arose in answer to people's demand for selfdetermination. Others, such as Czechoslovakia and Yugoslavia, were created not only to satisfy popular desire but also as punishment for the defeated powers, as buffers against communist Russia, or as safeguards against the possible revival of a Hapsburg monarch. Still others, such as the Kingdom of Iraq or the mandate of Syria, were established to serve as a cover for British and French influence.

This proliferation of nations created many new problems in subsequent decades. The establishment of an independent Finland, for example, proved relatively successful; but the creation or resurrection of many states fanned countless new irredentist problems and reinvigorated the spirit of nationalism that led to new friction and eventual hostilities. Czechoslovakia, for instance, was a strange concoction made up of Czechs, Germans, Poles, Ruthenians, Slovaks, and Hungarians—a condition which facilitated its dismemberment during the crises of the late 1930's. The new Polish state encompassed numerous Russian and German subjects, again a circumstance which served as a cause or pretext for wars. Similarly, the consolidation of mutually antagonistic states in the Near East, arising from the dismemberment of the Ottoman Empire and the creation of European mandates, was to present a serious problem of instability in the Arab world.

The war and the peace settlements left many scars. The unrealistic assessment of reparations payments, together with the failure to adjust inter-Allied debts, caused grave financial dislocations that ultimately contributed to the Great Depression of the 1930's. The failure to include Soviet Russia in the peace settlements, because the Western powers considered her a socialistic pariah, added to the growing distrust among the European powers. In fact, the question of maintaining, revising, or abolishing the peace treaties, either by persuasion or by force, remained a dominant theme in European history during the subsequent two decades.

SUGGESTED READINGS

Origins of the War

Fay, Sidney Bradshaw, *The Origins of the World War,* Vol. I, "Before Sarajevo;" Vol. II, "After Sarajevo" (Macmillan, 1967).
Lafore, Laurence, *The Long Fuse: An Interpretation of the Origins of World War I* (Lippincott, 1965).
Tuchman, Barbara, *The Guns of August* (Dell).

World War I

Falls, Cyril, *The Great War, 1914–1918* (Putnam, 1961).
Fischer, Fritz, *Germany's Aims in the First World War* (Norton, 1967).
Liddell Hart, B. H., *The Real War, 1914–1918* (Little, 1964). Military history.
May, Ernest R., *The World War and American Isolation, 1914–1917* (Quadrangle, 1966).
Roth, Jack J., ed., *World War I, A Turning Point in Modern History* (Knopf, 1967). Collection of essays.
Snyder, Louis L., *Historic Documents of World War I* (Van Nostrand, 1958).

Revolutions in Russia

Berdyaev, Nicolas, *The Origin of Russian Communism* (U. of Michigan, 1960).
Dmytryshyn, Basil, *USSR: A Concise History* (Scribner, 1965).
Florinsky, Michael T., *The End of the Russian Empire* (Macmillan, 1961).
Fueloep-Miller, René, *The Mind and Face of Bolshevism: An Examination of Cultural Life in Soviet Russia* (Harper, 1965).
Kennan, George F., *Russia Leaves the War* (Atheneum, 1967).
Luxemburg, Rosa, *The Russian Revolution and Leninism or Marxism?* (U. of Michigan, 1961).
Meyer, Alfred G., *Leninism* (Praeger, 1957).
Pipes, Richard, *The Formation of the Soviet Union: Communism and Nationalism 1917–1923* (Atheneum, 1968).
Reed, John, *Ten Days That Shook the World* (International, 1967).

Revolutions in Germany, Austria-Hungary, and Turkey

Antonius, George, *The Arab Awakening* (Putnam, 1965).
Armstrong, H. C., *Gray Wolf, The Life of Kemal Ataturk* (Putnam, 1961).
*Burdick, Charles B., and Lutz, Robert H., eds., *Political Institutions of the German Revolution 1918–1919* (Stanford, 1966).
Jaszi, Oscar, *The Dissolution of the Hapsburg Monarchy* (U. of Chicago, 1961).

The Peace Settlements After World War I

Birdsall, Paul, *Versailles Twenty Years After* (Shoe String, 1941).

Lederer, Ivo J., *The Versailles Settlement—Was It Foredoomed to Failure?* (Heath, 1960).

Mayer, Arno J., *Wilson vs. Lenin: Political Origins of the New Diplomacy, 1917–1918* (World, 1959).

*Noble, George B., *Policies and Opinions at Paris, 1919* (Fertig, 1967).

Wheeler-Bennett, J. W., *Brest Litovsk, The Forgotten Peace, March 1918* (St. Martins, 1957).

CHAPTER XXVI

✥ *The Search for Security*
(1919-1929)

The decade between World War I and the Great Depression was marked by strong currents of pessimism in Western civilization. The horrors of the war had helped undermine Western man's faith in reason. Irrationality now touched politics, literature, art, and man's assessment of himself in general. While people and governments searched for security from want and wars, new socio-political forces competed for the allegiance of the masses whom the war had catapulted into prominence.

The temper of the times

Absolutes had come to be questioned already in the last decades before the war, but in this postwar era, lack of certainty became a pervasive attitude in Western life. This new feeling manifested itself in many ways and seemed to fit the mood of the new generation. Sigmund Freud (1856-1939) had done his spadework around the turn of the century, and Freudian psychology with its emphasis on unconscious forces came into its own after the war. Thereafter, psychology, often in popularized and diluted form, exerted strong influence particularly on writers and artists, affecting both contents and style of their work. Symbolism and stream of consciousness, nightmares and mysterious unconscious forces, inner motivation, doubt, and self-despair marked much of the literature (André Gide, Marcel Proust, Franz Kafka, and James Joyce, for instance) that appealed to the postwar intelligentsia. In art, Dadaism, a short-lived movement started during the war, derided all accepted rules of painting in favor of madly haphazard composition. Dada's successor, Surrealism, leaned heavily on the Freudian unconscious to picture the mysterious and the incongruous. Increasing in popularity were the Cubists (Pablo Picasso and Georges Braque) who, like the physicists, recognized the fallacy of accepting the material world as seen by the human eye. Hence they sought to depict objects in component geometric patterns. The same rejection of traditional standards occurred in music when composers (Arnold Schoenberg, for example) abandoned conventional tonality and chord construction and instead adopted the twelve-tone scale.

Scientists discovered fallacies in the absolutes of the Newtonian universe and became resigned to the new proposition that science deals with hypotheses rather than with eternal "truths." The discovery of the quantum theory (Max Planck's principle that the molecular emission of energy is not continuous but occurs sporadically), Albert Einstein's (1879–1955) law of relativity, as well as the theory of indeterminacy (developed by Werner Heisenberg) sharply contributed to this lessening faith in scientific certainty. At the same time, the growing knowledge of atomic theory revolutionized man's concept of the physical universe and added to his perplexity, since matter turned out not to be the solid substance previously imagined but an agglomeration of energy perceivable by man.

While British philosophers elaborated a new analytical method, Logical Positivism, in hopes of endowing philosophy with mathematical certainty, Martin Heidegger (1889–   ) in Germany further developed existentialism. Avoiding traditional philosophical systems, existentialism stressed personal experience and commitment rather than principles. Man's anxiety, so the existentialists asserted, derived from his essential aloneness and his constant need to make decisions. Well attuned to the tenor of the 1920's, this new view of life was to become widespread after World War II.

Decreased confidence in rational solutions also characterized political behavior in many countries. Demagogues and dictators appealed to the emotions of the masses and vaunted their contempt for democracy, which they scorned as a product of eighteenth-century rationalism with its premise of rational behavior in individual citizens.

Besides indulging in neo-romantic escapism, novelists, dramatists, and producers of silent films engaged in vigorous attacks on persistent social inequities, on remnants of Social Darwinism, and on the tendency to glorify war. The futility of war, for example, was underscored in such typical novels as Erich Maria Remarque's *All Quiet on the Western Front* (1929). The misery and hopelessness of the lower classes was dramatized by Bertolt Brecht in his *Three Penny Opera* (1928) and was evoked in mimed pathos in Charles Chaplin's movies.

On the whole, the war had shattered the stable world of Victorian traditions. People felt more inclined to experiment, in the arts as well as in social mores. It is not surprising, for instance, that the jazz age abandoned the traditional dances to plunge into a multitude of new and bewildering steps, while the emancipation of women, especially in the more industrialized countries, fostered political and social equality of the sexes.

The quest for normalcy

The war left most ex-belligerents with a heightened desire for security. The return of peace, on the other hand, presented them with economic and social problems of a magnitude never before encountered. Unable to solve these problems through traditional means, many nations eventually resorted to totalitarian dictatorships.

Postwar readjustments

In most cases, the degree of suffering experienced during the war affected the amount of changes expected after termination of hostilities. The more people had suffered, the more they claimed compensation, either as a nation or as social groups within a given society.

The United States and her Latin-American allies had lost relatively little in the fighting; only eight Central and South American republics had actually declared war. Hence, the American states expected to return to normalcy, as if the war had been but an unpleasant interruption. The Republican majority in the United States (under Harding, Coolidge, and Hoover) sought to reduce the economic influence of the federal government, restore greater controls to private enterprise, and lessen the power of organized labor, partly out of fear of growing radicalism. Increasingly higher tariffs resulted in greater economic isolation, since such barriers prevented foreigners from earning dollars in American markets and forced others to rely heavily on American loans for the purchase of United States goods. A brief postwar recession was followed by mounting prosperity, spurred by installment buying and lower taxes. While "business as usual" was resumed, speculation on the stock market soon assumed unusual proportions.

Return to normalcy included a deep longing for moral purity, as seen in the enactment of prohibition. Yet, despite religious crusades for a spotless life of honesty and labor, the 1920's had their measure of scandals, of bathtub gin, and frenzied search for pleasure and fast wealth.

Feeling that they had wasted lives and other resources on a useless "European war," many Americans became more isolationist than ever. Strict quotas lowering immigration were enacted to reduce the "alien" strain in American life. The Senate refused to ratify the Treaty of Versailles, since it also contained the covenant for the League of Nations, which the isolationists did not wish to join. Instead, the United States eventually concluded a separate peace with Germany. Moreover, Washington tried to disassociate itself from Europe's financial and economic problems. During the war, America had extended to the Allies large loans, which were now expected to be repaid. The Allies, however, contended that the liquidation of their debts depended in part on Germany's payment of reparations, a contention stanchly rejected by Washington. In the end, a curious merry-go-round developed, with Americans lending money to the Germans, who used part of it to pay reparations to the Allies, who in turn took a portion to repay wartime loans to America. The Wall Street crash of 1929 soon put an end to this financial whirl.

In most Latin-American countries, the war brought about an expansion of trade, the growth of some local industry, and a sharp increase in foreign investments, particularly for the exploitation of raw materials. As a result, tension increased in the 1920's between the conservative "establishment" of landholders, church, army hierarchy, and upper middle class on the one hand and the growing proletariat (mostly agricultural) and lower middle class on the other. At the same time, nationalistic resentment against foreign companies increased.

Great Britain, for her part, experienced serious economic dislocation and suffered some destruction from air raids as well as heavy casualties. Yet, in contrast to most Continental states, British losses were light, and many Britons assumed that the nation could easily return to the comforts of prewar life. This attitude, reinforced by a temporary industrial boom and prosperity, complicated the task of postwar reconstruction.

The parliamentary elections of 1918, the first in which women participated, gave Lloyd George an overwhelming mandate to speak for Britain at the Versailles Conference. Proud of being once again on the winning side, the usually reserved Britons spiced their campaign with vengeful calls to "Hang the Kaiser" and to "Squeeze the [German] orange till the pips squeak." It was to be several years before these vengeful feelings subsided.

After the immediate postwar economic bubble burst, unemployment, labor unrest, strikes, and a slump in trade evoked the hesitant realization that new adjustments were required. These conditions, together with the spectacular growth of a more militant Labor party and the rapid decline of the Liberal party, led even the Conservatives to turn Britain from laissez faire and free trade to greater government intervention. Emergency doles to the unemployed, subsidies for miners, and protective tariffs were instituted to relieve distress among the workers and to aid industry.

The fact that the war had altered the status of imperial relations was also gradually recognized. The division of Ireland into Protestant Ulster in the North and Catholic provinces in the South, effected in 1920, failed to solve the perennial Irish problem. After years of repression and civil war between British troops and proponents of Irish independence (the Sinn Fein), the southern provinces were finally granted the status of a self-governing dominion within the British Empire and adopted the name of the Irish Free State in 1922. Nonetheless, friction continued between those Irish satisfied with dominion status and arch-republicans, led by Eamon de Valera (1882–   ), who rejected all ties to Great Britain and particularly the oath of loyalty to the king. While England and the Irish Free State engaged in a tariff war, hostile incidents multiplied between Ulster and the new Irish Free State. It was not until 1949 that Eire became a republic and achieved complete independence from Great Britain.

Relations with the British dominions that had contributed so much to England's war effort were discussed in a series of imperial conferences during the 1920's. In 1923, the dominions were granted the right to conclude foreign treaties on their own; three years later, they were awarded autonomous and equal status with England, all being freely associated in allegiance to the crown. The Statute of Westminster (1931) finally contained a complete outline for the British Commonwealth of Nations. Relations with India, however, were more complicated than those with European-populated Australia and Canada. After the British crown had taken over control of India from the East India Company (1858), Britain had initially done little to encourage the development of self-government. Only shortly before World War I had the Indians been awarded a considerable voice in legislative and executive councils, and their contribution to the war effort forced Britain to pay even greater heed to India's demands for more self-government. A year after termination of hostilities, a bicameral all-Indian parliament was established and some provinces were granted local governmental responsibility, although the British viceroy still retained wide powers of control. Since most Indians were dissatisfied with such minor concessions, nationalist independence movements grew in intensity. Some were violent, engaging in riots and massacres; others, led by Mahatma Gandhi (1869–1948) and Jawaharlal Nehru (1889–1964), preached nonviolent resistance to British authority. Provincial governments were given more self-government in 1935 and a federation of British and native-controlled states was suggested; yet no further changes were effected before the advent of World War II.

Like all capitalist countries, England faced the dilemma of relations with Russia's new Soviet regime. Fear of bolshevism, anger at Russia's unilateral repudiation of her foreign debt, and uneasiness over political repercussions at home were only partially balanced by desire for trade with Russia. Soon after the first Labor government under Ramsay MacDonald (1866–1937) was installed in 1924, *de jure* recognition was extended to Soviet Russia and commercial treaties with the Soviets were signed. When the Conservatives returned to power a few months later, the treaties with Russia were abrogated and diplomatic relations were again severed. Although relations with Russia were resumed in 1929, when MacDonald returned to the prime ministership, British distrust of the Soviet Union hardly diminished until Hitler's attack on Russia in 1941.

On the other hand, peoples that had suffered heavily from the war, as in France, Italy, Serbia, and Germany, expected to receive compensation for their losses. French industry, mines, and agriculture in the north were destroyed; France's foreign assets were lost, her trade ruined, and her currency undermined. Moreover, war casualties, a serious excess of civilian deaths over births, and a staggering total of disabled veterans added to the decline of population that further heightened French apprehension of a possible resurgence of German military power.

To speed up reconstruction, the French pressed for maximum deliveries of reparations from Germany, in raw materials as well as manufactured goods. They encouraged immigration and awarded state subsidies to large families in order to increase the population. To stabilize the franc, they resorted to new taxes, funded the national debt, and ultimately devaluated the currency. Yet none of the measures taken gave France socio-economic stability or the assurance that the sacrifices of the war had been worthwhile.

Bitterness among the Italians was even more pronounced, heightened as it was by the government's failure to fulfill promises made during the war in order to popularize the anti-Austrian campaign. Veterans could not find jobs; widows received inadequate pensions; inflation undermined the security of the middle class, with prices 800 per cent higher in 1920 than in 1913; nationalists felt that Italy's territorial gains from the war had been insufficient and that *Italia irredenta* was still not redeemed; and many Italians felt slighted by the Allies when not a single mandated German or Turkish territory was awarded to Italy. Yet, despite the discontent among the population, the growing street fighting between opposing factions, and the instability of Italy's democratic institutions, most professional politicians sought to conduct affairs of state in the usual manner. Such disregard of political realities left the field open for communist and fascist demagogues.

Serbia, which had suffered greater destruction per capita than any other state, was compensated by an increase in territory to more than twice its prewar size. The enlarged state, at first officially called the Kingdom of Serbs, Croats, and Slovenes, labored under great internal divergencies. Not counting smaller minorities, such as Italians, German-speaking Austrians, and Montenegrins, there were four major language groups: Serbs, Croats, Slovenes, and Macedonians. The peoples used two alphabets, both the Cyrillic and the Latin, and practiced three major religions: Greek Orthodox (48 per cent), Roman Catholic (37 per cent), and Moslem (11 per cent). It proved difficult to weld these divergent groups into a single state. The Serbs, proud of their century-old independence, favored a centralized government under their domination, whereas the Croats and other ethnic groups demanded a loose, federalized structure. Moreover, no social reforms were undertaken. The result was governmental instability and frequent political murder, until the king (Alexander, 1921–1934) established a royal dictatorship in 1929 and tried to apply force to shape his country into a unitary state, an attempt symbolized by changing the name of his kingdom to Yugoslavia.

Germany, for her part, had suffered little physical destruction, but her finances and economy were in ruin. Disillusionment and bitterness prevailed. Veterans who had spent years in rat-infested trenches returned to a defeated and truncated Germany and found themselves mauled in the streets as symbols of the militarism that had plunged the country into a losing war. Unable to find jobs, some veterans joined the free corps, paramilitary organizations formed by self-confident officers. Free corps units battled in the streets of Germany, participated in the Russian civil war, and fought in the Russo-Polish campaigns of 1920. Most of them fought for hire rather than for political ideals, but all opposed the status quo and the new Weimar regime.

Many Germans resented the onus of the Treaty of Versailles and unjustly blamed the Weimar government for having signed the treaty. In addition, the lower classes were not satisfied with the mere grant of political equality, but also expected social benefits. They were particularly disappointed that the Social Democrats, initially in control of the government, implemented no socialistic measures, despite their doctrinaire Socialist slogans. Workers were worried when the federal government, although dominated by left-wing and center parties, was induced by fear of communism to lean increasingly toward the conservatives. Soon runaway inflation, which reached its apex in 1923, undermined the confidence of the middle class and made them skeptical about the advantages of a democratic republic. The Weimar Republic thus was started on a tenuous footing.

Moreover, in most countries various social groups expected rewards for their contributions to the war or compensation for suffering. Widows insisted on pensions; unions sought more rights and greater job security; the handicapped and mutilated claimed government assistance; the middle class called for greater safety for their savings and investments. On the one hand, such demands gave a boost to the growing Socialist parties in many countries; on the other, they added to the widening appeal of various fascist movements.

The search for international security

Five discernible policies marked the nations' search for international security after World War I: isolationism, reliance on a balance of power, regional security pacts, collective security, and disarmament.

The first of these policies, reliance on neutrality or isolation, was practiced by those states that had benefited from neutrality during the war. Switzerland, Holland, and the Scandinavian monarchies continued to prefer non-alignment, though they all joined the League of Nations. Despite her stanch adherence to neutrality, even Switzerland subscribed to the League's compulsory arbitration clauses as early as 1920.

Although a belligerent, the United States went beyond neutrality into isolation. Notwithstanding Woodrow Wilson's initial pleas, the Republican majority in the Senate was determined to return America to a policy of non-involvement in international affairs. The Senate rejected Clemenceau's call for an Anglo-American-French alliance and voted against membership in the League of Nations. Wilson's stubborn attitude probably contributed to these decisions. Association with the Permanent Court of International Justice was also rejected, although participation in some non-political discussions sponsored by the League was later authorized.

Despite this preference for isolation from Europe, America remained alert to her interests in Latin America, in the Far East, and in naval matters. She participated in various conferences on Latin American affairs. In 1921, she signed the Four-Power Pact in regard to the Far East, whereby America, Britain, France, and Japan pledged mutual respect for each other's rights and interests—a maneuver partly designed to undermine Britain's special position in the Far East. The Nine-Power Pact of the same year, concluded by Japan and the colonial powers, was presumably intended to prevent Japan from gaining privileges in China. The United States moreover sponsored the Washington Conference on the Limitation of Armaments (1921), at which America, Great Britain, Japan, France, and Italy agreed on a fixed ratio of tonnage for capital ships. Aimed at easing the naval race and at reducing military expenditures, this agreement was followed by further naval conferences in 1927 and 1930, in which the United States participated.

Italy and Germany were caught in their own peculiar isolation. After Mussolini's seizure of power (see p. 483), he developed a "go-it-alone" policy based presumably on military and economic strength. World War I, he thought, had taught the Italians that allies could not be trusted. To be sure, he concluded treaties of friendship with most Balkan countries in order to extend Italian influence in that area; but, in essence, Mussolini sought to base Italy's security on internal strength. He abandoned this stand only in the mid-1930's and helped create the Rome-Berlin "axis," when he felt the need for firm outside support for his African and Mediterranean ventures (see p. 509).

Germany's isolation resulted largely from her postwar ostracism from the community of Europe. Except for cooperative friendship with Russia, another pariah, Germany remained without allies during the 1920's.

A second formula for international security, based on a balance of power, was adopted by Great Britain, who was also tempted to return to her insularity, although her world-wide imperial commitments rendered such a policy impossible. She became very active in the League of Nations and participated in many multilateral conferences, but refused to enter into binding alliances. As in previous periods, she expected to use her influence for bringing the balance of power into proper equilibrium. In the Far East, Britain tried unsuccessfully to smooth over the conflicting interests of Japan, China, and Russia. In Europe, British statesmen soon feared that Germany's apparent prostration in contrast to France's resurgence and continued attempt to further crush Germany might produce a serious dislocation of

European power. Hence, some of them began to favor Germany over France, an attitude that proved to be a dilemma for British policy after the rise of Hitler in the 1930's.

A third path to security involved alliances of the prewar type, aimed at regional security. This policy proved particularly attractive to France. Disappointed by American withdrawal from Continental affairs and wary of British intentions, the French sought safety by establishing their own security system outside of the League of Nations. In the course of the 1920's, the French government concluded bilateral alliances with Belgium, Poland, Czechoslovakia, Rumania, and Yugoslavia. Initially, these pacts were designed as safeguards against a possible resurgence of Germany, Austria, or Hungary. Over the centuries, the French had become accustomed to putting pressure on Central Europe by concluding alliances with states to the east— at first Turkey, Poland, and Sweden, and later Russia. Since France shunned a *rapprochement* with the bolsheviks, the new states of Eastern Europe now took the place of Russia. This alliance system initially helped the small states and spread French influence; but its inherent insufficiency was to become apparent in the 1930's. In addition to the military weakness of the smaller states in contrast to Germany and Russia, there was a fatal ambiguity in the alliances from the vantage point of the eastern states. They sought for themselves protection against penetration by Soviet Russia as well as against the revisionist policies of such defeated Central Powers as Hungary and Bulgaria. At the critical moment in 1938, Poland, Czechoslovakia, and Rumania in particular were hard put to decide whether the greater danger to their own security lay in Germany or in Russia.

Another example of regional security was established in Eastern Europe with the encouragement of France. The Czechs, Rumanians, and Yugoslavs, whose countries were largely carved out of the former Austro-Hungarian Empire, formed a Little Entente (1921) as reassurance against Hungarian revisionism. The three states naturally sought to keep the territorial status quo, whereas Hungary agitated for revision of the peace treaty and a return of the territories lost in 1919.

There were various other arrangements for regional security, some bilateral, others multilateral. Starting in 1922, Germany and the Soviet Union entered into several agreements involving mutual cancellation of debts, increased economic cooperation, and eventual military collaboration. The growing Red Army could benefit from German technology, while the German military could secretly use Russian soil for trying out weapons prohibited by the Treaty of Versailles. Although not a military alliance, this Russo-German cooperation afforded both states an added measure of security—at least until the advent of Hitler. Similarly, Soviet Russia began during the later 1920's to conclude non-aggression pacts with most of the states bordering on her frontiers. Such treaties were designed to draw Russia's neighbors away from the anticommunist camp.

The Locarno Treaties of 1925 represented attempts at regional security along the borders of Germany. In these agreements, Germany, France, and Belgium, with England and Italy as guarantors, consented to maintain the inviolability of the Rhineland boundaries as fixed by the Treaty of Versailles. The Germans however refused to extend similar guarantees in respect to their eastern frontiers, although they signed arbitration treaties with Poland and Czechoslovakia, which stipulated that these boundaries would not be changed by force. On paper at least, the Locarno Treaties thus added to the security of France and Belgium; for the Czechs and Poles, however, they did not provide the same reassurance against German desire to revise the boundaries set by Versailles.

A fourth path to international peace lay in collective security, a relatively new concept embodied in the League of Nations. According to the preamble of its covenant, the League, officially inaugurated in 1920, was "to achieve international peace and security by the acceptance of obligations not to resort to war." But it was handicapped from the first by the absence of three of the world's major powers—the United States, Soviet Russia, and Germany—and by the reluctance of powerful states to submit to international arbitration. Nevertheless, in its lifetime it was effective in handling some thirty minor disputes, and various organizations under its auspices worked on assuaging world-wide economic and social problems.

Although the League of Nations fell far short of becoming the international panacea envisioned by Woodrow Wilson, and failed dismally in the face of the major international crises of the 1930's, it set a valuable precedent for international cooperation. Despite the sneers of skeptics, its very existence furthered the realization that national sovereignty must bow to international law, if peace is to be preserved.

After the rise of Adolf Hitler in Germany (1933), however, the ideals of the League in part gave way to a new type of collective security, which in essence resembled the prewar system of alliances. Russia, which entered the League in 1934, assumed the lead in calling for the establishment of a grand antifascist bloc, directed chiefly against Nazi Germany and to some extent against Italy and Japan. Hitler, for his part, formed his Anti-Comintern Pact with Japan, Italy, and others, aimed at containing, if not ultimately eradicating, communism in Russia. Although many of the powers remained uncommitted, unsure whether communism or fascism represented the greater threat, this type of collective security soon split the world again into two hostile camps and recreated the dangers of 1914 (see p. 447).

Finally, a fifth road to international security lay in the idealists' quest for disarmament or the outlawing of war. The three naval conferences (see p. 477) temporarily slowed naval construction, but the two-year-long Geneva Disarmament Conference (1932–1934), in which sixty nations participated, failed to stem the armaments race in general. The visionary Kellogg-Briand Pact of 1928, co-sponsored by America and ultimately ratified by sixty-five states, required the signatories to renounce war "as an instrument of national policy." However, the nations could not agree on an acceptable definition of "aggression" and were unwilling to form an international army to restrain or punish a potential aggressor. Hence, the Kellogg-Briand Pact remained a paper hope. The Permanent Court of International Justice, for its part, successfully arbitrated some cases, but it could not enhance the authority of international law as a guarantor of world peace.

The confrontation of opposites

Whereas the nineteenth century had inclined toward compromise, the period between World War I and World War II was marked by the hard confrontation of opposites, if not extremes. Compromise was seen as a sign of weakness rather than wisdom, as the political and ideological "middle-of-the-road" lost its appeal. Resort to violence became more frequent in struggles between rightists and leftists, and greater tension soon developed between the "have" and "have-not" nations.

Left versus right

The socio-political struggle between the left and the right was hardly a new phenomenon, but after World War I it assumed a more organized and vehement form. The success of the Communist revolution in Russia, the first avowedly egalitarian regime to achieve lasting control of a major state, and the vaunted aim of the Third Communist International to achieve world-wide revolution naturally influenced all such confrontations.

In the United States this struggle remained in its mildest form, although it inspired many headlines and ruffled emotions. Communists gained influence in several unions and helped organize strikes, some involving violence. Fear of "radicalism" was rampant and an apprehensive public applauded the government's hunt of "reds" and deportation of foreign-born suspects. Yet, outright communism remained weak and lost ground with the return of prosperity. Even the Socialists, despite their moderation, polled less than a million votes in 1920, when Eugene V. Debs ran for the fifth time for the presidency, despite the fact that he was then in prison on a charge of treason. Four years later, the even more moderate Progressive Robert LaFollette carried only his own state of Wisconsin in the presidential elections.

In England, and especially in France, the confrontation between left and right was more vehement than in the United States, producing occasional clashes in the streets and weakening the political stability of the two states. After Lloyd George resigned in 1922, the Conservatives governed for slightly more than a year before being in turn supplanted by Ramsay MacDonald's Labor party. However, since MacDonald needed the support of the Liberals, he had no opportunity to get any Socialist legislation passed. Abroad he sought to steer a new course toward international harmony by working for a *détente* in Europe in cooperation with the leftist bloc in France under Edouard Herriot (1872–1957). Furor over a loan to Russia, designed to prime Anglo-Russian trade, coupled with rumors of Communist plots, soon brought about MacDonald's electoral defeat and resulted in victory for the Conservatives in late 1924.

This two-fold swing of the political pendulum in England was followed by five years of Conservative rule. Except for again severing relations with Soviet Russia (see p. 474), Prime Minister Stanley Baldwin (1867–1947) essentially continued Labor's policy of Continental collaboration. At home, his measures were conservative. Protectionist tariffs, an attitude of laissez-faire, and a return to the gold standard were supposed to strengthen Britain's industrial and financial structure. After some 2,500,000 members of the Trades Union Congress organized a General Strike in 1926 in solidarity with striking miners whose wages were threatened with reduction, the Baldwin government outlawed such strikes, but did little to improve the lot of the miners. The Conservatives' inability to solve the economic problems resulted in their defeat in 1929 and their replacement by a second Labor ministry under Ramsay MacDonald, whose task was complicated by repercussions from the New York stock market crash that occurred four months after his assumption of office.

Although unemployment was not severe, political fluctuations in France were even more pronounced than in England. Between 1920 and 1929, there were nineteen changes of ministries. The parties on the right, including revived monarchists, were mostly nationalistic, strongly pro-Catholic, and sometimes anti-Semitic. At home, they called for the restoration of rights to the Catholic Church and hoped to weaken the unions, especially the General Confederation of Labor (C.G.T.); abroad, they demanded strict enforcement of reparations payments from Germany and advocated a tight security system for the containment of Germany and Soviet Russia. The leftist parties, for their part, were anticlerical and demanded increased social legislation. Most of them favored amicable relations with the Weimar Republic and Soviet Russia and stanchly supported the League of Nations.

Soon after the signing of the Treaty of Versailles, which many Frenchmen considered too lenient, Clemenceau's wartime coalition fell apart. While the numerous parties resumed their traditional freedom of action, a right wing (*Bloc National*) and a left wing (*Cartel des Gauches*) were formed for the sake of election strategy, since no single party could hope to gain a majority. With the right wing in power between 1920 and 1924, relations with the Vatican were resumed, some properties restored to the Catholic Church, attempts made to strengthen the presidency, and the first treaties in the French security system signed. To extract faster payments of German reparations, Prime Minister Raymond Poincaré, who had been president of France from 1913 to 1920, sent French troops into Germany's highly industrialized Ruhr region in 1923—an ill-fated step which further embittered

Franco-German relations. German resort to passive resistance against the French occupation armies and the accompanying runaway inflation of the German currency further hampered the delivery of reparations. This failure of Poincaré's "tough policy" led to an electoral victory of the leftist bloc in 1924.

Under Edouard Herriot, the French government reinstituted anticlerical measures, sought to weaken the powers of the president, and tried to lessen international tension by recognizing Soviet Russia and by reducing friction in the Rhineland (Locarno Treaties). The patient labors of Aristide Briand (1862–1932)—prime minister eleven times between 1909 and 1930, and foreign minister from 1925 until his death—achieved a measure of international security, but the leftist bloc could not solve France's mounting financial crisis. In 1926, Poincaré returned to power at the head of a cabinet of national union, including representatives from the left and the right. The new government, which was granted the power to rule by decree, adopted measures to balance the budget and reduce the national debt, and eventually devalued the franc by 80 per cent. These steps brought some stability to French finances, at a time when the Great Depression was about to create new chaos on the international monetary market. While Briand pursued further conciliatory steps toward Germany, the government also began to construct the Maginot Line, a system of intricate fortifications from the Swiss border to the Belgian border that brought further stability to the Rhineland. Construction of the Maginot Line, however, should have alerted France's eastern allies that she planned a policy of pure self-defense and might not be willing to come to their aid in case of attack by Germany or Russia.

Whereas the confrontation of left and right was mild in the United States and more polarized in England and France, it assumed violent proportions in Italy and Germany. Strikes, riots, and street fighting marked the early years of postwar Italy. No party or electoral bloc could master a majority to form a stable government. The Socialists, the largest party in 1919, refused to cooperate with either the newly formed Communist party or with bourgeois groups. Fearful of the Bolsheviks' strident propaganda, some of the traditional and semiconservative forces, supported by the Catholic Church, formed the Popular party, a forerunner of today's Christian Democrats. In addition, various smaller and less cohesive parties joined in temporary and ineffective political coalitions. But nothing served to save the government from paralysis caused by growing interparty discord.

Such disorder presented fertile ground for the emergence of new groups, proffering extremist panaceas. Among these was Benito Mussolini's (1883–1945) black-shirted Fascist party, which, in 1919, issued an intensely nationalistic and opportunistic party program, "revolutionary and hence antidogmatic . . . new and beyond limiting principles." Mussolini, himself an ex-socialist, advocated enough democratic and socialistic measures, such as lowering the voting age, an eight-hour work day, a minimum wage, and nationalization of the defense industry, to attract many workers and lower bourgeois. On the other hand, he reassured the propertied classes with promises of economic stability, safety from communism, national glory, and "a role in international life." Organized along paramilitary lines, Fascist squads terrorized the country with punitive expeditions. Meanwhile their leaders blamed all chaos on the "reds" and promised to enforce order after their assumption of power.

In October, 1922, the Fascists staged a so-called March on Rome in order to put pressure on the central government. Rather than declare martial law and use the army to repress this threat, the perplexed king asked Mussolini to form a new government. This act saved the monarchy at the cost of Italy's tottering democracy. At the head of a new coalition cabinet dominated by Fascists, the flamboyant Mussolini was granted power to rule by decree for a year. Armed with this legal power and loyally supported by his blackshirted squads, the new prime minister gradually suppressed all opposition, by force or persuasion. The suspension of civil rights, the use of censorship, recourse to political tribunals, and the replacement of local leaders by Fascist appointees helped centralize all power in the head of the Fascist party. After widespread revulsion against Fascist methods threatened to erupt in unrest, Mussolini changed his prime ministership into an avowed dictatorship (1925). With Fascists assuming full control, *Il Duce* (The Leader), as he styled himself, then began to transform the state and its economy, to recast Italian social and intellectual life, and launch a new and more active foreign policy (see p. 509).

In Germany's Weimar Republic, internal strife also assumed violent forms during the early postwar period (see p. 476). Communists, nationalists, neo-monarchists, militarists, and assorted antidemocrats repeatedly used shock troops and staged putsches in attempts at toppling the republican regime in Berlin or overthrowing some of the state governments. Resort to force became an accepted form of political action. After the threat of sovietization declined, anti-Bolsheviks, anti-Semites, and antidemocrats continued to refine their tactics of political terror. Some whom they regarded as "traitors to the fatherland," liberals or advocates of compliance with the Treaty of Versailles, were condemned to death in secret meetings and were subsequently murdered. Significantly, the German courts, still staffed by conservative judges left over from the imperial period, were lenient with those seeking to assassinate the republic from the right, but reacted more severely against similar attempts from the left.

Despite a model constitution, the Weimar Republic continued to flounder in political instability. In addition to nine major parties, there were numerous small splinter groups, most of them representing social and economic interests of the right. Among them was the National Socialist German Workers' Party (NSDAP), which ultimately became Adolf Hitler's vehicle to power in 1933. Incapable of achieving financial solvency, of dealing with the demand for reparations in a manner that would satisfy France without enraging domestic public opinion, and of making the Treaty of Versailles more palatable, twelve hapless coalition cabinets followed one another at brief intervals between 1919 and 1924.

After the disastrous inflation of 1923, which wiped out the savings of the middle class and ruined the security of pensioners, widows, and disabled veterans, and after the failure of renewed leftist and rightist uprisings that almost destroyed the republic, the government launched a determined campaign for financial and political stabilization. Under Gustav Stresemann (1878–1929), who served as chancellor in the fall of 1923 and then guided Germany's foreign policy until 1929, a period of "fulfillment and stabilization" was inaugurated. The inflation was cut short by the issuance of a new currency. A more stable economy in turn lessened political friction. Recognizing that Germany was in no position to evade fulfillment of the obligations imposed by the Treaty of Versailles, Stresemann strove to promote a climate of international goodwill by accepting the Dawes Plan (1924) which scaled down Germany's annual reparations payments and by signing the Locarno Treaties (see p. 479). As a result, Germany was admitted to membership in the League of Nations in 1926. Stresemann hoped that readmission to the family of nations would quench German thirst for self-respect and might eventually permit a revision of the Treaty of Versailles in Germany's favor.

In several other states, antagonism between political extremes led to outright civil war. As we saw in the last chapter (see p. 464), Hungary was plunged into armed conflict between "whites" (anti-Communists) and "reds" when the Communist Bela Kun attempted to convert the country into a soviet republic, modeled on experiments then being made in Russia. Kun's defeat by the anti-Communist forces was followed by several months of "white terror" against all left-wing elements. Under Horthy's regency, the government then became increasingly conservative. Unhappy with the Treaty of Trianon and frightened by the civil war of 1919, the Hungarians also aligned themselves more and more with the revisionist and authoritarian forces of Europe.

Russia, for her part, was plunged into a longer and more destructive civil war. The Bolsheviks' seizure of power on November 7, 1917 (see p. 461) did not assure Lenin of control over the entire country, nor even over the Constituent Assembly which met in January, 1918. To gain the upper hand, the Bolsheviks set up a secret police, the *Cheka* (Extraordinary Commission for the Suppression of the Counterrevolution), and organized the Red Army, composed mostly of volunteers and directed by Leon Trotsky. While the *Cheka* used terror to extirpate counterrevolutionary elements, the Red Army was readied to defend Bolshevism. Most politically oriented Russians opposed Lenin's regime and particularly objected to the Treaty of Brest

Litovsk (see p. 453), which the Bolsheviks signed in March of 1918. The need for armed support to ensure the survival of the new government became all the more urgent when in June, 1918, the Allies sent expeditionary corps first into northern Russia, then to her Black Sea ports, while the Japanese undertook similar steps on the Pacific shores of Siberia. Officially, the British, French, and American contingents were dispatched to prevent Allied war material in Russia from falling into the hands of the advancing German armies. Actually, the Allies hoped to keep the Russian front against Germany open, or to reopen it, while at the same time supporting anti-Red forces to prevent the triumph of Bolshevism.

By late 1918, "white" armies and foreign troops controlled major portions of Russia. "White" governments were installed in various areas, a troop of released Czech prisoners of war seized control of the Trans-Siberian railway, and Japanese, French, British, and American contingents occupied strategic posts in the East, South, and North. By 1919, the Red Army was facing the additional task of fighting Poland over possession of Lithuanian, White Russian, and Ukrainian territory. In the face of this multiple onslaught, Russia seemed at first to disintegrate.

The utter confusion of these years may be illustrated by the fate of the Ukraine, which became an independent, moderately socialist, state in January, 1918. In February, the Red Army conquered most of the Ukraine, before having to abandon it in March to the Germans, who thereupon installed a conservative government. When Germany collapsed in November, 1918, Ukrainian Socialists overthrew the conservative regime. A month later, French armies seized the southern Ukraine and in February, 1919, the Red Army retook the northern areas. By April, the French were expelled and the Ukraine once again turned into a Socialist Republic, only to be captured by "white" Russian armies in the following August. Even after the Bolsheviks reconquered the state in December, 1919, the fate of the Ukraine was not yet sealed. In the following spring, Polish armies conquered the area in the course of the Russo-Polish War, but were driven out by a Bolshevik counteroffensive a month later. In the summer of 1920, the war-torn Ukraine was finally joined to the Soviet Union to become one of the Soviet Socialist Republics.

Victorious in the Russo-Polish War, the Red Army also emerged triumphant from the civil war. The "whites" were defeated, foreign troops were evacuated, and the Bolsheviks achieved control of Russia. The latter owed their success to Trotsky's superb organizational talents, to the fanaticism of their followers, and to the patriotism and loyalty of the peasants, who resented the foreign incursions and who were swayed by Lenin's promise of land. Moreover, the disunity among their opponents, "white" generals and foreign commanders alike, each fighting for their own purpose, facilitated the triumph of the Bolsheviks.

During this period, China also became engulfed in civil wars that were to last three decades. The revolution of 1911 had overthrown the Manchu rulers, whom the Chinese still resented as foreigners even though they had ruled China for over two and a half centuries. Impatient with the slow pace of reforms and the inability of the imperial government to resist continuing foreign encroachment, the Chinese declared a republic in 1912. But Sun Yat-sen (1866–1925), the revolutionary leader who advocated the three principles of "Nationalism, Democracy, and Social Progress," and his Kuomintang (Nationalist People's Party) found it difficult to establish an orderly central government in the face of semi-independent war lords who were assuming control in many provinces. Moreover, the Japanese opposed the emergence of a revitalized, republican China and sought to acquire the influence formerly exerted by the Western powers. During World War I, they had seized the German areas in China, extended their ascendancy over the northern provinces, and gained a share in the control of Chinese industry.

In the early 1920's, Soviet Russia helped Sun Yat-sen organize an army for the Kuomintang in support of his attempt to unify the country. After the death of Sun, who despite his failure became a national hero, General Chiang Kai-shek (1886–   ) took control of the Kuomintang and its army. Although the latter defeated some of the war lords, the Kuomintang could not extend its rule over the outlying provinces, including Manchuria, Tibet, and Outer Mongolia. Afraid of growing Communist influence among the peasants, Chiang finally split with them in 1927 and soon found himself in frequent armed clashes with the Communist forces led by Mao Tse-tung (1893–   ).

Taking advantage of these continued disorders in China and economically hurt by a Chinese boycott of Japanese textile goods, Japan invaded and seized the industrialized province of Manchuria in 1931. Despite this foreign threat, Communists and Kuomintang continued their civil war until 1937. In that year, new Japanese demands, whose rejection soon led to Japan's invasion of northeastern China, brought about renewed cooperation between Chiang and Mao. General Chiang meanwhile, at first a liberal revolutionary, began to develop an increasingly authoritarian regime to cope with the threat of Japan and of the remaining dissident war lords.

Although these world-wide confrontations between left and right did not all follow a similar path, they were characterized by the same general trend. In most countries, social and political antagonism increased in violence during the 1930's, partly as a consequence of the 1929 Depression. Violence was also heightened by the growing bitterness between the so-called have and the have-not nations.

Haves versus have-nots

International harmony was increasingly clouded by the demands of certain have-not nations. These states were not necessarily destitute, as the term might imply. On the contrary, Italy, for example, fared better economically than southern Europe in general, and Japan was by far wealthier than most areas of Asia. Yet, both states looked upon themselves as have-not nations. Hence they joined the camp of the revisionists, in particular Germany and Hungary, who called for revision of the peace settlements of 1919 and sought to redraw the map of the world in order to recoup their territorial losses after World War I.

The revisionists justified their demands on the basis of irredentism, of the need for living space for a growing population, or the claim that the world's riches should be shared more equitably. In the case of Japan's aspiration for a "New Order," in which she would exert economic and political control over China, Southeast Asia, and the Pacific Islands, it was simply a new form of imperialism.

The case of Fiume may serve as a typical example of irredentism. This Adriatic city, with a majority of Italian-speaking inhabitants, had belonged to the Austro-Hungarian realm since the fifteenth century. Italy's claims to Fiume were rejected at the Versailles Peace Conference and the area was instead awarded to Yugoslavia. Thereupon, the Italian war hero and nationalistic poet Gabriele D'Annunzio (1863–1938) seized Fiume with the aid of a band of devoted followers. Although the Italian government was embarrassed, Italian nationalists applauded D'Annunzio's audacity, and the powers met in conference and decided not to interfere. In late 1920, a bilateral Italo-Yugoslav agreement declared Fiume a Free City and the Italians sent troops to force D'Annunzio out of the city, much to the consternation of Italian patriots. In 1922, however, Italian Fascists overthrew the government of the Free City, and once again Italian troops seized the area, and a new Italo-Yugoslav treaty in 1924 finally awarded Fiume to Italy. Thus, another small portion of "Italia irredenta" had been redeemed through force and audacity.

Revisionist demands became more vehement during the 1930's, when nations showed less and less hesitation to use force to satisfy their aspirations. The have nations, for their part, countered all demands by insisting that the status quo was practically untouchable and showed little inclination to discuss or negotiate territorial changes.

Involvement of the masses

World War I, with its mobilization of millions for military and industrial service, had raised the masses to unprecedented importance. A new "mass" culture emerged, radically altering Western civilization, and, eventually after World War II, also the non-Western world.

Emergence of a mass culture

Although a relatively small group continued to dominate the governmental processes in most states, the introduction of universal suffrage, including the vote for women, and the development of large political parties increasingly involved the masses in the political life of the nations. This participation grew with the extension of literacy and education, and was made more meaningful through the rapid development of the mass media of communication. By 1930, for instance, there were 12,000,000 radios in American homes, and American studios produced over 4,000 features and short films for showing in some 23,000 motion picture theaters across the nation. And all along, daily circulation of newspapers multiplied.

The accelerated pace of industrialization also involved a majority of the population in Europe and North America. Assembly line production called for mass consumption. World industrial output doubled between 1921 and 1929. Transportation facilities expanded at a phenomenal rate, although the mileage of railroad tracks in use actually decreased in France, Germany, and England during the 1920's, as the trucking industry assumed greater importance. In the United States, where fewer than 200,000 cars, trucks and buses had been sold in 1910, such sales reached over 4,000,000 in 1925.

With the population engaged in industry rapidly growing—in America it more than doubled between 1900 and 1930—organized labor assumed·more importance. Large federations of unions, such as the General Confederation of Labor (CGT) in France and the Trades Union Congress (TUC) in England, became influential, although not yet very effective, pressure groups. England improved its unemployment payments in the early 1920's, and in 1930, France passed a National Workmen's Insurance Law which insured some 9,000,000 workers against sickness, old age, and death.

At the same time, the demand for mass entertainment increased at a fantastic rate. Weimar Germany built numerous municipal swimming pools and generously subsidized theaters and opera houses. Public parks and amusement centers abounded in Europe and national parks multiplied in the United States. Bicycle races and bullfights attracted millions of *aficionados*. In 1923, a crowd of 200,000 tried to get into the Wembley stadium near London to watch a soccer game; the 1928 season attracted 35,000,000 spectators to college football in the United States; and by 1929, 90,000,000 Americans per week attended movie theaters.

Greater involvement of the masses in the political, economic, and cultural life in the Western world accented their desire for a larger share in the benefits of an industrialized society. In many countries, these demands were skilfully exploited by dictators who appealed to the masses with promises of satisfying their claims.

New socio-political forms of government

During the 1920's, some twelve European and several Latin American and Asian states came under the rule of dictatorial regimes. Dictatorships were to be even more common during the 1930's. Whether led by a single man or by a group, dictatorships usually involved similar processes. Democratic and parliamentary institutions were either suspended or made meaningless. The nation's political life was more or less rigidly controlled, usually by a single party which loyally carried out the dictates of the leader. By monopolizing the effective means of mass communication, by using the police and the armed forces to suppress "enemies" of the regime and sometimes to attack arbitrarily selected scapegoats, and by directly or indirectly controlling the nation's economy, the dictators imposed their power on the entire population.

The goals of dictatorships varied. All aimed at achieving internal order; but some concentrated on economic reforms, others on a more aggressive foreign policy, on the suppression of dissident minorities, or on safeguarding the possessing classes from socialist expropriation. Moreover, many different types of dictatorships arose. Yugoslavia, for instance, experienced a royal dictatorship. Unable to achieve internal stability through democratic means, its king instituted himself as dictator in 1929. Spain, on the other hand, developed a military dictatorship under the aegis of a weak monarch, King Alphonso XIII (1886–1931). Postwar Spain was rent by disorder. Socialists, anarchists, and anticlericals contended with the entrenched class of landholders and the hierarchy of the Church; the Catalans again demanded autonomy. A military debacle in Spanish Morocco and revealed corruption in the army finally led King Alphonso to permit General Miguel Primo de Rivera (1870–1930) to establish a dictatorship in 1923. Although Rivera proved unable to solve Spain's social ills, his dictatorship heralded later Spanish developments (see p. 505).

Dictatorship in Poland took yet another form. Poland's position was precarious. In the East, she faced the Russians from whom she had taken some sixty thousand square miles as a result of the Russo-Polish War; and in the West, she occupied eighteen thousand square miles reclaimed by *revanchist* Germany. Moreover, Poland lacked internal stability. With little experience in self-government, burdened by the diverse heritage of century-long occupation by Prussians, Russians, and Austrians, and troubled by the presence of large White Russian, Ukrainian, and German minorities, the individualistic Poles formed some eighty political parties during the early 1920's. Their constitution, which sanctioned a weak executive and a strong legislature, rendered the government incapable of satisfying the peasants' call for land reform, or of reconciling the demands of the clericals on the one hand and the socialists on the other. In the face of this political chaos, General Jozef Pilsudski (1867–1935) assumed control of Poland in 1926. As a hero in the Polish independence movement prior to World War I and the commander of the Polish armies in the war against Russia (1919–1921), Pilsudski retained the loyalty of most of the armed forces. Although he never made himself a dictator in the formal sense, he controlled Polish affairs from behind a façade of officers and civilians who purportedly ran the state.

To be sure, all dictatorships involve appeals to some ideological concepts, be they nationalism, the belief in the future of the regime, or simply trust in the leader. But most dictatorships, whether run by a king, set up under a monarchy, or conducted by a group of army officers, were not characterized by strong ideologies. Hence, they were not totalitarian, and the governments did not try to control the totality of the lives of the people. Propaganda, for instance, played only a minor role in Yugoslavia, Spain, and Poland in the 1920's.

Italy and Russia, however, developed totalitarian dictatorships, in which ideology became a major motivating force for the construction of a radically new society. Here, elaborate socio-political pseudo-philosophies were expounded to effect a complete break with the past, to unify the country behind a common purpose, and to extend the nation's influence beyond its borders by ideological conquest, backed, when needed, by military pressure. Two major types of totalitarian dictatorships came to power during the 1920's: fascism and bolshevism. To avoid confusion, it should be stressed at the outset that fascism and bolshevism are alike only in that both used totalitarian dictatorships for the acquisition of power and the furtherance of their dogmas. Their ideologies were diametrically opposite.

Fascism favored the elite. According to Mussolini's own definition, it "affirms the immutable, beneficial and fruitful inequality of mankind." Communism, on the other hand, as advocated by the Bolsheviks, was egalitarian in its aims, theoretically working toward the abolition of all class distinctions. Fascism, as described by *Il Duce,* involved "the dictatorship of the state over many classes co-operating"; whereas communism sought to eliminate the bourgeoisie and establish a temporary dictatorship of the proletariat. Although declaiming anticapitalist slogans, the Fascists favored the capitalists, while Communists suppressed individual capitalism. Similarly, whereas the Communists nationalized the land and the means of production, the Fascists safeguarded the possessions of the landowning classes and the industrialists. Both systems however controlled industry for the purpose of creating a more powerful state.

After assuming complete dictatorial powers in 1925 (see p. 483), Mussolini gradually transformed Italy into a corporate state. Under this system, representation in the government was changed from geographic districts to economic interests. All productive forces—employers, employees, and self-employed professionals—were organized into syndicates, which were legally recognized as corporate associations. Their duties were to regulate production, to manage labor relations, and to act as advisers to the government. Their leaders, strictly supervised by the Fascist party, also were to see to the "moral and patriotic education of [the syndicate's] members." The four hundred deputies who represented the syndicates and acted as the supposed new Italian legislature were chosen by the Fascist Grand Council from a list of candidates submitted by the corporations. In 1938, Mussolini abandoned even this modest remnant of democratic procedures and empowered himself personally to appoint all "representatives." This corporate system, which was later imitated by the dictators of Spain and Portugal, served *Il Duce* as a useful instrument for controlling the political and economic life of Italy.

Mussolini also achieved greater power through indoctrination. Youths from the age of eight were encouraged to join the uniformed *ballila* troops, in which they were taught military discipline, patriotism, virility, and loyalty to *Il Duce*. Even the leisure time of adults was filled with Fascist propaganda through an organization called *Dopo Lavoro* (After Work). Like the Romantics who had espoused the notion of an organic state (see p. 377) that gave meaning and purpose to the life of its citizens, so Mussolini saw in the state "a spiritual and moral fact in itself." It was "the custodian and transmitter of the spirit of the people."

Stridently nationalistic, the Fascists built up the armed forces, including a sizable navy and air force, in preparation for turning the Mediterranean into an "Italian lake," if necessary by military aggression. After all, Mussolini asserted that "war alone brings up to its highest tension all human energy. . . ."

The Bolsheviks in Russia faced a much more difficult task in establishing their dictatorship than did the Fascists in Italy. A multi-ethnic, largely illiterate population, relatively poor communications, and a backward economy almost totally dislocated by the war made it harder to create a totalitarian regime. Moreover, as we saw (see p. 484), it took three years of civil and foreign war before Lenin's government, with its capital moved from Petrograd (renamed Leningrad in 1924) to Moscow, could gain control of Russia.

Despite the disorders of the civil war, Lenin sought to implement the socialist formula: From each according to his ability, to each according to his need. Private trade was outlawed by government decree; inheritances, interests, and all income not derived from work were abolished. Irrespective of the amount of labor performed, workers were paid in coupons, which they could exchange in government stores for the necessities of life, provided the needed goods were available. With little incentive for the workers to exert themselves, and the economy further disrupted by civil war, production fell to one-sixth its normal level and famines struck various areas.

Confronted by failure, the pragmatic Lenin decided on ideological retreat. In 1921, he adopted a new economic policy (NEP), which was essentially a compromise with capitalism and an accommodation with the peasantry that still harbored a "bourgeois acquisitive spirit." Under NEP, wages were again paid in money, small-scale private trade was permitted, and peasants paid an agricultural tax in lieu of the requisitions of all but their own essential food supplies that had been levied during wartime communism. Recognizing that without passing "through the period of Socialist accounting and control," as Lenin put it, "it would be impossible to pass even to the lowest stages of communism," he invited foreign engineers and capitalists to help build up Russian industry. For true communism could only be effected when production reached such proportions that everyone could indeed be supplied according to his need. Until that distant day, Russians would have to remain in the intermediary stage of socialism, which, according to Article Twelve of the 1936 Constitution, was guided by the principle: From each according to his ability, to each according to his toil.

Despite economic setbacks and changes in policy, the Communist party achieved total control of Russia by the mid-1920's. After Lenin's death in 1924, however, ideological differences rent the top echelon of the party. Ever since the revolution, the question had been debated whether bolshevism in Russia was merely a preliminary stage for world-wide communism, to serve as incentive for similar revolutions in more industrialized countries, or whether the primary aim of the revolution was to be a nationalistic rejuvenation of Russia for her own sake. In this ideological debate, Leon Trotsky, a firm believer in the theory of permanent revolution, stressed the primacy of world-wide revolution, whereas Josef Stalin emphasized the importance of strengthening Russia as a bulwark of socialism.

Another major difference of view concerned the peasantry. Although all land had theoretically been nationalized, the *kulaks* (the more affluent peasants) were acquiring large holdings under the NEP. Since the proletariat-minded Bolsheviks instinctively suspected the peasants' acquisitive mentality, they framed the Soviet Constitution of 1924 so as to allot rural districts only one-fifth as many votes as comparable workers' districts in the cities. Many Bolsheviks however wanted to go beyond partial disenfranchisement and demanded the complete elimination of the kulak class. The pragmatic Stalin admitted that the Kulaks constituted a "rural bourgeoisie," but he preferred to delay any drastic action in view of the temporary need for the kulaks' productive talents to feed the nation and supply grain for export. He was ready to brush aside ideological consistency, since exports were needed to pay for the import of machinery for the development of Russia's heavy industry.

In addition, Russia's leading circles were torn by personal rivalries, skilfully exploited by Stalin to further his assumption of total power. The best known of these struggles occurred between Stalin and Trotsky. The latter, more doctrinaire in his ideology and wary of the growing bureaucracy and concentration of authority in Stalin's hands, was eventually expelled from the Communist party (1927), exiled from Russia (1929), and finally murdered in Mexico (1940) by Stalinist agents. Such struggles for power, in which the loser was usually accused of ideological deviation, were to become a common feature in Russian political life.

Once in full control, Stalin decided to postpone further plans for immediate world-wide revolutions, to establish more friendly relations with capitalist nations, and to concentrate on building up Russia's strength. In 1928, he instituted the first of a series of Five-Year Plans. Meticulously designed by the State Planning Commission, this plan outlined the development of new industries, allocated all national resources and manpower, fixed prices and distribution, and assigned detailed production quotas for industry and agriculture. Primary emphasis was placed on heavy industry, with little attention paid to the production of consumer goods. To mechanize farming, the collectivization of land was given high priority. Although the goals of the first Five-Year Plan proved visionary in some aspects, Russian industry achieved considerable progress under its aegis.

SUGGESTED READINGS

General Books on the Twentieth Century

Cronon, David E., *Twentieth Century America, Selected Readings,* 2 vols. (Irwin, 1965, 1966).

Fung, Arthur Layton, ed., *Europe in the Twentieth Century, Source Studies on Contemporary Issues and Problems* (Irwin, 1968).

Graves, Robert, and Hodge, Alan, *The Long Week-end: A Social History of Great Britain 1918–1919* (Norton, 1963).

Havighurst, Alfred F., *Twentieth-Century Britain* (Harper, 1966).

Seuphor, Michel, *Abstract Painting* (Dell).

Snyder, Louis L., *Fifty Major Documents of the Twentieth Century* (Van Nostrand, 1955).

Taylor, A. J. P., *From Sarajevo to Potsdam* (Harcourt, 1967).

Wright, Gordon, *Rural Revolution in France: The Peasantry in the Twentieth Century* (Stanford, 1964).

International Relations

Brandt, Conrad, *Stalin's Failure in China: 1924–1927* (Norton, 1966).

Carr, Edward Hallet, *German-Soviet Relations Between the Two World Wars, 1919–1939* (Harper).

——, *Twenty Years' Crisis, 1919–1939: An Introduction to the Study of International Relations* (Harper, 1946).

Craig, Gordon A., and Gilbert, Felix, eds., *The Diplomats 1919–1939,* Vol. I, "The Twenties" (Atheneum, 1963). Diplomatic history.

*Dawson, Robert M., *The Development of Dominion Status, 1900–1936* (Shoe String, 1937).

*Dexter, Byron, *Years of Opportunity: The League of Nations, 1920–1926* (Viking, 1967).

Gruber, Helmut, ed., *International Communism in the Era of Lenin* (Fawcett, 1967).

Kennan, George F., *Russia and the West Under Lenin and Stalin* (New American Library, 1961).

Korbel, Josef, *Poland Between East and West, Soviet and German Diplomacy Toward Poland, 1919–1933* (Princeton, 1965).

Seton-Watson, Hugh, *Eastern Europe Between the Wars, 1918–1941* (Harper, 1967).

Shannon, David A., *Between the Wars: America, 1919–1941* (Houghton, 1965).

Wandycz, Piotr S., *France and Her Eastern Allies 1919–1925: French Czechoslovak-Polish Relations from the Paris Peace Conference to Locarno* (U. of Minnesota, 1962).

Wolfers, Arnold, *Britain and France Between Two Wars: Conflicting Strategies of Peace from Versailles to World War II* (Norton, 1966).

Socialism and Communism

Borkenau, Franz, *World Communism: A History of the Communist International* (U. of Michigan, 1962).

Brenan, Gerald, *The Spanish Labyrinth: An Account of the Social and Political Background of the Civil War* (Cambridge, 1960).

Isaacs, Harold R., *The Tragedy of the Chinese Revolution* (Atheneum, 1966). The years 1925 to 1927.

Lichtheim, George, *Marxism in Modern France* (Columbia, 1968).

Rigby, T. H., ed., *Stalin* (Prentice-Hall, 1966). Essays and documents.

Schapiro, Leonard, *Communist Party of the Soviet Union* (Barnes and Noble, 1966).

Seton-Watson, Hugh, *From Lenin to Khrushchev, The History of World Communism* Praeger, 1960).

Sharmon, Lyon, *Sun Yat-sen: His Life and Its Meaning* (Stanford, 1968).

Von Laue, Theodore H., *Why Lenin, Why Stalin? A Reappraisal of the Russian Revolution, 1900–1930* (Lippincott, 1964).

Wolfe, Bertram D., *Three Who Made a Revolution: A Biographical History* (Dell). On Lenin, Trotsky, and Stalin.

Weimar Germany

*Eyck, Erich, *History of the Weimar Republic,* Vol. I, "From the Collapse of the Empire to Hindenburg's Election"; Vol. II, "From the Locarno Conference to Hitler's Seizure of Power" (Wiley, 1967).

*Gatzke, Hans, *Stresemann and the Rearmament of Germany* (Johns Hopkins, 1954).

Halperin, S. William, *Germany Tried Democracy: A Political History of the Reich from 1918–1933* (Norton, 1965).

Turner, Henry Ashby, Jr., *Stresemann and the Politics of the Weimar Republic* (Princeton, 1965).

Wheeler-Bennett, J. W., *The Nemesis of Power: The German Army in Politics, 1918–1945* (Viking, 1964).

Cultural Changes

Mowry, George E., ed., *The Twenties: Fords, Flappers, and Fanatics* (Prentice-Hall, 1963). Collection of documents.

Ortega y Gasset, José, *Revolt of the Masses* (Norton, 1960).

Richter, Hans, *Dada: Art and Anti-Art* (McGraw, 1965).

Stern, Alfred, *Sartre: His Philosophy and Existential Psychoanalysis* (Dell, 1967).

CHAPTER XXVII

❧ The Era of the Great Depression
(1929-1938)

Despite the general pessimism of the decade, there had been an economic upswing during the later 1920's. More people had found employment, the middle classes had regained some self-confidence, within states there was less violence, and increased harmony marked international relations. But the accompanying brief mood of optimism was shattered by the Great Depression that started in 1929. It soon became evident how far the world was from achieving prosperity and international peace. Skyrocketing world-wide unemployment hurt the workers, and loss of their savings deprived the middle classes of their sense of security. To overcome their economic frustrations, classes and nations again resorted to force or the threat of violence.

The Great Depression

The crash of the New York stock market in October 1929, which resulted in a loss in stocks estimated at fifty billion dollars, initiated a long period of world-wide depression, from which many nations did not recover until the beginning of World War II. The United States soon suffered from grave unemployment, thousands of bank failures, and even more bankruptcies of businesses. While production in industry slumped, agriculture piled up surpluses that could not be exported. Between 1929 and 1933, the national income fell from eighty-seven to thirty-nine billion dollars.

The interlocking nature of international trade and finance soon turned the American depression into a world-wide phenomenon, producing similar effects in most countries. The recall of American short-term loans under-

mined European banks and industry, while world production and trade fell
sharply. By 1931, most areas of the world were in economic chaos. A continuing downward spiral developed. Lower production entailed the dismissal of
workers, which in turn reduced people's purchasing power; the resulting reduction in demand drove down prices and entailed still lower production. A
similar vicious circle was started by tariff wars. Some states sought to protect
their industries by restricting imports through high tariffs. Yet, the usual
effect was a further blow to their industry, since retaliatory tariffs of other
states lowered industrial exports. The excessive duties of America's Smoot-
Hawley tariff of 1930, for example, evoked retaliatory steps by some twenty-
five countries.

The depression also affected the non-industrialized countries of Latin
America and Asia, whose economies depended heavily on the export of a
few commodities. Malaya, Chile, Brazil, and Bolivia, for instance, derived a
major portion of their foreign earnings from rubber, nitrate, coffee, and tin
respectively. When lower production and reduced purchasing power decreased demand in the industrialized countries, world prices of raw materials
and commodities plummeted, ruining the non-diversified economies of the
Latin American and Asian states.

Diverse remedies were applied to reduce the harmful impact of the depression and reverse the deflationary trend. The repayment of international
loans and war debts and the fulfillment of reparations obligations were postponed as a result of a moratorium proposed by President Herbert Hoover in
1931. Although supposedly a temporary measure, this step effectively ended
Germany's reparations payments and led to the eventual repudiation of
many international debts. To combat the drain on their gold reserves, the
United States, Britain, and other countries abandoned the gold standard, an
action resulting in the devaluation of the currency and greater monetary
fluctuations. Moreover, countries producing primarily raw materials restricted production of commodities and placed quotas on their exports in
order to raise the world market price through scarcity. Malaya, Bolivia, the
Dutch East Indies, Nigeria, and Siam, for example, agreed to limit the production of tin, with the result that its price doubled between 1931 and 1934.
Similar agreements were made for rubber and copper, while Brazil decided
to destroy portions of its own harvest of coffee beans in order to raise the
price of coffee.

Some dictators sought to insulate their states against the depression by
creating relatively closed economies. Autarky (economic self-sufficiency),
they concluded, would render their countries economically, and hence also
militarily, less dependent on the rest of the world. Hitler's Germany became
a surprisingly successful example of autarky (see p. 500).

Finally, in many parts of the world, the depression was met by resort to
force and violence. Seriously hurt in her exports, especially of silk, and pressured by a rapidly expanding population, Japan conquered Manchuria in

1931 and established a protectorate over this area rich in raw materials and foodstuffs. This conquest was the first in a series of military aggressions through which the Japanese expected to solve their economic problems. Violence also occurred within many states. Of the estimated one hundred million unemployed throughout the world who had lost their jobs through the depression many engaged in street fighting and other acts of violence in futile efforts to effect a change in their economic plight.

Growth of the state

The central machinery of government had been growing for centuries, particularly in the wake of the industrial revolution. But, despite socialist pressure, a strong measure of laissez faire had continued to guide most statesmen. World War I, with its need for governmental concentration of power to conduct a total war, had hewn the first major breach in the hands-off policy of nineteenth-century liberalism. The Great Depression was to administer the coup de grace to laissez faire. Proponents of the New Deal in America, of socialist planning in Russia, and of Fascist controls in Italy all agreed on the need for state intervention in the economic life of their nations. The primary issue separating democrats from Communists and Fascists was the effect such economic controls would have on politics. The former insisted that political freedom could be safeguarded despite government involvement in economics, whereas the latter automatically combined economic and political controls.

Government intervention in the democracies

Even before the depression, governments had of course been involved in the economic, social, and financial affairs of their nations. Germany's government-sponsored social security system dated back to the 1880's; England had instituted old-age pensions for all indigent British subjects in 1909; and during the 1920's, the three Scandinavian monarchies had begun to develop a mixed economy, in which state and private enterprises competed but also cooperated with one another. In Sweden, under direction of several socialist governments, public works, including public housing, were stressed, while Denmark with its more agricultural economy emphasized the development of rural cooperatives.

Such governmental intervention and participation in the national economy greatly increased during the depression. Generally, the measures taken were inspired by a mixture of paternalism and Marxian principles of nationalization.

France, for instance, which had passed a National Workmen's Insurance Law in 1930, providing for sickness and old-age benefits, attempted far-reaching social and economic reforms under Léon Blum's (1872–1950) Popular Front government in 1936. Among other steps, Blum nationalized the Bank of France and the munitions industry, and decreed a forty-hour week as well as paid vacations for workers.

Paternalistic and socialistic ideas also helped shape the American New Deal, inaugurated by a flood of reform legislation during the first hundred days of Franklin D. Roosevelt's administration. In addition, the New Deal was in part a pragmatic application of Keynesian theories, a new economic philosophy that was neither Marxist nor paternalistic. John Maynard Keynes (1883–1946) was not the first economist to advocate government intervention in order to regulate business cycles, but his statements of the new theories were so convincing that he became the apostle of the new economics. Keynes argued that the level of employment in a nation was determined by the level of aggregate expenditures; and he believed that America could not pull itself out of the depression so long as business lacked the funds and incentive for expansion. Hence, the government should lend a helping hand by spending large amounts on investments. Such pump priming, even at the cost of deficit spending, should continue until the economy as a whole once again began to expand. Keynesian methods for regulating economies were ultimately adopted in many parts of the world.

The New Deal helped alleviate some of the worst ills of the depression, but it did not eradicate all unemployment. Only the advent of World War II, with its massive demand for armaments and industrial products, effected the inflationary expansion needed to bring back prosperity. On the other hand, the New Deal, with its penchant for government intervention, its plethora of new agencies to control and supervise the economy, and its tendency to favor labor, alarmed the business community. Distrust of the federal government became an increasingly powerful factor in American life, particularly at a time when European dictators, of the left as well as the right, gave the state full control over the economies of their nations.

National Socialism in Germany

Next to Russia under Stalin, the greatest concentration of power in the hands of the state occurred in Germany under Adolf Hitler (1889–1945), who was appointed Chancellor in 1933. By then, the relative stability and prosperity of the later 1920's in Germany had disintegrated under the impact of the depression. At the end of 1932, 43 per cent of Germany's labor force was out of work. The shock troops of various parties and unions, brown-shirts, red-shirts, green-shirts, and others, were terrorizing the cities. Parliamentary government had reached an impasse, blocked by the obstructionist tactics of the anti-Weimar parties which had gained a majority in the Reichstag in the elections of 1930. Chancellor Heinrich Brüning (1885–   ), therefore, ruled by decree, a device that further weakened the frail democratic institutions of Weimar. But neither Brüning nor his two successors could stay the economic collapse or achieve internal peace.

With the middle class longing for security and the workers clamoring for jobs, Hitler's popularity rose considerably. In the 1932 presidential elections, he received over thirteen million votes and his National Socialist German Workers' Party (NSDAP) became the largest party in Germany. Hitler attracted confidence by promising something to all Germans: full employment, a stable economy, renewed national self-respect, redemption of the lands lost through the Treaty of Versailles, rearmament, safety from communism, and a purification of Germany by the elimination of Jews and other "non-German" elements. Moreover, his movement was supported by certain financiers and industrialists who saw in it a bulwark against bolshevism, and he did not hesitate to use his storm troopers to silence political opponents.

Immediately after his assumption of the chancellorship—an event Hitler triumphantly called "the day of the national rising"—he began to "reconstruct the *Reich*" by converting Germany into a totalitarian dictatorship. Civil liberties were suspended, including the inviolability of home and property. Justice was turned into a political concept, with people's courts passing sentence on the basis of National Socialist doctrine rather than established laws. "Enemies of the state," that is those who opposed nazism, or the so-called November criminals who had helped establish the Weimar Republic in 1918, soon began to disappear into concentration camps.

In March 1933, Adolf Hitler was given the right to make laws without approval of the Reichstag. He then outlawed all political parties, leaving his NSDAP the sole legal party in Germany. As his shrewd Minister for Propaganda and Culture Joseph Goebbels (1897–1945) explained: "National Socialism requires all power and all responsibility."

By the summer of 1934, Hitler and his followers had achieved enormous power over the German people. Within his own party, he purged by assassination those of his subordinates he suspected of left-wing leanings. He also attained more influence over the German officer corps, many of whom looked with some disdain and distrust upon the rabble-rousing *Führer* (leader). After the death of President Hindenburg, the venerated, senile army hero of World War I, Hitler simply took over the presidency, made himself the commander in chief of the armed forces, and required its members to take an oath of "unquestioning obedience to . . . the *Führer* of the German *Reich* and people, Adolf Hitler."

As in Russia, totalitarian control involved all aspects of life. Labor unions were abolished and replaced by an All-German Labor Front under supervision of the state. Nazi ideology was to be spread through propaganda and a revised program in the schools. The aim of Nazi education was to shape youths "whose thoughts and actions are dedicated to serving the nation and to self-sacrifice, if needed." Literature, art, architecture, and all cultural activity were to glorify the state and "the German-ness" of its people. Consonant with their motto "One *Volk!* One *Reich!* One Faith!" the Nazis soon found themselves in conflict with the established churches. While clericals were harassed or arrested on trumped-up charges, some fanatic National Socialists sought to concoct a new "Aryan" religion, purged of all Hebrew-Christian influence. Children were taught in special Nazi youth organizations to worship the *Führer* as if he were the second Messiah, who had saved Germany from ruin and who infallibly knew what was best for the Germans.

In the realm of economics and finance, the Nazis were highly successful. By applying skillful economic planning, using a mixture of state ownership and free enterprise, and running roughshod over the rights of all "enemies of the state," they succeeded in pulling Germany out of economic chaos. The resulting renewed prosperity, together with Hitler's successful foreign policy (see p. 508), in part explain his popularity and the readiness of many Germans to overlook the sinister aspects of his regime.

Unemployment was eradicated. By 1938, in fact, Germany experienced a labor shortage. Men were taken off the labor market by being enrolled in labor service battalions, engaged in full-time para-military organizations, or drafted into the growing armed forces. Vacancies were created by dismissing Jews, communists, and socialists from their jobs. Moreover, the economy was rapidly expanded by massive government investment in heavy industry, armaments, and public works, including the construction of monumental government edifices, huge sports arenas, and superhighways.

To pay for this economic expansion, the Nazis assumed tight control over all areas of German finance. Hjalmar Schacht (1877–   ), the financial wizard who had helped stabilize the German mark in 1923, was made President of the Reichsbank and Minister of Economics. Schacht sealed off Germany's currency from other countries, so that its purchasing power could be maintained artificially at home, although it lost its value in relation to free currencies such as the dollar. The government alone could hold gold, foreign moneys or assets, and conduct imports and exports. The German mark was backed by industrial output and, as it were, by confidence in the *Führer*. To conserve sparse foreign assets, Schacht arranged for barter agreements with many states, whereby Germany supplied industrial equipment in exchange for food and raw materials. Such agreements also enhanced Germany's political influence, particularly in some Balkan states. To lessen the need for vital imports and to reduce the risk of a harmful blockade in any future war, the Nazis strove to achieve as much autarky as possible. Strategic goods were stockpiled and new synthetics, among them artificial fuels, rubber, and fibers, developed with all the speed and skill the German chemical industry could provide. Within Germany, high taxes, controlled prices and wages, and compulsory savings provided for relative financial stability. All these devices to control the German economy and to make Germany militarily strong were included in a series of Four-Year Plans, at first directed by Schacht and later by Hermann Göring (1893–1946), Hitler's much decorated associate, who was also Minister for the Air Force.

Finally, Nazi control of the masses was strengthened by insistence on total obedience, enforced through the vigilant secret police (Gestapo) and the ubiquitous storm troopers. All elements of the nation were hierarchically subordinated under Hitler, who swayed the masses with his oratory. Most Germans readily responded to his nationalistic appeals, his assertion that they belonged to a superior "race," and his promise to "make Germany the first military power on earth."

Fascism and other dictatorships

National Socialism was a peculiar type of fascism, more vehemently nationalistic and racist, more militaristic and aggressive, more tightly organized, and more anticlerical than Fascism in general. Moreover, the Nazis never sought to develop a corporate state. Yet, despite its doctrine of German superiority, nazism appealed to many people in other states who were tired of democratic instability and longed for the establishment of a "new order." Nazi-style parties and para-military organizations became important in a number of democratic states, including Holland, Belgium, France, and Austria. In some cases, as with the German-American *Bund,* these groups received funds and encouragement from Germany.

Most of those who advocated authoritarian solutions, however, looked for a model to Italy rather than to Germany. Mussolini's fascism had achieved order with somewhat less violence than was used by the Nazis. Despite *Il Duce's* vainglorious speeches from the balcony of the Palazzo Venezia in Rome, his regime appeared to outsiders to be more respectable than that of the rowdy Brown Shirts in Germany. Actually, Mussolini's economic program was far less successful than Hitler's, and Italy suffered considerably from the effects of the Great Depression. To earn the foreign exchange required to finance the import of raw materials that Italy lacked, the Italians redoubled their effort to encourage tourism and provided state subsidies for construction of a large passenger fleet. Inside Italy, Mussolini cut wages on the one hand while increasing public expenditures on the other. He ordered the draining of the Pontine Marshes near Rome to provide for more agricultural land and expanded the public building program of hydroelectric dams, ornate railway stations, superhighways, and general beautification of Italy's major cities. Nonetheless, Italians did not attain a great measure of prosperity.

During the 1930's, many new dictatorships were added to those already established during the first postwar decade. Soon all of eastern Europe, except for Czechoslovakia, and all of southern Europe were governed by more or less dictatorial regimes. In Portugal, for instance, which had been a military dictatorship since 1926, Antonio de Oliveira Salazar (1889–   ) converted the state into a fascist dictatorship, with corporate institutions based on the Italian model. Salazar's regime gradually achieved political stability, but failed to bring real economic relief to the masses of impoverished Portuguese.

Like Portugal, Austria sought to establish what has been called a clerical-corporative system, since its outstanding features were support for the Catholic Church and a corporate organization of economic life. During the 1920's, landlocked Austria, a rump state shorn of most of its productive areas by the Treaty of St. Germain, had suffered from economic stagnation as well as serious internal friction between Catholics and conservatives in the provinces and socialists and liberals in the capital of Vienna. Moreover, many Austrians resented that union with Germany, which would have been economically beneficial, was prohibited by the Western powers. In the wake of the depression, Austria went almost bankrupt and violence in the streets became a common occurrence.

In 1933, Chancellor Engelbert Dollfuss (1892–1934), a strong supporter of Catholicism and an admirer of Mussolini, suspended parliament and abrogated most constitutional freedoms. Equally opposed to the socialists on the one hand and to the Austrian Nazis on the other, he proscribed all political parties except his own Fatherland Front and issued a new fascistic constitution. Through a *rapprochement* with Mussolini, he hoped to safeguard Austria against Hitler's annexationist designs. This strategy proved useful in 1934 when Austrian Nazis, encouraged by Germany, attempted a coup d'état. Mussolini promptly indicated his intention of giving Austria military aid against any attempted German invasion, thereby forcing Hitler to withdraw his support from the Austrian Nazis. Austrian independence was thus preserved, but Chancellor Dollfuss himself was killed during the Nazi uprising. His successor in the Chancellorship, Kurt von Schuschnigg (1897–   ), continued similar dictatorial policies and began to build up the Austrian army. Yet, despite a slight improvement in the economic status of the country, Austrian Nazism grew and prepared the way for Hitler's eventual annexation of Austria in 1938 (see p. 513).

Beyond Europe, too, there were individuals and groups who admired or implemented dictatorial or fascistic systems. Huey Pierce Long (1893–1935) of Louisiana, for example, the demagogic governor and later senator, applied dictatorial methods to control his state, although his "Share Our Wealth" program was hardly fascistic. In Brazil, an outright dictatorship was established in 1937. Social and economic conditions, always a problem in Brazil, had been badly hurt by the depression. As a result, communist and fascist groups were growing during the 1930's, the one presumably supported by Moscow, the other by Berlin. To maintain internal peace and safeguard the property-owning classes, President Getulio Vargas (1883–1954) changed the constitution in 1937, transformed his presidency into a dictatorship, and adopted some corporative measures.

Japan also changed with the depression. During World War I, Japanese industry had expanded rapidly to meet military demands. As a result, middle-class political parties and labor unions had gained in significance. Moreover the fact that Japan had fought and won on the side of the democracies encouraged increased Westernization in cultural as well as political areas. This trend was sharply reversed by the depression, which discredited political and economic liberalism in the eyes of many Japanese. Although industrial methods continued to be based on Western models, cultural and political Westernization lost its appeal. Fear of communism and of the rising strength of labor unions, worry over increasing population density, and greater insistence on governmental economic planning provided the background for a strong resurgence of conservatism and nationalism.

As a result, more and more power came to be lodged in the hands of the emperor, the military, the nobility, and assorted chauvinistic groups, supported by much of the peasantry that distrusted the bourgeois and the workers of the city. The ancient code of the samurai was again stressed and other non-Western traditions revitalized. As in Germany, political murder and police repression of liberal elements was condoned by the ruling classes, and tighter government control over the economy was instituted. Thus, a gradual dictatorship was developed, not by a single man, such as Mussolini in Italy, but by a military-aristocratic oligarchy. The policy was militaristic and imperialistic, aimed at expanding Japanese holdings on mainland Asia, in order to obtain more raw materials, food, and space for Japan's excess population.

The establishment of a fascist dictatorship in Spain is of particular interest in view of the international involvement in the Spanish Civil War. Primo de Rivera's dictatorship (see p. 489), instituted in 1923, had roused so much discontent that in 1925 King Alphonso asked him to convert his regime into a less authoritarian system, in which Rivera ruled with a mixed military and civilian cabinet. Nonetheless, unrest continued and became more aggravated with the depression. After Rivera's resignation in 1930, in part because of ill health, the government sought to placate the people through conciliatory measures, but antiroyalist agitation increased rapidly and persuaded the king to leave Spain in 1931. Thereupon the republicans, under Alcalá Zamora (1877–1944), set up a provisional government, which promptly ordered elections for a constituent assembly. With republicans and socialists in the majority, the new assembly proclaimed Spain a republic and promulgated a new, liberal constitution.

Spain's constitution of 1931 was anticlerical, antimilitary, and inimical to the interests of the large landholders. Hence it aroused immediate opposition by the Church, the army, and the landholding grandees. The constitution stipulated religious freedom, secularized education, and nationalized ecclesiastical property; it ordered an end to the political activities of the military, and authorized a government commission to expropriate the large estates and divide them among the peasants; moreover it granted special privileges to the Catalonians, who had been demanding autonomy for centuries. But neither the new constitution nor the republican regime, with Zamora as its first president, brought tranquility to Spain.

The radical left, anarcho-syndicalists and Communists, staged uprisings in protest against the slow pace of social reforms, while the Catalonians demanded complete autonomy. Fear of radicalism in turn pushed the government toward greater conservatism and increased the solidarity of rightist elements: monarchists, clericals, fascists, military, and the Falange party, newly created by José Antonio de Rivera (1903–1936), the son of the ex-dictator. Uprisings and reprisals placed the country at the edge of civil war. To counteract the resurgent strength of the conservatives, the parties of the left, republicans, Socialists, syndicalists, and Communists, formed a Popular Front, which enabled them to win the elections of February 1936. The new liberal government under Manuel Azaña (1880–1940), who had been prime minister from 1931 to 1933, resumed the program of land reform that had been blocked after 1933. The prospect of further socialization and anti-clericalism in turn induced the conservatives to embrace fascist remedies and spurred a group of army officers to plot the revolt that in July 1936 plunged Spain into a three-year civil war.

The Spanish Civil War, a bloody conflict that caused well over a million deaths, started as an army revolt in Spanish Morocco. Various army and air force units on the mainland immediately joined the insurrection, whereas most of the navy stayed loyal to the government of Madrid. Within ten days, German and Italian airplanes arrived to ferry rebel units from Morocco to the mainland to help spread the rebellion. Soon most of the western half of Spain was in the hands of the insurrectionists, whose leadership was assumed by General Francisco Franco (1892–   ), a politically ambitious officer whom the Popular Front government had removed from Madrid by appointing him governor of the distant Canary Islands. Franco's forces received the active support of the Falange and other fascist groups, of the wealthy upper classes and the Church, and of the two major fascist powers, Italy and Germany. Mussolini sent Franco some eighty thousand or more soldiers as well as large amounts of equipment and logistical supplies; Hitler dispatched dive bombers, tanks, and technicians.

Contrary to Franco's expectations, however, the Madrid government did not fall. It retained control over most of the major cities and industrial centers, including Barcelona, Valencia, and Madrid itself, and was stanchly supported by middle-of-the-road and leftist groups and by the Basques and Catalonians. From abroad, the Loyalists, as those who sided with the legal government were called, received material aid and advisers from Soviet Russia. Moreover, some forty thousand volunteers from many countries, including the United States, went to Spain to fight for the Loyalists. These volunteers comprised for the most part Communists, liberals, and dedicated anti-fascists. The Civil War thus led to a severe international crisis (see p. 509).

In October 1936, Francisco Franco took the title of Chief of the Spanish State and soon became known as *El Caudillo* (the leader), even though he had by then conquered less than half of Spain. Seven weeks. later, the *Füh-*

rer and *Il Duce* extended diplomatic recognition to their new Fascist comrade. The war gradually turned into a grueling duel. Madrid was besieged, shelled, and bombed for twenty-nine months. With superior equipment, vast aerial superiority, and more supplies from abroad, the rebel forces slowly gained ground. Although fighting with greater conviction than their opponents, the Loyalist forces had less modern equipment and an inferior air force. Moreover, their ranks were at times weakened through disagreement between communists, anarcho-syndicalists, socialists, and republicans.

In the end, Franco triumphed. Barcelona fell in late January 1939, and two months later Madrid and Valencia surrendered unconditionally. Even before the fall of Madrid, Paris and London recognized the Franco regime and urged *El Caudillo* to show mercy to his vanquished opponents. But Franco acted ruthlessly against all opposition. Although tens of thousands of Loyalists succeeded in escaping to France, even more were imprisoned in Spain and an unknown number was executed. Franco did not seek conciliation; rather he wanted to impress on every Spaniard the fact that he had won. For years, he tried to keep alive the memory of the horrors of the Civil War in order to warn his subjects that if they did not support him, another and even more horrendous fratricidal conflict might ensue.

Once his armies were in control of Spain, Franco began to construct a clerical-corporative regime, partially based on the Italian model. Syndicates replaced the outlawed labor unions. Catholicism was made the state religion, and confiscated ecclesiastical property as well as control over education was handed back to the Church. Further land reform was halted, and most estates were returned to their former owners. The army, civil guards, and police were used to enforce political discipline and tight censorship, and the Catalonian autonomy movement was suppressed in the interest of greater centralization. Although all political parties but the Falange were outlawed, Spain's fascist regime was not built on a one-party dictatorship as those in Germany and Italy; rather, subject to control by Franco, it developed into a dictatorship by the same oligarchy that had dominated the country before the revolution of 1931.

Renewed recourse to force

In the late 1920's, most nations had benefited from several years of relative internal tranquility. Similarly, no serious armed conflicts had marred international relations. The "spirit of Locarno" marked by greater willingness to discuss and if possible adjudicate differences pervaded most foreign offices. Germany was admitted to the League of Nations (1926), the United States and Russia were more active in international conferences, and the hope was strengthened that the League, the Court of International Justice, and *ad hoc* commissions could after all achieve permanent peace.

This mood changed drastically in the 1930's. As we saw, force was again widely used by governments in efforts to establish internal order. In the international field, trust in the League and in collective security evaporated rapidly after 1931. It was symptomatic that, whereas only three states (Costa Rica, Brazil, and Spain) had withdrawn from the League of Nations in the 1920's, over a dozen, including Japan and Germany, did so between 1933 and the outbreak of World War II in 1939. At the same time, revisionism grew in ardor. Some states used armed aggression to satisfy their demands, and many began to rearm, in order to gird themselves for the possibility of another large-scale war.

Internal violence

As mentioned before (see p. 496), the effects of the Great Depression and the creation of more and more authoritarian regimes entailed violence inside most countries. To understand this breakdown of Western traditions, whether temporary or long-term, one must comprehend the magnitude of this phenomenon. Violent strikes, riots, and street fighting occurred in many countries. Political assassination became common again, as in Japan where prime ministers and other government leaders were murdered. Spain, as we saw, experienced almost five years of sporadic violence even before the outbreak of actual civil war.

Austria presents a typical example of the new ruthlessness. When Chancellor Dollfuss outlawed all political parties except his own Fatherland Front (see p. 502), the socialists called a protest strike. Dollfuss then had some of their leaders arrested, whereupon the socialists barricaded themselves in Karl Marx Stadt, a large municipal housing complex built by the city of Vienna. Rejecting any thought of negotiation, the chancellor simply used the army to bombard the dissenters into unconditional surrender.

France, too, experienced its share of violence. The left-wing bloc, victorious in the 1932 elections, was weakened by internal disunity and proved incapable of solving the growing economic problems resulting from the depression. The ensuing social unrest encouraged the growth of various right-wing groups, among them the *Croix de Feu* (Cross of Fire), an organization of veterans, students, and fascist sympathizers who denounced democratic institutions and demanded a strong executive. In the wake of a financial and political scandal that involved members of the government and led to the installation of yet another prime minister, Edouard Daladier (1884–), right-wing groups decided on force. In February 1934, they assembled shock troops to storm the French Chamber of Deputies. Daladier used police and national guards to defend the government. Although the rebellious right-wingers were defeated in fighting that resembled a minor civil war, Daladier's government fell. Thereafter, with the exception of the Popular Front of 1936, French politics assumed an increasingly authoritarian trend, a development which terminated with Marshal Pétain's fascist dictatorship of 1940.

In some states, the application of force became systematized, as in Russia where Stalin used it to control not only the political and economic life but also the thoughts and aspirations of its people. The first Five-Year Plan (1928) had called for prompt establishment of state farms (*sovkhozy*) and collectives (*kolkhozy*). State farms were owned and operated by the state, with peasants working as state employees. Collectives, on the other hand, consisted of land leased from the state, with the collective owning its own buildings, animals, and farming equipment, and, where needed, renting machinery from nearby government machine tractor stations. After paying taxes to the government, the members of the collective shared in the profits from the harvest on the basis of individual work performed.

Despite the security offered by this system, most peasants, particularly the wealthier kulaks, did not wish to lose the land they had so recently acquired. The government reacted with relentless severity to this challenge. Millions of peasants who resisted collectivization or failed to cooperate were simply driven from their land, exiled to Siberia, executed, or permitted to starve to death. At the same time, the secret police (NKVD) consigned uncounted numbers of those who resisted other phases of communist policies to concentration camps, in which the inmates had to perform hard labor on public projects, such as building canals and roads or working in mines.

Finally, starting in 1935, Stalin organized a series of purges within the Communist party. Both left-wing and right-wing deviationists, that is those, respectively, who thought Stalin not sufficiently revolutionary or too revolutionary, were put on trial and induced to confess such crimes as plotting counterrevolution, conspiring with foreign powers, or negotiating with the exiled Trotsky. Most of the accused were condemned to death. This elimination of several thousands of old-line Bolsheviks immensely fortified Stalin's monolithic power.

The application of violence took equally alarming forms in Germany. From the beginning of his regime, Hitler's stormtroopers and secret police used physical coercion to intimidate recalcitrants or eliminate opponents. Concentration camps were soon filled with tortured inmates, and political executions became more frequent. As the Nazis consolidated their power, brutality gave way to inhuman bestiality. Their policy toward "non-Aryans," specifically Jews, over the years progressed from disenfranchisement and harassment to persecution, deportation, and finally to extermination. During World War II, their conquests of wide areas of Europe brought millions of non-German Jews under Nazi control. After first throwing most Jews into special ghettos and concentration camps for use as slave labor, the Nazis decided on "the final solution of the Jewish problem" in 1942. Close to six million Jews were gassed, shot, or tortured to death in specially constructed extermination camps.

International tension

The 1930's saw a long series of international crises, most of them the result of piecemeal aggression by the revisionist powers. Japan's seizure of Manchuria in 1931 (see p. 496) was the first. The United States protested in vain against this violation of the Kellogg-Briand Pact, and when the League of Nations proposed a compromise that would have left Manchuria as an autonomous state within China but subject to Japanese economic control, Japan simply withdrew from the League. The latter's patent failure to make its decision respected bode ill for the future of collective security.

Hitler's determination to scrap the Treaty of Versailles provided the next crises. A Nazi electoral victory in the Free City of Danzig in May, 1933, foreshadowed later German annexation of this area, which had been taken from Germany in 1919. Also in 1933, Germany withdrew from the Geneva Disarmament Conference on the grounds that the powers would not allow her parity in armaments; moreover she left the League of Nations, which in Hitler's view was primarily a device for enforcing the Treaty of Versailles and preventing Germany's resurgence. Next came the attempted Nazi coup d'état in Vienna, which was supposed to effect the union of Austria and Germany (see p. 502). The return of the Saar to Germany at the beginning of 1935, though legally sanctioned by a plebiscite supervised by the League, was accompanied by strident German propaganda and signified another step in German resurgence. Soon thereafter, Hitler repudiated all armaments restrictions and publicly vowed that Germany would rearm. His announcement was in fact merely an open acknowledgment of steps initiated earlier.

Worried by German expansionism, Russia joined the League of Nations in 1934 and launched a concerted drive to form an antifascist collective security system. Moreover, at the Seventh Congress of the Communist International in 1935, the Soviets adopted a resolution asserting "that at the present historical stage it is the main and immediate task of the international labor movement to establish the united fighting front of the working class." The resolution urged all Communists to cooperate with Socialists and, if necessary, with bourgeois parties in all efforts aimed at stemming the rising tide of fascism and led to the formation of Popular Front governments in Spain and France. Italy, France, and England, for their part, met at Stresa to discuss united action against Germany. But all efforts at collective security proved abortive, and each power began to devise its own security measures. France and Italy tried a *rapprochement* to block further German expansion, an attempt soon vitiated by Mussolini's war against Ethiopia. France and Russia negotiated a defensive alliance, a useless gesture, since the French legislature never ratified it. England decided on accommodation with Germany, by signing a naval agreement that permitted the Germans to build a navy up to 35 per cent of the tonnage of Britain's fleet. This naval pact, which implicitly acknowledged the invalidity of the Versailles Treaty, profoundly disturbed France and Russia.

At this point, Mussolini seized the standard of active revisionism with his invasion of Ethiopia. *Il Duce* intended to wipe out the stain of Italy's defeat by the Ethiopians in 1896 and at the same time give the Italians glory and a greater share of colonial possessions. Surprisingly, Italy's armies and air force required six months of severe fighting to conquer this independent African nation. Although the League voted to impose economic sanctions on Italy, its impotence was again revealed when many nations failed to apply the sanctions effectively and refused to take other actions to save Ethiopia. Besides further discrediting the League, Italy's Ethiopian war led to a *rapprochement* between Hitler and Mussolini, for while France and England made futile gestures of disapproval, Germany supported Italy's colonial adventure. The resulting Italo-German friendship, leading to the so-called Rome-Berlin Axis, marked an end to Germany's isolation and an important step in the division of Europe into two antagonistic camps.

Taking advantage of Europe's preoccupation with the Ethiopian War and yet another cabinet crisis in France, Hitler remilitarized the Rhineland in March, 1936, contrary to the Versailles Treaty. Boasting publicly about his new war machine, he furthermore denounced the Locarno Treaties with the explanation that Russia and France had aggressive designs on Germany. Once again, the League, France, and England protested, but it seemed obvious that the Treaty of Versailles had been scrapped for good.

Hardly had the Ethiopian War ended when the Spanish Civil War plunged Europe into a new crisis in the form of an open armed confrontation between communism and fascism. Joseph Goebbels insisted that Franco's uprising "was in reality an act of self-defense on the part of the people" against a Communist revolt "planned in Moscow . . . organized from Moscow, and directed from Moscow." Stalin, for his part, feared that a Franco victory would add yet another country to the list of fascist states. Russia sent aid to the Loyalists, and Germany and Italy supported Franco, using Spain as a proving ground for their new war equipment. The democracies vainly called for non-intervention. The United States Congress voted to apply an arms embargo to both sides, an act which indirectly gave legal recognition to Franco's rebels. France and England sponsored a twenty-seven nation conference on non-intervention which organized an ineffectual sea blockade to keep war materiel out of Spain. Such efforts failed however to stop the flow of aid to the belligerents.

While Europe was occupied by the Spanish Civil War, Japan struck again. After the seizure of Manchuria, frequent Japanese military incursions into China had continued. Now, in 1937, Japan launched a full-scale invasion of northern China, accompanied by devastating aerial bombardment. Peking, Shanghai, and Nanking were conquered, and China north of the

Yangtze River occupied. Chiang Kai-shek moved China's capital inland to Chungking and organized military resistance to the Japanese for a war that was to last until 1945. Japan's aggression caused serious tension with the United States, England, and France.

Thus, by the end of 1937, the League of Nations had been dismally discredited, and efforts to establish effective collective security had proved fruitless. Instead, new antagonistic blocs of world powers were being formed in anticipation of another major war. Germany, Japan, and Italy joined in the Anti-Comintern Pact, ostensibly aimed at confining the spread of communism, while in reality directed against Russia. The Pact could also serve to provide mutual support to the revisionist powers in their search for new conquests. At the same time, England and France again drew closer together, although by no means agreeing on common policy. A major dilemma confronted the democratic states in Europe: they could not decide whether communism or fascism presented the greater threat and were usually loath to antagonize Hitler or Mussolini, since the fascist powers might prove to be convenient counterweights to Stalinist Russia. The Soviet Union found that she had to shift for herself and develop her own security as best she could. Meanwhile the United States, busily implementing New Deal legislation and happily ensconced between two oceans, retained her isolationist stance.

In view of the failure of the disarmament conferences and the increased tension and actual hostilities, the nations gradually began to rearm. Germany was feverishly at work building a highly mechanized war machine, stockpiling strategic matériel, and instilling a martial spirit in its population. Russia further developed production of tanks and heavy artillery, and increased her strength in paratroops. Unlike the French, who felt relatively safe behind their Maginot Line and seemed convinced that the same methods that helped them win World War I would suffice in a future conflict, the British also began to rearm. Although Neville Chamberlain (1869–1940), prime minister from 1937 to 1940, later became known as an apostle of appeasement, he saw to the development of tanks and to the expansion of antiaircraft defenses and of the Royal Air Force. These decisions proved of great importance during the so-called Battle of Britain in the early stages of World War II.

Although many people remained convinced pacifists and believed that peaceful solutions would be found, others began to warn that each crisis brought the nations closer to another world-wide catastrophe. It is noteworthy that as early as 1935 neutral Switzerland started to modernize her army, improve her air defenses, and stockpile food to prepare for the contingency of another war.

SUGGESTED READINGS

Economic and Social Reform

Burns, James MacGregor, *Roosevelt: The Lion and the Fox* (Harcourt, 1957).

Craig, Gordon A., and Gilbert, Felix, eds., *The Diplomats 1919–1939*, Vol. II, "The Thirties" (Atheneum, 1963).

*Diamant, Alfred, *Austrian Catholics and the First Republic: Democracy, Capitalism and the Social Order, 1918–1934* (Princeton, 1960).

Galbraith, Kenneth, *The Great Crash, 1929* (Houghton Mifflin, 1955).

Harrod, R. F., *The Life of John Maynard Keynes* (St. Martins, 1963).

Schlesinger, Arthur Meyer, Jr., *The Age of Roosevelt*, Vol. II, "The Coming of the New Deal" (Houghton, 1959).

*Werstein, Irving, *Nation Fights Back: The Depression and Its Aftermath* (Simon and Schuster, 1962).

Nazism

Allen, William Sheridan, *The Nazi Seizure of Power* (Quadrangle, 1965). Describes Nazi domination of a small town, 1930 to 1935.

Bullock, Alan L., *Hitler, A Study in Tyranny* (Harper, 1964).

Documents on German Foreign Policy, 1918–1945 (United States Department of State, Series C, 1959). Documents on Hitler's revision of Versailles, 1933–1937.

Meinecke, Friedrich, *The German Catastrophe* (Beacon, 1963).

*Schweitzer, Arthur, *Big Business in the Third Reich* (Indiana, 1964).

Shirer, William L., *The Rise and Fall of the Third Reich* (Fawcett).

Snell, John L., *The Nazi Revolution—Germany's Guilt or Germany's Fate?* (Heath, 1959).

Italy and Fascism in General

*Crowley, James B., *Japan's Quest for Autonomy, National Security and Foreign Policy, 1930–1938* (Princeton, 1966).

Fermi, Laura, *Mussolini* (U. of Chicago, 1961).

Greene, Nathanael, *Fascism, An Anthology* (Crowell, 1968).

Halperin, S. William, *Mussolini and Italian Fascism* (Van Nostrand, 1964).

*Harris, Brice, Jr., *The United States and the Italo-Ethiopian Crisis* (Stanford, 1964).

Payne, Stanley G., *Falange: A History of Spanish Fascism* (Stanford, 1961).

*Skidmore, Thomas E., *Politics in Brazil, 1930–1964* (Oxford, U.P., 1967).

Weber, Eugen, *Action Française: Royalism and Reaction in Twentieth-Century France* (Stanford, 1962).

Spanish Civil War

Borkenau, Franz, *The Spanish Cockpit* (U. of Michigan, 1963).

Orwell, George, *Homage to Catalonia* (Beacon, 1955).

Thomas, Hugh, *The Spanish Civil War* (Harper, 1961).

CHAPTER XXVIII

❧❧ *Another World War*
(1938-1947)

The starting dates for World War II differ from continent to continent. In Europe the conflict began with Hitler's attack on Poland in 1939. For the Americas the war started only in the winter of 1941-42, when, after Japan's attack on Pearl Harbor, the United States and most of the Latin-American Republics took up belligerency. In the Far East the Sino-Japanese War, which became an integral part of World War II, had erupted in 1937, one might even say as early as 1931 (see p. 508). In all three areas World War II terminated in 1945.

The approach of war

Despite the international crises that had threatened the general peace before 1938, few statesmen had feared a world-wide conflagration. The crises of 1938, however, produced a change of view among some observers. By September many American diplomats stationed in Europe were sending their families home, a sign that serious international troubles were expected. To some the question was no longer whether a war would erupt, but when.

The increase in international tension derived largely from Hitler's conviction that the time had come to solve Germany's "question of living space" (*Lebensraum*). Believing that "Germany's problem could be solved only by means of force," Hitler secretly informed his generals that a first step in satisfying Germany's space requirements "must be to overthrow Czechoslovakia and Austria simultaneously in order to remove the threat to our flank in any possible operation against the West." Early in 1938 he ordered a

512

vast expansion of Germany's economic and military production and called for detailed strategic planning in case of various war contingencies. He assumed the tightest possible control over the Ministry of Economics, the General Staff, and the Foreign Office by firing most independent or less ardent members of these three governmental agencies and replacing them with men more inclined toward his will. The official Nazi newspaper headlined these changes as "Strongest concentration of all powers in the *Führer's* hands." Such total command allowed Hitler to exploit all chances for expanding Germany and taking advantage of his opponents' hesitation.

The new international climate also resulted from the increasingly vociferous stand of other revisionist powers, such as Japan, Italy, and Hungary, all emboldened by the League of Nations' increasingly obvious incapacity to ensure world peace. At the same time, the powers who were pledged to maintain the status quo stood by seemingly paralyzed. France was plagued by internal instability; England under Neville Chamberlain preferred accommodation for the sake of peace; Belgium abandoned its alliance with France and retreated into neutrality; and the Little Entente (see p. 478) disintegrated in the wake of the West's failure to prevent the dismemberment of Czechoslovakia (see p. 515). Moreover, England and France's refusal to collaborate with Russia even in the face of Hitler's overt penetration into eastern Europe convinced Stalin that he had to find new ways to safeguard the interests of the Soviet Union. Thus Europe stood poised at the edge of war by the end of 1938.

The last prewar crises

By the end of 1937, Hitler had succeeded in scrapping various clauses of the Treaty of Versailles. He had not, however, extended Germany's boundaries beyond those established by the peace treaty. In the spring of 1938, he felt Germany strong enough for him to undertake a piecemeal revision of the map of Europe. Annexation of his native Austria was to be his first step.

The miscarried coup d'état of 1934 in Vienna (see p. 502) had taught Hitler that he could not readily annex Austria without first obtaining Mussolini's acquiescence. Germany's benevolent neutrality during the Italian conquest of Ethiopia had meanwhile improved Italo-German relations and led eventually to the establishment of the Rome-Berlin Axis. Hence, *Il Duce* agreed to let events in Austria "take their natural course," meaning that he abandoned his protectorship over the little republic. Although Hitler had given public assurances that Germany would not interfere in Austria's internal affairs, he now proceeded to encourage the Austrian Nazis to foment disorders so that, at an opportune moment, he might intervene to restore order. This stratagem was to become a favorite Nazi device. In February 1938, Hitler invited Austria's Chancellor Schuschnigg to his mountain retreat at Berchtesgaden in Bavaria and presented him with an ultimatum to admit a number of Nazis into his cabinet and to stop the "persecution" of

Nazis in Austria. In view of Hitler's threat to blow Austria's "ridiculous defense mechanism" to bits, Schuschnigg felt compelled to comply and turned the Ministry of the Interior over to the Austrian Nazi leader Arthur Seyss-Inquart (1892–1946). But systematic Nazi rioting continued, directed by Göring from Berlin.

By mid-March, with German troops massed at the border, Schuschnigg could no longer resist mounting Nazi pressure and transferred the chancellorship itself to Seyss-Inquart. Following instructions from Göring, the new chancellor promptly asked for German troops to help "restore law and order" in Austria. German forces immediately occupied the entire country, and the new Nazi government of Austria passed a law turning the state into "a territory of the German *Reich*." Three days after Schuschnigg's resignation, Hitler staged a triumphal visit to Vienna, while Nazi officials swiftly converted Austria into a German province. Paris, London, and the League reacted with polite protests to Hitler's first successful move to expand Germany.

Encouraged by the West's inaction and bolstered by his recent success, Hitler rushed Europe into the next crisis. Using techniques similar to those that had gained him Austria, he urged Konrad Henlein (1898–1945), the Nazi leader among the three and one half million German-speaking Sudetens living along the western borders of Czechoslovakia, to stage riots in support of their demand for autonomy. The *Führer* assured Henlein that he was prepared to support such demands with force. These steps led to the first Czech crisis in May of 1938. Czechoslovakia's President Beneš ordered partial mobilization to counter possible German moves, and Russia and France, albeit hesitatingly, assured the Czechs that they would fulfill their treaty obligations in case of aggression by Germany.

Not ready to face a general war, Hitler abandoned his demands temporarily, and the crisis abated. To prepare for later steps and perhaps to lull France into a false sense of security by pretending that German expansion was to be only eastward, he built the so-called Siegfried Line, a system of fortifications facing the French Maginot Line. Thus protected in the West, he felt more secure in the pursuit of further eastward expansion.

The second Czech crisis flared up in September of 1938, when the Sudetens intensified their riots and Henlein fled to Berlin to broadcast an appeal to his followers to "march home to the *Reich*." His demands on Beneš had progressed from autonomy for the Sudetenland to incorporation of the German-speaking areas of Czechoslovakia with Germany, demands fully backed by Hitler. When a military confrontation between the small, but well-armed, Czech Republic and Germany seemed imminent, England's Neville Chamberlain decided on personal intervention to save the peace. Twice he journeyed to Germany to mediate between Beneš and Hitler and to arrange for some scheme of self-determination for the Sudetens that might be acceptable to the German chancellor. At each conference the Nazi leader upped his demands. Finally Hitler warned that his troops would move unless the areas of Czechoslovakia with predominantly German inhabitants would forthwith be ceded to Germany. At the same time he insisted that Polish and Hungarian irredentist demands on Czechoslovakia had to be satisfied.

At this point, war was once again averted, through a conference that took place in Munich at the end of September. Hitler, Mussolini, Chamberlain, and French Prime Minister Edouard Daladier met at the Nazi headquarters in the Bavarian capital to discuss the German demands. Neither Czechoslovakia nor the Soviet Union, vitally concerned with Germany's eastward expansion, was invited. The participants gave Germany the right immediately to annex areas of Czechoslovakia deemed to be predominantly German-speaking, and they agreed to satisfy the Polish and Hungarian territorial demands on Czechoslovakia.

As a result of the Munich conference, Czechoslovakia was forced to cede large areas and millions of people to Germany, Hungary, and Poland. The revisionist forces had again triumphed, and Hitler was more convinced than ever that he was destined to redraw the map of Europe. Moreover, dismayed by British and French readiness to sacrifice Czechoslovakia to the voracious Nazis, many of the smaller European nations wondered whether it might not be wiser to befriend Hitler rather than rely on the dubious promises of assistance by France.

During the winter of 1938–39, Hitler prepared for further German expansion, despite his public assurance that there were "no further territorial problems for Germany in Europe." He fomented disorders in Slovakia, and, posing as the protector of the Slovaks against the Czechs, ended in March of 1939 by occupying all of Czechoslovakia for the ostensible purpose of restoring order. Once again the powers merely protested. Within a few weeks after the seizure of Czechoslovakia, Germany forced the Lithuanians to cede Memel, which they had acquired in 1923. Mussolini then joined the revisionists by invading and annexing defenseless Albania. At the same time, Hitler prepared for the annihilation of his next victim, Poland. Publicly he called merely for the return of Danzig and the cession of an extraterritorial strip across the Polish Corridor to connect East Prussia and the *Reich* with a German railroad and superhighway, whereas actually he sought "to round out our living space in the East and to solve our food problem."

This time, Neville Chamberlain realized that Germany's land hunger was not confined to territories inhabited by German-speaking peoples. Jointly with France, England concluded a mutual assistance pact with Poland and offered guarantees to other states potentially threatened by Germany. However, it proved impossible for Paris and London to form an anti-Nazi coalition with Moscow (see p. 517)—a step that might have put a damper on Hitler's expansionist plans.

The Nazi *Führer* took advantage of his enemies' inability to cooperate.

Untroubled by ideological scruples, he decided that a temporary accommodation with Communist Russia would allow Germany to conquer Poland. Even if the British and French were to assist the Poles—an eventuality he seriously doubted—the Germans at least would not have to face the massive Red Army in the East while fighting France in the West. Stalin, for his part, recognized the opportunities offered by an understanding with Germany: it would permit Russia to regain some of the areas along her eastern borders lost between 1917 and 1921 and assure her at least temporary safety from a Nazi attack. Hence, Stalin and Hitler concluded a non-aggression treaty on August 23, 1939. In a secret protocol appended to this Nazi-Soviet Pact, the two dictators agreed on a division of Poland and on respective spheres of influence in eastern Europe.

After the conclusion of this pact, Hitler immediately increased his pressure on Poland and, eight days later, hurled his tanks and dive bombers across her borders. Unlike the Czechs, the Poles attempted resistance, and England and France demanded immediate withdrawal of German troops from Polish soil. When Hitler refused to halt the advance of his armies, London and Paris declared war on Berlin. World War II had begun.

The dilemma of the antirevisionist states

The inaction of the antirevisionist states in the face of Japanese, Italian, German, and Hungarian expansion can be explained in many ways. For one, a good measure of blind self-interest marked the calculations of most foreign offices. For instance, the commercial interests of England and France lay mostly in southern China; hence, these states were not overly worried by Japanese seizure of China's northern provinces. On the contrary, they deemed that Japan's move would entail a welcome reduction of Russian influence in the Far East. Similarly, by concluding the 1935 Naval Pact with Germany (see p. 508) Britain had disregarded Russian interests, since a German fleet one-third the size of Britain's spelled an end to Soviet naval supremacy in the Baltic. One could point to many other examples of self-interest, such as America's non-involvement with the world as long as the Western Hemisphere seemed safe or Stalin's hope that a German war against England and France would lead to the destruction of both nazism and capitalism.

Another reason for inaction was a strong strain of pacifism. Mindful of the horrors of World War I, most Frenchmen were in no mood to enter a new holocaust. Moreover, they were still repairing the damage from the earlier conflict: restoration of the Cathedral of Rheims, for example, was completed barely a month before the outbreak of World War II. The popularity of the movie La Grande Illusion, with its theme of Franco-German reconciliation—a film that Goebbels banned in Germany—demonstrated the attitude among wide segments of Frenchmen. Pacifism was also particularly strong among British students. The so-called Oxford Movement, in which students took an oath that they would "in no circumstances fight for . . . King and country" found wide adherence in Britain and the Commonwealth.

Reluctance to take a firm stand and readiness to appease the revisionists were helped by the fascists' new methods of piecemeal aggression. As Hitler had predicted in *Mein Kampf,* if the Nazis shrewdly presented their demands "in installments," their opponents would "become characterless" and would "no longer find any sufficient reason in each of these detailed oppressions to take to arms once more."

Finally, perhaps the main reason for inaction was the inability of many to decide which was the greater danger to their security and their way of life: fascism or communism. This indecision had been evident in the attitude of the democracies toward the Spanish Civil War (see p. 509). It was particularly apparent in France. Gradually encircled by fascist states, many Frenchmen split sharply over the question of whether external security and internal stability could be better attained by France's going fascist herself or by rallying to the Soviet Union in an antifascist bloc.

The same dilemma was evident at Munich, when London and Paris did not insist on the presence of Russian negotiators at the 1938 conference. By thus snubbing Stalin and demonstrating that, at least for the moment, they were willing to appease Hitler at the expense of Soviet interests, they unwittingly drove the Russian dictator into a *rapprochement* with Hitler. Similarly, Poland and Rumania had to decide whether they feared communism and Russian imperialism more than Nazi expansion. During the fruitless negotiations in 1939 between Anglo-French and Russians over the security of eastern Europe, Poland and Rumania refused to adhere to any agreement that would permit the Red Army to cross their territory even in the event of German aggression. Such failure to agree on a common policy made it easier for Germany to attack her enemies one by one.

The course of the fighting

World War II can be divided into two distinct phases. During the first three and one-half years, from the summer of 1939 to the winter of 1942, the revisionist powers won an almost uninterrupted series of victories that made their military might seem well-nigh invincible. The second phase of the war, the two and one-half years from early 1943 to the summer of 1945, saw the gradual crushing of the revisionists, culminating in the final triumph of the Allied Powers.

The success of the revisionist powers

During the first phase of the war, Germany and Japan, the leaders among the revisionists, benefited from superior armaments, the bold use of new tactics, careful strategic planning, ruthless exploitation of conquered territory, and the readiness to resort to total war. In time they were joined by Italy, Hungary, Rumania, Bulgaria, and Finland. The Allies, for their part, initially consisted of only England, the British Commonwealth, France, and Poland, none of them well prepared for a modern war. In the course of the war, however, their ranks swelled to some forty-six states and, largely through Anglo-American scientific and industrial developments, their war machine developed into a formidable striking force.

At the onset of the war, Hitler's mechanized troops and air force crushed Poland's large army in less than a month, while Anglo-French forces contented themselves with broadcasting propaganda from behind the Maginot Line. Toward the end of the Polish campaign, Russia's Red Army cashed in on the Nazi-Soviet Pact by seizing a strip of eastern Poland and later occupying Lithuania, Latvia, Estonia, Bessarabia, and Bucovina. Only Finland resisted Russian expansion in a winter campaign of several months before finally agreeing to cede parts of Karelia and other areas to the Soviets.

After a relatively calm winter, during which Goebbels sought to convince the Europeans of the invincibility of the German army by distributing a film on the *Blitzkrieg* (lightning warfare) in Poland, Hitler was ready to strike again. In April of 1940, German forces suddenly seized Denmark and Norway. Neutrality, it became evident, no longer guaranteed safety in a total war. German strategy required occupation of the Norwegian coast to outflank the British naval blockade of the North Sea, to give German submarines better bases for preying on Allied shipping, and to enable the German airforce to strike at northern England and Scotland from airfields closer to their targets. (See Map 29.)

A month later the Germans used similar tactics of surprise to conquer Holland, Belgium, Luxembourg, and France. Dive bombers suddenly paralyzed Dutch cities and paratroopers dropped from the skies to seize strategic points while mechanized columns raced across the border. Holland capitulated within four days. Aided by some hastily dispatched British and French units, Belgium was able to resist just a little over two weeks. Then, while the British evacuated their expeditionary corps through the port of Dunkirk, German troops poured into France. In a maneuver that resembled their strategy in World War I, the German panzers by-passed the Maginot Line and entered France across her poorly defended northern frontier. With the French reeling under this onslaught, Mussolini, not to be outshadowed by Hitler, entered the war, although his troops took few immediate military steps. Five weeks after launching their attack on the Lowlands, the Germans captured Paris, and the demoralized French requested a cease-fire. Hitler arranged for the armistice to be signed in the same railroad carriage in which the Germans had been forced to accept the armistice of World War I.

So far, German successes had been dazzling, and the jubilant *Führer* became more convinced than ever of the infallibility of his political and military acumen. In less than a year Germany had smashed all but one of her enemies and acquired control over more than two hundred thousand additional square miles with valuable resources in food, raw materials, and manpower that could further strengthen her war machine. Like Napoleon, Hitler faced only one further task: defeating England and the British Empire.

German victories elicited political changes among the Allies. In England Prime Minister Chamberlain was replaced by the energetic Winston Churchill (1874–1965), who was doggedly determined not to come to terms with Hitler and to continue the struggle, no matter what the cost. France and her empire fell under three different jurisdictions. The North and the Atlantic coast to the Pyrenees were occupied by German forces and controlled by a German military governor. The Southeast was temporarily left as an independent state. With its headquarters at Vichy, a new French government under Marshal Henri Pétain established a semi-fascist, dictatorial regime that worked in relative harmony with Nazi Germany. Hitler hoped Vichy France could retain the loyalty of the large French colonial empire and prevent its falling into British hands. The third France, soon called "Free France," initially consisted of a small army of French volunteers organized on British soil. Led by General Charles de Gaulle (1890–   ), who had escaped to England, and aided by the British navy, it gradually gained control of several French colonies.

After the defeat of France, Hitler first directed his attack against the British Isles. When constant air bombardment and a submarine blockade of England failed to produce the expected British surrender, the Nazis turned their main attention to the Balkans in preparation for an eventual clash with Soviet Russia. With Hungary already firmly in the German orbit, the Germans used a mixture of political and economic pressure, subversion by native fascist sympathizers, and outright military invasion to gain control of Rumania, Bulgaria, Yugoslavia, and Greece.

Mussolini meanwhile had tried to convert the Mediterranean into an Italian lake. In September of 1940, his armies invaded Egypt, and a month later they crossed into Greece. But everywhere they suffered defeats: the Greeks pushed the Italians back into Albania, the British navy crippled the Italian fleet in Italy's home waters, and Commonwealth forces saved Egypt and plunged deep into the Italian colony of Lybia. Coming to the rescue of his fellow dictator, the *Führer* sent troops to seize Greece and Crete and dispatched the Africa Corps for a new invasion of Egypt. However, the Germans failed to get a foothold in the Middle East, where British and Free French forces seized Iraq, Syria, and Lebanon.

Thus, by June 1941, Hitler controlled most of what he liked to call "Fortress Europe." Only Sweden and Switzerland stayed completely neutral, while Portugal and the Irish Free State, though neutral, were friendly to England and Germany respectively. Spain and Finland cooperated with Hitler. On the Continent, essentially only the Soviet Union and the areas it had

annexed in 1939-40 remained outside of Hitler's grasp. With distrust between Stalin and Hitler constantly mounting in apprehension as to who
might strike first, the Nazi leader overruled the advice of his more cautious
generals and struck at Russia in June of 1941.

During these first two years of war in Europe, Africa, and Asia, the
United States kept its official neutrality, although American sympathy for
Great Britain increased rapidly. Starting in November 1939, the government
permitted belligerents to purchase American arms on a basis of "cash and
carry," a step clearly favoring the Allied Powers whose navies dominated the
Atlantic Ocean. In 1940, President Roosevelt expanded the army and navy,
instituted Selective Service, and gave England fifty destroyers in exchange
for bases in Newfoundland, the Bahamas, and other islands, in order to improve the defenses of the Western Hemisphere. Finally, the Lend-Lease Act
of 1941 allowed Roosevelt to supply Britain with arms, and new American
bases in Greenland and Iceland made it easier for American forces to help
patrol the North Atlantic.

At the same time Japan continued to expand her economic and military
influence. With Europe's colonial powers occupied by the war, only the
United States could potentially prevent further Japanese expansion. Yet
Washington merely protested and prohibited the export of iron and scrap
steel to Japan when the Japanese seized French Indo-China after the fall of
France. In 1940, the Allies began to suspect that Japan and Germany might
plan the joint conquest of Asia, particularly after Tokyo, Berlin, and Rome
concluded a pact, promising mutual aid in case one of them were "attacked
by a Power at present not involved in the European war or in the Chinese-
Japanese conflict." For Japan, this unnamed "Power" clearly was America;
for Hitler, however, it could also have meant Russia, despite the fact that the
Soviet Union was officially exempted in the pact. Yet, in 1941, Japan concluded a neutrality pact with Stalin, revealing her intention of expanding in
Southeast Asia rather than becoming involved in a conflict with the Soviet
Union.

Between the summer of 1941 and early fall of 1942, Germany and Japan
attained the pinnacle of their power and expansion. Despite an unusually
severe winter that enabled the Russians to launch a brief counter-offensive,
the German armies plunged deep into Russia's heartland, while a new offensive by the Africa Corps almost captured the Suez Canal. Similarly, Japan
followed its surprise attack on the United States Fleet at Pearl Harbor (December 7, 1941) with lightning sweeps that conquered the Dutch East
Indies, the Philippines, Thailand, Malaya, Burma, and the Pacific islands as
far south as the Solomons near Australia, some 3,500 miles from Japan itself.
The magnitude of these German and Japanese strikes can best be visualized
by studying maps of the two war zones. (See Maps 29 and 30.)

Thus, the war assumed global proportions in 1941, when Russia and the
United States, soon followed by Brazil and most other Latin American Re-

publics, were drawn into the conflict. Although not always agreeing on tactics or ultimate war aims, the Allies began to cooperate in order to reverse Axis successes. On January 1, 1942, twenty-two Allied governments—some of them governments-in-exile, such as those of Holland and Norway, whose homelands were occupied by the enemy—signed the United Nations Declaration, in which they pledged their resources to fight jointly until the defeat of Germany, Italy, and Japan. In the course of that year, the tide of war was to turn in favor of the United Nations.

Victory for the United Nations forces

In the fall and winter of 1942, the Axis powers experienced their first major defeats in Russia, North Africa, and the Pacific. In the Battle of Stalingrad, which lasted four and one-half months, the Germans lost some twenty-two divisions and forfeited the momentum of their advance. Aided by American war matériel shipped to Russia via Iran or the northern ports of Murmansk and Archangel, the Red Army then launched a highly successful counter-offensive which gradually drove the Germans out of Russia.

At the same time, the British resumed their offensive in North Africa and pushed the Italo-German forces out of Egypt, while an Anglo-American army landed in Morocco. After a brief scuffle with Vichy elements, the Allies seized Morocco and Algeria and penetrated into Tunisia, which had been hastily occupied by German troops. Further fierce fighting ensued, but by May of 1943, all of northern Africa had fallen into Allied hands. In retaliation for Vichy's failure to defend Morocco, the Germans occupied Vichy France.

Meanwhile the Germans at home got their first taste of total war as Anglo-American squadrons based in Britain mounted ever larger bombing raids on the German homeland. The Germans were also beginning to lose the Battle of the Atlantic. Most of their surface fleet had been sunk or damaged, and an elaborate Allied convoy system, improved antisubmarine defenses, as well as stepped-up American production of new ships had broken the attempted blockade of Britain and gradually assured Allied supremacy on the seas.

Although Roosevelt had assigned priority to the defeat of Germany and Italy, the Americans sent sufficient air, naval, and marine units to the Pacific to halt further Japanese conquests. After the naval victory off Guadalcanal in November of 1942, they began the slow process of driving back the Japanese, island by island.

In January 1943, Roosevelt and Churchill met at Casablanca and decided on total air war to effect "the destruction . . . of the German military, industrial, and economic system" and to end German capacity for resistance by "undermining the morale of the German people." To avoid the mistake of 1918, they determined to accept nothing less than unconditional surrender from Germany, a decision that may have stiffened German resistance during the last phases of the war and rendered the work of the German underground more hopeless. At Casablanca, as at other Allied conferences, there was disagreement on the question of a second front in Europe. Stalin had been pleading for an immediate Allied invasion of "Fortress Europe" to relieve German pressure on the Russian front. When Allied invasion plans were constantly postponed, he suspected the capitalist democracies of wanting to see Communist Russia bleed to death before they would attack Hitler themselves. Churchill, for his part, insisted on preparing for an invasion of the Balkans, whereas General George C. Marshall (1880–1959), the U.S. Chief of Staff, advocated an invasion of northwestern Europe, once sufficient forces had been assembled in Britain. Finally, Churchill and Roosevelt concurred on Italy as the first target.

Hence, American, British, and Canadian forces invaded Sicily in July 1943, a step which provoked the overthrow of Mussolini in Rome and the installment of a non-Fascist Italian regime which promptly initiated negotiations with the Allies for an armistice. During the protracted negotiations which culminated in an armistice only in early September, Hitler dispatched added divisions to Italy to fortify the peninsula against Allied penetration. He then rescued the imprisoned Mussolini and installed him as head of a Fascist Republic in northern Italy. Thus Italy became divided. The Allies seized the South and eventually accepted the liberated Italians as co-belligerents against Germany, but their northward advance was stopped by well-entrenched German lines between Rome and Naples. The ensuing bloody Italian campaign, with Germans and Italian Fascists fighting against the Allies and Italian partisans, was to continue until almost the end of World War II.

In the course of 1943, the German armies also encountered a new problem in the growing strength of underground forces: Russian partisans, Yugoslav and Greek guerillas, the so-called French Forces of the Interior (FFI), and others—many of them supplied by Allied airdrops—interrupted communications systems, destroyed war supplies, and helped in the escape of downed Allied fliers. The Germans had to divert many divisions in attempts to suppress this underground activity, troops they could ill afford to withhold from the battle areas.

In 1944, the pace of Axis defeats accelerated rapidly. The Red Army cleared the Germans out of the northern Balkans, invaded Poland and Finland, and advanced along the Baltic shore to East Prussia. By the end of the year, the Russians stood ready to invade Germany proper. In southern Europe, meanwhile, the Allies captured Florence and liberated Greece, and the Yugoslavs freed most of their own territory. In the West the massive Allied invasion of Normandy on June 6 under the command of General Dwight D. Eisenhower (1890–1969) led to the rapid liberation of France, Belgium, and Holland. At the same time, the Allies achieved air superiority even over Germany itself and could bomb targets with less and less interference.

Although some generals warned Hitler to "put an end to a hopeless struggle," the *Führer* remained determined to continue the battle, and his propagandists assured the German people that secret weapons would bring ultimate victory. Indeed, the Germans had developed improved rocketry and new turbojet fighter planes, but the atomic bomb, on which German scientists were feverishly working, was not completed before the total collapse. Some Nazis also hoped that the incompatibility between Communists and capitalists would shatter the anti-Nazi alliance and that the Germans could persuade the British and the Americans to join in a crusade to safeguard central Europe from domination by Soviet Russia.

The German anti-Nazi underground finally decided on a desperate attempt to overthrow Hitler before he dragged Germany down to total ruin. Several half-hearted attempts had been made previously to kill Hitler, but most army officers had frowned on such plots. They hesitated to commit treason and violate their oath to the *Führer;* moreover, they lacked assurance from the Allies that a non-Nazi German government could expect better terms than the announced unconditional surrender. Yet, the underground needed the support of the army to overcome Hitler's para-military units. When defeats on all fronts made the military situation hopeless and Hitler still would not listen to their counsel "to draw the proper conclusions without delay," several of the highest-ranking officers agreed to join the plot of July, 1944. But Hitler was only slightly wounded and prompt countermeasures by Goebbels and other Nazis foiled the plot. Those conspirators who did not commit suicide were summarily executed or thrown into concentration camps. Thereafter, most army officers stood loyally by Hitler until Germany's total destruction.

Japan, too, suffered constant defeats in 1944. Her air and naval power was crippled, although not yet eliminated, permitting the United States to deliver more and heavier air raids on the Japanese Islands. Meanwhile United States army and marine units, commanded by General Douglas McArthur (1880–1964), leapfrogged northward from island to island and reconquered the Philippines. On mainland Asia Chiang Kai-shek's forces based at Chungking, with some supplies from the Allies, continued to tie down a Japanese army of almost one million, while further south, British Commonwealth troops began the reconquest of Southeast Asia.

The end came in 1945 amid the worst destruction and casualties of the long war. After defeating Hitler's unsuccessful attempt once again to break through to the Channel—in the so-called Battle of the Bulge—Allied armies streamed into Germany from the West, while the Red Army concentrated on capturing Berlin from the East. In April the German armies surrendered in Italy, where partisans caught Mussolini trying to flee to Switzerland and summarily shot him. With much of Germany occupied by the enemy, with bombs raining incessantly from the skies and millions of refugees in flight, and with his capital surrounded and partially conquered by the Red Army,

Hitler ranted in his underground bunker in Berlin, still unwilling to spare his people the final suffering. Even the political testament he wrote shortly before his suicide on April 30 contained the exhortation that his people should "on no account give up the struggle" and that all good German soldiers should prefer "death to cowardly abdication or even capitulation." Nonetheless, his designated successor, Admiral Karl Doenitz (1891–   ), signed Germany's surrender on May 7 and then supervised the initial dismantling of the Nazi regime before the Allied Military Government took complete charge of all German affairs.

In the spring of 1945, Japan too was subjected to incessant bombardment by airplanes launched first from carriers, then also from bases on newly reconquered islands. Destruction of the Japanese fleet resulted in isolating Japan from most of her conquered territories. By then, the Japanese air force was so decimated that the United States fleet could steam into Japan's home waters and shell coastal cities. Still Japan refused to surrender. On August 6, the United States dropped an atomic bomb on Hiroshima, two days later Russia declared war on Japan and invaded Manchuria, and the following day the United States detonated a second atomic bomb over Nagasaki. These disasters led to Japan's capitulation. Soon thereafter American troops landed to initiate the military occupation of the Japanese islands.

The aims of the combatants

In earlier centuries the purposes for which wars were fought were usually easy to ascertain. A duke might seek to conquer a neighboring province, a king might claim a disputed inheritance, or the merchants of one state might try to wrest economic privileges from others. When after 1792 ideological warfare came to be stressed, war aims became more complex, even though most nineteenth-century wars were still fought on relatively clear-cut issues of economics and spheres of influence. World War I, as we saw (see p. 457), presented a more complicated issue with its vaunted appeal to make "the world safe for democracy." World War II, finally, inaugurated an age when ideological aims, both real and imagined, began to obscure the more traditional goals of power politics. Starting in World War II, governments devoted ever greater attention to propaganda in order to instill in soldiers and civilians an ideological motivation for prosecuting wars.

Expectations of the revisionist powers

In chapter XXVI we discussed the expectations of the have-not, or revisionist powers (see p. 486). Although never spelled out precisely, their war aims were widely broadcast. In the Tripartite Pact of 1940, for instance, Japan, Germany, and Italy promised mutual cooperation in order to "establish and maintain a new order of things calculated to promote the prosperity and welfare of the peoples" in "Greater East Asia and in the regions of Europe." The Japanese coined such slogans as "Asia for the Asians" and proclaimed they had come to Southeast Asia to liberate the people from European colonialism. Such appeals to Asian nationalism bore fruit only after the war, for in reality the Japanese acted as strict masters over the peoples they had conquered and ideological proselyting hardly figured in their war aims. Rather they were primarily interested in military power and economic benefits. From the vast colonial empire they had acquired by 1942 they hoped to extract oil, rubber, tin, and other raw materials needed for their industries.

Like the Japanese, the Nazis sought an expansion of military power and greater access to food supplies and raw materials. These were to be obtained first in Europe and later in colonial areas. Through effective collaboration with Nazi sympathizers in the Western Hemisphere, a few German leaders even believed that domination of that continent was feasible.

Nazi aims for military and economic expansion were, however, complicated by ideological and racist factors. Their dilemma was seen in their treatment of conquered peoples. On the one hand, they urged all Europeans to help establish a "New Order." In conquered areas they spread Nazi ideology, applied Nazi laws, and awarded supervisory assignments to local Nazi sympathizers. On the other hand, the Germans treated peoples who fell under their control according to Nazi racist ideas. "Nordic" peoples were given preference, "Latin" peoples were ranked lower, Slavs were considered barely human, and Jews, Negroes, and "racially mixed peoples" were regarded as subhumans.

Hitler had proclaimed his intention of ridding Europe, if not the entire world, of Jews and Communists. Until his death this remained one of his war aims. He had also stated his aim of increasing the "German *Volk*" so that "250,000,000 Germans will live on this continent in less than one hundred years." Such a feat was to be attempted by planned eugenics and by somehow bringing together all German-speaking peoples. This, too, became one of the Nazis' aims, although no consistent policy ever developed. The party philosopher Alfred Rosenberg (1893–1946) envisioned an eastward expansion by establishing colonial enclaves of peoples of "superior racial stock"—Germans, Dutch, Danes, and Norwegians—scattered in the agricultural areas of eastern Europe, surrounded by Slavic slaves who toiled for their German masters. The Gestapo chief Heinrich Himmler (1900–1945), on the other hand, sought to concentrate all ethnic Germans in Central Europe by repatriating them from wherever they could be found. This core of "ethnic purity" in Central Europe, in his view, could easily dominate the rest of Europe peopled by "racial inferiors."

Wartime conferences of the Allies

War aims among the United Nations were complicated and diverse. Despite dozens of conferences and consultations at the level of heads of state, foreign ministers, or lower echelons and despite many official communiqués purporting harmonious agreement, no real consensus ever developed beyond the obvious need to defeat the enemy.

A detailed analysis of inter-Allied wartime negotiations would make a fascinating study, revealing basic friction that later emerged in the cold war and in the anticolonial struggles of Africa and Asia. Disagreements ranged from such relatively small points, as whether Trieste should go to Italy or to Yugoslavia, to such major items as whether Russia would be allowed predominance over the Balkan Peninsula. To be sure, differences of views arose among all Allies, but those between Stalin and the Anglo-Americans were the most pronounced.

Officially, all the Allies except General de Gaulle subscribed to the Atlantic Charter, drawn up by Winston Churchill and Franklin Roosevelt in 1941 and incorporated in the United Nations Declaration of 1942. This declaration, with its "hopes for a better future for the world," was in many respects as idealistic as Wilson's Fourteen Points. The Allies also agreed that German Nazism, Italian Fascism, and Japanese totalitarianism should be destroyed and the three nations demilitarized, but there was no consensus as to what sort of new regimes to foster in the enemy states. The term "democratic," which frequently appeared in official releases, had different meanings to Communists, Socialists, and capitalists. Moreover, the economic and military destruction of the Axis powers was likely to create a power vacuum in strategic areas of Europe and the Pacific. The question remained as to who would fill these vacuums. Plans for the treatment of Germany were revised continuously, as the powers debated whether to dissect Germany into several separate states, whether to arrange for military occupation by a joint Allied force or by separate zones, whether to allow France a role in the control of Germany, what sort of reparations to demand, and what level of industrial production to permit the defeated enemy.

The delay of the British and Americans in establishing a major second front in Europe was more than a military question, since it involved the future political and military balance in Europe. Whoever "liberated" a given area from Nazi or Fascist domination was likely to exert long-term influence over the region's political development. Moreover, the cost of an invasion, in men as well as resources, could well affect the relative postwar strength of a nation such as England.

Among the many points frequently on the agenda of inter-Allied conferences was the question of Russia's postwar borders. Stalin insisted from the beginning on retaining the new frontiers of 1941, by which the Soviet Union regained most but not all of what she had lost in 1917–21. In addition, he clearly wanted to safeguard Russia's security by insisting on the installation of friendly regimes in neighboring states. There was even discussion of whether Russia should finally be allowed seizure of Istanbul (Constantinople), so as to permit ready Russian access to the Mediterranean. Stalin's demands for security were particularly concerned with Poland, the state over whose fate World War II had originated. The Soviets remained adamant about instituting a pro-Russian government in liberated Poland, whereas the West insisted on "free, democratic, elections."

Other disagreements involved Britain's role in the world. Roosevelt favored independence for India and other British dependencies and advocated a trusteeship for all colonies under the United Nations Organization which he hoped would be created after the war. Churchill, however, saw no need to dismember the British Empire. Then again, some Western statesmen encouraged England to establish military bases in northern and western Europe as a counterweight to Russia, since America was likely to retreat into isolation after the end of the war.

Finally, there were many other issues on which agreement was hard to achieve: the role of China in the postwar world, the decision of whether to subject the enemy leaders to war crimes trials, and the question of who would lead the future United Nations Organization and whether a veto should be allowed to the major powers.

The impact of the war

World War II affected the world more fundamentally than any previous armed conflict, more decisively perhaps than any other conceivable event in history. It involved more people and was fought over wider areas than World War I. It was infinitely more destructive, while at the same time unleashing hitherto unimaginable human and material energies. In 1945, few people thought that after such a war one could return to ante-bellum "normalcy."

The effects of the war

The loss and damage, both human and material, resulting from World War II were so staggering that the magnitude of statistics of casualties, destruction, and costs defies normal human comprehension. Military deaths among all combatants have been estimated at seventeen million; more than twelve million civilians were killed as a direct result of military action; some thirty-five million were injured; over six million were exterminated in Nazi concentration camps; and an untold number succumbed to epidemics and starvation. Alone, the five-day raid on Dresden by Anglo-American planes (February, 1945) killed some 135,000 people; and upward of 80,000 died in a single minute during the atomic bombing of Hiroshima.

Equally astronomical was the devastation caused by the war. Entire cities were leveled; millions of houses burned or reduced to empty shells; railroads, roads, bridges, and hydro-electric dams rendered useless; and factories and mines blown up. In many agricultural areas, in Russia, Poland, Holland, and elsewhere, much of the soil was ruined and livestock decimated. Starvation and disease were rampant in Europe and Asia. Masses of homeless were hoveled in whatever shelters remained usable or were housed in the barracks of former concentration camps or military stockades. And in the first cold winter after the end of the war, there was practically no fuel to heat homes, to drive machines, or to reactivate transportation systems.

The financial cost of the war also staggers the imagination. It has been estimated that the combined participants spent well over 1,100,000,000,000 dollars on weapons and armaments alone. United States Lend Lease Aid, most of which was never repaid, totaled over fifty billion dollars, and America's national debt, less than forty-five billion in 1940, rose to two hundred and seventy-five billion by the end of 1945. With these figures one must keep in mind the considerably higher purchasing power of the dollar at that time.

Not even at the time of the barbarian invasions of the Roman Empire had so many people, relatively speaking, been uprooted. Central and Western Europe were glutted with twenty to thirty million refugees, displaced persons, and expellees. The refugees had lost their homes or had fled from their homelands to save their lives or to escape political persecution—anti-Communists fleeing before the advancing Red Army, collaborators escaping with the retreating Nazis, or peoples forcefully evacuated by the military. The stream of refugees from Communist-occupied territories was to continue for years. Most of the refugees could not or would not return to their homelands and had to be resettled. Displaced persons were those uprooted by the war, usually because of military requirements. Many of them had been used as conscript labor on German farms or in German industry. These displaced persons had to be housed and fed until transport could be found to ship them back home. Finally came the expellees, mostly ethnic Germans, soon numbering over nine million. These were driven out of Poland, Czechoslovakia, Hungary, Rumania, and other eastern states as a result of strong anti-German feelings, with the official explanation that such a step would prevent a future Hitler from using the pretext of "liberating Germans" to justify a new eastward expansion.

Disease, devastation, and despair, coupled with the friction of military occupation during, as well as after, the war also frayed the moral fabric of the peoples of Europe and Asia. Shaken by the desolation about them, bewildered by the contrasts between Allied propaganda and former Axis indoctrination, and seeking desperately to find food and shelter, most people had little time for the niceties of civilized behavior. The black market flourished, and the normal respect for law and social conventions seemed to lie buried in the ashes of the war.

Not all the results of the war, however, were bleak and destructive. Spurred by the exigencies of military requirements and the people's willingness to pay for the necessary cost, science and technology advanced at an unprecedented rate. Thousands of new devices were invented, new materials produced, and methods of production improved, resulting in a veritable new scientific, technological, and industrial revolution. In one way or another, most of these inventions and improvements radically affected the development of world civilization in the second half of the twentieth century. One might mention the development of jet aircraft and rockets, the improvement of television, the perfection of synthetic fibers, and, of course, the splitting of the atom. Wartime requirements also accelerated the process of industrial and agricultural automation. The destruction of factories and machinery, particularly in Germany, Japan, and Russia, permitted the modernization of plants during postwar reconstruction, just as the increased productive capacity in England, America, and elsewhere after conversion to peacetime production resulted in greater availability of consumer goods. Finally, the need to regulate economic and human resources during the war further boosted the state's control over its peoples, in both totalitarian and democratic regimes. There may be disagreement whether this enhanced power of the state in the long run benefited a majority of the people, but no one can deny that this development strongly affected the lives of all people in the postwar decades.

Another postwar era

It is instructive to compare the immediate postwar years after 1918 and 1945. As a generalization, one might venture the conclusion that more leaders recognized the need for finding *new* solutions to national and international problems in 1945 than in 1918.

The difference may be seen in the programs of the political parties that came to power in many countries at the conclusion of the two wars. Soon after 1918, right of center or outright conservative parties or coalitions governed Britain, France, the United States, and many other countries. After 1945, however, the left of center factions tended to dominate, at least during the early postwar years. In Great Britain the Labor party won a decisive electoral victory in July 1945, forcing Churchill's resignation and bringing about England's first all-Labor cabinet under Prime Minister Clement R. Attlee (1883-1967), a government convinced that England's social dislocations could be remedied by far-reaching socialist measures. In France, communists, socialists, and the new liberal Popular Republican Movement (MRP) attained a majority in the Constituent Assembly that was given the task of creating the Fourth French Republic, and several Socialist-dominated governments ruled France until 1947. Similarly, leftist parties emerged strong in Holland, Belgium, Austria, Germany, Italy and Japan. And in the United States President Truman's Fair Deal sought to resume Roosevelt's New Deal, which had been held in abeyance during the war.

This resurgence of the left can be accounted for in many ways. For one, it was a natural reaction against fascism, which had dominated so much of the world. Moreover, the spectacular victories and expansion of the Soviet Union convinced many that communism might prove to be a viable and vibrant system, worth adopting elsewhere. The anti-Nazi underground and resistance movements had also been strongly influenced and, in many cases, led by socialists and communists, partly because they were better organized, more dedicated, and more determined foes of fascism. Their political orientation affected postwar restoration. When the various governments-in-exile returned or attempted to return to their liberated capitals, it became evident that some had grown out of touch with the changed needs of their war-plagued peoples. The resistance leaders, on the other hand, who had stayed behind and fought the enemy from precarious hide-outs, often displayed a better grasp of the immediate desires of the populace. Hence, their organizations—such as the National Council of Resistance in France, the National Liberation Front in Greece, and Marshal Tito's (1892–   ) National Liberation Movement in Yugoslavia—assumed great importance in the immediate postwar period. In France, their pressure led to the leftward orientation of the government, in Greece it entailed a civil war, and in Yugoslavia it ended in victory for the communists.

The liberal trend was also aided by a revival of Christian Socialism. While not radical in any sense, the new or reconstituted Christian Socialist parties in Italy, Germany, Austria, Holland, Belgium, and France (MRP) acknowledged the need for strong governmental measures to provide a minimum level for the people's living requirements. With the return of prosperity most of these parties were to grow more conservative.

Another major difference between 1918 and 1945 was the handling of problems of demobilization and reconversion to a peacetime economy. Despite the normal pressure "to get the boys home," Britain and America discharged their vast array of soldiers more slowly, so as not to glut the labor market. Moreover, careful provisions for veterans were made in all states that could afford such practices. Price controls, rationing, and other economic safeguards were retained for some time in order to avoid sudden inflation. Thus, although many economic and financial problems remained unsolved, the transition to peace was more strictly controlled than after 1918.

Furthermore, during the 1920's most nations had retreated into economic isolation through higher tariffs and other restrictive practices. After World War II, however, most influential leaders outside the communist orbit soon took cognizance of the world's economic interdependence. America's Morgenthau Plan, which advocated the de-industrialization and pastoralization of Germany in order to eliminate her potential for waging another war, was discarded after it became evident that one could not readily resurrect the economy of Europe without also rekindling that of Germany. Recognition of this economic interdependence led many governments to reduce tariffs, to enter into cooperative financial agreements between nations, and to explore programs for bilateral or multilateral economic integration (see p. 565).

Finally, the holocaust of World War II spawned a new international spirit unknown after World War I. The 1920's had on the whole been highly nationalistic. The era after 1945 was to be different in a curious way. On the one hand, few states retreated into isolation or neutrality. Many Europeans renounced nationalism and their traditional reverence for the sovereignty of nations by expressing their readiness to join in larger political units comprised of several states, all of Europe, or even the entire world. This new internationalism became an important force in postwar Europe. Even the United States recognized the need for collective security and relinquished its hemispheric isolation in favor of a new role of intense world-wide financial and military involvement. On the other hand, the colonial lands of Asia and Africa emerged from the war with new and vibrant feelings of national aspirations. This stirring among the colonial peoples, in part also attributable to World War II, effected another fundamental change in postwar world history with the creation of seventy new sovereign states between 1945 and 1968.

The United Nations and the peace treaties

At the San Francisco conference of the United Nations, April to June, 1945, the wartime cooperation of the anti-Axis coalition was officially converted into a formal international organization when fifty-one nations subscribed as original members to the United Nations Charter. The formation of such an organization had been discussed at many high-level inter-Allied meetings, and beginning in 1944, various preparatory and executive committees had elaborated detailed proposals. The U. N. was to succeed the defunct League of Nations and inherit its physical assets. As expressed in the Charter, its purpose was "to save succeeding generations from the scourge of war . . . to reaffirm faith in fundamental human rights . . . to promote social progress and better standards of life in larger freedom . . ." and "to maintain international peace and security."

Within the U. N. the Security Council of eleven members (increased to fifteen in 1965), with permanent seats for the Big Five—China, France, Great Britain, Russia, and the United States, each entitled to a veto power— was entrusted with "primary responsibility for the maintenance of international peace." The General Assembly, in which all member states had an equal vote, was to discuss any and all questions within the scope of the U. N. Charter. A Secretariat, headed by the U. N. Secretary General, was to supervise the day-to-day functioning of the organization. Three other integral parts of the United Nations were the Economic and Social Council, the Trusteeship Council, and the International Court of Justice, which supplanted the former Permanent Court of International Justice. In addition, numerous affiliated agencies were established, such as the United Nations Educational, Scientific, and Cultural Organization (UNESCO), the World Health Organization (WHO), the International Bank for Reconstruction and Development, and the International Monetary Fund.

At a meeting in London in the fall of 1945, a temporary executive committee of fourteen nations voted nine to three—with Canada and the United States abstaining—to locate the headquarters of the United Nations in the United States. France, Holland, and Britain preferred a European location, whereas the U.S.S.R. was among those favoring America.

At its first meeting in January 1946, the U. N. General Assembly began its long task of debating international problems and soon found itself confronted with such thorny issues as disputes in Indonesia, Greece, Palestine, Korea, and Kashmir, and the question of control over atomic energy. But the U. N. was not involved in writing the peace treaties for the defeated axis nations. This task was assumed by the Council of Ministers of the Big Five, composed of the foreign ministers of Russia, England, America, France, and China.

Reminiscent of the Congress System after 1815, this Council of Foreign Ministers met frequently after September 1945 to discuss areas of international friction and to draft peace proposals. Strong disagreements at once emerged between Russia and the three Western powers. Less concerned with European affairs, China stayed on the side lines. The views of the Big Four differed on many issues, among them reparations to Russia, internationalization of the Danube, withdrawal of occupation forces, and the composition and voting procedure of an eventual peace conference.

The twenty-one nation peace conference that finally convened in Paris from July to October, 1946, was marked by distrust and acrimony. The smaller states resented domination of proceedings by the Big Four; and the East-West split, foreshadowing the cold war, was evident in the usual voting alignment of fifteen to six in favor of the West. It proved impossible to reach agreement on treaties for Austria and Germany, but compromises were finally reached in regard to the five other defeated states. At another Paris conference in February 1947, peace treaties were signed for Italy, Bulgaria, Finland, Hungary, and Rumania.

The treaty for Italy stipulated some territorial losses to Greece, France, and particularly to Yugoslavia, abandonment of her colonies, reduction of her army, navy, and airforce, and payment of reparations to Yugoslavia, Greece, Ethiopia, and Albania. No agreement could be reached on the future of Trieste, a question that was settled only in 1954, when the city was awarded to Italy and most of the hinterland was assigned to Yugoslavia. The treaties for Bulgaria, Finland, Hungary, and Rumania all followed similar patterns, arranging for territorial readjustments, reduced armed forces, and reparations. (See Map 32.)

The Italians were particularly unhappy with the peace settlement. Since in 1944 that part of Italy not occupied by German troops had become a co-belligerent in the anti-Nazi coalition, the Italians resented being punished like other defeated Axis powers. Actually, except for the territorial clauses, the peace treaties soon lost their significance. As the cold war intensified, the

West turned to wooing Italy and urged her to disregard parts of the treaty, particularly the clauses limiting her armed forces. The treaties for Bulgaria, Hungary, and Rumania similarly lost meaning as these countries slipped into the orbit of Soviet Russia.

While the U. N. struggled to ease international friction and the Council of Ministers debated peace proposals, many new organizations, most of them governmental, some privately sponsored, labored to bring relief to the millions of starving and homeless and to reconstruct the economic, social, and financial structure of the world community. The United Nations Relief and Rehabilitation Agency (UNRRA), organized in 1943, with contributions from forty-eight nations—mostly from the United States—provided emergency food, clothing, medical supplies, farm implements, transport equipment, and whatever was needed to avoid disaster. The International Refugee Organization sought to find new homes for expatriates; the International Monetary Fund worked on stabilizing currency exchange rates; and the new World Federation of Trade Unions attempted to assist the revival of labor movements. Although theoretically reconstruction was to be undertaken on a world-wide basis, in practice priority was extended to Europe.

SUGGESTED READINGS

Approach of War

Feis, Herbert, *The Road to Pearl Harbor, The Coming of the War Between the United States and Japan* (Atheneum, 1962).

Goerlitz, Walter, *History of the German General Staff 1657–1945* (Praeger, 1955).

Loewenheim, Francis L., ed., *Peace or Appeasement, Hitler, Chamberlain, and the Munich Crisis* (Houghton, 1965). Collection of Documents.

*Presseisen, Ernst L., *Germany and Japan; A Study of Totalitarian Diplomacy, 1933–1941* (Fertig, 1958).

Rowse, A. L., *Appeasement: A Study in Political Decline 1933–1939* (Norton, 1961).

Snell, John L., *The Outbreak of the Second World War—Design or Blunder?* (Heath, 1962).

Wheeler-Bennett, J. W., *Munich: Prologue to Tragedy* (Viking, 1964).

The War

*Churchill, Winston S., *Memoirs of the Second World War* (Houghton, 1959).

Clark, Alan, *Barbarossa: The Russian-German Conflict, 1941–1945* (New American Library, 1964).

Ehrlich, Blake, *Resistance: France 1940–1945* (New American Library, 1964).

Hilberg, Raul, *The Destruction of the European Jews* (Quadrangle, 1961).

Langer, William L., *Our Vichy Gamble* (Norton, 1966). On United States-French relations during the war.

Langsam, Walter Consuelo, *Historic Documents of World War II* (Van Nostrand, 1958).

Snyder, Louis L., *The War: A Concise History 1939–1945* (Dell, 1960).
Warlimont, Walter, *Inside Hitler's Headquarters, 1939–1945* (Praeger, 1964).

War Diplomacy and Peace Treaties

*Armstrong, Anne M., *Unconditional Surrender: The Impact of the Casablanca Policy in World War II* (Rutgers, 1961).
*Cohen, Benjamin V., *The United Nations: Constitutional Developments, Growth, and Possibilities* (Harvard, 1961).
*Dunn, Frederick S., *Peace-Making and the Settlement with Japan* (Princeton, 1963).
Feis, Herbert, *Churchill, Roosevelt, Stalin: The War They Waged and the Peace They Sought* (Princeton, 1967).
——, *The Spanish Story: Franco and the Nations at War* (Norton, 1966).
*Opie, Redvers, and others, *The Search for Peace Settlements* (Brookings, 1951).
Snell, John L., *Illusion and Necessity: The Diplomacy of Global War, 1939–1945* (Houghton, 1964).

CHAPTER XXIX

✦ *Another Postwar Period*
(1947-1955)

Varied as they were in trends, the decades after World War II were marked by four major characteristics. On the one hand, the unprecedented proliferation of nations in Asia and Africa evoked a new wave of national pride and intransigence. On the other hand, increasing cooperation between the peoples of the globe was fostered for the sake of achieving a world community. Driven by economic and financial needs, motivated by the fear of a nuclear holocaust, and helped by instant communication and rapid transport, the nations of the world struggled toward the establishment of a global society, despite national rivalries and ideological differences. A third characteristic lay in vehement ideological confrontations, perhaps more pervasive than at any time in known history—rivalry between communist and capitalist power blocs, enmity between Buddhists and Catholics, between Moslems and Hindus, between Arabs and Zionists, and between black and white peoples.

Finally a fourth characteristic of the postwar period embodied a tragic irony in the divergence between technological advancement and the static condition of man's social and humanistic understanding. Scientists became capable of programming computers to operate entire factories, placing spaceships on the moon, exploring the depth of the oceans, and transplanting human hearts. Socially and politically, however, man has remained perilously close to Hobbes' state of nature. No computer could impose the rule of law on relationships between peoples or between nations. Violence has remained the order of the day, in Arab-Negro fights in the Sudan, in Republican-Monarchist battles in Yemen, in Hindu-Moslem outbursts in South

Asia, in Socialist-Conservative skirmishes in Latin America, in power struggles in China, in student uprisings in Europe, and in race riots in America.

Despite the lack of perspective toward recent decades, one can establish meaningful divisions for the postwar period: the years of reconstruction and the cold war to 1955, an era of transition in the late 1950's (see Chapter XXX), and the contemporary period of the 1960's (see Chapter XXXI). In this chapter we shall deal with the rehabilitation of the war-torn nations and the cold war.

Rehabilitation of the war-torn nations

In modern war, distinctions between victor and vanquished have become increasingly blurred. Russia, France, and China, for example, emerged on the side of the victors in World War II, yet they suffered more devastation than some of the defeated states. Similarly, no correlation existed between being on the winning side and the speed of postwar recovery. West Germany's economy, for instance, recovered rapidly, whereas economic reconstruction of France took much longer. Although different factors affected the progress of recovery in each area, two general inferences are possible: most countries received outside aid, particularly from the United States; and reconstruction in most instances was complicated by ideological rivalry between Marxism and anti-Marxism, coupled with the power struggle between Russia and America that emerged at the end of the war.

The former Axis states

In July 1945, the Allied Big Three (Stalin, Truman, and Attlee) met at Potsdam near Berlin to establish directives for the occupation of Germany. The resultant Potsdam Agreements, although intended as temporary measures, gradually assumed long-range importance, since the Allies could not agree on a formal peace treaty for Germany. According to the Potsdam Agreements, Germany was given her 1937 boundaries in the West, except for the coal-rich Saar, which was temporarily placed under French administration. In the East, the border of Germany was tentatively set at the Oder and Neisse rivers. The urban area of Königsberg was ceded to the Soviet Union, while the remaining former German territory east of the Oder-Neisse line was to be temporarily administered by Poland. Whether these eastern lands were to be considered as permanently lost to Germany was to become a thorny, emotional issue in postwar German politics and a complicating factor in international relations. (See Map 32.)

The defeated nation was divided into four zones, governed respectively by Russian, English, American, and French zone commanders who theoretically acted under the supervision of an Allied Control Authority (ACA). Similarly, the city of Berlin, deep inside the Russian zone, was split into four Allied sectors.

At Potsdam it was furthermore stipulated that Germany be demilitarized and de-Nazified, and that democratic ideals be encouraged. Reparations were to be paid by the removal of factories and industrial equipment, by the seizure of foreign assets, and by deliveries from current production. Ethnic Germans residing in Poland, Czechoslovakia, and Hungary were to be transferred to Germany. Moreover, German industry was placed under strict economic controls to prevent the manufacture of war materiel, to decartelize her industrial complexes, and to limit her level of production. No central German government was to be established until democratic institutions had been developed at the local level. However, Germany as a whole was to be treated as an economic unit, with a free flow of goods from one occupation zone to another, and "so far as . . . practicable," there was to be "uniformity of treatment of the German population throughout Germany."

Acting like a provisional legislature for all of Germany, the Allied Control Authority, representing the four occupying powers, passed ordinances to implement the Potsdam Agreements. Yet, wide differences soon developed between the four zones, since execution of such directives depended on the four zone commanders and their respective governments. Both France and Russia were interested in keeping Germany impotent. The French sought this end by pressing for a loose confederation of states, whereas the Russians favored a centralized state, which they hoped would be dominated by Socialist or Communist parties. Great Britain desired a unitary German state with some reserved local powers, and America called for a federal system.

Despite increasing inter-Allied disagreements, the Allied Control Authority struggled valiantly to accomplish its manifold tasks. It was easy to abolish the Nazi party apparatus and to dismantle German military installations, but it proved infinitely more complex to eradicate "nazism," or "militarism." The much publicized Nuremberg War Crimes Trials (1945–1946), in which twenty-two Nazi leaders and seven German organizations were tried on various charges including war crimes and crimes against humanity, were spectacular and perhaps precedent setting. Yet such trials contributed little toward the "re-education" of convinced Nazis.

Mounting tension between the three Western occupiers and the Soviet Union prevented agreement on reparations deliveries to Russia, on badly needed financial and economic reforms for Germany, and on an all-German peace treaty. Hence Great Britain and the United States, with the reluctant consent of France, merged their zones and proceeded with plans for the creation of a federal government for the three Western zones. By the spring of 1948, all four-power cooperation on the Potsdam model had ceased. The stalemate was soon climaxed with a total land blockade of Berlin by the Russians, who hoped to force the Western powers to lift their ban on reparations deliveries to Russia from the Western zones. The West successfully countered Russia's gambit with a dramatic eleven-month airlift of food and supplies for the Western sectors of Berlin. After the failure of this Berlin blockade, Russia and the West, even more than before, each went their own way in administering their respective areas of occupied Germany. Germany and the city of Berlin thus became divided into two states.

In the fall of 1948, the United States, England, and France authorized the election of a convention for their three zones to draft a provisional constitution, with the understanding that the Russian zone could join in at any time. Dominated by the new Christian Democratic Union (CDU) and the Social Democratic party (SPD) and guided by Allied advice, this constitutional convention eventually produced the so-called Basic Law, a provisional constitution for the Federal Republic of Germany. Subject to a special Occupation Statute and separate provisions for the industrial Ruhr region, Western Germany, with Konrad Adenauer (1876–1967) as Chancellor, was then given conditional self-government by the Western Allies on September 21, 1949. Two weeks later, the Russians transformed their zone into the German Democratic Republic, controlled by Walter Ulbricht's (1893–   ) Socialist Unity party (SED), a combination of Communists and Socialists.

Economic reconstruction had initially been hindered by zonal divisions, by the lack of a sound currency, by the influx of refugees and the uncertainty of Germany's political future. The currency reform of 1948 and the establishment of a stable government in 1949 quickly initiated a remarkable industrial resurgence in Western Germany. With American support in the form of the Marshall Plan and other aid programs, with new industrial equipment replacing that destroyed by bombing or dismantled as reparations, with a highly cooperative and skilled labor force, and with no expenses for rearmament, the West German economy revitalized itself miraculously. By 1955, West Germany had overcome severe agricultural shortages and assumed the third place among the world's industrial powers.

Despite Ulbricht's attempt to rebuild East Germany's industry and agriculture through a measure of nationalization and collectivization, her economy lagged conspicuously behind that of West Germany. Her currency remained weak and the large number of her people fleeing to the West depleted the supply of skilled labor. Food rationing and restricted allocation of raw materials continued, as did reparations deliveries to Russia. Chafing under the strict political supervision of an authoritarian regime, the workers of East Berlin resented the government's admonishment to work harder without enjoying more consumer goods. In June 1953, they staged a short-lived uprising which was crushed by Russian tank forces. Thereafter Walter Ulbricht achieved even more control over his docile state.

As the cold war (see p. 549) intensified and led to armed confrontation in Korea (1950), the two Germanies became increasingly absorbed into the opposing camps. The United States, in particular, sought the creation of a West German army that could contribute toward the defense of Western Europe against a possible Soviet attack. Despite strong misgivings among many Germans and serious reservations in France and Great Britain, the Bonn government of West Germany finally agreed to remilitarize. In return for building a new conventional army and joining the North Atlantic Treaty Organization, the Federal Republic was granted its sovereignty in May, 1955, just ten years after Germany's surrender to the Allies. In response, Russia stepped up the remilitarization of East Germany and incorporated her economic and military resources into the communist block of Eastern Europe. The division of Germany thus became frozen into the antagonism between the Western and the Communist camps.

Unlike Germany, Japan did not experience a divided occupation. The British, French, and Dutch took back Japanese War conquests, such as Hongkong, Malaya, Indochina, and Indonesia. Russians and Americans occupied Korea and some Pacific islands. In the Japanese home islands, however, General Douglas MacArthur, as Supreme Commander of the American occupation forces, exerted almost unchallenged control, although theoretically an Allied council was to supervise occupied Japan. From the onset, the Americans decided to disarm Japan, despite the risk that a prostrate Japan would create a political vacuum in the Far East. Furthermore, they undertook the democratization of Japanese political institutions. Notwithstanding his earlier acquiescence in imperialist ventures, Emperor Hirohito (1926–   ) was allowed to retain his throne, although he was stripped of his traditional divine prerogatives.

While many young Japanese welcomed the new wave of Westernization, Japan was soon caught in the dilemma of the cold war. The civil war in China, the inability of the British, French, and Dutch to reassert their former colonial control in the Pacific, and Russia's expanding influence forced the United States to revise her attitude toward Japan. American economic aid was sharply increased, restrictions on Japanese enterprises were lifted, and, by 1950, reparations removals were discontinued. The Korean War (see p. 550) accelerated this revision of policy. Japan was allowed to create a large police force as a preliminary step toward the creation of a defense force. In 1951, the United States and most of the former Allies signed a peace treaty with Japan, notwithstanding Russian and Communist Chinese objections. Moreover, an American-Japanese defense pact permitted the stationing of American troops in Japan as allies rather than occupiers, and decentralization of the economy was halted in the interest of furthering production. Thus, both Japan and Germany were built up as outposts of American influence against Russia. The strengthening of Japan was also directed against China, which by this time had been taken over by the Communists.

American aid, the Korean War, worldwide inflation, and native industriousness soon helped Japan to prosper economically. Gradually she reentered the world community, and, in 1956, was admitted to the United Nations. Yet the Japanese people were torn by grave dissensions. Many could not shake off traditional mores at the simple command of MacArthur's baton. Although Westernization had begun in the nineteenth century, the fast pace of the occupation period jarred established customs and evoked occasional anti-Western outbursts. Facing an uneasy relationship with Russia and Communist China and chafing under the tutelage of America, Japanese Socialists and Conservatives fought many political battles that frequently involved violence.

Postwar recovery among the lesser ex-Axis states was slower than in Germany and Japan. Austria, for example—although immediately permitted to form a central government, which prevented the kind of splintering that occurred in Germany—was unable to recuperate while under foreign occupation. Effective economic rehabilitation began only after 1955, when the first thaw in the cold war after Stalin's death led to agreement on a treaty for Austria. In return for accepting a status of "perpetual neutrality," the Austrians were granted complete independence, and all occupation troops were evacuated. Governed by a surprisingly stable coalition of the moderate Social Democratic party and the conservative People's party, Austria then regained relative prosperity, although she continued to be plagued by problems reminiscent of the 1920's. For one, many Austrians soon became jealous of West Germany's soaring wealth; and once again *Anschluss,* which would have been an economic boon, was prohibited by the powers.

Italy's postwar status was ambiguous, since she was both a defeated Axis power and a co-belligerent of the Allies. Large-scale destruction, lack of food and raw materials, inexperience with democratic processes, and distrust between former Fascists and ex-partisan fighters complicated the reshaping of Italy's political and economic life. After a popular referendum abolished the discredited monarchy, a new constitution, conservative in tenor and favorable to the Catholic Church, was promulgated in 1948. The subsequent elections were crucial for the future of Italy. A large Communist party, supported by left-wing Socialists, contended against Alcide de Gasperi's (1881–1954) conservative Christian Democrats and turned Italy's polls into a battlefield of the cold war. American promises of aid vied with communist charges of "American imperialism." When the electorate endorsed de Gasperi, Italy turned firmly to the West and eventually joined the North Atlantic Treaty Organization (NATO). Despite economic progress, however, political stability continued to be jeopardized by the weakness of the moderates in contrast to the strength of the Communist party, the largest outside the communist bloc countries.

Although not an avowed belligerent in World War II, Franco's Spain had flirted with Hitler and sent a Spanish division to fight against Russia. Hence the United Nations, in 1946, barred Spain from all U.N. organizations. With Spain a pariah, hardly recovered from the devastation of her civil war and unable to share in American aid, Franco received economic support and encouragement only from the dictators, Salazar of Portugal and Juan Perón (1895–   ) of Argentina. At home, he used his large army and police to impose an ever tighter control on his state, while placating monarchist opposition by theoretically restoring the Spanish monarchy. As in the case of Germany and Japan, the Korean War changed America's attitude. Spain was granted diplomatic recognition and economic aid and made a partner of American's overseas military establishment. Thereafter, the Western Europeans reluctantly admitted the dictatorial Franco regime into the world community. With Spain's economy slowly improving, Franco gradually loosened his dictatorship, although until the late 1960's, he retained full personal control of the government of Spain.

The former Allies

As in 1918, Great Britain and France emerged from a World War on the victorious side, but this time facing the painful acknowledgment that they no longer ranked among the first powers of the world. To be sure, most citizens were primarily concerned with the immediate problem of their material existence; also, the numerous socialists in both countries, traditionally international in outlook, were less worried about national prestige than were the more empire-minded conservatives. Yet, the morale of the British and the French depended to some extent on the skill of their governments in offering compensatory satisfactions at home as substitutes for the lost glory and the colonial empires that were slipping from their control.

England's Labor government under Clement Attlee (see p. 529) concentrated its efforts on raising the standard of living of the lower classes. It passed legislation to grant more power to labor unions, to provide free medical service for everyone (National Health Service Bill), and to nationalize, among others, the Bank of England, the coal and electric power industries, and the transport and communications facilities. Nationalization of basic enterprises resulted not only from the socialist dogma that such industries should be run in the interest of *all* the people. The Labor ministry also argued that only the government had sufficient funds to effect needed modernization and to increase productive capacity.

Britain's most pressing problem was the mounting deficit in her balance of payments. The government tried various devices. A program of austerity and rationing was to lessen the need for imports; production for export was stimulated; the pound was devalued to make British goods more competitive on foreign markets; and loans from the United States and Canada were used to increase foreign exchange. But neither the Labor ministry nor subsequent Conservative governments succeeded in finding permanent remedies to what had become a perennial problem for Britain: an excess of imports over exports.

Although Great Britain felt compelled gradually to dismantle her empire, first in Asia and then in Africa (see p. 555), and although she reluctantly recognized that in world decisions she carried only a secondary voice behind America and Russia, she attempted to safeguard a measure of world-

wide influence through skillful diplomacy and military preparedness. She retained the sympathetic support of most members of the former empire and
maintained a military presence through a far-flung chain of naval bases. Despite the cost, which she could ill afford, she temporarily continued to develop her navy and air force, instituted a peacetime draft, and built her own
hydrogen bombs. Although acting at times as mediator between Russia and
America, she in fact established extraordinarily close ties with the United
States, a relationship decried as tutelage by the left-wing members of the
Labor Party. Toward Continental Europe, however, her attitude remained
ambivalent. She joined various defensive agreements and other cooperative
arrangements with non-Communist Europe, and Churchill, while not in
power, eloquently supported attempts at European unification. Yet Britain
long remained reluctant to abandon her isolation and to tie her economy to
that of Western Europe. (See Map 31.)

With the decline of the Liberal party, the English drifted toward a two-
party system. Elections in 1951 returned the Conservatives to power for thirteen years, until the Labor party in turn regained control of the government.
Since the Laborites gradually substituted pragmatic measures for doctrinaire
socialism, and the Conservatives acquiesced in the basic ideals of the welfare
state and recognized the necessity to continue the dismantling of the empire,
these governmental changes produced few essential alterations in policy.

French postwar problems differed from those of Great Britain. In
World War II, France had suffered more destruction, and she had undergone the humiliation of foreign occupation as well as quasi-civil war among
Nazi collaborators, Vichy French, Communists, the French underground,
and de Gaulle's Free French. Furthermore, Britain still enjoyed a workable
political system and cohesion through loyalty to a popular monarchy,
whereas France, having scuttled the Third Republic in favor of Vichy's fascist regime, faced the task of writing a new constitution and constructing a
viable political framework. De Gaulle, who acted as provisional President,
favored the creation of a strong executive and resigned when his advice was
not heeded. The new constitution, which the feuding parties and a bewildered electorate finally adopted in 1946 as basis for France's Fourth Republic, retained the strong legislature that had characterized the Third Republic.
Once again ministerial instability, caused by bickering among numerous political parties, marked the French political scene.

The weak French coalition governments, succeeding one another in a
rapid ministerial merry-go-round, could not solve the nation's financial, economic, and imperial problems. Postwar recovery continued to be hampered
by inflation, lagging industrial production, an inequitable tax imposition, a
poor tax-collection system, and an inefficient, entrenched bureaucracy.

Attempts to transform her colonial empire into a French Union similar
to the British Commonwealth proved only a temporary expedient as a step
toward colonial independence. The North African possessions, Morocco,

Tunisia, and Algeria, agitated restlessly against French domination, even though Algeria was officially considered an integral part of France. In Indo-China—consisting of Laos, Cambodia, Cochin-China, Tonking, and Annam —where nationalistic feelings had grown steadily during the Japanese occupation, the French sought unsuccessfully to regain their former control through a mixture of force and concessions. Laos was granted sovereignty in 1949 and Cambodia proclaimed her independence in 1953. But in the newly created state of Vietnam, composed of Annam, Tonking, and Cochin-China, the French were soon plunged into a full-scale war against the nationalist and Communist forces of Ho Chi Minh (1894–1969). Although Vietnam was granted autonomy within the French Union, Ho Chi Minh, soon supported by Russia and Communist China, called for complete independence for Vietnam. The ensuing prolonged war seriously sapped French resources and intensified the rift in French public opinion. Finally in 1954, after Ho Chi Minh's Viet Minh forces inflicted a serious military defeat on the French army at Dien Bien Phu, France agreed to a compromise. At the Geneva Conference of that year, Pierre Mendès-France (1907–   ), the twentieth French prime minister since 1946, agreed to a division of Vietnam along the seventeenth parallel, the North to be independent under Ho Chi Minh, the South to remain temporarily within the French Union. Coupled with internal problems, such military humiliation in the colonial arena further discredited and weakened the Fourth Republic.

The United States, and to some extent Russia, emerged from the war with problems largely the reverse of those of England and France. Whereas the war had toppled the latter from first-power status, it had catapulted America and the Soviet Union to control over vast areas of the globe. Whether reluctantly or by imperialistic design, the two giant powers soon found themselves sharing in the responsibility for patrolling the world, a task previously exercised by Western Europe's colonial powers. Furthermore, unlike Britain and France, the United States exported considerably more than she imported and hence was the major creditor and financier of the world. The United States dollar had supplanted the British pound sterling as the preferred international currency (except for gold), a position it was to retain until the mid-1960's.

America's new attitude toward the world was illustrated by a series of financial, political, and military decisions approved by Congress during the presidency of Harry S. Truman. For one, the United States agreed to help finance the economic rehabilitation and development of much of the world. After the end of Lend-Lease in August 1945, America extended emergency aid to numerous countries, either directly or through such agencies as UNRRA, granted large-scale loans, and developed the Marshall Plan for European recovery as well as the Point-Four Program for aid to developing nations. Priorities of American concern can be measured by the fact that of almost forty-seven billion dollars in foreign aid granted between 1945 and

1954, over thirty-four billion were allocated to Europe, nine billion to Asia, and 1.1 billion to Latin America.

Secondly, America assumed firm political and military commitments on a global scale. Besides joining the United Nations, she occupied the forefront in various international cooperative organizations and entered into an array of military pacts. The Truman Doctrine of 1947, specifically aimed at bolstering the troubled governments of Greece and Turkey, summed up the new stand "that it must be the policy of the United States to support peoples who are resisting attempted subjugation by armed minorities or by outside pressure."

Finally, the American public became willing to spend huge portions of the national budget for a large military establishment in support of these new world-wide commitments. After first rapidly demobilizing, reconverting factories to the production of consumer goods, and selling surplus war matériel, the trend was sharply reversed in 1948. The Defense Department was reorganized, the peacetime draft instituted, and plans laid to develop a hydrogen bomb. At the same time, the United States government launched a propaganda offensive against Russia with Voice of America broadcasts.

At home, the Truman years were marked by economic problems and sharp clashes between liberals, who favored the Fair Deal, civil rights, and increased benefits to workers and farmers and conservatives who resented the growing power of the federal government. The removal of price and wage controls in 1946 was followed by inflation that boosted prices by some 32 per cent in a year. Inflation, in turn, evoked waves of strikes for higher wages. Labor unions thus grew in strength, despite conservative efforts to curb their power through the Taft-Hartley Act of 1947, which Congress passed over Truman's veto.

The Truman government made generous provisions for veterans through the so-called G. I. Bill of Rights, granted large subsidies to farmers, and attempted to slow the rapid growth of city slums through federal aid to housing, but most efforts to implement the Fair Deal and civil rights legislation failed to obtain congressional approval. The memorable Supreme Court decision banning racial segregation in public schools, which helped to accelerate the Negroes' drive for equality, was handed down only during the subsequent presidency of General Eisenhower (1954).

Nor was Truman able to assuage the fear of Communist subversion that gripped large segments of the American public. Made nervous by spectacular spy trials, by the conviction of the leaders of the American Communist party, the perjury trial of Alger Hiss, and the investigations of the House Un-American Activities Committee, and inflamed by such demagogues as Senator Joseph McCarthy, Americans plunged into a period of loyalty oaths, security investigations, and mutual distrust. A rash of Red fear had also characterized the early 1920's. But it was during these cold war days that many Americans espoused the myth which ascribed all ills in America and the world to the little understood phenomenon of communism, a myth that made American foreign policy relatively rigid in the ensuing decades.

Like the United States, Soviet Russia found herself with increased responsibilities beyond her borders. Despite the Bolshevik's initial vision of a world-wide communist revolution, Stalin had limited his aims to the development of a strong Russia. The opportunities and consequences of World War II, however, fundamentally altered this position. With Russian armies in control of the greater part of Eastern Europe and Communist forces gaining ascendancy in China, the Soviet Union, with her vast reservoir of resources and fast developing technology, suddenly became the sole competitor of the United States. It was a question of who would step into the power vacuum created by the war.

Russia had suffered staggering losses. In 1945, her western and southern provinces lay devastated. About seven and one-half million men had died in battle, and an estimated twenty-five million people had become homeless. The emotional strain of the war had also left deep scars on the Russian people. Nonetheless, Russia's psychological and industrial resilience astounded the world. Stimulated by Stalinist propaganda, the Russians felt an outburst of patriotic pride and newly won self-confidence with the realization that they had vanquished the enemy and had captured Berlin. In such a mood, the people readily supported the government's demand for security against future invasions.

During the war, the Soviets had hastily moved factories into eastern Russia to prevent seizure by the Germans, and they had built new industrial complexes in the Urals and Siberia, where they were closer to raw materials and safer from potential attack. After the war, this emphasis on the East continued with the construction of numerous modern factories in previously barren or agricultural regions. The Five-Year Plans of 1946 and 1952 stressed the expansion of heavy industry, the output of basic materials such as steel, coal, and hydroelectric power, and the production of armaments. Production of consumer goods continued to be neglected.

Despite occasional bureaucratic bungling and popular grumbling at the insufficiency of food and consumer goods, industrial recovery and progress were prodigious. Rapidly increasing industrial capacity and growing scientific know-how enabled the Soviet Union to build her own atomic bomb (1949) and thereafter led to a long series of technological leaps forward that were to place Russia frequently ahead of the United States in the development of missiles and the race to explore outer space. Soon Russia could afford to extend loans to selected countries, to export machinery, and to supply military equipment to the Communist Chinese, North Koreans, and some Eastern Europeans. Facilitated by an abundance of raw materials, this industrial progress also owed its success to unstinting hard work by Soviet men and women who labored under strict discipline in the hope of helping "the Party" build the communist world of plenty in which according to

Stalin's promise, there would be enough goods for all to enjoy equally. To spur this industriousness, Soviet officials further emphasized the system of "socialist competition," by which individuals and groups of workers who overachieved their production quotas were awarded medals, incentive pay, or free vacations. To perform some of the less desirable chores, such as mining, the Soviets used forced labor by political prisoners or prisoners of war, whom they retained in bondage long after the armistice of 1945.

Neither force, nor mechanization, nor scientific improvements, however, helped the Soviets solve the problem of agricultural underproduction. Collective farms were forcefully consolidated into larger units, experimentation with state farms was gradually abandoned, and new lands were opened to cultivation. Still, the Soviets could not produce enough to feed Russia's growing population and have surpluses left for export. The question of increased agricultural production was to remain the Achilles heel in the Soviet system.

Russia's industrial recovery and acquisition of international power and prestige did not alter the tyrannical aspects of the Stalinist regime. Concentration camps and strict political censorship, forced indoctrination and suppression of individualism continued to characterize the dictatorship of Joseph Stalin. The guarantees of basic rights, contained in the Constitution of 1936, remained conspicuously disregarded. At the same time, the increasing need for engineers, technicians, managerial supervisors, and professional experts, and the resulting greater differentiation in pay led to new class distinctions and the creation of a new upper class of managers and functionaries—thus further subverting the Marxist ideal of a classless society.

The Soviets meanwhile expanded Russian influence through military and economic pressure, appeals to communist ideology, and the use of the international links of the various Communist parties. By 1948, they had created a series of buffer or satellite states in Eastern Europe, including Albania, Bulgaria, Rumania, Hungary, Czechoslovakia, East Germany, and Poland. Added to the territory annexed between 1940 and 1945, these states presented a reassuring barrier between Russia and the West. Although ostensibly ruled by so-called Peoples' Governments in which local Communists had a dominant voice, these satellites were in effect governed from Moscow during the first postwar decade. With Communists controlling North Korea, Outer Mongolia, and major portions of China, Russia seemed to have achieved similar security in the East. At the same time, Stalin could hope that his influence over Communist parties in Italy, France, Indonesia, India, and elsewhere could help him gain a measure of control over these additional areas.

It gradually appeared, however, that communism was not identical in all countries. Where communist control had been imported by the Russians and supported by the Red Army, as in East Germany, Poland and Bulgaria for example, Moscow could exert a powerful voice in local affairs. However, where a strong native communist movement had risen to power and expelled the enemy without direct aid from the Red Army—as in Yugoslavia and China—Moscow's influence was precarious.

In Yugoslavia, Joseph Broz, later called Tito, had successfully organized his wartime Partisans into a guerilla army that helped expel the Germans. After the war he emerged as the most powerful political force in his country. Tito then changed the monarchy into the Federal People's Republic of Yugoslavia, organized along socialistic lines. Although a loyal Communist, partly trained in Moscow, Tito refused to subordinate Yugoslav economic interests to those of Russia. Unable to bring the Yugoslav maverick into line, Stalin expelled Yugoslavia from the Cominform (1948), the recently created Communist Information Bureau that served as a coordinating agency for Europe's Communist parties. Despite Russian and satellite pressure, Tito proved strong enough to weather Stalin's wrath and to maintain an independent Yugoslavia. He began to rebuild his country's economy with some American and British aid, emphasized federalism rather than centralism, devised a new constitution (1953) that contained some corporate features, and gradually loosened his dictatorial grip. Abroad, he successfully steered a neutral course between Russia and the West, acting at times as a leader of the so-called non-aligned third world. By shaping his own version of applied Marxism, Tito (along with Mao Tse-tung) thus became one of the first important Communists who successfully defied the dogma that Moscow was the Mecca and Rome of world communism. His actions marked the first crack in the monolith of international communism.

In China, which also emerged as a devastated albeit victorious state, Russia was eventually to experience a similar defection from communist solidarity. Although he accepted considerable Soviet aid, Mao Tse-tung, like Tito, the leader of a strong, native Communist movement, was heavily imbued with nationalistic fervor. The civil war between Mao's Red Army and Chiang Kai-shek's Kuomintang forces resumed almost immediately after the collapse of Japan. Although signing a treaty of friendship with Chiang's Nationalist Government, Stalin extended aid to Mao. The United States, for its part, vainly attempted to mediate an accommodation between Communists and Nationalists and granted about two and a half billion dollars of assistance to shore up Chiang's tottering government. Reconciliation between militant Communists and ultra-conservative Nationalists proved impossible. Despite occasional short truces, the civil war continued, with the Red Army gaining ground until Chiang's depleted forces fled to the Island of Formosa at the end of 1949. With his capital at Peking, Mao then formed the People's Republic of China and concluded a treaty of alliance and mutual assistance with Stalin. So long as China's new leader depended on Soviet aid, relative Russo-Chinese harmony prevailed. Yet, in retrospect, one can see that even then Mao intended to be master in his own house and that Peking's rejection of domination by Moscow was only a matter of time.

Asia's quest for identity

The desires of the peoples of Asia to resume control over their own affairs was strongly enhanced by the wartime promises extended by both belligerent camps. Hence, the drive toward independence in Asia assumed floodlike proportions in the immediate postwar years. Despite the varying degrees to which the colonial powers—France, America, England, Holland, and Portugal—had prepared their overseas subjects for the task of self-government, most Asian peoples achieved independence by 1954, with the exception of the Malay Peninsula and several sultanates in the Middle East. France terminated her mandates over Syria and Lebanon and eventually abandoned her control over Indo-China; the United States granted sovereignty to the Philippines, subject to residual American rights; Great Britain consented to the establishment of Hindu India, Moslem Pakistan, Buddhist Ceylon, and Hebrew Israel; Holland ceded her rights over Indonesia; only Portugal tenaciously sought to retain control over her small colonial holdings in Asia. (See Map 31.)

In most cases, decolonization was accompanied either by outright war between the colonial peoples and the Western "mother country," such as Indonesians against the Dutch or Vietnamese against the French, or by internal clashes between rival religions, competing cultures, or jealous tribes. The bitter animosity between Moslems and Hindus led to the violent death of hundreds of thousands and resulted in the partitioning of South Asia into India and Pakistan. Kurdish tribes fought Arabs in Iraq, Jews and Arabs battled in Palestine, Catholics and Buddhists vied for power in Vietnam. In fact, few of the new states of Asia enjoyed internal peace during the early years after achieving independence. While some of these conflicts remained localized, most of them sooner or later involved the open or clandestine entanglement of the major powers, in particular the United States, the Soviet Union, and Communist China.

Despite these internal animosities and mutual distrust, a measure of cultural solidarity marked the relations among many of the new nations of Asia. Yet, whatever cooperation developed often derived from political or military considerations or from a common feeling of frustration rather than from a genuine feeling of cohesion, such as had developed in Europe. The loosely organized Arab League, for example, reflecting a feeling of Arab affinity, owed its existence largely to a common antagonism toward the newly created state of Israel. Similarly, the amity between Asian and African nations that was proclaimed at the Bandung Conference (1955) and was frequently voiced at the United Nations, was motivated more by common resentment of the have-not nations against the haves and by their desire to establish a neutral third force between America and Russia than by a feeling of shared tradition. Other cooperative efforts were organized by outside forces, such as the Southeast Asia Treaty Organization (SEATO, 1954), created by the United States as an anticommunist alliance.

Most of the new nations of Asia soon found that independence might provide a new sense of dignity to their peoples, but that it brought no panacea to their myriad socio-economic and political problems. Plagued by overpopulation and food shortages, unable to industrialize for lack of capital and skilled labor, with a largely illiterate population restrained by religious taboos and traditional mores, most of the new states found themselves in continued economic dependence on the former colonial powers. Significant economic progress and substantial improvement in the standard of living of the masses were also prevented by the fact that a small landholding class, the owners of most of the wealth, controlled the new governments and generally ran them in their own interest. Moreover it is debatable whether the peoples of Asia can achieve a truly industrial society without first acquiring the mentality of acquisitiveness that characterizes the industrialized nations of the West.

Despite the urgency of reforms, the governments of the newly created states as well as of the older ones, such as Thailand and Iran, proved reluctant to upset the status quo. They sought to attain prestige, usually with outside help, by forming modern armies, complete with tanks and jet aircraft, but did little to further social reform. After the reforms of 1963, Iran was to become an exception in this respect. Where the colonial powers had instituted a measure of self-government prior to independence, as in India and the Philippines, governments enjoyed relative stability, despite social discontent. Where governmental participation had been minimal, as in Indonesia, Syria, and Iraq, the old guard was eventually ousted and replaced by more reform-minded younger leaders. Yet, there remains much political uncertainty in most Asian states, whether ruled by traditional regimes, such as Saudi Arabia, Jordan, and Thailand, or by new groups, as in Pakistan and Burma. Everywhere demands for accelerated reform are voiced by leftist and nationalist elements, receiving aid and encouragement from the outside, particularly Communist China.

Cold war and containment

Hostility between the Soviet Union and the United States affected most international issues as well as the internal development of most nations. Distrust, stemming from ideological suspicions, had marred Russo-American relations even during the war. When after the war America extended her domination over the Pacific and Western Europe, while Russia gained control over Eastern Europe and expanded her influence in East Asia, distrust turned into the enmity of the cold war.

The cold war assumed many forms. Russia sealed off her sphere of influence by an "iron curtain" to ward off hostile ideas and to prevent her subjects from fleeing abroad. In the United States, Communists were hunted and dismissed from sensitive positions. Both sides launched propaganda offensives against one another to garner the allegiance of the uncommitted peoples of the world. And at the United Nations, the two camps engaged in obstructive maneuvering that frequently prevented much-needed agreement on vital issues.

America and Russia expanded and consolidated their influence over other states through military and economic measures. The United States extended military assistance to anticommunist regimes and concluded regional military pacts, such as the North Atlantic Treaty Organization (NATO, 1949) and the Southeast Asia Treaty Organization (SEATO, 1954). Furthermore, American military bases were established around the periphery of Russia from Iceland and Spain to Japan to implement the policy of containment that was to prevent further expansion of Russian influence. Russia, for her part, countered with military and economic pacts of her own. The Council for Mutual Economic Assistance (COMECON, 1949) was designed to coordinate the economic policies of Eastern Europe, and the Warsaw Pact for Mutual Defense (1955) attempted to integrate the forces of the satellite states with those of the Red Army.

The conflict between Russia and America soon involved indirect violent confrontation. Greece was wracked by civil war between left-wing groups aided by the communist camp and conservatives helped by American military detachments. In the Philippines, peasants clamoring for land reform organized the "Huk" party which used communist help to launch guerilla attacks against American supported government troops. Similar confrontations occurred between the British and communist-supported nationalists in Malaya, and of course between the French and Ho Chi Minh's partisans in Vietnam.

But open warfare between Communist and non-Communist forces did not erupt until 1950 in Korea. At the end of World War II, the Korean Peninsula had been divided, with the thirty-eighth parallel serving as boundary between the American and Russian occupation zones. In view of the impossibility of reaching agreement on the establishment of an all-Korean government, the United States in 1948 had formed the Republic of Korea south of the thirty-eighth parallel, and the Soviets had turned their zone into the People's Democratic Republic of Korea. After both had withdrawn their occupation forces in the following year, a North Korean army, supplied with Russian equipment, suddenly swept across the parallel into South Korea in 1950 in an attempt to reunite Korea under communist auspices. With the support of the United Nations, President Truman swiftly dispatched American forces to counter this North Korean invasion. Under the command of General MacArthur, American units, soon supplemented by several other United Nations contingents, drove the invaders out of South Korea. However, when American forces broke deep into North Korea and reached the border of Manchuria, Communist China dispatched several hundred thousand "volunteer" troops to help throw back the United Nations army. After three years of heavy fighting, an armistice was finally concluded in 1953. The armistice, concluded shortly after Stalin's death, restored the border between North and South Korea along the thirty-eighth parallel. It also marked the end of open armed conflict in the cold war until its renewal under different· conditions in Vietnam.

The Korean War raised considerable debate within the United States whether indeed "containment" was an advisable policy. MacArthur's temporary conquest of parts of North Korea prompted critics of the Truman Administration to suggest that rather than "contain" communism America should attempt to "liberate" other peoples. Allusions to a policy of "liberation" marked the early years of the Eisenhower Administration and may have encouraged Chiang Kai-shek in his frequent announcements from Formosa that he intended to reconquer mainland China. The policy of "liberation" may also have added to the ferment in Eastern Europe in the early postStalin period, an unrest that ultimately erupted in revolution in Poland and Hungary (1956).

At the level of bilateral negotiations between Moscow and Washington, however, the cold war was gradually transmuted into the idea of co-existence. The Geneva Summit meeting of 1955 between President Eisenhower, Soviet Premier Nikolai Bulganin (1895–   ), and Russia's Communist Party chief Nikita Khrushchev (1894–   )—the first meeting between the heads of state of the two opposing camps since 1945—marked the first tenuous beginning of the idea of peaceful competition and co-existence that was to gain momentum in the 1960's.

SUGGESTED READINGS

General Works on Post-World War II Period

Aron, Raymond, *The Century of Total War* (Beacon, 1955).

Barker, Charles A., ed., *Problems of World Disarmament* (Houghton, 1963). Collection of lectures on atomic warfare and disarmament.

Cordier, Andrew W., and Maxwell, Kenneth, eds., *Paths to World Order* (Columbia, 1967). Collection of essays.

*Fischer, Eric, *The Passing of the European Age: A Study of the Transfer of Western Civilization and Its Renewal in Other Continents* (Russell, 1948).

Oliver, Roland, and Fage, J. D., *A Short History of Africa* (Penguin, 1962).

Sinai, I. Robert, *The Challenge of Modernization: The West's Impact on the Non-Western World* (Norton, 1964).

Postwar Germany, Japan, and Italy

*Balabkins, Nicholas, *Germany Under Direct Controls: Economic Aspects of Industrial Disarmament, 1945–1948* (Rutgers, 1964).

*Davidson, Eugene, *The Death and Life of Germany* (Knopf, 1959). Treatment of the American occupation.

Feis, Herbert, *Between War and Peace: The Potsdam Conference* (Princeton, 1960).

Grosser, Alfred, *The Federal Republic of Germany: A Concise History* (Praeger, 1964).

*Hornsby, Lex, ed., *Profiles of East Germany* (Barnes and Noble, 1967).

*Kawai, Kazuo, *Japan's American Interlude* (U. of Chicago, 1960).

Kogan, N., *The Government of Italy* (Crowell, 1962).

*Reuss, Frederick G., *Fiscal Policy for Growth Without Inflation: The German Experiment* (Johns Hopkins, 1963).

*Windsor, Philip, *City of Leave; A History of Berlin, 1945–1962* (Praeger, 1963). Deals with Berlin as well as the two Germanies and United States and the Soviet Union.

*Woetzel, Robert K., *The Nuremberg Trials in International Law* (Praeger, 1962).

United States

Goldman, Eric F., *The Crucial Decade—And After: America 1945–1960* (Random, 1960).

Perkins, Dexter, *The Diplomacy of a New Age: Major Issues in U.S. Policy Since 1945* (Indiana, 1967).

Potter, Charles E., *Days of Shame,* (New American Library, 1965).

Spanier, John W., *The Truman-MacArthur Controversy and the Korean War* (Norton, 1965).

Watson, Richard L., Jr., *The United States in the Contemporary World, 1945–1962* (Macmillan, 1965).

The Soviet Bloc

Brzezinski, Zbigniew K., *The Soviet Bloc* (Praeger, 1961).

Korbel, Josef, *The Communist Subversion of Czechoslovakia, 1938–1948* (Princeton, 1959).

*Neal, Fred Warner, *Titoism in Action: Reforms in Yugoslavia, 1948–1954* (U. of California, 1958).

Pethybridge, Roger W., *The Development of the Communist Bloc* (Heath, 1965).

Zaninovich, M. George, *The Development of Socialist Yugoslavia* (Johns Hopkins, 1968).

China, England, and France

Brandt, Conrad, Schwartz, Benjamin, and Fairbank, John K., *A Documentary History of Chinese Communism* (Atheneum, 1966).

*Bruce, M., *The Coming of the Welfare State* (Schocken, 1966).

Luethy, Herbert, *France Against Herself* (World).

Schoenbrun, David, *As France Goes* (Atheneum, 1968).

Simone, Vera, ed., *China in Revolution: History, Documents, and Analyses* (Fawcett, 1968).

Asia's Awakening

Campbell, Robert D., *Pakistan: Emerging Democracy* (Van Nostrand, 1963).

Fischer, Louis, *Gandhi: His Life and Message for the World* (New American Library, 1960).

*Hammer, Ellen J., *Struggle for Indochina, 1940–1955* (Stanford, 1966). On French attempt to retain colonial Indochina.

*Kahin, George McTurnan, ed., *Nationalism and Revolution in Indonesia* (Cornell, 1952).

Lamb, Beatrice P., *India: A World in Transition* (Praeger, 1966).
*Lenczowski, George, *The Middle East in World Affairs* (Cornell, 1962).
Spear, Percival, *India, Pakistan, and the West* (Oxford U.P., 1967).
Tinker, H., *India and Pakistan: A Political Analysis* (Praeger, 1966).
Von der Mehden, Fred R., *Religion and Nationalism in Southeast Asia—Burma, Indonesia, and the Philippines* (U. of Wisconsin, 1963).

Cold War and Containment

Feis, Herbert, *The China Tangle, The American Effort in China from Pearl Harbor to the Marshall Mission* (Atheneum, 1965).
Hartmann, Frederick H., *Germany Between East and West: The Reunification Problem* (Prentice-Hall, 1965).
*Leckie, Robert, *Conflict: The History of the Korean War, 1950–1953* (Putnam, 1962).
Schuman, Frederick L., *The Cold War, Retrospect and Prospect* (La. State, 1967).
Shulman, Marshall, *Stalin's Foreign Policy Reappraised* (Atheneum, 1965).
White, Theodore H., *Fire in the Ashes, Europe in Mid-Century* (Crowell, 1968).

CHAPTER XXX

✎✎ *Toward a New Era*
(1955-1960)

The mid-1950's represent a dividing line, marking the termination of the postwar era. The granting of sovereignty to the two Germanies and to Austria in 1955 signified a symbolic end to wartime enmity. In the same year, Winston Churchill became the last of the great wartime leaders to retire from active political life with his resignation from the prime ministership. It was also in 1955 that the Geneva Summit Meeting produced the first significant thaw in the cold war that had begun with the distrust between Russia and the West during World War II. Finally, the quest of the Asian peoples for independence, which had been stimulated by the events of the war, had achieved its aim by the mid-1950's. Most peoples from the Philippines and Indonesia in the Pacific to Syria and Israel on the Mediterranean had by then obtained or regained their independence.

After 1955, the world seemed pointed toward new directions. A new generation was coming into its own, young men and women who had been in their infancy at the end of World War II. Less troubled by the memories of the war, more enthralled with the opportunities offered by science and technology, more impatient about eradicating lingering colonialism and social injustice, the youth of the period looked forward to a new era. Nazism and Stalinism became a matter of the past; jet aviation and television were taken for granted. The headlines of the day featured new problems and new visions: school desegregation and freedom riders in the United States, atomic-powered submarines, exploration of outer space, de-Stalinization in Russia, the formation of a united Europe, social revolutions in Latin America, and African independence.

But the late 1950's remained a period of transition and the first full impact of the changes was not to be felt until the 1960's. The cold war, for example, lessened after Khrushchev's assumption of power and after the revolts in Hungary and Poland in 1956; yet co-existence as a true *modus vivendi* was achieved only after the Cuban missile crisis of 1962. Similarly, although Russia launched the world's first man-made satellite, Sputnik I, in 1957, the real space age opened only in the 1960's; just as Black Africa's drive for independence, initiated with Ghana's achievement of quasi-independence in 1956, gathered momentum only in 1960.

New faces and new forces

After the mid-1950's, Africa, Latin America, and Eastern Europe were stirred by revolutionary waves that inaugurated fundamental changes in the development of these areas. At the same time, France underwent yet another revolution that terminated her Fourth Republic. These changes were symbolized by the emergence of such diversely oriented people as Kwame Nkrumah (1909–   ), Gamal Abdel Nasser (1918–   ), Fidel Castro (1917–   ), Nikita Khrushchev, and Charles de Gaulle.

The awakening of Africa

"There comes a time in the history of all colonial peoples when they must, because of their will to throw off the hampering shackles of colonialism, boldly assert their God-given right to be free of a foreign ruler." This pronouncement by Nkrumah, the leader of the independence movement in Britain's Gold Coast Colony, sums up the sentiments of most Africans in the late 1950's.

The process of achieving independence differed considerably between the Moslem states of northern Africa and the black peoples of sub-Saharan Africa. By 1956, Egypt, Sudan, Libya, Tunisia, and Morocco had attained their independence, in all cases with relatively little violence. Only Algeria became involved in a protracted war (1954–1962) between her French masters and the Algerians' National Liberation Front. France's implacable determination not to relinquish control over Algeria stemmed in part from the fact that for well over a century Frenchmen had looked upon the Algerian area as an integral part of France, and that a million Frenchmen lived there and considered themselves to be native Algerians. The nine million Moslems of Algeria, on the other hand, resented the *colons* (French Algerians) who owned much of the best agricultural land and controlled most of Algeria's economy. Hence their resolve to fight for independence from Paris.

The political regimes of the newly independent North African states varied widely. Libya and Morocco emerged as relatively conservative monarchies; the Sudan became an unstable republic, plagued by dissension between its Arab and Black inhabitants; Tunisia abolished the monarchy and set up a moderate republic under President Habib Bourguiba (1903–   ). Egypt, where reform-minded army officers overthrew the monarchy in 1952, soon slipped under the centralized, semi-constitutional regime of Gamal Abdel Nasser, who endeavored to pursue a leftwing, but anticommunist policy. Algeria, finally, after obtaining independence in 1962, remained under the control of the former National Liberation Front in the guise of a Socialist dictatorship.

In general, these new states were faced by vast socio-economic problems and suffered from political inexperience. For example, no matter how fast the Egyptians opened new arable lands through irrigation, the increase in population offset all gains. Apart from lack of capital, the traditions of religious conservatism made industrialization difficult. Moreover, the new governments confronted perplexing problems in their foreign relations. They sympathized with the non-aligned world, while trying to obtain economic assistance from both the communist bloc and the Western powers, in particular America. Despite these problems, North Africa's emergence was facilitated by conditions not generally found south of the Sahara. The cohesiveness of the states along the southern shores of the Mediterranean benefited from the consciousness of a long and continuous history, as well as from religious, cultural, and linguistic unity. Furthermore, as evident in the Arab League, the North African states felt more affinity with the Moslem and Arab peoples of the Middle East than with sub-Saharan Black Africa, except for some cultural ties with African Moslems living in Mali, Mauritania, and elsewhere.

South of the Sahara, where only three independent states had existed at the end of World War II—Liberia, Ethiopia, and the Union (later, the Republic) of South Africa—the rush to independence gained momentum after 1956. By 1960, nineteen additional states had been created in sub-Saharan Africa; and by 1968, the number of states in all of Africa had risen to forty-two.

This rush toward independence often ill prepared and motivated by emotions in disregard of practical considerations, produced numerous problems for the new states of Africa. It was necessary, for instance, to determine future relations with the former colonial masters. At first, two distinct patterns of orderly withdrawal seemed to be started. Kwame Nkrumah decided to keep Ghana within the British Commonwealth, while Sékou Touré (1922–   ) of Guinea took his state out of the French Union. In the long run, however, Sékou Touré's solution was rejected by other independence leaders, and the new nations tended to retain friendly relations and close economic ties with their previous colonial masters.

Even more serious problems were involved in the creation of viable internal structures for the new states. Most of them lacked national cohesion. Their boundaries had been arbitrarily set by the colonial conquerors during the nineteenth century, or casually redrawn on the eve of independence, as for example combining the Ashanti Territories, the Gold Coast, and a part of Togo to constitute Ghana. The new states generally included many different, often hostile tribes. The Ashanti, for instance, many of them relatively affluent growers of cocoa, resented economic domination by Nkrumah's Ghanaians. Nigeria, with a population of 59,000,000 (1967), contained some 250 tribes, speaking different languages. Tribal antagonism led to frequent civil strife and attempts at secession, as in the case of the 8,500,000 Ibos who in 1967 revolted against the Nigerian government to set up their own state of Biafra.

The new African states also suffered from a lack of trained personnel in almost all fields—government, education, medicine, and technology. For those with advanced education, who had usually been trained abroad, it was relatively easy to assume positions of leadership; yet their foreign training often alienated them from their native cultures. It also proved difficult to establish grass-roots political support for the new governments. Violent clashes between political rivals, coups d'état, and resort to military rule became common substitutes for orderly government. Stability frequently relied not on political systems but on the presence of charismatic leaders who had been instrumental in the attainment of independence, such as Jomo Kenyatta (1900?–   ) of Kenya and Julius Nyerere (1921–   ) of Tanzania.

Despite all difficulties, the new states were proud of their independence, intent on stimulating nationalistic feelings, anxious to create some sort of African solidarity, and determined to make themselves heard and respected in the forum of the world, particularly at the United Nations. Yet their new status was fraught with frustrations, since their independence was frequently illusory. Although many Africans theoretically agreed with Nyerere's assertion that it would be better to be a "poorer free man" than a "wealthy slave," their economies continued to depend on outside help, frequently extended by their former colonial masters. English and French remained the common languages for communication in most of the sub-Saharan continent, and European political and cultural traditions predominated among the ruling classes. Russia, China, the United States, Israel, and others offered technical advice, financial aid, and military supplies in hope of acquiring new spheres of influence. Moreover, African governments found at times that their survival depended on foreign armies. In 1964, for instance, President M'Ba (1902–1967) of Gabon was restored to power by French troops after a revolution had toppled his government, and Julius Nyerere in the same year used British Marines to subdue rebellious elements within Tanzania's army. And in the long civil wars that bled the Congo after it unexpectedly received its independence from Belgium in 1960, much of the fighting was done by white mercenary troops hired by the government or by dissident elements fighting against it.

Finally one should note that overt colonialism continued to operate in some areas of Africa. By 1969, Spain still retained possession of several areas along Africa's West Coast; Portugal held a part of Guinea and the sizable colonies of Angola and Mozambique; and, despite protests from the United Nations, the Republic of South Africa dominated the former German colony of South West Africa. The white minority governments of the Republic of South Africa, which left the British Commonwealth in 1961, and of Rhodesia, which declared its independence in 1965, enforced strict separation of *apartheid* between the races and perpetuated essentially colonial privileges for the white man.

Changes in Latin America

Socio-economic problems in most Latin American countries were aggravated after World War II by rapid expansion of the population, not matched by commensurate growth of economic productivity. The decline in the price of agricultural products—sugar, coffee, bananas, and others—on which much of the economy of certain states depended, caused a severe lack of investment capital. The output of some raw materials, such as crude oil, rose significantly, but the resulting wealth continued to flow into the pockets of a select few, except in rare instances where nationalization had been effected, as was the case with most of the tin mines of Bolivia. Despite the gradual build-up of local industry, especially in Argentina, Brazil, and Mexico, the middle classes remained relatively small, while inflation and political instability undermined their incentive to forge ahead in industrial expansion. Poverty and illiteracy remained serious problems. The average annual per capita income in Colombia, for example, was 170 dollars (1966 figures); and by 1967 only a little more than half (56 per cent) of the school-age population of all of Latin America was enrolled in primary schools.

Assistance from abroad took many forms: loans from the Inter-American Development Bank, investments by private foreign interests, educational and technical help by philanthropic foundations, medical help from the World Health Organization, and, after 1961, financial assistance from the Alliance for Progress. Yet, in the final analysis, peoples of Latin America had to devise their own solutions if they hoped to achieve general prosperity and stability. On the whole, few fundamental changes were undertaken. Social and economic progress was hampered by the lack of significant land reform, by haphazard tax structures, and poor transport systems. Governmental stability suffered from violent antagonism between liberal and conservative parties, from frequent interference by the military, and from the perpetuation of inoperable political systems. Revolutionary unrest and military coups continued to be the norm in most countries, and constitutions were either disregarded or rewritten by more or less militant dictators. Only Mexico, which had begun a social revolution of sorts in 1910, seemed exempt from this pattern of political floundering.

A new twist had been added to the usual dictatorial system of Latin America by Juan Perón, who had been president of Argentina from 1946 until he was ousted in 1955. Perón mixed fascist ideas with Jacobin traditions, consolidated his power by appealing to the workers, and assumed a strongly nationalistic pose. In essence, however, he effected no fundamental reforms. Although his attempt to spread Perónism to other Latin American states was hampered by their fear of Argentine expansionism, similar ideas were espoused by political parties in all major Latin-American countries except Mexico and Colombia.

A year after Perón's downfall, a new revolutionary movement was launched by Fidel Castro and Ernesto "Che" Guevara (1928–1967) in the mountains of eastern Cuba. After an unsuccessful attempt in 1953 to overthrow the dictatorship of General Fulgencio Batista (1901–   ), Castro had trained a small band of guerrilla fighters, which he used to undermine the Batista regime. Two years of terrorism provided him with such strength and so many adherents that the government lost confidence in its ability to suppress the movement. At the beginning of 1959, Batista fled into exile and Castro assumed the post of prime minister. He promptly eliminated all possible opponents and established his own militant dictatorship, with absolute power to rule by decree. Together with his brother Rául (1930–   ) and with Guevara, he then launched a thoroughgoing socio-economic reform for Cuba. Within a short period, landowners were expropriated and peasants organized into collectives; United States properties were seized prior to general nationalization of all industry and housing. Guevara brought all business and labor under government control, and Castro's followers undertook far-reaching measures to wipe out illiteracy and to indoctrinate the Cuban people with revolutionary ideals.

Castro's early actions and his proclaimed intention of promoting proletarian revolutions throughout the Americas at first evoked enthusiasm among those who were disillusioned with the failure of military dictatorships or conservative democracies to bring about reform. This enthusiasm soon cooled, however, when Castro gradually revealed his communist connections. In 1960, he arranged for economic and military aid from Soviet Russia and extended diplomatic relations to Communist China. A year later, he declared Cuba to be a socialist state and announced his own adherence to Marxism. At the same time he stepped up revolutionary activity abroad by disseminating propaganda and dispatching agents and weapons to train and equip "national liberation" groups in other Latin American states. Antagonized by such subversive interference in their own affairs, an increasing number of Latin American governments broke relations with Cuba. The United States secretly supported the ill-planned Bay of Pigs invasion (1961), in which some fifteen hundred Cuban exiles attempted a landing in south-central Cuba in hopes of joining local anti-Castro elements and toppling the *massimo lider*. The ease with which Castro's forces repelled the attack allowed the Cuban dictator to assume even tighter control over his people.

Faced with Castroism, some Latin American governments sped up their own pace of reform, whereas others relied largely on military force to maintain the conservative status quo. Soon a third alternative emerged—particularly in Chile and Venezuela—with the growth of Christian Democratic parties, modeled to some extent on those of Western Europe. These left-of-center groups, firmly attached to democratic principles, sought to achieve social reform and economic development in cooperation with labor unions, progressive-minded members of the middle class, and liberal elements of the Catholic Church.

Despite such intense internal problems and common concern over Castroism and despite greater hemispheric economic cooperation, the nations of Latin America persisted in distrusting one another. Their mutual relations were marred by disputes over territories and by occasional armed border clashes. Hence, many of the governments entered into costly arms races, purchasing planes, tanks, and ships in efforts to impress their neighbors and to give added prestige to their own military establishments.

Changes in Europe

The death of Stalin in 1953 had left Eastern Europe and the communist world in uncertainty until Khrushchev's speech to the twentieth congress of the Communist party in 1956 inaugurated a new era, the period of systematic de-Stalinization. In this speech, which was at first kept secret from the public, Khrushchev denounced Stalin's resort to terror and purges and called for the abolition of the "cult of the individual." Russia's leadership henceforth was not to rely on a single dictator, but on collective leadership. Furthermore, Khrushchev made the significant admission that there might be various roads to socialism and that war, revolution, and violence were not necessarily inevitable. By rejecting rigid Stalinism, Moscow tacitly acknowledged the impending disintegration of the monolithic structure of international communism.

De-Stalinization was of course a slow process. It was five years before Stalin's embalmed body was removed from Lenin's great stone mausoleum in Red Square and interred in a simple grave along the wall of the Kremlin. Internal repression was slowly loosened, although political arrests and the dictatorship of the Communist party continued. Slightly more freedom of expression was allowed. While state economic planning continued to emphasize industrial and agricultural expansion, the advisability of producing more consumer goods was gradually recognized, and strict Marxian economics were abandoned to the point of modifying production and pricing to suit demand.

The removal in 1956 of Vyacheslav Molotov (1890–   ), who had guided Russian foreign affairs since 1939, marked the beginning of less rigid relations with other nations. Russia reduced her armed forces and effected a reconciliation with Tito's Yugoslavia. Among communist governments and parties, Moscow's new line evoked consternation and confusion. Discontented Poles and Hungarians promptly seized the opportunity to stage a revolution in hopes of reasserting self-determination, and various Communist parties in other states began to chart a more independent course from Moscow. Although the Polish and Hungarian revolutions were effectively quelled by Soviet armies, these developments set the trend for communism during the 1960's, when the Soviet grip on Eastern Europe was to loosen and when world-wide communism was to show less subservience to Moscow.

While Russia was undergoing ideological reorientation, France suffered from internal paralysis. The elections of 1956 had given the mutually antagonistic Right and Left a majority, thus preventing the moderate parties from governing effectively. The impasse of the Algerian war, however, demanded solutions that required a strong government. Afraid that the Paris government might abandon Algeria as it had Vietnam, elements of the French army and French *colons* in Algeria staged a revolution in May 1958, designed to topple the Fourth Republic. With civil war imminent, General de Gaulle emerged from retirement and announced his "readiness to assume the powers of the republic." Despite strong misgivings on the part of liberals and leftists, de Gaulle was soon recognized as the saviour in a time of need. After two weeks of maneuvering, the national assembly invested him as prime minister, with powers to rule by decree for six months and to write a new constitution for France.

De Gaulle used his special powers and his charisma to regain partial control over the rebellious groups in Algeria and to mollify the feelings of the *colons*. At home, he instituted a program of austerity and economic and fiscal reforms in order to promote confidence and stability. Within two months, he completed the formulation of a new constitution, which he then submitted to a referendum after touring France and many overseas territories in order to urge its acceptance. His draft constitution called for a strong presidency, a two-chamber parliament, and the reorganization of overseas territories and colonies into a community of autonomous states, bound together in common defense, with a joint policy on finance, economics, and foreign affairs. In the referendum of September 1958, Frenchmen overwhelmingly accepted the constitution, and overseas, all but Sékou Touré's Guinea voted to join the new French Community. In the following December, de Gaulle scored another triumph with his election as first president of the new Fifth French Republic.

De Gaulle was immensely self-assured in his conviction that he embodied the will and destiny of France and that he stood above the selfish squabbles of political parties. His influence over the new parliament was based on personal magnetism and the support of his new party, the Union for the New Republic (UNR), whose members had relinquished personal ideologies in favor of trust in de Gaulle's leadership. The new president exerted considerable pressure on the French public through skillful use of radio, television, press, and popular referendums. In 1962, he further enhanced his independence from parliament by instituting direct presidential elections, on the basis of which he was reelected for a second seven-year term in 1965.

Benefiting from unaccustomed political stability, the Fifth Republic prospered under de Gaulle's patriarchal dictates. Stringent governmental measures succeeded in reforming the tax structure and the tax collection system, stabilizing the franc, and shoring up gold reserves. Under a new system of national planning, affecting both private and public investments, industrial production rose markedly, foreign trade flourished, and full employment was achieved. Despite economic setbacks in some sectors, the French economy spurted upward and the standard of living improved measurably.

In foreign affairs, de Gaulle launched what he called "the process of taking our destiny in hand, which had, since 1940, been in the hands of others." In essence, this meant reawakening among Frenchmen their sense of national self-identity and implanting upon the world a respect for the grandeur and culture of France. To achieve this aim, de Gaulle proceeded to accelerate the construction of France's own atomic weapons, modernize her armed forces, and initiate a go-it-alone policy in regard to her former allies. Despite vehement opposition by the *colons* and by most conservative Frenchmen, he finally negotiated complete independence for Algeria (1962). While concluding a special treaty of friendship and cooperation with Germany, he tried to assume the role of spokesman for the Common Market (see p. 567), and posed as the defender of Europeanism against what he saw as Anglo-Saxon domination of the Continent by England and America. Although endorsing most attempts at closer European cooperation for the sake of Continental solidarity, he favored a Europe of cooperating states rather than the creation of a European state. His nationalistic appeals at times frustrated those intent on constructing a united Europe, and his gradual disengagement from NATO bewildered France's traditional postwar friends.

De Gaulle's Fifth Republic became an unusual phenomenon: authoritarian in nature, yet democratic in essence; anticommunist and at heart aligned with the West, yet decidedly independent and neutral in the East-West struggle; isolationist and yet striving to employ its good offices toward the solution of international friction.

The trend toward cooperation and integration

Notwithstanding ideological and national antagonisms, the old as well as the new nations felt compelled to examine their international relationships and commitments in view of the rapid scientific and technological changes in communications, transportation, and industrial production. Fear of a nuclear holocaust and visions of a new world polity both impelled people to seek new forms of internationalism.

A great variety of cooperative schemes was developed, some instigated by private organizations, others by governments. Among others they dealt with economic, cultural, educational, scientific, political, and military affairs. In scope, they ranged from specific technical devices to rather broad and vague ideals, from the pooling of electric power nets among nations to World Federalism. Generally speaking, the trend toward cooperation and integration was by far strongest in the economically developed areas of Europe and North America. In Latin America, the implementation of significant co-operative ventures was retarded by strong currents of national self-reliance. And among the emerging nations of Asia and Africa, newly gained national pride made such undertakings exceedingly difficult.

Most arrangements were cooperative in nature, in the sense that participating states retained complete jurisdiction over their own affairs; some, however, were integrative, involving the establishment of common institutions and a willingness on the part of the member states to grant a measure of sovereign control to such institutions.

It is well-nigh impossible to divide all existing schemes into neat categories for the sake of orderly discussion, and the plethora of bilateral and multilateral arrangements allows treatment of only a few examples.

Political and military organizations

Programs of a world-wide or regional scope were generally directed toward promoting world peace, developing continental rather than national policies, or helping the peoples of the world improve their standards of living. The World Federalists proposed the gradual dismantling of the sovereign prerogatives of nation-states through the substitution of a world government. Proponents of Atlantic Union, a concept often debated in the United States Senate and frequently praised by President John F. Kennedy, sought the gradual creation of a community embracing the peoples on both sides of the Atlantic.

The United Nations Organization, which by 1968 compromised 124 member states, became the best known arena for the discussion of international problems endangering the peace. Less known but perhaps more important in their impact were some of the fourteen intergovernmental agencies connected with the United Nations. The World Health Organization (WHO), for example, worked on improving hygiene and medical facilities in the less developed areas; the Food and Agricultural Organization (FAO) sought to increase food production and improve its distribution; the International Monetary Fund (IMF), which by 1967 had one hundred and twenty-two member states, devised methods to stabilize monetary exchange and discussed plans for the eventual creation of an international currency as a substitute for, or an addition to, gold, in order to satisfy the monetary needs of an expanding world economy.

Apart from the United Nations, numerous other organizations sprouted to deal with world-wide or regional problems. Among these, the Organization of American States (OAS, 1948) became one of the most active. Designed to promote hemispheric peace and security and to define the position of the Americas in world affairs, it was also concerned with cultural relations and economic development, particularly after the establishment of the Alliance for Progress. Following Fidel Castro's seizure of power in Cuba, the primary concern of the OAS was increasingly directed against the possible spread of communism in the Western Hemisphere.

Another regional organization, the Arab League (1945), which by 1966 included thirteen states, sought to coordinate Arab policy and promote greater economic cooperation. The League's effectiveness, however, was hampered by violent dissensions between its more conservative and more radical member governments. Equally ineffective was the thirty-eight member Organization of African Unity (1963), a loosely organized body dedicated to the promotion of African unity and development as well as to the eradication of all remnants of colonialism.

Cooperation was also stressed in Europe. In the immediate postwar years, Churchill and others repeatedly urged Europeans to cast aside their traditional separatism. In one speech Churchill asserted that "the safety of the world requires a unity in Europe, from which no nation should be permanently outcast." And in 1947, he proclaimed: "If we are to form the United States of Europe or whatever name or form it may take, we must begin now!" In response to such urging, ten European states, later augmented to fifteen, formed the Council of Europe in 1949, with the prescribed aims of achieving "a greater unity between its members for the purpose of safeguarding and realizing the ideals and principles which are their common heritage and facilitating their economic and social progress." With its headquarters at Strasbourg, the Council of Europe soon became an influential voice in the European movement, representing public opinion rather than its member governments. Although possessing no supranational powers, it assumed the prerogative of discussing a broad spectrum of social, political, cultural, and economic questions. In 1950, it adopted the European Convention on Human Rights, guaranteeing basic civil rights to all citizens of member states and their entitlement to seek redress before a special European Court of Human Rights. Despite the hopes of stanch supporters of the European movement, the Council of Europe did not become a true European parliament, which might have acted as the precursor of a European supranational government.

Military collaboration resulted at first from the West's determination to keep West Germany disarmed. Later, other multilateral defense organizations were created in response to the cold war. Unlike the old-style mutual defense pacts, most of these new arrangements included economic and political clauses and involved not only close coordination of strategic planning but considerable integration of war matériel, logistical systems, and command echelons.

One of the earliest treaties, the Dunkirk Pact (1947) between France and Great Britain was soon expanded to include Holland, Belgium, and Luxembourg (Brussels Treaty of 1948). The resulting Western Union, as it was called, was a fifty-year military alliance with a joint military staff and a Consultative Council for the coordination of military, economic, and political policies. When the Western powers decided to rearm West Germany, Western Union was further expanded to include West Germany and Italy. The new Western European Union (WEU), working in close harmony with NATO, was to supervise the rearmament of the German Federal Republic and to continue the integrative policies of standardizing armaments and developing combined staff planning. With Germany a partner in WEU, the *raison d'être* of this seven-nation organization clearly shifted. What had started as a security pact against Germany had become a defense alliance against Russia.

The North Atlantic Treaty Organization (NATO), however, was from its inception directed against the Soviet Union. Signed in 1949 at the time of the first major Berlin crisis, the North Atlantic Defense Pact stipulated "that an armed attack against one or more of [its members] in Europe or North America shall be considered an attack against them all." Under the pact, the twelve member states—later increased to fifteen with the addition of Greece, Turkey, and West Germany—set up a permanent Council, assisted by an international staff, and devised several integrated commands to coordinate planning and supervise the movements of all forces assigned to NATO. Within the framework of NATO, the United States and Canada constructed a joint defense system for the North American continent, including a Distant Early Warning line (DEW) near the Arctic Circle, completed in 1959, to prevent possible surprise attacks across the North Pole.

The Soviet Union reacted to the remilitarization of West Germany by concluding the Warsaw Pact (1955), a twenty-year mutual defense agreement with the seven communist states of Eastern Europe, including East Germany. Although a consultative political committee of all member states was to assist a Russian general in his command over the Warsaw Pact forces, less integration was achieved than existed within NATO.

Economic integration

Most of the schemes so far discussed, whatever their primary purpose, also involved economic matters. Some organizations, however, were primarily economic in nature. The earliest example of economic integration was an agreement by Belgium, the Netherlands, and Luxembourg to work toward a customs union even before the war in Europe had ended. The resulting Benelux Economic Union by 1948 set up common tariffs on imports and, for all intents and purposes allowed the free movement of goods and labor among the three states.

The Marshall Plan gave further impetus to European economic cooperation. The United States Congress stipulated that it would help finance European recovery only if the recipients of aid would pool their resources and closely coordinate their efforts for economic rehabilitation. Sixteen European states thereupon set up the Organization for European Economic Cooperation (1948), later joined by West Germany and eventually by Spain. Although not empowered with supranational authority, OEEC played a significant role in generating cooperation in matters of trade and finance.

By far the most successful and spectacular step was the formation of the European Economic Community (EEC), often labeled "the Inner Six." Its origins lay in a proposal of 1950 by French Foreign Minister Robert Schuman (1886–   ) to merge the coal and steel industries of France and West Germany and any other state willing to join such a venture. Schuman's hope was that such a step would render future Franco-German wars impossible, would speed up economic recovery, and lead toward the creation of a united Europe. The progress of such a united Europe, Schuman contended, would benefit "all lands, especially Africa, that look to the old Continent for their development and prosperity." Together with Jean Monnet (1888–   ), one of the principal architects of the European movement, Schuman looked forward to the eventual political unification of Europe, but chose the gradual, "functional approach . . . for the practical reason that it seemed wiser to begin with integration in a restricted technical sector of national life," in fields that "lie somewhat outside the areas of sharpest controversy." Italy, West Germany, and the Benelux states responded to his invitation and in 1951 established the European Coal and Steel Community (ECSC). Great Britain, however, decided against joining this new organization.

ECSC was placed under the control of nine directors who constituted the High Authority, a supranational body with power to control the coal and steel industries of the "Inner Six," to levy taxes, and to close down unprofitable mines. Within its prescribed limits, the High Authority thus acted like a sovereign entity. It was aided in its work by an Assembly, which performed the role of a parliament, by a Council of Ministers and a special Court of Justice. ECSC was so successful in furthering economic growth within the "Inner Six" and heightening the hopes of those seeking to create a United Europe, that the same six nations decided in 1957 to supplement it with two further functional institutions. By the Treaties of Rome of that year they set up an Economic Community Commission for the creation of a customs union and an Atomic Energy Community (EURATOM) for the development of atomic power for peaceful uses. Once again, Great Britain declined to join.

The new agencies began to function in 1958 and, together with ECSC, developed into the European Economic Community (EEC) or Common Market, as it came to be popularly called. Tariffs and quota restrictions among the Six were gradually abolished and uniform external tariffs erected, thus creating a single trade area for a population of 185 million (1967 figures). As Robert Schuman had hoped, integration within EEC soon went beyond purely economic areas. Free labor mobility led to attempts to bring social conditions in the six states to more nearly equal levels. Projects were undertaken to develop a "European" rather than a national education and to reconcile differences in the various legal systems. European television (Eurovision) was inaugurated and a new civil service arose, composed of the so-called Eurocrats who worked for the European Community rather than for a single government. Despite occasional difficulties and despite French reluctance in the 1960's to allow EEC to move toward greater political unification, the Common Market's success advanced the European ideal and made the "Inner Six" a powerful factor in the world market. By 1968, associate membership had been granted to Greece, Turkey, and eighteen African states.

Having failed in her attempt to persuade all members of OEEC to adopt a free trade policy, Great Britain in 1959 formed her own European Free Trade Association (EFTA), often called the "Outer Seven" (Britain, Norway, Sweden, Denmark, Austria, Switzerland, and Portugal). EFTA's aim was to abolish trade barriers on non-agricultural products only. Moreover it permitted member states to continue to set tariffs for trade with non-EFTA nations. Although stimulating trade in industrial goods, EFTA lacked the integrative impetus of EEC, and many of its members soon became interested in joining the more successful organization of the "Inner Six." Starting in 1961, Great Britain herself began to negotiate with EEC in regard to her possible admission as well as that of her EFTA partners. Initially complicated by her hesitation to abandon her special commercial relations with the Commonwealth, Britain's application was vetoed by France in 1963.

Steps toward economic collaboration were also taken in other regions. In 1949, the Soviet Union established the Council for Mutual Economic Assistance (COMECON) to coordinate the economies of the communist states of Eastern Europe. COMECON sought to assign production levels to the various states, but achieved little true integration. Moscow's demand that her partners concentrate on the production of raw materials, while retaining for herself primacy in industrial development, eventually disenchanted most of the members of COMECON.

Elsewhere, numerous diverse cooperational schemes emerged. The Inter-American Development Bank (1959), the Organization for Economic Cooperation and Development (1961), and the African Development Bank (1964), for instance, distributed financial assistance to developing countries.

The Scandinavian nations formed a joint commercial airline; five Central American Republics established a fairly successful common market; ten South American states strove for a free trade area (LAFTA); the twenty-three-nation Colombo Plan countries worked on economic development in South and Southeast Asia; and a twelve-nation West African Free Trade Union was created in 1967.

SUGGESTED READINGS

Africa

Benson, Mary, *South Africa: Struggle for a Birthright* (Funk, 1968).

Cowan, Laing Gray, *The Dilemmas of African Independence* (Walker, 1967).

*Cromer, Evelyn B., *Modern Egypt,* 2 vols. (Fertig, 1968).

Emerson, Rupert, and Kilson, Martin, eds., *The Political Awakening of Africa* (Prentice-Hall, 1965). Collection of sources.

Ferkiss, Victor C., *Africa's Search for Identity* (World, 1967).

Nielsen, Waldemar A., *Africa* (Atheneum, 1966).

Wallbank, T. Walter, *Contemporary Africa: Continent in Transition* (Van Nostrand, 1964).

Latin America

Barager, Joseph R., *Why Péron Came to Power* (Random, 1967).

Hamill, Hugh M., Jr., ed., *Dictatorship in Spanish America* (Knopf, 1965). Collection of essays.

Johnson, John, *Political Change in Latin America: The Emergence of the Middle Sectors* (Stanford, 1958).

Larson, David L., ed., *The "Cuban Crisis" of 1962: Selected Documents and Chronology* (Houghton, 1963).

Petras, James, and Zeitlin, Maurice, eds., *Latin America: Reform or Revolution?* (Fawcett, 1968). A Reader.

Schurz, William Lytle, *This New World, The Civilization of Latin America* (Dutton, 1964).

Szulc, Tad, *Latin America* (Atheneum, 1966).

Russia After Stalin

Brzezinski, Zbigniew K., *Ideology and Power in Soviet Politics* (Praeger, 1967).

*———, *Soviet Bloc: Unity and Conflict* (Harvard, 1967).

———, *The Anti-Stalin Campaign and International Communism; A Selection of Documents* (Columbia, 1957).

Jacobs, Dan N., ed., *The New Communist Manifesto and Related Documents* (Harper, 1964).

Werth, Alexander, *Russia Under Khrushchev* (Fawcett).

Zinner, Paul E., ed., *National Communism and Popular Revolt in Eastern Europe; A Selection of Documents in Poland and Hungary* (Columbia, 1956).

Fifth French Republic

Cairnes, John C., *France* (Prentice-Hall, 1965).

Harrison, Martin, *French Politics* (Heath, 1968). Collection of essays.

Maier, Charles S., and White, Dan S., eds., *The Thirteenth of May: The Advent of de Gaulle's Republic* (Oxford U.P., 1968). Collection of sources.

*Pickles, Dorothy, *Algeria and France: From Colonialism to Cooperation* (Praeger, 1963).

*Priestley, Herbert I., *France Overseas* (Octagon, 1966).

Schoenbrun, David, *The Three Lives of Charles De Gaulle* (Atheneum, 1966).

Willis, Roy F., ed., *De Gaulle: Anachronism, Realist or Prophet?* (Holt, 1967).

Cooperation and Integration

Benoit, Emile, *Europe at Sixes and Sevens, The Common Market, the Free Trade Association, and the United States* (Columbia, 1962).

Buchan, Alastair, *Nato in the 1960's: The Implication of Interdependence* (Praeger, 1963).

Cleveland, Harold van B., *The Atlantic Idea and Its European Rival* (McGraw, 1966).

Curtis, Michael R., *Western European Integration* (Harper, 1965).

Deutsch, Karl W., Edinger, Lewis J., and others, *France, Germany, and the Western Alliance: A Study of Elite Attitudes on European Integration and World Politics* (Scribner, 1967).

MacDonald, Robert W., *The League of Arab States: A Study in the Dynamics of Regional Organization* (Princeton, 1965).

Machlup, Fritz, *Remaking the International Monetary System, The Rio Agreement and Beyond* (Johns Hopkins, 1968).

Mayne, Richard, *The Community of Europe* (Norton, 1963). Brief survey.

Mitrany, David, *A Working Peace System* (Quadrangle, 1966).

Townley, Ralph, *The United Nations: A View from Within* (Scribner, 1968).

CHAPTER XXXI

᠉᠗ *The Contemporary World*

During the 1960's, the world became less rigidly divided into two camps. The two antagonistic power blocs loosened, and the neutral world gained greater self-confidence. At the same time, technology and science evolved so rapidly that man seemed capable of constructing a new world civilization. Yet the persistence of incalculable socio-economic problems and of violence between and within nations made it evident that the millennium was not about to appear.

Co-existence and the "third world"

"Peaceful co-existence," according to Russia's official Diplomatic Dictionary, "is a specific form of class struggle between socialism and capitalism" in which "the socialist system is victorious in world-wide competition with capitalism, because the socialist mode of production has a decisive advantage over the capitalist mode of production." This view generally characterized Khrushchev's administration. But the Russian leader was also intent on advancing the Soviet cause by a good measure of bluster and by sustained efforts at gaining a better foothold in the non-aligned nations comprising the "third world."

Prior to 1962, the easing of the cold war and the attainment of peaceful co-existence was marred by various crises that threatened the *rapprochement* between the two antagonists. Russia's launching of Sputnik I in 1957 upset the Russo-American balance in the race to control outer space, and proved the Soviets' temporary superiority in the development of ballistics. There were also repeated crises over Berlin, when Russia tried to dislodge the Western powers from that city and announced her readiness to conclude a separate peace with East Germany. These German crises finally subsided after Walter Ulbricht had a wall built around West Berlin in 1961 and ordered a plowed death strip constructed along the border with West Germany in order to prevent further flights of his people to the West. In 1960, a projected summit meeting between Khrushchev and President Eisenhower was aborted when an American U-2 spy plane was shot down over the Soviet Union and America subsequently admitted that its planes had made frequent surveillance flights over Russia and China. When similar intelligence flights over Cuba in 1962 revealed the presence of Soviet missiles on the island, a final showdown brought Moscow and Washington perilously close to war. Alarmed by the intrusion of Soviet power into the Western Hemisphere, President John F. Kennedy deployed a naval blockade around Cuba and warned that "any missile launched from Cuba against any nation shall be regarded as an attack by the Soviet Union on the United States, requiring full retaliation." The crisis abated when the Russians pulled back their missiles in return for Kennedy's promise not to send an invasion force into Cuba.

The Cuban missile crisis was followed by a genuine *détente* between Russia and America, a period when occasional verbal sparring and diplomatic jockeying did not obscure the fundamental decision of the two powers not to engage in thermonuclear warfare. The so-called hot line, a system of direct communications between the White House and the Kremlin, installed in 1963, was a symbolic as well as a practical step for reducing world tension. The treaty banning nuclear weapons tests in the atmosphere, in outer space, and under water, signed in the same year by Russia, America, and England, was also designed to lessen the possibility of nuclear warfare. More than one hundred nations subscribed to this treaty, with the notable exception of China and France, who were developing their own atomic striking forces. Next, Russia and America, with the encouragement of the United Nations, initiated drawn-out negotiations over the more difficult questions of disarmament and nuclear non-proliferation. At the same time, the two nations concluded various agreements on trade and cultural exchanges, eased travel restrictions, and undertook wary cooperation in other areas, as if to test one another's trustworthiness.

This change in attitude derived from many factors. Once the United States had caught up with Russia's advantage in missiles and ballistics, a nuclear stalemate had been achieved that made nuclear war unacceptable to either protagonist. Khrushchev's bluster had failed and he was deposed in 1964 and replaced by the new collective team of Communist party Chairman Leonid Breshnev (1906–   ) and Prime Minister Aleksei Kosygin (1904–   ), both representing the new generation of Communists that had come of age after the Bolshevik Revolution. Equally important as the nuclear stalemate, however, was the disintegration of the communist monolith. After 1960, Russia's break with China became rapidly accentuated, so that Moscow had to divide its resources between countering the West, casting a watchful eye on East Asia, and pursuing its growing role in the uncommitted "third world."

Among these developments, the Chinese-Soviet split was probably the most significant and therefore deserves further explanation. After gaining control of mainland China in 1949 (see p. 547), Mao Tse-tung and Prime Minister Chou En-lai (1898–   ) had at once launched a hasty program of forced internal reforms and of building up Chinese military strength. Although China still suffered from the aftermath of the long civil war, Mao promptly dispatched forces to regain control over Tibet and a month later sent several hundred thousand well-organized "volunteers" to eject General MacArthur's American and United Nations troops from North Korea. In the mid-1950's, Communist China made repeated attempts to dislodge Chiang Kai-shek's forces from the offshore islands and, if possible, from Formosa itself. These attempts, however, were thwarted by large-scale American military assistance to the Nationalist government on Formosa and by the interposition of the United States Seventh Fleet. Mao was thus frustrated in his desire to stamp out Chiang's pretension to speak for all of China. On the other hand, he expanded Chinese influence by supporting communist movements abroad, as in Indonesia, and by inciting "revolutionary warfare" against "the imperialists," particularly among the emerging peoples of Africa. In 1962, he launched a brief attack against India along the Himalayan frontier, and later furnished military aid to Pakistan in her conflict with India. Meanwhile, despite shortages at home, China increased her foreign aid to North Vietnam, North Korea, and elsewhere in an effort to undercut Russian influence over the communist world.

Within China, the Communists inaugurated Mao's shifting precepts for a permanent revolution. The landlord class was wiped out, and the first Five Year Plan of 1953 called for an ambitious program of forced industrialization, initially with Soviet financial and technical assistance. By 1958, Mao decided that the pace of modernization and collectivization should be hastened in a "Great Leap Forward." The second Five Year Plan called for the establishment of rural communes, social and politico-economic units that were to control and discipline the people and to help raise production and allocate distribution of consumer goods. Total dedication, hard work, and frugality were to be the shibboleths of the Chinese masses. Notwithstanding some economic progress, however, China could not produce enough food to support her skyrocketing population, which increased from an estimated 475 million inhabitants in 1946 to about 825 million by 1967. Hence, China was forced to import grain in order to avert starvation.

To cope with increasing unrest among his people, Mao relaxed his program of instant "communalization" in 1960 only to launch a new and different attack five years later in his purported "great proletarian cultural revolution." This time, Mao sought to eradicate all possible opponents of his own ideology and policies, both within and outside of the party. His wrath was directed particularly against intellectuals whom he accused of deviation from the strict party line. Despite the internal turmoil and power struggles that at times resembled minor civil wars, China made great economic and technological progress during the 1960's. In 1964, Chinese scientists exploded their first atomic device, while others worked feverishly to develop missiles that could carry the newly developed atomic bombs. With China thus rising to the level of a world power, the Peking government continued to be vexed by the refusal of the United States and a majority of the world's nations to extend it diplomatic recognition. To be sure, Great Britain, in accord with her usual policy of granting *de jure* recognition to a government with *de facto* control over a given state, had established diplomatic relations with the Communist regime in 1950, and France had followed suit in 1964. Yet, nineteen years after the Communists came to power in mainland China, Chiang Kai-shek's Nationalist government on Formosa, controlling a population of some thirteen million, was still recognized by a majority of the nations as the official spokesman for all of China and was permitted to retain its permanent seat on the Security Council of the United Nations. The rift between Peking and Moscow only aggravated this dilemma of Mao's foreign policy.

In 1960, Russia recalled her technical advisers from China and demanded the prompt repayment of short-term loans extended to the Chinese government. This breach of trust between the two regimes soon spiralled into virulent antagonism and mutual recriminations. The ensuing Sino-Soviet split had many causes. Ever since Russia's first determined penetration into the Far East during the nineteenth century, Sino-Russian rivalry had become inevitable. After World War I, these differences were at first assuaged by China's weakness and later temporarily patched over by communist solidarity. However, once the traditionally proud Chinese had regained power and self-confidence, Peking was not likely to accept second place, not even within the communist fold.

The usual power struggle for spheres of influence was soon aggravated by ideological differences. Mao accused the Soviets of having become a satiated, bourgeois-minded nation, and of having abandoned the concept of permanent revolution. He insisted that the policy of peaceful co-existence with the capitalist world was in fact a sell-out to the "imperialists," and that only a stepped-up program of "revolutionary warfare" could bring about the advent of world-wide socialism. With Moscow and Peking both claiming to embody the Marxist-Leninist tradition and accusing the other of being deviationists, a struggle for leadership of world-wide communism developed. In Europe, Albania lined up with Peking, and some of Russia's satellites made occasional flirtatious overtures to China as a means of gaining greater independence from Moscow. In the non-committed world of Asia, Africa, and to some extent in Latin America, the Soviets and Chinese rivaled each other for influence over local Communists and dissident elements, with Russia generally succeeding in retaining more sway.

The ebbing of the cold war and the Sino-Soviet rift had a profound influence on the cohesion of the two power blocs and the attitude of the neutral "third world." During the 1960's, the communist states of Eastern Europe felt increasingly emboldened to modify Marxist theory to suit their own requirements and to shape their foreign policy more independently of Moscow. They established closer trade contacts with the West and relaxed totalitarian restrictions in varying degrees. Among the Western powers, particularly the members of NATO, there was a similar relaxation. Less worried about a possible Soviet attack, Europe's NATO nations sought to lessen their subservience to Washington or to acquire a significant share in the formulation of NATO policy, particularly in regard to the deployment and use of atomic weapons. After various schemes for the sharing of control over atomic weapons failed to materialize, the cohesion of NATO was further reduced when Charles de Gaulle withdrew all French units from NATO's integrated command and expelled NATO headquarters from French soil in 1966. Although de Gaulle kept France theoretically within the NATO alliance, he made it clear that in time of peace France would pursue an independent stance.

Concomitant with the loosening of the two cold war blocs, there was a resurgence of European continentalism. With the Iron Curtain becoming more penetrable, peoples on both sides recalled their common heritage and began to call for cultural and economic exchanges, regardless of the differences in the socio-political systems under which they lived. France's de Gaulle sought a *rapprochement* with Russia and Eastern Europe. Even West Germany, hitherto reluctant to deal with communist Europe because of her own continued division, initiated commercial and diplomatic relations with Eastern Europe and began to disassociate herself more from Washington and devise her own foreign policy.

The "third world," too, was losing its anticipated cohesion. The leaders of the uncommitted world—Tito, Nasser, Jawaharlal Nehru of India, and Sukarno (1901–   ) of Indonesia—had hoped to act as a balancing force for world peace. Yet, such hopes gradually faded with the realization that the neutral nations were hopelessly divided. Intra-Arab dissension and continued Arab-Israeli enmity, angry discord between left-wing and moderate African governments, continued belligerence between Moslem Pakistan and Hindu India, and clandestine armed confrontation between Indonesia and her Southeast Asian neighbors made a sham of the much vaunted Afro-Asian solidarity first heralded at the Bandung Conference of 1955 and later reiterated at Belgrade in 1961.

Hence, by the mid-1960's, the world was no longer divided into two neat camps, with a "third world" vainly acting as mediator. With the communist protagonists sharply splintered and the Western powers somewhat diffident toward one another, with the neutral nations seemingly impelled in centrifugal directions, and with the prospect of increased atomic proliferation, the peace of the world no longer depended on a clearly defined balance of power but on whatever common sense and humanity might exist among the statesmen of the world.

An emerging world civilization

With instant communications and supersonic transportation, the world of the 1960's had grown so small that little could happen in one corner of the globe without evoking prompt repercussions in many other areas. Despite nationalistic tendencies, many people were recognizing that neither "Western" nor "Eastern" modes of living remained feasible as an exclusive way of life. The new realities of a global civilization called for a frank accommodation of past differences, based, so it appeared, on Western advances in science and technology. At the same time, this emerging world civilization was plagued by innumerable problems which neither efforts within states nor cooperation among states seemed capable of solving.

The unity of mankind

Recognizing that problems facing one nation or one group might eventually affect many others, most governments and peoples developed a feeling of international solidarity relatively unknown before. In case of sudden famines, epidemics, or natural disasters such as earthquakes, it became customary for the nations of the world to respond with prompt aid, where possible. Similarly, several United Nations organizations, governmental agencies of various nations, as well as private groups initiated world-wide programs in such diverse areas as combating illiteracy, furthering international understanding, and developing birth control plans. Some of the more prosperous nations sent volunteers or conscripts abroad in programs similar to that of the United States Peace Corps. These corpsmen assisted underdeveloped countries by improving agricultural methods, promoting primary education, expanding transport facilities, or undertaking other activities designed to raise the general standard of living. To be sure, such programs did not lack ulterior motives. De Gaulle's envoys were to promote greater appreciation for French culture; Bonn's Development Helpers sought to rehabilitate Germany's repute in the eyes of the world; Israeli technical advisors in various African states helped break Israel's isolation in the Mid-East. The over-all effect of these programs, however, was to enhance the similarity of views among the world's people, particularly in regard to basic standards of living.

Expanding world trade and the increasing internationalization of business enterprises also brought greater similitude to the material and organizational aspects of various areas of the globe. The United States in particular was eagerly extending its economic influence, exporting not only its merchandise but also its business methods, spreading, as some critics complained, its Coca-Cola imprint around the world. Supermarkets and chewing gum appeared in the most implausible places. Such giants as Standard Oil of New Jersey operated in 110 countries, and General Motors with its affiliates ran production or assembly plants in sixteen nations. Industrial, commercial, and financial crossing of international boundaries was also undertaken by many other countries. Russian engineers constructed the Aswan Dam across the Nile in Egypt and built steel mills in India; Italy's Fiat Company set up an automobile plant in Russia; and Imperial Chemical Industries of Great Britain owned subsidiary or associated companies in forty-five countries. As a result, the middle classes of the world were becoming more alike in their commercial practices.

The space race proved to be another arena in which the world could draw close together. Not only could communication satellites provide instant contact, but space ventures required global tracking stations and called for cooperative arrangements for the recovery of astronauts. Moreover, the scientific exploration of outer space became a global enterprise transcending national boundaries. By 1968, eighty-three countries were cooperating with America's National Aeronautics and Space Agency (NASA) in conducting scientific space programs. Unquestionably the participants were motivated partly by desires to further their national prestige; yet another motive surely was man's common urge to explore the universe. This feeling was also in evidence when many hailed the space feats of Russia and America not so much as the victory of a particular nation but as miraculous accomplishments of twentieth-century man.

Other types of cooperation included religious ecumenical movements among the world's one billion Christians. The World Council of Churches labored to break down barriers between denominations, to secure worldwide religious freedom, and to promote social and psychological health through cooperation with other agencies. Pope Paul VI (1963–   ) held conferences with heads of other Christian churches and authorized the Vatican's Secretariat for Promotion of Christian Unity to collaborate with other Christian churches on a project to produce a common Bible. Beyond the body of Christendom, there were stepped-up attempts at inter-faith collaboration between Christians and Jews, and the World Fellowship of Buddhists tried to overcome doctrinal differences among the various Buddhist sects. However, no apparent reconciliation took place between Moslems and Hindus or between Moslems and Jews.

In the field of culture, too, the world was growing closer together. World-wide tours of symphony orchestras, dance groups, or theatrical companies became commonplace. New movements in art quickly transcended national boundaries, and best sellers in one country were promptly translated into countless languages. Modern architectural styles became international, with similar skyscrapers emerging in Abidjan on the Ivory Coast, and in Milan, Italy. Movies, television programs, and popular magazines the world over reflected this cultural assimilation, despite centuries of different backgrounds.

This outward *rapprochement* among the world's people entailed serious strains, particularly among the underdeveloped nations. The idea of progress, a concept associated with Western Enlightenment of the eighteenth century and the industrial development of the nineteenth, assumed a controlling role among the emerging states. In disregard of traditional values, religious mores, and social customs, the peoples of Africa and Asia sought to adopt Western ideologies and standards, often ill-suited to their own socioeconomic conditions. The establishment of a national airline, for example, became a symbol of national prestige, just as Western dress and social customs became the norm among the aspiring peoples of the world.

The major powers added to this trend through their attempts to prescribe ready-made remedies for the socio-economic and political ills of the developing world, remedies not always suited to local conditions. The peoples of Asia and Africa were swamped with patented solutions: American style free enterprise and representative institutions, Soviet collectivism, and Chinese wars of liberation. Rare indeed were attempts at developing indigenous solutions to the problems of modernization, like those being carried on in Mexico.

Notwithstanding differences and friction, the emerging world civilization was characterized by a gradual *rapprochement* in thought and attitudes. The meditative life of the East, as exemplified for instance by Zen Buddhism, came to be somewhat better understood in the West, while Western secularism spread to other areas. Materialistic philosophies, stemming from the nineteenth century, strongly enhanced by Marxian doctrines and the acquisitive standards of Western middle classes, gained growing influence. The "God is dead" movement popular among some segments of Western society was but a polarized version of an increasing general secular trend. Everywhere, be it among Jews, Moslems, or Hindus, the "orthodox" found themselves engaged in desperate rear guard skirmishes against the forces of secularization.

A similar common trend marked the attitudes toward life, particularly among the younger generation. By the 1960's, the stress on "experience" or on an existentialist type of "commitment" was becoming the credo of more and more young people. Heralded in philosophic theories, illustrated in literature, and expressed in popular music and art, this new spirit manifested itself increasingly in everyday life. Student protests became a familiar phenomenon in America and Europe as well as in Asia. As standards of traditional morality loosened, the youth groped for new experiential values, sometimes found in drug-induced hallucinations or in the thrills of juvenile delinquency. Whether in Poland or the United States, in Communist China or Chile, there was no shortage of causes to which the youth could rally in protest.

Unsolved problems

World-wide cooperation in some areas and a new sense of human unity, however, did not suffice to solve a plethora of problems that continued to mar man's social and economic existence. Worst among these was continued reliance on violence and war.

The decades after World War II, rather than embodying years of international peace, in fact turned into an age of undeclared wars and perilous truces. Fifteen years after the official end of the Korean conflict, only a tenuous and frequently violated truce agreement existed between North Korea and the United Nations. A mere armistice separated the forces of Pakistan and India in their repeated clashes over the possession of Kashmir; and even after three wars between 1948 and 1967 there was no peace between Israel and her Arab neighbors. One might also add that no conventional peace had as yet been concluded between Germany and the Allies of World War II. Mere armistices had seemingly become the norm in an age of international friction.

Since the chimera of a nuclear holocaust made war between the major military powers unacceptable, so-called localized wars fought with conventional weapons came to be the favored methods for seeking to settle international disagreements. Such conflicts, no matter how bloody and prolonged the fighting, were never officially labeled as wars nor accompanied by declarations of war. Rather they were called border conflicts, colonial revolts, police actions, guerrilla uprisings, or extended civil wars. Although most of these conflicts, whether in Vietnam, the Near East, or the Congo, were secretly or openly supported by some of the major powers, the device of localization temporarily shielded the world from a third world war.

Faced with such numerous instances of resort to warfare, the United Nations Organization frequently intervened to procure armistices. Such actions coincided with other world-wide efforts to secure the rule of law rather than of violence in the preservation of basic human rights. The U.N. established peace-keeping forces, border patrols, and observation teams, consisting of military units made available by member states such as Norway, India, and Ethiopia. These U.N. troops were used on Cyprus, in Egypt, Kashmir, and other trouble spots and sometimes succeeded in shortening the fighting or preventing further outbreaks of violence. The U.N., however, could act effectively only if the major powers cooperated. Moreover its efficacy was weakened through its restricted membership. Although involved globally in the matter of keeping peace, its membership was not universal. In fact, those areas that produced more than their share of crises were not admitted to the U.N.: Communist China and the three divided states, East and West Germany, North and South Korea, and North and South Vietnam.

A further reason for the U.N.'s difficulties was the nebulous origin of many of the armed conflicts. During the postwar decades, violence marked the internal affairs of many states. In fact, revolutions afflicted a majority of the nations—from Greece, Poland, and France to Iraq, Lebanon, and Egypt; from Indonesia, Burma, and Vietnam to Nigeria, Ghana, and the Congo; from the Dominican Republic and Nicaragua to Argentina and Brazil, is but a brief sampling. Remarkably few countries escaped revolutionary upheavals. Many of these revolts—the rebellion of Katanga province against the new government of the Congo, for example, or the overthrow of President Ngo Dinh Diem of South Vietnam—involved foreign complications. For the U.N. it was difficult to distinguish between purely internal affairs, which according to its charter do not fall within its jurisdiction, and external affairs that threatened the peace between nations.

Violence also became common in the form of rioting and government suppression of dissident groups. Mass killings, such as occurred on Formosa, in India, China, the Congo, South Africa, and elsewhere, whether for political, religious, or economic reasons, evoked surprisingly little shock in world opinion. Incongruous as it might seem in an age of increasing humanitarianism, the violent death of anonymous masses often hardly troubled people who otherwise worried over the saving of a single life through some spectacular rescue operation or the use of a new drug.

Finally, deep animosity and frequent violence were caused by racial and religious hatreds, derived from economic disparity or simple bigotry. The Afrikaners of South Africa propounded *apartheid* (segregation), Moslems slaughtered Hindus in South Asia, and Buddhists fought against Catholics in Vietnam. Discrimination against whites and blacks, Jews, Chinese, Indians, and other groups was widespread in almost all areas of the world. Despite an emerging world civilization, suspicion and hate toward groups that somehow differed in color of skin, religious customs, or traditional mores continued to motivate the actions of people.

Besides violence, a further problem was illiteracy among much of the world's exploding population. In 1967, twenty-seven countries reported a literacy rate of less than 50 per cent and only nine states claimed 100 per cent literacy. The inability of millions of people to read and write naturally impaired their potential for developing modern industrial societies. Educational progress and economic improvements were of course closely tied to the population explosion which marked the postwar decades. By the late 1960's, the world's population was growing by a net of some 170,000 people a day, with the heaviest growth in the less developed countries. Some nations, such as Japan, established fairly effective birth control programs, but despite efforts by the United Nations and other organizations, many others found it impossible to check their rate of growth. Religious mores, traditional patterns of life, or sheer ignorance and indifference made the distribution of birth-control drugs and devices futile in many areas.

The population explosion caused frequent famines in the underdeveloped nations and infinitely complicated the process of raising their standard of living. Existing commercial practices and nationalistic restrictions on trade did not permit the natural flow and distribution of surplus agricultural products, where they existed. In case of extreme emergencies, America sent food to India and Algeria, and Canada sold wheat to China. But in ordinary times, American farmers were paid by the federal government not to plow their lands and not to sow their crops, while millions in Asia barely subsisted on starvation diets. Despite the explosive danger of such maldistribution, world-wide economics were still based largely on regional and national interests.

The population explosion and residual economic nationalism also accounted for an increasing disparity between the rich and the poor nations. Even though developing nations gradually improved their standards of living, the growth in their national product was in many cases more than offset by an increase in the population. Hence the improvement in income per head was very slow, and such countries could hardly hope to catch up with the galloping economic advances in Europe and North America. As a result, the gap widened between the emerging and the established nations, despite foreign aid and technical assistance. Similarly, despite progressive income taxes, the disparity between the affluent and the impoverished in most capitalist countries increased, giving greater urgency to the growing demands of the underprivileged for equality.

The population growth, urbanization, industrialization, and automation also added to the plight of the cities. With the continuing influx into urban areas, the desperate need for metropolitan planning was at last recognized in many countries. But despite the affluence of the developed nations, slum clearance in many areas could hardly keep pace with the growth of new ghettos. And despite man's scientific and technical capabilities, people seemed unwilling to pay the price required to clean the air of their smog-filled cities and purify their polluted streams. Notwithstanding his infinite capacity for technological development, man found himself dominated by the industrial system he had created.

Toward the twenty-first century

Even though mankind had not overcome its primitive impulse to resort to violence, man's physical environment, particularly in the developed nations, was changing at a phenomenal rate. Scientific breakthroughs and technological innovations occurred so rapidly that it was no longer possible to predict what man's life might be like in the twenty-first century.

Basic to this continuous opening of new horizons was the development of new and vastly more powerful sources of energy. Atomic fuel was used to power ships, produce electricity, and desalinate sea water. Solid fuel rockets propelled space ships to the moon and exploratory satellites as far as Venus, while laser beams served as tiny scalpels in surgery.

New power, coupled with the refinement and miniaturization of electronic devices, radically altered systems of transportation and communication. Supersonic flights placed every area on earth within at most six and a quarter hours of any given point. Man-made satellites circled the earth to relay global phone conversations or television programs, to report on atmospheric weather conditions, or to spy on military activities in other countries. Having only recently surveyed the arctic regions and having just begun the exploration of outer space, scientists also developed highly sophisticated techniques for examining the bottoms of the oceans in expectation of finding new resources. A measure of the change that had taken place in a hundred years can be seen when one recollects that in 1869, Americans marveled at the engineering accomplishment when the "golden spike" was driven to complete the first transcontinental railroad. A century later, people took it almost for granted that an engineer could push a button on earth in order to activate a soil sampling machine on the moon and check on it by means of television cameras.

The improvement of solid state, integrated circuits in electronics permitted rapid improvement in computer technology. More versatile computers were capable of reading handwriting and playing games, and could be made small enough for installation in missiles as auto-guidance systems.

Developments in medicine and biochemistry may in the long run prove to be of greater significance than a rendezvous of astronauts in space and manned missions to the moon. Most noticeable was the advance in preventive medicine, such as antibiotics and vaccines, and in surgery. Transplants of eyes, kidneys, and other organs had become common, and by 1968 surgeons struggled to perfect techniques for their ultimate achievement, the use of artificial or transplanted hearts. Such medical developments not only reduced human suffering, but also greatly prolonged human life spans. Whereas the average life expectancy in the United States had been fifty-six years at the end of World War I, it had risen to seventy-four by 1967. The socio-economic and psychological consequences of such prolongation of life can barely be fathomed. Potentially even more revolutionary were the discovery of the genetic code and current investigations in neurology.

Given man's potential for scientific advance and technological improvements, contrasted with his apparent inability to solve social, economic, and psychological problems, it is manifestly impossible to predict the course of man's further development. When surveying the last four millennia, one discovers a constant capacity for change. Technology advanced gradually, then spurted to a gallop in recent years; standards of morality changed gradually;

and religion became slowly more demythologized. But, for whatever reason, man's reliance on violence, albeit with more sophisticated weapons of destruction, remained much as it had been in prehistoric times.

SUGGESTED READINGS

Lessening of Bi-Polarity

Dallin, Alexander, ed., *Diversity in International Communism; A Documentary Record, 1961–1963* (Columbia, 1963).
Djilas, Milovan, *The New Class: An Analysis of the Communist System* (Praeger, 1957).
Fischer-Galati, Stephen, ed., *Eastern Europe in the Sixties* (Praeger, 1963). Collection of essays.
Lerche, Charles O., Jr., *Last Chance in Europe, Bases for a New American Policy* (Quadrangle, 1967). On problems of NATO.
Liska, George, *Imperial America: The International Politics of Primacy* (Johns Hopkins, 1967).
London, Kurt, ed., *Eastern Europe in Transition* (Johns Hopkins, 1966). Collection of essays.
Planck, Charles R., *The Changing Status of German Reunification in Western Diplomacy, 1955–1966* (Johns Hopkins, 1967).

The "Third World"

Bhagwati, Jagdish, *Economics in Underdeveloped Countries* (McGraw, 1966).
Durdin, Tillman, *Southeast Asia* (Atheneum, 1966).
Liska, George, *Alliances and the Third World* (Johns Hopkins, 1968).
Martin, Laurence W., ed., *Neutralism and Nonalignment: The New States in World Affairs* (Praeger, 1962).
Tutsch, Hans E., *Facets of Arab Nationalism* (Wayne, 1965).
Wilcox, Wayne A., *India, Pakistan and the Rise of China* (Walker, 1964).
Wolpert, Stanley, *India* (Prentice-Hall, 1965).
Zinkin, Taya, *India* (Walker, 1966).

China

Houn, Franklin W., *A Short History of Chinese Communism* (Prentice-Hall, 1967).
Lewis, John Wilson, *Leadership in Communist China* (Cornell, 1963).
Liu, William T., ed., *Chinese Society Under Communism, A Reader* (Wiley, 1967). Collection of articles.
Zagoria, Donald S., *The Sino-Soviet Conflict 1956–1961* (Atheneum, 1964).

International Problems of the 1960's

Adams, Thomas W., and Cottrell, Alvin J., *Cyprus Between East and West* (Johns Hopkins, 1968).
Aron, Raymond, *On War* (Norton, 1968).
Dougherty, James E., and Lehman, J. F., Jr., eds., *Arms Control for the Late Sixties* (Van Nostrand, 1967). Collection of essays.
*Fall, Bernard B., *The Two Vietnams: A Political and Military History* (Praeger, 1966). On United States involvement in Vietnam.

Fulbright, James William, *The Arrogance of Power* (Random, 1967). On Vietnam.

Hilsman, Roger, and Good, Robert C., eds., *Foreign Policy in the Sixties* (Johns Hopkins, 1965). Collection of essays.

*Jenks, C. W., *Prospects of International Adjudication* (Oceana, 1963).

Kerr, Malcolm, *The Arab Cold War, 1958–67; A Study of Ideology in Politics* (Oxford U.P., 1967).

Marshall, Charles Burton, *Crisis Over Rhodesia: A Skeptical View* (Johns Hopkins, 1967).

Technology and Science

*Ashford, Theodore A., *Physical Sciences: From Atoms to Stars* (Holt, 1967).

*Asimov, Isaac, *New Intelligent Man's Guide to Science* (Basic Books, 1965).

Buckingham, Walter, *Automation* (New American Library, 1961).

Oppenheimer, J. Robert, *The Open Mind* (Simon and Schuster, 1960). On science, the atom, and general culture.

Socio-Political Questions

*Brown, Robert McAfee, *Ecumenical Revolution* (Doubleday, 1967).

Dechert, Charles R., ed., *The Social Impact of Cybernetics* (Simon and Schuster, 1967). Collection of essays.

Haworth, Lawrence, *The Good City* (Indiana, 1963). On urban renewal.

Josephson, Eric and Mary, eds., *Man Alone: Alienation in Modern Society* (Dell). A collection of writings.

Kostelanetz, Richard, ed., *Beyond Left and Right, Radical Thought for Our Times* (Crowell, 1968). Essays on the future.

Mitau, G. Theodore, *Decade of Decision: The Supreme Court and the Constitutional Revolution, 1954–1964* (Scribner, 1967).

Ng, Larry K. Y., and Mudd, Stuart, eds., *The Population Crisis, Implications and Plans for Action* (Indiana, 1965). Collection of essays.

Reed, Edward, ed., *Peace on Earth* (Simon and Schuster, 1965). World response to Pope John XXIII's encyclical.

Theobald, Robert, *The Challenge of Abundance* (New American Library, 1962).

*Wolfgang, M. E., and Ferracuti, F., *Subculture of Violence* (Barnes and Noble, 1967).

Bibliography

COLLECTIONS OF SOURCE MATERIALS

NOTE: All books listed are available in paperback editions. For some reprints, dates of publication are not readily ascertainable.

Amann, Peter H., ed., *Western Society: Institutions and Ideals,* Vol. III, "The Modern World: 1650–1850" (McGraw, 1967).

Bagley, John J., and Rowley, P. B., *A Documentary History of England,* Vol. I (Penguin).

Baltzly, Alexander, and Salomone, A. Williams, eds., *Readings in Twentieth-Century European History* (Meredith, 1950).

Bernard, Leon, and Hodge, Theodore B., eds., *Readings in European History* (Macmillan, 1962).

Bierck, Harold A., ed., *Latin American Civilization: Readings and Essays* (Allyn and Bacon, 1967).

Black, Eugene C., and Levy, Leonard W., eds., *Documentary History of Western Civilization* (Harper).

Burke, Richard J., Jr., ed., *The Ancient World: 800 B.C.–A.D. 800,* Vol. I (McGraw, 1967).

Caldwell, Wallace E., and McDermott, William C., *Readings in the History of the Ancient World* (Holt, 1952).

Carroll, Harry J., Jr., Embree, Ainslie T., and others, *The Development of Civilization: A Documentary and Interpretive Record,* 2 vols. (Scott, 1961, 1962).

Cherno, Melvin, ed., *Western Society: Institutions and Ideals,* Vol. IV "The Contemporary World: Since 1850" (McGraw, 1967).

Clough, Shepard B., and Moodie, Carol G., eds., *Documents and Readings: Major Developments from the End of the Middle Ages to the Present* (Van Nostrand, 1965). European economic history.

Cohn-Haft, Louis, ed., *Source Readings in Ancient History* (Crowell, 1965). Near East and Greece.

Downs, Norton, ed., *The Medieval Pageant: Readings in Medieval History* (Van Nostrand, 1964).

Erickson, Arvel B., and Havran, Martin J., eds., *Readings in English History* (Scribner, 1967). Pre-Norman Britain to the present.

Goerner, E. A., ed., *The Constitutions of Europe* (Regnery, 1966). England, France, Germany and Russia.

Judd, Gerrit P., ed., *Readings in the History of Civilization* (Macmillan, 1966).

McGary, Daniel D., and Huhl, Clarence L., Jr., eds., *Sources of Western Civilization*, Vol. I, "From the Ancient World to the Reformation Era"; Vol. II, "From the Seventeenth Century to the Present" (Houghton, 1962, 1963).

Mosse, George L., Hill, Henry Bertram, and others, *Europe in Review–Readings and Sources Since 1500* (Rand McNally, 1957).

Powers, Richard H., ed., *Readings in European Civilization Since 1500* (Houghton, 1961).

Rowen, Herbert, gen. ed., *Sources in Western Civilization,* 10 vols., Vol I not yet completed (Macmillan, 1965).

Snyder, Louis L., gen. ed., Anvil Books (Van Nostrand). Brief texts with appended documents.

———, ed., *Documents of German History* (Rutgers, 1958).

Stearns, Raymond P., *Pageant of Europe, Sources and Selections from the Renaissance to the Present Day* (Harcourt, 1961).

Straka, Gerald M., ed., *Western Society: Institutions and Ideals,* Vol. II, "The Medieval World and Its Transformations: 800–1650" (McGraw, 1967).

Weber, Eugen Joseph, ed., *The Western Tradition, From the Ancient World to the Atomic Age* (Heath, 1965).

White, Donald A., ed., *Medieval History: A Sourcebook* (Irwin, 1965).

Williams, E. N., ed., *A Documentary History of England,* Vol. II (Penguin).

PHILOSOPHY, LITERATURE, AND GENERAL CULTURE

Black, Eugene C., ed., *Modern European Intellectual History: A Sourcebook* (Irwin, 1964).

Cantor, Norman F., gen. ed., *Ideals and Institutions in Western Civilization,* Vol. I, "The Ancient World: to 300 A.D."; Vol. II, "The Medieval World: 300–1300"; Vol. III, "Renaissance and Reformation: 1300–1648"; Vol. IV, "From Absolutism to Revolution: 1648–1848"; Vol. V, "The Modern World: 1848 to the Present" (Macmillan, 1968, 1968, 1963, 1968, 1968).

Chadwick, H. M., and Chadwick, Nora K., eds., *The Growth of Literature,* Vol. I, "The Ancient Literatures of Europe"; Vol. II, "Russian, Yugoslav, Early Indian, Early Hebrew"; Vol. III, "The Tatars, Polynesia, Some African Peoples, General Survey" (Cambridge U.P., 1968).

Commins, Saxe, and Linscott, Robert N., eds., *Man and Man: The Social Philosophers* (Simon and Schuster). From Plato to Dewey.

———, eds., *Man and Spirit: The Speculative Philosophers* (Simon and Schuster). From St. Augustine to William James.

———, eds., *Man and the State: The Political Philosophers* (Simon and Schuster). Eighteenth and nineteenth centuries.

Greer, Thomas H., gen. ed., *Classics of Western Thought,* Vol. I, "The Ancient World"; Vol. II, "Middle Ages, Renaissance, and Reformation"; Vol. III, "The Modern World" (Harcourt, 1964).

Hacker, Andrew, gen. ed., *History and Sources of Western Political Thought,* 6 vols. (Macmillan).

Horowitz, Irving L., ed., *The Anarchists* (Dell). Selections from Diderot to Camus.

Johnson, Oliver A., *Man and His World: Introductory Readings in Philosophy* (McKay, 1964).

Knoles, George H., and Snyder, Rixford K., eds., *Readings in Western Civilization* (Lippincott, 1960).

The Mentor Philosophers Series (New American Library).

THE WORLD BEYOND EUROPE

Aston, William G., trans., *Nihongi, Chronicles of Japan from the Earliest Times to A.D. 697* (Allen and Unwin, 1956).

Bartlett, Ruhl J., ed., *The Record of American Diplomacy, Documents and Readings in the History of American Foreign Relations* (Knopf, 1964).

Chamberlain, Basil H., trans., *Kojiki or Records of Ancient Matters* (J. L. Thompson, 1932). On Japan.

De Bary, William Theodore, *Sources of Chinese Tradition,* 2 vols., (Columbia, 1964).

———, ed., *Sources of Indian Tradition,* 2 vols. (Columbia, 1964).

———, *Introduction to Oriental Civilizations,* Vol. I, "From Earliest Records of Japan to Eighteenth-Century Rationalism"; Vol. II, "The Shinto Revival to the Japanese Tradition in the Modern World" (Columbia, 1964).

Fitzgerald, Gerald E., ed., *The Constitutions of Latin America* (Regnery, 1968). Six constitutions.

Handlin, Oscar, ed., *This Was America: As Recorded by European Travelers to the Western Shore in the 18th, 19th, and 20th Centuries* (Harper).

Heffner, Richard D., ed., *A Documentary History of the United States* (New American Library, 1950).

Keen, Benjamin, ed., *Americans All: The Story of Our Latin American Neighbors* (Dell, 1966). Selected sources from the Aztecs to the present.

———, ed., *Readings in Latin-American Civilization: 1492 to the Present* (Houghton, 1967).

Lach, Donald F., and Flaumenhaft, Carol, eds., *Asia on the Eve of Europe's Expansion* (Prentice-Hall, 1965).

Legge, James, trans., *The Chinese Classics,* 5 vols. (Hong Kong, 1961).

Lensen, George Alexander, *Russia's Eastward Expansion* (Prentice-Hall, 1964). Accounts of participants.

Meyers, Marvin, Cawelti, John G., and Kern, Alexander, eds., *Sources of the American Republic, A Documentary History of Politics, Society and Thought,* 2 vols. (Scott, Foresman 1961, 1967).

Oliver, Roland, and Oliver, Carol, eds., *Africa in the Days of Exploration* (Prentice-Hall, 1965). Reports of travelers from the tenth to the nineteenth century.

Rappaport, Armin, ed., *Sources in American Diplomacy* (Macmillan, 1966).

Saunders, John J., ed., *The Muslim World on the Eve of Europe's Expansion* (Prentice-Hall).

Sheer, George F., gen. ed., *Documents of American History,* 7 vols. (World).

Wallbank, T. Walter, ed., *Documents of Modern Africa* (Van Nostrand, 1964).

Wuest, John J., and McAree, James G., eds., *Modern Asia in Conflict: Readings and Documents,* Vol. I "China and Japan"; Vol. II, "India, Pakistan and Southeast Asia" (McKay, 1967).

SOURCES FOR HISTORICAL PROBLEMS

De Bary, William Theodore, *Problems in Asian Civilizations* (Heath).

Greenlaw, Ralph W., and Lee, Dwight E., eds., *Problems in European Civilization* (Heath). Many titles in this series.

Hill, Henry Bertram, gen. ed., *European Problem Studies* (Holt). Many titles in this series.

Kagan, Donald, ed., *Problems in Ancient History,* Vol. I, "The Ancient Near East"; Vol. II, "The Roman World" (Macmillan, 1966).

Lieuwen, Edwin, ed., *Problems in Latin American Civilization* (Heath).
Rozwenc, Edwin C., ed., *Problems in American Civilization* (Heath).
Schaefer, Ludwig, Fowler, David, and Cooke, Jacob, eds., *Problems in Western Civilization; The Challenge of History* (Scribner, 1965).
Source Problems in World Civilization (Holt). Many titles in this series.
Spitz, Lewis W., and Lyman, Richard W., gen. eds., *Major Crises in Western Civilization* (Harcourt, 1965).
Tierney, Brian, Kagan, Donald, and Williams, L. Pearce, gen. eds., *The Random House Historical Issues Series, Twenty-Four Individual Pamphlets* (Knopf, 1968).

REFERENCE WORKS AND BOOKS ON PARTICULAR AREAS

REFERENCE WORKS

Boyd, Andrew, *An Atlas of World Affairs* (Praeger, 1964).
Bulfinch, Thomas, *Bulfinch's Mythology* (Dell).
Kingsbury, Robert, and Pounds, Norman J. G., *An Atlas of Middle Eastern Affairs* (Praeger, 1966).
Shepherd, William R., *Historical Atlas* (Barnes and Noble, 1964).
Steinberg, Siegfried H., ed., *Historical Tables* (St. Martins, 1967).
Williams, Neville, *Chronology of the Modern World: 1763 to the Present Time* (McKay, 1967).

SERIES

The American Universities Field Staff, *The Developing World: A.U.F.S. Readings* (American University, 1966).
Berkshire Studies in European History (Holt).
Mazlish, Bruce, ed., *Main Themes in European History* (Macmillan).

PARTICULAR AREAS

Benedict, Ruth, *The Chrysanthemum and the Sword: Patterns of Japanese Culture* (World).
Cady, John F., *Thailand, Burma, Laos and Cambodia* (Prentice-Hall, 1966).
Chai, Ch'u and Winberg, *The Changing Society of China* (New American Library, 1962). From ancient dynasties to communism.
Charques, Richard D., *A Short History of Russia* (Dutton, 1956).
Clissold, Stephen, ed., *A Short History of Yugoslavia, From Early Times to 1966* (Cambridge U.P., 1966).
Clubb, Oliver Edmund, *Twentieth Century China* (Columbia, 1963).
Dimont, Max I., *Jews, God and History* (New American Library, 1964). Jewish contribution to other civilizations.
Fagg, John Edwin, *Cuba, Haiti, and the Dominican Republic* (Prentice-Hall, 1965). From the sixteenth century to the present.
Halecki, Oscar, *The History of Poland* (Regnery, 1966).
Hitti, Philip K., *A Short History of the Near East* (Van Nostrand, 1966).

Jelavich, Charles and Barbara, *The Balkans* (Heffer, 1965). Early national movements and creation of states.
Learsi, Rufus, *Israel: A History of the Jewish People* (World).
Legg, John D., *Indonesia* (Prentice-Hall, 1964).
Li, Dun J., *The Ageless Chinese: A History* (Scribner, 1965).
Muller, Herbert J., *The Loom of History* (Oxford U.P., 1966). A history of Asia Minor.
Nehemkis, Peter, *Latin America: Myth and Reality* (New American Library, 1964).
Nutting, Anthony, *The Arabs* (New American Library, 1963). From Mohammed to Nasser.
Pendle, George, *History of Latin America* (Penguin, 1963).
Rodriguez, Mario, *Central America* (Prentice-Hall, 1965).
Schurz, William Lytle, *Latin America, A Descriptive Survey* (Dutton, 1964).
Smith, Wilfred Cantwell, *Islam in Modern History* (New American Library, 1959).
Webb, Herschel, *An Introduction to Japan* (Columbia, 1957).
Wright, Arthur F., *Buddhism in Chinese History* (Atheneum, 1965).

POLITICS AND ECONOMICS

Arendt, Hannah, *The Origins of Totalitarianism* (World, 1966).
Hielbroner, Robert, *The Worldly Philosophers: The Lives, Times and Ideas of the Great Economic Thinkers* (Simon and Schuster, 1961).
Lubasz, Heinz, ed., *The Development of the Modern State* (Macmillan, 1964).
McIlwain, Charles H., *Constitutionalism, Ancient and Modern* (Cornell, 1958).
Nadel, George H., and Curtis, Lewis P., Jr., *Imperialism and Colonialism* (Macmillan, 1964).
Nomad, Max, *Aspect of Revolt* (Twayne, 1959). On nineteenth and twentieth century radical groups.
Pike, Frederick B., ed., *The Conflict Between Church and State in Latin America* (Knopf, 1964).
Rossiter, Clinton, *Constitutional Dictatorship: Crisis Government in the Modern Democracies* (Harcourt, 1963). On ancient Rome, modern France, England, Germany, and America.
Ruggiero, Guido de, *The History of European Liberalism* (Beacon, 1959).
Schumpeter, Joseph Alois, *Capitalism, Socialism and Democracy* (Harper, 1950).
Wormser, René, *The Story of the Law* (Simon and Schuster, 1962).

SCIENCE AND TECHNOLOGY

Butterfield, Herbert, *The Origins of Modern Science: 1300–1800* (Macmillan, 1965).
Hall, A. R., *The Scientific Revolution, 1500–1800* (Beacon, 1966).
——, and Hall, M. B., *A Brief History of Science* (New American Library). Emphasis on pre-nineteenth century.
Hughes, Thomas Parke, ed., *The Development of Western Technology Since 1500* (Macmillan, 1964).
Landes, David S., *The Unbound Prometheus: Technological Change and Industrial Development in Western Europe from 1750 to the Present* (Cambridge U.P., 1968).
Marsak, Leonard M., ed., *The Rise of Science in Relation to Society* (Macmillan, 1964).
Pledge, Humphrey T., *Science Since 1500: A Short History of Mathematics, Physics, Chemistry and Biology* (Peter Smith).
Usher, Abbott Payson, *A History of Mechanical Inventions* (Beacon, 1959).

ART AND MUSIC

Artz, Frederick B., *From the Renaissance to Romanticism, Trends in Style in Art, Literature, and Music, 1300–1800* (U. of Chicago, 1962).

Brockway, Wallace, and Weinstock, Herbert, *Men of Music* (Simon and Schuster, 1958). From Palestrina to Stravinsky.

Christensen, Erwin O., *The History of Western Art* (New American Library, 1959).

Compass History of Art, 12 vols. (Viking). Each on a special period of Painting.

D'Espezel, Pierre, and Fosca, François, *A Concise Illustrated History of European Painting* (Simon and Schuster, 1961).

Janson, Horst W., and Janson, Dora Jane, *The Picture History of Painting* (Simon and Schuster, 1961).

Mumford, Lewis, *Art and Technics* (Columbia, 1960). On the relationship between the artistic and the technical.

PHILOSOPHY AND RELIGION

Allen E. L., *From Plato to Nietzsche* (Fawcett).

Bahm, Archie J., *The World's Living Religions* (Dell).

Baker, Herschel C., *The Image of Man: A Study of the Idea of Human Dignity in Classical Antiquity, The Middle Ages and the Renaissance* (Harper, 1961).

Bolgar, R. R., *Classical Heritage and Its Beneficiaries: From the Carolingian Age to the End of the Renaissance* (Harper, 1964).

Bouyer, Louis, *The Spirit and Forms of Protestantism* (World).

Brinton, Crane, *The Shaping of Modern Thought* (Prentice-Hall, 1963). Surveys Western ideas from the fifteenth century on.

Bronowski, J., and Mazlish, Bruce, *The Western Intellectual Tradition: From Leonardo to Hegel* (Harper, 1960).

Burrell, Sidney A., ed., *The Role of Religion in Modern European Society* (Macmillan, 1964).

Cohn, Norman, *Pursuit of the Millennium: Revolutionary Messianism in Medieval and Reformation Europe and Its Bearing on Modern Totalitarian Movements* (Harper).

Cornford, F. M., *From Religion to Philosophy: A Study in the Origins of Western Speculation* (Harper, 1957).

Dean, Vera M., *The Nature of the Non-Western World* (New American Library).

Eliade, Mircea, *Patterns in Comparative Religion* (World).

Finegan, Jack, *The Archaeology of World Religions,* Vol. I, "The Background of Buddhism, Confucianism, and Taoism"; Vol. II, "The Background of Shinto, Islam, and Sikhism" (Princeton, 1965).

Liu, Wu-Chi, *A Short History of Confucian Philosophy* (Dell).

Russell, Bertrand, *A History of Western Philosophy* (Simon and Schuster, 1945).

Seznoc, Jean, *The Survival of the Pagan Gods: The Mythological Tradition and Its Place in Renaissance Humanism and Art* (Harper, 1961).

Sohm, Rudolph, *Outlines of Church History* (Beacon).

Wach, Joachim, *The Comparative Study of Religions* (Columbia, 1961).

Wells, Donald A., *God, Man, and the Thinker: Philosophies of Religion* (Dell).

Whitehead, Alfred North, *Religion in the Making* (World, 1956).

INDEX

Abbassid dynasty, 107, 136
Abelard, Peter, 142
Abraham, 17
Absolutism, 231-32, 242, 247, 252, 272, 289; England, 184-85, 237, 258, 274; France, 183, 221, 223, 242-44, 253, 255-56, 276-78, 282, 289-90, 292, 376; *H. R.E., 247, 292-93; Ottoman Empire, 234; papal, 240-41; Prussia, 284-85, 292; Russia, 233, 294-95; Scotland, 245; Spain, 235, 298; Sweden, 256, 296-97
Abyssinia. See Ethiopia
Académie Française (1635-), 255-56
Achilles, 46
Act of Settlement (1701), 300
Act of Union (1707), 300
Actium, Battle of (31 B.C.), 65
Adages (Erasmus), 214
Adams, John, 353
Address to the Christian Nobility, 209
Adenauer, Konrad, 538
Adrianople, Battle of (378), 79
Aegean civilization, 6, 20
Aeneid, 67
Aeschylus, 41-42
Age of Reason, The (Thomas Paine), 309
Agincourt, Battle of (1415), 172
Ahriman, 25
Ahura (Ahura-Mazda), 21, 25
Akbar (Mogul of India), 181
Akkadians, 7, 14
Alaric (Visigoths), 81, 94
Alberti, Leon Battista, 195
Alcántara, Order of (Spain), 148
Alcuin of York, 115
Alexander (Serbia), 475
Alexander I (Russia), 360-62, 376, 380
Alexander II (Russia), 404, 418-19
Alexander III (Russia), 419
Alexander III (Pope), 127
Alexander VI (Pope), 191, 198, 204-05
Alexander the Great, 22, 25, 38, 44-48, 75, 106
Alexis (Russia), 267
Alexius Comnenus (Byzantium), 139
Alfred the Great (England), 130
Algeria, 391, 543, 555-56, 561
Ali, Mehemet, 391

All Quiet on the Western Front, 471
Allied Control Authority (ACA), 536-37
Alphonso XIII (Spain), 489, 503
Alva, Duke of, 248
Amadeus of Savoy, 138
Amenhotep IV (Ikhnaton, Egypt), 18-19
America, pre-Columbian, 5
American Revolution, 302, 332-33, 336, 353, 372, 386
American War of Independence. See American Revolution
Ammon, 18-19, 46
Anabaptists, 212
Anglo-French Entente (1904), 439, 443
Anglo-Japanese Alliance (1902), 439, 441, 447
Anglo-Russian Entente (1907), 433, 443
Anglo-Saxons, 80, 94, 96-99, 130-32
Anne (England), 301
Anne (France), 254, 276
Anne (Spain), 236
Anti-Comintern Pact, 479, 510
Antigone, 16
Antigonid dynasty, 48
Antony, Marc, 62, 64-65, 68
Apollo, 32, 40, 70
Appian, 61
Aquinas, Thomas, 143, 145, 149, 167
Aquitaine, 96, 130
Arab League, 548, 556, 564
Aragon, 125, 134-35, 150, 163, 175, 185, 226, 235
Arc, Joan of, 173
Archimedes, 50
Arianism, 77-79, 85, 94-96, 98
Ariosto, 196
Aristarchus, 50
Aristophanes, 42
Aristotle, 33, 43, 45, 108, 143, 149, 193, 303
Arius, 77-78
Armenia, 21, 24, 69
Arrian, 46
Aryan, 15-16, 20-21, 25
Asiento, 227, 320
Asoka (India), 26-27, 48
Assyria, 7, 19, 21, 24-25, 69
Asura, 21

* H.R.E. refers to Holy Roman Empire

591

* c. refers to century